PRINCIPLES OF
**COMPUTER NETWORKS
AND COMMUNICATIONS**

PRINCIPLES OF
COMPUTER NETWORKS
AND COMMUNICATIONS

M. BARRY DUMAS
Baruch College
City University of New York

MORRIS SCHWARTZ
Baruch College
City University of New York

PEARSON
Prentice
Hall

Upper Saddle River, NJ 07458

Library of Congress Cataloging-in-Publication Data

Dumas, M. Barry.
  Principles of computer networks and communications / M. Barry Dumas,
Morris Schwartz.
  p. cm.
  Includes index.
  ISBN-10: 0-13-167264-9
  ISBN-13: 978-0-13-167264-2
  1. Computer networks.   I. Schwartz, Morris (L. Morris)   II. Title.
  TK5105.5.D8925 2009
  004.6—dc22

                     2007042135

Executive Editor: *Bob Horan*
Editor-in-Chief: *David Parker*
Product Development Manager: *Ashley Santora*
Assistant Editor: *Kelly Loftus*
Editorial Assistant: *Christine Ietto*
Marketing Manager: *Anne Howard*
Marketing Assistant: *Susan Osterlitz*
Senior Managing Editor: *Judy Leale*
Project Manager: *Kelly Warsak*
Manager, Rights & Permissions: *Charles Morris*
Operations Specialist: *Carol O'Rourke*

Senior Art Director: *Janet Slowik*
Interior Design: *Jodi Notowitz*
Cover Design: *Jodi Notowitz*
Cover Photo: *Zap Art/Image Bank/Getty Images*
Illustration (Interior): *ICC Macmillan Inc.*
Composition: *ICC Macmillan Inc.*
Full-Service Project Management: *Leo Kelly/ICC Macmillan Inc.*
Printer/Binder: *Edwards Brothers Incorporated*
Cover Printer: *Phoenix Color Corp.*
Typeface: *10/12 Times*

Pearson Prentice Hall™ is a trademark of Pearson Education, Inc.
Pearson® is a registered trademark of Pearson plc
Prentice Hall® is a registered trademark of Pearson Education, Inc.

Pearson Education Ltd., London
Pearson Education Singapore, Pte. Ltd
Pearson Education, Canada, Ltd
Pearson Education–Japan

Pearson Education Australia PTY, Limited
Pearson Education North Asia Ltd
Pearson Educación de Mexico, S.A. de C.V.
Pearson Education Malaysia, Pte. Ltd.

10 9 8 7 6 5 4 3 2 1
ISBN-13: 978-0-13-167264-2
ISBN-10:   0-13-167264-9

Dedication

To my wonderful family, my wife, Laura, and our sons Steve and Dave, for the unparalleled meaning and perspective they have given my life.

For past, present, and future students—what would I have done without you?

M. Barry Dumas

This book is first and foremost dedicated to the many students whom I have taught, who have made me appreciate the many struggles they face in learning network technology without the benefit of a thorough grounding in the sciences. They have caused me to seek ways by which to crystallize and clarify the often-complex concepts and render them in terms that are familiar and related to their everyday lives. The book is also dedicated to the many colleagues with whom I have worked and taught, who have provided this author with an environment that stimulated a constant flow of ideas and who had the intellectual capital to deal with the ideas.

Morris Schwartz

Brief Contents

Contents

Preface

This book is designed for undergraduate and graduate students majoring in information systems and for students in other business disciplines who would like a grounding in telecommunications, either from a standalone elective or as part of a minor in information systems. It also is suitable for business professionals who want an introduction to the field or to refresh their knowledge.

Many books have been written on the subject of data communications and networks. What, therefore, could possibly energize an author to undertake writing yet another tome? This is precisely what we asked ourselves as we searched for a suitable text for the undergraduate and graduate courses we have been teaching for many years in the Computer Information Systems Department of Baruch's Zicklin School of Business.

The major challenge for networking and telecommunications courses in schools of business comes from equipping the students to deal with three related workplace issues:

- **Comprehension:** knowing how to determine when there is a need to install, upgrade, reconfigure, expand, or otherwise redesign networks
- **Focus:** keeping up with the latest developments and evaluating them with regard to the reality of the situations in question
- **Balance:** avoiding the tendency to overspecify, thereby boxing out future options while not underspecifying in an attempt to keep options wide open

From a student perspective, this means developing an understanding of the technology, not simply amassing a collection of facts. Without this, the ability to integrate those facts into meaningful assessments is problematic. But integrative skill is precisely what is essential in business. For example, typical network-related job tasks require evaluating need, discovering and weighing options, and selecting from among those options.

To do this successfully, whether working solo or, more likely, with a team, means being able to make appropriate comparisons of the various technologies available, which in turn requires something more than a surface grasp of terminology. Even when a project is contracted out rather than developed in-house, the subsequent proposals and bids must be evaluated—that takes the same kind of ability and understanding.

Too often, students think of telecommunications topics as a series of isolated subjects. Making the transition from that mode to an integrative one is not easy. It requires developing an appreciation for the field and a comprehension of the subject matter, which is quite different from learning terminology, rules, and procedures.

We believe that the text to support this effort needs to provide balance between discourse and technical depth, while taking an historic, developmental approach. We should not assume that students in these classes cannot manage technical detail; neither should we expect them to become engineers. Yet a text without technological underpinning provides explanations too vague to be sufficiently meaningful. The business student with no prior background in the subject will not have the technical context within which to comprehend and assimilate what appear to be high-level concepts, whereas the more experienced student or professional is not provided with the possibility of deeper insight.

In our courses, we have seen that when we take the typical approach of treating topics by discussing their general dimensions without the support of the underlying basics, we are doing our students a disservice. This becomes clear later on when a problem is confronted, or when the student is questioned a year, or even a semester, later.

We have developed a pedagogy that, in our experience, works quite well for business students, whether information systems majors or not—a blend of foundation material and historical context that follows a developmental approach to understanding networking and communications technology. Accordingly, we searched for texts supporting that pedagogy.

What we found was a variety of approaches:

- Texts that combine basics and applications in each chapter, an organization that forces piecemeal treatment of the foundation material, with a concomitant loss of effectiveness
- Texts that treat topics mostly in isolation, without a connective flow
- Texts that follow a network architecture model as a framework for discourse although the student has no basis for truly comprehending what an architecture is, why it is, or what it actually does
- Texts that presume that business students cannot handle much in the way of technical detail or that don't mesh well with the background expected of the students

Many authors now follow the protocol stack as a logical and natural way to develop and unfold the material. Given that these days students already are familiar with the Internet, following a TCP/IP stack exposition seems to make sense. In our experience, that approach doesn't work well.

Yes, the students may know how to surf the Web, and some may even have knowledge of HTML and various Web tools. Yet they often have little understanding of what is going on in the networks they are using. Getting students to grasp the meaning of an architectural model such as OSI or TCP/IP right at the beginning, and appreciate what it does, is largely impossible—they don't understand what a network is, what it means to move information through it, or the mechanisms by which information is carried. How, for example, can a description of the data link layer's functionality be meaningful under this scenario? The upshot is that the student is left without much context or basis to value, let alone really comprehend, the subject.

Features

Technologies do not arise spontaneously. Instead, each builds upon what preceded it, guided, prodded, and molded by performance necessity, business concerns, political issues, and engineering capabilities. In our text, we take the same view, noting how the field developed in response to a variety of pressures and, thereby, how each step led to the next. At the same time, we follow a discourse that keeps the business student's needs squarely in mind.

This historical developmental approach leads to a broad understanding of the field that also provides the basis for further study, whether in the classroom or on one's own. We believe so strongly in this approach that we have explored certain topics more than might at first glance seem warranted. For example, we have found that it is far easier for the student to appreciate the need for digital signaling after understanding the impact of noise on analog signals, just as it is simpler to comprehend the benefits of an ATM network after looking at X.25 and frame relay. In addition, we present the more complex aspects of the material with a balance of rigor and commonplace examples.

We believe that our text's organization, content, and style is highly effective pedagogically, supporting students in the development of true appreciation of the field and comprehension of the issues—those aha! moments that we all seek to instill in our students. Once the foundation is laid, technologies become more than terms to memorize, network architectures can be appreciated for their organizational proficiency, and the Internet, with its robustness and openness, will have meaning far beyond an easily accessed widespread network.

Every chapter begins with an overview and ends with a summary. End-of-chapter problems consist of short-answer, fill-in, multiple-choice, and true-or-false exercises that students can use to check their understanding of the material. These are followed by expanded questions that call for some exploration and deeper thinking.

To further help the student, chapters include sidebars of varying length. These provide amplifications and historical, business, and technical expansions of text material. For the more inquisitive student, technical extensions with detailed information on various topics also are incorporated. Additional material on a variety of topics appears in appendices.

Another pedagogical device is the use of cases that deal with the application of networking and communications technologies. Two kinds appear—independent standalone cases that relate to particular chapter issues, and an ongoing business case based on a business world scenario that also relates to chapter issues but that develops as the book proceeds. Each successive iteration builds on what came before. Cases are first introduced in Chapter 9, as the prior chapters don't lend themselves to applications cases.

MOSI Running Case

The running case deals with a fictitious but realistic company, Metropolitan Outpatient Services, Inc. (MOSI). The basic description of the company that follows serves as a reference for the specifics in the chapters and should be read by the students:

> Metropolitan Outpatient Services, Inc. (MOSI), founded by two social workers, launched operations as a one-stop source for the medically related outpatient needs of people discharged from hospitals. The social workers own the company and are its managers.
>
> Here is their initial business model: MOSI works with area hospitals and with a list of freelance providers who take care of various outpatient needs on a fee-for-service basis. For a patient nearing discharge who will need some type of home care or assistance for a period of time, the discharging hospital calls MOSI, which locates appropriate available care providers from its list and assigns them to the case. MOSI pays the freelancers for their services and in turn receives payments from the patient's insurance company, Medicaid, Medicare, self-pay, or some combination.
>
> Upon launch of the business some time ago, MOSI had agreements with two area hospitals and a list of about 50 care providers covering registered and practical nursing, physical therapy, psychological and social work, counseling, and shopping and transportation services. They employed three full-time on-site schedulers to take calls from hospitals and arrange for service placements and a full-time accountant to handle all the internal and external paperwork. All their records were kept on paper and stored in file cabinets.
>
> In each chapter where the case is relevant, particular situations and issues are described. Further, each case statement ends a series of questions, including something similar to:
>
> > *Before you begin (to resolve the issue at hand), what questions would you ask of the managers, other employees of MOSI, or other parties?*
> > *Think about what you need to know before you investigate options.*

As the case builds, MOSI grows, creating an in-house care staff, adding other sites and feeder hospitals, linking to feeder hospitals, and so on. Each stage in MOSI's development requires incorporating various networking and communications technologies. We leave it to the instructor to specify the growth in numbers of different personnel, facilities sizes, demand levels, and so on. This allows tailoring the case to particular classes.

What also works very well is to have students make reasonable assumptions about the dimensions of these factors or show how different assumptions lead to different designs and conclusions. We have found this approach to be particularly effective, as it requires more critical thinking on the part of the students. Furthermore, their diverse assumptions and conclusions are themselves fertile ground for class discussions. This applies whether assignments are for individual students or for student teams.

Book Organization

Our text is suitable for a one- or two-semester undergraduate or graduate course. Rather than making the text encyclopedic, we have carefully selected topics for inclusion that we believe will serve to give students a sound foundation of understanding and prepare the interested student for a life of learning as a professional for further formal study.

The first chapter presents a big-picture view of the field, introducing students to the relevant areas in the context of an historical overview. This sets the stage for the next six chapters, which cover the foundation material necessary to understanding what networks and telecommunications are all about—the basics of signaling, encoding, error control, connections, and digital communications.

Chapter 8 provides another overview—this time of the various networking technologies themselves. This serves to orient the students to the applications covered in the next eight chapters. There we see how the fundamentals are applied to create circuit and packet switched networks, local and wide area networks, wired and wireless networks, and the Internet, which receives special emphasis. We also discuss network security and network management, both from a business perspective. The last two chapters explore how to plan, design, and implement networks, and what the future may hold.

A more specific picture of our approach to content and organization can be seen in the detailed table of contents. Here is a brief overview of the chapters:

- Chapter 1 provides an easy-to-read historic overview of voice and data communications, showing how the fields began and grew in a developmental process. Architectural models are introduced as a natural follow-on. The topics are presented in an integrated fashion, illustrating how the field has evolved.
- Chapter 2 looks at how electricity and light carry signals, the media they travel on, and the impairments they are subject to. The latter are explained as a consequence of the characteristics of the signal carriers and the media. We also consider changing electrical to light signals and vice versa, required by the mixed systems prevalent today.
- Chapter 3 deals with signal types, analysis, and bandwidth. We explore what signals are, how they are characterized, and what bandwidth really means, both technically and intuitively.
- Chapter 4 covers the four categories of signal encoding: digital data/digital signals, digital data/analog signals, analog data/digital signals, and analog data/analog signals. In addition, we see why those combinations are needed, where they come into play, and their performance implications.
- Chapter 5 focuses on error control: detection and correction. We look at various methodologies, comparing techniques to situations and effectiveness. Both forward and backward error correction are covered, as well as consideration of the circumstances in which they make sense.

- Chapter 6 explores the different types of communications connections, why particular connection methods arose, and how and where they are used. This includes the varieties of multiplexing, network topologies, and addressing basics.
- Chapter 7 investigates digital transmission techniques. We discuss why bits are packaged for transmission, how asynchronous transmission came to be, why synchronous transmission became dominant, and the pros and cons of each. We also delve into the need for flow control and how it is done.
- Chapter 8 provides an overview of the variety of network types that are covered in greater detail in the remaining chapters. Methods of classifying networks are covered, along with the ideas behind circuit, packet, message, and cell switching, and wired and wireless systems.
- Chapter 9 covers local area networks, physical and virtual, their topologies, operating characteristics, and applications, when segmentation is indicated, and how to interconnect them. We also show how and why they evolved over the years.
- Chapter 10 details circuit switching, exploring the telephone systems that formed the basis for and influenced development of today's communications systems. The need for multiplexing becomes evident here and is revisited in somewhat more detail. Also discussed is why DSL came about and how it works, broadband cable and alternatives for phone service, and SONET as a model for optical networks.
- Chapter 11 investigates packet switched wide area networks, covering the variety of services and the historical growth and development of packet switching WAN technologies.
- Chapter 12 looks at internetworking in general and the Internet in particular, again from an historical developmental viewpoint. The Web is discussed along with addressing types and issues. This brings up the need for the move from IPv4 to IPv6 and a discussion of the ways in which companies may make that transition.
- Chapter 13 explains and probes further into the Internet, detailing TCP/IP and associated Internet protocols, routing, quality of service, and VoIP.
- Chapter 14 delves into wireless networks, including WLANs, WPANs, and WiMAX. The evolution of cellular telephony is explored, and the same treatment is given to satellite links. In each of these subjects, we consider issues related to providing reliable and secure service.
- Chapter 15 examines network security from a business perspective. Different types of network threats are discussed, along with methods for dealing with them. Encryption also is covered. We look at certifications, compliance, and cyberlaw as well.
- Chapter 16 explores the problems of network management, planning, and structuring. FCAPS is examined as one de jure model. Business issues are considered as fundamental in designing a management strategy and implementation.
- Chapter 17 looks into the ideas behind planning and implementing a new network or modifying an existing one. We cover traffic analysis, reliability and maintenance considerations, finding providers, managing proposals and bidding processes, and testing and acceptance. This chapter has a practical orientation and covers material not usually found in networking texts.
- Chapter 18 takes a look at what the future of networking and telecommunications might hold. We reflect on such areas as fiber to the home, the growth of optical networks and power line networks, and the next generations of the Internet and the Web, among others.
- Appendices are provided for students who wish to probe deeper into the technological aspects of many of the chapter subjects.

Supplements

The following resources are available to adopting instructors.

- Instructor's Manual—contains a chapter outline and answers to all end of chapter questions for each chapter of the text.
- PowerPoint Presentations—feature lecture notes that highlight key text terms and concepts. Professors can customize the presentation by adding their own slides or by editing the existing ones.
- Test Item File—an extensive set of multiple choice, true/false, and essay questions for each chapter of the text. Questions are ranked according to difficulty level and referenced with page numbers from the text. The Test Item File is available in Microsoft Word format and as the computerized Prentice Hall TestGen software, with WebCT-and Blackboard-ready conversions.
- TestGen—a comprehensive suite of tools for testing and assessment. It allows instructors to easily create and distribute tests for their courses, either by printing and distributing through traditional methods or by online delivery via a Local Area Network (LAN) server. TestGen features Screen Wizards to assist you as you move through the program and the software is backed with full technical support.
- Image Library—a collection of the text art organized by chapter. This collection includes all of the figures, tables, and screenshots from the book. These images can be used to enhance class lectures and PowerPoint slides.

Acknowledgements

This book would not have been possible without the contributions of many people. We would like to thank our editor, Bob Horan, for his support throughout, and the hard work of Ashley Santora and Kelly Loftus, who made this text a reality. The production team of Kelly Warsak, Renata Butera, Carol O'Rourke, and Arnold Vila also deserve special mention for their commitment and dedication to this project.

And a special thanks to Dave Dumas for his invaluable suggestions on phrasing and grammar.

Many reviewers were involved as this text progressed. We thank them sincerely for their meticulous assessments and valuable suggestions:

Hans-Joachim Adler, *University of Texas at Dallas*
James Gabberty, *Pace University*
Charletta Gutierrez, *Northern Illinois University*
Rassule Hadidi, *University of Illinois at Springfield*
Vasil Hnatyshin, *Rowan University*
Hassan Ibrahim, *University of Maryland College Park*
Khondkar Islam, *George Mason University*
Virginia Franke Kleist, *West Virginia University*
Turgay Korkmaz, *University of Texas at San Antonio*
Sunita Lodwig, *University of South Florida*
Frank Panzarino, *Stevens Institute of Technology*
George Scheets, *Oklahoma State University*
Wayne Summers, *Columbus State University*
Dwayne Whitten, *Texas A&M University*
Richard Wolff, *Montana State University*
Yue Zhang, *California State University, Northridge*

Family and friends are last in the list, but foremost in our hearts.

About the Authors

M. Barry Dumas is professor of computer information systems at Baruch College, City University of New York. He developed and taught the first networks courses given by the department and, among other courses, has been teaching networking and computer communications at both the undergraduate and graduate levels ever since.

His professional experience includes consulting at area hospitals and firms regarding networking, computer communications, and systems design issues. He designed and installed the first local area network at Mount Sinai Hospital, New York, for the Social Work Services Department, a design that subsequently was repeated in several other departments. He also developed large-scale simulation models for experimenting with integrated system designs, several of which were implemented.

From 1990 to 1996, Professor Dumas was associate provost at Baruch College, where he also held the position of director of academic computing and educational technology. In that role, he initiated and oversaw the elimination of the College's mainframe computers and their replacement via installation and integration of campus-wide networks. He also planned and led the merging of the College's separate educational and administrative computing centers into what became the Baruch College Technology Center.

Professor Dumas received his Ph.D. in computing and quantitative methods, with a minor in marketing, from the Columbia University Graduate School of Business.

Morris Schwartz is a professional engineer licensed in New York State and a senior member of the IEEE. He has been teaching data communications and networks on graduate and undergraduate levels for 10 years in the Computer Information Systems Department at Baruch College of the City University of New York. He was formerly the chief communications engineer for the New York City Transit System. He led the design of the packet and message switching protocols teams during the development of one of the first commercial packet switched networks based on the original ARPANET design for the International Telephone & Telegraph Company (ITT), and he developed Value Added Network (VAN) applications at the General Electric Company. He has also taught a variety of graduate and undergraduate classes in multimedia technology, Web design, and e-commerce. He received the Bachelor of Engineering (Electrical) and the Master of Engineering (Electrical) degree from the City College of New York, the Professional Degree (EE) from New York University, the Master of Computer Science degree from the Polytechnic Institute of New York, and the M.B.A. (Finance) degree from the New York Institute of Technology.

PRINCIPLES OF
COMPUTER NETWORKS
AND COMMUNICATIONS

1

Introduction

1.1 Overview

Communication is at the heart of humankind's ability to disseminate ideas and information, coordinate complex tasks, and build cohesive societies. In effect, communication provides both the fundamental underpinnings of civilization and an important mechanism for its growth and development.

In this chapter, we will look at communication from an historical and a developmental perspective. We will see how technologies developed in response to market-driven performance demands and attempts to overcome technological limitations. We also will see how shortcomings of particular methodologies moved developments in response to competitive pressures, and how advances in data networks and computer communications often are the result of business decisions.

By way of introduction and to provide an overview, many concepts and terms are introduced here. These will be explored fully in subsequent chapters, where we will investigate how the communications systems of today work, how they developed, and how they evolved in response to the demands placed upon them; we also will examine how they have changed and have been changed by the way we work, commute, shop, and play.

1.2 The big picture

For much of history, communication has been strictly between people. If they were within hearing distance, people could simply speak to each other; if not, some means of remote communication was needed. From the earliest development of writing and for thousands of years thereafter, such communication was the province of the written word, with transmittal aided in recent history by the postal system. As societies matured and became industrialized, this type of communication suffered because it was overly slow, particularly where business decisions were concerned. Much later, the advent of the computer and the need for inter-computer communication necessitated something else altogether.

A major leap forward in distance communication had its roots in the discovery of electricity and the development of several of its applications. As a result of the early work of Samuel Morse on the telegraph, Alexander Graham Bell on the telephone, and Thomas Alva Edison on the electromechanical recording of sounds, electricity became the favored means by which people, and later, computers, could communicate quickly even over very long distances. In this role, electricity and electromagnetic waves became the principal underlying carriers of communications. Although they continue in this role today, light as a communications carrier has taken over some of this task and is growing in importance in many arenas.

The spectrum of electromagnetic waves is described by frequency and wavelength. The spectrum covers a wide range, from long-wavelength, low-frequency radio waves to short-wavelength, high-frequency gamma rays. (The higher the frequency, the shorter the wavelength.) Roughly in the middle of the spectrum and occupying a very small part of that range is light—infrared, visible, and ultraviolet.

Thus far, communication technology has utilized the lower half of the spectrum, from radio waves to infrared. At the bottom of the communications spectrum are radio waves, with frequencies below about 3×10^9 hertz (Hz) and wavelengths of at least 10^{-1} meters; microwaves come next, with frequencies up to about 3×10^{11} Hz and wavelengths down to about 10^{-3} meters; infrared follows, with frequencies up to about 4×10^{14} Hz and wavelengths as short as 7×10^{-7} meters.

For more information, see

http://imagine.gsfc.nasa.gov/docs/science/know_l1/ emspectrum.html.

AMPLIFICATION

The relationship between the number of telephones, N, and the number of wire pairs needed to fully interconnect them is $(N)(N-1)/2$. For example, 1,000 telephones would need $(1000)(999)/2 = 499,500$ wire pairs.

1.3 Voice communications: an historical perspective

By 1880, four years after their invention, about 30,000 telephones were installed in the United States, but the telegraph, which by then had been in use for about 35 years, was still dominant for real-time distance communication. Telephone communication received a major boost in 1880 from the formation of the American Bell Company, founded to develop and promote the telephone as the preferred means of real-time communication over a distance. From a practical business perspective, achieving that goal meant creating an economical and affordable system—and that required many technological innovations that were yet to come.

In the earliest stages of telephone use, to call one telephone from another required the two telephones to be directly connected by a pair of wires carrying electricity. But actually interconnecting every telephone to every other by such "dedicated" wire pairs quickly proved to be both impractical and expensive. With two telephones, just one wire pair is needed; for three telephones, three pairs suffice. But adding a fourth telephone doubles the requirement to six wire pairs. Fully interconnecting 100 telephones takes 4,950 pairs, and connecting 1,000 telephones takes nearly half a million; every pair must be connected to every phone as well—clearly an impossible task. (Figure 1.1 illustrates some of these interconnections.)

FIGURE 1.1

Wire pairs needed for full
interconnection

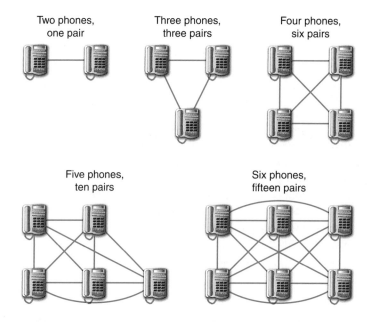

Even if you ignore the unwieldiness of having a huge number of wires attached to each telephone, the scale, cost, and management effort of such an endeavor would multiply rapidly because the phones could be hundreds, if not thousands, of miles apart. Reducing the magnitude of the interconnection problem, thereby making the connection of individual telephones practical and manageable, called for a different way to make connections.

The solution was to link every telephone to a ***central office (CO),*** instead of directly to every other phone. At the CO, the wire pair from each ***subscriber*** (customer) telephone was ***terminated*** at (connected to) a ***switchboard.*** There, any two telephones could be physically connected by an ***operator*** who would plug a short ***patch cord*** between the termination points of those telephones, thus linking them directly. The operator ended the call by unplugging the patch cord.

With a CO, many different pairs of telephones could be connected simultaneously, yet each would need just one wire pair to the CO to be fully connected to every other phone. (See Figure 1.2.) So, for example, instead of the 499,500 wire pairs noted earlier to fully interconnect 1,000 phones, just 1,000 wire pairs are needed with a CO, the same as the number of phones.

FIGURE 1.2

Telephone connections
using a central office

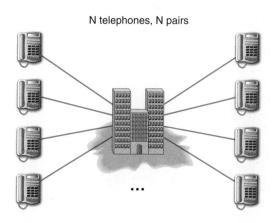

As economical as this system was, the growing number of phone installations and increasing usage meant more and larger switchboards and greater numbers of operators, resulting in higher infrastructure expenditures and operating costs. Consider also that an operator could connect or disconnect only one call at a time, which had an impact on connection timeliness. Once again, increasing cost and demand for more and better service pushed for another solution. (See "Historical note: Telephone operators reach a limit.")

The next improvement came about in 1891, when Almon Brown Strowger patented the dial telephone together with a switchboard replacement that used electromechanical switches to automate the process of connecting and disconnecting telephones. (Why was Strowger, an undertaker, spurred to create this invention? It was a business strategy. See "Historical note: Strowger outfoxes a competitor.")

This sped up the connection process, removed the "personal touch," and reduced the need for operators. The Strowger switch was installed in the Bell system in 1920. Although it was faster than operators, it produced *noise* (interference) on adjacent connections every time it *switched* (created) a new connection. In 1938, the Bell system introduced an improved central office device, the *crossbar switch.* Also electromechanical, it further sped up the switching process and increased reliability while introducing less noise.

HISTORICAL NOTE
Telephone operators reach a limit

The invention of a practical telephone in 1876 was followed two years later by the hiring of the first female telephone operator, Emma Nutt. From about 1881 through the middle of the 20th century, nearly all telephone operators were women, and by 1900, the telephone company was the largest private employer of women in the United States.

According to Mr. Eckert, who ran a telephone company in Cincinnati in the early days of the industry, this was in part because, "Their service is much superior to that of men or boys. They are much steadier, do not drink beer nor use profanity, and are always on hand." (See http://www.cclab.com/billhist.htm.)

As more telephones were installed, the size of the switchboards grew, and the demand for more operators reached a point at which it was becoming untenable. The impending practical limits on telephone operators as a connection methodology was apparent. (If we continued to use the switchboard system and followed Mr. Eckert's advice today, there would be so many switchboards that the entire female population of the country would have to be employed as telephone operators.)

For an interesting overview of telephone operator history, see

http://www.pbs.org/wgbh/amex/kids/tech1900/phone.html.

Bringing wires into COs and switching connections on demand was a dramatic improvement, but it did not entirely solve the problem of wire proliferation. It was easy enough to connect calls between telephones wired to a particular CO, but what about phones that were too far away from that CO to be wired there feasibly? As telephones grew in popularity, more COs had to be installed, keeping pace with the growth in telephones as they spread across the country. For every telephone to be able to connect to any other telephone, the COs had to be connected. So what was once a problem of interconnecting individual telephones became a problem of interconnecting COs—namely, one wire pair for each telephone in every CO had to be connected to each telephone in every other CO. Once more, the wiring situation became untenable and a better solution was needed.

Further thought led to the conclusion that the probability of every subscriber at one CO wanting to be connected to every subscriber at another CO at the same time was extremely low. It was much more likely that only a small percentage would need to be connected simultaneously. If, for example, only 10 percent of a 50,000-subscriber CO would place calls to an adjacent CO at any one time, then instead of 50,000 CO-to-CO wire pairs, just 5,000 would be enough to do the job. Of course, this meant that the 5,001st simultaneous call could not be connected until someone else hung up. Still, it was clear that relatively few interconnecting pairs would provide sufficient connectivity almost all the time. So a business decision was made to avoid the cost of satisfying every interconnection request no matter what, at the risk of being unable to connect every call attempted during peak demand periods.

As promising as this premise was, there was room for improvement. Even with such significant reductions in CO-to-CO wiring, construction and maintenance costs were still quite substantial, because the wires had to be carried over some distance on poles or buried in underground ducts. Furthermore, as the telephone subscriber population increased, the number of simultaneous calls attempted increased, creating consumer pressure for more CO-to-CO wiring. Once again, meeting demand was fast becoming overly costly and impractical, leading to the next logical step, wire sharing—a method for carrying more than one conversation over a single wire pair at the same time. The first successful wire-sharing technique was called *frequency division multiplexing (FDM).*

HISTORICAL NOTE
Strowger outfoxes a competitor

Almon B. Strowger (1839–1902) was not the first to create an automated telephone switch—that honor goes to M.D. Connolly, T.A. Connolly, and T.J. McTighe, who applied for a patent for their automatic switch in September 1879 and received it in December of the same year. But Strowger was the first to develop *and market* a *practical* switch that became a commercial success. In fact, it was the only successful switch out of many that were created in the decade ending in 1900.

Interestingly and at first glance strangely, Strowger was not a professional engineer or mechanic, but an undertaker living in Kansas City. That an undertaker should develop such a system makes sense when we discover that the wife of a competing undertaker was a telephone operator who transferred calls meant for Strowger to her own husband's establishment instead and, for good measure, kept Strowger's line "busy" for much of the time. Removing the human operator from the system was, according to the story, Strowger's motivation.

Together with his nephew Walter S. Strowger, Almon produced a working model of the switch in 1888, a patent for which was granted in October 1891. At about the same time, Almon and two partners, Joseph B. Harris and Moses A. Meyer, formed the Strowger Automatic Telephone Exchange (SATE). In 1901, after Almon retired, partner Harris licensed the technology to the Automatic Electric Company (AEC). Seven years later, SATE and AEC merged. Over the years, the company evolved into AG Communications Systems. Now a subsidiary of Lucent, which has partnered with Alcatel, the company provides advanced network-based solutions.

For more information about Alcatel-Lucent, see

http://www.alcatel-lucent.com/wps/portal.

FDM is the same technique that allows multiple radio and television stations to transmit their programs simultaneously over the same medium (the air), yet allows an individual radio or television set to tune in a particular broadcast apart from all the others. FDM allows multiple telephone conversations to travel simultaneously between COs over the same wire pair, without interference from each other. The number of simultaneous calls that one wire pair can carry depends on its **bandwidth** (capacity) and the bandwidth needed by each of the calls—the less bandwidth each call uses, the more calls a single wire pair can carry. On the other hand, the less bandwidth used for a call, the lower the speech quality, because not all of the frequency components that make up voice sounds will be transmitted.

To achieve maximum practical wire sharing, telephone companies had to determine the minimum bandwidth required for a conversation to be of reasonable quality. Human speech has a frequency range of about 100 to 7,000 Hz, but experimentation established that a range of 300 to 3,400 Hz (called the **voice band**) provided acceptable, intelligible (though "tinny-sounding") speech quality. Accordingly, it was decided that this reduced bandwidth would do the job. So telephone companies installed equipment that limited the bandwidth of a conversation prior to transmitting it through the telephone system over the shared wires.

As a compromise between voice quality and line utilization, the restricted voice band was quite reasonable. But this decision, made at a time when computers were essentially unknown, had the unintended consequence of being extremely limiting for the computers to come that would want to utilize the very same telephone system for communication. This constraint was a major factor leading to the development in the 1970s of separate **data networks.**

Although FDM greatly increased CO-to-CO wire pair utilization, it was not without shortcomings. FDM uses **analog signaling** techniques to carry telephone conversations. When analog electrical signals are corrupted by noise from another electrical force, such as energy radiated from a conversation on an adjacent pair of wires in a cable bundle, a power surge, or a bolt of lightning, it is impossible to completely remove the noise at the receiving end. This means that the signals cannot be fully restored to their original state. Furthermore, FDM equipment is relatively large, requiring considerable building space.

Once again, a growing number of subscribers meant more and more space and equipment, pushing up the cost of providing phone service. Moreover, the analog signaling techniques of FDM did not allow telephone companies to take full advantage of computer technology for call transmission, routing, and management.

As before, when it was faced with reaching the practical limits of a technology, the telephone companies sought methods to go beyond those limits. This time the next step was a revolutionary technique called **time division multiplexing (TDM).** Introduced in the early 1960s, it was based on **digital signaling** techniques. Digital signals can be made to be highly resistant and insensitive to interfering electrical phenomena; in most cases, a corrupted digital signal can be fully restored. TDM equipment uses the same technology as the ordinary microcomputer and takes advantage of the same strides in miniaturization and cost reduction that this technology has produced. TDM equipment therefore is far smaller and less expensive than FDM equipment with similar capabilities.

Of course, TDM was not without its complications. Spoken words, being analog in nature, are most easily depicted as analog signals. To utilize TDM, a process was needed to convert analog sounds into the digital signals required by the TDM system. This process was **pulse code modulation (PCM),** developed at the Bell Laboratories of the American Telephone and Telegraph Company in the 1930s, based to a large extent on the seminal work of Dr. Harry Nyquist (1889–1976, physicist and electrical engineer).

At the time of TDM's introduction, communication between computers was a rarity. Because the incredible growth in computer technology and usage that ensued was not envisioned, the technical needs of vast numbers of inexpensive high-speed computers were not considered when constructing the TDM design. As it turned out, this became another reason for the development of data networks designed to deal exclusively with computer communications.

Nevertheless, for some time after its introduction, TDM was wonderfully suited to the needs of telephone companies, bringing efficiency to carrying the spoken word. Using digital signals, the *lingua franca* of computers, allowed telephone companies to fully utilize computer power in the communications process. Yet even the immense increase in wire utilization realized was not enough to keep pace with the extraordinary demand for telephone service prompted by fax machines, Internet activity, and e-mail usage.

Pushed again by technology limitations, in 1975 telephone companies in the United States and Europe began trials of a new connection medium, ***optical fiber.*** Optical fiber consists of very thin strands of glass that can guide light for long distances with very little loss, with a much larger practical capacity than wire. By 1980, optical fiber transmission systems were being deployed actively.

Glass fibers can carry very large numbers of calls simultaneously. Using a technique called ***wavelength division multiplexing (WDM),*** one strand of optical fiber can carry as many as 129,024 conversations at the same time. With recent advances, using a method called ***dense wavelength division multiplexing (DWDM),*** that number can be increased by a factor of 256, for an extraordinary total of 33,030,144 simultaneous telephone calls on a single optical fiber strand! One fiber strand could transmit 350 copies of the entire *Encyclopaedia Britannica* from New York to San Francisco in one second.

Today, most of the telephone systems around the world use computer-based switching and multiplexing equipment that has given rise to a tremendous increase in the number and quality of services provided. It has even allowed the expansion of these services to a wireless telephone system, a development that some expect may overtake the cabled telephone system in the not-too-distant future.

1.4 Data communications: an historical perspective

Mainframes, the first business computers, were physically large units that were expensive to purchase and maintain, requiring special temperature- and humidity-controlled rooms designed to be run by trained technicians. Work was brought to the "computer center," and that is where the results had to be picked up. As mainframe use grew, the inconvenience of this arrangement became more apparent, leading to the idea of ***distributed access,*** also called ***remote access.*** Devices called ***terminals,*** attached to the mainframe over a ***communications link,*** allowed submission of jobs to the computer from distant locations; sometimes the "distant" location was the room next door. These terminals, simple input/output (I/O) devices that did not have any computing capability themselves, were called ***dumb terminals.*** Later terminal versions did have some computing capability, mainly to aid in communications processing. Even so, they still functioned primarily as I/O devices.

Computers, of course, do not possess voices. Their exchanges involve transmitting the bits (0s and 1s) that represent computer data. Because of this, the name ***data communication*** was adopted to distinguish it from voice transmission between people.

The key to this new form of communication—between geographically separated computers or between a computer and a remote data terminal—was the communications link. To enable two or more computers to communicate, especially when separated by great distances, an effective connection infrastructure was needed. Because the existing telephone system already spanned the globe, it seemed like a natural to fill the need. However, that presented a problem.

As we discussed earlier, telephone systems were designed to carry voice traffic, not bits. To make the system usable, a device was needed to translate the digital signals' bits into a form compatible with the analog telephone system. (Note that this is different from PCM, a method for analog-to-digital conversion. Here we are talking about converting digital signals to analog.) In 1955, such a device was first described in the *Bell System Technical Journal* in a paper by Ken Krechmer, A.W. Morten, and H.E. Vaughan: "Transmission of Digital Information over Telephone Circuits." By 1958, AT&T deployed it: the ***modem.***

So it appeared that a good solution to the data communication problem had been achieved. However, once more it became apparent that this solution was not ideal. Early modems were relatively slow, running at 110 to 300 bits per second (bps). Because connection time was often lengthy and involved long-distance calls, user expenses quickly mounted. This dilemma worsened as the amount of data exchanged between computers grew immensely. Customers demanded better.

Delivering this increasing load in a timely fashion without runaway costs meant designing ever faster modems and better software. Under this pressure, modem speeds gradually migrated from 110 bps to 56 kilobits per second (Kbps). But at that point, speeds bumped into the natural limit imposed by the standard telephone system. The telephone company decision mentioned previously to limit the voice band to 4 kilohertz (kHz) had the unintended consequence of limiting the maximum speed achievable by modems over standard telephone lines to approximately 34 Kbps.

TECHNICAL NOTE
56-Kbps modems

The so-called 56-Kbps modems actually do not work entirely through standard telephone system connections. To operate at or near their advertised speed, they must be used under special circumstances and with particular software (although 56 Kbps is an exaggeration even then). Otherwise, they operate at a maximum speed of 33.6 Kbps.

Ironically as well, the telephone company's decision to improve the efficiency of voice communications over its inter-CO links by implementing line sharing using TDM actually proved to be a very inefficient way for most computer-originated traffic to share those links, because such traffic comes in short bursts rather than as a continuous stream of data. When not bursting, line capacity reserved for that computer goes unused, in effect raising the cost of every bit of information sent.

There is yet one more aspect of data communication that requires special attention. During a telephone call, people can usually fill in gaps caused by poor reception. If not, they can easily ask the speaker to repeat the missed piece. In data communication, computers are the "speakers," and they do not inherently have the intelligence to fill in missing bits.

These deficiencies spurred the search for an alternative to the telephone network infrastructure. The result, based on a variation of TDM called ***statistical time division multiplexing (STDM),*** was the ***packet switched network,*** focused from the start on robust, computer-based data transmission. In 1969, the first packet switched network began operation. Known as the ***ARPANET*** because its development was supported by ARPA, the Advanced Research Projects Agency of the U.S. Department of Defense, it connected computers at Stanford University and the University of California at Los Angeles. (See "Historical note: Network pioneers and the ARPANET.")

The ARPANET was improved and greatly expanded over a period of more than two decades, eventually interconnecting hundreds of universities, research centers, defense contractors, and related businesses. Toward the end of the 1980s, the ARPANET was opened to the general public, and from there the development of the Internet ensued.

In the early days of the computer revolution, the initial demands for data communication were driven by the very high cost of computers, which were physically large mainframes that were expensive to purchase, operate, and maintain—all in all very costly business tools. To justify the business expenses of computers, companies had to make the most of them, which meant making computer services available to a large number of employees, few of whom were likely to be in the same building as the computer, or even in the same geographical area. A terminal with a keyboard and monitor, connected to the computer for in-building users and by modem through the telephone system to the computer for outside users, provided access.

Initially the telephone connection was made by either dialing the remote computer or using a ***leased line*** (a fixed, direct, telephone line connection). Although this did allow computer resource sharing, these connections were themselves very expensive. Terminals sent one character at a time by a rather inefficient scheme called ***asynchronous communication*** whose use was dictated by the limiting nature of the telephone networks. Though widely used for some time, a situation was again developing in which, despite technological advances, the business case for using the telephone system for computer communications was growing weaker.

The potential of the ARPANET juxtaposed with the high costs of data transmission over the telephone system spurred a great deal of activity in creating networks specifically geared to the needs of data communication. By 1974, the company Bolt, Berenak, and Newman (BBN) had developed a practical packet switched network that would be to computers what the telephone company's communications system was to voice. Other vendors entered the market with their own packet switched network offerings, differentiating themselves by various ***value-added services,*** such as protecting data against transmission loss or providing ***protocol conversion*** (translations to allow dissimilar systems to "talk" to one another).

HISTORICAL NOTE
Bolt, Berenak, and Newman

Formed in 1948 by two MIT professors, Richard Bolt and Leo Berenak, as an acoustical consulting firm and joined by Robert Newman in 1949, BBN became closely involved with the development of the ARPANET in 1968. The firm is credited with many "firsts" in computing and telecommunications and continues in business today, now as a subsidiary of Verizon Communications.

The biggest advantage of these data-oriented networks, called ***public packet data networks (PDNs),*** was cost: it was generally far less expensive to send computer data over a PDN than over the regular telephone network. For the latter, transmission cost was typically based on distance and call length. For a PDN, cost was a function of the amount of data transmitted, not distance, and most often not even time.

This is an important distinction. As briefly mentioned, computers do not talk to each other continuously. Rather, one computer will send some data to another and then wait while the receiving computer performs some action to compose a response. The same cycle happens in reverse when the response is sent, and so on. In other words, transmissions are sporadic, occurring in bursts of activity, analogous to bursts of wind that appear momentarily in gusts, then disappear, only to reappear again a few moments later. So, we describe this type of transmission as "bursty."

HISTORICAL NOTE
Network pioneers and the ARPANET

Len Kleinrock, then a Ph.D. student at MIT delving into the new field of data networks for his dissertation, wrote the first published paper on the theory of packet switching. It appeared as part C: "Information Flow in Large Communications Nets" in the July 1961 RLE Quarterly Progress Report (MIT Research Laboratory of Electronics) and was updated as part D in the April 1962 report. His dissertation thesis, also completed in 1962, was published two years later by McGraw-Hill (New York, 1964) as *Communication Nets: Stochastic Message Flow and Delay*.

This work described the basic concepts of packet switching networks, wherein data to be transmitted is subdivided into small chunks (packets), each of which is routed through the network, thereby enabling use of alternate routes to avoid congested or inoperative links. These basic principles are followed to this day, leading to the description of Kleinrock as the father of modern data networking. His work progressed during his subsequent professorship at UCLA's Computer Science Department, where he continued to develop packet switching technologies and provided much of the seminal work that was subsequently used in configuring the original ARPANET and the Internet that followed. For further information, see

http://www.lk.cs.ucla.edu/internet_history.html.

Paul Baran joined the RAND Corporation in 1959 as a researcher working on creating data networks that were robust enough to keep operating in the face of link outages. Sponsored by the United States Air Force, his work was first published in August 1964 as RM-3420-PR (RAND Memorandum), "On Distributed Communications Networks."

Baran described using message blocks (packets of data) to send information across a digital communications network consisting of switches connecting links that provided a variety of paths between two end points, similar to the way a network of roads and highways provides a variety of ways to drive between two places. Furthermore, this type of network had no central point of control. Rather, packets would be routed over the links independently by each node in turn, thus enabling avoidance of any single point of outage. As with Kleinrock, much of Baran's work was also key in development of the ARPANET and, subsequently, the Internet. For further information, see

http://www.ibiblio.org/pioneers/baran.html.

Although some of the terminology has changed, many of the concepts that Kleinrock and Baran developed are still relevant today.

Because the connection between computers is idle for significant amounts of time, it takes longer to transmit a given amount of data than it would if it were sent continuously. This makes the regular telephone cost model, which charges for connection time whether the link is used or not, much more expensive than the PDN model that charges only for the amount of data sent. PDNs also can accommodate multiple users on some parts of the same links, sharing the links by making the idle moments available to other computers—not the case with the standard telephone system. This efficiency allows PDN providers to spread the cost of a connection over a larger number of customers, thereby further reducing the cost to individual customers. It is easy to see why PDNs became a very attractive alternative to the standard telephone system.

Over the years, the approaches taken to sharing a common connection changed, reflecting the types of connections available, the nature of the data to be transmitted, the state of hardware and software technology, and the kinds of devices that were to be connected. At first and for some 20 years thereafter, PDNs were used overwhelmingly for the transport of computer data alone; after all, that was why they were created. But that meant that business customers needed two distinct networks: the telephone system for voice and a PDN for computer connections.

The expense of using and maintaining two separate networks became onerous. It often necessitated duplicate equipment, less-than-optimal utilization of either network, and the need to have two groups of technicians, one knowledgeable in voice technology and the other in data network technology. Moreover, as time passed there was an immense growth in the amount of data transported, propelled by the increasing use of computers in businesses and homes and by a change in the nature of "data." This led to dramatic modifications in design that made it possible to use just one "data" network for all communications needs. Here is how that happened.

At first, data meant a coding of bits to represent either *text* or *binary* values sent to and from the computer. Internally these corresponded to software and the values needed for computations and executing instructions. The nature of these data did not require them to be delivered in a steady stream. For example, it does not matter to the computer receiving an e-mail message if its bits arrive immediately one after the other, or whether the first few bits are delivered, then a pause before another group of bits, and so on until the entire message has arrived. The person receiving the e-mail message will see it only after it has been completely received and assembled. The fact that it may have taken a little longer than if it was received in a steady stream is not critical. The same may be said of file transfers, in which the data are just a fixed file such as a customer transaction record.

The picture changed dramatically with the introduction of digital video and digital audio. The volume of data involved and the time sensitivity of its bits precluded the collect-bits-and-wait technique suitable for e-mail and static files.

Representing audio and video digitally requires very large numbers of bits. For substantial transmissions, collecting all the bits before acting on them is impractical because of the disk space required and the waiting involved. Even more importantly, if the audio or video is occurring in "real time," as with an online broadcast or live conversation, the data must be delivered as they occur—"on the fly." For practical listening or viewing of video over a communications network, the bit stream must be delivered and acted on continuously and smoothly without interruption. Otherwise, the audio will drop sounds and the video will appear jerky, with missing spots and artifacts.

Yet again, developments on the demand side impelled developments on the communications side—in this case for faster data networks together with more efficient ways to process the data. Meanwhile, as the pressure on data networks was growing, the telephone network was carrying more and more voice in digital form. The growth in the capabilities of these networks led to the recognition that "digital voice data" could be carried over the same networks used for computer data. By the 1990s, the result was the **_convergence_** of the different network types into those that were capable of effectively carrying all data forms, including telephone call traffic.

1.5 Standards and architectural models in the design of networks

Standards are all around us. Because of electrical standards, we can plug any standard lamp into any standard outlet and it will work; we can get into the driver's seat of a car and expect the accelerator pedal to be on the right and the brake pedal to be on the left; we can send an e-mail message with one e-mail program and the recipient using different e-mail software can read the message. Life without standards would be much more confusing, to say the least.

In the world of networks, standards come about as new developments impel advances in they way things work. There are many well-established standards organizations that work in particular areas of concern, forming expert committees that seek the opinions of developers, users, and other interested parties, synthesizing and publishing the results. Such standards are called ***de jure*** (by right). Other standards evolve in the community of users. They are not the work of standards organizations, but they become standards simply by force of popular use. These are called ***de facto*** (by fact, in reality).

It is important to note that no networking standards of any type are enforced by law. However, from a business perspective, a product that does not conform to standards is not likely to succeed in the marketplace. Of course, there are exceptions. Company-based standards, called ***proprietary,*** can become global standards if the company has enough clout, marketing savvy, and a product that catches the public fancy. A prime example of this is the Microsoft Windows operating system.

Many standards apply to networking and telecommunications. Two major standards are reference model architectures; one is a *de jure* standard, the other a *de facto* standard. To learn how they came about and the logic behind them, let's first look at a non-computer example.

Suppose we need to send a message to a person some distance away. We may construct the words of a message from the letters of an alphabet and a language that both of us understand and write the words on a medium such as paper to create a note. These words are strung together using grammatical forms, sentences and paragraphs that help the reader understand the meaning we wish to convey.

When the note is complete, we must decide how to deliver it, and this decision is based on a variety of criteria—speed of delivery, reliability of service, security in transit, cost, convenience, availability, and ease of use are examples. Which criteria are more important may differ from time to time according to factors such as the urgency of the message, its confidentiality, its size, and its distance from the recipient. We may seek a delivery service that combines at least some minimum level of several of these factors. So we may choose to use a courier, the postal service, a private delivery service, or a personal employee, to name some options.

The choice of delivery method will dictate how the note must be packaged and addressed so that it can be delivered securely in a timely fashion without being damaged in transit or marked undeliverable. Different services are likely to have different requirements for packaging and addressing. Finally, if we need to be certain that the recipient did indeed receive the note, we may require an acknowledgment of delivery.

So we see that even for this simple process, there are several steps that must be carried out to send a note between two parties at a distance from each other:

1. Choose an appropriate alphabet.
2. Select a form for the alphabet, such as block or script.
3. Select a mutually understood language.
4. Follow the grammar and rules of the language.
5. Select a medium to carry the words of the note.
6. Place the words on the medium to create the note.

7. Choose a method for sending the note.

8. Package and address the note accordingly.

9. Require an acknowledgment from the recipient, if desired or required.

Of course, the process of composing a note in this way is so familiar to us that we rarely stop to consider the steps we carry out. Yet from the earliest development of writing and for thousands of years thereafter, this was, in essence, how people communicated with each other whenever they were unable to meet in person.

Now let's think about communication over networks. There is great complexity entailed in the design and operation of a network. Moreover, many companies are involved in developing and producing hardware and software to run, and to run on, networks. Typically, each of these products deals with only some of the aspects of a complete network, perhaps being an end user application such as e-mail, a circuit board used to connect a computer to a network cable, a program for transferring files from one network node to another, or software that runs devices that route messages over a system of networks.

If we want designers to exercise their creativity to come up with better ways of accomplishing network tasks or to conceive of new applications or systems, they need some degree of free reign. At the same time, their creations must be able to function in combination with existing hardware and software systems and with other new innovations if we expect our networks to operate smoothly. The implication is that to ensure compatibility we need standards to which products must conform, but this conformity must not inhibit change—seemingly contradictory objectives.

The key to unraveling the contradiction lies in the way network standards are specified. First, we break down the various tasks that a network has to perform into separate logical procedures. Just as in the preceding example, in which we separated the process of creating and sending a note into nine steps, we can similarly divide network operations into a number of functions. Then we can group those functions and specify how the groups interface. In that way, the means for carrying out the tasks of a functional group are left to the designers, while the connections between particular groups are standardized so that they can operate smoothly together.

Two approaches for grouping network functions are in popular use today. They are known as the ***Open Systems Interconnection (OSI)*** reference model and the ***Transmission Control Protocol over Internet Protocol (TCP/IP)*** reference model. The OSI reference model, a *de jure* standard of the ISO standards organization, views networks as having seven distinct functional groups, called layers, whereas the TCP/IP reference model, a *de facto* standard, has five layers. (See "Technical note: OSI and TCP/IP layers.") Whether we divide the functions that a network must perform into seven, five, or any other number of layers is strictly a matter of perspective and convenience. For example, we could reduce our nine-step model for sending a note to an eight-step model by deciding that steps 1 and 2 (choose alphabet, select alphabet script) should be considered as one step (choose and select alphabet script).

AMPLIFICATION

ISO is an international organization for standardization whose members comprise organizations from many countries worldwide. Despite citations to the contrary, ISO does not stand for International Standards Organization. Rather, it is derived from the Greek word *isos*, meaning equal. To learn more about ISO, visit

http://www.iso.org/iso/en/ISOOnline.frontpage.

TECHNICAL NOTE
OSI and TCP/IP layers

The following table outlines the functional groupings of the OSI and TCP/IP model architectures. The meanings of the various functions and how they are carried out are explored throughout this book in the chapters that deal with those aspects. The table is presented here primarily as an introduction to the terminology.

OSI	Functions	TCP/IP
1. Physical	Hardware; transmitting bits over a link; mechanical, electrical, and light characteristics	1. Physical
2. Data link	Reliable data transfer; frame synchronization, error control, flow control	2. Data link
3. Network	Message addressing, switching, routing, congestion control	3. Internet
4. Transport	End-to-end error and flow control	4. Transport
5. Session	Establishing, maintaining, and terminating communication connections between computers	
6. Presentation	Data transformations to standard applications interfaces; common communications services such as encryption and compression	5. Application
7. Application	Services that directly support applications, such as file transfer and e-mail	

Note the use of the word *reference* in both OSI and TCP/IP. It indicates that they represent the models to which we ought to refer as we proceed to design a network or some hardware or software component of a network. You may hear people refer to OSI and TCP/IP as architectural models, as in the OSI architecture or the TCP/IP architecture, because reference models provide a structure and overall plan for a network just as blueprints describe a building's architecture.

Other parallels can be drawn between a network reference model and a building architecture. In new housing developments, model homes are built to represent a variety of features, colors, and styles. You may want your home to have different colors and styles and fewer or more features than are displayed in a particular model, but overall, each home in the development retains the main architectural features seen in the model. Furthermore, every home has certain functional components—kitchens, bathrooms, bedrooms, and so on. Although the particulars may differ from home to home—for example, gas or electric stoves, plain or whirlpool bathtubs—the functionality of each room is predefined; how the functions are carried out can vary.

In a network, each device or its software also need not contain all the functions described in a reference model's architecture, but the functions it does possess should conform to the dictates of that reference model. For example, a switch that transfers data in a local area network (LAN) does not need all the functions required by a router that moves data along in a wide area network (WAN), and the programs that run the router need different functionality than those of a switch. In fact, the programs that run one company's router can be different from those of another company. Yet we can connect a switch to a router as part of our network, and if they conform to a common architecture they will work together.

What are some of the functions that network reference models explicitly include? They describe such physical things as how two communicating devices are to connect to one another, what the connectors should look like, and how many wires should be used. They also explicate *protocols* (rules) for functions like how data exchange is to be started, how transfers are to be accomplished, and how data can be protected against corruption during transmission. In sum, they deal with hardware and software issues, protocols and procedures.

One important concept in these reference models is that of *transparency,* implemented via *encapsulation.* The idea is that each network layer should be able to operate without knowing what is going on in any other layer or how any other layer accomplishes its jobs; *adjacent* layers need to pass data between them according to the model protocols.

Here is a simple description of what happens. (As you read, refer to Figure 1.3, which illustrates the ideas using a simple four-layer model.) The sending computer starts with data at the topmost layer, adds a *header* containing information particular to the control and operation of that layer, and sends the package down to the next layer. There the process is repeated, and so on down all the layers to the bottom (always the physical) layer, which adds nothing but treats the entire package as a collection of bits to be transmitted. The next-to-the-bottom layer may also add a *trailer* for additional control purposes.

On the receiving end, the package travels up through the layers, each one looking at the header corresponding to its layer, taking appropriate action, and removing it before sending it up to the next higher layer. In this way, each layer needs only to look at its header data and does not need to interpret what is inside the package—the layers are transparent to each other.

There is much more to reference model architectures than is covered in this introductory description. In subsequent chapters, we will refer to particular aspects of the OSI and TCP/IP architectures as they apply to the chapter material, and we will expand on the surprising significance they have on the availability and cost of network devices.

FIGURE 1.3

Encapsulation

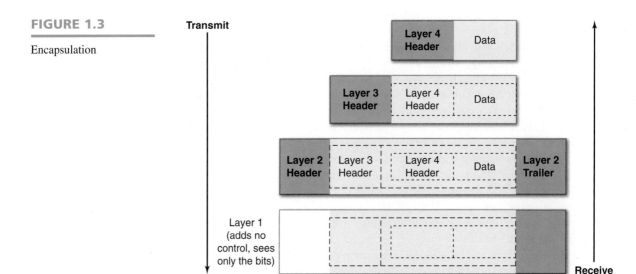

1.6 WANs, MANs, and LANs: an historical perspective

Thus far, we have tacitly used the word *network* to describe a broad variety of communications facilities. More precisely, the term network describes a hardware and software communications system formed by the interconnection of three or more devices; these may be telephones, PCs, routers, or any of a number of other devices that are described in later chapters. The general idea of a network is to allow multiple devices to communicate concurrently, to allow communications to proceed at the highest achievable speeds, and, very importantly, to reduce the cost associated with their interconnection.

How a particular network achieves these goals depends in part on the network's physical architecture—how the network is physically constructed and connected, not to be confused with the architecture of a reference model, which is a verbal paradigm—and that, in turn, is largely determined by the availability and costs of connection media and transmission services, as well as the capabilities of the communicating devices. Of these, the most profound influences on network architectures are usually the connection type and cost, and these, in turn, generally depend on the geographic *span* of (distance covered by) the network.

Over the years it has become common practice to classify network types by their geographic span. Though rather imprecise, the result is three broad categories:

- A network confined to an office, building, or small cluster of buildings (often called a campus), is considered to be a *local area network (LAN)*.
- A network whose reach is limited to a neighborhood or city (a metropolis) is called a *metropolitan area network (MAN)*.
- A network that spans a large geographic region, perhaps an entire state, several states, a country, or even the entire world, is referred to as a *wide area network (WAN)*.

Some make a fourth distinction, calling a network that spans the world a Global Area Network.

With the advent of wireless networks (discussed in detail in Chapter 14, "Wireless networks"), some new terminology has been added to describe what is roughly a similar span breakdown: *wireless personal area network (WPAN), wireless local area network (WLAN),* and *wireless wide area network (WWAN).* One of the most recent wireless technologies (called Bluetooth), designed for short distance links, adds *piconet* and *scatternet.*

Within each of these categories, the precise maximum geographic distance achievable is determined by the protocols that govern the communications between the devices, by the *media* (wired and wireless) that connect them, by considerations of signal impairments, and by power requirements and limitations.

It would seem logical that the first computer networks were small LANs and that the larger ones grew from those. In fact, the opposite occurred. Historically, the first computer networks grew out of the need to utilize mainframe computers economically. As has been discussed, the mainframe was at one location and the computer users might be anywhere in the world. To provide access to the mainframe, then, a large geographical network was necessary. Thus, the WAN was born.

Later, the growing appeal of PCs in business led to the need to interconnect those in one office and, subsequently, in one building. This newly defined class of networks had to run at very high speeds relative to the WAN, because they were to share printers and hard disks over the network; slow WAN-type speeds would create large bottlenecks. This meant that techniques different from those used in WANs were needed. As a result, there arose the LAN.

The increasing popularity of LANs gave rise to the need to interconnect LANs in different buildings, but within the same city. Ergo, the MAN was born.

Another significant and perhaps even more relevant factor generally distinguishes LANs from both WANs and MANs. A LAN lies entirely within a private domain—such as a floor in a business office. This means that the LAN media are completely within the private domain. No public areas like streets or parks need to be crossed. If a company owned two buildings on either side of a public street, it would not be possible to create a single wired LAN for the buildings because the wires would have to cross a public area over which the company had no rights. On the other hand, if the two buildings were on a college campus or a private business development such as an office park, the devices in the buildings could be interconnected solely within the realm of private access, subject, of course, to the distance limits of the particular protocols used.

Taking this illustration a bit further, if the two buildings were separated by a public domain, we could create an individual LAN in each building and then interconnect them by, for example, using a telephone line. The telephone company, which has legal authority to place wire in the public domain, could provide the connection. However, as will be described in later chapters, this greatly limits the speed with which the two LANs can communicate. (Referring back, the interconnection of individual LANs within a city-wide geographical area is a MAN. If the individual LANs are in buildings separated not by streets within a city, but by many cities, their interconnection via the telephone company is a WAN.)

MANs and WANs almost always depend on telephone companies for interconnections precisely because the public domains and large distances separating the various devices make it either impractical or illegal to run one's own wire. But it is important to understand that a telephone company does not literally provide specific individual wires to span the public domains. Rather, it provides a ***connection service***—a service with a defined set of protocols and speeds.

To use the service, we must follow those protocols and speeds even though they fall short of what may be needed to achieve maximum LAN operation. Traditionally, telephone companies have not been very fast to introduce new technology. Historically, this was due to the monopolistic, regulated nature of the business. Although monopolistic control has been reduced recently, innovation still is slow in coming, primarily due to the immense capital investments made in older technologies, thus making rapid changeover too costly. For some years the result was that LANs operated at much higher speeds than MANs and WANs. It is only fairly recently that WAN speeds have surged ahead.

So here is the crux of the matter. In addition to the role that cost plays, we must consider the following:

- In designing MANs and WANs, we are very dependent on the telephone companies for our connections and therefore are limited to whatever speeds and media types they make available.
- For LANs, which do not require telephone company connections, our network designs are limited solely by the availability of technology.
- For wireless, we are subject to limitations imposed by the Federal Communications Commission (FCC) in its distribution of the wireless spectrum.

The impact these factors impose on the design of different networks will be highlighted throughout the text.

Local area networks

Microcomputing, which got underway quite modestly in the 1970s, began to hint at its potential with the introduction of the IBM PC in 1981. Previously, what is now called ***office productivity software,*** then primarily word processing and database applications, was the province of minicomputers, mainframes, and dedicated word processing equipment. When these products were redesigned for the microcomputer, and especially when a new class of software called ***spreadsheets*** was introduced, PC computing took off. (See "Historical note: Spreadsheets, the 'killer app.'")

At first microcomputers were focused on the business office market. ***File sharing*** and ***peripheral sharing,*** already possible with minicomputers and to some extent with mainframes, had to be carried down to the microcomputer level. It was not feasible to have individual users keep separate copies of spreadsheet and database files on each of their machines, because the data in those files would quickly become out of sync—a data change made at one machine would not be reflected automatically in the others. At the same time, peripherals such as hard disks and business-quality printers were quite expensive, too expensive to outfit every computer with printers and multiple drives.

HISTORICAL NOTE
Spreadsheets, the "killer app"

The earliest reference to computer spreadsheets appeared in a paper by Professor Richard Mattessich (University of California at Berkeley, "Budgeting Models and System Simulation," *The Accounting Review*, July 1961: 384-397). Three years later, in a book by Mattessich (*Simulation of the Firm Through a Budget Computer Program*, Homewood, IL: R.D. Irwin, Inc., 1964), a spreadsheet program for the mainframe, written in FORTRAN IV by Tom C. Schneider and Paul A. Zitlau, appeared. This presaged the initial microcomputer spreadsheet programs.

The earliest successful one of those, considered to be the first "killer application" for microcomputers, was VisiCalc (Visible Calculator), authored by Dan Bricklin and Bob Franksten, originally designed for the Apple II and released in 1979. Interestingly, it was never patented. (To see why, visit http://www.bricklin.com/patenting.htm.) Subsequent versions of VisiCalc were released for the Radio Shack TRS-80 and the IBM PC.

VisiCalc was followed in short order by SuperCalc (Superior to VisiCalc), produced by Sorcim (which happens to be micros backwards). It was designed to run with the then-popular CP/M operating system rather than for a particular computer, and later was released for MS-DOS (used by the IBM PC, among others) and Apple-DOS. In 1981, IBM released Multiplan, a spreadsheet program that was produced in versions capable of running on more microcomputers than any other, although it did not attain the popularity of its competitors.

Mitch Kapor and Jonathan Sach created Lotus 1-2-3, so named because it was originally intended to be three integrated programs in one package—spreadsheet, graphics, and word processor. But the equipment available at the time was not up to the task, so they concentrated on the spreadsheet. Lotus 1-2-3, released by Lotus Development in 1983, soon became the best-selling spreadsheet program on the market. That lasted until Microsoft Excel came along.

So the pressure for sharing files and peripherals grew, similar to the way it did for utilizing mainframes and minis. But there was a big difference: PCs were not simple terminals connected to a single computer—they were computers in their own right. Connecting independent computers required something different, more sophisticated, than terminal connection. This was what came to be called a LAN.

As it happened, from the early 1970s much of the work that would be needed to create LANs was going on at Xerox PARC (Palo Alto Research Center), the source of a great many developments in computing that would later become commonplace. PARC was where some of the very first PCs were made and also where the first laser printer was developed.

Although Xerox's computers were not destined to become commercial successes, they were used extensively by Xerox for its own office and engineering computing. The urge to connect them, for the usual reasons of file and peripheral sharing, was made stronger by the desire to share the printing speed and prowess of their breakthrough laser printer. Although there were methods for connecting a handful of PCs, Xerox was talking about connecting hundreds. The result of their efforts was **Ethernet,** first described in 1976, released as a *de facto* standard in 1980, and subsequently released in slightly modified form by the IEEE (Institute of Electrical and Electronics Engineers) as the 802.3 *de jure* standard. (See "Historical note: Robert Metcalfe, Ethernet, and 802.3.")

Meanwhile, IBM was working on a different LAN system, called token ring. They presented their idea to the IEEE 802 committee in 1982, which released it in 1985 in slightly modified form as the 802.5 *de jure* standard.

The release of the 802.3 and 802.5 standards prompted the marketing of conformant hardware and software that coincided quite well with the rapidly developing boom in business use of the PC. Although Ethernets and token rings were not the first commercial LAN systems—they were preceded by, among others, the 1977 release of DataPoint's ARCnet (Attached Resource Computer network)—they soon became the most commercially viable. To this day, Ethernet in its various forms continues to lead the pack as the system with the most installations, widest support, and greatest sales.

HISTORICAL NOTE
Robert Metcalfe, Ethernet, and 802.3

At Xerox, the task of developing what was needed to connect their computers fell to a team led by Robert Metcalfe who, over a period of about three years, created the idea of a LAN, described in a paper published in 1976 entitled "Ethernet: Distributed Packet Switching for Local Computer Networks." The first Ethernet put into operation by Xerox connected more than 100 of their workplace computers with servers and printers. It ran at a nominal speed of 2.94 megabits per second (Mbps), over a 1-Km coaxial cable.

"Metcalfe's first experimental network was called the Alto Aloha Network. In 1973 Metcalfe changed the name to Ethernet, to make it clear that the system could support any computer, not just Altos, and to point out that his new network mechanisms had evolved well beyond the Aloha system. He chose to base the name on the word 'ether' as a way of describing an essential feature of the system: the physical medium (i.e., a cable) carries bits to all stations, much the same way that the old 'luminiferous ether' was once thought to propagate electromagnetic waves through space. Thus, Ethernet was born." (From Charles E. Spurgeon, *Ethernet: The Definitive Guide*, O'Reilly and Associates, 2000.) For additional information, see

http://www.ethermanage.com/ethernet/ethernet.html.

Metcalfe's influence led the DIX (Digital Equipment Corporation, Intel, Xerox) consortium to standardize Ethernet. In 1980, DIX released a 10-Mbps version as a *de facto* standard that became the basis for the IEEE standards organization's work on Ethernet. In 1983, the IEEE released the official Ethernet standard, called 802.3 after the designation of the workgroup that developed it. (Actually, Ethernet and 802.3 are slightly, but not crucially, different.) Metcalfe went on to found 3COM, a highly successful manufacturer of Ethernet-related equipment. Ethernet development continues to this day, with versions now running at nominal speeds of 10 Gbps. It is by far the predominant LAN standard and is moving into the MAN arena. For more information on the history of IEEE 802, see

http://grouper.ieee.org/groups/802/.

Whereas Ethernet and token ring provided the physical connections between computers (OSI layer 1) and the logic to manage access to the LAN system (OSI layer 2), they were not concerned with managing the resources of the LAN or with the user interface. Those tasks are the province of ***network operating system*** (NOS) software. Akin to the computer's operating system (OS), NOS software mediates between operations handled by the PCs and those carried out by the network, directing them as appropriate. A NOS was needed that would work with a large variety of hardware and applications software.

As it happens, there was a company working on exactly that need—Novell, founded in 1983. Not the only company engaged in NOS development, Novell was unique in that its NOS, called NetWare, was designed from the beginning to support a wide variety of hardware and applications, and it was the first LAN software based on dedicated file server technology, a networking system that designated one machine to manage the network and control access to shared devices such as disk drives and printers. At the time, other developers wrote proprietary NOSs to support their own hardware; these were not compatible across manufacturers.

The confluence of NetWare, Ethernet, token ring, and the PC came at just the right time, resulting in a boom in LAN installations and sales of PCs, and the rapid ascension of Novell, 3COM, and IBM to overwhelming market dominance in the LAN arena.

AMPLIFICATION

Novell Data Systems Incorporated (NDSI) began life in 1979 as a computer manufacturer and maker of disk operating systems. In January 1983, Raymond J. Noorda and Safeguard Scientific, a venture capital firm, reincorporated NDSI as Novell, Inc. to design and market software and hardware used for data networks.

The Internet

The Internet is the latest offspring in a family tree that began life as the ARPANET, the result of a network project sponsored by ARPA, the Advanced Research Projects Agency of the United States Department of Defense. The agency has changed its name periodically, shifting back and forth between ARPA and DARPA (Defense ARPA). The last change was to DARPA in 1996.

ARPA was interested in the development of a robust network system that could continue operating even in the face of significant outages. (See "Historical note: The birth of the ARPANET.") Some sources relate that the ARPANET was to be designed to function in the event of a nuclear war. That was not the case, but it probably started as a rumor because the RAND Corporation, one of the original ARPA contractors, released a study on a secure voice system that did mention nuclear war. This is but one of the many "inside stories" that are woven through the history of data networking and telecommunications.

By the 1970s, networks based on the ARPANET were springing up in many venues. As relevant to the Internet to come, the most important of these were:

- CSNET (Computer Science Network)
- NSFNET, initially funded by the National Science Foundation for use by academics and professionals, which served as a backbone network for the early Internet

- USENET, a widely used network promoted by AT&T based on UNIX, later to become the foundation operating system of the Internet
- BITNET, a system linking academic mainframe computers

These, their progeny, and several from other countries eventually interconnected and merged into the Internet. Because this was a gradual evolution, there is no "official" date on which we can say that the Internet was born. However, the turning point usually is considered to be the creation of TCP/IP by Vincent Cerf and Bob Kahn during the 1980s, as it became the *de facto* standard for the common interconnection protocols of all computers on the Internet. This, together with the boom in PCs during the late 1980s, followed by the release in 1993 of Mosaic, the first graphics-based browser, led to the rapid growth of the Internet in the form familiar to us today.

HISTORICAL NOTE
The birth of the ARPANET

The earliest published reference to the basic ideas of what might be called a worldwide computer network was a series of memos written by J.C.R. Licklider (1915–1990) in August 1962 while at MIT. These describe what he called a "Galactic Network." Built upon this work and that of Len Kleinrock and Paul Baran in packet switching, the ARPANET first came to life under the guidance of Lawrence Roberts, who was the ARPANET program manager.

ARPANET's precursor began quietly and simply in October 1965 when the TX-2 computer at MIT's Lincoln Laboratory "talked" to the SDS (System Development Corporation) Q32 computer (built by IBM) in California, in one of the world's first digital network communications. The ARPANET itself is considered to have begun in September 1969, when a team at UCLA's Network Measurement Center, headed by Len Kleinrock, connected one of their SDS Sigma 7 computers to an Interface Message Processor, thereby becoming the first node on the ARPANET and the first computer on what became the Internet. Other computers connected that year were on the campuses of Stanford, UC Santa Barbara, and the University of Utah.

1.7 Summary

This chapter provided an historical overview of the development of voice and data communications and the networks that support them. We saw how the desire to achieve particular communications goals fostered the development of techniques to fulfill those goals and how solving the problems that arose in that quest resulted in the path that computer-based communications followed. We also can glean from this history the hints of what the future might bring.

In the following chapters, we will describe the details of communication and network technology, continuing with the evolutionary historical perspective evoked in the preceding sections. In this way, beyond an understanding of the technology itself, you will gain a perspective on how the developments in communications and networking evolved in response to user demands, networking deficiencies, competitive pressures, and even political influences.

END-OF-CHAPTER QUESTIONS

Short answer

1. Describe the wiring dilemma of fully connecting telephones.
2. Why do COs not guarantee that every call attempt will be successfully connected?
3. What is distributed access computing?
4. How did the decision to limit call bandwidth to the voice band affect data communication via modems?
5. What is the business case for voice and data network convergence?
6. How do *de jure* and *de facto* standards differ?
7. Besides span, what major factor distinguishes LANs from both MANs and WANs?
8. Why did network development proceed from WANs to LANs instead of the other way around?
9. Explain the concept of encapsulation.
10. Why is noise a problem with analog signaling?

Fill-in

1. _____ multiplexing is based on digital signaling techniques.
2. One process used to convert analog to digital signals is the _____.
3. The device used to convert digital signals to analog signals is the _____.
4. _____ multiplexing for optical fiber systems is analogous to _____ multiplexing for electrical wire systems.
5. Computer communications are characterized by _____ rather than by continuous transmission.
6. Two network reference model architectures are _____ and _____.
7. _____ is a seven-layer model architecture, whereas _____ is a five-layer model.
8. Developed at Xerox PARC, _____ has become the most popular LAN standard.
9. Software that mediates between operations handled by the PCs on a LAN and those carried out by the LAN is called _____.
10. To fully interconnect 500 telephones without a CO requires _____ wire pairs, whereas with a CO, _____ wire pairs are needed.

Multiple-choice

1. Analog signaling
   a. is used by FDM
   b. cannot be used for computer communications
   c. is the basis for TDM
   d. is no longer used
   e. all of the above

2. Telephone voice networks grew inadequate for data communications because
   a. their end user cost became untenable as a business expense
   b. they were inefficient from a provider perspective
   c. they did not reach all the desired locations
   d. they did not allow transmission of digital data
   e. both a and b

3. Public packet data networks
   a. are limited in span
   b. have a more expensive cost model than telephone networks
   c. were designed from the beginning to transport digital data
   d. operate only within metropolitan areas
   e. all of the above

4. *De jure* standards
   a. legally bind providers to follow their provisions
   b. are established by standards organizations
   c. must be followed completely
   d. guarantee the quality of conforming products
   e. can accommodate proprietary standards

5. Office productivity software
   a. had no impact on the demand for business LANs
   b. made file sharing much simpler compared to stand-alone computers
   c. resulted in the decline of mainframe computing
   d. allows computers to communicate without human intervention
   e. all of the above

6. Token ring
   a. is a proprietary system
   b. was initially developed by IBM
   c. is sanctioned as the 802.3 IEEE standard
   d. has become the most popular LAN standard
   e. also is applied to WANs

7. The Internet
   a. was an outgrowth of the ARPANET
   b. became a reality with the creation of TCP/IP
   c. does not operate under *de jure* standard protocols
   d. can be thought of as a global network
   e. all of the above

8. UNIX
   a. stands for United Network International exchange
   b. is a foundation operating system of the Internet
   c. is implemented in hardware
   d. is a high-level programming language
   e. none of the above

9. The voice band defined by the telephone company is the range of frequencies from
   a. 100 Hz to 7,000 Hz
   b. 100 Hz to 4,000 Hz
   c. 300 Hz to 3,400 Hz
   d. 300 Hz to 4,000 Hz
   e. 300 Hz to 7,000 Hz

10. TDM
    a. is based on digital signaling techniques
    b. was introduced about 45 years ago
    c. uses equipment that is much smaller and cheaper than that of FDM
    d. requires analog-to-digital conversion for voice transmission
    e. all of the above

True or false

1. Frequency division multiplexing is a technique for simultaneous sharing of communications links.
2. The decision to limit the bandwidth of individual telephone calls was a compromise between voice quality and line-sharing efficiency.
3. Optical fiber transmission systems have been in use only in the last five years.
4. The first packet switched network was the ARPANET.
5. PDNs can facilitate line sharing by making idle moments available to other computers.
6. WANs, MANs, and LANs are strictly defined by their geographic spans.
7. The first computer network was a LAN.
8. NetWare is a network operating system.
9. ARPA developed the ARPANET.
10. TCP/IP is a *de jure* standard.

Expansion and exploration

1. Go to the ISO Web site and make a list of the network standards committees and their areas of interest.
2. Search the Web for information on the convergence of voice and data networks. Compare early reports of convergence with later reports of progress.
3. Create a timeline for the major developments in computer communications and networking.

The modern signal carriers: electricity, light, media, and impairments

2.1 Overview

All modern computer communications depend on two fundamental physical phenomena: electricity and light. They are the vehicles that make it possible and practical to move a wide variety of information and data quickly between just about any points in the universe.

Electricity and electromagnetic waves (such as radio frequency and light waves) carry data as *signals* that travel over a physical path consisting of one or more types of transmission *media* connected by switching and other equipment. Electricity flows over metallic wire cables; light runs through glass or plastic fiber-optic cables; radio waves and higher-frequency electromagnetic radiation travel through air and space.

Signals progress along a medium by a process called *propagation.* Signals propagating through cables are confined to the cables and therefore follow the route the cables do; cables are called *bounded* or *guided* media. Signals traveling through air or space are not confined; air and space are called *unbounded* or *unguided* media.

In this chapter, we will explore some of the basic characteristics of electricity and light, the media through which they travel, and some of the impairments that adversely affect our transmissions. We also will look at factors to consider when there is a choice of medium and, as always, how we got to where we are.

This material is the foundation upon which computer communications are built. By understanding it, you will be able to make sense of the methods that are used for communications, the issues involved, and the roads taken on the continuing journey for improved communications systems.

2.2 Properties of electricity and electrical media

Electricity consists of a flow of electrons called a *current,* whose magnitude is measured in *amperes* and strength (pressure) in *volts.* The process of electron flow is called *conduction;* opposition to flow is called *resistance.* Materials such as copper and aluminum that easily accommodate electrical flow are called *conductors.* Materials such as rubber, plastic, and air that strongly resist electrical flow are called *insulators.* Within those two categories are a range of good to poor conductors and good to poor insulators. *Semiconductors,* the basis of computer chips, widely used in communications systems, usually act as insulators, but we can make them behave as conductors.

Perspective: communicating by light and electricity

Light-based optical fiber transmission systems are a relatively new development, so it would seem that electricity was the first means of communications over a distance. If we think about it, though, whether directly or indirectly, people have been using light to send messages since the dawn of civilization. Primitive man waving his hand to signal his hunting partner was using light indirectly—without daylight, his hand signal would not have been seen. Smoke signals, another indirect use of light, were employed by many early cultures; some put different combustibles in the fire to color the smoke for added information. Even today, boaters use orange and red smoke to signal distress.

An early cave dweller reflecting sunlight off a shiny surface to signal a companion some distance away was using light directly. Soon after the discovery of fire, signal flares on mountain tops sent messages to distant communities—especially effective at night. Early seafarers depended on shipboard and lighthouse oil-fired signal lamps, and even modern sailors still use electric signal lights and pyrotechnic flares to communicate with other ships and the mainland. (For examples of interesting attempts at sight-based distance communication, see Claude Chappe in "Historical note: communicating with light—some early efforts.")

The success of these light/sight-based methods was circumscribed by their limited range, human vision, and lack of security for signals "broadcast" over the air that anyone within range could see. Soon after electricity's discovery, therefore, it quickly overshadowed light as the preferred high-speed, long-distance carrier of information.

For over 125 years, from 1839 with the introduction of the telegraph in Great Britain to the mid-1970s, electrical communications reigned supreme. By the end of this period, however, an increasing prosperity that drove up the demand for telephone service caused rapid growth in other communications devices and computer networks, which caused a powerful market push for greater communications capacity and speed, ratcheting up the development and implementation of light-based communications systems. Although electricity still is a major force, if the telecommunications companies of today relied on electricity alone, they would be hard-pressed to keep pace with demand.

Resistance is directly proportional to wire length and indirectly proportional to wire thickness, purity, and consistency.

HISTORICAL NOTE
Three pioneers

The *ampere,* a unit of measure of the magnitude of electrical current, is named after André Marie Ampère (1775–1836), a French mathematician, chemist, and physicist. Among his numerous accomplishments were his investigations into electricity and magnetism, about which he published several treatises.

The *volt,* a unit of measure of electrical potential or pressure, is named after the Italian physicist Alessandro Giuseppe Volta (1774–1827), who did much pioneering work in electricity. Among his many contributions to electrochemistry was the invention of the electric battery (1800), originally called the voltaic pile.

The *ohm,* a unit of measure of resistance to current flow, is named after Georg Simon Ohm (1789–1854), a German mathematician who investigated electricity and magnetism. His treatise covered many aspects of electricity, including what became known as Ohm's law: voltage equals current times resistance.

The type of electricity most relevant to telecommunications is *alternating current (AC)*—the kind that utility companies provide. The other type is *direct current (DC)*—the kind that comes from batteries. *Alternating* refers to the fact that the current continually changes direction and magnitude at a regular rate, moving smoothly one way while increasing in strength to a set maximum, subsiding to zero strength, then repeating in the opposite direction. For example, the electricity delivered to your home usually has a set maximum of 120 volts.

For simplicity, we refer to direction as positive and negative strength. One complete journey from zero through positive and negative strength and back to zero is called a *cycle* and traces out a *sine wave* pattern. This important pattern comes up repeatedly in computer communications for building signals using both electricity and light waves.

TECHNICAL NOTE
Perspective: the oddity of alternating flow

It seems strange to think of electricity flowing back and forth along a conductor, rising and falling in power, especially when we see a lamp running on AC glowing steadily, but that is what it does. Typical household AC runs at 60 cycles per second, so even discounting the fact that a glowing light bulb filament does not stop glowing instantaneously when the power goes to zero, the flicker that we might expect to see from the back-and-forth nature of AC does happen, but too quickly for us to perceive.

Figure 2.1 shows the AC sine wave pattern, with voltage on the vertical axis and time on the horizontal.

The sine wave pattern of AC is also the pattern with which we build signals.

A sine wave with constant maximum voltage (±V) also showing one cycle

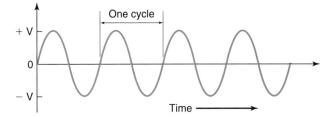

FIGURE 2.1

Alternating current

If you want to explore this topic further, see Appendix B.

Electricity as it moves and changes: implications for wired and wireless transmission

We have noted that electricity can carry signals over wires, but how can signals travel through air or space? The answer is, by the phenomenon of *radiation.*

If we run a *varying* current through a wire, magnetic and electrical forces are produced. Together these create *electromagnetic waves* that *radiate* from the wire and that *mimic the pattern of change* of the current in the wire. If we lay another wire, with no current running through it, parallel to the first, waves radiating from the first wire will intersect the second wire, causing a current flow in that wire whose varying pattern *mimics that in the first.* We have *induced* a similar current in the second wire without any physical connection between the two!

Now if the pattern of variations in our first wire is carrying a message (signals), the radiating electromagnetic waves will carry that message to the second wire without a physical connection—wireless transmission!

Because the radiation effect happens without physical contact, we can use it to carry information through the air or even through the vacuum of outer space. With enough energy, radiated waves can travel considerable distances.

Now the question is, *What purpose do we want our wire to serve?*

- **If our wire is meant to carry signals within our own wired network,** we want to conserve signal energy (minimize radiation) and protect our signals from currents induced by other wires.
- **If our wire is meant to be a transmitting antenna,** we want it to radiate as much signal energy as possible.
- **If our wire is meant to be a receiving antenna,** we want it to absorb as much of the radiated signals as possible.

Not all of the first wire's electrical energy is converted to radiation, and not all the radiated energy is converted to electricity in the second wire. So no matter what, the flow induced in the second wire will not be as strong as that in the first wire.

The power of radiated energy depends in part on the power of the current that creates it. Because power drops off (attenuates) as it travels, the farther the current goes in our wire the weaker it gets; hence, the weaker its radiation. In addition, radiated waves spread out as they travel, which also dilutes their power. The more they spread, the more they attenuate.

Induced current always is weaker than the current that induced it.

HISTORICAL NOTE
Three more pioneers

Michael Faraday (1791–1867) was a British physicist and chemist who made many discoveries concerning the nature of electricity. One of the most significant in its later applications to communications technology was the phenomenon of electromagnetic induction (based on the earlier work of Hans Christian Oersted (1777–1851), a Danish physicist).

James Clerk Maxwell (1831–1879), another prolific mathematician and scientist, was born in Scotland. He extended the work of Faraday to show the relationship between the behaviors of electric and magnetic fields. In particular, he showed how a changing electric field induced a changing magnetic field, and vice versa—the

basis for electromagnetic waves and radiation. He also discovered that the propagation speed of an electromagnetic field was the same as the speed of light and, by extension, that light is a form of electromagnetic radiation.

Heinrich Rudolf Hertz (1857–1894) was a German physicist who expanded upon the work of Maxwell. He proved that electricity could be propagated as electromagnetic waves, that these waves had many of the same properties as light, and that they could be used to transmit information. Subsequently, this led to the development of radio and other wireless transmission. "Hertz" (Hz) came to be the term used to denote cycles per second.

Waves and wavelength basics

Many network choices and design factors involve *wavelength,* an important property of electricity, light, and signals. For example, efficient antennas have to be at least one quarter the size of the wavelength they are meant to transmit or receive. Cell phones would not be practical if the wavelengths they used required long antennas. To understand wavelength, we need to understand waves.

A wave is a regularly recurring pattern that moves away from the force that creates it. We can see wave patterns by dropping a stone into a pond—the ripples that radiate out from where the stone was dropped are water waves. We know that all electromagnetic radiation consists of particular wave forms—*sine waves* (also called sinusoids), the same wave form we saw for AC and the basis for all signals. The time it takes for a sine wave to trace one complete pattern is called its *period* (or *cycle*). (See Figure 2.1.) Because the period pattern keeps repeating over time, sine waves are *periodic.*

The number of times the pattern repeats itself in one second is the wave's ***frequency*** denoted in cycles per second, or Hertz (Hz). Cycle time T and frequency f are inversely related: $T = 1/f$. For example, if one wave cycle takes 1/2 second, its frequency is 2 cycles per second.

The ***distance*** a wave travels in one cycle is its ***wavelength.*** We can calculate this distance by using the standard relationship between distance d, velocity v, and time t: $d = vt$. For electromagnetic radiation, it is traditional to write this formula as: $\lambda = v_m T$, where λ is wavelength, v_m is the velocity of light in a given medium, and T is one period, in seconds.

In communications work, it is common to replace cycle time by its frequency equivalent ($T = 1/f$), giving us: $\lambda = v_m/f$. (See Figure 2.2.)

Wavelength is the distance traveled by the wave in one cycle

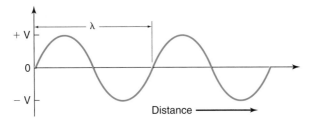

FIGURE 2.2

Sine wave and wavelength

AMPLIFICATION

In a vacuum, all electromagnetic radiation travels at the speed of light, which is nearly 300,000 kilometers per second (about 186,000 miles per second). In different media, electromagnetic radiation travels at different, somewhat slower, speeds than it does in a vacuum.

2.3 Signal impairments in electrical transmission

Impairments are caused by noise and distortion; they change and deform the signals carrying our information. If impairments are severe enough, the receiver will not be able to interpret our signals correctly.

Noise is unwelcome energy appearing in our transmission media. Picture yourself in a room full of loudly talking people. If you want your friend standing next to you to understand what you are saying, you need to speak louder than the level of the "noise" coming from all the other conversations in the room. Similarly, if we expect the receiver to properly interpret our signals, the received signal energy must exceed the energy of the noise in the line.

Distortion is unwanted changes in signal shapes due to interactions between the signals and the media. If you stand in front of a funhouse mirror, your image will be distorted because of the way the mirror is bent. Media can distort our signals.

There are many types of noise and distortion impairments; we will discuss the most common.

Attenuation is a form of distortion in which signal energy is lost as it travels—signal shapes get smaller and smaller, flatter and flatter. (See Figure 2.3.) Attenuation is primarily due to the resistance of the medium to electrical flow. Overly attenuated signals will not be recognized by the receiver.

FIGURE 2.3

Attenuation of a sine wave

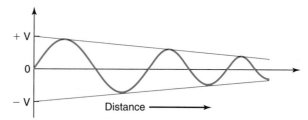

A sine wave with attenuating maximum voltage (±V)

Thermal noise, also called background noise, white noise, Gaussian noise, and hiss, is unwanted energy in our transmission line caused by random movements of electrons of the media (and, in fact, in all electronic devices) and *cannot be eliminated.* Thermal noise is distributed uniformly over the entire electromagnetic spectrum, proportional to temperature and the bandwidth (capacity) of the line, but independent of line length and signal frequencies.

Because thermal noise cannot be eliminated, it is a major factor in electrical signal transmission, limiting the distance that a signal can travel before it attenuates too much to be distinguished from the noise.

Electromagnetic interference (EMI) is unwanted energy induced in our line by radiation from any external source of electromagnetic energy. Examples include crosstalk and impulse noise. EMI also affects wireless signals.

Crosstalk is the result of energy induced in one wire by signals radiating from another. You may have experienced this phenomenon when talking on a telephone and suddenly hearing a conversation from a phone call between two other parties.

Impulse noise, also called spikes, is different from crosstalk and thermal noise in that the latter two are reasonably predictable, rather continuous, and of fairly constant power, whereas impulse noise is unpredictable, usually of very short duration, and composed of large, sudden power surges. It typically comes from nearby electrical equipment (such as an elevator motor), electrical faults in the communications system, lightning strikes, and induction from power surges in the electrical system.

Delay distortion stems from the way wires affect signal velocity. If we send various frequencies down our wire, we will see that they travel at different speeds. Because signals are composed of a range of frequencies, their frequency components arrive at the receiver at somewhat different times, even though they were transmitted at the same time. If the delays are large enough, our signal will be distorted beyond proper recognition.

Because delay differences are magnified by distance, delay distortion is another limiting factor of network cable length.

Intermodulation distortion is the result of non-linearities in a communications system. The output of a linear system is a simple multiple of the input. The output of a non-linear system contains powers of the input.

Signals from a non-linear system contain multiples of the original frequencies (called *harmonics*) that were not present in the signals to start with. Harmonics may have some of the same frequencies as other original signals traveling in the system. If so, they act as particularly troublesome noise to those signals because they can't be distinguished from them. Similarly, harmonics from other signals can be noise to our signals.

2.4 Common guided electrical media

All guided electrical media have metal conductors surrounded by insulation and possibly protective jackets. The metal is almost always copper; insulators are some form of rubber, plastic, or even air; jackets usually are some form of plastic or rubber as well. We will discuss the two most common types of guided electrical media: twisted pair and coaxial.

Twisted pair

Currently, the most commonly used guided electrical medium in network communications systems is *twisted pair.* One wire carries the signal, and the other is the ground. The wires are insulated and twisted around each other in a spiral fashion. The number of twists per inch is the *twist rate.*

Twisting reduces crosstalk from external radiation, because induced currents are weakest where wires are not parallel. Within a cable bundle, which may contain anywhere from two pairs to many thousands of pairs, the greater the twist rate difference between pairs, the less intra-cable crosstalk.

AMPLIFICATION

A ground wire, or simply *a ground*, is a return path for the electricity, so that a circuit is created.   Without a circuit, no current will flow.

Twisted pair comes in two basic varieties—unshielded (*UTP*) and shielded (*STP*). UTP is the most common, widely used for telephone connections and Ethernet local area networks (LANs) in offices and other buildings. Although the twists in UTP are often sufficient to alleviate external noise effects, adding conductive shielding is even more effective. This is STP, the most popular of which was developed by IBM for their token ring networks.

In STP, a conductive wire mesh or foil is wrapped around the twisted pair bundle. The shielding works in two directions, stopping external EMI from distorting its signals and preventing EMI from the cable from distorting signals in other cables. Because of this, STP is often preferred in certain electrically "noisy" environments or where especially sensitive equipment that could be affected by EMI is in use.

AMPLIFICATION

An electrically noisy environment is one with strong EMI. Where heavy-duty electrical machinery is in use, networks need protection from EMI. Networks in offices with large copier machines, mailers, sorters, and the like also may need protection.

Hospitals have equipment that can interfere with or receive interference from network transmissions. Some newer equipment is shielded to prevent interference; other equipment and older devices can be problematic.

Although IBM STP cable types are robust and perform well, they also are thicker and harder to work with than UTP. More telling, token ring networks have largely fallen out of favor; Ethernet, the preferred LAN scheme, specifies UTP.

Coaxial

In contrast to UTP, the two conductors in coaxial cable (*coax*) are concentric. A wire conductor running through the center of the cable (axially) is surrounded (co-axially) by a conducting braided metal or foil shield, protected by an outer jacket. As with STP, the shield operates in two directions, intercepting external radiation and absorbing internal radiation. Individual coax cables can be bundled together.

The wire and the shield are electrically isolated by the space between them, kept constant either by an insulating filler or by washer-like spacers that use the air between the two conductors as the insulating filler. The type of filler and the amount of space greatly affect the bandwidth and noise resistance of the cable.

From one perspective, coax is preferable to twisted pair: it offers much greater capacity for carrying signals and is relatively immune to external sources of interference. But even in its thin version, coax is considerably more bulky than any variety of twisted pair. As such, it is more difficult to install. It has a larger minimum bend radius, the sharpest bend that the cable can make without damage, making it harder to snake around obstacles. It also weighs more. Coax also is more costly and more difficult to modify when changes to the network are necessary. Because of these drawbacks, coax lost favor among network designers, who concentrated on using twisted pair. But it wasn't always so. The original Ethernet LAN, for example, specified coax cabling.

Even today, cable TV companies use coax in home installations for TV and broadband Internet access. Coax is still common in other parts of the television distribution system and in long-distance telephone transmission, though it is steadily being replaced by fiber-optic cable. (Even the vaunted twisted pair is being replaced by fiber in many applications.) Far less common for networks than it used to be, coax still is found in many building network backbones.

AMPLIFICATION

Generally speaking, a backbone is a high-capacity common link to which networks and communications devices are attached. A typical office building has several local area networks connected by a common backbone. To handle inter-network traffic successfully, the backbone must have significantly greater capacity than the networks it connects. There are several forms of backbones, ranging from a simple cable to a complete network.

TECHNICAL NOTE
Wire grades and connectors

UTP ratings are signified by grading schemes, the most common comprising a number of wire categories (cats) currently ranging from 1 to 6, with 6 being a relatively recent addition—TIA/EIA (Telecom Industry Association/Electronic Industry Associates) Standard 568. The cat 6 standard was released in June 2002. Cat 7 is now under consideration.

The higher the cat number, the more capable the wire is of carrying higher-speed data signals reliably and the more it costs. For computer communications, cats 3 and 5 still are prevalent because of existing (legacy) installations. Cat 5e (5 enhanced) and cat 6 are rapidly gaining as the demand for speed continues to grow—they are typical for new installations.

UTP connectors are denoted by RJ (radio jack) numbers. All UTP cables to date use the same connector, called an RJ-45. This looks like the connector commonly found on home telephones (called an RJ-11) but is designed to accommodate four wire pairs and is therefore somewhat wider than the two-wire-pair home phone connector.

STP originally was a bulky cable, in which each wire pair of a four-pair bundle was shielded. It evolved into a somewhat slimmer cable, with shielding around the bundle instead of each pair. IBM designed eight variations, called types; they were given numbers from 1 to 9 (type 7 was never specified). The most common were type 1 (two-pair) and type 2 (which added four voice pairs to the type 1 configuration).

IBM STP connectors are comparatively large and cumbersome, but they are unique in being neither male nor female, so they can be joined together directly. Other connectors, like the RJ-45, are male on the wire and require a female port or a female segment on the wire to be joined.

Coax is graded by RG (radio government) numbers, primarily based on impedance, a measure of total opposition to electrical flow, of which resistance is one component. Impedance, like resistance, is measured in ohms. RG 58 (50 ohms) and RG 59 (75 ohms) are common, the former (called thin coax) used in radio transmission systems and older local area networks, and the latter used for video and some long-distance applications. RG 11 (50 ohms, also called thick coax) is used in backbone layouts and older legacy local area networks. Network coax uses BNC connectors, rotating cylinders that lock with one-quarter turn, making secure contact with the central conductor and the shielding.

AMPLIFICATION

There are several versions of what BNC stands for. Among them are: **B**ayonet **N**eill-Concelman **C**onnector, named after an Amphenol engineer; **B**ritish **N**aval **C**onnector; and the most descriptive, **B**ayonet **N**ut **C**onnector.

2.5 Unguided media and antennas

All unguided media use antennas for transmission and receipt of signals. The word *antenna* conjures up images of thin metal wands extending from automobile fenders, tall towers with rectangular panels for cell phones, satellite TV dishes, and the like. Indeed, all these are antennas, but as we have seen, so is anything that conducts electricity and therefore

AMPLIFICATION

According to the FCC Web site (http://www.fcc. gov/), the FCC "is an independent United States government agency, directly responsible to Congress. The FCC was established by the Communications Act of 1934 and is charged with regulating interstate and international communications by radio, television, wire, satellite and cable. The FCC's jurisdiction covers the 50 states, the District of Columbia, and U.S. possessions."

Electrical cable installation and costs

Purchase price is only one part of the cost of wiring, and a relatively minor one at that. Therefore, when you install new wiring, it makes sense to use the highest grade available, even though its purchase cost per foot is higher. By the same token, because fire laws in most locales specify that cables running through plenums (enclosed air spaces such as dropped ceilings or shafts) be specially coated to prevent noxious fumes emanating from the cables in the event of a fire, and because cables might be relocated to plenums even if they are not initially installed there, it is a good idea to use coated cables.

The largest cost component is for installation and testing labor. For that reason, it is a good idea to install some extra wire for future expansion, because labor costs for adding wire later on are much higher. Some disruption to your business during added installation is also likely.

Whether new, expanded, or replaced, cable installation always should be done by qualified professionals. Improperly installed cables will not operate as expected. For example, to connect UTP to a patch panel, some of the twist has to be undone and some of the insulation stripped away. If this is done to excess, considerable crosstalk will occur. Similarly, to connect STP, the shielding must be properly attached to the connector or its shielding capabilities will be lost.

Contracts should require full labeling of all wire runs, connectors, and ports, performance guarantees, and warranties. More expensive than anything else is correcting and maintaining poor installations after the fact.

Following these simple ideas will help ensure that your installations are reliable. Further, as connectivity needs increase, technology improves, and greater speeds become possible, your wiring will remain viable longer, thereby postponing the day when wiring additions and upgrades will be needed.

can be the transmitter or recipient of induced radiation. In fact, even your body can act as an antenna. You can experience this phenomenon by touching a radio antenna connection or a TV rabbit-ears antenna—weak reception may improve.

Antennas come in a wide variety of shapes and sizes, designed for specific applications based on the portion of the electromagnetic radiation (EMR) spectrum that is used. The EMR spectrum, much of which is regulated by the Federal Communications Commission (FCC), has been divided into **bands** described by EMR frequency ranges or their associated wavelengths. Broadly speaking, there are three EMR groupings relevant to communications: radio waves, microwaves, and infrared light. In this grouping, radio waves have the lowest frequencies and longest wavelengths, and infrared light has the highest frequencies and shortest wavelengths. (See Table 2.1.)

TABLE 2.1   EMR frequency bands for communications

	Frequency (Hz)	Wavelength (m)	Type
Radio	Less than 3×10^9	10^{-1} and greater	Omni-directional
Microwave	3×10^9 to 3×10^{11}	10^{-1} to 10^{-3}	Line of sight
Infrared	3×10^{11} to 4×10^{14}	10^{-3} to 7×10^{-7}	Line of sight
Visible*	4×10^{14} to 7.5×10^{14}	7×10^{-7} to 4×10^{-7}	Line of sight

*Visible light is shown for comparison; it is not used in optical transmission systems.

The higher the frequency of the EMR, the more directional and focused the radiation. As a result, lower-frequency EMR is ***omnidirectional***—propagating in all directions at once. Higher-frequency EMR tends to travel in straight (though spreading) lines, called ***lines of sight*** (see Table 2.1); in principle, their transmitting and receiving antennas have to be aimed at each other such that if you were to draw a straight line from one, it would connect to the other.

The natural limit to line-of-sight antennas is the horizon, but we can extend the horizon by putting antennas on towers—the taller the tower, the farther the horizon extends. Of course, tower height has limits, especially considering the neighborhoods where they would need to be built. Then there is the terrain—distance to the horizon is one thing on a plain, another in the mountains, and still another in cities.

The line-of-sight requirement is eased somewhat by reflection, refraction (bending), diffraction, and gravity. Gravitational force attracts EMR as it does everything else. Microwaves, for example, tend to be pulled toward the earth as they travel. Therefore, though ostensibly traveling in straight lines, they actually curve somewhat. Although this bending is not enough to force microwaves to fully follow the curvature of the earth, it does allow microwave antennas to be farther apart than is required by a strict line-of-sight imperative.

AMPLIFICATION

When an electromagnetic signal hits the edge of an object that is large compared to the signal's wavelength, the signal propagates in many directions, with the edge as the apparent source. This is called ***diffraction.***

Depending on the material involved, EMR can pass through, be refracted, be diffracted, or be reflected. This means that two antennas whose line of sight is obstructed may still communicate. Consider these examples:

- Most television remotes use infrared beams. Although they ostensibly require line of sight, you can reflect the beams off of ceilings and walls to reach the television indirectly.
- Cell phones transmit in the microwave range. Their signals pass through some objects and also depend on reflection and diffraction to reach relay station antennas that are not in an unobstructed line of sight. (The next time you use a cell phone, look around to see if you can spot a relay antenna—chances are you can't.)

Unfortunately, reflection and diffraction can cause problems in distinguishing which received signals are appropriate, which are overly delayed, and which are duplicates. This is made all the more difficult by the fact that reflected and refracted signals take different routes, and so signal components and duplicate signals can arrive at different times, which can result in distortions or misinterpretations.

2.6 The basic nature of light

Over the centuries, people have struggled to understand what light is. So elusive this quest has been that a great many theories have been proposed, only to be discarded. About 2,000 years ago, the characteristics of light were defined by the way it *behaved* under a variety of conditions (***geometric optics***). The premise was that light consists of rays that move outward from their source in straight lines as long as they are traveling in a consistent medium (air, water, space, or glass, for example). When a ray of light hits another medium, as when sunlight strikes the surface of a lake, it may be reflected or refracted (bent).

This premise was good enough for some time, but it concentrated on descriptions of behavior rather than explanations. We now accept two complementary explanations. One considers light to be *waves of energy* (***wave optics***), which explains interference and diffraction. The other depicts light as *particles* (***quantum optics***), which explains how we can produce light by imposing electrical energy on some materials and how we can produce electricity by shining light onto others. We may consolidate these theories by thinking of light as a particle whose motions are wavelike. When we wish to describe a particular phenomenon, we use that aspect of light that most easily lets us analyze the situation.

Light diffraction, a wave phenomenon, has a direct application in communication by light: We use a diffraction grating to separate a light beam into its component wavelengths, each of which can carry information independently and simultaneously. This greatly multiplies the transmission capacity of light-based systems in a process called wavelength division multiplexing.

If you are interested in learning more about light and light phenomena, see Appendix C, "Light."

2.7 Common media for use with light

Light is a form of electromagnetic radiation that can be carried by both guided and unguided media. Although light rays can be beamed through the air and space just as radio waves and microwaves can, this is rarely done; hence, we will focus on guided media. (However, see Edison in Appendix G, "Communicating with light—some early efforts," for an extremely clever invention to transmit voice through the air by using light beams.)

The notion that light could be guided by a medium at all first "came to light" in the 1840s when John Tyndall found that a narrow stream of water could direct a beam of light along its trajectory. (See Tyndall's light pipe in Appendix G.) Realistic use of light to carry signals had to await the development of a more useful medium than water.

By the late 1880s, glass rods were used to guide light, but it wasn't until 1970 that the first practical use of glass for communications systems was demonstrated (by Corning Glass Works), using glass drawn into very fine strands called ***optical fibers.*** Optical fiber is not drawn from ordinary window glass, which contains many impurities and attenuates the light too quickly for use in communications systems. Instead, it is made of highly refined pure silica and has very low attenuation rates. (See Table 2.2.) For communications, we need optical fiber with carefully controlled optical densities and specific attenuation rates.

Table 2.2   Comparative purity of glass

Type of glass	Distance to reach half power point
Window	1 inch thick
Eyeglass	10 feet thick
Optical fiber	9 miles long

AMPLIFICATION

When discussing fiber-optic cables, we concentrate on glass. Some cables are made of plastic fibers. Although they are cheaper and easier to work with, they attenuate light more quickly. Most plastic fiber is used only where runs are very short.

The silica used to make glass optical fiber is a form of silicon, a very common element comprising about 28 percent of the earth's crust where it occurs mainly as silicates and oxides. Silica is a component of ordinary sand. Silicon is used in many computer components and gives its name to Silicon Valley, California. Silicon is different from silicone, a man-made inorganic polymer not found in nature.

It is revealing to note that historically, the development of light sources and optical media progressed along independent lines. As a result, they often did not correspond well to communications needs. One particularly vital issue was matching the wavelengths of the light that could be produced with the wavelengths that the fibers could carry best. Rather than wait for the perfect match, less-than-ideal combinations were used. For a time, this delayed the deployment of optical systems for communications. Now that light sources and fiber are more closely compatible, implementation is growing rapidly.

Attenuation of light is the primary way we measure the relative purity of different kinds of glass. A common criterion for attenuation is the ***half power point***—the point in its travel at which a signal, in this case a light beam, has lost half of its original power. To give you an idea of the purity of optical fiber, we compare its half power points to those of window glass and the glass used in eyeglasses. This table shows typical values.

We see that light can travel 570,240 times as far through optical fiber as it can through window glass (9 miles = 570,240 inches) and 4,752 times as far as it can through eyeglass (9 miles = 47,520 feet), highlighting the optical purity of glass fiber.

Optical fiber cables

In an optical fiber cable, the signal-carrying fiber, called the ***core***, runs through the cable axially. It is surrounded by ***cladding*** designed to reflect light to keep it within the core; a ***coating*** layer covering the cladding absorbs light rays that escape the core and are moving out through the cladding.

Typically, hundreds and even thousands of fibers are bundled together. Because the extremely thin fibers are easily broken, strengthening and protective material is added to the cable—non-light-conducting material such as Kevlar and steel wires. Each strand or the entire cable may be jacketed as well. (See Figure 2.4.)

FIGURE 2.4

Optical cable construction
for a single fiber

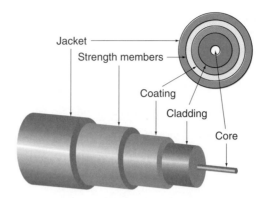

The core has a greater *index of refraction* (is more optically dense) than the cladding so that between the two, *total internal reflection* occurs. This keeps the light beam in the core as it travels along. Now we can understand how Tyndall's light pipe worked—the optical density of a water stream is much greater than that of the surrounding air, so the light rays are contained within the stream.

If you want to learn more, refraction and total internal reflection are explained in Appendix C.

Optical fiber types

Two basic types of optical fiber are *multimode* and *single mode.* Historically, multimode fibers were the first to be produced. They have relatively large core diameters—50,000 nm (nanometers), 62,500 nm, and 100,000 nm (or 50 μm (micrometers), 62.5 μm, and 100 μm)—so light rays can enter the fibers at many angles relative to the core axis; shortly, we will see why this is an issue.

The two varieties of multimode cores are *step index* and *graded index.* Step index core density is constant from the center to the edges, so there is an abrupt change (step) in density at the interface between the core and the cladding. Graded index core density is greatest at the center of the core and decreases (is graded) toward the edges, so rays of light traveling at an angle are more likely to refract toward the center of the core, keeping them contained.

Single-mode core is uniformly dense but has very much smaller diameters than multimode fiber (typically ranging from 8 μm to 10 μm, although a diameter of just 7 μm is now available), so small that relatively few wavelengths of light can pass through. At these diameters, rays can enter the core at essentially only one angle—the one that goes straight through the core axis.

Table 2.3 shows the diameters of the different fiber types and, for comparison, of human hair. We see that step index core diameter is about the same as a human hair,

Table 2.3 Fiber-optic cable diameters (See Figure 2.5.)

Fiber type	Typical core diameter (μm)	Total diameter* (μm)
Step index multimode	50	250
Graded index multimode	62.5	250
Single-mode	7–10	250
Human hair	50	50

*core + cladding + coating

whereas single-mode fiber core is about 1/5th the diameter of a human hair. This highlights the technical difficulties of producing a light source small enough that it can be physically coupled to the fiber, yet can emit a powerful beam of light.

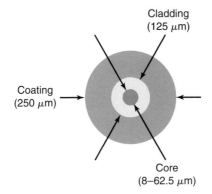

Cladding
(125 μm)

Coating
(250 μm)

Core
(8–62.5 μm)

FIGURE 2.5

Fiber optic cable diameters

Business NOTE — Fiber-optic cable installation and costs

Fiber-optic cable installation requires even more care and expertise than electrical cable installation and should be done only by fully qualified professionals. It is critical not to curve the cable more than its specified minimum bend radius to avoid damaging the fiber, which will substantially reduce its effectiveness. Even if the bend is not too severe, the sharper the curve, the more likely that light beams will be refracted into the cladding, and therefore lost to the transmission.

Careful attention must be paid to avoid excess stretching. Simply lowering a cable down a shaft, if not done properly, can cause it to stretch too much just from its own weight. Aside from breaking the fibers, even moderate stretching narrows the fiber, which increases attenuation. Special devices are used to avoid this problem. Joining (splicing) fiber cables and attaching them to connectors also requires special care and devices.

All in all, installation of fiber-optic cable is an exacting and expensive proposition. On the other hand, correcting a poor installation is a much more expensive proposition. Because labor cost is the biggest expense item, extra fiber should be installed; adding more at a later date will be much more costly as well as potentially disruptive to normal business. Finally, no job should be accepted or final payment made until the installation is fully labeled, tested, and proved to be functioning properly.

For additional information, see Appendix D, "Optical fiber."

2.8 Light sources for computer communications

As in all communications systems, there are three related components: a source of the signal, a medium to conduct signals, and a receiver to accept information. For optical communications systems, signals are carried by light created by *LEDs* and *lasers,* the medium is *optical fiber,* and the receiver is a *light detector.*

Optical communications systems have to deal with more complex issues than do electrical communications systems. The technology available to economically manufacture lasers or LEDs that produce particular light wavelengths is a limiting factor in the communications chain. To further complicate the issue, the behavior of light in optical fiber varies dramatically with different wavelengths.

The extreme thinness of optical fiber magnifies the problem of manufacturing light sources—coupling a light source to these fibers requires that the source's output dimension be comparable to fiber core diameters. This is a major practical issue, because not only do we need the source to create an exceedingly narrow beam of light, the beam must also be powerful enough to make a long journey through the fiber.

Whatever the source, we need to match the wavelengths of light that the light source can produce to the properties of the available optical media. Currently, only LEDs and lasers that produce light beams in the infrared range fill the bill.

AMPLIFICATION

Radio frequency and light are part of the electromagnetic spectrum, a continuous ordered range of radiated frequencies, about half of which is used in computer communications. Sometimes the entire spectrum is referred to as "light," and sometimes it is referenced by its components (for example, radio waves, microwaves, infrared, visible light, and so on), which occupy different parts of the spectrum.

Our eyes are sensitive to a range of light wavelengths called the **visible spectrum.** Particular wavelengths in that range determine the colors we see. Infrared light used in optical communications systems has wavelengths outside the range detectable by the human eye.

If you want to explore LEDs and lasers further, see Appendix C. For more information, see

http://imagine.gsfc.nasa.gov/docs/science/ know_l1/emspectrum.html

2.9 Lighting up the core

Step index multimode core diameters are huge compared to light wavelengths. Thus, source light rays can enter the core at many different angles. As Figure 2.6A shows, there are three possibilities:

- The light ray points straight through the core.
- The angle of refraction is at least 90° at the core/cladding interface, so we have total internal reflection (see Appendix C)—the light ray reflects off the surface of the cladding repeatedly as it zigzags down the fiber core. (If the angle of incidence is precisely 90°, the light ray travels straight through the core after the first reflection.)
- The angle of refraction is less than 90°—the light ray is refracted into the cladding and absorbed by the coating.

The first possibility is the ideal, because the rays follow the shortest path through the fiber. The third situation is the worst, because all the energy of the rays refracted into the cladding is lost to the signal. The second result is the most complex; rays following a zigzag path travel farther than those that go straight through. Moreover, the steeper a ray's angle of reflection, the farther it has to travel, so the longer it takes to reach the receiver.

Why does the second result matter? Because it can cause signal distortion or loss. Light beam signals are composed of many rays. Each ray, being part of the same beam,

FIGURE 2.6

Optical fiber cables

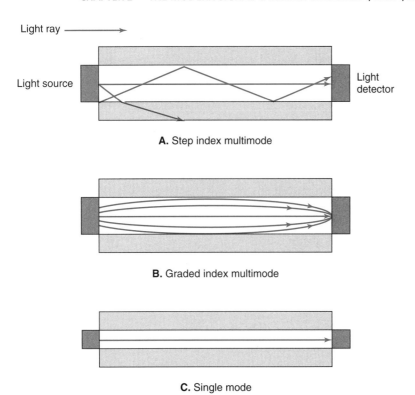

Light ray

Light source

Light detector

A. Step index multimode

B. Graded index multimode

C. Single mode

carries the same information. Because rays traveling different distances reach the receiver at different times, the receiver may not be able to distinguish between a late-arriving ray and a ray from the next piece of information.

The longer the cable, the greater the time difference, so the greater the likelihood of signal distortion or loss. This is one factor that limits the practical length of step index multimode cable. Others have to do with the light sources typically used and light absorption. Still, under the right conditions and where cable runs are relatively short, the low costs of the cable and light source make step index multimode a good choice.

Another consideration: Rarely can cables be installed in completely straight lines. Rather, they must be curved around various obstacles and follow layouts. The more sharply a cable is bent, the greater the likelihood that as the reflecting ray hits the curve it may be refracted into the cladding rather than reflected within the core.

Graded index fiber was designed as a partial solution to the zigzag and curved cable problems. Because its core density decreases from center to edge, light rays entering at an angle refract toward the more dense center of the core before they reach the cladding (see Figure 2.6B). This means that more of the original rays carry through the fiber, so there is less loss of signal strength than with step index. Refraction of the differently angled rays also reduces the distance they have to travel, which in turn reduces signal distortion. Capacity is much greater as well.

Although graded index relaxes cable length limits somewhat, as distances and speeds increase, even small time differences in the arriving rays are enough to confuse the receiver. For these situations, what we need is a core through which essentially all light rays travel down its center. This is what single-mode fiber is about.

Single-mode fiber has such small diameters that issues of zigzag paths disappear. Essentially only one ray of light enters—the one that travels straight through the core (that is, a single mode). As shown in Figure 2.6C, by using a low-density, narrow-diameter core and a highly focused light beam, in essence all the light rays take the straight-through path and experience very little attenuation. Capacity is much greater as well. Single-mode fiber cables should be used for long-distance transmissions and very high-speed communications.

TECHNICAL NOTE
Caution: lasers and safety

Lasers of many different types have found their way into a wide variety of applications. Lasers can cut steel, repair torn retinas, improve vision, play our CDs and DVDs, and make very good pointers. They also produce the light beams that carry our information in optical communications systems.

Whether laser light is in a visible wavelength range or not, even the relatively low-powered lasers used for communications can severely damage an unprotected eye and can even cause blindness. Therefore, never look into an optical fiber (or any laser-producing device) without proper eye protection unless you know with *absolute certainty* that no laser light is being transmitted!

For a great deal of specific information on laser safety, visit

http://www.repairfaq.org/sam/lasersaf.htm.

Business NOTE
Choosing the right components

Optical fibers carry light best at particular wavelengths and attenuate different wavelengths at different rates. Light sources produce light of particular powers and wavelengths. Optical detectors need a certain amount of light to function properly. How can you go about selecting a fiber-optic system that will perform successfully in light of these various requirements? How can you ensure that a design you commission is appropriate? The answer to both these questions is: by constructing an **optical link loss budget.** Appendix D explains.

2.10 Signal impairments in light transmission

One of the great advantages of optical fiber and light waves is that they are not subject to interference or distortion from electrical or magnetic forces, nor do they radiate any electrical or magnetic disturbances. But just as with any electromagnetic radiation, as light travels it loses power (attenuates). This is the principal source of optical transmission impairment. The four main causes of light attenuation are absorption, scattering, bends, and coupling.

Absorption results from various impurities that find their way into the fiber during its manufacture. Chief among these is water. Although it seems odd, glass fiber does contain water molecules. At the typical light frequencies used for communications, water molecules can absorb light. The more water, the more absorption and the greater the attenuation.

Wavelength also plays a role in absorption: The shorter the wavelength, the more energy is absorbed. So attenuation is greater for the shorter wavelengths used with multi-mode cables than for the longer ones used with single-mode cables—one more reason why multimode cables are useful only for short distance transmissions and single-mode cables are appropriate for long distances.

Scattering is caused by small contaminants and density differences in the core. Scattered light can be reflected back to the source or refracted into the cladding. Either way, the power of the transmitted beams is attenuated.

Bends are classified as macro and micro. Macro-bending is the kind you can easily see—when the cable is curved around some obstacle or when extra cable is hung in loops. Instead of terminating every cable at the precise length needed to reach its end connection, extra length is often left to allow for access, such as when equipment has to be pulled. (This applies to electrical cable, too.) Nominally, light travels in straight lines, so to follow a bend the beam must reflect off the cladding. If the bend is sharp enough, the light will refract into the cladding instead of following the bend. With step-index multimode fiber, even small bends can result in power loss; with single-mode fiber, a bend that is too sharp will cause all light to be lost to the cladding! (This is apart from the minimum bend radius, which also takes into account physical damage from a bend that is too sharp.)

Micro-bending is usually the result of mishandling, which produces very small kinks or sections where the cable was compressed. These deformities may be difficult to see with the unaided eye. Micro-bends also can result in light refracting into the cladding.

Coupling refers to splicing (joining) cables and attaching cables to connectors. This is much more complex than the comparable processes for electrical cables. Any fiber coupling that is even slightly out of alignment or incompletely joined will result in significant power losses, severe enough to disrupt communications. In fact, no matter how well the coupling is done, there is always some loss of light in the transition from one spliced section to the next or from the fiber to a connector.

2.11 Mixed systems: converting electricity to light and vice versa

Today's computers and computer-based communications equipment create and process electrical signals. This means that where optical communications systems come into play, there must be a conversion from electricity to light at the sending end and light to electricity at the receiving end—or, in fact, any place in between where electrical and light systems must join. At every such location, additional equipment is needed and extra processing must take place.

Even more to the point, the overall speed of communication is limited by the electrical pieces of the system, which react more slowly, and transformation processing. So although light over fiber can achieve far higher speeds than electricity over copper, communication speed still is constrained by having to make conversions between light and electricity and having to handle electrical signals at slower rates.

Here we have another example of need propelling development; there is a substantial research effort underway to build equipment that can process light directly, which would enable an entire communications system to function with light signals alone. For now, focus is on the specialized computers used within communications systems. Today they operate entirely electrically, but IBM and Bell Laboratories have demonstrated the possibility of operating a computer via light signals. When this becomes a reality, the sky is the limit for the speed of communications systems!

2.12 Summary

In this chapter, we explored the basic natures of electricity and light, uncovering some of their properties that are relevant to carrying information over network communications systems. We looked at several of the impairments encountered as we send signals via electricity and light, how they affect our transmissions, and what might be done about them. We also discussed the most popular media for carrying electrical and light-based signals and examined important installation considerations.

We considered electricity's long reign as the preferred carrier of high-speed communications and noted the growing emergence of light-based transmission, already a major player in long-distance links, for general communication. As light technology develops in response to mounting pressure for faster and more capable communications systems, light will succeed electricity as the dominant carrier of information. The replacement of electronic computing by light computing will lead to skyrocketing growth in optical communications systems.

If you wish to explore these topics in greater detail, read appendices B and C.

In the next chapter, we will explore signals—what they are, how they are created, and their characteristics.

END-OF-CHAPTER QUESTIONS

Short Answer

1. Describe the effects of attenuation on electrical or light signals.
2. What does the plus and minus voltage of alternating current indicate?
3. Describe the process of radiation as it relates to sending a signal through the air or space.
4. List the names of the EMR frequency bands used for communications.

5. How does a line-of-sight requirement affect communication tower locations?
6. Why is thermal noise a particular problem?
7. Discuss the ways in which light has been described and explained.
8. Describe the three types of optical fiber.

9. Why is professional installation of electrical and optical cable systems a good idea?
10. Describe the four main causes of attenuation in optical fiber.

Fill-in

1. The type of electricity most applicable to networks is _____.
2. The three EMR groupings relevant to communications are _____, _____, and _____.
3. Hertz (Hz) denotes _____.
4. Frequency is _____ related to period.
5. The distance a wave travels in one cycle is its _____.
6. The two categories of signal impairments are _____ and _____.

7. The two types of light source for optical fiber systems are _____ and _____.
8. The fiber-optic cable whose density decreases from the core axis is _____.
9. The type of optical fiber best suited for long-distance communications is _____.
10. _____ fiber has about the same diameter as human hair, whereas _____ fiber's diameter is about one-fifth that of human hair.

Multiple-choice

1. A material that strongly resists electrical flow is called a(n)
   a. conductor
   b. insulator
   c. medium
   d. semiconductor
   e. cable

2. The number of times a sine wave repeats itself in one second is its
   a. cycle
   b. period
   c. frequency
   d. amplitude
   e. wavelength

3. The signal impairment caused by induction of energy in one wire from signals in another wire is
   a. thermal noise
   b. impulse noise
   c. delay distortion
   d. crosstalk
   e. intermodulation distortion

4. The signal impairment that results from non-linearities in a communications system is
   a. thermal noise
   b. impulse noise
   c. delay distortion
   d. crosstalk
   e. intermodulation distortion

5. The purpose of the twists in UTP is
   a. to reduce crosstalk
   b. to allow more pairs to be bundled in one cable
   c. to keep the wire pairs separated from each other
   d. to eliminate thermal noise
   e. to strengthen the cable

6. Fiber-optic cables
   a. have less capacity for carrying data than copper cables
   b. use visible light as the message carrier
   c. attenuate light signals
   d. are extremely flexible
   e. are easier to install than copper cables

7. The material in a fiber-optic cable that absorbs light rays escaping the fiber is the
   a. core
   b. cladding
   c. coating
   d. jacket
   e. sheath

8. The material in a fiber-optic cable the carries the signal is the
   a. core
   b. cladding
   c. coating
   d. jacket
   e. sheath

9. The minimum bend radius of a cable
   a. indicates how much to bend a cable coil
   b. exists only for electrical cable
   c. exists only for optical fiber cable
   d. cannot be exceeded without damaging the cable
   e. is a measure of cable diameter

10. In long-distance communications systems today
    a. conversions between electrical and light signals are required
    b. most transmission lines are fiber optic
    c. twisted pair wiring is not used
    d. communications speed is limited by the electrical components and the need for signal carrier conversion
    e. all of the above

True or false

1. All conductors offer some resistance to electrical flow.
2. A sine wave is aperiodic.
3. Resistance is directly proportional to wire length and indirectly proportional to wire diameter.
4. Reflection, refraction, and diffraction enable cell phone communications in areas where line-of-sight is not practical.
5. Thermal noise can be eliminated by shielding the cable.
6. Impulse noise is avoidable because it is predictable.
7. Delay distortion is one factor that limits cable length.
8. Multimode optical fiber admits light rays at many angles to the core axis.
9. The larger the minimum bend radius, the more sharply a cable can be bent without damage.
10. Graded index fiber was designed to ease the zigzag problem of step index fiber.

Expansion and exploration

1. Suppose your company is contemplating rewiring its in-house networks. What would you consider to decide between a copper-based scheme and an optical fiber-based scheme?

2. Investigate the phenomenon of total internal reflection. Why is this important for the operation of optical fiber communications systems?

3. Go to the IEEE Web site (http://www.ieee.org); what is the status of the cat 7 twisted pair standard? Describe cat 7 twisted pair.

3

Signal fundamentals

3.1 Overview

Before we can send information over a communications network, it must be transformed into something the network can handle—that is, into *signals.* There are two basic forms of *information—analog* and *digital.* Analog information is produced by real events, such as a speaker's voice or a band playing music. It is called analog because it is always in some way analogous (similar) to the event that caused it. As such, it may take on any values created by the event: potentially an infinite number of values. Digital information is produced by computers, which work with bits. Hence, digital information is composed of just two values: 0 and 1.

To represent information of any type, signals must change shape over time—without change, no information can be carried. There are two basic types of *signals—analog* and *digital.* Either type of information can be represented by either type of signal. Thus, there are four possibilities: we can carry analog information as analog signals or as digital signals, and we can carry digital information as analog signals or as digital signals.

The information type, signal type, and how information is transformed have great impact on how successfully the signals travel through a communications system. In this chapter, we will look at basic signal properties, signal types, and their implications for transmission quality. In Chapter 4, "Encoding," we will explore a variety of encoding techniques that are used create the signals that carry our data.

3.2 Analog signals

Analog signals have two major characteristics:

- They are continuous and hence take on whatever shape or power is needed to represent information—an infinite number of values may come into play.
- They cannot change shape instantaneously, although the change can happen in an extremely short amount of time.

As an example of an analog signal, a portion of the signal representing the sound waves produced by someone speaking may look like the patterns shown in Figure 3.1. The "up and down" variations closely follow the speaker's voice patterns. In B, we can see that the seemingly sharp peaks of A actually are rounded—very fast but not instantaneous change.

A. A small part of a sound signal

FIGURE 3.1

Sound waves: an example
of analog signals over
time

B. Zooming in on a very small part of the signal in A

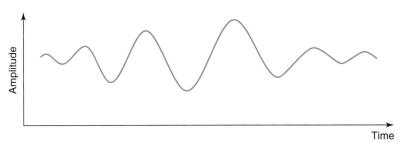

Of the infinite possible analog signal shapes, the class of **sinusoids** (sine waves) has a special place. Sinusoids are perhaps the simplest of all signal shapes found in nature; in one form or another they are omnipresent in our modern society. Most importantly for communications, sine waves are the building blocks of *all* signals!

All signals are combinations of simple sine waves.

Figure 3.2 illustrates the three characteristics of sine waves, expressed at any time t by the equation $s(t) = A \sin(2\pi f t + \varphi)$: maximum amplitude A, frequency f (the number of times the sine wave pattern repeats per second), and phase φ (its angular point relative to time $t = 0$). For a derivation of this equation, as well as a full discussion of sine wave characteristic components, see Appendix A, "Sine waves: basic properties and signal shifting."

AMPLIFICATION

Figure 3.2 is typical for sine waves formed by electricity, in which case amplitude is measured by voltage. We recall from Chapter 2, "The modern signal carriers," that positive and negative voltage refers to direction of flow; hence in the figure, we use positive and negative amplitude.

HISTORICAL NOTE
Analog signals and the phonograph

Thomas Alva Edison (1847–1931) was a renowned inventor whose discoveries dramatically changed the world we live in. Among his many accomplishments, the phonograph is of interest in our discussion of analog signals.

In the earliest versions of this invention, sound captured by a megaphone caused a needle to vibrate analogously; as it did, it moved around a wax recording surface, cutting grooves that corresponded to its vibrations—analog signal representations of the sounds. To re-create the sounds, a needle traveled inside the grooves, which caused it to vibrate as the recording needle had. These vibrations created analogous sound waves, amplified by a megaphone. (In later models, vibrations created an analogous electric current that was amplified and sent to speakers to re-create the sounds.) If we strongly magnified the grooves, we would see patterns like the ones shown in Figure 3.1A.

In Figure 3.2A, we see two sine waves with the same frequency and phase but different peak amplitudes; 3.2B shows two sine waves with the same peak amplitude and phase but different frequencies; 3.2C has two sine waves with the same amplitude and frequency but different phases. Although each of these illustrations shows variation of just one characteristic at a time, any combination of characteristic variations is possible—for example, changes in both amplitude and phase with frequency constant, or even changes in all three.

FIGURE 3.2

Sine wave characteristics: amplitude, frequency, phase

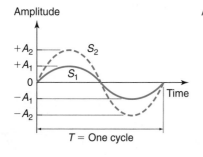

A. Two sine waves with the same frequency and phase but different amplitudes

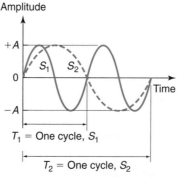

B. Two sine waves with the same amplitude and phase but different frequencies

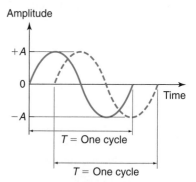

C. Two sine waves with the same amplitude and frequency but different phases

In simplest form, to represent the 0s and 1s of digital data we need to vary just one characteristic of the sine wave. For example, we could represent 0 and 1 bits by peak amplitudes A_1 and A_2, or by frequencies f_1 and f_2, or by phases φ_1 and φ_2. The resulting signal is a composite sine wave. For reasons we will see in Chapter 4, we also may want to vary combinations of these characteristics, creating more complex composite signals.

Although it might seem logical that analog data could be transmitted directly, that is not the case, because doing so would vastly underutilize analog transmission systems (as we will see when we discuss multiplexing in Chapter 6, "Communications connections"), and this would not work at all with digital transmission systems. Composite sine waves come into play here as well.

The analog signals that carry analog or digital data comprise composites built from combinations of simple sine waves.

The following are some advantages of analog signals:

- They provide a very faithful copy of analog information.
- Conceptually, they are a straightforward way to represent real events.
- They usually can travel quite far before showing appreciable shape distortions due to the properties of the medium.
- They are easy to create and handle.

However, analog signals have one major disadvantage that, especially for computer communications, outweighs all their advantages—susceptibility to damage from noise.

Noise adds to a signal, resulting in a composite signal that no longer closely corresponds to the original signal's shape. To recover the original signal, the noise would have to be separated out, possible only if the receiver knows either the original signal shape or the shape of the noise that added to it. But the receiver does not know the original shape—if it did, there would be no need to send the signal in the first place—and there is no way to guess at what it might have been because, as we have noted, an analog signal can take on any of an infinite number of shapes.

The noise effect cannot be known accurately, either, because noise shapes and strengths are random. Therefore, the receiver cannot precisely reconstitute the original signal. We can take steps to reduce noise, but we cannot eliminate it. Hence, the problem remains.

Reconstructing a noise-deformed analog signal exactly is an impossible task.

3.3 Digital signals

The noise susceptibility of analog signals, a direct consequence of the infinite possible values that analog signals can take, leads to the concept of using a different type of signal, one that needs only a very small set of very simple shapes. Examples of digital signal shapes are shown in Figure 3.3.

FIGURE 3.3

Some digital signal shapes

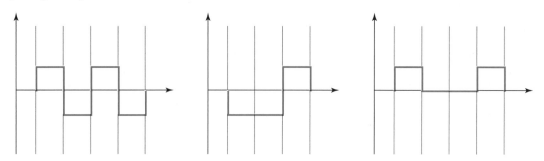

Because of the limited number of shapes, even if they are corrupted by noise it usually is possible to guess, with a high degree of confidence, what the original signal was. We could further improve our guess if the signal shapes were chosen to be very different from each other, making it highly unlikely, although not impossible, that noise could alter one shape to such an extent that we might be fooled into thinking it could have started out as another (see Figure 3.4). This is precisely what is done in digital signal representation of information.

Digital signals have two major characteristics:

- They are discrete, so their voltage is limited to a vary small set of values.
- *Theoretically,* when the value of the digital signal needs to change, it changes instantaneously—for example, when amplitude changes from +5 V to −5 V, the change theoretically happens in *zero* time, as represented by the sharp corners in the shapes of Figure 3.4. However, no physical phenomenon can change instantaneously. See Figure 3.5 and "Technical note: The nature of instantaneous change in digital signal values."

AMPLIFICATION

The word *digital* derives from the word for fingers—*digits*. Just as the digits of our hands are discrete and limited in number, so too are digital signal shapes.

FIGURE 3.4

Noise altering the amplitude (power) of a digital signal

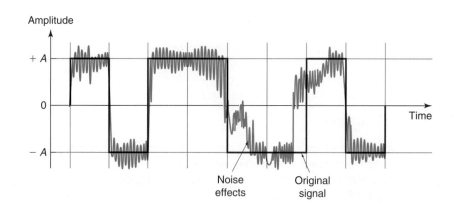

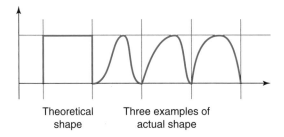

FIGURE 3.5

Instantaneous change—
theoretical and actual

Theoretical
shape

Three examples of
actual shape

Because digital signals are not direct analogs of real physical events, such as the sounds of a person speaking or a band playing, such analog information can only be approximated. With appropriate techniques, the approximations can be quite good. When the original information is digital to begin with, as it is for computer-generated data, approximations are not necessary. However, transformation still is needed to put the data in a form that can travel over the digital communications system. Throughout the text of this chapter, we will discuss applications of these techniques and provide examples that illustrate these concepts.

TECHNICAL NOTE
The nature of instantaneous change in digital signal values

Theoretically, digital signal values change instantaneously in zero time. In the "real" world, nothing can actually change in zero time. But the idealized digital signals that do so are useful in simplifying our study of complex real systems. Further, the change is so rapid that to a very good approximation we can consider it to be instantaneous. This simplification greatly reduces the effort needed to study the behavior of digital signals as they make their way through a variety of communications systems.

The following are two advantages of digital signal representation:

• Even when corrupted by noise, digital signals usually can be restored to their original shapes, making them a robust way of carrying information.
• Digital signals are a natural and intuitive way of representing bit-based computer information—a straightforward transformation process. As an example, we could use +10 V to represent a 1-bit and +5 V to represent a 0-bit (see Figure 3.6). (In Chapter 4, we explore the details of signal creation and data representation.)

The following are two disadvantages of digital signal representation:

• Although digital signals accurately represent computer data, they never exactly represent real-world (analog) phenomena. Therefore, the best that we can hope for is a close approximation. We are willing to live with approximations, because the noise immunity provided outweighs the loss in accuracy.

- Everything else being equal, digital signals cannot travel as far along a medium as analog signals can before being unacceptably distorted due to the properties of the medium. This is related to the abrupt changes that occur as digital signals make the transition from one value to another value in essentially zero time. Electrical media, and even optical media to a lesser extent, do not handle these rapid transitions well.

FIGURE 3.6

Representing bits with digital signals—an example

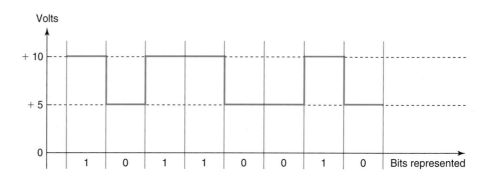

The technology needed to create and handle digital signals is more complex than for analog signals. However, with the amazing strides made in the miniaturization of electronic components and the accompanying dramatic drop in their cost, this is no longer an issue. Digital signaling has become the norm for communications.

Digital signal representation is standard in computer communications.

3.4 Signal amplification and regeneration

All signals suffer some attenuation as they travel. Without any help, a signal traveling a long distance could arrive at its destination in a state too weakened to be recognized reliably, if at all. Because of this, signals are intercepted at points where they are still accurately recognizable, strengthened, and sent on. The number of points needed depends on the type of signal, the media characteristics, and distance. In any case, strengthening is done by amplification for analog signals and by regeneration for digital signals.

Analog signals and amplifiers

When a signal of a given shape is sent through an ***amplifier,*** it exits with the same shape and increased strength. But in its journey to the amplifier, the signal will not have stayed pure; it will have been affected by noise and other distortions. So when it enters the amplifier, the signal is actually a composite of the original signal plus the corruptions.

The amplifier boosts *all* composite components—the signal, the noise, and any other distortions—equally, and there is no way to know which part is the original signal, which part is noise, and which part is other distortions (see "Technical note: Amplification and analog signals"). This unfortunate consequence of analog signals, as we have seen, is a shortcoming that led to the introduction and increasing popularity of digital signaling.

TECHNICAL NOTE
Amplification and analog signals

We can see the effect of and problem with amplification by an example, using the equation for a sine wave:

$$s(t) = A \sin(2\pi ft + \varphi)$$

Suppose our signal has maximum amplitude of 5 V and phase is 0. That is:

$$s(t) = 5 \sin(2\pi ft)$$

If we put that pure signal through an amplifier with an amplification factor of 10, what emerges (ignoring distortions produced by the amplifier itself), is:

$$s(t) = \underline{50} \sin(2\pi ft)$$

But before reaching the amplifier, noise and other distortions have been added, resulting in the composite signal:

$$s(t) = 5 \sin(2\pi ft) + \text{noise} + \text{other distortions}$$

And because all components of this signal are amplified equally, what actually emerges is one inseparable composite signal:

$$s(t) = \underline{50} \sin(2\pi ft) + \underline{10}\,\text{noise} + \underline{10}\,\text{other distortions}$$

Digital signals and regenerators

Because it often is possible to deduce the original digital signal shapes even in the face of various distortions, we can use a strategy different from a simple power boost to strengthen them—*regeneration.* The regenerator does its job in two steps:

1. Discern the original shapes of the signal that actually enters the regenerator.
2. Re-create the signal accordingly, and send it on with its original shape and power.

Thus, the issue of amplifying a distorted signal vanishes and the regenerated signal is a perfect copy of the original. Here's how this works: The regenerator uses a rule that depends on how bit values are represented to determine the original shapes of an incoming signal. For example, we may call a received pulse between +1 V and +3 V a 0-bit and a pulse between −1 V and −3 V a 1-bit. The "between" rule is meant to account for noise and attenuation. Thus, if we send a +3 V pulse that attenuates to +2.7 V, or due to a noise pulse of −1.5 V arrives as +1.5 V, it still will be properly recognized.

There is no foolproof decision rule; some values of noise and other distortions can always result in a mistake. The gap (in this example between ±1 V) in this type of rule is designed so that a high percentage of the distortions do not change a signal to a value on the wrong side of the gap. If a signal falls in the gap, we would rather have the regenerator make no choice and call the arriving signal an error to be dealt with by other means. How high is a high percentage? That depends on the nature of the transmission system and the requirements of the designer. We need to take this into account when deciding where to place the regenerators. But no matter what, errors still are possible. (Error detection and correction is explored in Chapter 5, "Error control.") Figure 3.7 illustrates these ideas.

FIGURE 3.7

Correct and erroneous
received digital signals

(For clarity other signal
distortions are omitted)

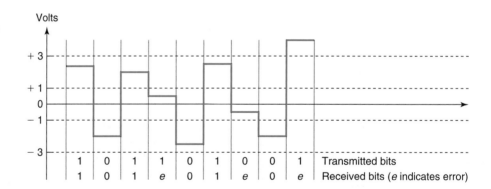

| | 1 | 0 | 1 | 1 | 0 | 1 | 0 | 0 | 1 | Transmitted bits |
| | 1 | 0 | 1 | *e* | 0 | 1 | *e* | 0 | *e* | Received bits (*e* indicates error) |

TECHNICAL NOTE
Regenerators and repeaters

In the world of communications systems, two devices sometimes are confused—the regenerator and the repeater. The regenerator re-creates a weakened digital signal. The repeater is simply a pass-along device that does not enhance the signal in any way; it is used to send signals to parts of a communications system that otherwise would not have access to them. A hub, used in some Ethernet local area networks (LANs), is a repeater. The confusion probably arises because some devices called repeaters have a regeneration function added to them. Though properly called "regenerating repeaters," they sometimes are referred to as just repeaters.

3.5 Signal analysis

Signals that carry our information through the communications systems may travel over thousands of miles of media, passing through a variety equipment that may re-direct and/or strengthen them. The media and equipment interact with the signals in ways that are entirely dependent on the signal shapes. For a communications system to be useful, these interaction must not change signal shapes beyond proper recognition, for if they do, the information they carry will not be recoverable and the system will be useless for communications.

To ensure that our communications systems will deliver our signals successfully, we need to take into account how signals and systems interact. With an infinite number of potential signal shapes, this seems like an impossible task. If we were to analyze how a particular system interacts with one shape, how could we draw conclusions about any other shapes? Yet, if we attempted to study interactions with every possible signal, the task would never end. Luckily, the work and insight of several investigators provide us with the tools necessary to tackle this problem.

Signal decomposition

Newton realized that white light (sunlight) was actually a blend of the ***primary colors*** of light—**R**ed, **G**reen, and **B**lue (***RGB***) and that all the colors we see also are blends of the primary colors (see "Historical note: Newton and sunlight"). Jean Baptiste Joseph Fourier, and later James Clerk Maxwell, demonstrated that all time-based signals are a blend of appropriate combinations of basic sine waves called ***elementary signals.*** (See "Historical note: Fourier and the decomposition of signals.")

When a beam of light is separated into its component colors, the resulting array of colors is called the ***beam's spectrum;*** when a signal (analog or digital) is separated into its elementary signals, the resulting collection of sine waves is called the ***signal's spectrum.***

HISTORICAL NOTE
Newton and sunlight

Isaac Newton (1642–1727), often regarded as the most important figure in the development of science, invented the calculus, developed the theory of gravity, constructed the basis of classical mechanics, and provided crucial insights into the nature of light. The last item provides an apt analogy to the way we approach the analysis of signals.

The well-known tale of an apple falling from a tree in Newton's garden, landing on the unsuspecting man's head, is offered as the inspiration that led him to the idea of gravity. A somewhat more whimsical story tells of Newton's discovery of the composition of light. While having breakfast one fine, sunny morning at a table near a window, Newton was amazed to see that rays of sunlight streaming in from the window and passing through a triangular glass dish on the table emerged from the other side of the dish as a rainbow of colors. Where had the colored lights come from, he wondered? Sunlight (also called *white* light) entered the glass dish, and yet all those colors were leaving it!

Pondering the mystery, he repeated the event under controlled conditions and came to the conclusion that white light actually was composed of all the colors blended together; the triangular glass dish (a prism) separated (decomposed) the white light into its constituent colors. He also noted that when the colors were passed through an inverted prism, they were recombined into white light. But when he tried to decompose the constituent colors by passing them through a second prism, he found that they were not further divisible; he called them primary colors.

He further determined that by blending together an appropriate number of primary colors, any other color of visible light could be created. Today, the set of primary light colors, red, green, and blue (RGB), is used in varying intensities to create the myriad colors produced on our computer monitors and television screens. The flip side of this is that a ray of light whose color is not one of the primaries can be decomposed into the set of primary colors RGB.

We can use two methods to determine the spectrum of a particular signal:

- Mathematical analysis—techniques developed by Fourier enable us to describe any signal by a mathematical expression.
- Spectrum analyzer—the spectrum of a "live" signal can be determined by feeding it into a spectrum analyzer, which produces a graphical display showing the sine waves that make up the spectrum.

We can infer a signal's behavior as it travels through a communications system by the behavior of its sine wave components. This is a far easier task than trying to determine a signal's behavior directly. As a practical matter, most of the time we do not actually need to determine the spectrum of an individual signal. Rather, we design our communications systems to work with a class of signals of a particular bandwidth.

HISTORICAL NOTE
Fourier and the decomposition of signals

Jean Baptiste Joseph Fourier (1768–1830), a mathematician and scientist, was obsessed with the study of how heat flows through solid materials. Visitors to his apartment remarked on how uncomfortably hot he kept his rooms even while he wore a heavy coat.

Fourier realized that heat flows were a form of signal flows—after all, a signal is just something that carries information—and was able to express those flows mathematically as a combination of sinusoids (sine waves). Amazingly, he proved that *any* signal (in fact,

any expression containing a variable), could be constructed by a combination of appropriate sinusoids. The combination came to be called a **Fourier series** for periodic signals and a **Fourier transform** for aperiodic signals. Fourier's techniques thus led to a practical and relatively straightforward way to decompose signals and to determine the particular collection of sine waves needed to construct any signal. Fourier's methods are widely used today and are especially relevant in communications system design and analysis.

3.6 Bandwidth

To see how a signal evolves over time, we use a two-dimensional *time domain view* such as those shown in Figure 3.1; the horizontal axis represents time and the vertical axis shows signal strength. To focus on the simple sine wave components that create a signal's spectrum and hence show its bandwidth, we use a two-dimensional *frequency domain* view, such as that shown in Figure 3.8; the horizontal axis represents frequency and the vertical axis shows signal strength of the various frequency components.

Bandwidth is a rather confusing term used in many applications: signal transmission in networks, audio, video, antenna design, and circuit design to name a few. Its definition depends in part on context. We could simply say that bandwidth describes a range of frequencies, but although this is the essence of the term, it does not help us much because it's too general. The problem is that bandwidth is a word that is often bandied about in a casual manner that belies its true nature and does not lead to understanding. To get a good handle on what bandwidth is about, we will start with a simple question: *Why bandwidth?*

We have seen that we use sine waves to create the signals that convey information. This means that we need to be able to create as many different signal shapes as there are different potential messages or kinds of information to be sent. Because there is no

FIGURE 3.8

Frequency domain view

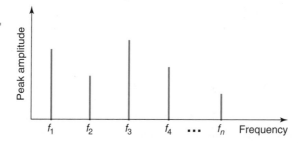

discernible end to the variety of information that we may want to transmit, neither is there an apparent limit to the number of signal shapes—there is an infinite variety of possibilities.

Now suppose that we have to put together a network system. How do we know that it will be able carry the variety of signals that we may have to send? We could attempt a brute force test by sending every possible signal through the network to see whether each one makes the journey successfully. Faced with the potential of an infinite number of possible signals, that is not a practical procedure.

Because we know that all signals are composed of a combination of simple sinusoids, perhaps we only have to test the performance of our system with regard to the sinusoids. Then we can infer how the system will handle any signals. This seems like an elegant solution to our problem, but wait a minute—aren't there an infinite number of sinusoids, and isn't a signal potentially composed of an infinite number of them? The answer to both questions is yes! So it seems like we have gained nothing.

For the solution to our dilemma, let's look at a little history. When telephone companies began designing their networks, they started with the premise that only voice signals had to be carried, which is not surprising considering the state of technology at the time. By eliminating any other signals from the system, only a limited number of signals had to be dealt with. To further simplify carrier requirements, even that limited number was reduced to just a part of the frequency range producible by human voices. As a result, telephone system performance could be tested with just a small range of sinusoid signals, and that made testing practical.

Well, we have made some progress—we now can say that we can characterize a system by its ability to handle some set of sinusoids, and we can characterize a signal by the collection of relevant sinusoids that it is composed of. What we need now is a compact way of referring to these characteristics—and so we arrive at the concept of **bandwidth.** As general statements, we can say:

> For a signal, bandwidth is the significant range of frequencies in its spectrum. For a system, bandwidth is the usable range of frequencies it can carry.

We need to talk about what "significant" and "usable" mean, but first, we see that we can now easily state the relationship between network (system) capability and signal requirement as follows: if B_m is the bandwidth of the signals we need to carry and B_s is the bandwidth of the network system, then ostensibly:

> If $B_m \leq B_s$, the network can successfully carry the signals.
> If $B_m > B_s$, the network cannot successfully carry the signals.

There is, however, more to the story.

Bandwidth of a signal

What is the significant range of frequencies in a signal's spectrum? Denoting the highest significant frequency in that spectrum by f_h and the lowest by f_l, we can define the signal's bandwidth B_m as:

$$B_m = f_h - f_l$$

Figure 3.9 illustrates this concept, using a frequency domain view to show sample frequencies of an arbitrary signal. Frequency components below f_l and above f_h are not

FIGURE 3.9

Signal bandwidth—
significant range of
frequencies

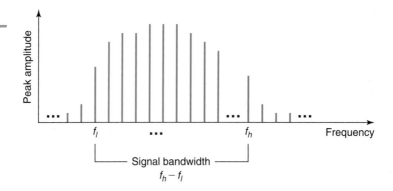

considered significant because their peak amplitudes are too low to make a significant contribution to the signal, so they are not considered as part of the signal's bandwidth.

The frequencies contained in the bandwidth are the signal's spectrum. Interestingly, bandwidth does not tell us what the spectrum is—it only gives us the width of the spectrum. Two different signals, with two entirely different ranges (spectra), may have the same bandwidth. For example:

Signal 1: $f_h = 10,000\,\text{Hz}; f_l = 5,000\,\text{Hz} \rightarrow B_m = 10,000 - 5,000 = 5,000\,\text{Hz}$.

Signal 2: $f_h = 100,000\,\text{Hz}; f_l = 95,000\,\text{Hz} \rightarrow B_m = 100,000 - 95,000 = 5,000\,\text{Hz}$.

Still, we see that the word *bandwidth* is an apt description of the concept. It measures the *width* of a *band* (range) of frequencies.

Recalling that a system's bandwidth refers to the usable range of frequencies it can carry, we see from the preceding example that we will not know whether a system will be able to carry a particular signal simply from knowing the signal's bandwidth. We must know more about its spectrum and about the bandwidth of a system.

Bandwidth of a system

The bandwidth of a system is analogous to but different from the bandwidth of a signal. For a signal, bandwidth is concerned with the range of its useful frequencies. For a system, bandwidth is concerned with the range of frequencies that it can carry successfully.

For our signal to pass through a communications system successfully, all the frequencies in its spectrum must be able to pass successfully.

Experimentally, we can find the lowest such frequency and then test a sequence of higher frequencies until we reach one that cannot traverse the system successfully. We then can use the range that we have discovered to define the bandwidth of the system (B_s):

$$B_s = f_h - f_l$$

Comparing this equation with the one for signal bandwidth reveals that they look the same. The difference is in the meaning of their terms. For the system, f_h and f_l represent the highest and lowest frequencies the system can successfully pass; for the signal, they represent its highest and lowest significant frequencies. Just as two signals of differing spectra may have the same bandwidth, two entirely different systems that pass different frequency ranges may have the same bandwidth. Therein lies some of the confusion.

To see how we determine the bandwidth of a system, let's consider a wire—the simplest component of a system. Its bandwidth relates to its response to transmitted signals—how it reacts to and affects whatever signals are sent through it. The wire's bandwidth is defined in terms of those effects, the primary one being attenuation. The bandwidth of a system is similarly defined.

Attenuation is not uniform for all frequencies. Typically, frequencies at the ends of a signal's spectrum attenuate more quickly than those in the middle, and higher frequencies attenuate more quickly than lower ones, although the degree of attenuation for various frequencies is a characteristic of the wire itself.

Suppose we take a fixed length of wire, send various single frequencies of a fixed power over it one at a time, and measure how much of the power of each frequency survives the trip. The question becomes, For which frequencies has attenuation lowered the power to an insufficient level? If we have a rule that defines how much attenuation we will tolerate, we can answer the question and determine the wire's bandwidth.

Engineers have concluded that a practical power-limit value is one half—that is, to be called usable, the power of the frequency received should be at least one half of the power sent. The same half-power rule applies to signals as well and is used to determine which frequency components of a signal are significant. (For additional insight, see "Technical extension: The $-3\,\mathrm{dB}$ point.")

The wire's bandwidth, then, is the difference between the highest and lowest frequencies received whose powers are at least one half of that sent.

In the frequency domain view shown in Figure 3.10, all frequencies are sent with power P. The arrows indicate the power at the receiving end of the wire. We see that for this example, the 20-kHz frequency's power has dropped to one half its original strength; higher frequencies have attenuated even more. The lowest frequency of at least $1/2P$ is 5 kHz. Subtracting 5 kHz from 20 kHz, we would say that this wire has a bandwidth of 15 kHz.

In general, if f_l is the lowest half-power frequency (which may even be 0 kHz) and f_h is the highest, then the bandwidth of the wire B_s is $f_h - f_l$. The bandwidth of other media and of systems is analogously defined.

Each frequency is sent with power P; the arrow heights indicate frequency power at the receiving end of the wire.

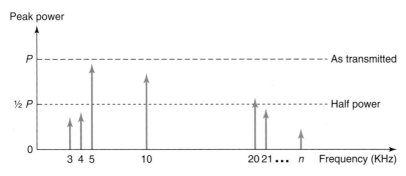

Peak power

FIGURE 3.10

Attenuation of frequency power sent through a wire

TECHNICAL EXTENSION
The –3 dB point

The half-power cutoff point for bandwidth is often referred to as the −3 dB (minus 3 dB) point. Here's why: The Bel, originally defined by A. G. Bell (a Scottish-U.S. scientist, 1847–1922) to measure the relative intensity (loudness) of a sound, is calculated as the logarithm to the base 10 of the ratio of the power of the sound to the power of a reference sound. Later on, the Bel was used to measure other power ratios, signal power among them. One modification often used is to change the units of measure from the Bel to the decibel (dB), which is one tenth of a Bel. In decibels, then, the measurement is 10 times the logarithm of the power ratio. As noted, bandwidth cutoff is defined as the point at which the received signal power is one half the sent power. In decibels, we have:

$$10 \log_{10}(P_{received}/P_{sent}) = 10 \log_{10}(1/2) = -3\,\text{dB}$$

The ratio in this expression sometimes is written the other way around, as power sent divided by power received. In that case, the result is 3 dB, rather than −3 dB. The concept remains the same.

Bear in mind that attenuation is a function of distance. We started this example with a fixed length of wire. If we change its length, we also change its bandwidth. Everything else being equal, as we increase its length we decrease its bandwidth and vice versa.

Continuing with this example, suppose we want to send a signal with a bandwidth of 10 kHz and a spectrum of 1 kHz to 11 kHz through our wire, which has a bandwidth of 15 kHz and a spectrum of 5 kHz to 20 kHz. Although the bandwidths of the signal and the wire are compatible, their spectra are not; hence, we could not send this signal through the wire. By shifting the signal's spectrum up by 7 kHz, to 8 kHz to 18 kHz, the spectra become compatible. (Note that we cannot shift the spectrum of the wire—it is a characteristic of the wire itself.) After it has been received, we can shift the signal's spectrum back to its original value.

If you are interested in how signal shifting is accomplished, see Appendix A.

3.7 Summary

In this chapter, we explored analog and digital signals, looking at their characteristics, strengths, and weaknesses. We also saw how any signal is no more than a combination of basic sine waves, a fact that makes their construction and analysis much simpler than would otherwise be the case.

After we discovered the nature of signals, we were able to delve into the concept of bandwidth. We saw that signal and system bandwidths, though similar in concept, are different in fact. We noted that signal bandwidths had to be compatible with system bandwidth for the system to carry the signals successfully. We also briefly noted that signal spectra could be shifted to fit into system spectra, provided that their bandwidths were compatible.

In the next chapter, we will see how signals are encoded for transmission.

END-OF-CHAPTER QUESTIONS

Short answer

1. What are the four combinations of information form and signal type?
2. What is the major disadvantage of analog signals?
3. Explain why analog signals cannot be recovered after distortion from noise, whereas digital signals often can.
4. What does the bandwidth of a signal mean, and what does it tell us?
5. What does the bandwidth of a system mean, and what does it tell us?
6. Explain how we can vary single characteristics of sine waves to represent digital data.
7. Why do we not transmit analog data directly, without transforming it into analog or digital signals?
8. Draw an illustration of how noise and other distortions can affect a digital signal enough to result in erroneous received data.
9. What is a composite sine wave?
10. What is the "between rule" for digital signal regeneration?

Fill-in

1. Two basic forms of information are _____ and _____.
2. Two major characteristics of analog signals are _____ and _____.
3. Two major characteristics of digital signals are _____ and _____.
4. After an analog signal is sent, its power can be increased by _____.
5. After a digital signal is sent, its power can be increased by _____.
6. To depict a signal as signal strength over time, we use a _____ view.
7. To depict a signal by the peak amplitudes of its frequency components, we use a _____ view.
8. Sound waves are an example of _____ signals.
9. Digital signals can represent _____ data accurately but can represent _____ data only approximately.
10. If we call a received pulse between +2 V and +5 V a 0-bit and we call a pulse between −2 V and −5 V a 1-bit, what does the receiver do if it gets a pulse of +1 V?

Multiple-choice

1. In the equation for a sine wave,
   $s(t) = A \sin(2\pi ft + \varphi)$, φ represents
   a. frequency
   b. amplitude
   c. phase
   d. period
   e. cycle length

2. Which of the following are advantages of analog signals?
   a. They provide faithful copies of analog information.
   b. They are a conceptually straightforward way to represent real events.
   c. They can usually travel quite far without undue attenuation.
   d. They are easy to create and handle.
   e. All of the above are advantages.

3. Which of the following are advantages of digital signals?
   a. They usually can be restored to their original shapes, even after they are distorted by noise.
   b. They are a natural way to represent digital data.
   c. They can travel farther than analog signals without boosting.
   d. They can exactly represent analog phenomena.
   e. both a and b

4. The bandwidth of a signal is determined by
   a. the number of frequencies it contains
   b. the highest and lowest significant frequencies in its spectrum
   c. the peak amplitudes of its strongest frequency components
   d. the average amplitude of its frequency components
   e. the highest and lowest amplitudes of the frequencies in its spectrum

5. The bandwidth of a system is determined by
   a. the number of frequencies it can carry
   b. the highest and lowest frequencies whose amplitudes are not less than the half-power point
   c. the maximum power it can handle

   d. the range of frequencies that can be generated by the sender
   e. both b and d

6. To use analog signals to carry digital data, we can
   a. vary the frequency while keeping the amplitude and phase constant
   b. vary the amplitude while keeping the phase and frequency constant
   c. vary the phase while keeping the amplitude and frequency constant
   d. vary the amplitude and phase while keeping the frequency constant
   e. use any of the above

7. Signal decomposition refers to
   a. the distortion that results from media effects on the signal
   b. the effect of noise on the signal
   c. expressing a signal in terms of its component sine waves
   d. creating a signal from sunlight
   e. both a and b

8. A spectrum analyzer
   a. shows the accuracy of a signal's spectrum
   b. shows the distortions of a signal's spectrum
   c. shows the components of a signal's spectrum
   d. shows how closely a signal represents data
   e. both a and d

9. The equation $B_m = f_h - f_l$ refers to
   a. the bandwidth of a signal
   b. the bandwidth of a system
   c. the components of a signal
   d. the basis of a medium
   e. both a and b

10. The instantaneous change, in zero time, of digital signals is
    a. precisely how they do change
    b. only a theoretical construct
    c. a convenient and effective way of representing the signals
    d. a requirement of digital transmission systems
    e. both b and c

True or false

1. Signals cannot carry information if they do not change shape over time.
2. Sine waves are the building blocks of all signals.
3. No signal can change its shape instantaneously.
4. Analog signals are not susceptible to noise distortion.
5. Digital signals are not susceptible to noise distortion.
6. Regeneration and amplification are equivalent processes.
7. If we know the bandwidth of a signal, we know its spectrum.
8. If we know the bandwidth of a system, we know how many signals it can carry.
9. If a system's bandwidth is at least as wide as a signal's bandwidth, the system has the ability to carry the signal.
10. Digital signals, as square waves, are not representable by sine waves.

Expansion and exploration

1. Why is bandwidth a useful concept? How is it applied in different usages?
2. Make a list of the analog and digital devices that are in your home. Which ones are involved with data transmission or receipt?
3. Sketch composite sine waves made up of the following three component sine waves:
   a. amplitudes 2 V, 5 V, and 7 V, all with frequency 5 Hz and phase 0°
   b. frequencies 2 Hz, 4 Hz, and 6 Hz, all with amplitude 5 V and phase 0°
   c. phases 90°, 180°, and 270°, all with amplitude 5 V and frequency 4 Hz

CHAPTER 4

Encoding: representing information

4.1 Overview

For information to be transmitted over a communications system, it must be in a form that the system can handle, whatever its original form—that is, it must be **encoded** to create the signals that carry the information. We saw in Chapter 3, "Signal fundamentals," that signals are physical representations of information. We can extend that description here to say that signals are physical representations of encoded information.

Because the original form of our information can be text, voice, audio, images, or video data in any combination—that is, analog and digital data—we need encoding schemes that will permit our analog and digital systems to handle any of these. Thus, we consider how to transform analog data into analog or digital signals, and digital data into analog or digital signals.

Table 4.1 shows these combinations along with a usage example of each.

TABLE 4.1 Information types and signal types

		Signal type	Usage example
Information type	Analog	Analog	AM radio
		Digital	CD music recording
	Digital	Analog	Modem
		Digital	Local area network

There are a great number of encoding schemes. We will look at some of the most common and instructive ones for illustrating encoding concepts.

No matter what the encoding scheme, a signal can carry information only if its elements are demarcated. For example, when we speak, we create words (encoding according to some language), but to produce (signal) those words, we modulate the tone of our voice, we form different sounds, we make those sounds for different lengths of time. If instead we just emitted a steady hummmmmm, we could not convey any information.

The same is true with computer communications, where signals are formed by electricity and light. For signals to carry information, they must be demarcated by changes in their characteristics. As we look at different encoding schemes, we will see that the choice greatly affects how well the information will travel through a communications system, or more drastically, whether it will succeed in traveling through the system at all!

Encoding is different from encryption. The latter is to render information unreadable by unauthorized recipients; the former is to transform information into a form that a communications system can handle.

Encoding schemes tell us how to represent raw data; the resulting signals are the manifestations of those representations.

4.2 Digital data/digital signals

Digital signals by definition can take on only a limited set of values. If the number of values is just two, we have a *binary* signal; the bits in a computer are similarly limited to two values: 1 and 0. So we need to consider how to represent those bits.

Common character codes

ASCII (American Standard Code for Information Interchange), a widely accepted character code standardized by ANSI (American National Standards Institute) and ISO (an international standards organization), is a 7-bit code that can represent 128 combinations (2^7) of 0-1 bits. The first 32 are non-printing control characters. Because ASCII was designed for teletypes, some of these characters are irrelevant today and are not used in their original meaning. The rest of the code represents grammatical symbols, numbers, and letters. Table 4.2 has a sample of ASCII codes.

TABLE 4.2   Some ASCII codes

Character	Binary representation
A	1000001
a	1100001
1	0110001
9	0111001
{	1111011
BS (backspace)	0001000
NAK (negative acknowledge)	0010101

For a complete list, see http://www.neurophys.wisc.edu/www/comp/docs/ascii.html.

HISTORICAL NOTE
ASCII

The first version of ASCII was introduced by AT&T in 1963 (and therefore called ASCII-1963). It was revised in 1967, changing some control characters and adding some rudimentary graphics characters. ASCII-1967 is still in use today.

Although for some time 128 characters were all that were needed, things changed in the mid-1980s with the introduction of the Windows operating system and its graphical user interface (GUI). This event highlighted ASCII's lack of graphical character representation and led to Microsoft creating its own version of extended ASCII that accommodated 256 characters (see "Technical note: ASCII—why a 7-bit code?"). But as the Internet expanded globally, even extended ASCII could not accommodate myriad different alphabets and the extensive use of non-textual information. Consequently, another code, called *Unicode,* was developed (see "Historical note: the development of Unicode").

Unicode is a 16-bit scheme that can represent 65,536 symbols, a number sufficient to handle the characters used by all known existing languages, with spare capacity left over for newly developed character sets. Unicode is not a single encoding scheme. Rather, there are several standardized versions. Each one uses the 16 bits differently to represent various characters and is called a *Unicode Transformation Format (UTF).*

Which UTF to choose depends on needs. For example, to preserve ASCII coding and to make the transition from ASCII to Unicode easier, UTF-8 is used. UTF-8 encodes each character as a variable number of bytes. By encoding ASCII characters with just one byte, UTF-8 ensures that Unicode and ASCII have the same character representation. Using appropriate translations, it is possible to transform a character from one UTF encoding scheme to another UTF encoding scheme.

TECHNICAL NOTE
ASCII—why a 7-bit code?

Traditionally, most computers were designed to handle bits in groups of 8 (a byte or an octet), yet ASCII was designed in rather "unnatural" 7-bit groups. This was done so that error detection, via an 8th "parity" bit, could be accommodated. (Parity is discussed in Chapter 5, "Error control.") For systems that do not use parity, the 8th bit can be utilized to expand the number of characters representable to 256. Called extended ASCII, it exists in several versions—that is, it is not standardized.

For interesting histories and descriptions of a variety of character codes, see http://tronweb.super-nova.co.jp/characcodehist.html.

Timing considerations and bit synchronization

After a bit scheme is chosen, the bits themselves must be encoded. That is, whatever code we use, the bit values must be translated into voltages or light pulses suitable for transmission over the systems in question. As a simple example, we could use two voltage values, say +5V for a 1-bit and 0V for a 0-bit. Thus, to send the data sequence 10101010, we would create a signal with voltages +5 0 +5 0 +5 0 +5 0. Graphically, this would look like Figure 4.1A. Other examples are shown in Figures 4.1B and 4.1C.

HISTORICAL NOTE
The development of unicode

Unicode grew out of early attempts by researchers at Xerox in 1986 to develop fonts for Japanese and Chinese characters. This soon evolved into the idea of developing a code that had sufficient combinations to represent any known set of characters. Through the collaboration of linguists, technicians, and interested computer-related companies, the first Unicode specification was published in 1991.

Unicode is now an official joint standard of ISO and IEC (International Electrotechnical Commission). The Unicode Consortium, in parallel and in cooperation with ISO/IEC, is a private not-for-profit association of computer- and software-related manufacturers that promotes and designs worldwide character sets.

For more information on Unicode, see

http://www.unicode.org/.

HISTORICAL NOTE
EBCDIC

While ASCII was being developed in the early 1960s, IBM produced an encoding scheme for its mainframe computers. Introduced in 1965 and called **EBCDIC** (Extended Binary Coded Decimal Interchange Code), it was based on the Hollerith punch card code, punch cards being the principal means of mainframe job entry at the time. EBCDIC is essentially proprietary

to IBM, unlike standard ASCII. Although it is still used for its mainframes, even IBM uses ASCII in its PCs.

EBCDIC is a full 8-bit code and does not allow for parity error detection. For a brief history of EBCDIC as well as a table of the codes, see

http://www.terena.nl/library/multiling/euroml/section05.html.

We can see from the figures that there are some issues here. In Figure 4.1B, how is the receiver to know that we have sent eight 1-bits and not just one 1-bit? In figure 4.1C, how is the receiver to know we have sent anything?

The reason the signal in 4.1A is clear to us is because the signal value changes for each successive bit and a bit voltage value lasts for a fixed amount of time, called the *bit duration.* Note that bit duration is the inverse of bit rate (transmission speed). For example, if we transmit at 100 bps, bit duration is 1/100 of a second.

If the receiver knows the bit duration used by the sender, it can tell how many bits are represented in 4.1B, *provided that the receiver also knows when to start measuring time.* So there are two components—sender and receiver clocks that beat at the same rate and whose beats occur at the same time. This is called ***synchronization,*** illustrated in Figure 4.2.

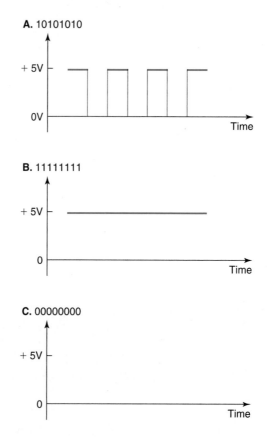

To get a sense of the critical nature of timing, consider this example: If we are transmitting at a rate of 10 Mbps, rather moderate in today's world, the bit duration is just 10^{-7} seconds—one ten millionth of a second—not very much time for a receiver to recognize a bit properly. You can imagine that timing that is off by even a minuscule amount can lead to errors.

Not synchronized—Different beat rates and different timing:

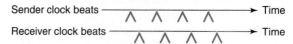

Not synchronized—Same beat rate but different timing:

Synchronized—Same beat rate and timing:

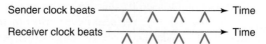

For successful communications, there must be some means for synchronizing the sender and receiver.

After clocks are synchronized, to the receiver, Figure 4.1B would "look like" Figure 4.3.

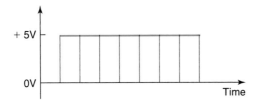

FIGURE 4.3

A string of 1-bits with clocking

What about Figure 4.1C? Even if clocks are synchronized, how does the receiver know if we are sending eight 0s, the transmission link failed, or we are sending nothing? In the absence of other information, the receiver doesn't know. If it assumes we are sending 0s, its clocking would demarcate the bits. This doesn't seem very satisfactory.

Suppose we change our signaling scheme a bit, denoting a 0-bit by –5V. Then the examples in Figures 4.1A and 4.1C will look like those in Figure 4.4. (Figure 4.1B will look like Figure 4.3.) We see in 4.4B that the ambiguity of 4.1C is removed.

We have made some progress, but we need to answer two key questions—how are clocks synchronized and, because clocks can drift, how is synchronization maintained throughout the transmission? There are two possibilities—use a separate line for a clocking signal, or incorporate a clocking signal in the encoding scheme.

Before we address these, let's review what a clocking signal is. We have seen that to convey information, a signal must vary. This is true for a clocking signal as well. It is regular, consistent, fixed-interval, repetitive signal change. For example, the signals of Figure 4.1A or Figure 4.4A, whose shapes are called square waves, could be clocking signals.

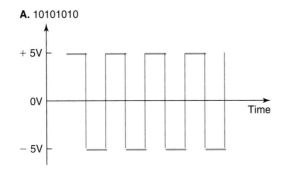

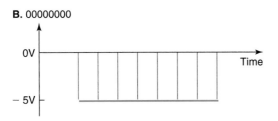

FIGURE 4.4

An alternate encoding, with clocking

To use a separate line for clocking, we send a continuous stream of square waves. This wave train produces repetitive voltage transitions that coincide with the beginning and ending of the bit duration used by the line carrying the data signals. Each transition acts as the tick of a clock and is used by the receiver to tell when each data signal bit begins and ends; the receiver does not need to depend on its own clock.

This seems to solve the synchronization problem, but there are two serious flaws:

1. The additional line, particularly over long distances, significantly raises cost.
2. To be useful, the clock signal and the information signal must arrive at the same instant. If they do not, we still have a timing problem. Physical variations in a transmission link can alter the speed of electricity flowing in it. Because the clock and data signals travel on different lines, even small variations in speed between the two lines can result in timing differences (recall that we are talking about very short bit durations), which results in misinterpreted data.

For a very short link, such as between a PC and a printer or between a PC and a modem, the difference in arrival time between the two signals will be so small as to be irrelevant. However, over connection lengths used in local area networks (LANs) and wide area networks (WANs), even very small differences in arrival times between the two signals will cause bit errors.

A separate clock line is never used in local or wide area networks.

Another approach is to use codes that provide clocking information along with the data. These are called *self-clocking codes.* For these, clocking information is provided by the sender according to its bit timing and applied by the receiver to synchronize its clock. The receiver's clock is used to interpret bits according to that timing. Because clocking and data are carried along together, a separate clock line is not needed.

S elf-clocking codes are a small subset of the very large number of possible codes, but because of their synchronization capabilities, they are preferred.

A key issue is how frequently clocking information is provided. During the intervals when there is no clocking information, the receiver is completely dependent on its own clock to separate the received bits correctly. For short intervals, we assume that the receiver's clock will not drift significantly from the sender's clock, so no timing errors will be made. Long intervals are another story.

The goal of all self-clocking codes is to find a way to reduce these long intervals. With perfect self-clocking, they are reduced to zero. As always, there is a tradeoff: Self-clocking schemes increase signal bandwidth; a communications system that can accommodate wider bandwidths is more costly.

RZ and NRZ codes

As an introduction to the considerations that come into play with clocking, we discuss two broad code classifications: *return-to-zero (RZ)* and *non-return-to-zero (NRZ).* As the names imply, RZ voltages must return to zero within each bit time, whereas NRZ codes do not necessarily do so. NRZ codes are simple and do not make large demands on system bandwidth, but they can be problematic in terms of clocking: When strings of bits with the same value are sent, clocking may be lost. In contrast, the return to zero in each bit time of RZ codes provides perfect clocking, but they extract a bandwidth penalty. (Figure 4.5A shows an example of RZ encoding.)

Two common NRZ codes—**NRZ-L** (L for Level) and **NRZ-I** (I for Invert)—illustrate the clocking issue. Figures 4.1, 4.3, and 4.4 all are examples of NRZ-L codes, wherein bit values are denoted by voltage values. These suffer potential clocking losses when there are strings of 0-bits or strings of 1-bits.

NRZ-I differs from NRZ-L in that it is not the voltage value that denotes bit value, but whether the voltage changes. This is called a differential code. We might specify, for example, no change for a 0-bit, change for a 1-bit; figure 4.5B illustrates this.

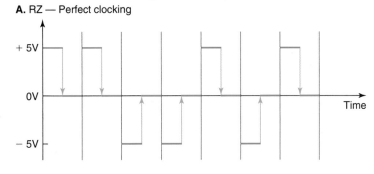

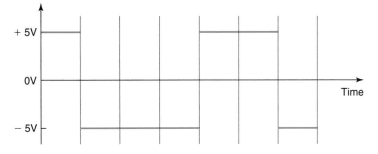

FIGURE 4.5

RZ and NRZ encoding

Block coding schemes, discussed later in this chapter, are a means of taking advantage of the simplicity of NRZ encoding while minimizing the likelihood of losing synchronization.

Differential codes represent bit values by signal element changes—either by the presence or absence of a change or by the direction of a change.

Non-differential codes represent bit values by the values of the signal elements themselves.

Alternate mark inversion

One of the first widely used digital codes to include clocking information was *alternate mark inversion (AMI).* The word "mark" reaches back to the days of the telegraph, when a mark was a click of the key. Today, mark refers to a 1-bit. In AMI, 0-bits are denoted by 0 voltage, whereas successive 1-bits are encoded by alternate ± voltages. Figure 4.6 has an example, and "Historical note: AMI and clocking" provides some background.

FIGURE 4.6

Alternate mark inversion

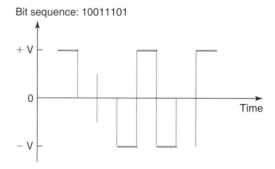

The alternating voltage for 1-bits provides the self-clocking feature of this encoding method. We can see a problem here: If we send a long string of 0s, there is no alternating voltage, hence no clocking.

AMI provides perfect clocking information when 1-bits are sent, but no clocking information when 0-bits are sent.

HISTORICAL NOTE
AMI and clocking

AMI was developed in the 1960s when electronic and computer technologies were in their infancy. For the sake of simplicity and to keep required bandwidth narrow, thus lowering cost, the number of different voltage levels used to encode bits was to be kept to a minimum. (As a general rule, the more times a signal's form changes per second, the greater the resulting bandwidth.)

In that era, almost all information was textual and often represented by the ASCII code. A sampling of ASCII files showed that, on average, most data consisted of fairly long sequences of 1-bits interspersed

occasionally with 0-bits. Therefore, the thinking went, if clocking is provided for 1-bits, the majority of time clocking information would be provided. As 0-bits arise for only short periods between very long strings of 1-bits, the receiver will use its own clock to ride out these short intervals.

The use of AMI became very widespread, because it was used in the telephone system when individual telephone signals first began to be combined (multiplexed) digitally in a service called T-1. AMI encoding, enhanced by later clocking improvements, is still used for the ever-popular T-1.

Bipolar 8-zeros substitution

At the time, AMI was a good compromise between the need to keep bandwidth low and the need to provide frequent clocking information to the receiver. Progress in the development of the digital facsimile (fax) machine in the 1970s began to upset the balance of 1-bits and 0-bits that the developers of AMI depended on for its successful operation. To appreciate why this happened, let's take a quick look at how fax machines convert information on a page to bits.

A fax machine sees a sheet of paper as many lines of individual dots. Each dot is either white (blank space) or non-white. To deconstruct the page, the fax machine represents a white dot's value as a 0-bit and a non-white dot as a 1-bit. As a typical page is mostly white space (between the words, between the lines, and as the border), the result is very long sequences of 0-bits. Transmitting these bits using AMI encoding presented a serious clocking problem and a potential stumbling block for fax transmissions

To avoid discarding AMI entirely or introducing new voltage levels that would add complications and cost, a relatively simple modification was made to AMI to solve the problem. The modified scheme was called **bipolar 8-zeros substitution (B8ZS).** Bipolar refers to the use of two voltage polarities (positive and negative) for encoding. There are many bipolar schemes, including several that do not use the word bipolar in their names. AMI is one example.

B8ZS designers considered that a string of seven consecutive 0s was as much as could be tolerated before clocking information has to be sent. Accordingly, B8ZS follows the AMI scheme until it comes across a string of eight 0s. Then, specific code violations are created that incorporate timing. (A violation is simply a bit representation that does not follow the standard AMI encoding rule for 0-bits.) The receiver recognizes these violations and reinterprets them. Existing AMI voltage values are used, so new values do not have to be accommodated.

The violation pattern depends on the value of the last 1-bit before the string of eight 0s:

1. The first three 0s are encoded as 0 volts each (as with AMI).
2. The fourth 0 is given the same voltage as the last 1-bit (an AMI violation).
3. The fifth 0 is given the opposite voltage of the fourth 0.
4. The sixth 0 is encoded as 0 volts (as with AMI).
5. The seventh 0 is encoded the same as the fifth 0 (another violation).
6. The eighth 0 is given the opposite voltage of the seventh 0.

So, if the string is . . . 1 0 0 0 0 0 0 0 0 . . . and the 1-bit was a +V, the encoding would look like this: +V 0V 0V 0V +V −V 0V −V +V. (See Figure 4.7.) In standard AMI encoding, every 0-bit would be encoded as 0 volts; here, the + − − + voltages substituted for the four 0-bits that come after the first three 0-bits violate that AMI rule.

The additional voltage transitions serve as a clock signal; the receiver recognizes the violations and restores the original string. After the substitution is made, the count of 0s begins again. Thus, for a string of 12 0s, the first eight would be substituted and the next four left as is. For a string of 19 0s, the first and second groups of eight would be substituted and the remaining three left as is.

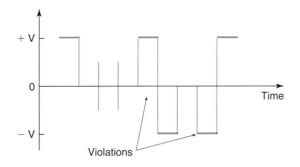

FIGURE 4.7

B8ZS

Although B8ZS offers substantial improvement over AMI in synchronizing sender and receiver clocks, it comes with a cost. Because of the increased number of signal (voltage) transitions from the violation substitutions, a B8ZS signal has a larger bandwidth than the AMI signal for equivalent bit strings when there are many runs of 0s. However, the improvement in synchronization is very significant, so the increase in bandwidth can generally be tolerated over the same media used by AMI.

Manchester encoding

As network speed increased and bit duration decreased, timing and synchronization grew in importance. The introduction of high-speed (10 Mbps) Ethernet LANs in the early 1970s called for a synchronization scheme more reliable than B8ZS—one that incorporated clocking within each bit signal. Called **Manchester encoding,** the voltage level changes every mid-bit, providing a clocking signal no matter what the bit value. The direction of the voltage change is used to indicate the bit value: For a 1-bit, the transition is from negative to positive voltage; for a 0-bit, the change is positive to negative. (See Figure 4.8.)

FIGURE 4.8

Manchester encoding

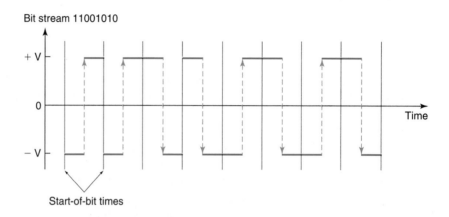

Differential Manchester encoding

One practical problem with Manchester encoding has to do with polarity. Because bit values are represented by voltage directional transitions (negative to positive and vice versa), if the wire pairs are misconnected, reversing the electrical polarity, every bit will be interpreted incorrectly. **Differential Manchester encoding** avoids this situation by representing bit values by the presence (for a 0-bit) or absence (for a 1-bit) of a transition at the bit start. (See Figure 4.9.) Thus, polarity is irrelevant because direction of change has no

FIGURE 4.9

Differential Manchester encoding

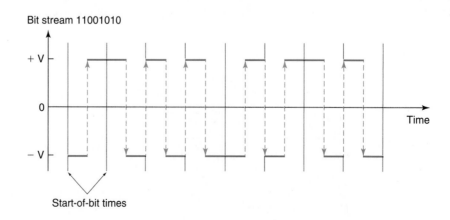

meaning; the clocking signal remains as a mid-bit transition, whose direction also has no meaning. Differential Manchester encoding is used in token ring LANs.

Business NOTE   Manchester and differential Manchester encoding

Both versions of Manchester encoding provide excellent clocking, and both produce much higher bandwidth signals than either AMI or B8ZS. For LANs, this is not an issue because the media, owned by the company where the LANs are installed, are designed to support the bandwidths. But WAN links typically are provided by telephone companies. Bandwidth may not be available, and even if it is, it will be very costly. Hence, although a compromise in terms of clocking, AMI and B8ZS are typical for WANs, whereas the Manchesters are not.

Block codes

Block code schemes are a different approach to providing clocking information without incurring as big of a bandwidth penalty as the Manchesters or RZ codes. At the same time, some measure of error detection is incorporated.

All of the block code schemes are based on replacing one sequence of bits with a somewhat longer sequence (the block code). Although it seems contrary to common sense to transmit more bits than are present in the raw data, by replacing the troublesome (for clocking purposes) long sequences of 0-bits with blocks that avoid those sequences, sufficient clocking information is carried without needing to supply clocking along with every bit. Then, relatively simple NRZ bit-encoding schemes can be used for signal creation.

Let's look at a specific example. The *4B/5B* block code replaces 4-bit sequences with 5-bit sequences. Suppose the original data stream is 0100 1000 1001 1111. Each of these 4-bit blocks will be converted to 5-bit blocks as shown in Table 4.3, resulting in the transmitted sequence 01010 10010 10011 11101.

The receiver reverses the process, re-creating the original data stream.

How does this incorporate error detection? There are 32 possible 5-bit sequences (2^5) and 16 possible 4-bit sequences (2^4); hence, 16 of the 5-bit sequences are valid blocks and the other 16 are invalid. If any of the invalid blocks are received, an error is indicated. Block codes are chosen to be as different as possible from one another so that errors in bit transmission are unlikely to result in one valid block being converted to another valid block. (This idea is discussed further in Chapter 5.)

TABLE 4.3   An example of 4B/5B encoding

Original data	Encoded data
0100	01010
1000	10010
1001	10011
1111	11101

4B/5B is used for 100Base-FX (Fast Ethernet for fiber-optic media) and FDDI (a fiber-based metropolitan area network design). These are discussed in subsequent chapters. For more about 4B/5B, as well as other encoding schemes, see http://www.rhyshaden.com/encoding.htm.

4.3 Digital data/analog signals

Although it seems perfectly logical to represent digital data by digital signals, this is not always viable. A case in point is sending digital data over the analog telephone network, accomplished by a device called a *modem.* Even today, when almost all of the telephone network is digital, local loops (the links from customer premises to telephone-switching end offices) are still predominantly analog.

The word *modem* is derived from *mo*dulation *dem*odulation. Modulation is a process that embeds information in an analog signal by varying some characteristic of the signal. A modem performs this task by changing some characteristic of that special analog signal, the sine wave, in accordance with the digital data it will represent. Demodulation reverses the process. The modem, in a single package, performs both functions.

HISTORICAL NOTE
The modem

In the 1950s, digital computers started to find their way into the business environment, bringing with them the need to have computers communicate with each other and with terminals. This required a network, and the most connected network at the time was the telephone system. To use this analog system for computer communications, engineers at what was then known as the Bell Laboratories of AT&T created a device called a modem that would transform digital signals into analog forms compatible with the telephone system. Although modems became popular from this usage, they can be employed in any situation where digital signals must be carried in analog form.

The design of the telephone system, developed over 100 years ago, places rather severe restrictions on the bit rates (bits per second) achievable by modems connected to telephone lines. At the most basic level, a modem represents each bit by one sine wave whose frequency must be in the range 600 Hz to 3,000 Hz (see "Technical note: Modem bandwidth limitation"), a bandwidth of only 2,400 Hz (at least in the local loop); this is the primary factor limiting modem speed, as follows.

The bandwidth of a signal, hence the bandwidth required of a system, is directly related to the rate at which the signal's shape changes to represent bits. That rate, measured in changes per second, is called the *baud rate.* (Baud rate also is referred to as the number of signal element changes per second, the symbol rate, or the modulation rate.)

Key to understanding this definition is what a signal change is: a change in one or more of the characteristics of the sine—peak amplitude, frequency, or phase. If all of those characteristics are constant, the signal is not changing, even though the sine continues its wavelike motion. (We will see examples of signal changes in subsequent sections.) So, the faster the bit rate we want, the wider the bandwidth must be. With just 2,400 Hz to work with, we run out of bandwidth at relatively low bit rates.

TECHNICAL NOTE
Modem bandwidth limitation

For the local loop, the telephone system allocates 4 kHz for analog voice, from 0 Hz to 4,000 Hz, which includes guard bands associated with the voice band of 300 Hz to 3,400 Hz. However, the system's response to frequencies in that range is not uniform, with power dropoffs on both sides of a flat response region. For data transmission via modem, frequencies are limited to that flat range: frequencies of 600 Hz to 3,000 Hz.

The baud rate equals the number of signal changes per second. The greater the baud rate, the wider the signal's bandwidth.

We can see a dilemma in the making. If we represent one bit value by one signal value, then as we increase transmission speed (bit rate), we increase baud at the same rate (double the bit rate, double the baud), concurrently increasing the signal's bandwidth. At some point, the resulting signal bandwidth will be greater than that of the system. As we have seen, when the system involves the narrow bandwidth telephone network local loop, the speed limit will be reached fairly quickly. To do better, we need schemes that increase the bit rate without increasing the baud rate.

For three of the four principal modulation schemes used for digital data/analog signals, namely amplitude shift keying (ASK), frequency shift keying (FSK), and phase shift keying (PSK), the bit rate and baud rate are equal. Quadrature amplitude modulation (QAM) is a popular scheme whose bit rate is faster than its baud rate; some of the other techniques that also achieve that result are noted in this chapter.

AMPLIFICATION

The word *keying* comes from the days when the telegraph was popular. To send a message, the telegraph operator would press a key to signal various letters. With modems, keying means sending a bit.

Amplitude shift keying

As the name implies, Amplitude Shift Keying (ASK) uses amplitude changes to represent bit values, while keeping frequency and phase constant. For example, we could signal a 0-bit and a 1-bit by sine waves with respective peak amplitudes of 2 volts and 5 volts, both with frequency 1,800 Hz and phase 0°.

An example of ASK is shown in Figure 4.10. The main advantage of ASK is that it is a very simple encoding system. Its baud rate equals its bit rate—each time the voltage changes from one value to another is a signal change, and each signal change denotes one bit value. Its main drawback is susceptibility to noise.

FIGURE 4.10

ASK

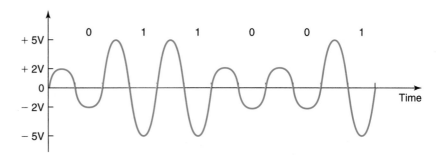

Noise corrupts the amplitude of signals. Because ASK representations are by amplitude, bit damage caused by noise is more likely than with other schemes. In particular, modern modems no longer use ASK alone. Instead, QAM, which combines ASK with PSK, is the preferred method.

Frequency shift keying

Frequency Shift Keying (FSK), true to its name, modulates the frequency of a sine wave to represent bit values, while keeping amplitude and phase constant. For example, we might use frequencies of 1,200 Hz and 1,800 Hz to signal a 0-bit and a 1-bit respectively, both with amplitude 7 volts and 0° phase. Figure 4.11 shows an example.

FSK's major advantage over ASK is its immunity to noise. As noise does not corrupt the frequency of signals, the reliability of the information embedded in frequencies is far greater than that embedded in amplitudes. But this advantage comes at the cost of a considerably higher bandwidth requirement. Because two frequencies are used, the bandwidth required for FSK is significantly greater than for ASK when both are running at the same bit rate-baud rate. This is FSK's major disadvantage and typically results in turning to PSK where bandwidth is at a premium.

FIGURE 4.11

FSK

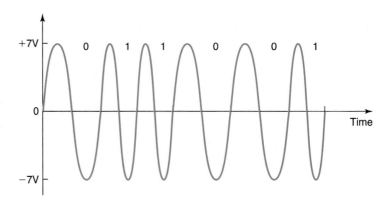

Phase shift keying

As you would now expect, Phase Shift Keying (PSK) modulates the phase of a sine wave to represent bit values, keeping amplitude and frequency constant. For example, we might use phases of 0° and 180° to represent a 0-bit and a 1-bit respectively, both with amplitudes of 7 volts and frequencies of 1,200 Hz. Figure 4.12 shows an example.

Because frequency is fixed, the system bandwidth required is determined primarily by signaling speed—that is, the bit rate—as is the case with ASK. Hence, PSK's bandwidth requirement is significantly less than FSK's. PSK also is immune to noise because noise will not affect phase. These factors combine to make PSK a popular choice.

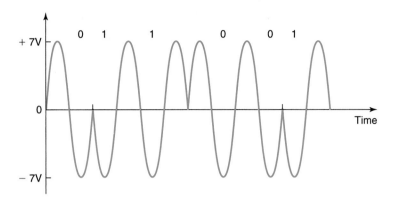

FIGURE 4.12

PSK

In ASK, FSK, and PSK, the baud rate equals the bit rate.

Increasing the bit rate/baud rate ratio

Implicit in our discussion of bit rates, baud rates, and bandwidth is the notion that in our quest for faster speeds (that is, higher bit rates), we are faced with limits in available system bandwidth. (Recall that the higher the baud rate, the wider the bandwidth required.) Thus, our quest leads to two questions:

- How can we increase the bit rate for a given baud rate (or alternately, how can we decrease the baud rate for a given bit rate)? We answer this question next.
- Is there a limit to the achievable bit rate? We resolve this question later on.

Let's look at the first question by considering the following modification of ASK. Instead of using just two peak amplitude (voltage) values, we use four, with each value representing two bits instead of one. For example, see Table 4.4.

Suppose we transmit at a bit rate of 4 bps. With the simple ASK scheme of two voltage values, one for each 0-bit and 1-bit, the baud rate also is 4—because each voltage value represents one bit, the sine wave shape (peak amplitude) has to change at the same rate at which the bits change. But with four-level ASK, each sine wave shape represent two bits, so the shape needs to change only half as often as the bits change—here, two times a second to represent 4 bits per second. In other words, this encoding scheme's bit rate is twice its baud rate. That is, our new scheme yields the same bit rate as simple ASK but at half its baud rate, thus reducing demand on system bandwidth.

Alternatively, by keeping the baud rate at 4, our new scheme will yield a bit rate of 8 bps, compared to the 4 bps of simple ASK. Thus, we can double the bit rate of simple

TABLE 4.4   Four-level ASK

Bit combination	Sine wave amplitude (peak volts)
00	+2
01	+4
10	+6
11	+8

ASK while using the same baud rate. After we decide what we want to do—increase the bit rate for a given baud rate or decrease the baud rate for a given bit rate—we can calculate the number of bits that each baud must represent; that is, the number of different signal shapes needed.

 The number of different signal shapes needed to represent *n* bits is 2^n.

We call the 2-bits-per-signal scheme 4-ASK, because it requires four different signal levels. With 3 bits per signal, we have 8-ASK; with 4 bits per signal we have 16-ASK, and so on. We could make the same types of modifications to FSK and PSK, using each frequency or phase value to represent multiple bits, with the same impact on bit rate-baud rate. The terminology carries through as well, giving us 4-FSK, 8-FSK, 16-FSK, 4-PSK, 8-PSK, 16-PSK, and so on.

 Given the cap on bandwidth, and therefore baud rate, we can increase the bit rate by using multi-valued encoding schemes.

TECHNICAL NOTE
Bits, bauds, and modem speeds

The *bit rate* and the *baud rate* are related through the number of bits per baud:

$$\text{bits/second} = \text{bits/baud} \times \text{baud rate}$$

For example, if a modem's baud rate is 4,800 and there are 4 bits per baud, then the modem's bit rate is $4 \times 4,800 = 19,200\,\text{bps}$.

Depending on the encoding scheme, the bit rate may be less than, equal to, or greater than the baud rate.

It would seem that we have a universal solution to the bandwidth issue. Simply by increasing the number of bits represented by a signal level or sine wave, we could increase the bit rate as much as desired without a bandwidth penalty. Unfortunately, that is not the case.

With ASK, we either would have to use higher and higher voltage values, which at some point will reach the limits of the electrical system, or use finer and finer differences between voltage values, which soon will be too close to be reliably distinguished in the face of noise distortion. Although FSK is not affected by noise, the more frequencies we use, the higher the bandwidth—whatever the baud rate; further, increasingly fine distinctions between frequencies also creates a detection problem. PSK is not affected by noise, either, but similar to FSK, the finer the phase distinctions, the more difficult it is to recognize differences. (We will delve further into this issue subsequently.)

This dilemma leads to the idea of combining modulation methods, changing more than one characteristic of the sine wave at a time. For example, we could combine ASK and FSK, PSK and FSK, or ASK and PSK. Because any technique with FSK extracts a higher bandwidth penalty, the last of these combinations is the most desirable. It is called QAM.

Quadrature amplitude modulation

Quadrature Amplitude Modulation (QAM) combines amplitude shifts with phase shifts. This can provide a large number of signal elements—a large number of bits per baud—with tolerable separation between individual amplitudes and between the different phases. For example, it is common for each signal element to represent 9 bits at a time; this requires 512 (2^9) different signal elements. With a 3,200-baud modem, the bit rate would be 28,800 bps (3200×9).

Various combinations of amplitudes and phases are possible. Because the amplitude components are subject to noise corruption, commonly used versions have more phases than amplitudes. As with the shift key methods, QAMs are labeled by the number of signal values, hence the number of amplitudes times the number of phases. For example, with two amplitudes and two phases, we have 4-QAM; with 2 amplitudes and 4 phases, we have 8-QAM.

To help visualize the signal combinations and bit representations, we create a graphical design called a ***signal constellation.*** Each point on the constellation has as its radius the amplitude of the particular signal element, and the angular position of the point represents the phase of the same signal element. Each point is labeled with the bit combination it represents. For example, for 8-QAM with amplitudes of 2 and 4 volts and phase angles of 0°, 90°, 180°, and 270°, the constellation appears as shown in Figure 4.13.

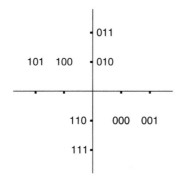

FIGURE 4.13

8-QAM constellation

Maximum bit rate over a transmission system

Now that we've explored techniques for increasing the bit rate/baud rate ratio, we can look into the second question: Is there a limit to the achievable bit rate? This issue was first addressed by Dr. Harry Nyquist while working at Bell Laboratories of the American Telephone and Telegraph Company. (H. Nyquist, "Certain Topics in Telegraph Transmission Theory." *Trans. AIEE* 47 (April 1928): 617–644.)

He began by assuming that signals are traveling through a noiseless system whose bandwidth is B_s and he discovered that the maximum achievable bit rate C (which he called the system's Capacity) is directly related to B_s and the number of signal levels L used in bit encoding, according to what was called Nyquist's Theorem:

$$C = 2B_s * \log_2 L \text{ (maximum bit rate in a } noiseless \text{ system)}$$

HISTORICAL NOTE
Dial-up modems and standards

Modems operate in a variety of ways; it is possible for two modems to operate at the same speed and yet not understand each other. This was a problem with the introduction of the so-called 56K modems. Two competing camps championed their own method for achieving this speed: A team led by Rockwell used a scheme they labeled K56flex, and a group led by U.S. Robotics had its own method called X2 technology. Eventually, an international group under the auspices of the International Telecommunication Union (ITU) introduced a common standard called V.90. The situation prior to the V.90 standard was chaotic because some people were using K56flex while others were using X2, and the two could not communicate. This points to the importance of having accepted standards that manufacturers follow to assure the widest interoperability.

As technology evolves, so must standards. It often is desirable for newer standards to be backward compatible—the ability of a newer device to also operate according to an older standard. For a list of the most common modem standards, see

http://searchnetworking.techtarget.com/sDefinition/0,,sid7_gci213282,00.html.

This indicates that for a given B_s we can increase the bit rate without limit simply by increasing the number of levels, which hardly seems realistic. Yet this is the result when noise is omitted, a point addressed 20 years later by another researcher at Bell Labs, Dr. Claude Shannon, who established one of the most fundamental and important relationships in communications. (C. E. Shannon, *The Mathematical Theory of Information*. Urbana, IL: University of Illinois Press, 1949.)

Taking into account the immense impact of noise on the number of levels that can be used, while keeping the baud rate consistent with the bandwidth of the given system, he created what came to be called Shannon's Capacity Theorem:

$$C = B_s * \log_2(1 + S/N)\,(\text{maximum bit rate in a system with noise})$$

where S is the signal strength and N is the noise strength. Thus, he demonstrated that for a given bandwidth, the key factor is the ***signal to noise ratio (SNR)***. Now it would seem that we have an easy way out—increase signal strength to increase the SNR, thereby increasing the bit rate. Whether this works depends on where we do it.

If we transmit a higher-power signal, we do increase the SNR. Of course, there are limits to how much power we can give to the original signal before we damage the transmission system. On the other hand, as we have seen in Chapter 3, if we amplify the power of an analog signal along its route, we also boost noise power inherent in the transmission system by the same amount—so, alas, the SNR remains unchanged.

As it happens, Shannon's equation does not take into account all the types of noise that may plague a communications system. Therefore, the result provides an upper bound to the achievable bit rate, but not necessarily the one that can be realized in a particular system. (For additional insight, see "Technical extension: Shannon's and Nyquist's capacity theorems.") For an example of how this affects modem speeds, see "Technical note: Modems and Shannon's theorem."

TECHNICAL NOTE
Modems and Shannon's theorem

Early telephone line modems operated at what today are considered very low speeds. Over a period of some 30 years there was a steady speed progression, from 300 bps in 1962 to 1,200, 2,400, 9,600, 14,400, 28,800, and finally 33,600 bps in 1995. Since then, no further increase has been achieved. To see why, let's apply Shannon's theorem to the telephone system.

The voice band of the telephone system is 3,100 Hz (B_s) and its SNR is 3,162. Using these parameters in Shannon's equation, we obtain:

$$C = 3,100 * \log_2(1 + 3162) = 36,023 \,(\text{maximum})\, \text{bps}$$

As we stated earlier, Shannon's equation does not take into account all noise sources, so the preceding result is greater than can actually be achieved. Yet it does reflect why modem speeds have peaked at 33,600 bps. The so-called 56-Kbps modems (a misnomer) introduced in the late 1990s were meant for use specifically with the Internet and assume very particular operating conditions. Even then, they do not operate at 56 Kbps. See "Technical extension: 56K modems, sampling, and Shannon's theorem."

Note: These observations are based on the raw bit content of transmissions. By using various compression schemes, the information content can be increased, making the perceived bit rate larger than the actual bit rate.

TECHNICAL EXTENSION
Shannon's and Nyquist's capacity theorems

Shannon's Capacity Theorem, $C = B_s * \log_2(1 + S/N)$, tells us the maximum bit rate a given channel can support, but not how to achieve that rate. For example, if $B_s = 500$ Hz and $S/N = 1,000$, then substituting these values in the equation yields $C \approx 4,984$ bps.

Fourier analysis reveals that the spectrum resulting from a simple ASK encoding at this bit rate has a bandwidth far greater than 500 Hz. Hence, to use this channel we must move beyond simple ASK and use additional signal levels to represent our bits. Although Shannon's formulation, unlike that of Nyquist, does not explicitly include signal levels, we can see from the preceding example that signal levels are implied when we actually try to apply Shannon's result.

Shannon recognized that although Nyquist's capacity theorem does include signal levels, because it does not account for noise, the result could require such small differences between levels that the noise in the system would make it impossible to distinguish properly between levels. In other words, given a baud rate compatible with the system's bandwidth, as we add levels to raise the bit rate, the difference between each level becomes ever smaller; noise then can potentially overwhelm those small differences, changing a signal from one level to another. Thus, noise limits the number of levels and therefore the maximum bit rate.

Shannon sought to correct Nyquist's result by representing noise statistically (after all, noise is a random event) and calculated the impact the noise had on the actual value of the levels measured by the receiver. This led to a reformulation in which the levels of Nyquist's formulation are subsumed in the signal-to-noise ratio. To keep his calculations reasonable, Shannon did not incorporate all noise sources, so his equation still overstates the maximum bit rate actually attainable.

4.4 Analog data/digital signals

Digital encoding of analog data is common. When you scan an image or use an Internet phone, the analog image or your analog voice are converted into digital signals. Because analog data is continuous and can take on any of a potentially infinite number of values, and digital signals are discrete with a limited number of values, there cannot be a direct translation from one to the other. Instead, to create digital signals, the analog data is first *sampled;* next, the samples are converted to digital data, a process called *quantizing;* then the digital data values are *encoded* as a digital signal. A device called a *codec* (*co*der/*dec*oder) performs the analog-to-digital translation on transmission and reverses the process on receipt. Two popular techniques for digitizing analog data are *pulse code modulation* and *delta modulation.*

Pulse code modulation

In the sampling step for pulse code modulation, the amplitude (voltage) of the analog signal is measured (sampled) at fixed intervals of time, a procedure called *pulse amplitude modulation (PAM).* Each PAM sample voltage value is quantized by converting it to a binary value representing the sample value. Then the binary value is encoded for transmission.

Two factors determine the quality of the result:

* The *PAM sampling rate* (the number of signal samples per second)
* The *sampling resolution* (the number of bits used in the binary representation of the actual sample values)

Let's look at the sampling rate first. If we sample too slowly, we will miss many analog values (see Figure 4.14); if we sample too quickly, we will be creating more sample data than we need, hence more data to store, encode, and transmit.

Nyquist's sampling theorem tells us that if we sample at a fixed rate that is at least twice the highest signal frequency in the analog source's spectrum, the samples will contain all the information of the original signal. In other words, by sampling at the Nyquist rate, we can completely reconstruct the original signal from the sample values.

AMPLIFICATION

The fixed rate requirement means that the interval between successive samples is constant. For example, if we sample 8,000 times per second, we must take a sample every 1/8,000th of a second.

The sampling rate determines how well the sample values represent the original values. Nyquist: Sample at a fixed rate that is at least twice the highest frequency in the analog source's spectrum to capture all the information of the original signal.

Now let's look at sampling resolution. If there are more voltage levels in our samples than we can transform into their binary equivalents, we cannot accurately represent all of our sample values. For example, if we use 5 bits for quantizing, we can represent 32 voltage values; if the samples have more than 32 values, they all cannot be represented uniquely. That is, in such an instance, even if our samples contain all the information of the original signal, we cannot quantize (translate into binary) all those values. This is called *quantizing (or quantization) error.*

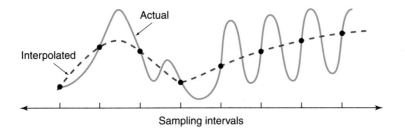

FIGURE 4.14

PAM: sampling rate too slow

Quantization error can be thought of as adding noise to the resultant digital representation. In fact, quantization error is also called quantization noise and factors into the noise value in Shannon's equation.

We know that with n bits we can represent 2^n voltage levels. How many levels do we need to be able to represent? Let's start with the sampling rate and as an example use a rate of 8,000 samples per second.

In the first second, we take 8,000 samples. In the worst case, each sample has a different value, so we need enough bits n to satisfy $2^n \geq 8,000$—that is, 13 bits. ($2^{12} = 4,096; 2^{13} = 8,192$). But wait—the next second could give us 8,000 more values that also are different; now we need n to satisfy $2^n \geq 16,000$—and so on for each subsequent second, requiring more and more bits for sample values. Although this is the worst case scenario, analog signals can take on an infinite number of values, so an extremely large number of bits is not out of the realm of possibility.

Here we face one of those tradeoffs: quantizing error versus amount of data—the more accurate we want the representation to be, the more bits we need; the more bits we need, the more we need to store, encode, and transmit. Often the capabilities and characteristics of the transmission system are overriding, but in great part, if we know the nature of the analog signals, we can arrive at a reasonable estimate of the range of voltages in the original data and use this to judge the accuracy we can achieve with various numbers of bits. In practice, this determination typically is made by experimentation.

TECHNICAL NOTE
Two industries—two sampling choices

Telephone companies and the music recording industry make extensive use of sampling. Each has experimentally determined a suitable sampling rate and sample accuracy for its purpose. The telephone companies sample 8,000 times a second using 8 bits per sample value, whereas the music industry samples 44,100 times a second using 16 bits per sample value.

Delta modulation

As we have seen, the dilemma of PCM is the tradeoff between sampling resolution and volume of data: The greater the resolution (the more bits used), the greater the accuracy of the quantized values (the less the quantizing noise), but the greater the file size, storage requirements, and transmission volume and time. To resolve this dilemma, delta modulation takes a different approach.

TECHNICAL EXTENSION
56K modems, sampling, and Shannon's theorem

56-Kbps (56K) modems seem to promise higher communications speeds through the telephone system than our earlier calculations indicated were possible. Have we been misled by advertising, or has our previous discussion been wildly mistaken?

The 56K modem, intended for use mainly with the Internet, requires that the link from the modem to the telephone company switching office be via a standard *analog* line, whereas the link between that office and the Internet (your ISP) must be via a *digital* connection. It is designed to operate nominally at 56K only in the downstream direction; upstream, its maximum speed is 33.6 Kbps. (If connected to a source other than the Internet and that source is not connected to the telephone system via a digital link, both upstream and downstream maximums are 33.6 Kbps.)

Why the speed difference? Upstream, when the analog signal from the modem reaches the switching office, it must be sampled to convert it to a digital signal, which adds quantizing noise. This contributes to the SNR of 3,162 that we saw in "Technical note: modems and Shannon's theorem," which limits maximum modem speed to about 36 Kbps. Downstream, data coming from the Internet already is in digital form, so no sampling is needed, hence no quantizing noise is added.

The result is a higher SNR, which Shannon's theorem shows us results in a faster maximum speed. Even then, 56K is not realized. For this to happen, the SNR would have to be increased further than the gain caused by the lack of quantizing noise, by increasing initial signal power. But the Federal Communications Commission (FCC), wary that a more powerful signal could interfere with nearby equipment, limits modem speed to 53 Kbps. For the higher speed to be realized upstream, the line from the computer to the switching office would have to be digital, a costly proposition for the individual customer even if it were available.

Today we have alternatives, the most common being DSL from the local telephone company and cable modems from a cable TV provider.

Instead of measuring (sampling) actual analog amplitudes, it attempts to *track the changes* in the signal values via a **step function** that at each time interval moves up or down one step—that is, one fixed voltage amount. Thus, only the step direction needs to be recorded, and that is easily and precisely quantized as a single bit, say with a 1-bit for a step up and a 0-bit for a step down. Thus, the quantizing and encoding processes and the transmission requirements are vastly more efficient than PCM. But as always, this technique is not without drawbacks.

The key determinants of the accuracy of delta modulation are the **stepping frequency** (analogous to the sampling rate) and the **step size.** We cannot use the Nyquist sampling rate calculation because Nyquist's theorem is based on measuring actual signal levels. Delta modulation does not measure actual values; rather, it attempts to predict the direction of the next value based on the current value and cover that value with a step.

As for step size, if the analog signal level is rising or falling more quickly than the step can cover, we will be tracking below or above the actual levels—that is, lagging or leading the signal values. This is called **slope overload noise.** On the other hand, if the signal level is rising or falling more slowly than the step height, we will be tracking above *and* below the actual levels—that is, we will be hunting back and forth over the actual levels. This is called **quantizing noise.** Figure 4.15 illustrates these circumstances.

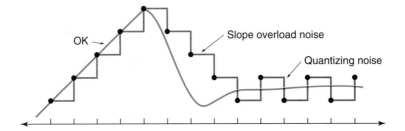

FIGURE 4.15

Delta modulation
sampling errors

As with PCM, if we know the characteristics of the analog signal, we can adjust the tracking parameters to give us the best results; even so, these may not be all that good, especially when the signal contains combinations of rapidly rising, falling, and flat components. We can somewhat moderate the error effects by increasing the stepping rate and reducing the step size. Rapid stepping and a small step generally will track more accurately than a slower rate, whatever the step size. The tradeoff here is accuracy versus quantity of data—greater accuracy means more data to calculate, store, and transmit. We also could say that for a given signal, the tradeoff is between slope overload noise and quantizing noise, because reducing one will usually increase the other.

TECHNICAL NOTE
Comparing PCM and delta modulation

PCM remains the standard against which other analog-to-digital conversion methods are compared. It is the method used in traditional telephone networks and in the music recording industries. Its main drawback lies in the large number of bits the process generates. When this is a particular issue, as when we try to integrate voice and data on the same data network, we turn to delta modulation, which typically generates vastly fewer bits. For example, when we use the Internet as a telephone system, as in VoIP (Voice over IP), a minimum digitized voice bit rate is necessary to achieve a reasonably smooth flowing conversation; because of bandwidth limitations, delta modulation is preferred.

Which method provides the best performance depends on the source and strength of the analog signal and how the digitized signal will be used:

- Voice and television signals fare better when encoded by delta modulation, whereas music signals perform better using PCM.

- Because delta modulation's quantization levels are smaller, quantization noise may actually be less than in PCM.
- PCM signals are relatively easy to convert between different PCM versions, such as are used by telephone systems in different parts of the world, whereas conversion between different delta-modulated signals is far more complicated.
- PCM encoding and decoding requires only one codec for all 24 channels of a T-1, whereas delta modulation, which tracks a specific signal, requires one codec per channel.
- To convert from PCM to PCM, it is necessary to translate just one codeword at a time, whereas to convert from delta to delta requires decoding a substantial part of the signal and then re-tracking it to re-encode it.

4.5 Analog data/analog signals

Just as we asked the question, "why does digital data need to be encoded to send digital signals?" we ask the question, "why do we need to modulate analog data instead of just transmitting it the way it is?" There are several reasons; here are some of the more important ones:

- The transmission system may require the signal to be in a different frequency range than it is originally. Modulating the signal shifts its spectrum into the proper range.
- Modulation is the basis of frequency division multiplexing (FDM), a technique for combining several analog signals onto a single communications link for simultaneous transmission. (Multiplexing is discussed in Chapter 6, "Communications connections.")
- For efficiency, transmitting antennas should be equal to at least 1/4 the length of the lowest frequency wavelength in the signal. An audio signal whose lowest frequency is 20 Hz would need an antenna almost 2,400 miles long. Modulating the signal to move it into a higher-frequency range alleviates this problem.
- An amplitude-based analog source signal is much more susceptible to noise than a frequency-based signal; changing the modulation scheme reduces noise distortion.
- FCC requirements for wireless transmission necessitates that we modulate our analog signals to use and stay within particular frequency bands.

The three basic analog modulation techniques are ***amplitude modulation (AM), frequency modulation (FM),*** and ***phase modulation (PM).*** As their names imply, these methods modify the named characteristic of sine waves while keeping the other two characteristics constant. In essence, this is quite similar to that of the shift keying modulation methods ASK, FSK, and PSK, but there is a major difference. Shift keying methods deal with digital data; hence they create analog signals that need to represent only two values: 0 and 1; in contrast, AM, FM, and PM must create analog signals that represent the full range of the original analog source information.

ASK, FSK, and PSK modulation methods need to represent only the two values of the digital information source, 0 and 1. AM, FM, and PM need to represent all the values of the analog information source.

Amplitude modulation

In amplitude modulation (AM), as in ASK, the amplitude of a carrier sine wave is varied so as to represent the information carried by the source, whereas the carrier frequency f_c and phase φ_c are fixed (see Figure 4.16). The AM signal $m(t)$ is produced simply by multiplying the sine wave carrier $c(t)$ by the original analog source signal $s(t)$:

$$m(t) = s(t) * c(t)$$

Substituting $A \sin(2\pi f_c t + \varphi_c)$ for $c(t)$ and then multiplying gives us:

$$m(t) = s(t) A \sin(2\pi f_c t + \varphi_c)$$

$s(t)$ multiplies the carrier's original amplitude, so $m(t)$'s amplitude varies with that of the source signal.

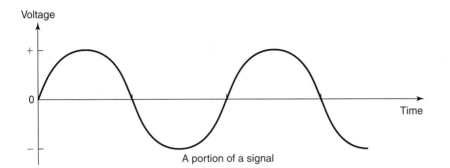

Voltage

A portion of a signal

FIGURE 4.16

Amplitude modulation

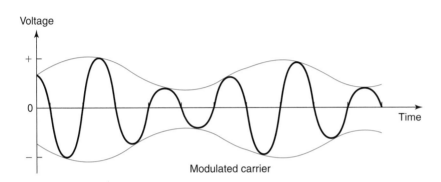

Voltage

Modulated carrier

If we next substitute the sine expression for $s(t)$ and carry out the multiplication, the result will show that all the frequencies in the original signal $s(t)$ are shifted above and below the carrier frequency f_c. (Signal shifting is explained in detail in Appendix A, "Sine waves: basic properties and signal shifting.") Therefore, the bandwidth of the resulting modulated signal, $m(t)$, is twice the bandwidth of the original signal $s(t)$.

The range of those frequencies in $m(t)$ that are below the carrier frequency f_c is called the ***lower sideband of m(t),*** and the range of those above the carrier frequency is called the ***upper sideband of m(t).*** Importantly, each of those sidebands contains all the information of the original signal. This means that we can reduce the bandwidth of the modulated signal by eliminating one of the sidebands, which is often what is done, resulting in a ***single sideband system.***

TECHNICAL NOTE
AM radio

Radio stations broadcasting on the AM band use amplitude modulation, which is why they are called AM stations. The FCC has set aside the range of frequencies from 530 kHz to 1,700 kHz for the AM band. In that band, the FCC allocates a 10-kHZ bandwidth to each station and mandates a 10-kHz guard band between adjacent stations to avoid interference between them. (Guard bands are discussed in the frequency division section of Chapter 6.)

FIGURE 4.17

Frequency modulation

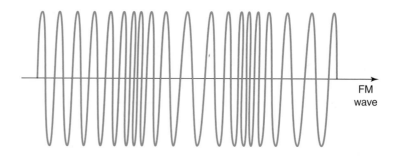

FM
wave

Frequency modulation

Similar to FSK, in frequency modulation (FM) the frequency of a carrier sine wave is varied to represent the information of the original analog signal, while keeping the carrier's amplitude and phase constant (see Figure 4.17). The modulated signal is:

$$m(t) = A \sin(2\pi[f_c + s(t)]t + \varphi_c)$$

$s(t)$ is added to the carrier frequency, so $m(t)$'s frequency varies with the source signal.

As with AM, varying the carrier frequency f_c causes the frequencies of the original analog signal to shift above and below f_c. However, the distribution of the shifted frequencies is considerably more complex than is the case for amplitude modulation and results in a bandwidth 10 times that of the original signal. Although this is a heavy bandwidth penalty, we gain a substantial benefit in terms of noise immunity.

TECHNICAL NOTE
FM radio

Radio stations broadcasting on the FM band use frequency modulation, which is why they are called FM stations. The FCC has set aside the frequencies between 88 MHz and 108 MHz for the FM band. Each station is allocated a bandwidth of 200 kHZ with a mandated guard band of 200 kHz between adjacent stations to avoid interference between them.

Phase modulation

As with PSK, in phase modulation (PM) the phase of the carrier sine wave is varied according to the changes in the original analog signal (see Figure 4.18). Just as in PSK, neither the amplitude nor the frequency of the carrier is modified. Hence,

$$m(t) = A \sin(2\pi f_c t + s(t))$$

$s(t)$ replaces carrier phase, so $m(t)$'s phase varies with the source signal.

The analysis of a phase-modulated signal is entirely the same as that for a frequency-modulated signal, and the results are essentially the same. Varying the phase results in a similarly complex distribution of frequencies around the carrier frequency. Once again, the bandwidth is 10 times that of the original signal. Also as with FM, PM gives us the same substantial benefit in terms of noise immunity.

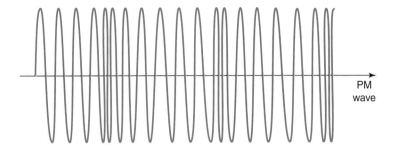

FIGURE 4.18

Phase modulation

AM produces a signal with twice the bandwidth of the original analog source. FM and PM produce signals with 10 times the bandwidth of the original analog source. FM and PM provide noise immunity; AM does not.

4.6 Summary

This chapter follows from the foundation laid by Chapter 3, where we discussed signals as they originate and as they are characterized. In this chapter, we explored the four data/signal encoding combinations: digital data/digital signals; digital data/analog signals; analog data/digital signals; analog data/analog signals.

We saw the importance of sender/receiver synchronization and the pros and cons of various encoding schemes. There are many more encoding schemes than we have covered, but the ones we discussed are among the most popular and, more importantly, they illustrate the principal concepts behind all encoding methods.

No matter what encoding method is used, errors can creep in during transmission. Error control, a topic of major importance in computer communications, is explored in the next chapter.

END-OF-CHAPTER QUESTIONS

Short answer

1. What are the four combinations of information types and signal types?
2. Why do sender and receiver clocks need to be synchronized?
3. What are the disadvantages of a separate clock line?
4. For the bit string 1110001010, sketch the graph for encoding via RZ, NRZ-I, AMI, Manchester, and differential Manchester.
5. Explain the logic behind substitution codes.
6. Explain the logic behind block codes.
7. How is baud rate related to signal bandwidth? How can the bit rate be increased without increasing the baud rate?
8. How are Nyquist's theorem and Shannon's theorem related? How do they differ?
9. Contrast ASK with AM, FSK with FM, and PSK with PM.
10. Explain the tradeoffs involved when considering the number of bits used for quantizing, representation accuracy, and the amount of data to be transmitted.

Fill-in

1. _____ schemes tell us how to represent raw data.
2. With a 7-bit code, we can represent _____ characters.
3. The two requirements for clock synchronization are _____ and _____.
4. Two methods for achieving synchronization are _____ and _____.
5. Codes that provide clocking along with the data are called _____.
6. In _____ encoding, the voltage level changes every mid-bit and the direction of the change indicates the bit value.
7. Two digital encoding schemes that provide perfect clocking are _____ and _____.
8. The _____ is the number of signal changes per second.
9. Four methods for encoding digital data with analog signals are _____, _____, _____, and _____.
10. The graphic representation of QAM is called a _____.

Multiple-choice

1. One of the 7-bit character code is known as
   a. EBCDIC
   b. ASCII
   c. extended ASCII
   d. Unicode
   e. Baudot code
2. To be useful for synchronization, a signal must
   a. alternate between plus and minus voltages
   b. produce repetitive transitions at regular intervals
   c. consist of square waves
   d. run on a separate line
   e. all of the above

3. Encoding schemes in which bit values are represented by changes in voltages rather than by voltage levels are called _____ codes.
   a. return-to-zero
   b. non-return-to-zero
   c. differential
   d. self-clocking
   e. pulse

4. Substitution codes
   a. increase the bandwidth requirements of the signal
   b. work by purposely creating code violations
   c. improve the clocking characteristics of the signal
   d. allow use of analog signals for digital data
   e. all but d

5. In _____ encoding, there is a mid-bit transition in every bit.
   a. NRZ
   b. RZ
   c. differential Manchester
   d. AMI
   e. B8ZS

6. QAM combines
   a. FSK and PSK
   b. ASK and PSK
   c. ASK and FSK
   d. both b and c
   e. both a and b

7. If a signal has a bandwidth of 4 kHz and a lowest frequency of 1 kHz, the Nyquist sampling rate is _____ samples per second.
   a. 2,000
   b. 4,000
   c. 5,000
   d. 8,000
   e. 10,000

8. The sampling technique that attempts to track the signal is
   a. PAM
   b. PCM
   c. delta modulation
   d. Nyquist's rule
   e. both a and b

9. A signal with four amplitudes and four phases would be called
   a. 8-QAM
   b. 16-QAM
   c. 8-PSK
   d. 16-PSK
   e. either b or d

10. If the interval between samples is 125 μs, the sampling rate is _____ samples per second.
   a. 125,000,000
   b. 125,000
   c. 12,500
   d. 8,000
   e. 8,000,000

True or false

1. To carry information, signals must be demarcated by changes in their characteristics.
2. Sender and receiver clocks that beat at the same rate still may not be synchronized.
3. Unless a code is self-clocking, it is not useful for data transmission.
4. AMI provides perfect clocking information.
5. Block codes trade extra overhead for the ability to use simple encoding schemes.
6. A 3-bit symbol can account for six data levels.
7. The bit rate cannot exceed the baud rate.
8. If we sample at a rate three times the highest frequency in the source's spectrum instead of twice that frequency, we can improve the accuracy of a PCM signal.
9. Quantizing error results when we sample at too slow of a rate.
10. PCM and delta modulation involve converting digital data to analog signals.

Expansion and exploration

1. Using the bit string 000011110101, discuss the advantages and disadvantages of the analog and digital encoding schemes described in this chapter.
2. Write a brief explanation of the following encoding schemes: pseudoternary, 8B/6T, HDB3.
3. Contrast the various digital encoding schemes discussed in this chapter.

5

Error control

5.1 Overview

Whenever we transmit information over a communications network, errors may occur. Measures taken to deal with transmission errors fall under the heading of ***error control,*** which comprises ***error detection*** and ***error correction.*** As the names imply, error detection is a class of techniques aimed at discovering whether there was a transmission error; error correction is a class of techniques dealing with what to do if an error is discovered.

There are two major kinds of errors—those in which transmitted information is lost or destroyed in transit, and those in which the receiver interprets data incorrectly. For the former, the only course of correction is to retransmit the data, which presumes some mechanism to alert the sender that the information was not received. For the latter, the word "interprets" is an important one: Just because a transmitted signal is altered in some way during transmission does not mean that it will be interpreted incorrectly. Depending on the signal type (analog or digital), the cause of the alteration, and the extent of the alteration, a signal may or may not be interpreted correctly.

A different type of error occurs when the receiver or the sender mistakenly concludes that retransmission is required; retransmitting correctly received data means unnecessary use of the transmission system and processing capacity. For example, this can happen if the sender is waiting for an acknowledgement of receipt from the receiver, but it is not forthcoming. Even worse, retransmitted data may confuse the receiver or may itself become faulty in transmission. So too, appropriate retransmission of a faulty signal is not totally reliable, because the retransmitted signal may have errors that go undetected.

Of course, as always, there is a tradeoff—the more accurate and reliable the error control schemes, the more overhead is required in the transmitted signal and the more processing is needed to carry out the schemes. To make a tradeoff decision, the costs of errors, which depend on the probability of their occurrence and the kind and value of the information being transmitted, should be balanced against the costs of the control schemes, a standard business decision-making approach.

Before we begin, there is another point to note. All non-trivial networks are composed of multiple nodes. Particularly in wide area networks, there will be a very large number of intermediate nodes that a signal traverses while moving from the original sender to the final receiver. Error control exists in two domains: between two directly connected nodes (point-to-point) at the data link layer and between the original sender and receiver (end-to-end) at the transport layer. In this chapter, we will focus on point-to-point error control.

As we explore the topic, keep in mind that each node in non-trivial networks acts as both a sender and a receiver, because it must receive data from a connected node and send it to the next one in the path. End-to-end communication, then, is a series of point-to-point communications. Therefore, these techniques relate to both point-to-point and end-to-end error control. The special considerations that come into play in the latter are explored in Chapter 11, "Packet switched wide area networks," as part of the discussion of congestion and flow control in wide area networks.

There is no completely foolproof method for error detection or error correction. Although some techniques prove highly reliable, we still must be aware that error control measures may themselves lead to erroneous results.

5.2 Errors in analog transmission

We learned in Chapter 3, "Signal fundamentals," that electrically transmitted analog signals suffer from impairments caused by electromagnetic interference (EMI) and thermal noise, resulting in a composite wave from which separation of signal and noise is impossible. To varying degrees, we can protect analog transmission systems from EMI noise. If we are transmitting voice or music, some noise distortion may be tolerable. On the other hand, if we are transmitting data, the distortions may render the data unusable.

As is the case with any transmitted signal, analog signals suffer from attenuation. We can ameliorate the effects of attenuation by amplifying the signal, but as we also have seen in Chapter 3, the noise gets boosted as much as the data component. Recall further that thermal noise is irreducible; as original signal power attenuates, thermal noise power becomes an increasingly greater component of the total power. Hence, if amplification waits until the original signal power attenuates too much, distortion will be too great.

By careful calculation of attenuation per unit of distance, we can place amplifiers so that this doesn't happen, but the basic problem—the impossibility of separating noise from data—does not go away. No matter where we place amplifiers, the fact remains that we cannot restore the signal to its original form. Thus, for data transmission, analog systems are not very satisfactory.

Because of this, digital signaling, whose bit-forms usually can be restored, has become preferred for data transmission. If you had occasion to use an analog cell phone and then switched to digital service, you probably noticed an improvement in voice quality. This was due in large part to the differences in the way the two signal types are affected by noise and what can and cannot be done about it. (Also see "Historical note: Analog and digital television.") In this chapter, we will focus on error control for digital systems.

What about light signals, which are not affected by EMI or thermal noise? See "Technical note: Errors in light signal transmission."

TECHNICAL NOTE
Errors in light signal transmission

Compared to digital electrical transmission systems, digital optical systems have vastly fewer bit errors from transmission impairments. Nevertheless, they are not error-free. Bit errors can be caused by the effects of dispersion, scattering, attenuation, and delay phenomena (see Chapter 2, "The modern signal carriers"). What is of interest in this chapter is not what caused the errors, but how to detect and possibly correct them. Whether we are considering electrical signals or light signals, the same error detection and correction methods are used.

HISTORICAL NOTE
Analog and digital television

The first standards for television in the United States were approved by the Federal Communications Commission (FCC) in 1941. These outlined the protocols for black-and-white analog broadcasts. Thirteen years later, the National Television Standards Committee (NTSC) added parameters for color analog television.* These broadcasts were transmitted over the air and received by rooftop antennas. Reception often was plagued by ghost images and distorted shapes caused by reflections, image fade caused by attenuation, and interference from noise. Clarity also was problematic when broadcast and receiving antennas were more than a few miles apart.

Reception problems were one of the great motivators for the move to cable television, which, even when transmitting analog signals, was much less affected by these impairments because of the signal protection afforded by shielded cables. Although many of the external interference problems of broadcast over the air disappeared, there still were problems of attenuation and image clarity, much of the latter caused by the effects of system noise on analog signals. Whether via cable or over the air, the farther the signal had to travel, the greater the proportion of noise power was to original signal power, hence the greater the image impairment.

The push to resolve these problems led to the advent of digital television, all of whose signals are digital in form. Regenerators eliminate almost all of the noise effects, thus restoring the original forms. About 10 percent of overhead is added to the signal for error correcting code; even with over-the-air broadcasts, this enables the distance between digital transmitting and receiving antennas to be about 10 times as far, with the same clarity, as cable analog signals.

*Television images are created by a process called scanning, whereby each image is traced onto the picture tube or screen as a series of horizontal lines. Typically, each image is created by scanning every other line and then repeating the same image, scanning the remaining lines—a process called interlacing. By rapidly and continuously rescanning (refreshing), the brightness of still images is maintained and the illusion of motion is created for changing images. The NTSC standard calls for 525 interlaced horizontal scan lines, refreshed every 1/60th of a second, for an overall refresh rate of 1/30th of a second. The corresponding standards for European television are Phase Alternate Line (PAL) and Sequential Couleur Avec Memoire (SECAM), which are similar to but not compatible with the NTSC.

5.3 Errors in digital transmission

The sources and types of errors in digital systems were discussed in Chapters 2 and 3. Here we will focus on techniques for error control—detection and correction. Error detection methods depend on calculations based on redundant information that the sender adds to the transmission. Error correction falls under two general headings: ***repeat request (RQ),*** methods that remediate detected errors by requiring repeat transmissions, and ***forward error correction (FEC),*** a collection of methods by which a receiver node can correct certain errors without the participation of the sender node.

Detection: simple parity check

The most basic digital error detection technique is called ***simple parity check,*** also referred to as serial parity check, linear parity check, and vertical parity check. *Parity* refers to whether a data frame (a grouping of bits treated as a unit for transmission) contains an odd or even number of 1-bits. A single bit, called the parity bit, is added to each frame. It is given the value 1 or 0 so as to make the total number of 1s in the frame (including the added parity bit) either odd or even, depending on which parity rule is used.

For example, suppose we are using odd parity and we want to transmit the following two frames: 1101100 and 1001100. Because the first frame has an even number of 1-bits, we have to add a parity bit with value 1, thus making the total number of 1-bits in the frame an odd number. The second frame already has an odd number of 1-bits, so we give the added parity bit a value of 0. The two frames are now 11011001 and 10011000. The receiver counts the number of 1s in each frame. If that number is odd, the frames are considered to be correctly received; if the number is even, an error is indicated and the sender will have to repeat the transmission.

To assess the accuracy of this technique, we must consider the errors that might occur. If there is a ***single-bit error,*** that is, just one bit in a transmitted frame is inverted (changed from a 1 to a 0 or from a 0 to a 1), the parity check will indicate that an error has occurred, although it will not detect which bit is faulty. Consider this example, still with odd parity: We send 11011001 (including the parity bit), but 11001001 is received. Because the received number of 1s is even but parity is odd, we know there is an error. However, because we do not know what was originally sent, we do not know which bit was inverted.

Multiple-bit errors are more common than single-bit errors, because the most common cause, noise burst, lasts a long time compared to the time a bit lasts; the faster the data rate, the shorter the bit duration and the greater the potential for bit errors from a given burst. For example, suppose our transmission is hit by a burst of EMI that lasts 3 ms (.003 seconds). If we are transmitting at the fairly slow rate of 1 Kbps, the noise burst could cause as many as 3 bit errors ($1,000 \times .003$)—but at the faster rate of 1 Mbps, there could be up to 3,000 bit errors, and at a rate of 1 Gbps as many as 3,000,000 bit errors. Because not every bit will be affected enough by the noise to change values, these numbers are maximums.

Noise during a burst is not constant. Hence, it is not unusual to find non-sequential bit inversions—multiple burst errors. A burst error is a string of contiguous error bits, so errors separated by correct bits are considered to be separate burst errors even when caused by the same noise event.

How effective is the simple parity check technique in catching burst errors? If the number of inverted bits is odd, regardless of whether odd or even parity is used, the fact that the frame is erroneous will be detected; on the other hand, if the number of inversions is even, the frame will look error-free. Here is an example, still using odd parity:

Sent:	11001101
Received:	10011001, which has three inversions. The receiver is expecting an odd number of 1s but gets an even number. The frame is invalid.
Sent:	11001101
Received:	10101101, which has two inversions. The receiver is expecting an odd number of 1s and that is what it gets, so the errors go undetected.

Simple parity check will detect any odd number of bit inversions, but it will miss any even number of bit inversions. Thus on average, it will successfully detect bit errors only about 50 percent of the time.

Detection: block parity check

The *block parity check,* also called longitudinal parity check, parallel parity check, and two-dimensional parity check, was developed as a fairly straightforward extension of the simple parity check. The intent was to improve on the performance of the latter in the face of even numbers of bit errors.

At the sending node, frames are arranged in blocks in which each row is one frame whose parity bit is calculated by the simple method. The bits of each column are treated as additional bit strings to which parity bits also are appended, creating an extra row (frame) to which its own parity bit is appended. Here is an example with even parity:

	Original frames	*Parity bit*
	1 0 1 1 0 1 1	1
	0 1 1 0 0 1 1	0
	1 0 0 1 1 0 1	0
Parity frame	0 1 0 0 1 0 1	1

The receiver performs simple parity checking on each frame, including the parity frame. (To use block parity checking, the receiver must know the block size. Otherwise, it will have no way of knowing that the added (parity) frame is not a regular data frame.)

The block parity check method will detect erroneous frames for single-bit and multiple-bit errors, whether an even or odd number of bits have been inverted. The only exception is when precisely 2 bits in one frame and 2 bits in another frame in the same column positions are inverted, an extremely rare occurrence.

You might have noticed that if there is a single-bit error, there will be a parity violation in both the row and column where the error occurred; the intersection would tell us which bit was inverted. Unfortunately, we cannot use this procedure to correct errors because multiple-bit errors also cause row and column parity violations, so we would not know whether the violations we see were caused by single-bit or multiple-bit errors.

In summary, block parity checking is much more accurate than simple parity checking, but it also involves more computation and requires transmitting one extra frame (the parity frame), for each block. Furthermore, it is likely that most transmissions will not comprise a number of frames that will fill up every block. For example, suppose we have 20 frames to transmit and were are using a block size of 6 (excluding the parity frame). We will have three full blocks and one with only two frames. That means we will have to include dummy frames to fill out the block—more overhead.

Block parity check detects almost all single-bit and multiple-bit errors, but at the cost of added transmission overhead.

This leads us to investigate error detection methods that offer far greater accuracy than simple parity check, but whose error detection bits are self-contained within a single frame. These methods append to the frame a series of bits called a ***frame check sequence (FCS).*** Two major such methods are checksum and cyclical redundancy check; what differentiates them is the means by which the FCS is constructed.

Detection: checksum

The ***checksum*** method is based on simple arithmetic. The process involves dividing the bits of a frame into equal segments, adding all segment values together, and placing the complement of the sum in the frame's checksum FCS field. The number of bits in the checksum is the same as the number of bits in a segment. (See Appendix E, "Error detection and correction," for details.) The receiver performs the same calculation and checks the sum to determine whether the same result is obtained. If so, the frame is considered error-free.

Checksums will detect all single-bit errors, but they can miss burst errors when particular multiple-bit inversions cancel each other out, because in those cases the sums will not change. The likelihood of such a cancellation is rather low, but it can happen. Checksums usually outperform simple parity checks but not block parity checks (although checksums have the advantage of not requiring block assembly and an extra frame). Because only a single checksum field is added to the frame, there is relatively little increase in transmission overhead bits. The processing effort required for each technique is more or less the same.

Checksums are most common in end-to-end (transport) error checking.

For more details and an example of the checksum process, see Appendix E.

Detection: cyclical redundancy check

To keep the concept of a single error detection field per frame but improve on error detection capability, ***cyclical redundancy check (CRC)*** is used. The tradeoff for superior error detection is computational complexity, involving manipulating polynomials. As it happens, though, rather simple hardware can handle the task. This makes CRC eminently feasible for use in communications equipment, typically at the node-to-node (data link) level.

The technique involves dividing the frame's message bits by a given divisor and placing the remainder, which is the CRC, in the frame's FCS field. The divisor has one more bit than the FCS field. The receiver uses the same divisor but on the entire frame, including the FCS. If the frame is error-free, the receiver's remainder will be zero; if it is not, the frame is considered to be faulty. The frame size is expanded by the number of bits reserved for the remainder, which depends on the divisor used. In general, the larger the divisor, the more reliable the error detection. Here again we have a tradeoff—reliability against added overhead.

If you wish to delve further into the details of this technique, see Appendix E.

Correction: backward error correction

The simplest and most widespread error correction method is retransmission. This is triggered by information that the sender gets (or fails to get) from the receiver. The sender looks for *acknowledgements (ACKs)* from the receiver, which indicate that a frame was received correctly (or more accurately, that a frame was received for which no errors were detected).

Retransmission methods take note of the fact that it is possible for an ACK to be lost or damaged, by incorporating sender-timers—after some time passes without an ACK, the sender assumes retransmission is needed. For some methods, negative ACKs (NAKs) are sent to signal an error.

A NAK, a missing ACK, and a damaged ACK all act as a *request to repeat* the transmission—hence, *repeat request (RQ),* also called *automatic repeat request (ARQ).* Because these methods involve sending messages in the opposite direction of the original transmission, they are called *backward error correction techniques.* Discussed in Chapter 7, "Digital communication techniques," as part of flow control, they are comparatively simple to implement, trading repeated and sometimes unnecessary transmissions for computational ease.

AMPLIFICATION

Unnecessary transmission will occur if the receiver's ACK is destroyed or damaged in transit. The resulting retransmission after the wait time expires means the repeat transmission is a superfluous use of system capacity. Further, if the duplicate message is damaged in transmission, the receiver might not recognize the message as a duplicate and could ask for yet another retransmission.

Correction: forward error correction

Another group of methods involves having the receiver correct transmission errors without recourse to or knowledge of the sender. Because we are dealing with just two possible bit values, 0 and 1, when the receiver determines which bits are in error, correction is easy—simply flip the faulty bits. The key to success, then, is correct identification of those bits. Methods for doing this involve *block codes;* because they are done in the forward path of the transmission, they are called *forward error correction techniques.*

So that the receiver can determine which particular bits are in error, we must add even more bits to the frame than are required for detection techniques—the more erroneous bits per frame we want to be able to identify, the more redundant bits we need to add. Once again, we meet a tradeoff. On one hand, we have additional overhead that can be quite large and is useless when there is no transmission error, and we have additional computational effort. On the other hand, if the receiver can correct faulty frames, we don't need to notify the sender of a transmission error, we don't need retransmission, and we eliminate retransmission of correctly received frames whose resending is triggered by lost acknowledgements.

Over the years, guided media transmission systems have improved markedly, to the point where system-induced errors are relatively rare. Further, such errors that do occur most often come in bursts that affect only one or two frames out of many. Hence, frame retransmission is the practical way to go in most cases: the extra overhead and processing needed for forward error correction is not cost effective in systems with such few transmission errors. Wireless is another story; because of the numerous sources of frame-damaging interference that pervade unguided media, there is a fairly high likelihood of transmission errors in many frames. This makes the use of error correcting codes a much better tradeoff for wireless systems than for guided systems.

Backward error correction is most practical for guided transmission systems. Forward error correction is most useful for wireless transmission systems.

The first question we encounter is, how many redundant bits do we need? To answer this question, let's look at a simple example.

Suppose we have a 4-bit message. Any of the 4 bits can be in error, so we need enough redundant bits to represent each of those bit positions. Because each extra bit can represent two positions, we need to add 2 bits. But what about errors in the redundant bits themselves? We need to add 1 more bit to account for those two positions. Finally, we need to account for the possibility of no errors. In this example, the 3 bits we've added can account for eight values, which is enough for our needs: four message bit positions, three extra bit positions, and one no-error condition.

We can calculate the number of redundant bits needed for any given message block size. Let m be the number of message bits and r be the number of redundant bits. We need to find the smallest r such that $2^r \geq m + r + 1$ (the message bits plus the redundant bits plus the no-error condition). In our example, we found that we need $r = 3$, which satisfies $2^3 \geq 4 + 3 + 1$. (See Appendix E for a more detailed explanation.)

Here are the values for r for several values of m:

m	r	$m + r + 1$	2^r
4	3	8	8
12	5	18	32
18	5	24	32
24	5	30	32
48	6	55	64

We can see that the overhead we add to the message bit string may be a significant proportion of the total data block, but that as the size of the message string increases, the proportion decreases. We also can see that our extra bits are likely to have unused reference capability. In the preceding table, for example, the 5 redundant bits we need to account for the states of 12 message bits can account for 32 states ($2^5 = 32$), although we need to account for just 18. That is another of the tradeoffs we must make.

When we insert our added bits into the message, the resulting n-bit bit string is called a ***codeword.*** We can calculate two related efficiency measures for codewords: ***code redundancy,*** which is the ratio of extra to total bits, and ***code rate,*** which is the ratio of message bits to total bits. The following table expands the preceding table to include these measures:

m	x	$m + x + 1$	2^x	Code redundancy	Code rate
4	3	8	8	3/7 (42.9%)	4/7 (58.1%)
12	5	18	32	5/17 (29.4%)	12/17 (70.6%)
18	5	24	32	5/23 (21.7%)	18/23 (78.3%)
24	5	30	32	5/29 (17.2%)	24/29 (82.8%)
48	6	55	64	6/54 (11.1%)	48/54 (88.9%)

The inverse of the code rate shows the additional transmission capacity needed to accommodate the redundant bits. For example, if the code rate is 3/4, we need 4/3 (33.3 percent) more capacity than the no-redundant-bits case.

The next question is how to use the additional bits. One possibility relies on the concept of ***Hamming distance.*** If we compare two equal-length bit strings, the Hamming distance is defined to be the number of bits by which they differ. The receiver calculates the Hamming distance of the received erroneous frame compared to each legitimate codeword and chooses as the correct string the codeword whose Hamming distance is smallest.

The "minimum distance codeword approach" assumes that the fewest bit errors occurred, which is not necessarily the case. With this simple approach, there is no way to know whether that assumption is justified. Furthermore, we may receive a codeword that is faulty because one or more of its bits flipped to the pattern of another legitimate codeword, but not the one we originally sent. This error will go undetected, so the approach is not very robust. We can expand the technique to make our error correction more rigorous.

Examining codeword properties a little more closely, we can see that the bit-error identification abilities of a codeword set depend on the *set's* Hamming distance, H_d—the ***minimum H*** over all possible two-codeword combinations in the set. If two *legitimate* codewords are Hamming distance H apart, it would take H single-bit flips to convert one to the other. This means that to detect e bit errors, we need a codeword set whose H_d is $e + 1$, because in such a set e bit errors cannot change one valid codeword into another—at least $e + 1$ flips would be needed to do so.

To *correct* errors, however, we need much greater redundancy. In fact, we need a codeword set whose H_d is $2e + 1$, because with such a set it can be shown that even if there are e bit errors, the received erroneous codeword is still closer to the originally transmitted codeword than any other codeword in the set. If we want to be able to correct *all* possible bit errors in a frame of size n, then e in $2e + 1$ must equal n.

For a discussion of Hamming codes and error correction, along with examples, see Appendix E.

A more precise single-bit error correction technique places the redundant bits in particular positions within the codeword rather than adding them as a group or placing them in arbitrary spots in the bit string. The sender assigns values to these bits based on parity, using the values of the message bits. The receiver recalculates parity for the entire codeword. If there are no single-bit errors, all the added bit values will be 0; otherwise the value of the redundant bit set will be the position of the faulty bit.

For an explanation of how this technique is derived and used, see single-bit error correction in Appendix E.

As we saw when considering simple parity checks, this technique fails when there are multiple-bit errors. We resolve this issue in the same way. That is, instead of sending single codewords, the sender constructs blocks of n-bit codewords and sends one bit from each codeword in the block as a string (that is, all first bits in the codewords of the block as a string, all second bits as a string, and so on). Then a burst error will likely affect just one of those strings, hence a single-bit position in any of the codewords. After the block is received, each n-bit codeword is treated as a string with a potential single-bit error. As with block parity checking, this does not eliminate the possibility of multiple-bit errors within one codeword, but it does make it extremely unlikely, especially if the block size is fairly small.

HISTORICAL NOTE
A pioneer of error-correcting codes

Richard Wesley Hamming (1915–1998), born in Illinois, was a mathematician who did much revolutionary work in the mathematics of computing. In 1945 he joined AT&T's Bell Labs, where he did much of his work. Though not Hamming's only contribution to the field, it was his work on error detection and correction codes that made him famous. He published the fundamentals of the methodology in 1950, creating a new domain within information theory. To this day, Hamming codes are widely used, fundamental to the operation of error-correcting data codes.

5.4 Summary

We have explored error control from the perspective of error detection and error correction, with special reference to point-to-point connections. In the process, we have seen that there is a tradeoff between accuracy and overhead, as is typical in the field of data communications. The most basic error detection technique, simple parity check, also is the least capable; the most complex technique, cyclical redundancy check, is the most reliable. No matter what, there is no foolproof error detection technique.

When it comes to error correction, the simplest technique, ARQ, also is a bandwidth hog because of the many repeated transmissions that are required when the transmission system is not particularly reliable, as is the case with wireless transmission. On the other hand, for highly reliable wired systems, its simplicity makes it preferable. More complex systems are involved in forward error correction, which also introduces significant overhead. But for the more error-prone wireless systems, the added overhead is much less than what would be required for the large volumes of repeat transmissions that otherwise would be needed. That makes the computational complexity a good tradeoff.

In the next chapter, we will discuss various ways to connect senders and receivers, what a network is, and how we connect the devices that make up our network—that is, the ways in which networks are arranged to accommodate various types of communications.

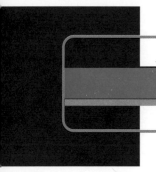

END-OF-CHAPTER QUESTIONS

Short answer

1. When analog signals are distorted by noise, why can we not restore them to their original form?
2. What are burst errors? Give examples.
3. What is the difference between backward and forward error correction?
4. Repeat the 3-bit inversion example of burst error discussion in section 5.3, using even parity.
5. How is the size of the checksum field related to the segment size we can use to group the bits of a frame?
6. Using even parity and a segment size of 8 bits, construct the block parity check frames for the following bit sequence:
   111000111110110100000000011111111

7. Calculate the number of redundant bits needed for forward error correction for message block sizes of 4,000, 8,000, 12,000, and 16,000 bits.
8. Calculate the code rates for each of the block sizes in the previous question.
9. What is the Hamming distance; how is it used in error correction?
10. Explain how parity is used to find the location of single-bit errors in the forward error correction technique.

Fill-in

1. The error detection method in which the frame is divided into a number of equal size segments is _____.
2. The error detection method that uses simple arithmetic is _____.
3. The error detection method that uses polynomials is _____.
4. The simplest error detection technique is _____.
5. The _____ error detection method achieves great reliability while using just one error detection field per frame.

6. Backward error correction depends on the receiver _____.
7. Forward error correction is handled by the _____ independently of the _____.
8. The error correction technique that relies on matching sums is _____.
9. For error correction in a frame with m message bits and x extra bits, x must satisfy the inequality _____.
10. If two codewords are a Hamming distance H apart, it takes _____ bit inversions to convert one codeword into the other.

Multiple-choice

1. The output of an amplifier is
   a. the restored original signal
   b. a multiple of the original signal
   c. a multiple of the attenuated signal
   d. a multiple of the attenuated signal and noise
   e. a multiple of the attenuated signal minus noise

2. Longitudinal parity check is based on
   a. the number of sequential 1-bits in the frame
   b. whether the number of 0-bits in the frame is odd or even
   c. whether the number of 1-bits in the frame is odd or even
   d. whether the total number of bits in the frame is odd or even
   e. whether the last bit in the frame is a 0 or a 1

3. Vertical parity check
   a. can detect almost all single-bit and multiple-bit errors
   b. has less overhead than longitudinal parity check
   c. detection accuracy depends on the size of the frame
   d. is most often used for analog transmission
   e. works best with odd parity

4. The number of bits in the checksum is
   a. one more than the number of bits in the segment
   b. equal to the number of bits in the segment
   c. one less than the number of bits in the segment
   d. $2m$ bits, where m is the segment length
   e. $2n$ bits, where n is the frame length

5. CRC
   a. trades computational complexity for increased error detection capability
   b. is easily implemented in hardware
   c. relies on the value of a remainder
   d. discards the quotient
   e. all of the above

6. Assuming the header and message part of a frame is m bits long and the CRC field is $n - m$ bits long, the divisor is
   a. m bits long
   b. $m + 1$ bits long
   c. $n - m$ bits long
   d. $n - m + 1$ bits long
   e. n bits long

7. Assuming that the frame is n bits long and the header and message part of the frame is k bits long, the CRC field is
   a. n bits long
   b. k bits long
   c. $n - k$ bits long
   d. m bits long
   e. $n - m + 1$ bits long

8. The "minimum distance codeword approach" to error correction
   a. is the quickest method for burst error correction
   b. assumes that the fewest bit errors occurred
   c. disregards bit strings that are not legitimate codewords
   d. will detect bit inversions that result in legitimate codewords
   e. is an alternative to Hamming distance methods

9. Forward error correction
   a. calls for additional overhead that is useless if there are no transmission errors
   b. saves overhead by largely eliminating the need for frame retransmission
   c. is principally used in wired transmission systems
   d. relies on the CRC to detect errors
   e. both a and b

10. Forward error correction
    a. is used in conjunction with longitudinal parity check
    b. is used in conjunction with vertical parity check
    c. is used in conjunction with checksum
    d. is used in conjunction with CRC
    e. none of the above

True or false

1. When we use amplifiers to extend the distance over which analog signals are transmitted, we employ filters to remove the noise components.
2. Because digital optical systems are so reliable, we do not need to use error detection mechanisms.
3. Digital transmission systems are preferred over analog systems for data transmission because we usually can restore the bit-signals in the latter, even after they have been altered by noise.
4. Longitudinal parity check can detect transmission errors only when an odd number of bits are faulty.
5. Vertical parity check improves on the detection of multiple-bit errors because a block of bits is less likely to have errors than a string of bits.
6. Checksum usually outperforms longitudinal parity check but not vertical parity check.
7. FCS is an error detection method.
8. Forward error correction depends on inserting redundant bits into the frame.
9. Forward error correction is principally used in wireless transmission systems.
10. Without using codeword blocks, we cannot correct multiple-bit errors.

Expansion and exploration

1. The CRC via polynomial in the example in Appendix E stops after calculating the CRC value. Continue this example to show the receiver calculations when there are no bit errors; repeat after introducing 1-bit errors and 3-bit errors.
2. Investigate Reed-Solomon codes. Why are they considered to be the foundation of forward error correction? To what are they applied?
3. Investigate "bit error rate." How does it relate to choosing between error detection and error correction?

6

Communications connections

6.1 Overview

Communication involves at least two entities—a sender and a receiver. In broad terms, those entities may be people, computers, other types of equipment, or some combination. How is this communication set up? Must there be only one sender and one receiver? Is one allowed only to send and the other only to receive? Can both transmit and receive? One at a time or simultaneously? Must a line be used for just one transmission at a time, or can multiple transmissions take place simultaneously?

In this chapter, we will discuss the answers to these questions. After we sort these out, we will explore what a network is and how we connect the devices that make up our network—how networks are arranged to accommodate various types of communications. You will learn about direction of transmissions, modes of connections, combining signals over a single connection, and the physical arrangements of networks.

6.2 Direction of data flow

When you listen to a radio newscast, the newscaster is the sender and you are the receiver (as are all of the other people listening to that station). You can listen to the broadcast, but you can't respond to the broadcaster.

If you have a cell phone with "walkie-talkie" capability, you can carry on a conversation with another person who has a similar phone. However, only one person can talk at a time. In order to speak (transmit), you press a button, which gives you control of the communication path. When you are finished, you release the button to signal the other person, who then can speak in the same way.

When you connect your computer to another over a telephone link, the computers can communicate with each other simultaneously, each transmitting and receiving at the same time. In a telephone conversation between two people, etiquette and practicality dictate that only one person should speak at a time, although the circuit established for the telephone call does not demand that etiquette. Of course, if both parties speak at once, their voices will be blended and, just as if they were speaking face to face, they won't understand each other.

What we are describing here are different modes of data flow. In the first instance, data flows in one direction only—from the radio station to the listener. This is called a *simplex* mode. Other examples of simplex communications are the links between a fire alarm or security alarm and the fire station or police station, between a remote control and a television set, and between a thermostat and a furnace.

In the second instance, information flows in both directions between the parties, but in only one direction at a time. This is called a ***half duplex*** mode. Other examples of half duplex communications are radio traffic between a pilot and the control tower, and the interplay between a computer and an attached DVD recorder.

In the last instance, information flows in both directions at the same time—this is called a ***full duplex*** mode. Full duplex communications are found in some modems and the TCP protocol used on the Internet, as well as in some local area networks (LANs) and most high-speed network connections.

What is the impact of a mode choice? It is an issue of physical and logical paths, and bandwidth. Simplex, being a one-way connection, means either that there is no need for a receiver response over the link (as with a fire alarm) or that two simplex links must be employed for two-way communication. Half duplex is useful where two-way communication is necessary but bandwidth is limited—because the single link is used one way at a time, bandwidth sufficient for one direction is enough for both. Full duplex, permitting simultaneous two-way communication, requires either greater bandwidth or duplicate links—one in each direction.

6.3 Using connections

What do the following examples have in common?

* You connect your computer to your printer via a cable.
* You press a button on your remote to control your TV.

In both cases, there is a direct link between the two devices and the full capacity of that link is dedicated to those devices. In this type of ***point-to-point*** connection, there is no intermediary between the devices (see Figure 6.1A).

Now what do these examples have in common?

* Twenty terminals in a room are communicating with a mainframe.
* A 15-workstation bus LAN incorporates a database server.

In both cases, there is a *single link shared* by multiple devices in communicating with another device. This type of connection is called ***multipoint*** (see Figure 6.1B). Connection types are explored in greater detail later in the chapter.

What is the impact of a connection choice? With point-to-point connections, link management is simpler and the link's full bandwidth is available for the use of the attached devices. With multipoint connections, link management may be more complex and, because bandwidth is shared, communications between any two devices may be slower than if they had a point-to-point connection.

FIGURE 6.1

Connection types

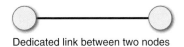

Dedicated link between two nodes

A. Point-to-point

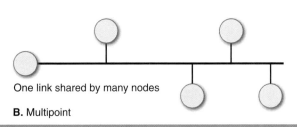

One link shared by many nodes

B. Multipoint

Managing shared links

All shared link methods have one goal in common—to reduce the amount of wiring required by point-to-point connections. There are two possibilities for link sharing. In one, the entire communications channel is taken by a single device but for a limited time (time sharing), after which it is available to other devices. In the other, channel capacity is divided over several devices that can then use the channel at the same time.

However sharing is accomplished, one hurdle must be overcome before it can take place: managing the sharing so as to avoid chaos in the system. That is, we need to consider *multiple access protocols*—*multiple* because many devices will share the link; *access* because what needs to be managed is how a device gets to use the link; *protocols* because what is established are the rules for managing multiple access.

In *centralized management* of link sharing, one device controls the access of all the other devices. This makes multiple access management straightforward and relatively simple to implement, because the controlling device is a single point of link usage coordination. On the other hand, it also means that there is a single point of failure—should the controller fail, the attached devices would not be able to use the link.

A prime example of centralized management is *polling*—the controlling device queries the other attached devices in turn and grants access, one at a time, according to which ones want to use the link. There are versions of polling that operate as first come, first served and versions that incorporate priorities. There also are limits as to how long a device can use the link before having to relinquish it, usually controlled by limiting the amount of data that can be sent in one link access period.

A similar control technique is a *reservation system.* In a restaurant, a manager keeps track of patron requests for dining reservations, which gives them access to tables; in a transmission system, the attached devices request permission to use the link and a central controller manages the requests, granting access to the communications link according to various algorithms.

A different approach to centralized control is *multiplexing.* It also is a different approach to sharing, because it focuses directly on the link's capacity, which is allocated over the attached devices to use as needed. The methods to do this divide link capacity based on frequency, wavelength, or time. Access to the shared link is the province of the *multiplexer,* which combines transmission requests from the attached devices and sends them out over the shared link, and also distributes incoming data to the appropriate devices.

In sharp contrast to centralized management, *decentralized management* (also called *distributed management*) of link sharing is based on protocols that the individual devices follow to manage themselves when seeking access to the link. Common in LANs and some wide area networks (WANs), such protocols are found in Ethernet and token ring LANs (see Chapter 9, "Local area networks"), among others.

Centralized access methods

In *polling,* one of the connected devices, called the *primary* or *master station,* controls access by having all data transfers go through that station. Further, transfers by the other devices, called *secondary stations,* can take place only after getting polled by the primary. In this process, the primary polls one of the secondaries. If the polled station has no data to send, it responds with a *NAK* (**n**egative **ack**nowledgment) message. If it does have data to send, it transmits the data to the primary, which will *ACK* (**ack**nowledge) receipt of the data. The primary forwards that data to the appropriate secondary.

Polling is a common control method used for mainframes and minicomputers. In those setups, secondary stations typically talk only to the primary (the mainframe or mini) and not to each other. When data is destined for the primary, the process ends there. If the data is meant for (addressed to) a different secondary station, the primary *selects* that station and forwards the data to it. The primary also can send messages to all stations.

AMPLIFICATION

The controller is a device attached to the mainframe or minicomputer. A secondary sending data to the computer actually sends it to the controller, which selects the computer and forwards the data. Similarly, a secondary requesting data from the computer will have that request forwarded by the controller. Then the data is sent from the computer to the controller, which forwards it to the secondary.

As noted, the main advantage of polling is that it is straightforward and simple to implement, although the master is a single point of failure. A significant drawback to polling is high overhead, a situation that worsens as the number of attached stations increases, which causes the number of polling messages to grow. Overhead is measured by the number of bits of control data sent compared to user data and the amount of time spent on controlling compared to the time spent transmitting user data. Because the ultimate purpose of communications networks is to send user data, control bits and control time are deemed to be overhead.

Propagation time can be a drawback as well. If the polled stations are far apart—for example, when a satellite is the primary—round-trip propagation time is relatively long. That means that the time it takes to poll is long, forcing stations to wait until they get permission to transmit. In those cases, reservation systems may be preferred.

The reservation process is based on dividing access time over the attached stations. Very small mini-slots of time are set aside by the primary to carry reservation messages from the secondaries. The primary collects reservation requests and then allocates regular-size time slots to the reserving stations. Because reservation requests come only from those stations that need to use the link, stations that have nothing to send do not need to participate in the access process, thus saving time for all. After the slots are used, the process repeats.

One of the reservation schemes, called *packet-demand assignment multiple access (PDAMA),* has the secondaries competing for reservation slots via a contention method—for example, first come, first served. This is like announcing concert ticket sales to a group of people who can reserve tickets by calling in; requests are granted in the order received until no tickets are left.

In another scheme, called *fixed priority-oriented demand assignment (FPODA),* one reservation mini-slot is assigned to each secondary station for use as needed; certain stations may also be given priority—for example, a server might have priority over a workstation, or a store-file request might have priority over a print request. This is like selling season tickets to a performance series; you can use your tickets or not, and if not, the seats remain empty; those who have purchased season tickets in the past may get priority for the next season over those making new requests.

Another form of central access control is the *queuing* model. When data packets (ordered groups of bits) arrive at a network device faster than they can be processed, they queue to wait for processing. The network device employs various schemes to prevent the queues from growing too long. Hence, though not central in the sense that there is just one device controlling all access, the queuing model is central in the sense that for the portion of the network involved, control is by the device and not directly by the transmitting stations. Chapter 7, "Digital communication techniques," discusses this type of control in greater detail.

The access methods just discussed all are packet based. That is, they deal with link sharing on a packet-by-packet basis. You may get access for one packet and then have to wait for access for another packet, depending on link usage. (Packet switching is explored in Chapter 8, "Comprehending networks.") Another form of centralized control is based on a circuit switching model—that is, after you have gained access to a link, you keep it until you are finished using it. (Circuit switching also is examined in Chapter 8.) A prime example of this is cell phone systems. Within a cell, a mobile switching station manages access centrally. However, when a phone is given access within a cell, it keeps it until the caller hangs up. (Cell phones are discussed in Chapter 14, "Wireless networks")

Multiplexing can be classified as a centralized control scheme in the same sense as queuing. Because of its importance and prominence in communications, we have given multiplexing its own section in this chapter.

Decentralized access methods

What do these two examples have in common?

- To enter a highway, you drive up the on-ramp and look to see if traffic will allow you to move onto the main roadway. If there is room to merge, you drive onto the highway; otherwise, you wait.
- You come to an intersection and stop at the stop sign. You would like to make a left turn, so you check for traffic on the intersecting road and for traffic on your road coming from the opposite direction. If all is clear, you turn left; otherwise, you wait.

In both of these examples, you (and all the other drivers) control access to various roadways yourselves by following the rules of the road. Use of the roadways is randomized—that is, there is no way to determine who will come along and want to travel on a particular road at a particular time. Anyone wishing to use a road must ***contend*** (compete) with all the other drivers who also want to use the road at that time.

This analogy applies to link sharing. Each station (device) gains access to the medium by contending for time according to some rules. One such rule is as follows: When a station wants to use the link, it listens for traffic on the link. Hearing none, it may use the link; otherwise, it waits. As with the automobile example, medium access demands by any particular station occur unpredictably, so such contention is called a ***random access method.***

One problem with contention is that even though stations follow the wait-until-clear rule, they still may attempt to gain access at the same time. For example, suppose two stations listen and hear no traffic, so they both transmit. Their transmissions ***collide*** and are destroyed. This is analogous to your driving across an intersection whose crossroad is a blind curve—you think the road is clear but another car is rounding the curve and you collide with it. Contention access protocols methods are explored in greater detail in Chapter 9.

With ***token passing,*** individual stations also manage their own access, but by very different, non-contention, rules. A special frame called a token is passed from station to station. The token is like an admission ticket to the shared link, and because only one station at a time can hold a token, only one at a time can use the link. Thus, access is controlled and collisions are prevented. This procedure is followed in the token ring LAN. Each station is linked to two others, called predecessor and successor stations. Data flows only in one direction, from station to station, and the stations form a ring. Additional rules prevent monopolizing the ring. (Token rings are explored in Chapter 9.)

AMPLIFICATION

Token rings can be called mixed centralized/decentralized access control. This is because in addition to the self-managed access process, one specific station on the ring acts as a monitor, ensuring that the ring is operating properly and taking specific action if it is not. Thus, it manifests a type of central control.

One problem with any of the token-passing schemes is their complexity, which means that a significant amount of computer time is spent on link management. Another issue can be round-trip time—the time it takes for a token to make a complete trip around the link before becoming available to the next station. On the other hand, as opposed to random access, performance in token passing schemes is deterministic. That is, when we know how many stations are involved, we can calculate how long it will take before the token works its way back to a given station under various conditions, ranging from no station wanting to use the link to all stations wanting access.

6.4 Multiplexing

As we saw in Chapter 1, "Introduction," early in the development of the telephone system the cost pressure of adding and managing an increasing number of telephone wires led to the development of methods by which the phone wires could be shared so that multiple simultaneous conversations could be carried over a single link. Such techniques are called *multiplexing,* the most widely used of all link-sharing methods.

The idea is to combine signals from several slow-speed links into a single signal for transmission over a high-speed link. Why would we want to do that? Simple economics. Although low-speed links cost less than high-speed links, the total cost of multiple low-speed links is greater than the cost of a high-speed link whose capacity equals that of the combined low-speed links.

Each end of the link has a *multiplexer (mux)* to which the communicating devices are attached. On transmission, the mux merges multiple signals onto a single line; at the other end, the receiving mux separates the combined signal into its original components, a process called *de-multiplexing.* (See Figure 6.2.) Typically, the two functions, multiplexing and de-multiplexing, are combined in a single box, which is simply called a multiplexer.

Frequency division multiplexing

The first successful multiplexing technique, introduced in about 1925, was *frequency division multiplexing (FDM).* At the time, all telephones were analog devices: Human voices, which are composed of combinations of sinusoidal sound waves, were carried over the wires as their electrical parallels (analogs), combinations of sinusoidal electric waves.

Very early on, phone companies, realizing that it was not necessary to carry the entire spectrum of the human voice (about 100 Hz to 7,000 Hz), calculated that restricting the range of vocal sounds transmitted to 300 to 3,400 Hz—the so-called *voice band*—would

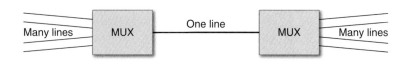

FIGURE 6.2

General multiplexer arrangement

produce acceptable quality for phone conversations and be less demanding on the communications system. Thus, a bandwidth of 3,100 Hz (3,400 − 300) was used to carry one conversation.

As it happens, phone wires have a much greater bandwidth than 3.1 kHz, so the phone companies began to explore ways to use that extra bandwidth to enable multiple simultaneous conversations to be carried over a single path. If this could be achieved, a great amount of the demand for phone service could be satisfied without an equivalent amount of additional wiring. (To be more precise, phone companies were looking for ways to share links beyond the local loop, which would remain unshared subscriber access. As we have seen, FDM was the technique first chosen.)

Suppose that a single wire pair could actually carry a 1 MHz range of frequencies, and suppose that, instead of 3,100 Hz, we were to allocate 4 kHz to each phone conversation (we will see where this number comes from shortly). That means that one wire pair could potentially carry 250 simultaneous conversations (1 MHz/4 kHz = 250). But every one of those conversations would begin as a human voice transmitted by the telephone in the same 300- to 3,400-Hz range—if they were all put on the shared wire as is, they would overlap, interfering with each other so that no conversations would be intelligible.

Each conversation's spectrum must therefore be shifted into its own frequency range for transmission, each using an equal size but a different subrange of the 1-MHz overall range. For example, the frequencies of one conversation could be shifted up to the range of, say, between 4 kHz and 8 kHz, those of another conversation to between 8 kHz and 12 kHz, still another conversation to between 12 kHz and 16 kHz, and so on. With each conversation occupying its own section of the bandwidth, all could be carried simultaneously (multiplexed) without interfering with the others.

So why 4 kHz instead of 3.1 kHz?—to avoid interference from frequency overlap of adjacent conversations. The extra bandwidth between each conversation's allocation is called a *guard band.*

Now, for the sounds to be intelligible to the people at either end, each transmitted range of frequencies must be converted back (demultiplexed) to its original 300- to 3,400-Hz range. This up and down frequency shifting is the essence of FDM.

To accomplish the shifting, we need to *modulate* (modify) an analog *carrier* so that it imitates the original frequency patterns of the voice (within the voice band), but at the carrier's higher frequency—carrier frequency typically is much higher than modulating signal frequencies. We establish a carrier sine wave, say of frequency f_1, for one conversation and then transform it by adding that conversation's voice frequencies to it. Then we use another carrier frequency, say f_2 (where $f_2 - f_1$ equals the subrange bandwidth), for another conversation, and so on. The *modulating signals*—those that have the information we want to transmit—are called *baseband signals.* So the transmit multiplexing process takes each input baseband signal and uses it to modulate individual carriers, thereby recreating the patterns of the baseband signals in the higher frequency ranges. (Appendix A, "Sine waves: basic properties and signal shifting," explains how frequency shifting modulation is accomplished.)

The carrier modulation process, carried out by the mux, is what divides the bandwidth of the line into discrete partitions called *channels,* each of which carries a separate conversation. (See Figure 6.3.) For transmission, the mux combines all the signals by adding them together, creating the single composite signal that is sent over a single wire pair, thus transmitting all conversations at once. (Because the separate conversations are combined in the composite signal, the partitions actually are channels.)

The process is reversed at the receiving end. First, *filters* re-create the separate channels (see "Technical extension: Bandpass filters"). For example, if we apply a filter that will pass signals only in the 8-kHz to 12-kHz range, that channel is re-created. The last step is

TECHNICAL NOTE
Dealing with the infrastructure

In the earlier days of telephone systems, almost all the wire was unshielded twisted pair (UTP). Not only was there no shielding, but the twists were what might be called informal, if they even existed—they often served more to identify particular pairs than to reduce crosstalk. Although this was fairly suitable for voice communications, transmitting the higher-frequency multiplexed signals would be problematic because attenuation and crosstalk become more severe as frequency increases.

Even after much old wire was replaced, the use of *loading coils* and *bridge taps* on the local loops presented direct limitations. Loading coils reduce the attenuation affects of the wire, thereby enabling a signal to travel much farther before becoming too weak. Developed early in the 1900s, they are still in common use. However, although loading coils improve transmission of signals in the voice band, they also add noise and distortion in frequencies above those in the voice band that are used for data transmission. Hence, the broader bandwidth and higher frequencies needed for FDM are unavailable in lines with loading coils.

Bridge taps are connections to the local loops that were used to create party lines—telephone lines whereby two or more customers shared the same telephone number. Bridge tapped lines are not in a direct path between customer premises and the central switching office. Because of this, an impedance mismatch is created in the transmission line, resulting in signal reflections. Although this is usually not a problem for basic phone service, reflections cause significant interference in the high-frequency ranges needed for fast data communications services. (For example, DSL, discussed in Chapter 10, "Circuit switching, the telcos, and alternatives," allows the local loop to carry signals of much higher frequency at higher speeds.) Even when the party lines are disconnected, as long as the taps remain in place, so does the effect.

Loading coils can be removed and bridge taps can be isolated, but they have to be located first. Records of their installation were not always accurate or complete, so finding them often involved much time-consuming testing and detective work, making it difficult and costly to provide DSL service to some households. It is one of the reasons that DSL is still not available in every locale.

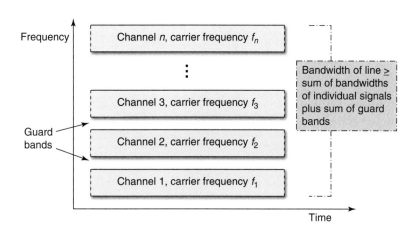

FIGURE 6.3

Frequency division multiplexing (*n* devices)

FIGURE 6.4

The FDM process
(*n* devices)

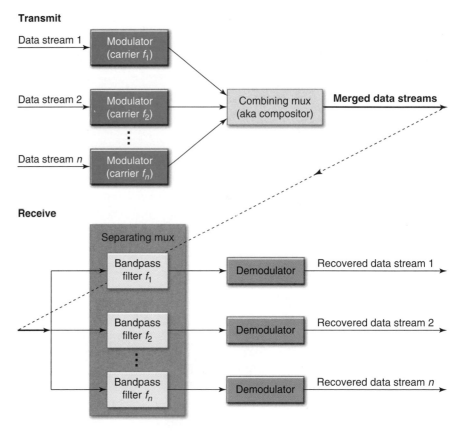

to drop the frequencies of the signals in each channel down to their original 300-Hz to 3,100-Hz range, re-creating the original voices. Figure 6.4 illustrates this process.

FDM can combine only analog signals. This is because FDM must limit the bandwidth of the signals it carries so that the link's overall bandwidth can be subdivided into bands that can be used separately and simultaneously. Analog signals can be band-limited even if they are not band-limited to begin with. Digital signals cannot be band-limited readily. FDM can be applied to any analog transmission link with suitable bandwidth. Cable television relies on FDM, as do AM and FM radio broadcasting (see "Technical note: FM radio").

FDM is appropriate for any analog system where the total of the bandwidths of the individual signals plus the guard bands is not more than the overall bandwidth of the system.

Wavelength division multiplexing

The unused line capacity issue that we saw for electrical transmission of analog signals applies to light signals as well: The capacity of optical fiber is much greater than what is needed to relay one transmission. Unless we can utilize it, most goes to waste. Hence, it is natural to turn to multiplexing.

Because optical fiber bandwidth is so large, dividing that bandwidth with an FDM approach seems appropriate—but with light as the carrier, we focus on wavelength rather than frequency. Recall from Chapter 2, "The modern signal carriers," that wavelength and frequency are inversely related, as indicated by the equation $\lambda = v_m/f$, where λ is wavelength, v_m is the speed of light in medium m, and f is its frequency. Also recall that whereas

TECHNICAL EXTENSION
Bandpass filters

A bandpass filter is an electronic device that passes only frequencies of a particular range. The ideal filter would pass full signal power for all frequencies in the range and zero power for all others. In practice, filters usually are designed to the half-power rule—output power of the low (f_1) and high (f_2) cutoffs will be half their input power; frequencies between will quickly move toward full power; frequencies outside will be less than half power and quickly approach zero. Figure 6.5, called a *spectral plot*, is an example.

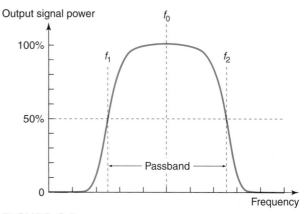

FIGURE 6.5

Bandpass filter, spectral plot

TECHNICAL NOTE
FM radio

FM radio stations use FDM to transmit their signals. The Federal Communications Commission (FCC) defines FM radio as having a 20-MHz bandwidth whose range is 88 MHz to 108 MHz. Within that bandwidth, partitions (channels) of 200 KHz, including guard bands, are assigned. The carrier for each channel is centered in the channel's frequency range.

When you tune in an FM station, say 104.1 (actually 104.1 MHz), you are selecting the carrier frequency that defines the particular channel over which the station is broadcasting. Because each partition is 200 kHz, successive carrier frequencies (and therefore radio dial numbers) above 104.1 are 104.3, 104.5, 104.7, and so on up, and below 104.1 are 103.9, 103.7, 103.5, and so on down; each is 200 kHz apart, with the carrier frequency in the center of the range. For example, the range for 104.1 extends from 104.0 to 104.2, the range for 104.3 extends from 104.2 to 104.4, and so on. Because of this arrangement, the lowest FM carrier frequency that can be assigned is 88.1 (with a range of 88.0 to 88.2); this is why all FM station numbers are odd.

The 20-MHz overall bandwidth can support 100 different stations (20 MHz/200 kHz = 100). But there are thousands of FM stations across the country. How are they supported? The answer is that station broadcast power is limited, so that within a predefined distance a station's signals attenuate to a point where the same carrier frequency can be used by another station beyond that distance, normally without interference. Unfortunately, attenuation also depends on atmospheric and other conditions. Therefore, under the right (or wrong?) conditions, the signals from two stations broadcasting on the same carrier frequency could potentially interfere with each other.

HISTORICAL NOTE
Some of FDM's progenitors

In 1862, Hermann Ludwig Ferdinand von Helmholtz (1821–1894), a German scientist, mathematician, and philosopher, described the *Helmholtz resonator* that could pick out particular sound frequencies. When excited by an electrically driven tuning fork, it could be used to produce messages that could be received by a similarly tuned resonator. This idea was incorporated by *Alexander Graham Bell, Emile Baudot,* and *Elisha Gray* (1835–1901) to send multiple Morse code telegraph messages simultaneously on the same wire. Helmholtz, whose interests lay elsewhere, did not pursue that avenue.

Bell's early experiments replaced tuning forks with tuned reeds. At the sending station, each reed would produce a signal on a different frequency; reeds at the receiving station tuned to the same frequencies would reproduce those signals. Bell later shifted to electrically tunable metal reeds that could be made to vibrate at many different frequencies. This was the basis for the device used to transmit the historic "Mr. Watson—come here . . ." message.)

In 1876, Bell received a patent for multiplexing Morse code. Called *harmonic-frequency multiplexing,* it was based on those electrically tunable reeds. Although in theory voices also could be transmitted using this system, it could not support the frequency range that would be necessary.

In principle, all these efforts were early forms of FDM.

frequency is determined by the light source and does not change, wavelength is determined by the speed of light and does change. Color is determined by wavelength as well. Thus, the idea is to use different wavelengths of light as carriers of the data transmissions that we want to multiplex, a technique called *wavelength division multiplexing (WDM).*

Conceptually, WDM is similar to FDM. We divide the bandwidth of our fiber-optic link into sub-bandwidths centered on particular wavelengths, $\lambda_1, \lambda_2, \lambda_3, \ldots, \lambda_n$ (our carriers), thus creating n transmission channels. Then we shift our original n signals into those different wavelengths (see "Separating the wavelengths of light" in Appendix C, "Light"). These are combined into a single composite signal for simultaneous transmission over a single-fiber link. At the receiving end, the process is reversed: The composite signal is separated into n channels and their signals are converted to their original wavelengths, thereby recovering the original data.

As with FDM, the channels created for WDM are separated by guard bands to keep signals in adjacent channels from interfering with each other. Some WDM systems use more closely spaced carriers and smaller guard bands to fit more channels into a given bandwidth. This is called *dense WDM (DWDM),* although often all systems are referred to simply as WDM. As yet, there is no accepted definition for drawing the line between WDM and DWDM. One rule of thumb is that WDM systems handle up to eight signals per fiber, whereas DWDM systems go up from there.

Time division multiplexing

FDM is an analog technique, not efficient for digital transmission. Yet for digital signals the goal is the same—transmitting multiple digital signal streams over a single transmission path. To that end, another technique was developed: *time division multiplexing (TDM),* also is known as *synchronous TDM.*

HISTORICAL NOTE
WDM, then and now

Practical single-transmission fiber-optic transmission systems date back to the mid-1970s, but the first successful WDM demonstration did not occur until 1985; it combined only two signals over a relatively short distance. Five years later, Bell Labs was able to transmit a 2.5 Gbps signal over 7,500 km without needing regeneration. Although it was a single signal, it demonstrated that light transmission over long distances was practical.

The next step was multiplexing. By 1998, Bell Labs demonstrated a system that transmitted 100 simultaneous 10 Gbps optical signals over a single optical fiber for a distance of 400 km (about 250 miles). A little calculating reveals that the overall data rate of this transmission was 1 Tbps (1 terabit per second, or 10^{12} bits per second). Commercially available systems today can handle 160 channels of 10 Gbps signals. Experimental systems have been able to transmit 256 39.8 Gbps channels over a single 100 km fiber link. These will likely reach the marketplace in the near future.

WDM systems are popular with telecommunications carriers because they can expand the capacity of their existing installed optical fiber. That is, by upgrading their WDM multiplexers, they can carry more data without adding any more fiber. On the downside, higher-performance equipment is complex and costly (but in most cases less costly than adding fiber). Only recently have standards been adopted (see ITU-T G.694.1) that make it easier to integrate WDM with older systems, particularly SONET (discussed in Chapter 10).

Although TDM operates as simultaneous transmission from the viewpoint of the senders and receivers, it actually is a ***sequential transmission*** technique. Instead of dividing a broad bandwidth into narrow sub-bands, time on a single connection is sliced into small, fixed-length, full-bandwidth segments (time slots) that are allocated to the attached devices in rotation (see Figure 6.6). The combination of slots creates a ***frame.*** Frames are transmitted sequentially without delay.

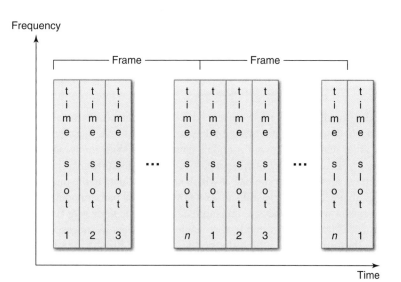

FIGURE 6.6

Time division multiplexing (*n* slots)

TABLE 6.1   **TDM efficiency vs. number of devices**

(8-bit slots)	2 devices		10 devices		24 devices	
	Control bits	Overhead	Control bits	Overhead	Control bits	Overhead
No frames	2	11.1%	10	11.1%	24	11.1%
Frames	1	5.26%	1	1.23%	1	0.52%

Data from the attached devices are sent to the mux buffers; a *scanning sequencer* transfers data to their corresponding time slots. If there is no data for a particular slot, it remains empty. Each time slot holds very little data, perhaps 1 byte or even 1 bit. Thus, many cycles are required to accommodate the data streams to be transmitted. However, the slots cycle so quickly that data appear to be transmitted continuously.

The key to TDM's simplicity lies in having each device assigned to a particular slot in the frame. At the receiving end, the same number of devices are similarly attached and assigned appropriate slots. Thus, sending device 1 and receiving device 1 are connected, as are sending device 2 and receiving device 2, and so on. Because of this arrangement, distribution of data requires almost no processing.

This system of frames and buffers saves a lot of overhead and processing. Were they not used and a device's bits sent out as they arrived, control information would have to be sent for each device's transmissions. This would increase both overhead and processing load. With the frame-buffer system, just one mini control slot is necessary for the entire frame, no matter how many slots it contains (and therefore no matter how many devices are attached). This is why frames are used in TDM systems.

For example, Table 6.1 illustrates the gain in efficiency (drop in overhead) as measured by overhead percentage for 2, 10, and 24 devices. For simplicity, we assume that without frames, each device needs just one extra bit for control.

AMPLIFICATION

Carrying information in frames requires that frames be properly demarcated. That is, for proper transport of the frame, receiving devices must be able to determine precisely when the frame begins. This is called *frame synchronization.* The first bit is the synchronization bit (also called a framing bit, flag, or start frame delimiter) that highlights the start of the frame. Note that this type of synchronization is distinct from *bit synchronization,* which is concerned with synchronizing the sender and receiver clocks to the bit times. Frame and bit synchronization are discussed in Chapter 7.

Typically, the data that a node must send requires many slots. Because the mux sends out each node's data a little at a time, it takes several slots (and therefore several frames), possibly a great many, to transmit a node's data stream. With many nodes sending data, how is it that from a node's view this appears to be continuous transmission?

To see how, let's consider the rate at which nodes send data to the mux buffer. Suppose, for example, that each node transmits at a rate of 100 bytes per second and we have 1-byte slots. If the rate at which frames are transmitted matches the *node rate* (in our example that would mean 100 frames per second), then each node's slots in successive frames will be available at the same rate at which the nodes are transmitting to the buffers. Hence, to the nodes, it looks like slots are available continuously without delay. For this to work, the capacity of the shared link has to equal or exceed the sum of the node data rates.

With TDM, the frame rate must match the node transmission rate.

(For a more thorough explanation, see "Technical note: Node rates and frame rates.")

As with FDM, whatever is multiplexed on the sending end must be demultiplexed on the receiving end. Recovering the data sent by a node requires collecting the data in that node's slot for each frame involved and recombining those data into the single stream that the node sent to the transmit mux in the first place. This must be done for each attached node—each slot. One node may have needed 12 frames to send all its data, another node three frames, another node 200 frames, and another node no frames (that is, no data to send). A *scanning resequencer* in the receiving mux removes data from each time slot and buffers it for reassembly into the original stream, which is held in the mux's outgoing buffers until it can be sent on to the appropriate attached device (see Figure 6.7).

TECHNICAL NOTE
Node rates and frame rates

Because TDM muxes transmit multiple data streams sequentially, not simultaneously, how can it be that node data is transmitted in what, to the node, appears to be a continuous stream?

Suppose we have just two nodes, each transmitting at 800 bits per second, and frame slots are 1 byte each. The mux constructs frames with two 8-bit slots and adds 1 bit for control, giving each frame 17 bits. For the moment, let's ignore that control bit and think of the frame as just 16 bits. To be able to transmit frames at the node's bit rate, we need the frame rate to match the node rate—here, 100 frames per second. Because our frames have 16 bits, the frame bit rate is 1,600 bits per second, which matches the combined rates of the nodes (2 × 800 bits per second).

The nodes and the mux use electricity to transmit the bits, and electricity travels at the same speed for both. We can't have the mux use faster electricity—it doesn't exist. How, then, can the mux transmit at a faster rate than the nodes? Only by decreasing its bit duration.

In this example, the bit duration for each node is .00125 seconds (1/800); the bit duration for the frame is

.000625 seconds (1/1,600), which is half the bit duration of each node. So by the time a node "looks" for its next slot (.0125 seconds later), an entire two-slot frame is sent out and the next slot is available. Recall that the nodes send their data to the mux buffer, so they do not actually look for a slot—the point is, slot availability and data transmission happen at the same pace at which the node is sending data. That's why the nodes are able to transmit continuously.

We do have to make a slight adjustment to this example—we must bring back that control bit that we temporarily ignored. This gives us a 17-bit frame and a frame bit rate of 1,700 bits per second, for a bit duration of .000589 seconds. So the bit rate is slightly more and the bit duration slightly less. Still, the preceding result applies. For *n* nodes connected to the mux, the frame bit rate must equal the node bit rate and the frame bit duration will be slightly less than 1/*n* times the node bit rate to account for the control bit.

One more point: For the mux to work properly, all nodes must be operating at the same bit rate. If they are not, we must pad (add dummy bits to) the faster nodes so that, in effect, they slow down. Thus, the speed of the slowest node is the governing factor.

FIGURE 6.7

The TDM process
(*n* slots)

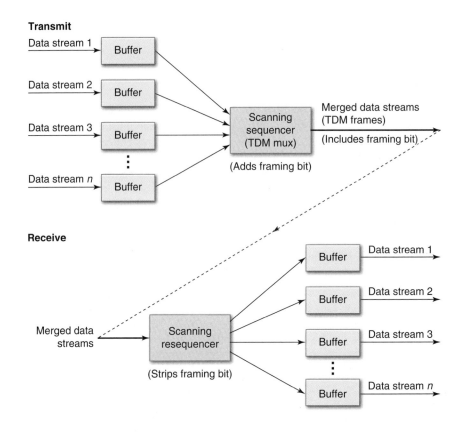

If we look at the mux from the viewpoint of any one of the devices, we see a sequence of slots into which the data goes. That sequence, then, is a conduit for data transmission, or in other words, a data transmission ***channel.*** (This is analogous to calling each FDM sub-band a channel.) The data from the combined sequence of a node's slots appear to arrive at the receiving end as though there were a single connection between the sender and receiver, that is, as though there were a direct channel. Because of the fixed slot assignments, the transit time for each attached device is predictable. Add relatively simple operating rules, and we can see why TDM is a widely used technique. For example, TDM is the basis for the widely used T-carrier and SONET systems (discussed in later chapters).

The principal drawback of TDM is that the slot assigned to one node cannot be used by another, even if the one has nothing to transmit. This results in transmission of empty slots, wasting transmission capacity (see Figure 6.8). Such an event is not uncommon. Typically, some nodes have a lot of data to transmit or they transmit frequently, whereas

FIGURE 6.8

A TDM example with one-character slots

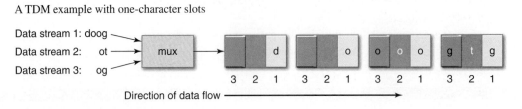

others have little or nothing to send or transmit infrequently—the bursty transmission typical of computers.

To address this problem, another version of time division multiplexing was developed, called *statistical TDM (STDM),* also known as *asynchronous TDM.* (Synchronous TDM, the first to be developed, is usually referred to simply as TDM.) This method assigns fixed-size slots according to device transmission needs. Thus, if a node has no data to transmit, its slot can be used for another node, thereby reducing the likelihood of empty slots. Even with this procedure, though, it is possible that there is not enough data to fill the whole frame. The STDM mux incorporates logic in the scanner to reassign slots according to its buffer contents.

The efficiencies gained by STDM come at a cost. As noted with TDM, each time slot is assigned to a particular node at each end of the transmission, so routing slot data to the proper receiving node is simple. With STDM, slots are assigned by need, so one node's data could be in several slots, and not even the same ones in successive frames.

The only way the receiving mux can know which device the incoming data is meant for is to include device addresses along with the slot data. In addition, other management data is desirable. For example, we may want to include extra bits for error checking. In sum, then, both STDM frames and device slots must be longer than those of TDM. Thus, not only is more transmission capacity lost to overhead, but more complex processing is required (which requires more costly equipment and results in more time lost to processing).

As an example, let's look at the implications of addressing. A key question is, how many slots do we want in a frame? (In other words, how many nodes will be attached to the mux?) Suppose we have just two. Then we need only 1 bit for addressing. What if we have four? Then we need 2 bits for addressing. With 3 bits we can handle up to eight addresses, and with 4 bits we can handle up to 16. In general, with n bits, we can address 2^n nodes—simple enough. But remember that these bits must come from each slot, so if we have 8-bit slots and, say, 16 nodes, we have to use half of each slot just for addresses.

Clearly this is an intolerable overhead burden, yet multiplexing 16 nodes doesn't seem like much to desire. The solution lies in increasing the number of bits per slot. If we want to keep overhead bits to a given percentage, the slot size must be increased accordingly. Let's say we want no more than 10 percent overhead for address bits. Then for every address bit we need 9 data bits, or a 10-bit slot.

In general, for an x percent overhead ratio, we need $n_a/n_t = x\%$, where n_a is the number of address bits and n_t is the total number of bits in the slot. If we have 24 slots, then to address 24 nodes we need 5 address bits ($2^4 = 16, 2^5 = 32$), and for 10 percent overhead, that means 45 data bits per slot. Similar results apply for other percentages.

Well, this is an easy calculation, but as usual, there are tradeoffs. The bigger the slot size the bigger the frame, hence the longer it takes to transmit a frame, so the longer it takes before the next round of slot filling can take place and the greater the delay potential for any node. We could reduce slot size by settling for a higher overhead percentage, but then we would be transmitting relatively less data per frame. If we want less overhead, we can either reduce the number of attached nodes so we don't require as much address space, or we can increase slot size further, settling for slower transmission times. Figure 6.9 shows a typical STDM frame without noting component sizes.

One aspect of STDM mitigates our tradeoff dilemma somewhat. The concept of STDM relies on the observation that not every node has data to transmit every time. This means that the capacity of the shared link does not have to equal or exceed the sum of the node data rates as it does with TDM. Instead, we can make an assumption about how many

FIGURE 6.9

STDM frame components

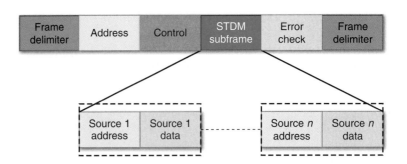

nodes are likely to be transmitting at any one time and base our number of slots on that figure, which presumably is less than the total number of nodes.

This situations is analogous to the CO-to-CO telephone issue noted in Chapter 1. In that chapter, we gave an example of 5,000 lines between two COs; when all 5,000 were engaged by callers, the 5,001st could not make an inter-CO call until someone hung up. Here, a node's data that does not find an empty slot must wait in a buffer until one comes up. Because of this, the TDM requirement that the number of nodes on each end must be equal is not a requirement for STDM. On the other hand, we now have a buffer management issue to contend with. If more data is waiting to be sent than can be accommodated, some nodes will have to wait before their data is acted upon.

Buffers are finite. As long as there is room in the buffer for incoming data, to the sending device it looks like the transmission succeeded. Whether the data is transmitted in the next cycle or in later cycles is not known to the device, and is usually not relevant. But what if the buffer is full? Then any incoming data will be refused and the device will experience a delay—that is, the device will know that transmission did not occur. That data will have to be re-sent. So we have another decision to make—trading off buffer size for delay potential.

There is an even more complex STDM scheme that allows for variable-length slots. For that, along with device addresses, individual slot lengths must be carried. As you would expect, this exacerbates the overhead problem.

Inverse multiplexing

The multiplexing techniques we have been discussing until now all have one purpose—to combine several low-speed channels into one high-speed channel, so that data streams from those multiple channels can share a smaller number of common connections. What can we do if we have a high-speed data source but only low-speed channels for transmission? We may do the inverse—that is, band together several low-speed channels so that they act as one high-speed channel, thereby allowing transmission at a much higher data rate than would be possible with any of the low-speed channels alone. Appropriately, the device to do this is called an *inverse multiplexer* (or *inverse mux*). An inverse mux could, for example, couple two 64-Kbps lines into one 128-Kbps line, as is done in ISDN (Integrated Services Digital Network) systems.

Just as with regular multiplexing, whatever happens at the transmitting end must be reversed at the receiving end. The process is quite different from de-multiplexing, because the input streams that a mux combines are not related to each other; with an inverse mux, a single input stream is separated into sub-streams that are transmitted over the bundled channels, so every channel's data is part of one data stream. That data stream has to be re-created (de-inverse muxed) at the receiving end. Similar to multiplexers and de-multiplexers, the inverse multiplexer and de-inverse multiplexer typically are combined into one box called an inverse mux.

Multiplexing and full duplex connections

Link access, or as we also call it, channel access, most often is a two-way affair. That is, communications across a channel go in both directions. As we have seen, this mode of communication is called *duplex,* simply another word for two-way. We also have seen that "two-way" may mean one way at a time (half duplex) or both ways at the same time (full duplex). If we use TDM to transmit signals in both the forward and reverse directions, and full duplexing to separate the outbound and inbound signals, we have *TDD* (time division duplexing); if we do the same with FDM, we have *FDD* (frequency division duplexing); for optical systems, we have *WDD* (wavelength division duplexing).

To provide full duplexed circuits for TDD, FDD, or WDD, we need separate paths for the two directions. For digital signaling and TDM, this is accomplished with a four-wire connection—two wires for outbound and two for inbound (see Figure 6.10). Each wire pair provides a simplex (one-way) circuit, and the two paths are physically separate. For analog signaling and FDM, this can be accomplished with one wire pair, the transmissions in each direction being carried on separate sub-bands. Wireless transmissions can operate in full duplex mode if sufficient bandwidth is assigned so that different sub-bands can be used for outbound and inbound signals. For optical systems, full duplex operation can be accomplished with a single fiber pair (one fiber in each direction), with one optical fiber and DWDM.

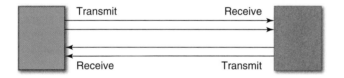

FIGURE 6.10

Full duplex, two wire pairs

6.5 Networks and topologies

When applied to computers, the term *network* encompasses many things. The purpose of a computer network is *communications*—that is, we create networks to provide a vehicle for *transferring information* from one place to another.

For this to happen, the *devices* (components) of the network must be *connected* to each other in a systematic way, using agreed upon *protocols,* so they can *understand* each other.

A computer network is a system of interconnected, comprehending, communicating hardware and software, designed to facilitate information transfer via accepted protocols.

In the next sections of this chapter, we will look at different layouts for physically connecting the components of a network—*physical topologies*—and the ways in which those connections may be operated—*logical topologies.* We will see that a network may be physically connected in one way and yet operated in another, and we will see why that may be a good idea.

TECHNICAL NOTE
Node/media placement

We indicate node connections by showing node-link patterns. But when it comes to installing a network, the actual placement of nodes and the media that connect them will vary considerably. In a business, for example, computers are placed in offices, carrels, and so on; cables must be laid in accordance with floor layouts, walls, columns, and building designs. Although the diagrams we show are not realistic in terms of actual cable runs and node placements, they do illustrate how nodes are linked to each other.

Point-to-point physical topologies

Let's start with a general characterization of physical topologies as *point-to-point* or *multipoint.* The usual definition for a physical point-to-point network is that each device can communicate directly only with those devices to which it is directly connected, and that those direct links are not shared. Figure 6.11A shows an example of two point-to-point links; nodes A and B communicate directly with each other, as do nodes C and D.

If we put a link between nodes B and C, as shown in Figure 6.11B, we create the possibility of, say, node A communicating with node C. But this can happen only if node A uses the point-to-point link between nodes B and C. From a strictly physical viewpoint, in this new configuration any of the links can be used by any of the nodes, so those links are shared and this is no longer a true point-to-point network.

On the other hand, we can look at this situation from the viewpoint of link access control. For example, if node A wants to send a message to node C, with the arrangement shown in Figure 6.11B the message must go from A to B, and it is node B that sends the message to node C; that is, access to the B-to-C link is controlled by B and C alone. Hence, we could say that the directly connected nodes, B and C, still have their dedicated link. From that perspective, Figure 6.10B is an example of a point-to-point network, too. This illustrates that physical connections are one thing, and access is another.

The same dual view may be taken for another physical topology, the mesh network. Here, many links directly connect two nodes that also may be used (shared) by many other

FIGURE 6.11

Point-to-point links

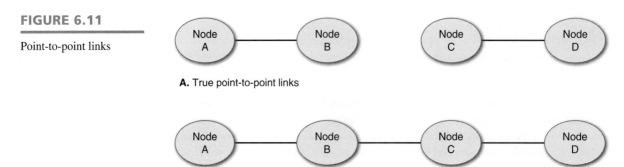

A. True point-to-point links

B. A chain of point-to-point links

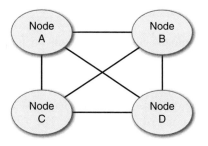

A. A four node full mesh network

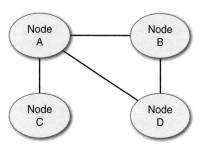

B. A four node partial mesh network

FIGURE 6.12

Mesh networks

nodes. In the ***full mesh*** design shown in Figure 6.12A, every node has a direct connection to every other node. In the ***partial mesh*** design shown in Figure 6.12B, the node A-to-C link is the only true point-to-point connection from the physical viewpoint, all the other links being usable by nodes A, B, and D as well. Once again, though, the nodes involved in the direct pairings, A-B, B-D, and A-D, control access to those links. The same applies in the full mesh of Figure 6.12A.

The full mesh needs much more cabling than the other configurations, and each node needs multiple connectors to accept those cables. Although partial meshes alleviate that situation somewhat, mesh designs always use more cable and connectors than others.

Another variation of a point-to-point network is a ***tree*** structure. In this topology, multiple nodes are connected in a branching manner, as illustrated in Figure 6.13. Once more, we see direct links between pairs of nodes (each node is connected only to its immediate neighbors) and indirect links (going through intermediate nodes) that can create a path between any two nodes.

Tree structures add a complication: Each node that branches in more than one direction (here, nodes A, C, E, and F) needs to know something about the nodes on those branches so that messages flowing down the tree can be properly directed. In effect, those nodes rank higher in order compared to the other nodes on the branches, with the node at the top (here, node A) having the highest order. For this reason, tree structures also are called ***hierarchies.***

It is possible to envision a protocol wherein any node getting a message meant for some other node simply passes it on to whichever nodes it is attached (a procedure called ***flooding***). This eliminates the need for a node to know what the tree looks like beyond its

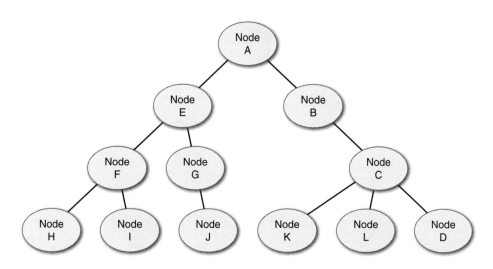

FIGURE 6.13

A tree (hierarchical) network

immediate neighbors. It also adds to the volume of traffic on the network, because messages will be sent down irrelevant paths.

Still another physical topology is the **ring.** As with the other point-to-point configurations, each node in a ring is directly attached only to its immediate neighbors. The ring differs in that the attachments form a complete loop, as illustrated in Figure 6.14. Another difference is that rings are **unidirectional**—that is, messages travel around the ring in only one direction. Thus, nodes must pass on any message intended for another node. We have seen that this requirement applies to other point-to-point structures as well. The ways in which nodes may circulate messages—that is, control over point-to-point links—are the subject of **link access management.**

FIGURE 6.14

A ring network

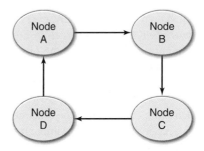

Finally we come to the star structure, illustrated in Figure 6.15. In this configuration, a central device creates the appropriate path between two nodes. In essence, that device makes each node an immediate neighbor of every other node. Therefore, a message from one node travels directly to another (via the central device) and does not have to go through any other nodes.

The central device may be a simple pass-along **hub** that sends an incoming message out to all connected nodes, or a **switch** that can direct messages along particular paths. Once more, we come to link access management and logical topologies, a subject we explore in greater depth later in the chapter.

Multipoint physical topologies

Physical **multipoint** networks (also called **multidrop** networks), are characterized by *shared* communications links—that is, every node is attached to a *common link* that all must use.

The simplest of these is called a **bus** structure. The bus is the common link shared by all nodes, as shown in Figure 6.16. A message from any node to any other travels along the bus in both directions. Link access control—gaining access to the bus—is the responsibility of each node. Thus, access control is decentralized.

FIGURE 6.15

A star point-to-point network

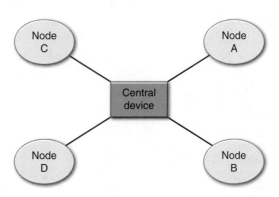

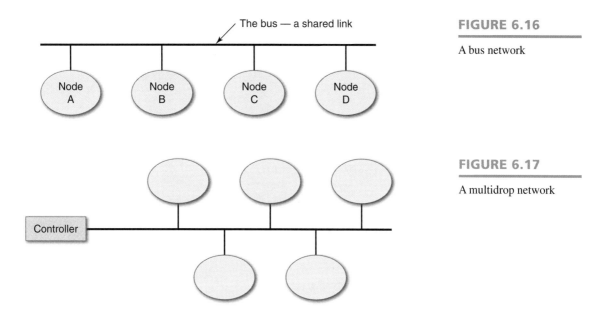

FIGURE 6.16

A bus network

FIGURE 6.17

A multidrop network

Although this arrangement looks similar to the point-to-point network shown in Figure 6.11, in the bus, messages do not pass *through* each node. Instead, messages travel from a node to the common bus and reach all other nodes via their taps into the bus.

In a similar-looking structure, nodes also are attached to a common link as in the bus arrangement, but link access is governed by a single additional node (a controller). This is called centralized access control. Figure 6.17 shows this configuration.

Hybrid physical topologies

It is possible to create *hybrid* networks in which different physical topologies are combined. For example, we can lay out a tree network with bus extensions, as shown in Figure 6.18A. You can think of other combinations as well.

One common hybrid configuration is used with *satellite* networks. Communications from a land-based node to the satellite (called *uplink*) typically are point-to-point; the node can reach only a particular satellite. On the other hand, communications from the satellite (called *downlink*) often can be received by more than one land-based station, the air (or space) being the common medium (Figure 6.18B). Satellite networks are discussed in Chapter 15.

Logical topologies

Many physical topologies can operate differently from the way they are connected. For example, a physical star network, the most versatile, can be run as a ring, as a bus, or as point-to-point links. We noted briefly in the discussion referring to Figure 6.15 that we could set up a star with either a hub or a switch as the central device. A hub simply passes on to all other nodes the message it receives from one node. Those other nodes ignore messages not addressed to them. So, in effect, the hub behaves like the bus shown in Figure 6.16, and we are *running our physical star as a logical bus*.

If instead of a hub we use a switch as the central device in our star, the switch recognizes the destination address of the node that a message is intended for and makes the connection between the sending node and the destination node. Because any pair of nodes can be connected in this manner, the switch turns the star into a collection of direct

FIGURE 6.18

Hybrid networks

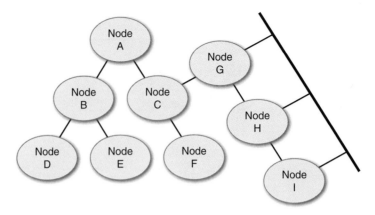

A. Tree/bus

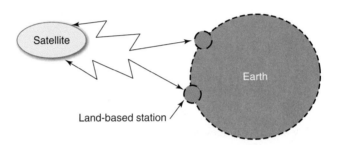

B. Point-to-point uplink/mutipoint downlink satellite hybrid network

point-to-point links by which each node can have a direct connection to any other node. Thus, *our physical star is operating logically as a pseudo mesh*. It is a full mesh in the sense that every node has a direct connection to every other node (*n* nodes, *n* − 1 links), but it is not a true mesh because there are no paths that involve more than two nodes; thus, there are no alternate routes between two nodes as there are with a true mesh.

We even can run our star as a ring. All we need is a central device that treats each attached node as a neighbor of two other nodes and passes a message from one to another. (The ***multi-station access unit (MAU)*** used in IBM Token Ring LANs is such a device—the token ring is physically constructed as a star but operates logically as a ring.) Figure 6.19 illustrates this setup. For example, a message from node A to node C would travel from A to the switch, then to B and back to the switch, then to C. In this instance, *the physical star is a logical ring*.

Because star wiring requires a cable run from every node to the central device, stars need more cable than all of the other configurations except the mesh. Yet, for local and building-wide networks, the star-wired topology is the most prevalent configuration scheme used. Why is this so?

Primarily, it has to do with issues of maintenance and ease of reconfiguration:

- **Maintenance:** Each node has a single link to a central point, so node faults are easy to trace.
- **Ease of reconfiguration:** Adding or relocating a node simply means one cable run to the central device, whereas removing a node is accomplished by simply unplugging it from the central device—no other cables or connections need to be disturbed or changed.

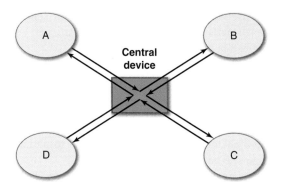

FIGURE 6.19

A star-wired ring

More complicated topologies are used for wide area networks—primarily hierarchies and meshes, mostly because the numbers and locations of the nodes that need to be connected are widespread, numerous, and variable, and because alternate routes between nodes are vital both for robustness and routing efficiency.

Interestingly, the mainframe-to-terminal topology can be thought of as a star, because the mainframe acts as the central device through which all messages must travel. However, most single-location terminals are not wired directly to the mainframe but instead share links in a multidrop fashion. Therefore, mainframe-to-terminal topology is actually a hybrid topology.

In Chapter 1, we saw a full mesh design for interconnecting telephones, wherein each telephone or phone switch was connected to every other one. We also saw that the amount of wiring required by such meshes grew extremely rapidly, to the point at which such a scheme quickly became infeasible. Therefore, partial meshes, in which not every phone or switch is fully connected, along with tree designs are blended to create most of the wide area interconnections of telephone carriers and the Internet.

6.6 Finding your way around a network

Now that we have seen the basic network topologies, we can look at the ways in which messages reach their destinations in those topologies.

Addressing basics

You mail a letter, send an e-mail message, make a telephone call. For these communication mechanisms to work, the system carrying the messages must be able to identify the communicating parties. Hence, there are postal addresses, e-mail addresses, and telephone numbers. These identifiers, though quite different looking, have two characteristics in common:

- They *uniquely identify* the communicating parties, so that a message is sent to the intended recipient and not someone else.
- There are *consistent rules* for their establishment and use, so that the systems in question know how to formulate and interpret addresses.

The same is true of computer networks. For one node to reach another, the system needs an addressing procedure that uniquely identifies the communicating nodes and follows consistent rules. Actually, many different addressing schemes are used in computer networking, each designed for a particular type of system. For example, there is one system for Ethernet LANs, another for Internet e-mail, another for frame relay wide area networks, and so on. Within a given system, all devices must follow and understand the addressing procedure. Between systems that use different schemes, some method is needed to convert one system's addresses to another's. (Particular addressing and conversion methods are explained in subsequent chapters.)

No matter what addressing scheme is used, schemes fall into one of two basic forms: *flat* and ***multipart*** (also called ***multilevel*** and ***hierarchical***). In a flat address, only one piece of identifying information is used. One example is a product serial number; it identifies a particular instance of that product, but nothing more. Another is the automobile VIN, a unique number that identifies a particular vehicle. Neither of these identifiers carries any indication as to where the item is at any time. If we want to find a particular product or vehicle, flat addresses are no help at all.

Each PC that is a member of a LAN has a ***network interface card (NIC)*** that contains a unique flat address assigned by the NIC manufacturer. This address is called a ***medium access control (MAC) address.*** Although MAC addresses uniquely identify every PC, there is no logical connection between one MAC address and another. Hence, like the VIN, knowing a machine's MAC address tells you nothing about where that machine is located.

AMPLIFICATION

Actually, a MAC address has two parts. One is a manufacturer code, called an ***organizationally unique identifier (OUI),*** that is administered and assigned by the IEEE (Institute of Electrical and Electronics Engineers) and is different for every manufacturer. The other is a serial-like number created by the manufacturers themselves. Because the OUIs are unique, and the serial-like numbers for any given manufacturer are unique, the MAC addresses are unique.

In networks in which MAC addresses are used, the whole address is treated as a single number that uniquely identifies a machine but not its location. Hence, it is a flat address. MAC addresses are discussed further in Chapter 9, "Local area networks," along with Ethernet.

By contrast, multipart addresses do contain location information, typically in a hierarchical form. The information you put on an envelope is such an address, with name, street name and number, city, state, and ZIP code all being separate parts that serve not only to uniquely identify the intended recipient, but also identify where that person resides.

The addressing schemes used in wide area networks also are multipart. In simplest form, one part identifies the network where the destination machine resides and the other part identifies the machine itself. Other multipart schemes have additional levels.

It is not necessary for every node in a system to know all the addressing information of every other node. In large networks that use multipart addresses, intermediate nodes add addressing information to the basic addresses provided by the source nodes, so as to route the message from device to device and on to its destination. We discuss routing schemes in Chapters 13 and 15.

WAN addressing considerations

As we have seen, we need to assign addresses to network nodes so that they can be found, either as end destinations or as intermediate points in a route from the sender to the recipient. When it comes to WANs, the number of nodes can range into the millions (as in the Internet). How can all these addresses be assigned, and how can they be managed?

Consider the postal system once more. Each piece of mail may be routed through many different locations to find individual destinations. These locations may be within particular geographical areas, in which there can be a great many street names that have many different building numbers, which may include private houses, apartment complexes comprising many apartments, commercial edifices with numerous offices, and so on, within which many people can be located. So a mailing address has a ZIP code, state, city, street name and number, and perhaps other information such as an apartment number, a floor, a company department, and a name—multi-level addressing.

The name of the friend you are mailing a letter to is not likely to be unique—a great many people may have the same name. But it is much more likely that there is only one person with a particular name, ZIP code, and street address. So too, with a WAN. If we demarcate subsections of the network and further divide those into sub-sub-sections and so on, we can create a system whereby every node has a unique multi-level address—a network address, a sub-network address, a local network address, a machine address. In fact, that is precisely what is done. The scheme is implemented in several different ways. We will see specific examples in later chapters.

Process addressing

Until now, we have considered physical addressing issues—how to identify a particular machine in a network. We also need to think about what goes on within a single computer. Your network computer is likely to be running more than one application (*process*) at a time. You may be downloading the latest anti-virus data, sending a query to a remote machine, receiving e-mail messages, transmitting a photo to a friend, writing a document, and perhaps engaging in an instant messaging conversation. When information from all of these activities arrives at your computer, how does it know which application gets what information?

Just as your machine must have a unique physical address so that it can be found, each application running on it must have a unique address so that information can find it. These addresses are called *service access points (SAPs)* in the OSI model architecture and *ports* in the TCP/IP model architecture. They serve the same purpose for applications that physical addresses do for machines. When you start an application, an SAP or port number is assigned to it by the operating system; when the application is terminated, that address is released so that it can be made available to another application. Process addressing is discussed in greater detail in subsequent chapters.

6.7 Summary

In this chapter, we discussed communications connections from several viewpoints—the direction of data flow and the way links are connected, accessed, and managed. We spent some time delving into methods for utilizing one link for multiple simultaneous transmissions (frequency and time division multiplexing), how this is accomplished, and the ramifications of the processes.

We also looked at network topologies and saw that a network could be connected one way (the physical topology) and operated another way (the logical topology). Then we considered addressing, one key to finding our way through a network.

In the next chapter, we will look at encoding schemes that make transmission of our data via electricity and light possible.

END-OF-CHAPTER QUESTIONS

Short answer

1. Describe simplex, half duplex, and full duplex data flow modes.
2. Discuss the relationship between data flow mode and bandwidth.
3. What are the advantages and disadvantages of centralized management of link sharing?
4. What are the advantages and disadvantages of decentralized (distributed) management of link sharing?
5. How do contention methods address link access?
6. Why is it not possible to directly transmit multiple telephone conversations over a single line simultaneously?
7. Why does TDM give the illusion of simultaneous transmission?
8. How does WDM make use of diffraction?
9. Explain the relationship between the data rates of the inputs to a TDM and the data rate of the output.
10. What is the relationship between physical and logical topologies?
11. Distinguish between flat and hierarchical addresses.

Fill-in

1. The link between a fire alarm and the fire house is an example of a _____ mode of data flow.
2. In _____, the controlling device queries the other attached devices in turn and grants access, one at a time, according to which ones want to use the link.
3. A NAK from a polled station indicates _____.
4. A _____ results when two devices attempt to use a link at the same time.
5. The bandwidth of the voice band is _____.
6. The multiplexing technique that transmits multiple signals simultaneously is _____.
7. The multiplexing technique that transmits multiple signals sequentially is _____.
8. _____ is the minimum bandwidth needed for a line to simultaneously carry 25 100-kHz channels with 10-kHz guard bands.
9. For _____ multiplexing, the number of lines on the receiving side must _____ the number of lines on the sending side.
10. The physical topology that requires the most wire is _____.

Multiple-choice

1. A single link can be shared by several devices by:
   a. giving each device a limited amount of time on the full link
   b. giving each device a portion of the link's capacity
   c. slowing down the devices' data rate
   d. speeding up the link's data rate
   e. both a and b
2. Multiplexers manage link sharing based on
   a. time
   b. frequency
   c. wavelength
   d. all of the above
   e. a and b only

3. Compared to contention access methods, token passing
   a. is less complex
   b. is always faster
   c. guarantees access within a fixed period of time
   d. is less adept at handling large demand volume
   e. all of the above

4. The voice band is
   a. 100 Hz to 4 kHz
   b. 0 Hz to 4 kHz
   c. 300 Hz to 3.4 kHz
   d. 300 Hz to 1 MHz
   e. 0 Hz to 1 MHz

5. FDM
   a. is a technique for analog or digital transmission
   b. can combine only analog signals
   c. does not require guard bands
   d. is widely used with data networks
   e. both b and c

6. Bandpass filters are needed for
   a. FDM   d. both a and b
   b. TDM   e. both b and c
   c. STDM

7. WDM is similar to
   a. FDM   d. both b and c
   b. TDM   e. none of the above
   c. STDM

8. STDM
   a. attempts to make better use of time slots than TDM does
   b. requires that the number of sending and receiving lines be equal
   c. is used only with analog transmission
   d. has the same overhead as TDM
   e. all the above

9. A star physical topology
   a. can operate as a logical ring
   b. can operate as a logical bus
   c. requires more wire than a physical bus
   d. is the most widely used topology for local area networks
   e. all of the above

10. WAN addresses
    a. cannot be flat
    b. are analogous to ZIP codes
    c. are assigned by the end users
    d. are 8 bits in length
    e. are not used with logical topologies

True or false

1. A TV remote control is an example of a multi-point link.
2. All shared link methods have the common goal of reducing the amount of wiring that would be needed for point-to-point connections.
3. Multiple access protocols are concerned with managing sharing of a common link.
4. Contention methods of link access guarantee access within a given time period.
5. Multiplexing is the most widely used method of link sharing.
6. Loading coils make FDM more efficient.
7. For FDM, the bandwidth of the line must equal the sum of the bandwidths of the individual signals.
8. TDM is widely used in the T-carrier system.
9. Transmissions are unidirectional in a ring topology and bi-directional in a bus topology.
10. A service access point (SAP) is an application address.

Expansion and exploration

1. Find three manufacturers of frequency and time division multiplexers. Compare specifications and prices.
2. Describe the Helmholtz resonator, invented by Hermann Ludwig Ferdinand von Helmholtz. Do the same for Alexander Graham Bell's harmonic-frequency multiplexer. How do they relate to FDM?
3. Develop and graphically illustrate a multipart addressing scheme to find a particular product in inventory by warehouse number, section number, product type, model number, and serial number.

Digital communication techniques

7.1 Overview

A major benefit of representing communication information in digital form is that the information can be manipulated by standard computer techniques. In digital transmission, we can think of the data as simply a collection of bits sent serially in a stream over a single electrical or optical communications path (link) that connects the sender and receiver. Because the data are binary, they are represented by two physical states: as one example, positive and zero voltages. Depending on the speed of the connection, there may be thousands, millions, or even billions of bits darting along a link every second.

As this sea of bits arrives at the other end of the link, the receiver must very quickly:

- Determine whether a 1 or 0 was received.
- Parse the bits into meaningful information units.
- Determine whether the information units are complete and error free.
- Uniquely identify each individual information unit from among the many that constitute the entire transmission.

For these receiver functions to be performed automatically under computer control, we need some means of ensuring that they are done correctly in spite of problems that may occur during transmission. In the remainder of this chapter, we will examine how to take advantage of the digital representation of data to resolve these communication issues.

Before proceeding, we should make an important distinction between *digital transmission* and *digital communication:*

- Digital transmission deals with representing bits by discrete values of electricity or light and ensuring that a receiver can definitively distinguish the individual bits correctly. Among other things, this requires a mechanism for bit synchronization, described in Chapter 4, "Encoding." In addition, we need to consider frame synchronization, which we will explore in this chapter.
- Digital communication, on the other hand, considers a far broader range of issues that flow from digital representation of data. Of the four bulleted items described in the preceding list, only the first is a digital transmission issue; all four fall under the purview of digital communication. The first is covered in Chapter 4; the last three are the subject of this chapter.

7.2 Packaging bits for transmission: framing

Let's assume that an appropriate bit synchronization scheme has been used so that the 1s and 0s can be read accurately. As the sea of bits travels down the link from the sender to the receiver, the transmission system has to handle a variety of other issues to manage the flow; control information is added, to be read and interpreted by the receiver.

To be useful, control information must be added in an organized manner. Practicality requires that first the sea of bits be subdivided into relatively small groups called *frames.* The control information becomes part of each frame. (As we shall see in later chapters, various processes operating within the sender or the receiver may manipulate a frame. Depending on the process and what is being done, a frame alternatively may be called a *packet,* a *cell,* or a *datagram.* For the time being, we will use the term "frame" to refer to any of these.)

For a frame to be created, its bits must be delineated—distinguished from all the others in the stream; that is, frame boundaries must be clearly defined. How to do so becomes an issue because, after all, any bit patterns we wish to use for delineation will be composed of 1s and 0s, just as will all the original data of the frame. So the challenge facing us now is how to make sure that the pattern of delineating bits is recognized definitively and consistently as marking the frame's beginning and end, and that it is not confused with the frame's other bits. In other words, how is *frame synchronization* accomplished?

Whereas bit synchronization can be achieved by embedding periodic signal changes (clocking) in a particular bit-encoding scheme, frame synchronization requires demarcating the beginning and end of the data that make up the frame. If these framing bits are independent of any particular larger character set, such as ASCII or EBCDIC, the frame synchronization method is known as a *bit-oriented communications protocol.* Otherwise, it is known as a *character-oriented communications protocol.*

Frame synchronization is accomplished by surrounding the data we wish to frame with a unique collection of bits.

There is no universal definition for frame size. Each framing protocol defines its own rules for sizing. The smallest frame may comprise just 10 bits. Much larger frames also are possible, consisting of thousands of bits.

Character (byte)-oriented protocols

Most written languages have physical symbols that represent the alphabet of that language. In addition to these, special symbols are used as aides in understanding writing—grammatical symbols and features such as the comma, colon, space, and period. These symbols help group the alphabet into meaningful, easily understood words, sentences, and statements.

In the digital world of the computer, the entire alphabet must be based on just two physical symbols: 0 and 1. Because two symbols alone are not sufficient to comprise a meaningful alphabet, it is necessary to define *sequences of 0s and 1s* to represent a larger alphabet of *logical symbols.* One popular way of sequencing bits is known as the ***American Standard Code for Information Interchange (ASCII).*** This is a 7-bit code from which it is possible to define 128 (2^7) distinct characters, representing the digits 0 through 9, the uppercase and lowercase letters, grammatical symbols, and other special-purpose symbols.

AMPLIFICATION

An extended version of ASCII, also called ASCII-2, has 8 bits, providing an additional 128 possibilities. These are used for special-language characters and graphics symbols. In 7-bit standard ASCII, an eighth bit is used for parity error checking. It is this bit that is taken for extended ASCII, eliminating the possibility of parity checks.

You can find tables of both ASCII and extended ASCII at

http://www.lookuptables.com/.

Character-oriented protocols generally draw their control symbols (communications control characters) from a code such as ASCII. For example, the control symbol that indicates the start of a frame in some character-oriented protocols is the ASCII bit sequence 0010110, which is given the name SYN (for synchronize). Other communications control characters, similarly defined by fixed 7-bit ASCII sequences, are added to frames to perform functions such as error detection and to identify particular types of frames. These control characters are *overhead* bits in the transmission stream; that is, they are not part of the *payload* (the data we want to transmit). The more control characters we need to add, the lower the transmission efficiency.

Character protocols, though overhead-heavy, originally achieved popularity because of the speed with which they could be processed, a result of their simplicity—all the control characters are the same 7-bit size, and they operate independently of any bit patterns the payload may contain.

As computing power increased over the years, the ability to handle more complex and more efficient protocols grew. Accordingly, the importance of processing simplicity declined and the value of transmission efficiency increased. As a result, the popularity of character-oriented protocols waned to the point where they were no longer widely used. As this was happening, the appeal of bit-oriented protocols grew. Now they predominate.

Bit-oriented protocols

We generally try to minimize the number of overhead bits added to transmissions because they use space on the communications link that otherwise could be used to send additional data. Just as within a business organization where we try to reduce overhead because it does not directly produce revenue, we do the same within a communications system because it detracts from the data-carrying capacity of the system.

Because the focus in bit-oriented protocols is on bits, any character structure that might be part of the data is transparent to bit-oriented protocols. Bit protocols define the *positions* within the frame of the addresses, control bits, payload bits, and error-detection bits. So by knowing where the frame starts and ends, we can work out the position of each element in the frame. We can recognize them for what they are without the need for any other control bits. Therefore, bit-oriented protocols generally need to define only one control string, the one used to identify both the start and end of a frame. Usually called a *flag,* it is defined independently of character codes, such as ASCII or EBCDIC, and is not a member of those code sets. This approach means that many fewer overhead bits must be added to the frame compared to character-oriented protocols.

The calculations needed to decipher the frame structure and to manipulate its bits demand more processing power than is needed for character-oriented protocols. In the 1970s, when bit-oriented protocols were first proposed, computers were not sufficiently fast to do the necessary processing without slowing down the communication system. As is so often the case, implementation of bit-oriented protocols was delayed until demand pressure led to a solution—the development of specialized hardware. Today, processing power is no longer an issue and bit-oriented protocols are dominant.

7.3 Your data, my data, control data: transparency

In general, communications systems are not, nor should they need to be, aware of the content or structure of the *user data* being transmitted. (User data is the data that the user wishes to transmit, as distinguished from any control data that must be sent for the communications system to operate properly.) In fact, a good communications system should be able to transmit *any* user data, regardless of the control scheme used. Such a communications system is called ***transparent,*** meaning that its operation is in no way affected by user data. This implies that if the communications system needs to impose some structure on the data being transmitted, the symbols used to do so had better be so different that they could never be mistaken for part of the user data. Otherwise, dire consequences would follow.

To maintain framing scheme transparency, both bit- and byte-oriented protocols have an additional complexity that, when needed, adds to transmission overhead. Bit-oriented protocols achieve data transparency through a technique called ***bit stuffing.*** Byte-oriented protocols use a similar method called ***character stuffing.*** Both are explained later in this chapter.

7.4 Asynchronous and synchronous framing

In this section, we will examine two broad approaches used to build a frame. One, historically the first, is used within asynchronous communication; the second is used within synchronous communication.

Historically, asynchronous communication viewed information as being composed of "text" characters, such as the letters of the alphabet. Asynchronous framing focuses on packaging individual characters. Each character is represented by a grouping of bits defined by a code—for instance, 7-bit ASCII. Such frames, therefore, are very small in size (10 bits after the control bits are added).

What, then, is done with digital information that is not characters—that is, not represented as a 7-bit code? Commonly, it is divided into groups of 7 bits, and for transmission, each group is treated as though it represented a character. At the receiving end, these bits are re-associated with one another to re-create the original information.

How does asynchronous communication manage bit and frame synchronization transmission requirements? Because asynchronous communication was introduced early in the development of electronic technology, providing precise synchronization of each transmitted bit was not viable. Instead, the idea was that, because there are so few bits in a frame, by synchronizing the sending and receiving clocks at the start of the transmission of each character (frame), the sending and receiving clocks would remain synchronized for the time it took to send a single character.

Synchronous frames, on the other hand, tend to be very big, containing hundreds or thousands of bits. With such large frames, relying on frame synchronization would not work. If we only re-synchronized clocks at the beginning of each frame, the receiver's clock would be certain to have drifted significantly out of step with the sender's clock before the entire frame was received, causing the receiver to make substantial errors in decoding. That is why it is crucial for synchronous transmission to use a bit encoding scheme that is self-clocking, or, less preferably, to use a separate clocking line.

Efficiency implications

One factor to consider when assessing the effectiveness of a communications scheme is transmission efficiency. Although the framing of individual characters fills the dual role of frame and bit synchronization, the process adds many overhead bits. A high level of overhead also means that the time needed to transmit a complete message is significantly increased.

We can measure efficiency by the proportion of user data bits to total bits transmitted. For example, suppose we are sending X user data bits, but to send them we have to add an additional Y overhead bits. The efficiency, E, of the communication scheme is:

$$E = X/(X + Y)$$

With asynchronous communication, we have to send *3* overhead bits for each *7*-bit character transmitted—two for framing, as noted, and one for parity (a simple error-detection method discussed in Chapter 5, "Error control"). Hence:

$$E = 7/(7 + 3) = 7/10 \text{ or } 70\%$$

A surrogate measure of efficiency is the time spent transmitting the user data of a frame compared to the time it takes to transmit the entire frame. Whereas transmission time depends on transmission rate, the ratio of data time to total time is independent of the transmission rate. Here is an example: With a low data transmission rate of 300 bits per second (bps), the duration of each bit is 1/300th of a second. Therefore, to send one 10-bit frame takes $10 \times (1/300) = 1/30 = .0333$ seconds.

The 7-bit data portion of the frame takes $7 \times (1/300) = 7/300 = .0233$ seconds. The ratio of data time to total time is $.0233/.0333 = .6997$. So again, we could say that efficiency is about 70 percent.

A transmission efficiency of 70 percent means that 30 percent of the transmission time is taken up by overhead. Efficiency this low may be acceptable if transmission volume is low, but as the amount of information we need to send grows, such high overhead becomes intolerable.

As a different measure of efficiency, we can examine the number of overhead bits added per second of transmission. Although the asynchronous data frame has three overhead bits, because we are focusing on framing, let's just look at the two framing bits added. At low data rates, only a few bits are added per second of transmission, so the previously noted inefficiency is tolerable. At high data rates, however, the number of framing bits added per second increases dramatically, as the following examples illustrate.

At the low data transmission rate of 300 bps, the number of frames (characters) transmitted in one second is:

$$300 \text{ bps}/10 \text{ bits per frame} = 30 \text{ frames per second}$$

And the number of framing bits transmitted each second is:

$$2 \text{ bits per frame} \times 30 \text{ frames per second} = 60 \text{ framing bits per second}$$

At the higher data rate of 1,544,000 bps, a common rate in wide area transmission, the number of framing bits transmitted per second is:

1,544,000 bps/10 bits per frame = 154,400 frames per second

2 overhead bits per frame × 154,400 frames per second = 308,800 framing bits added per second

We can tolerate the added burden of 60 overhead bits per second, but 308,800 bits per second is another story.

Synchronous communication was introduced to fix several shortcomings inherent in asynchronous communication, the framing bit inefficiency problem in particular. To correct the latter, synchronous communication packages a very large number of bits in every frame, so the ratio of control bits to data bits is quite small. Synchronous communication schemes typically use 8 bits to define the beginning of a frame and another 8 bits to define the end of the frame. Many thousands of data bits can be held in between. These are viewed as a continuous stream without regard to any implied logical grouping that the sender may have intended.

For purposes of comparison, let's look at the two preceding examples from the perspective of synchronous communication. Suppose we use a 12,000-bit frame, a common size in local area networks. For transmission at the low rate of 300 bps, we sent 30 frames (30 characters) asynchronously in one second. With a synchronous frame, we could send those 30 characters as a continuous string of 210 bits (30 × 7 = 210), to which we need add only 8 framing bits at the beginning of the frame and another 8 bits at the end. So instead of 60 framing bits, we need only 16. This is not a dramatic difference because the data rate is so low—another illustration that at low data rates, asynchronous inefficiency is not critical.

For transmission at the higher rate of 1,544,000 bps, we sent 154,400 frames (1,080,800 7-bit characters) asynchronously in one second. Fitting these into our 12,000-bit synchronous frame requires breaking them into 91 frames (1,080,800/12,000 = 90.07). Because each frame requires 16 framing bits, we need add only 1,456 framing bits (91 × 16 = 1456), compared to the 308,000 needed by the asynchronous technique. That is a dramatic difference.

Now let's look at the history and details of the pioneer—asynchronous communication.

7.5 Asynchronous communication

The word *asynchronous* seems to imply an absence of synchronism. For data communication, that is somewhat misleading. As we have seen, there are two types of synchronism involved—bit level and frame level. These apply equally to asynchronous and synchronous transmission. What distinguishes the former is that it comprises character-at-a-time transmission *that can start and stop at any time between characters*. That is, there is no time relationship between the arrival of one character and the arrival of the next. Asynchronous, then, refers to the lack of this time relationship.

Origin: the Teletype

Asynchronous communication was introduced early in the history of data communications, well before the development of the first digital computers. The need at the time was to communicate data that was entirely textual—information in the form of the alphabet and other symbols found on a typewriter. For transmission, the message was entered on a typewriter-like keyboard of a device called a **Teletype,** which also had a mechanism to send the keystrokes electrically over wires to another Teletype machine.

Each individual keystroke was sent out independently as a sequence of bits as soon as a key was pressed. At the receiving Teletype, the bit sequence was interpreted and the corresponding keystrokes that represented text (as opposed to control) characters were printed one at a time on a roll of paper.

After each keystroke was received, the Teletype would wait for the next one to arrive. When that would happen was entirely dependent on the person typing the message at the sending side. With a fast, smooth typist, keystrokes would appear quickly one after the other in fairly regular fashion. But if the typing was irregular or the typist stopped in the midst of the message for a break, the time between strokes could vary considerably and it could be some time before another character arrived. Yet, whenever the next stroke was sent, the receiving machine had to be ready to accept it.

The mechanism of the Teletype was designed with this unpredictable nature in mind. It used special signals called start and stop bits to achieve the necessary frame synchronization. ("Technical extension: The Teletype," describes how it worked.)

Because of the start/stop nature of the transmission, this scheme of sending characters came to be known as **asynchronous communication.** Although there was no requirement for a regular fixed time between the arrival of one keystroke and the next, there was, in fact, a requirement for synchronization within the entire bit sequence of each keystroke. Asynchronous communication also has come to imply that we precede the code representing an individual keystroke, or, more generally, a character, with a start bit and follow it with a stop bit. For this reason, asynchronous communication is also called **start/stop communication.**

Years later, the start/stop concept was adapted for use in communication between a computer terminal and a remotely located computer. Subsequently, the same technique was used to provide the means for a PC to communicate with a remote computer.

TECHNICAL EXTENSION
The Teletype

Teletypes encoded keystrokes with a 5-bit Baudot code.* One keystroke caused 5 bits to be sent out on the wire sequentially. To create the 5-bit pattern for a particular keystroke, a mechanical disc rotated to allow or prevent electrical flow on the transmission wire, representing 1 and 0, respectively, for each of the 5 bits in turn.

That took care of the sending end, but what about the receiving end? To re-create a keystroke, the receiving device used five two-position switches to "remember" the 5 bits in the order in which they were sent. Setting the switches properly required the receiver's disc to rotate in step with the sender's. That is, it had to be *synchronized*. A special signal, called a start bit, caused the receiving Teletype's disc to start spinning and position itself correctly to receive a character.

After start was sent, the 5 bits of the keystroke followed. The receiver's disc would spin in concert with the

sender's as the latter transmitted electrical signals representing the 5 bits, and the receiver could set its five switches properly and print the character represented. Then the receiver's disc would slow down and come to rest. In the small amount of time that took, the sender had to be prevented from sending another character, because that would catch the receiver's disc out of position (that is, out of sync). Hence, the sender had to transmit another special signal, called a stop bit, which kept the sender from transmitting another 5-bit character long enough to ensure that the receiver's disc had come to a stop.

*For a brief biography of Jean-Maurice-Emile Baudot, as well as descriptions and pictures of his teletype machines, see http://profiles.incredible-people.com/jean-maurice-emile-baudot/. For the code itself, see http://foldoc.doc.ic.ac.uk/foldoc/foldoc.cgi?Baudot.

Next step: the terminal

The first computers to be used extensively by businesses were mainframes. Not only did their purchase cost run into the millions of dollars, they also had very high operating costs. Maintenance required highly trained, expensive technicians. Operations were complicated, and well-paid systems and software engineers were employed for that purpose. The huge quantity of heat that the mainframe's electrical components created had to be dissipated to prevent the machine from melting. This meant running coolant pipes throughout the system and housing it in an air-conditioned room as well. All in all, owning a mainframe was a very costly proposition, and even when leased it was rare for any company to have more than one.

To maximize the utility of the mainframe and distribute its costs, its reach had to be company-wide. That meant making a single mainframe available to employees throughout geographically separated work locations. So the issue to be resolved was how to provide *remote access.* A fairly obvious candidate to link the remote users with the mainframe was the widely available telephone system. To connect to it, special devices called *terminals* were developed. Through them, remote users could issue commands that the telephone system would carry to the mainframe.

In many ways, the terminal was similar to the Teletype. Both had a keyboard and a process for conveying textual information to a remote machine over a communication facility. Just as the Teletype was not capable of dealing with more than one character at a time, the terminal, because of memory limitations, also could deal with only one character at a time. It therefore made perfect sense to adapt Teletype's start/stop asynchronous communication technique for the terminal.

In addition to having almost no memory, early terminals also lacked processing capability. They therefore came to be called *dumb terminals.* As technology developed and cost declined, it became feasible to add processing power and memory. These upgraded devices were called *smart terminals.* Later still, when the personal computer (PC) arrived, it became possible to have a PC act as a terminal via appropriate software. Operating in that mode, PCs were called *intelligent terminals.* This was somewhat of a misnomer, however, because when the relatively "intelligent" PCs were emulating terminals, they actually were operating in a "dumbed down" mode.

The introduction of smart and intelligent terminals led to the possibility of developing techniques that could take advantage of their increased power, thereby significantly surpassing the limits of asynchronous communication. These improved methods were based on synchronous communication techniques, described in the next section.

To adapt asynchronous communication for the terminal-to-computer connection, some changes had to be made. For one, the Baudot code was not sufficient to provide representations for the variety of characters required when communicating with a computer. The 5-bit Baudot code could represent only 32 ($2^5 = 32$) characters. An extended version of the Baudot code was created that utilized the "shift" character to enable reuse of the 5 bits by signaling a shift to another set of character definitions. Even with this ability to represent additional characters, there still were not enough characters for computer communications. This problem was resolved simply, by replacing Baudot with the 7-bit ASCII code, capable of representing 128 ($2^7 = 128$) characters.

Another consideration was transmission errors. An error caused by character corruption during Teletype transmission would usually be obvious to the person reading the printed result. Because the message was meant to be printed and directly read by a person, this was not much of an issue. On the other hand, terminals were meant to communicate with an inanimate object—the computer. Corrupted characters might not be recognized as such and therefore would be misinterpreted, leading to results that, though erroneous, might not look wrong to the computer. This problem was addressed by appending a *parity check bit* to the transmission of each character, thus providing a simple automatic error detection capability.

A subtle adaptation difference was in how start and stop bits were used. In both the Teletype and the terminal, they served as synchronizing mechanisms. In the Teletype, these bits controlled initial positioning of the remote Teletype's disc and allowed time for the disc to stop rotating. For terminals, which had no such mechanical parts, these bits were used to frame each 8 bits transmitted (that is, the 7 bits of the character plus the parity bit). The stop bit signaled the start of the frame, and the stop signaled its end. As was noted earlier, the start/stop framing bits also provide for bit synchronization. The start bit is an event that the receiver cannot easily miss, for it causes the electrical flow on the line to change abruptly. This triggers the receiver to reset its clock so that it is, at least for the duration of the character transmission time, running in step with the sender's clock.

Waking the dozing computer

Because asynchronous transmission is sporadic, periods when nothing is being transmitted are frequent. Theoretically, during these periods of idleness no electricity need be sent along the line. But consider a traffic light. Theoretically, we need only one light to control traffic—say a red light. When the light is on, traffic has to stop; when the light is off, traffic can flow. The problem with this approach is that the light may be off because the bulb is burned out or the electricity failed. In other words, the situation is ambiguous.

Now consider the terminal. Suppose we signal a bit value of 1 by sending a positive current down the line and a bit value of 0 by sending no current. Further, when there is no data to send, we also send no current. When the receiver senses no current, is a stream of 0s being sent, is nothing being sent, or is there a problem on the line?

We could introduce a third signal, say a negative current, to represent an idle state. But remembering that simplicity was a major driving force in this technology, another solution is called for, one that uses just the two signals—positive and zero current. The answer lies in the form of the start and stop bits. When the line is idle, instead of sending no current, suppose we keep electricity flowing. That is, we send a constant stream of 1 bits. To let the receiver know that we are leaving the idle state and are about to send a character, we have to change from the idle signal state. Because the only other signal available is the one representing 0, the start bit is always the same as a 0—that is, no current. The receiver, sensing the drop in current, synchronizes its clock and counts digits. To signal the end of the frame, we have to return the line to the idle state, if only for a moment. (Recall that asynchronous transmission means character at a time, start/stop. Even if the sender transmits one character right after the other, each character is treated as a separate entity.) That means going back to the 1 signal, so the stop bit is always the same as a 1.

7.6 Synchronous communication

We previously discussed how the word *asynchronous* refers to the absence of a timing relationship between the characters (frames) that make up the transmission. *Synchronous* communication, on the other hand, dictates a precise time relationship within the frames—hence, the use of the word *synchronous* to describe this framing technique.

Synchronous communication takes a large number of bits and sends them one after the other, without any gaps between them. To alert the receiver that this large group of bits is on its way, the sender precedes the transmission by a special symbol. When that symbol arrives, the receiver knows that the bits will follow immediately, one after the other, until the sender transmits another special symbol (often the same symbol is used) to indicate that all bits have been sent.

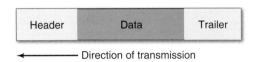

FIGURE 7.1

Generic frame

The mechanisms to ensure accurate bit timing (that is, bit synchronization) were discussed in Chapter 4. In the detailed discussion of synchronous communication that follows, we will concentrate on the framing aspects of this technique.

Synchronous communication techniques

Synchronous communication frame sizes vary considerably, from only 16 or 24 bits in control data frames to many thousands in general data frames. For example, frames as large as 12,000 bits are used in Ethernet local area networks, and frames as large as 32,768 bits are used in wide area frame relay networks.

Generically, synchronous frames are delineated by *encapsulating* (surrounding) the data portion with a *header* preceding the data and a *trailer* following the data (see Figure 7.1). Encapsulation procedures are handled by protocols. Different protocols call for different header, data, and trailer constructions. (Think back to asynchronous transmission once more: Although its transmitted block is generally not referred to as a frame, it can be considered as a frame whose header is a start bit, data is one 7-bit character, and trailer is a parity bit and a stop bit.)

Synchronous protocols can be subdivided into two types: character oriented and bit oriented. The major difference between the two is in the framing bits, with the former using characters from a defined code set and the latter using a simple 8-bit string not associated with any character set. We explore these two types of protocols in the next sections.

Character-oriented protocols

Character (byte)-oriented protocols are used much less than they once were. Although the data stream (payload) of character-oriented protocols may or may not be an undifferentiated train of bits, frame demarcation and control is based on byte representations from specific encoding schemes and is more complex than the simple 8-bit frame demarcation of bit-oriented protocols. Nevertheless, the same issues of bit recognition and bit synchronization must be addressed. After all, because a byte is simply an organized group of bits, to be read correctly its bits must be read correctly.

The framing characters of byte-oriented protocols are created using a code such as ASCII or EBCDIC. This is in contrast to bit-oriented protocols, to which no particular character codes apply because framing bits do not have to be grouped into bytes. The most commonly used byte-oriented synchronous protocol, and a prime example of the type, is BSC (Binary Synchronous Communications), developed by IBM.

BSC supports two frame types: control (Figure 7.2A) and data (Figure 7.2B). For either type, the frame begins with two 1-byte *synchronous idle (SYN)* characters (00010110) to demarcate the frame, thereby establishing frame synchronization, and ends with a *block check count (BCC)* for error detection, 1 or 2 bytes depending on the method used. (Block check counts are described in Chapter 5.)

In a *control frame,* the characters to establish and terminate a connection, control data flow, and correct errors reside between the SYNs and the BCC. In a *data frame,* the SYNs are followed by a *start of text (STX)* character (00000010), which, in turn, is followed by the data bytes. The end of data is marked by an *end of text (ETX)* character. Then comes the BCC. Because the start and end of the data section are explicitly marked, a variable amount of data can be accommodated. All control characters including SYN and BCC are in the binary range 00000000 to 00011111.

FIGURE 7.2

BSC frame types

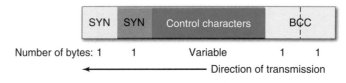

Number of bytes: 1   1   Variable   1   1

⟵ Direction of transmission

A. BSC control frame

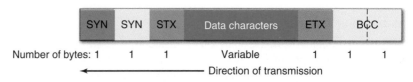

Number of bytes: 1   1   1   Variable   1   1   1

⟵ Direction of transmission

B. BSC data frame

HISTORICAL NOTE
Some IBM protocols

In 1964, IBM published the byte-oriented Binary Synchronous Communications protocol (BSC, also known as bisync). In 1967, IBM released it with its new mainframe, the 360/25. By the 1970s, BSC had become a de facto standard for file transfers. It was also used in such diverse applications as radar devices, automatic teller machines, and cash registers. By the 1980s, there was a huge installed base of equipment using BSC. Although there is still a significant remnant of this base, BSC's demise was foretold when IBM released its Systems Network Architecture (SNA) protocol in the 1970s. SNA incorporated a bit-oriented protocol, Synchronous Data Link Control (SDLC), which itself was the precursor of today's bit-oriented High-Level Data Link Control (HDLC) protocol.

An important question arises at this point. What if we need to transmit a data character that that is the same as a control character? That is, if a sequence with the same bit pattern as a control character must be transmitted as part of the message, how do we ensure that it is not interpreted as a control character? This is the problem of transparency noted earlier. Because we are dealing with a byte-oriented protocol, the solution lies in *byte stuffing,* also called character stuffing or byte insertion/deletion.

Here is how it works: The byte to be stuffed is a *data link escape (DLE)* character (00010000). The DLE is inserted before both the STX and ETX characters to demarcate the bit sequence for the transparent byte—that is, the byte in the data section of the frame that is not to be looked at for control information. Figure 7.3A illustrates this coupling.

Thinking ahead, we can envision a situation wherein the bit patterns of a DLE-STX or DLE-ETX combination are meant to be part of the transparent frame section. Once again, the same byte stuffing procedure applies.

If DLE-STX is the intended sequence, we insert another DLE before the first, creating the sequence DLE-DLE-STX. When the receiver encounters a DLE character, it examines the next character in the sequence. If that character is another DLE, it is deleted and the remaining pair is treated as data. If, instead, the next character is STX, no deletion occurs and the DLE-STX pair is treated as control.

FIGURE 7.3

Byte stuffing

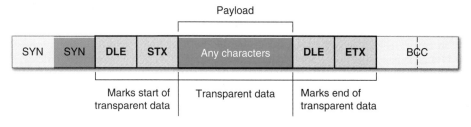

A. Byte stuffing for transparency — demarcating the transparent section

Transparent data section already containing a DLE-ETX sequence

The sender stuffs a DLE byte:

The receiver, seeing two sequential DLEs, removes the second and treats the remaining DLE as part of the data.

B. Byte stuffing for transparency — keeping the transparent data transparent

The same applies for a DLE-ETX sequence, illustrated in figure 7.3B. For extended combinations of either sequence, the same stuffing process is used. In this way, control or any other "non-data" characters can be transmitted without confusion, maintaining transparency.

Bit-oriented protocols

The most commonly used synchronous protocols are bit oriented. As the name implies, all data in bit-oriented transmission are transmitted as a stream of bits without regard to any particular coding scheme, although they are organized into frames. All of the current synchronous bit-oriented protocols are related to HDLC protocol, and many are directly based on it. Hence, we will use HDLC to illustrate the major features of this type of protocol.

HISTORICAL NOTE
Synchronous protocols

IBM was the progenitor of synchronous bit-oriented protocols, with the introduction of its Synchronous Data Link Control (SDLC) in 1975. That was followed by High-level Data Link Control (HDLC), a superset of SDLC, published in 1979 by the ISO standards organization.

Since then, several other link access protocol standards, offshoots of HDLC, have emerged, in addition to several proprietary protocols. It is safe to say that all current bit-oriented synchronous protocols are related more or less directly to HDLC, which, in turn, owes its existence in large part to SDLC.

As is usual, for successful receipt of a transmission, the receiver needs to recognize each bit in the frame and the boundaries of the frame itself. Hence, we are again talking about two synchronization needs: bit synchronization, which requires in-step clocking, and frame synchronization, which requires recognition of a unique bit pattern to detect the beginning and end of each frame—the 8-bit sequence 01111110, called a *flag,* is that pattern. Self-clocking schemes maintain bit synchronization throughout the transmission.

There are three basic synchronous frame types: *control* (or *supervisory*) frames carry information for the network to control flow and errors; *management* (or *unnumbered*) frames carry information used in network management; and *data* (or *information*) frames carry user data. In each frame type, the initial flag is followed by an address field and a control field carrying information such as frame type (control, management, or data), status, and sequence numbers used to keep track of each frame. Each type also ends with an error-checking field called the *frame check sequence* (FCS, explained in Chapter 5), followed by the second appearance of the same flag. In some protocols, the ending flag also serves to demarcate the start of the next frame, saving another 8 bits of overhead.

AMPLIFICATION

HDLC has a unique feature that enables it to piggyback some control information onto the data frame. In particular, this allows sending data receipt acknowledgments with data frames, thereby increasing efficiency compared to BSC (which cannot piggyback) by reducing the total number of frames sent.

A control frame has no other fields (see Figure 7.4A). In a data frame, the control field is followed by the main event, the data field—also called the *payload* because it contains the information that is the purpose of the transmission in the first place (see Figure 7.4B). In a management frame, that position is occupied by the management information field—we do not consider this as payload because it does not carry user data (see Figure 7.4C).

The payload can be quite long and can vary in length from frame to frame, but as we learned, it must be completely *transparent* to the transmission system. Because the payload is an arbitrary sequence of bits, why is a 01111110 pattern in the payload not interpreted as a flag? Or conversely, how is the ending flag recognized as such and not as part of the preceding payload? So once again the question arises: How do we maintain transparency of the data block?

The solution lies in *bit stuffing,* also called zero-bit insertion/deletion. An extra 0 is inserted by the sender after any five successive 1s in the payload of a frame and removed by the receiver. Thus, the flag is the only place in which a sequence of six 1s can appear.

Here are two examples: In the payload bit sequence 0110**011111**101101, the bold digits have the same bit pattern as the flag. On seeing this sequence, the sender will insert (stuff) a 0 bit between the fifth and sixth 1, resulting in the sequence 0110**0111110**101101. The receiver, on counting the sequence of five 1s, will examine the next bit. If the next bit is a 0, it will be removed, restoring the sequence to its original form. If it is another 1, it will be retained, indicating a flag.

What about the non-stuffed bit sequence 0110**0111110**101101, which has the same pattern of 0s and 1s as the bit-stuffed sequence in the preceding example? The bold digits highlight that it already has a 0 following five 1s. However, we do not want the receiver to remove that 0 because it is part of the data stream, so the sender, on counting five 1s, will

FIGURE 7.4

HDLC synchronous bit oriented frame formats

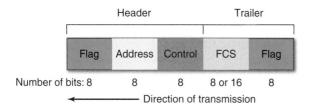

A. An HDLC control frame

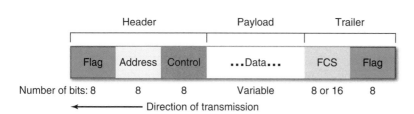

B. An HDLC data frame

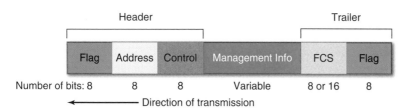

C. An HDLC management frame

again insert a 0, transmitting 0110**01111100**101101. As in the first case, the receiver examines the bit after the five 1s and, seeing a 0, removes it, restoring the original sequence.

Again we need to ask, what happens when there is no data to send? More specifically, what happens to the clocks when the line is idle? We could simply transmit nothing and allow the clocks to drift out of sync, but if idle times are intermittently dispersed throughout periods of data transmission, a more effective answer is to transmit an ***idle state signal*** to maintain clock synchronization. This signal (01110101), which has enough signal changes (0 to 1, 1 to 0) to maintain bit synchronization, is repeated as long as the line is idle. It is not confused with a data signal because it comes after a frame-ending flag and before the next start-frame flag.

An interesting example of how need drives technology and technological limitations drive development occurred historically at the intersection of asynchronous and synchronous communications technologies. See Appendix F, "Echoplex and beyond."

7.7 Flow control

As indispensable as it is, synchronization is not enough for maintaining proper data communication. Another situation, congestion at the receiver, arises when the receiver cannot process transmissions as fast as they arrive. This happens because the receiver has to handle other processing demands, because of transmissions to and from other devices, or simply because the receiver's processor is slower than the sender's. Whatever the reason, if the incoming data flow overwhelms the receiver, the data will be discarded. To resolve this problem, we must make sure that the senders do not transmit data faster than the receiver can handle it. That is, we need *flow control.*

Most flow control methods require the sender to get feedback from the receiver regarding its ability to handle incoming data. The two major methods of flow control, which differ primarily in how that feedback works, are:

- *Stop-and-wait protocol:* having the receiver tell the sender when to transmit a single frame of data
- *Sliding window protocol:* having the receiver indicate how many frames it is prepared to receive

In any non-trivial network, the initial sender and final receiver devices (nodes) generally are not connected directly to one another. Rather, they communicate through intermediate devices (also called nodes) that relay data frames from one to another until they finally reach their destination. Hence, we can think of a frame as traveling from the sender to the receiver along a succession of links, each link connecting a pair of nodes.

In this scenario, every node acts as a receiver when taking in a frame and as a sender when transmitting the frame to the next node. Thus, data flow typically needs to be controlled between each connected pair of nodes along these links, as does the overall flow between the initial sender and final receiver. (When discussing transmission and flow control concepts, we generally refer to any two directly connected nodes as the sending node and the receiving node. We denote the end nodes as the initial or original sender and the final or original receiver when it is necessary to make the distinction.)

In the discourse that follows, the emphasis will be on flow control between any two directly connected nodes, called *data link flow control.* Furthermore, although any node may be directly linked to many other nodes in a network, the flow control procedures described apply independently to each individual connection between each pair of nodes. The exception is when multiple links between two nodes are bundled (via inverse multiplexing, as discussed in Chapter 6, "Communications connections"), in which case it is common to apply flow control to the composite communications link. Figure 7.5 illustrates these connections.

End-to-end flow control between the initial sender and final receiver, also known as *transport flow control,* is achieved with similar mechanisms, although other factors come into play. These are discussed in Chapter 13, "TCP/IP, associated Internet protocols, and routing," where we will consider methods for dealing with congestion in wide area networks.

Any data handling procedure has its costs, and flow control is no different. The costs of flow control involve degree-of-processing complexity, speed of operation/transmission, link capacity, and the level of systems and computer resources required. Various methods of flow control trade one cost for another. For example, if we employ a method with simple processing and low memory requirements, we usually pay for it with poorer communication link utilization. We will highlight some of the relevant tradeoffs as we proceed.

Stop-and-wait flow control

One of the oldest and least costly flow control methods is also one of the most basic. The algorithm for this procedure calls for the sending node to transmit a single fixed-length frame and wait for an acknowledgement (ACK) of receipt from the receiving node. This ACK is the signal for the sending node to transmit another frame. The receiving node can delay transmission until it is ready simply by not sending an ACK. Because the sending node stops transmitting while it waits for the ACK, this technique is called the *stop-and-wait protocol* or *stop-and-wait ARQ (Automatic Repeat reQuest).*

FIGURE 7.5

Links between nodes

A. Single direct link   **B.** Multiple individual direct links   **C.** Multiple bundled direct links

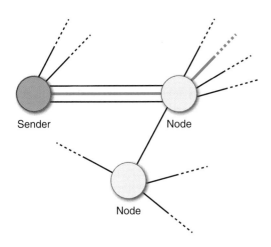
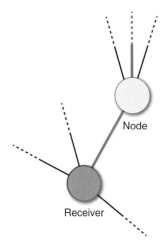

D. General case — sender, intermediate nodes, receiver — direct link between each pair of nodes along the connection path

With this technique, data to be transmitted from a device is first deposited in its buffer, a temporary storage area, from where it is sent out onto the physical communications link. Similarly, data to be received by a device is read from the physical link into its buffer, where the data is held until the receiving device has time to process it and remove it from the buffer.

The transmit-receive cycle depends on buffer space availability in the sending node to hold the frame for transmission, and subsequently on buffer space availability in the receiving node to hold the frame for processing.

If the receiving node is not ready to accept a frame, whether because it has not yet processed the prior frame and its buffer has no free space, or because the node is busy with some other operation, we do not want the transmitted frame to be rejected by the receiving node. Therefore, we require the sending node to wait for an ACK from the receiving node before transmitting the next frame.

Relying solely on ACKs is not sufficient. The transmitted frame may be lost or damaged in transit, and therefore no ACK will be forthcoming, and the ACK itself may also be lost. To prevent transmissions from being permanently halted, the sending node will retransmit the same frame after some time passes without an ACK. Because we do not know in advance whether that will be necessary, we cannot allow the sending node to free its buffer before receiving the ACK—if it did, the frame would be lost and could not be reconstructed for retransmission.

In an ACK-lost or ACK-not-yet-sent case in which the sender retransmits the frame, we need to consider how the receiving node will know that it has received a duplicate. Comparing one frame's bit pattern with another is not an option, because any bit pattern can be sent at any time; it is not unusual for two successive frames to have the same bit pattern.

This potential dilemma can be handled by a simple frame-numbering procedure. Because we have to deal with just two frames at any time (the one sent and the next one to be sent), we can number successive frames as 0 and 1. This means that we need just one extra bit to carry frame numbers.

Here's how this works: Suppose frame 0 is transmitted and received, but the ACK is lost. After the timeout period, the sender will retransmit frame 0. But the receiver will be expecting frame 1 because it already has acknowledged frame 0. The retransmitted frame 0 alerts the receiver that the frame is a duplicate; it will be discarded, and another ACK will be sent.

What are the pros and cons of the stop-and-wait approach? The algorithm is relatively simple, and processing is straightforward. Because the sending node can transmit only one frame at a time, only one outstanding frame must be tracked. Further, each node in the end-to-end path has only one buffer to manage for the connection. The cost for this simplicity is poor link utilization, as the link will have to remain idle between data transmission and ACK. Even under the best of circumstances, there will always be some delay before the ACK is received by the sending node. Hence, there is an opportunity cost—the lost opportunity to send more data during that time. The following example illustrates these ideas.

Assume that node A is transmitting frames to node B, and that A and B are directly linked. Node A may be the original sender or any intermediate node; node B may be the original receiver or any intermediate node. The following steps take place:

1. Node A *reads* a frame into its buffer. No transmission occurs until the buffer is loaded; if the buffer is not free because node A is waiting for an ACK or because node A is busy, this step is delayed. In any case, the *link is idle*.
2. Node A *transmits* a frame. The *link is utilized* as data is transmitted and loaded into node B's buffer.
3. Node A *waits* for node B to process the data and send an ACK. If node B is busy, ACK issuance will be delayed. The *link is idle* until the ACK is sent.
4. Node B *transmits* ACK. The *link is utilized,* but for an overhead transmission—*the link is not available for data transmission.*
5. Node A *processes* the ACK. The *link is idle* until node A begins processing and while node A is processing. Go to step 1.

All but the second step represent opportunity costs caused by idleness or unavailability of the link for data transmission.

The other two occasions during which no frame transmission is possible result when no ACK is received, causing node A to wait and the link to remain idle. After a set timeout has passed, node A will retransmit the frame.

3a. Nodes *wait* because of a lost or damaged frame. The *link is idle* during the wait for an ACK and *utilized* during frame retransmission, but the original transmission of that frame is an opportunity cost because *the link was ineffectively utilized.*
4a. Nodes *wait* because an ACK is lost, damaged, or excessively delayed by node B. The *link is idle* during the wait for an ACK and *utilized* during frame retransmission, but because that frame was already sent and received, *this is "false" utilization*—node A has no way of knowing that the retransmission is unnecessary. Hence, this also is an opportunity cost.

At low transmission speeds, not much data can be sent during the wait/link idle times, so the opportunity cost is small. For example, suppose the transmission rate is 300 bps and the ACK delay is half a second. The opportunity cost, measured by the number of bits that could have been transmitted in the link idle time, is 300/0.5 or 150 bits.

At higher speeds, the story changes. With a T-1 line (transmission rate 1,544,000 bps), again using an ACK delay of half a second, the opportunity cost is 1,544,000/0.5 or 772,000 bits—quite a different picture. Depending on how busy the receiving node is at the time the frame arrives, there may be an even greater delay with correspondingly higher opportunity cost. Furthermore, the higher the link speed, the greater the opportunity cost—and T1 is not nearly the fasted link speed available today.

In the early years of computer data transmission, equipment was relatively slow, memory was quite limited, and both were costly. Transmission rates of 300 bps were common, and even slower rates were not unusual. Simplicity was an overriding concern, and simple transmission algorithms that did not need complex, high-speed, memory-intensive processing were the only practical ones—trading simplicity for link utilization made the most sense. As computing power and memory availability increased while costs decreased, the tradeoff went the other way. High-speed links could be justified if they were highly utilized. The reduction in opportunity cost realized by greater link efficiency could more than offset the cost of added complexity—adding algorithmic complexity to gain efficiency made the most sense.

Today, it is a rare system that uses a stop-and-wait protocol, link efficiency being a paramount consideration. The technique commonly in use now is called *sliding window flow control.* Interestingly, as we will see in the discussion to follow, stop-and-wait can be viewed as a special case of the sliding window procedure.

Sliding window flow control

An obvious way to improve link utilization beyond that achievable by stop-and-wait is to reduce the number of ACKs that must be sent to manage flow. If the sending node could transmit K frames without waiting for each one to be acknowledged and the receiving node could send a single ACK to indicate receipt of all K frames, there would be far fewer stoppages. Pushing this idea a bit further, suppose the receiving node could send an ACK for some of those frames, say k < K before it processed all K of them and before the sending node had transmitted all K. Then the sending node, allowed to have a total of K unacknowledged frames outstanding at any one time, could transmit even more frames (here, k more) without hesitation.

Here is an example. Let's say that we allow six (K = 6) frames to be transmitted one after the other without requiring the sending node to wait for an ACK. Then the receiving node has to send only one ACK for the six instead of the six ACKs that stop-and-wait requires. But suppose that even if the receiving node is busy for the first few frames, it finds enough time to send an ACK for the frames it has already received, before the sending node has transmitted the sixth frame. Say only four (k = 4) of the six have been sent. Then sending continues without a stop beyond the fifth and sixth frames—an additional four frames can be sent before having to wait for an ACK.

To say this another way, instead of forcing the sending node to stop and wait after each transmitted frame, we allow it to send up to six frames before having to receive an ACK for *any* of the frames. What is more, we allow the sending node to *add continuously* to the frames that it is allowed to send, as long as there are never more than six consecutive frames that not have not been acknowledged. So if the receiving node has sent four frames and receives an ACK for those four, it can send not just the next two frames, but four more, keeping the unacknowledged total at six.

The rate at which a node can accept data often is not a constant. Although its upper limit is a function of its buffer size and data processing speed, it is important to keep in mind that the actual rate varies depending upon what else the node is doing. Recall that incoming frames are read into the receiving node's buffer, from where they are read *when it is ready to process the frame.* After a frame is processed, its buffer space is cleared. Meanwhile, more frames can be accepted only if there is sufficient buffer space; otherwise, acceptance has to wait—any frames arriving during that time are discarded.

A sending node that could obtain feedback information about the receiving node's buffer would be able to take that into account along with other factors to adjust the number of frames sent, varying from zero to the maximum number readable into the receiving node's buffer at that time. Because frames discarded due to full buffers are a wasteful use of the receiving node's time and the link's capacity, such feedback would substantially increase transmission link efficiency.

A technique that takes all of these considerations into account, allowing multiple-frame transmission and utilization of feedback information, is the ***sliding window protocol.*** The sending node maintains a window (actually, a list of frame numbers), whose *maximum size is established at the outset* of transmission. This size dictates the maximum number of unacknowledged frames that can be outstanding at one time, or in other words, the maximum number of frames that can be transmitted before having to stop and wait for an ACK. The window uses frame sequence numbers to indicate which frames have been sent but not acknowledged. Messages from the receiving node trigger the sending node to adjust the contents of the window and, depending on the particular protocol, its size, as transmission proceeds.

Two factors determine the maximum window size:

- The largest unique number that can be represented by bits reserved in the frame header for sequence numbers.
- The maximum number of buffers that can be made available at the sending and receiving nodes.

There are several sliding window protocol versions. In all of them, the contents (position) of the window change dynamically during transmission as frames are received and acknowledged. In some versions, the size of the window changes as well, based on feedback from the receiving node.

Sequence numbers and window size

Although we have just introduced the sliding window concept as a flow control mechanism, its need actually originated as a solution to a more fundamental and practical requirement. As we have seen, synchronous protocols place user data into frames. These are transmitted independently of one another, and it is possible that one or more frames may be corrupted or lost in transit and need to be resent. Because of this, individual frames must be tracked at each node throughout the transmission process. This requires the ability to identify individual frames uniquely. To do so, the original sending node places frame sequence numbers in the frame header.

Every node in the path beyond the original sender up to the final receiver also is a sending node in the pass-along sense. These nodes also use sequence numbers to identify frames, but because they receive packets from many original senders, the data link numbers they assign relate only to sequences of frames that, from the node's viewpoint, are not related to any particular message. The original node's transport layer numbers relate directly to the frames of a single message. This is discussed further in Chapter 11, "Packet switched wide area networks."

The sliding window concept originated as a means for sequencing independently transmitted frames. Its use has been extended to include point-to-point flow control.

Frame sequence numbering is a simple process in theory, but practical considerations make it a bit more complicated. Suppose we have a set of 10 frames to send. To uniquely identify each frame and its sequence position, we can number them, let's say from 0 to 9 decimal, and add each frame's number to its header.

Because we are adding information to the frame header, we need to know how much space to reserve for carrying that information—that space will determine the largest sequence number that can be carried. Remember that this number, along with everything else in the frame, must be in binary form. To represent the 10 decimal values in this example, we need four binary digits. In other words, we must add 4 bits of information to the frame. Recall that because these bits are not user data, they are overhead. (General rule: Because we start numbering from 0, the highest decimal value that can be represented by n binary digits is $2^n - 1$. Thus, for $n = 3$, $2^3 - 1 = 7$; for $n = 4$, $2^4 - 1 = 15$, and so on.)

Now suppose we need to send 100,000 frames. With continuous numbering, this requires 100,000 sequence numbers, 0 to 99,999 decimal. It takes 17 binary digits ($2^{17} - 1 = 131,071$, whereas $2^{16} - 1 = 65,535$) to represent those numbers, a much greater addition to overhead.

Different systems use different frame sizes, so depending on the particular size used and the number needed for a given amount of data, the impact of sequence number space on overhead varies. We could reserve space according to the number of frames we need to send, but because that number varies so much, the processing burden would become onerous. To simplify processing, we fix space for sequence numbers at one value for a given system. The question then becomes, what should that value be? It would seem that we could establish the value as the maximum number of frames expected to be handled, based, say, on user patterns. But two problems arise:

- Even if that maximum value is only moderately large, the space required in the frame header may add more overhead than we would like.
- Realistically speaking, no matter how much space we reserve, a sequence of frames could come along that requires greater numbers than would fit.

Practically speaking, we have no choice but to limit sequence number space, and this, in turn, appears to mean limiting the number of frames that can be handled. But regardless of overhead considerations, a good communications system should not impose such limits. Yet, as we have seen, as the number of frames grows, the number of bits needed for their sequence numbers grows as well.

Resolving these conflicting considerations requires modifying the sequence numbering scheme and using frame receipt notifications according to the following stratagem:

Fix the number of header bits reserved for sequence numbers based on the characteristics of the transmission system and the desired limit on the addition to overhead. This determines the largest decimal sequence number, call it S_{max}, that can be represented in binary. For example, if the number of sequence bits is fixed at 3, then $S_{max} = 7$ ($2^3 - 1 = 7$). Because we start numbering at 0, the 3 bits can hold the binary equivalent of the eight (2^n or $S_{max} + 1$) decimal numbers, 0 through 7. (The binary equivalents of the eight decimal numbers 0 through 7 in order are: 000, 001, 010, 011, 100, 101, 110, 111. This uses all of the 0/1 possibilities for three-binary digits.)

Number the frames as if there were no restrictions. If there are more than S_{max} frames, convert the unrestricted frame numbers to values that do not exceed S_{max} by *reusing* the numbers up to S_{max} as many times as needed. Thus, the 10 frames of the prior example would be numbered as follows:

Ten unrestricted sequence numbers	0 1 2 3 4 5 6 7 8 9
Ten converted sequence numbers	0 1 2 3 4 5 6 7 0 1

Because we are reusing sequence numbers, we must take steps to ensure that the sending node does not transmit a frame with a reused number until it knows that the previous frame carrying that number was correctly received. In the preceding example, if the sending node were allowed to immediately send all 10 frames, the receiving node, having gotten two frames marked 0 and two marked 1, could not distinguish between each of the two and would not know whether they were duplicates.

Similarly, if a frame were damaged in transit and another frame with the same sequence number were sent, the receiving node would not know whether it was a replacement for the damaged frame or another frame altogether. (You can see the parallel between this situation and the one for stop-and-wait, which had to deal with the same issue but for just two frames.)

This means that we have to limit the number of frames that can be sent at one time—that is, the number of unacknowledged frames that can be outstanding at any given moment. At first it would seem that the limit should be equal to the number of frames representable by the highest sequence number available—in the preceding example, eight frames. But this, too, can lead to problems.

Suppose the sending node transmits eight of the 10 frames in the example. With the available sequence numbers exhausted, transmission of the remaining two frames must wait for confirmation that the first eight were received properly. But what if the confirming ACK is lost? As we have seen, transmission systems include a timeout feature that prevents the sending node from having wait forever. In this example, after a predetermined amount of time elapses without an ACK, the sending node will resend the original eight frames.

The receiving node, having sent an ACK for frames 0 through 7, expects that the next group of frames will begin with frame number 0. The re-sent frames do start with frame 0. So the receiver has no way of knowing that these eight are re-sent frames and will assume that they are the next batch. This obviously would lead to a major mishandling of the user data. (Some sliding window protocols allow the receiving node to request retransmission of just those frames that were lost or damaged. Because the converted sequence number of those frames also will duplicate what was thought to be acknowledged, the problem remains.)

We prevent this from happening by reducing by one the maximum number of unacknowledged frames allowed to be outstanding at one time—that is, to $2^n - 1$, which again equals S_{max}. To see how this corrects the problem, consider the example once more, but this time suppose that the sending node has transmitted only $S_{max} = 7$ frames (0 through 6), instead of the previous eight. The receiving node sends an ACK, and again it is lost. The sending node, after the timeout, resends frames 0 through 6. But now the receiving node knows that these are duplicates because the expected next frame number, 7, is missing. This can only mean that the ACK was not received and the old frames were re-sent. The general discussion of sliding window to follow further illustrates these points.

Although the preceding procedure is the basis for the sliding window protocol, the size of the window (that is, the maximum number of unacknowledged frames) is dictated by our decision to fix the number of bits reserved for sequence numbers, and not by flow control considerations. We must do this whether or not we choose to implement flow control, but the same sliding window process also serves to control flow—because the sending node cannot reuse a sequence number before ACK receipt, the sending node must wait after all available sequence numbers have been used.

A flow control mechanism is inherent in the sliding window scheme.

Beyond transmission restrictions caused by sequence number considerations, for flow control purposes we may restrict transmission even more. For example, the window size could be altered *dynamically* according to the receiver's available buffer space as it varies during transmission. Furthermore, before file transmission begins, the sender and receiver can negotiate a mutually acceptable maximum window size that may be smaller than what the sequence number header space would allow. *No matter what the case, sequence numbering must be based on the header space reserved for those numbers.* With *n* bits reserved for sequence numbers, the maximum (decimal) sequence number is always $2^n - 1$.

We may now generalize the sliding window numbering scheme:

- If *n* is the number of bits reserved for sequence numbers, then 2^n decimal numbers can be represented in binary.
- Beginning numbering with 0, $2^n - 1$ is the largest decimal sequence number representable in binary.
- The ostensible *maximum* window size (the number of frames that can be sent at one time before receiving a confirmation—the maximum number of unacknowledged outstanding frames allowed) also is $2^n - 1$.
- For the purpose of flow control, the actual window size may be reduced to something less than the maximum.

Sliding window technique

Although sliding window is a fairly straightforward concept, it can be rather confusing to visualize. Let's examine more closely a version in which the size of the window changes and an acknowledgement covers several frames. In doing so, we will refer to the sequence numbers that we would use for the frames if there were no limit on number size as *unrestricted sequence numbers (USNs)* and the converted sequence numbers as *window-related numbers (WRNs)*. The latter are relative to the maximum window size, which, as we have seen, depends on the space reserved in the frame header.

Let's look at an example to illustrate sliding window operations, keeping in mind that although we use decimal numbers in this example, they must be carried as binary numbers in the frame header. To simplify notation, we will refer to the sending node as S and the receiving node as R. Assume that we reserve 3 bits in the frame header for sequence numbers. Supposing that our data comprises 18 frames in all, the numbers will be:

```
USN: 0 1 2 3 4 5 6 7 8 9 10 11 12 13 14 15 16 17
WRN: 0 1 2 3 4 5 6 7 0 1  2  3  4  5  6  7  0  1
```

To avoid the lost ACK problem described earlier, we set the window size to $S_{max} (2^n - 1)$ Hence, the initial (and maximum) window size is $2^3 - 1$, or 7 in the example.

At the outset, the window of node S is set to seven and covers frames 0 through 6:

```
USN: 0 1 2 3 4 5 6 7 8 9 10 11 12 13 14 15 16 17
WRN: 0 1 2 3 4 5 6 7 0 1  2  3  4  5  6  7  0  1
```

TECHNICAL NOTE
Converting USNs to WSNs

We convert unrestricted frame sequence numbers by using modulo division. (The result of X modulo Y is the remainder of X/Y expressed as a whole number. For example: 5 modulo 3 = 2; 9 modulo 3 = 0; 12 modulo 7 = 5.)

Given the USN, the WRN is USN modulo k, where $k = 2^n$, the maximum number of decimal numbers expressible in binary by the n bits reserved in the frame for sequence numbers. In the example where 3 bits are reserved, WRN = USN modulo 2^3—that is, USN modulo 8, which produces numbers from 0 to 7.

Node S begins transmission of these seven frames. As they arrive, they are collected in node R's buffer and processing begins. Let's say that S has transmitted all seven frames; S stops transmitting to wait for the ACK. R sends an ACK 7, indicating that it has processed the seven frames 0 through 6 and is now expecting frame 7. (Note that the ACK always signals the next number expected.) S will slide its window seven to the right so that it covers the next seven WRNs, 7 through 5, and begin transmitting again.

```
USN: 0 1 2 3 4 5 6 7 8 9 10 11 12 13 14 15 16 17
WRN: 0 1 2 3 4 5 6 | 7 0 1 2 3 4 5 | 6 7 0 1
     └─────────────┘
     sent and acknowledged
```

Suppose that R processes the first three of these frames (WRNs 7 through 1) and sends back an ACK 2 (indicating that 2 is the next frame expected), while S is still in the process of transmitting. When S gets the ACK, it will slide the window three to the right to account for the three acknowledged frames. S knows what it has already sent, so even if by the time the ACK 2 arrives S has sent more of those seven frames, it will not resend them. But now it can continue transmitting not just the frames up to WRN 5 that it has not yet sent, but three more as well, corresponding to WRNs 6, 7, and 0 in the shifted window.

```
USN: 0 1 2 3 4 5 6 7 8 9 10 11 12 13 14 15 16 17
WRN: 0 1 2 3 4 5 6 7 0 1 | 2 3 4 5 6 7 0 | 1
     └───────────────────┘
     sent and acknowledged
```

Going back to the start, suppose that frames 0 through 6 are sent and acknowledged (ACK 7), but the ACK is lost. After the timeout, frames 0 through 6 are retransmitted. Because the receiving node expects frame 7 next and does not get it, the re-sent frames are recognized as duplicates and discarded. A repeat ACK 7 is sent.

In some versions of the sliding window protocol, if R is getting too busy to handle frames at the same rate, it can change the window size to slow down the sending node without having to stop it completely. Suppose that after receiving the first seven frames, R does not want to get seven more frames for the time being. Then in addition to ACK 7, it would send back a reduced window size notice, say to four. S would slide the left side of the window seven to the right according to the ACK 7, but slide the right side of the window only four—now only four unacknowledged frames can be outstanding, at least until a different window size notice is sent. Instead of the result shown in the second example, we have the following:

USN: 0 1 2 3 4 5 6 7 8 9 10 11 12 13 14 15 16 17

WRN: *0 1 2 3 4 5 6* **7 0 1 2** 3 4 5 6 7 0 1

sent and acknowledged

What if R does want to stop transmission completely? R can withhold sending an ACK for a short time, but if the timeout period passes, retransmission occurs. We do not want to burden the link with repeated retransmissions when there is no need for them. To accommodate this situation, R can send back a window size of 0. This forces the window to be empty, so nothing more can be transmitted until R notifies S to expand the window.

In summary, the sending node window changes dynamically according to what is happening on the receiving side of the connection. For every frame acknowledged, whether singly or as a group, the left side of the window slides to the right. If in addition the overall window size has not been changed, the right side of the window also slides to the right the same amount. If the allowable window size has been reduced, the right side of the window slides less than the left. If the window size has been increased, the right side slides more than the left. Activity at the receiving node determines the feedback that is sent. If buffer readout is going smoothly, R will keep the window size at its maximum. If congestion is building, the window size will be reduced.

For sliding window protocols that do not allow window size to be changed dynamically, two more feedback messages are added—Receiver Not Ready (RNR) and Receiver Ready (RR). By sending an RNR, the receiver can halt transmission without timeout retransmissions occurring. When the receiver is ready for more frames, it sends an RR. These notifications have the same effect as reducing the window size to 0 and later expanding it to its maximum. Note also that if the maximum window size is set to 1, sliding window is equivalent to stop-and-wait.

In addition to flow control, sliding window protocols have error detection and resolution capabilities alluded to in the preceding discussion.

7.8 Summary

In this chapter, we distinguished between digital transmission and digital communication. We delved into the concept of framing—what it is and why it is needed. Then we looked at byte- and bit-oriented protocols and how they present different framing issues. A comparison of asynchronous and synchronous framing, with special attention paid to efficiency, followed.

After this background was established, we looked into asynchronous communication, its origins in the Teletype machine, its simplicity, and its problems. This was followed by an exploration of synchronous communication, developed as an answer to the shortcomings of asynchronous communication. In that discussion, we saw the need for data transparency and how that is accomplished within the two protocol classes of synchronous communication—bit oriented and byte oriented.

Finally, we discovered the need for point-to-point flow control and looked at the two basic methods for establishing it—stop-and-wait, and sliding window.

This chapter completes the foundation material of the text. In the remaining chapters, we will see how this material is put into play to form and run the networks of today, and where the next generations of communications systems are likely to go.

The next chapter begins this foray with a general discussion of networking and communications systems. These are revisited in greater detail in subsequent chapters. Thus, the next chapter serves as an introduction to the remainder of the text.

END-OF-CHAPTER QUESTIONS

Short answer

1. What are the four functions that a receiver must perform?
2. Explain the difference between bit synchronization and frame synchronization.
3. Why is bit stuffing needed? How does it work?
4. Why is byte stuffing needed? How does it work?
5. What was the Teletype's principal contribution to communications development?
6. Explain how stop-and-wait is a special case of the sliding window protocol.
7. How can the sliding window protocol be made to act like the stop-and-wait protocol?
8. Describe how synchronous transmission protocols accommodate variable length data sections in their frames.
9. Explain how bit-oriented protocols can transmit characters.
10. How did declining equipment costs and increased processing speed contribute to the shift from asynchronous to synchronous protocols?

Fill-in

1. In _____ protocols, special characters are used to demarcate frames.
2. _____-oriented protocols require fewer overhead bits than _____-oriented protocols.
3. _____ transmission uses 10-bit frames.
4. Of the 10 bits in an asynchronous frame, _____ are data bits.
5. If the overall transmission rate is 2 Mbps, asynchronous transmission will be sending _____ overhead bits per second.
6. If the overall transmission rate is 4 Mbps, bit-oriented synchronous transmission using 10-kilobit frames will be sending _____ framing bits per second.
7. DLE-ETX indicates that STX is _____, whereas DLE-DLE-STX indicates that STX is _____.
8. Bit-oriented protocols use _____ to demarcate frames.
9. Character-oriented protocols use _____ to demarcate frames.
10. Asynchronous frame sizes are _____ than synchronous frame sizes.

Multiple-choice

1. Frames are needed because
   a. transmission systems cannot deal with large numbers of bits
   b. they are the only way to synchronize bits
   c. they provide an organized way to add control information
   d. without them, receivers would not know whether a 1-bit or a 0-bit was received
   e. all of the above
2. In asynchronous transmission
   a. there is no relationship between the time when one bit is sent and the time when the next one is sent
   b. there is no time relationship between the time when one frame is sent and the time when the next one is sent
   c. there is no synchronization requirement for any bit

d. all of the above
e. none of the above

3. With bit-oriented synchronous transmission
   a. the number of overhead bits is directly proportional to frame size
   b. different flags are used to mark the beginning and end of each frame
   c. byte stuffing is never required
   d. there is a 12,000-bit maximum frame size
   e. none of the above

4. A positive voltage is used to designate an idle asynchronous line because
   a. it avoids confusion between an idle line and a non-functioning line
   b. 1-bits are always represented by positive voltage
   c. 0-bits are always represented by positive voltage
   d. it's a tradition started by the Teletype machine
   e. it's easier to do

5. HDLC
   a. has three frame types
   b. declined in popularity after asynchronous techniques were released
   c. is used only in LANs
   d. has fixed data length segments
   e. eliminates the need for bit synchronization

6. Node-to-node flow control
   a. can be used to speed up slow senders
   b. reduces link utilization

c. requires enlarging buffer space
d. depends on feedback from receivers
e. all of the above

7. The maximum sliding window size is limited by
   a. the number of bits reserved for frame numbers
   b. the size of the receiver buffer
   c. the size of the sender buffer
   d. the speed of the transmission line
   e. all but d

8. Sliding window flow control
   a. facilitates more efficient use of link capacity
   b. prevents transmission of duplicate frames
   c. can be used only with bit-oriented protocols
   d. requires each frame to be acknowledged
   e. all of the above

9. The three basic components of a frame are
   a. frame delimiter, data, and flag
   b. header, data, and trailer
   c. flag, BCS, and FCS
   d. start bit, check bit, and stop bit
   e. header, trailer, and controller

10. HDLC data frames
    a. have no control data
    b. do not need flags
    c. are character oriented
    d. can transmit any bit pattern as data
    e. none of the above

True or false

1. Parallel transmission is preferred in data transmission systems because 8 bits can be sent at once.
2. The sequence of bits used for bit-oriented frame demarcation is chosen to be a bit pattern that could never happen in the data section of the frame.
3. Transparency means the transmission system can transport any sequence of bits in the data section of the frame, regardless of the control scheme used.
4. The STX-ETX character pair is used to provide transparency.
5. Synchronous transmission techniques preceded asynchronous techniques.
6. To maintain data transparency, byte stuffing is used in bit-oriented protocols, and character stuffing is used in character-oriented protocols.
7. The simplicity of the stop-and-wait protocol makes it the preferred flow control technique.
8. The bigger the sliding window, the greater the number of frames that may have to be retransmitted.
9. Before transmitting the first frame, the sender must wait for an ACK from the receiver.
10. Frame sequence numbering is required only because of the need to control flow.

Expansion and exploration

1. Write a brief history of the Teletype. During what time period was it popular? How long did it last before being replaced? What replaced it?
2. Suppose that one node of a network is directly connected to three other nodes. Show how sliding window flow control would operate.
3. Trace the history of IBM's BSC and HDLC.

8

Comprehending networks

8.1 Overview

This chapter serves as an introduction to the remainder of the text. Some of the topics have been introduced in earlier chapters and are mentioned again for cohesiveness. Other topics are noted for the first time; they are discussed in general terms and will be revisited in greater detail in subsequent chapters.

In this chapter and Chapters 9 through 14, we will see how the network basics we have covered in the preceding chapters come into play to form and run the networks of today. We will see how various network forms began and how these precursors led the way to current communications technologies, from the venerable wired telephone systems to the Internet and the proliferating wireless networks of today. In Chapters 15 through 17, we will see what it takes to manage networks, learn how to identify and address security issues, and discuss how to plan, design, and implement networks. Finally, in Chapter 18, we will take a look at what the future may hold.

8.2 Extending network classifications

There are many ways to classify networks. Deciding how to do so depends on one's point of view. In Chapter 6, "Communications connections," we classified networks by link management, access methods, and topologies. Here we add classification by span, owner-ship, protocols, and traffic handling. Let's see what these added viewpoints tell us.

Span

Span is a geographic classification. Local area networks (LANs) cover small spans—an office, a floor, several floors, or perhaps a small campus—whereas wide area networks (WANs) cover distances that can range from around the block to around the globe. Some classify metropolitan area networks (MANs), actually small-span WANs, as an intermedi-ate step between LANs and WANs. Now that we can easily interconnect LANs to span large areas and connect LANs to WANs to form internetworks that reach substantial distances, span is becoming less useful as a classification.

Ownership

Quite often, a more relevant characteristic than geographic span is link ownership—LANs and their links are wholly owned by the companies they reside in. WAN links are most often provided by **public access carriers** (also called **common carriers**). WAN links are contracted for by those who need the service (but see "Technical note: Corporate WAN ownership"). The links comprising MANs also are frequently owned by carriers.

The carrier infrastructure, comprising media, a great number of switches, and software, often is referred to as a **cloud.** This nomenclature indicates that the details are not evident to the user, who merely connects to the cloud. LANs are connected to a WAN cloud by appropriate interface devices. For example, at home you connect to the Internet cloud via an intermediary—an **Internet service provider (ISP);** a business may connect to a WAN cloud through a router. Within the cloud, WAN media are linked by switches that relay information from sender to receiver.

Ownership difference relates not only to costs and fees, but also to options and control. In the LAN sphere, a business may select from whatever network technology is available and purchase what is deemed appropriate; as owner of the LAN, the business controls its use, access, and the administration of all its nodes and links. In the WAN arena, businesses can select only from the links offered by the carriers available to them and generally cannot exercise control over how carriers set up and use the links.

TECHNICAL NOTE
Corporate WAN ownership

The ownership issue of WANs is largely an issue of **right-of-way.** For example, if you want to connect your company networks in New York with those in Chicago, you cannot run cables because you have nowhere to run them. Public access carriers have rights-of-way for cable runs, and they have much infrastructure in place. The universal fact of life seems to be that if you want a WAN link, you contract with a common carrier.

In some realms, though, this universal fact is not so universal. Some corporate entities do own rights-of-way that they can exploit without having to use public access carriers. Here are a few examples:

• The Port Authority of New York and New Jersey has cables used for WAN links running through their tunnels and over their bridges. They also have installed wireless access points that travelers and Authority employees can use.

• Many county, state, and federal agencies lease rights-of-way along their roadways to corporations that install their own cables for WAN links. Railroads do the same.

• Large corporations with substantial capital, faced with high WAN usage, can, at times, construct microwave transmitters to create their own wireless WAN links without using any common carrier rights-of-way, especially when distances are not too great.

Despite these possibilities, private ownership of WAN links is a very slow-moving trend because it is not an option for most businesses—they don't own nor can they afford access to suitable rights-of-way, and wireless solutions are either too limiting or too costly. The vast majority of WAN traffic still flows over common carrier links and is likely to do so for many years in the future.

Protocols

From the protocol viewpoint, circuit switched networks operate at the physical layer of the OSI-TCP/IP model architectures; LANs function at the two lowest layers, physical and data link. When information heads for packet switched WANs, layer 2 addressing is insufficient. Hence, the third layer, the network layer, comes into play. Figure 8.1 illustrates this.

WAN software typically implements a variety of protocols in packet switched and cell switched networks, the most common of which are X.25, frame relay, asynchronous transfer mode (ATM), switched multimegabit data service (SMDS), and synchronous optical network (SONET). Internet protocols overlay WANs—that is, the Internet utilizes its own protocol suites running on top of those of a variety of WAN systems.

FIGURE 8.1

Architecture layers in LANs and WANs

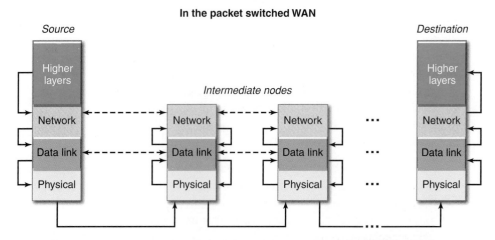

Recall that there is *virtual communication* between like layers in linked nodes (dashed arrows) and *physical communication* between the physical layers of linked nodes and between adjacent layers of a given device (solid arrows). For example, the network layers of the source and the first intermediate node communicate virtually; the physical layers of the source and the first node communicate physically; the data link and network layers of the source communicate physically. This is the nature of layered network architectures. For a review, see Chapter 1.

Traffic handling

Traffic is handled by one of four modes of operation: *circuit switching, message switching, packet switching,* and *cell switching.* Circuit switching provides dedicated bandwidth; packet and message switching do not provide dedicated bandwidth but are more flexible and efficient; cell switching combines some features of both circuit and packet switching to provide high-speed transport. We look at overviews of these modes next.

8.3 Circuit switching

It is no surprise that the first attempts to connect remote computers turned to the telephone companies (telcos); their network infrastructure already was in place. These are *circuit switched* networks, so named because switches create a circuit from the calling party to the called party by connecting a series of links leading from one to the other. The end-to-end circuit switching process is the same, regardless of whether the parties are people or computers and whether they are next door or across the country. Formally called *public switched telephone network (PSTN)* and informally called *plain old telephone service (POTS),* charges for their services are called *tariffs.*

Circuit switching has three phases: *setup*—the circuit is established; *hold open*—the circuit is kept available whether used or not; and *termination*—the circuit is released. Because the connection over which all traffic flows must be created and maintained until terminated, circuit switching is called a *connection-oriented service.*

Multiplexing is applied to improve circuit switched network efficiency. For telcos, synchronous time division multiplexing (TDM) is used after the customer's local loop reaches the first network edge switch, which resides in a telco central office. Thus, although it is convenient to think of a circuit as a long end-to-end cable, it is not actually the cable that is dedicated to the circuit, but some amount of capacity (called a *channel*) assigned to the user over a multiplexed link for the duration of the connection.

AMPLIFICATION

The local loop is the cable from a customer's telephone to the nearest central office (also called an end office). The switch in that office that is connected to the local loop is called an edge switch, because it is at the edge of the telco network.

Although telco networks were suitable for voice communications, as we have seen, the relatively narrow width of the voice band along with the inefficiency of TDM links for data transmission made them problematic for data communications. Eventually, this led to a different infrastructure—the *data network.* (See "Historical note: divergence and convergence.")

8.4 Message switching

In a typical WAN, to form a path from the original sender to the final receiver, a series of links must be traversed. These links frequently are connected by switches in a partial mesh—there are several routes between any two points, but not a direct connection between every two switches. According to how a message is routed, it can travel along any of the connected links as it wends its way through the network.

Upon reaching a switch, the entire message is stored until it can be sent out (forwarded) on the next link—a *store-and-forward* system. Because the switches treat each message as a single unit, the process is called *message switching.*

Recall that circuit switching operates at the physical layer, simply transmitting data bits without regard to what may or may not be message boundaries or transmission starts and stops. In contrast, message switching treats messages as distinct data blocks and therefore, unlike circuit switching, has to understand frame structure. This requires operation at least at the data link layer. Moreover, each intermediate switch treats each message independently.

Messages stored at a switch are forwarded either on a first come, first served basis or according to a priority scheme whereby waiting messages with higher priority are forwarded ahead of those with lower priority. Even when the outgoing link is free, the entire message is still stored at the switch before it is forwarded. Storage is on the switch's hard disk, which makes storage and retrieval relatively slow compared to packet switches, where storage always is in the much faster RAM.

If traffic volume is high, a message may have to wait at a switch before it can be forwarded over the next link. When the WAN is congested, delays can be considerable. Even worse, messages arriving when switch memory is full are discarded. Controlling flow to prevent this from happening, then, is an important aspect of this service.

HISTORICAL NOTE
Divergence and convergence

In the early days of WANs, most business traffic was voice oriented. Data transfers made up a fairly small proportion of network usage, so businesses were content to have data service ride along the telephone networks. As demand for fast, inexpensive data communications grew, data weighed more and more in terms of total traffic and cost. It became apparent that traditional telephone networks were not up to the task. The solution was divergence—independent voice and data networks. By the early 1980s, most corporations had both. Investment in these systems was in the billions.

Although this worked well from a performance perspective, several disadvantages were revealed over time. Cost was in the lead: for duplicate staffing, because telco and data network experts are different people; for maintaining two networks; for the inability to take advantage of a combined economy of scale. By the year 2000, data traffic had grown to an overwhelming percentage of business communications, so it became logical to focus on data networks and have voice traffic go along for the ride—that is, convergence. This reversal of the earlier trend has led, among other things, to the growing popularity of Voice over IP (VoIP) on the low- to no-cost Internet.

As a fairly new development, VoIP is not without performance problems. In addition, it must compete with other convergence technologies that can carry mixed traffic—frame relay and fast switching ATM are examples. Other convergence issues also come into play:

- With the global reach of networks, *compatibility* is especially important.
- Service providers competing for business must offer more and more **value-added services** to distinguish themselves.
- **Real-time transport** needs for voice and video add to pressure for high-performance networks.

As we have noted, demand for service quite often pushes technology. Once causing the divergence that resulted in the creation of separate voice and data networks, it now is precipitating advanced development of all-purpose converged networks.

8.5 Packet switching

Handling a large amount of data as a single unit is not efficient. If it is damaged in transit, the entire unit must be retransmitted, even if the damage is just to a few bits; this is a poor use of bandwidth. Additionally, when a small unit of information comes to a switch after a large unit has begun forwarding, it will have to wait a relatively long time before it can be forwarded—the time it takes to transmit the large unit—potentially delaying high-priority data. Of course, a large unit may be marked as high priority as well, meaning even more potential delays for small units.

Packet switching is designed to avoid the large unit issue, although varying packet sizes can still cause queuing delays. For transmission, large data units are broken into small units, which are assembled by protocol stacks into packets consisting of three organized parts: a header, a data section, and a trailer. (Packet size depends on the particular protocols being used.)

When the packets reach their final destination, they are reassembled into the original large data units. There is no guarantee that the packets of a given large unit will arrive in the order in which they were sent. Some may travel different routes with different transit times. Even if all packets of a group follow the same route, some may be damaged and need to be retransmitted—out of original order. Therefore, packets must contain sequence numbers so that they can be reassembled properly. Although this adds to overhead, the efficiencies gained are more than worth that cost.

Limits placed on addition to overhead restricts how many sequence numbers can be carried in a packet header. This and how sequence numbers are used are important performance issues that affect network traffic flows, delays at switches, and the potential of discarded packets. Already discussed with regard to sliding window flow control in Chapter 7, "Digital communication techniques," we will revisit these issues in later chapters.

Packet switching, based on statistical time division multiplexing (STDM), was a boon to the carriers because it allowed them to allocate their resources over a multitude of users more efficiently than did circuit switching. It also was a boon to the users because carrier efficiencies meant lower cost to the consumer. Whereas a dedicated circuit switched service is paid for as long as the circuit is open, whether or not it is used, packet switching payment depends on how many packets are sent. It also was typical for circuit switched rates to depend on distance; packet switching has no distance charges.

Packet switched networks provide two kinds of services: ***datagram*** and ***virtual circuit.*** Datagram service treats packets as independent units that are switched from link to link on their way to their destination addresses. Routing decisions are made on a per-packet basis according to various protocols, usually based on network traffic and route costs. For virtual circuit service, a path through the network is set up before any packets are sent. All packets from a given group follow that path. From the user perspective, it looks as though a dedicated circuit is in place—thus the name *virtual circuit*. Packets on virtual circuits move through the switches faster than datagrams, because after the circuit is established the switches do not need to make any routing decisions.

Datagram service

Datagrams are packets that are sent without prior circuit setup. Thus they are **connectionless.** Switching decisions are made independently for each datagram. This means that datagrams must carry full destination addressing information so the switches can make appropriate routing decisions as each datagram reaches them. (See Figure 8.2A.) This substantially increases overhead.

Datagram switching happens at the network layer (layer 3), providing what is called ***best effort delivery.*** There is no notification of delivery failure, so it often is referred to as an unreliable service. However, if reliable service is desired, transport layer (layer 4) protocols can be used to handle failures, thereby delivering datagrams reliably. Transmission control protocol (TCP), a major Internet transport layer protocol, is an example of a connection-oriented service that does guarantee datagram delivery.

TECHNICAL NOTE
Packets and frames

The terms *packet* and *frame* can be confusing. In essence, they both refer to an arrangement of information into a cohesive unit. In that sense, they mean the same thing. Usage conventions have resulted in the terms being employed differently, though not necessarily distinctively. For example, it is common to refer to data assembled by protocol layers above data link as a packet;

when the packet is encoded for transmission by the data link layer, it is called a frame. Yet traveling over a WAN, the frame may be moving through a packet switching network where it also can be called a datagram. One packet switching technique is called frame relay.

More important than the term is the idea that in all cases, the unit consists of control data, or of user or management data surrounded by control data.

Virtual circuit service

Virtual circuits are created as logical paths between network nodes, where each packet of a transmission follows the same route. Hence, virtual circuits are **connection oriented,** just as is circuit switched service. (See Figure 8.2B.) As with any such service, a problem anywhere on the route affects the entire service.

It is important to note that, in contrast to circuit switching, the physical route followed in a virtual circuit is simply an artifact of the packet-by-packet switching process. Packets follow that route because it was predetermined and is employed by each switch. There is no open circuit and no preallocated bandwidth, as is the case with circuit switching. Even though they all follow the same route, each packet is handled independently. This adds much less overhead than is the case with datagram service.

To create the virtual circuit, the end-point destination address is used to determine which switches will be used to form the path. Each switch in that path enters in its table the outgoing port for the path along with a virtual circuit identifier. Every packet using the circuit carries that identifier, so when a packet reaches a switch, a quick table lookup is all that is needed for next hop routing.

Although the route is pre-assigned to the virtual circuit, any part of that route still can be used for packets from other sources, whether they are part of another virtual circuit or sent as independent datagrams. Terminating a virtual circuit means removing the identifiers from the switch tables.

In circuit switching, the channel set aside for the circuit is not available for any other transmissions, whether that circuit is being used or not. In packet switching, any link channel may be used for any packet, even when the link is part of a virtual circuit.

FIGURE 8.2

Datagram and virtual circuit services

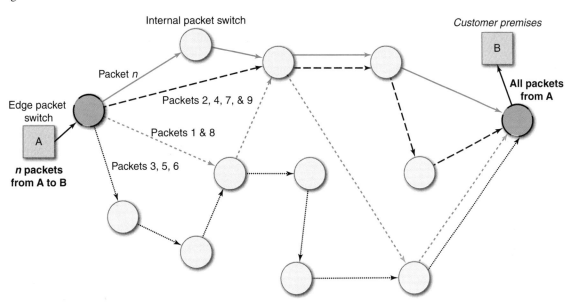

A. Datagram service: Each packet travels independently and may or may not travel the same route or the same links. All switches are store and forward. In this example there are *n* packets in the original data unit.

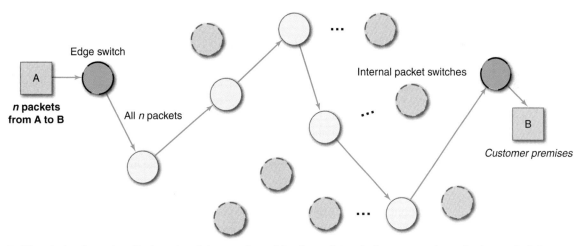

B. Virtual circuit service: Each packet of the *n* packets of the data unit travels the same predetermined route. Switches may be cut through or store and forward.

There are two types of virtual circuits: ***switched (SVC)*** and ***permanent (PVC).*** An SVC is created on demand and terminated when transmission is finished, similar to the way a telephone call works. SVCs are most often used where data transmission is sporadic, so the circuit is not needed for long. PVCs are set up by a network administrator. After the circuit is established, it exists whether or not it is used. When it is no longer desired, it will be terminated by a network administrator. For situations in which there is a fairly large and steady stream of data to transmit, PVCs are a good option, because repetitive delays for circuit establishment and termination and concomitant use of bandwidth are eliminated.

Statistical multiplexing

It is desirable for packets from many users to intermingle as they travel on the links of the network. To achieve this, multiplexing is employed, which increases network efficiency. Synchronous time division multiplexing (TDM) is impractical because the likelihood of many unused channels would be high. Instead, statistical time division multiplexing (STDM) is employed on packet and message switched links. On optical links, further efficiencies are obtained via wavelength division multiplexing (WDM) and dense wavelength division multiplexing (DWDM).

8.6 Cell switching

Cells are extremely small packets. Processing is simplified because cells are fixed in size, so they can be switched through a WAN at very high speeds by fast hardware, rather than by considerably slower software processing. Further, on a cell switching network, *delays are bounded* because a cell cannot get stuck in a queue behind a larger packet or message.

Cell switching, also called *cell relay,* is similar to packet switching in that blocks of data are broken into small units; it also is similar to circuit switching in that cell switching is a *connection oriented service.* A virtual circuit is set up before cell transmission begins, and every cell using that circuit follows the same path through the WAN. As we have seen, though, connection orientation means that a problem on the path affects the service. This contrasts with connectionless packet switching, in which alternate links can be selected automatically to route around problems.

The International Telecommunication Union (ITU) standard for cell switching is called *asynchronous transfer mode (ATM).* To increase efficiency further, ATM also uses statistical multiplexing. In fact, the *A* in ATM stands for "asynchronous TDM" (that is, statistical TDM).

8.7 Wired and wireless

With all the publicity wireless has been receiving lately, it would seem to be a very recent development. Yet wireless communications have been around since the end of the 19th century. As far back as 1896, Guglielmo Marconi demonstrated a wireless telegraph, and in 1927, the first radiotelephone system began operating between the United States and Great Britain. Even automobile-based mobile telephones were offered in 1947. That same year, microwave transmission was employed for long-distance telephone calls, obviating the need for cabled trunk lines on many routes. In 1964, the first communications satellite, Telstar, was launched, and soon after, satellite-relayed telephone service and television broadcasts became available. Satellite and wireless traffic have exploded since then.

Despite these early developments, wired networks were the standard for many years, especially in corporate environments, and even with the latest movements toward wireless, they remain so. As the newer wireless technologies mature, this picture is slowly changing. Now, although wired corporate networks still predominate, it is not unusual for businesses to have both wired and wireless networks. In the mobile world, wireless can provide "last mile" connectivity to wired networks.

AMPLIFICATION

"Last mile" refers to a connection between a WAN and a local site—that is, a link to the WAN infrastructure. When the WAN is the telco network, the last mile is the local loop.

In today's corporate climate, it makes sense to view wired and wireless networks as complementary, rather than competing, using each type where it makes the most sense. The growing capabilities of wireless networks are leading to another kind of convergence trend: networks that integrate wired and wireless technologies. This is especially true for wired and wireless LANs.

Wired and wireless networks both have their strengths and weaknesses. The following table shows a brief comparison.

Wired	Wireless
Dedicated or shared bandwidth	Shared bandwidth
Moderate to high data rates	Low to moderate data rates
High resistance to interference	Low resistance to interference
Relatively secure	Possibly insecure
Immobile, relatively inflexible	Mobile, relatively flexible
Installation usually straightforward	Installation potentially problematic
Coverage and access known and fixed	May present coverage and access problems
Accommodates a large number of nodes	Accommodates a moderate number of nodes
Very large existing infrastructure	Small but growing infrastructure

Wireless LANs and links

With the dramatic drop in the cost of laptop computers and ever-shrinking personal communications devices, businesses are installing *wireless LANs (WLANs)* in growing numbers. Mobility usually is offered as the explanation for the increasing popularity of wireless in the corporate world, although mobility within business offices predates WLANs—an appropriately configured laptop can be plugged into any open access port on a wired LAN, for example. We can say that wireless capability eliminates the need to find a wired port, but a more compelling explanation for the rise of wireless is flexibility.

WLANs can be configured and reconfigured on the fly, facilitating establishment of ad hoc temporary membership networks for special functions, such as might be useful for group meetings or project team communications. They also provide access points that employees can tap into from outside the corporate walls, in effect extending the reach of the WLAN throughout the world. Of course, this also can be done from many locations via wired access points, such as hotel rooms, but as wireless grows, the locations and availability of wireless access points will blossom. Many hotels now offer both types of access.

A WLAN can be a completely separate entity, not connected to any corporate network, or it can be linked to a wired LAN through a stationary access point connected to the wired LAN by one port and to the WLAN via an antenna. In either case, WLAN members can come and go, subject to protocol-based maximums on the number of active nodes.

The key feature is *flexible connectivity,* a highly prized goal that was not always so simple to achieve. Before 1999, there was no universally accepted standard for WLANs; commercially available systems were not necessarily compatible with hardware, software, or protocols. In 1999, the IEEE *802.11b* WLAN standard filled that need. Although it operated at a maximum data rate of 11 Mbps (slow compared to wired networks at the time), it provided the universality that boosted interest in WLANs and made sense for corporate investment. A growth spurt followed that pushed competition; production volume grew and prices dropped, further impelling growth.

As always, after the technology was proven, pressure for greater speed ensued. Two other standards provided that: *802.11a* offers a maximum data rate of 54 Mbps, but it suffers from lack of backward compatibility with the "b" standard; *802.11g* provides the same speed as "a" but also is compatible with "b." It has become the dominant protocol for new installations. The latest version is *802.11n,* which promises speeds up to four times those of "g." It has recently been released. (See "Historical note: 802.11").

These speeds are dramatic for WLANs. Although they lag considerably behind high-speed Ethernet, now readily available with gigabit and multigigabit rates, their combination of flexibility, mobility, and speed makes them a valuable corporate asset for many business applications. They also are a growth area for home installations that include broadband access.

HISTORICAL NOTE
802.11

The original wireless standard, *802.11,* was released in 1997, but it ran at a maximum data rate of only 2 Mbps and used infrared for transmission. Because of poor performance, equipment using the standard was not produced commercially.

802.11b, released in 1999, was a commercial success, not only because its data rate was 11 Mbps, but also because of the switch to radio wave communications, which has better performance characteristics than infrared.

802.11a was also released in 1999, but chip availability problems kept it out of the market until 2001. By then, the "b" standard had gained a strong foothold, and even though "a" had a maximum data rate of 54 Mbps, its range was shorter and it was not backward compatible with "b," which kept adoption at a low level.

802.11g was released in 2003. It had the same data rate as "a" but was backward compatible with "b," although not always smoothly. It created a big splash in the market and soon became the dominant 802.11 standard.

Products with a "g" version, dubbed "super g," came out in late 2004. Super g uses several proprietary enhancements that are not part of the standard. Operation generally requires that all components in the wireless system come from the same manufacturer and use the same enhancements. Although the claim is that the products are cross-manufacturer and cross-version compatible, this is not always the case.

An IEEE subgroup working on *802.11n* has recently released its specifications. It is backward compatible and should be able to capture a large market in the business sector. Prices of "b/g" equipment should drop accordingly.

Bluetooth and personal area networks

Bluetooth is a wireless technology that uses radio waves for transmission over a very short range, on the order of 30 to 40 feet. Recent developments have extended the range to nearly half a mile under the right atmospheric conditions by using special antennas. This is far beyond the original design and as yet has been operating only in demonstration situations.

The original impetus for Bluetooth was to replace the clutter of desktop cables by creating wireless connections between keyboards and computers, computers and printers, headphones and sound cards, and the like. Soon that concept expanded to the creation of mini-networks among devices in very close proximity.

Bluetooth networks operate with a master/slave relationship—one device automatically assumes the role of master through which all communications travel; assignment is ad hoc. Bluetooth-enabled devices, including laptops, cell phones, digital cameras, and PDAs, can join an existing group or form a new one just by being turned on.

A Bluetooth group is called a *personal area network (PAN).* Its members can come and go on the fly, although no more than eight devices can be active members at any one time. A single PAN also is called a *piconet.* Piconets can be linked via their masters to form more extensive networks called *scatternets.* (See Figure 8.3.) Although piconets in a scatternet can communicate with each other, they still operate as independent networks. As with WLANs, piconets and scatternets can be connected to wired networks.

Radio wave communication

Master: ⬤ Slave: ○

A. The smallest piconet—one master, one slave

FIGURE 8.3

Piconets and scatternets

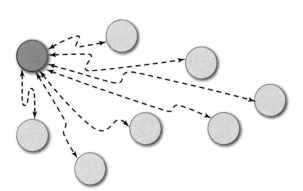

B. The largest piconet—one master, seven slaves

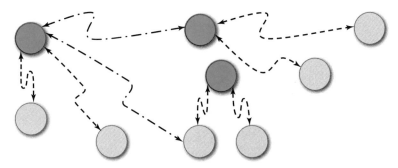

C. Linking three piconets to form a scatternet

Satellites

Satellites have become commonplace in everyday life. We get weather reports based on satellite imagery, receive television programs through satellite dishes, see correspondents reporting live over satellite links, and find our way around with the satellite-based global positioning system (GPS). Less visible to most of us are satellite communications used for newspapers and magazines to speed content collection by beaming articles over satellite links, geographical mapping based on satellite imagery, and shippers tracking their cargo via GPS. Even cable TV companies transport programs over satellite links to their wired networks. And these are only some of the myriad applications.

For data communications, satellites are relay stations that receive signals on one set of frequencies and transmit them on another set. Transmissions travel from ground-based stations to the satellites and back, and between satellites. For ground–satellite communications to work, the satellite must be "visible" to the ground station.

Visibility can be achieved in two ways. One is to place the satellites in a **geosynchronous earth orbit (GEO).** When a satellite orbits 35,786 kilometers (about 22,240 miles) above the earth in a band on either side of the equator from about 75 degrees north latitude to 75 degrees south latitude (an equatorial orbit), it is synchronized with (matches) the rotation of the earth. Hence, to a person (or station) on the ground, it appears to be motionless in the sky. Because of that, these satellites also are called **geostationary.**

Because the earth is a sphere, a single GEO satellite cannot "see" around it. Several satellites at appropriate distances from each other are needed (see Figure 8.4). Even then, GEOs cannot communicate with stations outside the latitude band.

To expand communication capacity, more than the minimum number of satellites are used. The upper limit is determined by interference—if the satellites are too close to each other, their transmissions will conflict.

Satellites in orbits other than the geosynchronous one do not appear stationary, nor do they need to follow equatorial orbits. As any one of these moves through its orbit, it will have contact with a given ground station for only a limited time. Therefore, to maintain communications, a train of such satellites following the same orbital path is needed. As a satellite passes out of a ground coverage zone, it hands off its communications with that zone to the next satellite in the train, which at that point is entering the zone. In this way, a given ground station always has one of the satellites "in sight." Again, to increase capacity, there can be more satellites in the train than the minimum needed for coverage, but not so many as to interfere with each other.

FIGURE 8.4

GEO satellites

To an observer on the ground, GEO satellites appear stationary.

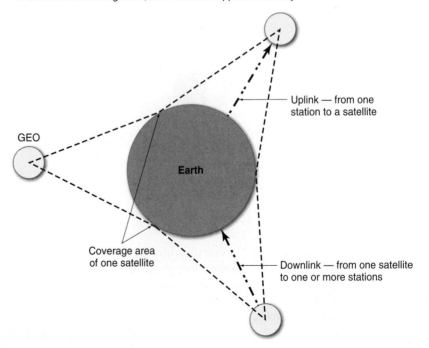

FIGURE 8.5

GEO, MEO, LEO, and HEO orbits

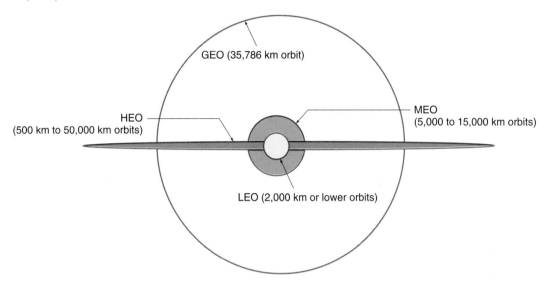

Not to scale. The earth is in the center of these orbits.

Satellites in orbits ranging from about 100 to 2,000 kilometers (almost 100 miles to a bit over 1,240 miles) above the earth are called *low earth orbit (LEO)* satellites; those with orbits from about 5,000 to 15,000 kilometers (roughly 3,100 to 9,300 miles) are called *medium earth orbit (MEO)* satellites. Note that all of these orbits are much closer to the earth than that of the GEOs.

GEOs, MEOs, and LEOs have orbits that are nearly circular. Another satellite type, called *highly elliptical orbit (HEO),* travels as close as 500 kilometers and as far as 50,000 kilometers (nearly 311 miles to over 31,000 miles) above the earth and is used to cover areas that GEOs, LEOs, and MEOs miss. To get a better idea of the relative scale of these orbits, see Figure 8.5.

Satellite communication uses microwaves and can carry analog or digital data. There are five different frequency bands ranging from 1.5 GHz to 20 GHz, in bandwidths from 15 MHz to 3,500 MHz. *Uplink* signals (from ground station to satellite) use different frequencies and sub-bands than *downlink* signals (from satellite to ground station).

8.8 Summary

In this chapter, we covered a broad range of technologies whose features and characteristics derive from the communications basics we explored in earlier chapters and whose details will be described in subsequent chapters. We saw several ways to characterize networks, looked at local area networks, and contrasted the two broad wide area network classes—circuit switched and packet switched. Within the packet switched realm, we discussed message and cell switching, and we noted datagram and virtual circuit services. Wireless communications systems, including local area networks, Bluetooth networks, and satellites, were surveyed as well.

In the next chapter, we will examine local area networks in greater detail. Subsequent chapters do the same for wide area networks, the Internet, and wireless communications.

END-OF-CHAPTER QUESTIONS

Short answer

1. How are networks characterized by ownership?
2. Explain "right-of-way."
3. What is a connection-oriented service?
4. What is a connectionless service?
5. What are the advantages of virtual circuits?
6. Contrast switched and permanent virtual circuit services.
7. With regard to wireless networks, what does "flexible connectivity" mean?
8. What makes 802.11g preferable to 802.11a?
9. What kinds of devices can participate in a Bluetooth group?
10. List some of the communications applications of satellites.

Fill-in

1. _____ is a geographic network classification.
2. Datagram service is a type of _____.
3. Statistical multiplexing is used to _____.
4. Switches in a packet switched network operate in a _____ mode.
5. The three basic components of a packet are _____, _____, and _____.
6. The three steps involved in using an SVC are _____, _____, and _____.
7. 802.11 a, b, and g are standards for _____.
8. Another name for a single personal area network is _____.
9. Interconnected piconets form a _____.
10. To a ground station, a GEO satellite will appear to be _____.

Multiple-choice

1. LANs function at the _____ protocol level(s)
   a. physical
   b. data link
   c. data link and network
   d. physical and data link
   e. physical, data link, and network

2. WANs function at the _____ protocol level(s)
   a. physical
   b. data link
   c. data link and network
   d. physical and data link
   e. physical, data link, and network

3. The public switched telephone network provides a _____ service.
   a. connection-oriented
   b. connectionless
   c. cell switching
   d. datagram
   e. virtual circuit

4. Virtual circuits are
   a. connection oriented
   b. connectionless
   c. datagrams
   d. public switched telephone networks
   e. LAN emulators

5. Message switching
   a. is a virtual circuit service
   b. breaks data into small packets
   c. is often used for e-mail
   d. avoids store-and-forward switches
   e. all the above

6. Cell relay
   a. is the same as cell switching
   b. is a connection-oriented service
   c. is the basis of ATM networks
   d. uses statistical multiplexing
   e. all the above

7. WLANs can be
   a. reconfigured on the fly
   b. independent of corporate networks
   c. accessed from remote locations
   d. connected to wired LANs
   e. all the above

8. A Bluetooth network
   a. has a limit of eight active members
   b. is composed of one or more piconets
   c. cannot be connected to a wired network

   d. uses microwaves
   e. all the above

9. MEO satellites have orbits _____ above the earth.
   a. no more than 2,000 kilometers
   b. from 5,000 to 15,000 kilometers
   c. 35,786 kilometers
   d. from 500 to 50,000 kilometers
   e. none of the above

10. For continuous communication between a ground station and a LEO satellite
   a. the LEO must be orbiting at a height of 35.786 kilometers
   b. the ground station must be located at one of the poles
   c. the ground station must be between 75 degrees north latitude and 75 degrees south latitude
   d. there must be a train of LEOs following the same orbital path
   e. the downlink speed must equal the uplink speed

True or false

1. In packet switching, all packets follow a predetermined route.
2. In circuit switching, all packets follow the same route.
3. Cell switching combines some of the features of datagram and virtual circuit services.
4. Datagrams can be routed around network trouble spots.
5. Message switching is a connectionless service.

6. Wireless communications have been available only in the last 25 years.
7. Wireless LANs cannot be connected to wired LANs.
8. A piconet operates on a master/slave basis.
9. Cable TV companies use satellites to relay some programs to their cable systems.
10. GEOs cannot orbit around the poles.

Expansion and exploration

1. Investigate network divergence and convergence. What led to network divergence? What is leading to convergence? In what direction is convergence taking us?
2. Discuss wired and wireless communications as corporate network implementations. In what situations would one be better than the other? Search the Web to get data on the dollar volume of sales for business expenditures on wired and wireless networks.
3. Create a timeline of communication satellite milestones.

Local area networks

9.1 Overview

A *local area network (LAN)* is a computer network whose span is relatively small—perhaps confined to a business office, one or two departments, a modest building, a small campus, or a home. In Chapter 1, "Introduction," we saw that business use of LANs grew out of the rise of office PCs and microcomputers in the early 1980s. After computers were on desktops, the next step was to connect them to each other. Although connecting computers was initially driven by the economics of sharing expensive peripherals, it soon became evident that the ability to effectively share data access was an even more valuable aspect of LANs. Now LANs can grow to incorporate hundreds of stations and can be interconnected to encompass thousands of stations.

Despite the traditional classification of LANs by span, a more relevant classification is link ownership. When a business sets up a LAN, it owns the equipment and the media, so LAN designs can be based on whatever protocols and link technologies are available and make the best business case. Decisions regarding type of LAN, how it is configured, operating speed, operating system, interconnections, access, and so on are under the control of the LAN owners, who can choose the setup that achieves whatever goals they desire—subject, of course, to cost and other practical considerations. Wide area network (WAN) links, in contrast, are almost always owned by public carriers. When we need to use those links, we are limited to what the carriers provide and their fee structures.

A further implication of ownership is that if we want to connect two of our LANs that reside in different buildings separated by a public thoroughfare such as a city street, in most cases we must use the services of a public carrier. Where distances between buildings are small and there is good line-of-site, we can set up our own wireless link between the two buildings to connect our LANs. If we don't mind occasional interference problems, a wireless link can be a low-cost solution and one that is under our control. Wireless links are discussed further in Chapter 14, "Wireless networks."

Two basic LAN classifications are *dedicated-server* (also called *server-centric*) and *peer-to-peer.* In the latter, each station is an equal (peer) of any other station. The essence of this definition is functional; it does not mean that every machine must be physically the same. Subject to setup, any computer can access files on any other and can take on the duties of a server, although special functions often are assigned. For example, one station can operate as a print server for all the stations, including itself, while still functioning as a user station on the LAN.

The original classifications of networks focused on span—the geographical distance, or "area," covered by each type of network. Thus, we had wide area, metropolitan area, and local area networks. The naming convention has continued, with such designations as PAN (personal area network), SAN (storage area network), and CAN (cluster area network), even though "area" has little meaning in these instances.

LAN links are privately owned; WAN links typically are owned by public carriers.

In dedicated-server LANs, the servers function only as servers—they cannot operate as user stations—and at least one of them must be a file server. These LANs also may utilize specialized servers to handle printing, database operations, Web sites, modem access, and other such functions. The vast majority of LANs in businesses are dedicated-server LANs, because they are better controlled and secured and can efficiently handle many more stations and servers. We will focus on this type of LAN.

AMPLIFICATION

Dedicated-server LANs often are called client-server LANs, because the stations (clients) request and receive services from the servers. More properly, client-server refers to a mode of operation. Thus, peer-to-peer LANs can operate in a client-server mode, too. So to keep the distinction clear, we will avoid that usage.

Within the realm of dedicated-server LANs, distinctions are made on the basis of protocols contained within the network operating system, physical and logical topologies, and media. We discussed media in Chapter 2, "The modern signal carriers," and topologies in Chapter 6, "Communications connections." In this chapter, we will focus on LAN protocols and interconnections.

9.2 LAN hardware and software

LAN hardware and software are the concern of the two lowest layers of the Open Systems Interconnection (OSI) and TCP/IP model architectures: layer 1, the physical layer, and layer 2, the data link layer.

As we saw in Chapter 1, layer 1 deals with transmitting and receiving bit streams via electricity or light, and physical specifications for device connection. Layer 2 involves frame assembly and disassembly, frame synchronization, point-to-point flow and error control, physical addressing, and medium access. In other words, the two layers handle all the protocols and specifications needed to run the LAN. Higher layers are involved only in processing information and when LANs are interconnected.

Except for the network operating system (discussed later in this section), almost all of the LAN protocols are embedded in hardware and firmware on a ***network interface card (NIC),*** which has ports to accommodate connectors for the medium being used, and which must be installed in each node of the LAN. Here, *node* means any device directly connected to the LAN medium or directly addressable on the LAN; it does not include devices indirectly connected. For example, a printer connected to a station is not a LAN node, but a printer with an NIC is. An NIC can be a separate card plugged into the system board, a chip set built into the system board, or a PC card for laptops.

Layer 2 addresses

A layer 2 address uniquely identifies each addressable LAN device. For the vast majority of LANs in use today, this is the ***medium access control (MAC) address*** defined by the IEEE (Institute of Electrical and Electronics Engineers). A MAC address is a *physical* address that is different for each NIC, hard-coded by the manufacturer, and read into RAM on initialization. Every MAC address is unique, predetermined, and permanent. (See "Technical note: The uniqueness of MAC addresses.")

AMPLIFICATION

In the OSI model architecture, layer 2 (data link) is subdivided into a lower sub-layer, Medium Access Control, and an upper sub-layer, Logical Link Control (LLC). The MAC sub-layer takes care of addressing and access; the LLC was intended for upper-layer compatibility with the MAC sub-layer, but it is not relevant in today's LANs.

The MAC scheme uses ***flat addresses.*** Although flat addresses uniquely identify individual machines, they do not have any information as to where the machines are or, for that matter, any relation to each other. An NIC with address 123 . . . 001 may be located in an office in New York, whereas an NIC with address 123 . . . 002 may be in a school in London. When we interconnect LANs and connect LANs to WANs, higher-level addresses must come into play. In Chapter 13, "TCP/IP, associated Internet protocols, and routing," we discuss how these are mapped to the MAC addresses.

TECHNICAL NOTE
The uniqueness of MAC addresses

The seemingly monumental task of insuring globally unique MAC addresses is made simple as follows:

MAC addresses are 48 bits long. The first 24 bits are assigned by the IEEE and are exclusive to each manufacturer; this is called the Organizationally Unique Identifier (OUI). The last 24 bits are assigned by each individual manufacturer (enough for 16,777,216 unique addresses per manufacturer ID) and are unique for each NIC it makes—typically, these are serial numbers or serial-like numbers. Because each NIC MAC address begins with an OUI, MAC addresses from different manufacturers will be unique even if they happen to have the same serial number appended.

MAC addresses sometimes are called *burned-in addresses (BIAs)* because they are stored in read-only memory (ROM) on the NIC.

Computers

Computers function as user stations and as LAN servers. Server computers differ from those used as stations by being faster and configured with much more memory and disk space. The number and types of servers employed depend on the usage demands of the LAN. In a business office that primarily runs word processing, spreadsheet, and simple database software but does not have any large volumes of data to transmit or manipulate, a single file server may be sufficient to hold all the shared files of the office and to run the network printers as well.

If there is a lot of database activity, a specially configured database server should be added to store and retrieve data and, importantly, to do most of the required data manipulations. This offloads work from the local stations, which are much less adept at database operations than a specialized server.

An office with large volumes of printing and many high-speed monochrome and color printers should install a print server. Print servers use a technique called spooling, whereby print jobs from the LAN stations are put in a queue on the print server's hard disk and sent to the appropriate network-attached printer when it is ready to receive a print job. This offloads print management tasks from the stations. Spooling software also can accommodate priorities so that urgent jobs are printed ahead of others.

The network operating system

The **network operating system (NOS)** mediates between the stations of the LAN, the LAN resources, and the processes being run, much the way a **computer operating system (OS)** mediates between the computer's resources and the software being run. In other words, whereas an OS controls the local hardware and software of a computer to achieve the actions required, the NOS controls the remote hardware and software of the LAN to achieve the actions required of the LAN.

Some OSs, such as the newer Windows and Mac operating OSs, include the basic functions of a NOS. UNIX and Linux OSs have NOS functions built in. Full-blown specialized NOSs, such as Microsoft Windows Server and Novell Netware, are installed separately from the computers' OSs. Small segments of the NOS are installed on each station; the complete NOS resides on the LAN file server. (For an exception, see "Technical note: NetBooting.")

A key NOS small segment is the **redirector.** It examines actions initiated on the local station, directing those that are local (such as saving a file on the station's disk) to the computer's OS, and redirecting those that call for a network resource (such as saving that file on the file server) to the LAN NOS. It also channels incoming actions to the local OS for handling.

The following are the functions of the NOS:

- Incorporates the protocols needed to operate the LAN
- Provides a consistent means for software running on the LAN to utilize the hardware of the LAN and for software running on the stations to interoperate with the LAN
- Controls operations of all server types
- Manages network disk access, file storage, and server memory
- Manages file security
- Provides tools for network administrators to manage the LAN

Media

The media are the physical links that tie the components of a LAN together. Taken as a group, LANs run on all the media types discussed in Chapter 2, namely varieties of coaxial and twisted pair cables, fiber-optic cables, and wireless. Each type is paired with appropriate connectors. For wireless, this means transmitting and receiving antennas. All are the province of the network architecture physical layer. Although there are some options for particular LANs, quite often the choice of LAN type and topology comes with a medium requirement. As we discuss various LANs, we will note the media specified.

TECHNICAL NOTE
Best effort delivery

Although LANs operate with extremely low bit error rates, errors can occur. LANs do not guarantee error-free data delivery, a deliberate design decision to keep complexity and cost low. Instead, LAN protocols are designed to give data frames a good chance of surviving the trip intact and provide receivers with a means for determining whether a frame is error-free. This is called *best effort delivery.* LANs rely on higher-layer protocols if more precise error detection and recovery is required.

TECHNICAL NOTE
NetBooting

In NetBooting, the entire OS of a station on the LAN is run from a NetBoot server, which can handle all the computers on the LAN simultaneously. No OS or NOS segments are installed on the stations, except what is needed to boot to the NetBoot server. To the users, it appears as though they are running their computers with the usual desktop operating system installed; the LAN functions are transparent.

Although NetBooting has been around for some time under the UNIX system, it now is available for Apple Macintosh computers running appropriate Open Firmware on a LAN operating under Mac OS X Server installed on a Power Mac. It cannot handle as many stations as can NetBooting running under UNIX. NetBooting has the advantages of offloading memory and computing activity from the local stations and simplifying installation and updating on the local side, but it creates more traffic on the LAN, potentially slowing down operations.

Some years ago, diskless stations had a modicum of popularity. Touted as a means of enhancing security (without local disks, files could not be saved or copied locally), these stations also booted from the server. They are no longer in vogue.

AMPLIFICATION

Technically, the medium for wireless is air or space; the signals travel through air and space analogously to electrical signals traveling through a wire or light signals traveling through a fiber-optic cable. In practice, though, the medium is referred to as "wireless medium," or simply "wireless."

9.3 Ethernet: the once and future king

Ethernet was not the first commercially successful LAN—that honor goes to ARCnet, released in 1977—but it has grown to become by far the most widely installed LAN (see "Historical note: the Ethernet genesis"). Periodically throughout its history, it has been dismissed as being on its last legs, becoming outmoded, about to be superseded by a better technology, and so on, and yet it remains the preferred choice in a tremendous variety of applications. Of course, as we shall see, Ethernet has changed considerably since it was first marketed in 1981.

To foster an understanding of Ethernet's operations and appreciation for its popularity, we will first look at the originally released Ethernet, also called traditional Ethernet. Then we will discuss its enhancements as it changed to meet growing business needs.

HISTORICAL NOTE
ARCnet

ARCnet (Attached Resource Computer network) was designed as a token passing bus running at a nominal data rate of 2 Mbps. Released in 1977, it had early success in office applications but was rapidly overshadowed by Ethernet. However, ARCnet has found its niche in real-time control networks for communications between embedded microcontrollers. For additional information, as well as a history of ARCnet, see the ARCnet Trade Association Web site: http://www.arcnet.com/.

Traditional Ethernet operation and the Ethernet frame

IN THE BEGINNING   The first commercial Ethernet was designed to run as a logical bus on a shared thick coax physical bus to which each station was attached. It was denoted as *10BASE5,* a label that signified a 10-Mbps data rate, baseband signaling, and a 500-meter maximum segment span. One segment could have up to 100 nodes. Overall span could be increased by adding up to four repeaters; connecting five 500-meter segments with four repeaters results in a maximum overall span of 2,500 meters.

Thick coax provides a wide bandwidth and good resistance to electromagnetic interference (EMI); the 500/2,500 meter span is long for a LAN. But thick coax, which has a diameter similar to a garden hose, is heavy and has a large minimum bend radius. To connect a station, the cable must be tapped—typically with a vampire tap that pierces the cable rather than severing it—and a device called a *medium attachment unit (MAU)* is connected to the cable and to the station. In sum, thick coax is difficult to work with, and its layout designs are rather inflexible.

THE ORIGINAL ETHERNET PROTOCOL   When a station transmits a frame, it includes the MAC address of the destination station. The frame travels along the bus in both directions. Each station reads the frame's destination address and discards any frame not addressed to it. Stations operate independently of each other—there is no central controller. To avoid chaos, each station follows a layer 2 protocol that guides access to the bus. That protocol is called *Carrier Sense Multiple Access with Collision Detection (CSMA/CD).* To handle multiple access, a station wanting to use the medium first must listen for activity on the bus; if the bus is being used, the station will hear the transmission (sense the carrier) and have to wait; if the bus is idle, the station can transmit immediately.

In essence, this procedure is a free-for-all. Any station can transmit a frame any time it gets to the medium before any other station. In other words, each station contends for access—hence, CSMA/CD is a *contention protocol.* After a station transmits one frame, it must stop and repeat the CSMA/CD procedure. This prevents it from monopolizing the LAN by transmitting continuously, which would block access by other stations.

It could happen that two stations listen for activity at the same time and, hearing none, transmit at the same time. Because both transmissions travel on the same bus, the frames will *collide,* destroying both. To recover, as soon as one of the stations "hears" the collision, it stops transmitting its original frame and sends out a *jamming signal*—a high-voltage signal that any station recognizes as collision notification. On hearing that signal, the other station ceases transmission.

We can imagine a scenario in which, after stopping, the two stations immediately sense the medium, find it idle and transmit again, only to collide again, ad infinitum. To avoid that paralyzing result, each station must wait a random time (called the *backoff*) before beginning the carrier sense process again. These steps are illustrated in Figure 9.1.

The Ethernet frame has five fields, illustrated in Figure 9.2. (The preamble and start frame delimiter are for synchronization and do not carry any information; they are not considered part of the frame but are shown with the other fields for completeness.) The maximum frame size is 1,518 bytes, which is reached when the data field is a full 1,500 bytes. (The size count begins with the destination address field.) The reason for a maximum is to prevent one station from monopolizing the LAN; it also limits the amount of data that must be retransmitted if the frame is damaged.

The minimum frame size, which results when the data field is just 46 bytes, is 64 bytes. If there are fewer than 46 bytes of data, the field is padded with zeros. (In some renditions, a PAD field is shown after the data field; the size of the PAD varies from 0 to 64 bytes.) The reason for a minimum has to do with collision detection, described next.

FIGURE 9.1

CSMA/CD

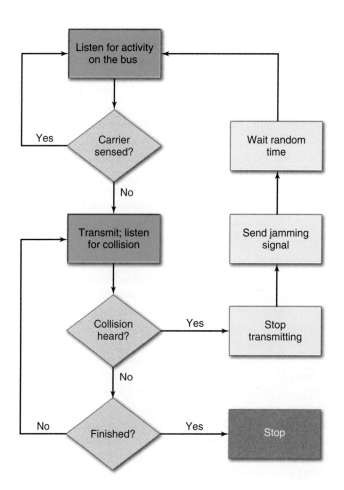

Preamble	SFD	Destination address	Source address	Type/ length	Data PDU	FCS
7 bytes	1 byte	6 bytes	6 bytes	2 bytes	46 to 1,500 bytes	4 bytes

FIGURE 9.2

The Ethernet frame

Preamble: 10101010 repeated seven times, for frame synchronization.

SFD (Start frame delimiter): 10101011 completes synchronization; alerts receiver of frame start.

Destination address: MAC address of recipient.

Source address: MAC address of sender.

Type/length: If its value is less than 1,518, it indicates the length of the data field; if greater than 1,536, it indicates what the network layer protocol is; for example, a value of 2,048 indicates an IP protocol.

Data PDU: Variable-length field containing the LLC PDU — all data from higher layers.

FCS (Frame check sequence): Uses CRC for error detection, based on all but preamble and SFD.

HISTORICAL NOTE
The Ethernet genesis

Robert Metcalf and David Boggs worked on the creation of Ethernet at the Xerox Palo Alto Research Center (PARC). Their first success came on May 22, 1973, when their LAN, running at a data rate of 3 Mbps, transmitted its first data frame. After three more years of diligent work, their experimental network connected 100 stations. They called their network Ethernet. The story is that Metcalf named Ethernet after the "luminiferous ether," the substance the ancient Greeks believed to be the medium for light propagation. This makes the name choice rather odd, as Ethernet was not designed as a light-based system. It could be reasoned that at its inception, Ethernet was as mysterious as the luminiferous ether.

Three more years passed before the Digital Equipment Corp., Intel, and Xerox consortium (DIX) was formed to further improve Ethernet and to manufacture the NICs. At the same time, they brought the Ethernet design, now running at 10 Mbps, to the IEEE for consideration as a standard. Most importantly for the acceptance and development of Ethernet, they wanted it to be an open industry standard that would permit anyone to manufacture Ethernet hardware and create software

(including operating systems) that would run it. Metcalf himself left Xerox soon after, and in 1979 he formed 3COM as a manufacturer of Ethernet hardware. (The name 3COM derives from the company's focus on three "coms"—computers, communication, and compatibility.) 3COM shipped its first products in March of 1981.

The IEEE had formed the 802 group to study and recommend various LAN standards. After receiving the DIX proposal, they created the 802.3 subgroup and assigned it to Ethernet. In 1983, the IEEE published a somewhat revised Ethernet standard, designated by the subgroup name 802.3. To support their desire for an open standard, Xerox turned over all its Ethernet patents to the IEEE. In 1989, the 802.3 standard was approved by ISO, thus gaining international approval. They called it Standard 88023.

The groundwork was done. Ethernet's simplicity and effectiveness, combined with a standard that was worldwide and open, led to the growth of its use by leaps and bounds. It quickly became the most popular LAN technology. With steady improvements, it has outpaced all competing LAN technologies and continues to grow, now even beginning to move into the WAN arena.

The collision window concept

Ethernet does not use acknowledgments. When Ethernets are connected to networks that do use acknowledgments, higher layers of the network architecture must come into play.

Non-use of acknowledgments has implications for the contention process. Suppose a station at one end of the bus sends out a small frame and finishes transmitting before the first bit of the frame reaches the other end of the bus; furthermore, suppose that the station at the far end of the bus listens for the carrier and, because the first bit has not reached it yet, senses no activity and starts to transmit its frame. The ensuing collision will not be heard by the first station, because it has finished transmitting and therefore stopped listening. In fact, even if the station continues to listen and hears a jamming signal, it will have no way of knowing that its frame was the one involved.

What is relevant here is called the *collision window*—the length of time it takes for a frame to travel from one end of the LAN to the other; this also is called the *slot time*. To avoid the ambiguous situation just described, Ethernet limits the maximum span of the LAN (and therefore the size of the collision window) and mandates a minimum frame size of 64 bytes.

For 10 Mbps Ethernet, the slot time is 512 bit times; 512 bits divided by 8 bits per byte is 64 bytes. That is large enough so that the station is still transmitting, and therefore listening for a collision of its own frame, during the time it takes the frame to reach the far end and for a possible jamming signal to travel all the way back—that is, twice the collision window. (Some references define the collision window as twice the slot time, rather than just the one-way trip.)

The key factors here are station *bit rate* and *propagation speed*. Propagation speed—how fast a bit travels on the bus—determines how long it takes for the bits to travel the length of the bus; bit rate determines how long it takes for a station to transmit a complete frame. We have two design elements that we can adjust to ensure that a station is still in the process of transmitting for at least twice the slot time: the maximum length of the bus and the minimum frame size. Ethernet designers struck a balance with a 500-meter maximum length and 64-byte minimum frame size. Although attenuation also becomes an issue as length increases, we can overcome that with repeaters. So, propagation speed and frame size remain the key determining factors.

Persistence strategies

Persistence strategies are the ways in which stations can act after the carrier sense step. With *1-persistence,* if the medium is idle, the station sends almost immediately. A very small amount of time, called the *interframe gap (IFG),* must pass between successive frames transmitted from a workstation. This provides time for the NIC to prepare a frame for transmission. For Ethernet, the IFG is 96 bit times.

The 1-persistence strategy has the highest incidence of collisions—whenever more than one station is sensing at the same time, an idle line result will yield a collision.

To reduce the chance of collisions, *p-persistence* requires that after finding the medium idle, a station transmits with probability p, and therefore does not transmit with probability $1-p$. Because each station generates a send-decision randomly based on p, it is much less likely that the stations will transmit at the same time and, accordingly, less likely that a collision will occur. The lower the p value, the lower the odds of stations transmitting or colliding, but the longer stations will wait before transmitting, on average, even when few or no other stations want to use the medium. We can see that if $p = 1$, p-persistence is 1-persistence.

Another idea is the *non-persistence* strategy. On finding an idle medium, a station will wait a random amount of time and then sense the line again. If it still is idle, the station will send the frame. Although this also reduces the likelihood of collisions, it means added delays in transmitting, even when no other station wants to use the medium.

9.4 Improving traditional Ethernet

The first improvement, a relatively modest one, reduced the problems of working with cumbersome thick coax by moving to thin coax, which also was much less costly. Later, the focus shifted to topology changes that eased management and reduced or eliminated the collision problem. Then the quest became increasing speed.

Thinnet

In 1985, the IEEE released a thin coax version of Ethernet, officially designated as *802.3a.* LANs using thin coax were called *thinnets* or *cheapernets;* thick coax LANs were retroactively named *thicknets.* With a diameter about that of a pencil, thin coax maintains the EMI resistance of thick coax but offers many advantages over its thicker counterpart.

The principal benefits of this move were:

- Easier installation. Thin coax is much more flexible, weighs considerably less, has a significantly smaller minimum bend radius, and is easier to tap.
- Elimination of a separate piece of equipment. The MAU that sits between the thicknet bus and the station was incorporated in the NIC rather than being a separate device.
- Cost reduction. Purchase, installation, and maintenance costs were lower than with thicknet.

The tradeoff was a reduction in the maximum segment span of the LAN because of the higher attenuation rate of thin coax. Designated *10BASE2,* segments cannot exceed 185 meters. No more than 30 nodes are allowed per segment, and only four repeaters can be used, extending span to a total of 925 meters. Quite often this was sufficient, as the small office LAN was predominant.

TECHNICAL NOTE
Names and numbers

As originally designed, maximum segment span of thinnet was 200 meters with a total maximum span of 1,000 meters, hence the designation 10BASE2. But transmission proved to be unreliable, so segmente span maximum was reduced to 185 meters and total maximum span to 925 meters. However, the designation 10BASE2 was not changed.

The numbers are less mysterious than it might appear. Thicknet maximums are 500/2,500 meters. The original thinnet maximum segment length of 200 meters is 40 percent (2/5) of thicknet; hence, maximum span is 2/5 of 2,500, or 1,000 meters. When it became clear that 185 meters was the practical segment limit, overall span maximum was reduced to 37 percent (185/500) of 2,500, or 925 meters.

Star wiring

The next improvement was more substantial: moving from a physical bus to a *physical star.* In this configuration, a central *hub* distributes signals from one station to all of the others, thus maintaining operation as a *logical bus* (see Figure 9.3). Most hubs also are repeaters, regenerating the signals that come to them. These are called active hubs. Passive hubs do no regeneration; they simply distribute signals the way a splitter for a TV cable does. Except for very small LANs, active hubs make more sense.

FIGURE 9.3

Bus and hub comparison

Both physical topologies operate as logical buses.

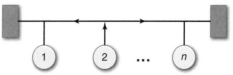

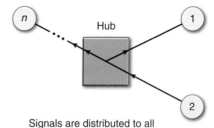

Signals on the bus propagate in both directions, reaching all stations.

Signals are distributed to all stations by the hub.

Cabling changed to the thinner, lighter, and more flexible unshielded twisted pair (UTP), and the designation changed to *10BASE-T.* This nomenclature maintained the meaning of the 10BASE part, but lost the indication of maximum span; the T refers to twisted pair. (As we will see, no subsequent versions of Ethernet designations have a span reference; it was replaced by an indicator of media type.)

Stations are connected to the hubs with two pairs of UTP, run in half duplex mode. One pair is for transmission, the other for receipt and collision detection.

Several advantages accrued:

- Reliability improved. With a physical bus, any break or disruption in the bus brings the LAN down; with a physical star, a break in any station's link to the hub brings down only that station's connection to the LAN.
- Management improved. With a physical bus, tracking down a faulty station is difficult, because there is no central point of access; with a physical star, the hub is the central point from which each station can be traced via a simple network management protocol (SNMP) module installed in the hub.
- Maintenance improved. To add a station to a physical bus requires cutting into the bus cable; to add a station to a physical star requires only running UTP from the station to the hub.

On the other hand:

- Physical stars require much more cable than physical buses; the latter need only a short drop line from the bus to each station, whereas the former need a cable run from each station all the way to the hub (see Figure 9.4).
- The speed and span of the LAN remain the same.
- Although the hub is a central point of access, it also is a single point of failure—hub failure brings down the entire LAN. In essence, the hub is the bus. Just as bus failure brings down the LAN, so does hub failure.
- Moving to 10BASE-T from a coax LAN requires complete re-cabling.
- Collisions still are possible.

 **A place for hubs**

It is worth noting that hubs have become very inexpensive and quite reliable. Although there now are better ways to wire a LAN, small office LANs still can benefit from a simple, inexpensive star-wired/hub setup.

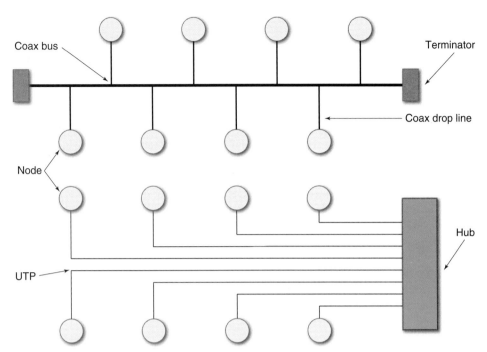

FIGURE 9.4

Bus and star cabling comparison: 8 nodes

These diagrams typify an office environment in which offices are arranged along a central corridor. Although standard depictions of a bus show all nodes on the same side of the bus and those of a star show the hub at the center with nodes circling it, these depictions display cabling length differences more realistically. Bear in mind that specific building features make such neat layouts unlikely.

A fiber-optic version of 10BASE-T, called *10BASE-FL,* has the same star configuration and data rate as 10BASE-T, but it uses two multimode fiber-optic cables in place of UTP, along with light-based hubs and NICs. This can be a costly upgrade, but its principal advantages, immunity from EMI and greater span, make it a worthwhile alternative to shielded twisted pair (STP) in situations where EMI is particularly troublesome.

TECHNICAL NOTE
Hubs

Hubs come in a variety of sizes, denoted by the number of ports they contain. Common sizes are 8-, 12-, 16-, and 24-port hubs. If more ports are needed, either at initial installation or because stations are added later on, hubs can be linked together via in/out ports included for that purpose.

Stacking hubs are designed so that when they are linked, they are viewed by hub management software as a single unit. This is a considerable advantage available at very little extra cost.

Switches

A more dramatic improvement came from replacing the hub with a ***switch.*** (Because the central device is not part of the 10BASE-T designation, it refers to either configuration.) The switch connects stations in pairs and will not connect a transmitting computer to a busy one. This means that the LAN no longer operates as a bus because the stations do not contend for medium access.

The following are advantages of switches:

- Collisions are eliminated. There is no simultaneously shared medium because each station has its own link to the switch, and the switch will not connect a station to one that is already connected to another station.
- Compatibility is maintained. Although CSMA/CD is not needed, stations still can operate as though it is; the MAC layer is not altered, assuring backward compatibility.
- The traditional Ethernet requirement of one station transmitting at a time is dropped; the switch can connect multiple pairs of computers at the same time. Theoretically, this provides a tremendous boost in throughput potential, but see "Technical note: Connections on a switched Ethernet."
- Upgrading is simple. To move from a hub to a switch, you need only remove the hub and plug all the cables into the switch.

In a switched LAN, there is no contention, and therefore there are no collisions and no length limits due to collision window considerations.

Disadvantages of switches include the following:

- They are more expensive than hubs, although not a lot more.
- They are a single point of failure for the LAN, as are hubs.

The advantages of 10BASE-T over the coax standards were so substantial that in short order it became the preferred Ethernet configuration. Except for some backbones, installation of coax Ethernets ceased.

TECHNICAL NOTE
Connections on a switched Ethernet

Although a switch has the potential of making $n/2$ simultaneous connections in a LAN with n nodes, compared to just two in a hub-LAN, this happens only under the rarest of circumstances. The vast majority of LAN traffic is between stations and servers. With one file server, most traffic is still limited to a pair at a time. This situation improves when specialized servers are used and when the speed of the link to the switch is increased, thus making more simultaneous pairwise connections more likely. In addition, some servers can accommodate multiple NICs. This means that each one appears to the switch as a different station, allowing multiple stations to connect to the server at the same time.

Fast Ethernet

Although in the early 1990s 10 Mbps was a relatively fast data rate (for context, modems for WAN connections were running at 1,200 bps and General Electric had leapt ahead with 4.8-Kbps "high-speed" links to its servers), after Ethernet technology was in place and stable, the quest for increased speed began. The first increase in actual data rate was a tenfold jump from 10 Mbps to 100 Mbps. Dubbed *fast Ethernet,* its official designation is *100BASE-TX.* This increase came with more rigorous media requirements: 10-Mbps stars can run on cat 3 pairs, but to run at 100 Mbps, two pairs of cat 5 UTP or STP are needed. In addition, NICs and switches have to be replaced. Once again, the MAC layer is left alone for backward compatibility. Fast Ethernet became an IEEE standard, called *802.3u,* in 1995.

To achieve a 100-Mbps data rate, bit duration was reduced. Encoding was changed from Manchester to a two-stage scheme: 4B/5B block coding is applied first; the result is encoded using MLT-3 (multiline transmission –3 level). (See Figure 9.5.) This is similar to NRZ-I, but it uses three signal levels ($\pm$ volts and 0 volts) instead of two; there is a start-of-bit transition for a 1-bit and none for a 0-bit.

The following are the advantages of 100BASE-TX:

- Speed boost is considerable.
- It is backward compatible; 10- and 100-Mbps stations can run on the same LAN, so the entire LAN does not have to be converted at once; NICs come in 10/100 versions. Often, the first step is to boost the server NICs to 100 Mbps while leaving most stations operating at 10 Mbps. Those stations with high file transfer activity would be upgraded first. To allow mixed speed configurations, *autonegotiation* was added. This allows nodes to agree on a data rate; point-to-point node links will operate at the rate of the slower node.
- Upgrade is simple if cat 5 UTP or STP is already installed; the NICs must simply be swapped.

Disadvantages include the following:

- Rewiring is required if cat 5 UTP or STP is not installed.
- NICs and switches must be replaced.
- Maximum segment length is 100 meters and total span to 250 meters. Because the slot time for fast Ethernet (512 bit times) and the minimum frame size (64 bytes) remained the same but bit duration was reduced, the maximum span had to be reduced accordingly.

Another format, *100BASE-FX,* is the multimode fiber-optic version of 100BASE-TX. (The designation 100BASE-X is used to refer to both 100BASE-TX and 100BASE-FX.)

Aside from the switch to optical transmission and equipment, the only other change is encoding: In the two-step process, MLT-3 is replaced by NRZ-I. (Diagrammatically, it looks the same as shown in Figure 9.5.) As with 10BASE-FL, 100BASE-FX is immune to

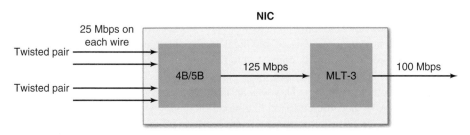

FIGURE 9.5

100BASE-TX

4B/5B is block encoding that represents 4-bit blocks as 5-bit blocks; the effective data rate is 100 Mbps on the receive side (see Chapter 4). MLT-3 is a line encoding scheme.

FIGURE 9.6

100BASE-T4

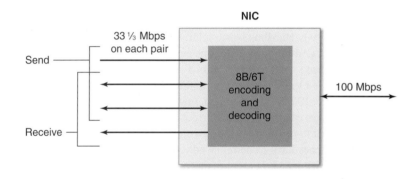

EMI. Another advantage over the copper standards is an increase in maximum span to 400 meters when running half duplex and 2 kilometers (over 1.2 miles) with full duplex. Full duplex is discussed in the next section.

One other version, *100BASE-T4,* was designed to run on cat 3 UTP, a considerable amount of which was in place in the mid-1990s. To achieve 100 Mbps with the lower-quality cable, four pairs are required: Two of the four pairs are run full duplex and two are run unidirectional. The signals are split among the pairs to reduce the load on each. Three pairs (two full duplex and one unidirectional) are used to transmit; the same two full duplex pairs and the other unidirectional are used to receive. Each pair runs at the relatively slower speed of 33⅓ Mbps, for a combined 100 Mbps in each direction. In addition, the more efficient 8B/6T block encoding replaces 4B/5B. (See Figure 9.6.) Maximum segment length is 100 meters.

100BASE-T4 was really an interim strategy. New installations and upgrades used higher-grade cabling than cat 3. Realizing this, businesses often opted to rewire rather than go to a short-term upgrade solution. As a result, the market for 100BASE-T4 was never very large and soon dwindled.

100BASE-X quickly became popular. Although at first it was used mainly to support building backbones and high-volume data access, it became increasingly common for new installations of large LANs and as an upgrade for older installations. The reason is simple: For no more than twice the cost of 10BASE-T, 100BASE-X yielded ten times the nominal data rate and was backward compatible as well.

Full duplex

By the mid-1990s, a different idea to increase Ethernet speed came up—a full duplex mode of operation. Published by the IEEE in 1997 as the *802.3x.* standard, it had the potential to double the speed of any half duplex Ethernet. At least theoretically, because full duplex stations can send and receive at the same time, throughput is doubled.

Technically, this was a simple enough upgrade, but it required replacing the switches and NICs with full duplex versions. With a lot of stations, that could get expensive.

There was one more stopping point as well. Full duplex works only over point-to-point connections; it is not applicable to physical buses. That meant that only star-wired switched LANs could be directly converted to full duplex.

On the other hand, switch functioning eliminated collisions, as was the case in the upgrade from hubs to switches. This was an important consideration for heavily loaded non-switched LANs, because collision likelihood increases with load. Importantly, it was possible to move to full duplex in just those sections of the LAN that needed greater throughput, as long as the switches had dual capability—full and half duplex—although that added complexity to the network.

Gigabit Ethernet

Late in 1995, the IEEE began looking into another tenfold jump in speed, to 1,000 Mbps, called *gigabit Ethernet.* In June 1998, the *802.3z* standard for fiber-optic media was released, followed about a year later by standard *802.3ab* for copper media.

Just as fast Ethernet built on the design of 10BASE-T, the same principle was followed in designing the gigabit standard: Leave the frame and MAC layer alone to ensure backward compatibility. Because bit duration is extremely short at gigabit speeds, the minimum frame size was increased from 64 bytes to 512 bytes. For gigabit Ethernet, the slot time is 4,096 bit times. Hence, the minimum frame size is 512 bytes (4,096 bits divided by 8 bits per byte is 512 bytes).

To bring the minimum to 512 bytes, the 802.3z standard adds an extension field that appends bits to the end of the frame if needed. Aside from this, the frame format was left the same.

The two basic classifications of gigabit Ethernet are *1000BASE-T* and *1000BASE-X.* 1000BASE-T runs on cat 5 UTP, uses 4B/5B encoding, and has a maximum span of 100 meters. 1000BASE-X uses 8B/10B encoding and is further subdivided into three versions: *1000BASE-CX,* a copper standard using twinax or quad cabling, with a maximum span of about 25 meters; *1000BASE-LX,* a fiber-optic standard using 1,300-nm signals, with a maximum span of 300 to 550 meters with multimode fiber and over 3 kilometers (almost 2 miles) with single-mode fiber; and *1000BASE-SX,* a fiber-optic standard using 850-nm signals, with the same span limits as LX.

AMPLIFICATION

Twinax cable is similar to coax except that it has two inner conductors instead of one; both are surrounded by conductive shielding. Quad cable has four inner conductors.

The fiber-optic specifications in the 802.3z standard are based on a variation of the Fibre Channel physical media standard, which is defined by the American National Standards Institute (ANSI) in the ANSI X3T11 specification. For more information about Fibre Channel, see

http://www.fibrechannel.org/.

So far, principal demand for gigabit Ethernet on copper media and on multimode fiber is to support high data rates on backbones and in storage area networks (see "Technical note: SANs"). It also is finding an audience in small LANs that process and share large amounts of data, such as for video imaging and special effects.

Gigabit Ethernet has become a strong competitor to ATM (asynchronous transfer mode, discussed in Chapter 11, "Packet switched wide area networks") on the local side because it more than matches ATM's speed but at a much lower cost. Based on past Ethernet migration trends, it is likely that these Ethernets will find their way into more and more LANs, just as fast Ethernet did. The ability of gigabit Ethernet running over single-mode fiber to span longer distances is making it a player in the high-speed MAN/WAN arenas as well.

10 gigabit Ethernet

The latest approved-standard development in the Ethernet world is 10 gigabit Ethernet (*10GBASE-X*), released by the IEEE in June 2002 as *802.3ae.* In a manner similar to its predecessors, it builds on the prior release (gigabit Ethernet) and mostly leaves the frame and MAC layer alone. It departs from lower-speed Ethernets in that it runs only in full duplex mode on fiber-optic media, of which there are seven types. This variety gives

TECHNICAL NOTE
SANs

A storage area network (SAN) is a high-speed specialized local network that connects a variety of storage devices designed to serve users on one or more LANs much more effectively than traditional LAN file or database servers. It is worthwhile for LANs where data volume and access needs are extensive.

For more on SANs, see

http://www.commsdesign.com/showArticle.jhtml? articleID=192200416.

10GBASE-X viability for use in LANs, MANs (metropolitan area networks), and WANs. The seven versions are as follows:

- *10GBASE-SR* (short range) and *-SW* (short wavelength) use 850 nm multimode fiber (MMF), intended for distances up to 300 meters.
- *10GBASE-LR* (long range) and *-LW* (long wavelength) specify 1,310 nm single-mode fiber (SMF), for distances up to 10 kilometers.
- *10GBASE-ER* (extended range) and **10GBASE-EW** (extra long wavelength) versions are for 1,550 nm SMF, for distances up to 40 kilometers.
- *10GBASE-LX4* uses wavelength division multiplexing to carry signals on four wavelengths of light over one MMF or SMF 1,310 nm pair. Distances are up to 300 meters on MMF and up to 10 kilometers on SMF.

In all versions, distances within ranges depend on cable type and quality. With appropriate signaling and cable quality, most of the distance limits noted in the preceding list can be extended.

Because of its speed, 10 gigabit Ethernet is cost effective as a high-speed infrastructure for segments up to 100 meters for both SANs and network-attached storage (NAS). In those applications, it is highly competitive with ATM, OC-3, OC-12, and OC-192. (These technologies are discussed in Chapter 10, "Circuit switching, the telcos, and alternatives," and Chapter 11.)

AMPLIFICATION

N etwork-attached storage is based on servers dedicated solely to file sharing. It does not provide any of the other services of typical LAN file servers.

NAS disk capacity can be added to a server-based LAN without shutting it down. One or more NAS servers can be located anywhere on the LAN.

Added to 10GBASE-X is a *WAN Interface Sublayer (WIS)* to provide compatibility between Ethernet and SONET STS-192c, which has a payload capacity of 9.58464 Gbps. 10GBASE-LR and 10GBASE-EW are designed to connect to SONET equipment. (SONET is discussed in Chapter 10.)

For additional information on 10 gigabit Ethernet, visit the IEEE 802.3ae Ethernet Task Force site at http://grouper.ieee.org/groups/802/3/ae/index.html.

9.5 Token ring

Token ring was created and patented by Olof S. Söderblom in the late 1960s. He licensed it to IBM, where the token ring LAN was developed and commercialized. In the 1970s, it was positioned as a LAN that did not suffer from throughput degradation due to collisions and that had predictable and acceptable performance under all loading conditions, accomplishments that the Ethernet of that era could not match.

Though initially proprietary to IBM, the design was subsequently submitted to the IEEE, which published it in somewhat modified form as standard *802.5* in 1983. In 1982, a year before token ring's release, IEEE published specifications for the token bus (802.4). Its principal use was on manufacturing floors for equipment control in electrically noisy conditions.

Although quite a bit more expensive and technically complex than Ethernet, token ring enjoyed a large following in the late 1980s and early 1990s in situations where reliable and predictable delivery of frames was paramount and where LAN loads tended to be high. Nevertheless, it was overtaken by Ethernet, whose steady improvements, low cost, simplicity, ease of installation, and widespread cadre of knowledgeable practitioners led to token ring's decline. These days, token ring has a rather limited audience, although there is a very significant installed base. Token ring equipment still is being sold, but it is not a big player in the market. Still, for historical perspective we will discuss the major characteristics of token ring.

Business NOTE — Token ring

For most businesses today, token ring makes sense only when adding to an existing token ring LAN or upgrading from an older version to a higher-speed version. For new installations, Ethernet is quite likely to be the best choice in nearly every situation.

Configuration and operation

The most common configuration of token ring, popularized by IBM, is a physical star/logical ring formed by connecting each station to a *multistation access unit (MAU)* at the star center. Cabling usually is STP, although fiber also is possible.

Logical topology requires operation as a point-to-point link between each node and its two immediate neighbors, which we can think of as predecessor and successor nodes. This logical linkage forms a ring that can be implemented as a physical ring, bus, or star. IBM's implementation is a physical star/logical ring; 802.5 does not specify physical topology.

A small packet called a *token* controls medium access—a station must have possession of a token to send a data frame, and there is only one token in circulation. Operationally, the token circulates around the ring, visiting each station in turn. When a station receives a token, if it does not have a frame to transmit, it regenerates the token and sends it on; otherwise, it creates a *data frame* and sends that out—when a data frame is circulating, there is no token.

As a data frame circulates around the ring, it is read by each station in turn and, if destined for another station, is *regenerated* and sent out. At the destination station, the frame is marked as read and sent back out again. It works its way around the ring to the original

FIGURE 9.7

Basic token ring operation

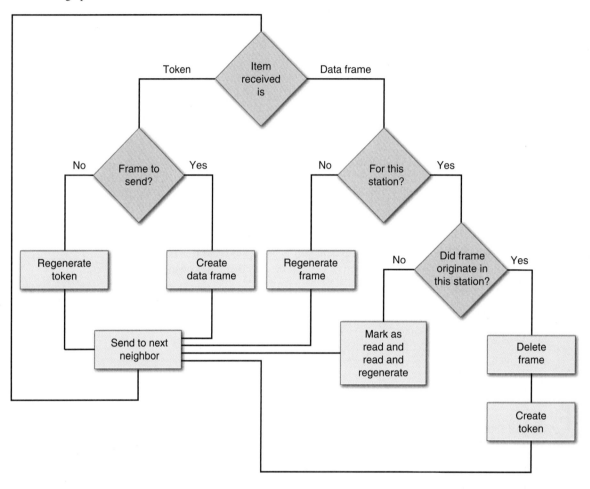

sender. That station must remove the frame, create a token, and send it out; this prevents any station from monopolizing the ring. The flow chart in Figure 9.7 illustrates basic ring operation.

For the ring to operate, there are many more processes needed than those noted so far and shown in Figure 9.7. Here are some examples:

- To start a ring—initial token creation
- To add a station—on ring startup and after the ring is operating
- To recover from a destroyed token—the ring will cease operating if there is no token
- To deal with a frame whose destination station is down—to prevent its circulating forever
- To deal with a frame that was read and is returning to a down originator
- To handle single station shut-down, so that ring operation continues

Most of these duties and others are the province of one station that acts as a monitor; the monitor station is chosen automatically on ring startup—another process. There also must be a process for reassigning a monitor station if that station shuts down.

It is clear that token ring operation is far more complex than Ethernet; this is the price for its deterministic, collision-free performance even when under load. At the same time, its complexity and its attendant cost implications have made token ring less attractive for the vast majority of business applications and have added to its cost as well.

Speed

The original token ring operated at a nominal data rate of 4 Mbps. Although this seems slow compared to the original 10 Mbps Ethernet, token ring was actually faster in operation under heavy loads. This is because there are no collisions, and every station gets a turn at a token. As Ethernet speeds increased, token ring attempted to keep pace. In 1989, the nominal rate was boosted to 16 Mbps and the possibility of two tokens circulating at the same time was incorporated. By then, however, Ethernet's destiny was clear and token ring declined in popularity.

A subsequent attempt to regain market share came after the High Speed Token Ring Alliance was formed by a group of manufacturers in 1997 to push IEEE for higher speed standards. One result was 100 Mbps token ring, released in 1998. But it was too late. It didn't have much of an impact in the typical business environment, because by then Ethernet had eliminated the collision issue and was operating at higher speeds. Later, a 1-Gbps token ring standard was published: It didn't find many takers.

Frames

There are three frame types: token, data, and command. These are shown in Figure 9.8. Note that the formats of data and command frames are the same; data frames have user data in the data field, whereas command frames carry control data.

The frame fields and their functions are:

- SFD (start frame delimiter): alerts the station to the arrival of an item; the field contains particular code patterns (differential Manchester encoding is used for token ring frames) so that frame type can be determined readily
- AC (access control): subdivided into priority (3 bits), reservation (3 bits), and token indicator (2 bits)
- FC (frame control): indicates data frame or control frame and type of control

FIGURE 9.8

Token ring frames

The token

The data/control frame

SFD: Start frame delimiter
AC: Access control
FC: Frame control
EFD: End frame delimiter

- EFD (end frame delimiter): end of frame; also used to indicate damaged frame and last-in-sequence frame
- Frame status: used to indicate that a data frame has been read; also terminates the frame
- Source and destination addresses: MAC addresses that follow the same format as Ethernet (and, in fact, all 802 MAC addresses)
- Data PDU: 0 bits for token frames, up to the maximum allowed by the particular implementation (based on ring speed); maximum total frame size is 18 kb
- FCS: uses CRC, as does Ethernet

If you would like to learn more about token ring, visit http://www.cisco.com/univercd/cc/td/doc/cisintwk/ito_doc/tokenrng.pdf.

9.6 LAN segmentation and interconnection

Consider the following two scenarios:

- As a business grows, its LANs also are likely to grow. At some point, LAN size results in a drop in efficiency and response time because of the demands of large volumes of traffic.
- Businesses are likely to have more than one LAN, and, at least some of the time, users on one LAN will need to access information or resources on another LAN or communicate with someone on another LAN.

In the first case, LAN segmentation is a solution; in the second, the solution is LAN interconnection. Bridges are a simple and economical way to accomplish both. Other methods include backbones and FDDI (discussed later in this chapter).

LAN segmentation

The goal of segmentation is to reduce overall congestion by grouping stations together (segmenting) according to traffic patterns; a segment will comprise stations that most often need to communicate with each other, with a common data source, or with a common resource. After the LAN is appropriately segmented, traffic is largely isolated within each segment, reducing overall traffic.

AMPLIFICATION

Segmentation sometimes is referred to as creating separate collision domains. This is true to some extent, as traffic local to a segment will not collide with traffic local to any other segment. However, because Ethernets can be set up as collisionless, this terminology is not as useful as in the past.

Often, segmentation begins by restructuring a large LAN into department groups—say one for accounting, one for marketing, and so on. But it also extends to situations in which activity can be logically grouped within a department—perhaps marketing can be segmented into sales, advertising, and research—or across departments where there is a common interest and communication need—for example, a research team with members from each of several departments.

It is important to note that each segment must be a LAN in itself, with its own file server, hub/switch, and possibly other shared equipment as well. After they are segmented, the newly created LANs can be interconnected to keep everyone in communication.

In a segmented LAN, each segment must be a complete, independent LAN.

Here is an example of how segmentation increases overall performance. Suppose we have a 40-station 10-Mbps LAN. On average, each station will be operating at 250 Kbps (10 Mbps/40 = .25 Mbps = 250 Kbps). Now let's reconfigure the LAN as two 20-station segments. Then, on average, each will be operating at 500 Kbps, double the rate.

Of course, these averages are only approximations, and segments are not always equal in size. Moreover, we did not account for having to add a file server to one of the segments, meaning that instead of 20 and 20 stations, we actually have 20 and 21. Finally, there are likely to be some occasions on which traffic from one must go to the other. All of these situations reduce the net gain somewhat. Nevertheless, the concept is clear, and when LANs are properly segmented, gains can be dramatic.

Bridge operation and bridge types

A bridge is a traffic monitor. Sitting between and connected to two LANs, say A and B, the bridge has a port for the A-side connection and another for the B-side connection. Thus, the bridge is a component of each LAN.

The bridge acts as a filter to keep local traffic local and send crossing traffic across. For example, when a frame from LAN A reaches bridge port A, if its destination address is a station in LAN B it will cross the bridge, but if the address is that of a LAN A station it will not. Looking at it from a cross-communications view, were the two LANs simply merged into one instead of being bridged, the traffic on both would be added together, with concomitant congestion. From a segmentation viewpoint, bridging reduces overall traffic by localizing segment traffic.

To filter traffic, the bridge must know which addresses are on both of its sides. It keeps these addresses in a forwarding table. How bridge address tables are established is one feature that distinguishes different bridge types. For the most basic bridge, tables must be manually loaded. This is a tedious process, even for small LANs, and it makes sense only in those that are unlikely to change—where stations are rarely added or NICs rarely replaced and where technical support to set up the tables is readily available. Instead, *learning bridges* can be used. These create the tables on their own, automatically.

There are two versions of the learning process, both of which are simple. In one, when a frame shows up at port A, the bridge puts the *source* address of the frame in side A of its forwarding table. The same happens for frames arriving at port B. In the other, the bridge sends a special frame to the LANs on each side, which is repeated to every station. This is called *flooding.* The response frames come back to the bridge, and the source addresses are entered into the table, as in the first version.

When fully constructed, the bridge table will have a two-column list of all the side A and side B addresses. Subsequently, when a frame from port A arrives, its *destination* address is compared to the side A column; if it's there, the frame stays on side A because its destination is a side A machine; if not, it crosses to side B. The same procedure applies for frames coming to port B.

Learning continues dynamically afterwards. In one case, if a station is added, when the first frame it sends reaches the bridge, the bridge sees that it is not in its address table and adds the frame's source address. A bridge also can be set up to periodically flood the LANs so that it can refresh its address table. This is especially useful when the LANs are frequently reconfigured.

One bridge can connect more than two LANs. The bridge will have one port for the connection to each LAN and one column in its address table for each port. Operation is a simple extension of the two-port model.

In operation, these bridges are ***transparent.*** That is, the stations act as they normally do and are not aware of the functioning of the bridge. The term "transparent bridge" often refers to a learning bridge, even though the two ideas, transparency and learning, are distinct.

Which type of bridge is better? The only virtue of basic bridges is low cost, but this is much less a factor than it used to be, as the price differential has narrowed considerably. Because learning bridges operate smoothly on their own, it makes little sense to bother with basic bridges.

Another distinction is that these bridges can connect LANs only if their layer 2 protocols match—for example, two Ethernets or two token rings. To connect those with different protocols, ***translating bridges*** are needed; they are limited to connecting 802.x LANs. Because of the work they do, translating bridges are operationally quite complex. Consider, for example, that for a frame to pass from an Ethernet LAN to a token ring LAN:

- The Ethernet frame must be deconstructed and reassembled according to token ring frame requirements.
- The bridge must wait for a token before it can transmit the frame.
- After it is read, the frame must be removed by the bridge and a token must be generated for the ring.
- If there is a response going back to the Ethernet side, the token ring frame must be deconstructed and an Ethernet frame must be created.

As it happens, Ethernets almost always use transparent learning bridges. Token rings use source routing bridges, in which the sending station determines the route the frame will take through the internetwork. Because the route is defined by the bridges in the path, source routing bridges must have addresses. Those addresses must be included in the frames, so the bridges are not transparent to the stations.

One type of translating bridge for connecting the two LAN types, called ***source routing transparent bridging,*** follows IEEE standard ***802.1d;*** the bridge has a transparent/learning side for Ethernet and a source routing side for token ring. Although this is but one of several interconnection solutions, it is the most straightforward.

Redundancy and the spanning tree

It is good practice to build some redundancy into networks; this allows continued operation in the face of some component failures. For bridged LANs, this means having more than one bridge between LANs. However, there can be *only one active path* between the two LANs for the network to operate properly; if there is more than one, ***loops*** are created, which results in duplicate frames and possibly endless looping. Figure 9.9 illustrates this with two simple examples.

The internetwork shown in Figure 9.9B is quite robust. Frames have several routes to reach their destination. For example, a frame can travel from LAN 1 to LAN 2 by these routes:

L1 – B1 – L2

L1 – B6 – L3 – B2 – L2

L1 – B5 – L5 – B6 – L3 – B2 – L2

L1 – B5 – L5 – B3 – L3 – B2 – L2

L1 – B5 – L5 – B4 – L4 – B3 – L3 – B2 – L2

Aside from the duplicate frames problem that these routes can create, another major potential problem is that of ***infinite looping.*** As one example, a frame from LAN 1 destined

FIGURE 9.9

Redundant bridges,
multiple frame copies, and
loops

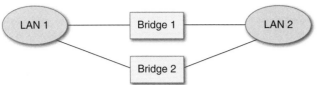

A. A frame from LAN 1 going to LAN 2 will cross both bridges. Two copies reach LAN 2.

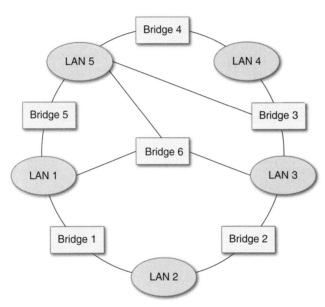

B. The situation gets more complex when more than two LANs and bridges are involved,
as shown in this internetwork of five LANs and six bridges.

for LAN 2 also follows the route L1 – B6 – L3 – B3 – L4 – B4 – L5 – B6 – L3 – B3 and so
on, round and round forever, clogging up the network. To achieve the robustness that
comes from redundancy, a method is needed to circumvent these occurrences. For Ethernet
LANs, that method is called *spanning tree.*

The spanning tree concept works like this:

- Set up the bridge ports so that there is only one route from each LAN to every other
LAN.
- Hold back the redundant routes until needed because of route failure.

A tree structure is overlaid on the network. One bridge is designated as the *root
bridge.* The port on each bridge over which frames may flow is called the *designated port,*
and the others are called *blocking ports.* An example is shown in Figure 9.10, which
repeats the internetwork of Figure 9.9.

In Figure 9.10, Bridge 1 is the root bridge. Allowed links are shown in bold, and the others are blocked links. The designated ports are those connecting the allowed links; blocking
ports connect the others—they are held in abeyance in case a designated route is disabled.

The ports are set up as follows:

- Each bridge has an ID; the one with the lowest ID becomes the root bridge.
- Each bridge sends special frames called *bridge protocol data units (BPDUs)* out of
all of its ports; the root bridge calculates the "shortest path" from each bridge back to
itself. The ports connecting these paths are called *root ports.*

FIGURE 9.10

Spanning tree

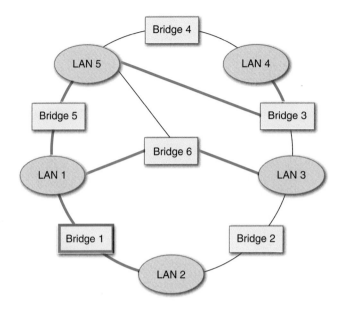

- The collection of allowed links will have paths between every pair of LANs but no redundant paths, and therefore no loops. Ports on disallowed paths will not forward frames—these are the blocking ports. Ports on allowed paths will forward frames—these are the designated ports.
- In the event of link or bridge failure, blocked ports can become designated ports; this happens by the same process as the original setup, resulting in a reconfigured internetwork.

The good news is that all the work of setting up and maintaining the spanning tree is handled by software and is carried out automatically after the metric for shortest path is selected.

AMPLIFICATION

The meaning of "shortest path" depends on the metric used. It may be actual distance; it may be some measure of cost, in which case the shortest path means the least cost path; or it may be speed, in which case shortest path means fastest. In other words, any metric can be applied, which makes the concept very flexible. The path is chosen by applying the metric in the **shortest path algorithm,** which makes the determination.

Backbones

In many businesses, especially those that occupy several floors in a building, a more efficient way to interconnect LANs is through a **backbone** rather than simple bridging. The difference is that with simple bridging, LANs and bridges connect directly, whereas with backbones, all interLAN links traverse the backbone.

Backbones may be linked to the LANs by bridges, they may be based on routers, or they may even be LANs themselves. Whatever method is used, the LAN stations connect to the backbone via their LAN hubs or switches, and the backbone serves as a high-speed pathway among all the LANs, thereby interconnecting them. Figure 9.11 shows two examples: a bridged backbone and a star-wired backbone.

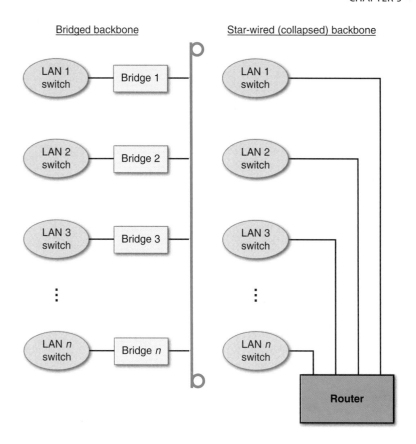

FIGURE 9.11

Backbone examples

In the bridged backbone, each bridge has one port for connection to the backbone bus and a another for connection to its LAN switch. A bridge will forward to the bus only those frames from its LAN that are destined for a non-local LAN and will forward from the bus only those frames destined for its LAN.

In the star-wired backbone, each LAN switch is connected to a router that has tables of LAN addresses and will send frames from one LAN to another according to frame destination addresses. In this configuration, the actual backbone is considered to be shrunk into the router itself; for this reason, it also is called a ***collapsed backbone.***

Collapsed backbones are very popular configurations because routers (which basically are switches that can operate with layer 3 addresses):

- Have powerful address-switching capabilities.
- Can be connected to external links as well as internal links.
- Can be placed anywhere that is convenient.
- Provide a single source for traffic management.
- Can incorporate ***remote monitor (RMON)*** devices and ***simple network management protocol (SNMP)*** software to permit easy traffic management.

The drawback, as with any single-source device, is that if the router fails, the backbone fails, leaving the LANs unconnected. Installations where reliable continuous service is paramount will have a spare configured router readily available to replace the failed unit.

A backbone LAN operates on the same principle as the star-wired backbone, except that a LAN takes the place of the router. Point-to-point connections are made between each LAN switch and the backbone LAN switch. Each connected LAN becomes a node on the backbone LAN. Figure 9.12 illustrates this concept.

FIGURE 9.12

Backbone LAN

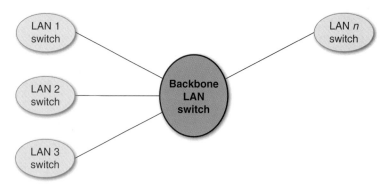

To avoid cluttering the figure, the LAN nodes are not shown. For the backbone LAN, the individual LANs are its nodes.

FDDI

In the mid-1980s, demand for higher-speed, more reliable LANs was building. In addition to being a prod to improve Ethernet, that pressure also took designers in a different direction—toward combining the high bandwidth, low attenuation rate, and interference immunity of fiber-optic media with the predictability of a token passing protocol. This led to development of the *Fiber Distributed Data Interface (FDDI),* which was published as ANSI standard X3T9.5 and subsequently incorporated by ISO in a compatible version. FDDI runs at 100 Mbps; stations can be as much as 2 kilometers (about 1¼ miles) apart with multimode fiber and 60 kilometers (about 37¼ miles) apart with single-mode fiber. As with token ring, each station acts as a repeater.

Reliability was boosted by designing FDDI as a dual ring in which each ring operates simultaneously but with traffic moving in opposite directions (*counter-rotating*). With this robust configuration, if a station shuts down or if a link on one ring crashes, the other ring picks up with virtually no time lost, thus preserving ring operation. In effect, the ring folds back on itself (a process called *wrapping*) and becomes a single ring until the station rejoins or the link comes back up. Wrapping and reconfiguration are handled by the *dual attachment concentrator (DAC)* that attaches each station to the rings.

Figure 9.13 shows the rings under three conditions: all stations and links operating; station failure; and link failure. When there is a failure, the DACs switch the port traffic from the failed route on one ring to the operational route on the other ring.

FDDI has been used somewhat successfully as a backbone for forming a MAN—in the days of 10 Mbps Ethernets and 4 Mbps token rings, it was the first technology available to build high-performance interconnections (internetworks) between buildings. However, even though it had the advantage of a frame structure that was compatible with 802 LAN frames, at the time it also was a high-cost solution because of the optical infrastructure required.

For cost relief, a copper wire standard of FDDI called *CDDI* was published by ANSI and ISO, designed to run on either cat 5 UTP or type 1 STP. However, because of the greater attenuation of copper, distance between concentrators was limited to only 100 meters. This meant that CDDI was not suitable for MAN applications, but it did work well in backbone setups and was especially useful where the cabling already was in place. Using CDDI also meant that there was no conversion from electricity to light and back; thus, CDDI equipment was less complex as well as less costly.

Since its brief popularity in the early 1990s, FDDI has been essentially superseded by higher-speed versions of Ethernet. Even though Ethernet cannot provide the predictable delivery of the token passing scheme or the robustness of the dual ring configuration, its

FIGURE 9.13

FDDI in operation

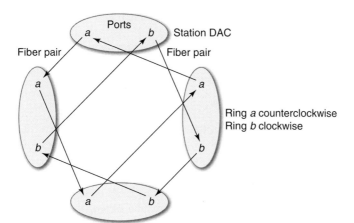

A. Fully operational

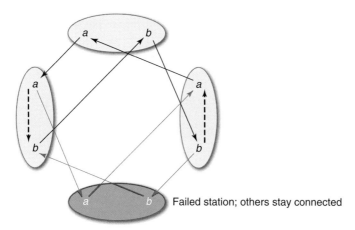

B. Station failure

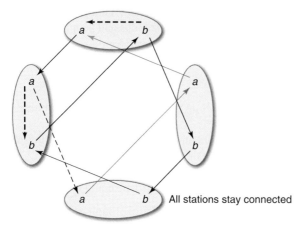

C. Link failure

speed, ready availability, cadre of technical experts, and great cost advantage once again have by and large won the day.

If you would like to learn more about FDDI, visit http://www.cisco.com/univercd/cc/td/doc/cisintwk/ito_doc/fddi.htm.

9.7 VLANs

Suppose a project is being put together that requires personnel from several different areas of the company. For the duration of the project, its members need to have access to particular data and resources and must be able to communicate with each other smoothly. Were they all part of the same LAN, this would be simple, but let's say they are in different LANs. To move the staff or create a special physical LAN or segment for the duration of the project makes little sense. Instead, we can create a *virtual LAN (VLAN)* that accomplishes the same thing via software. (The IEEE VLAN standard *802.3ac* was published in 1998. We can see from the ".3" in its designation that it applies to Ethernet LANs.)

VLANs are grouped by station or switch characteristics, or frame protocols, without changing physical LAN memberships or links. It doesn't matter whether the stations are in the same LAN or different LANs, as long as there are physical connections (such as backbones or bridges) among them.

 VLANs are the logical counterparts of physical LANs.

VLANs have four major benefits:

- Security. Messages and data transfers within a VLAN are not accessible to people who are not members, even if they are on the same physical LANs.
- Traffic reduction. Broadcast and multicast traffic that otherwise would travel to all stations can be restricted to the subsets of stations for which the traffic is relevant.
- Flexibility. VLANs are easily set up and easily disbanded, memberships are simple to add and remove, and stations can be part of more than one VLAN at the same time.
- Cost savings. In both money and time, the cost of creating a VLAN is minuscule compared to the cost of physically moving stations and people, especially because the need arises most commonly for temporary workgroups or groups whose memberships change frequently.

VLANs also come with caveats:

- Just because a VLAN is easy to set up does not mean that the resulting VLAN will be a well-designed sub-network.
- You should be wary of too many members who are on too many physical LANs, especially when those LANs are in different buildings.
- You should be rigorous in defining which members must be on a VLAN; those who need only occasional communication with a group should not be part of the group.

Oversizing a group and creating complex VLAN groupings can lead to the following problems:

- Congestion. Unnecessary traffic on the connecting links can slow down all the stations using those links, whether or not they are VLAN members.
- Network management difficulty. Problems can be tedious and time consuming to trace, especially when the physical components are widely scattered.

FIGURE 9.14

Switches and VLAN membership

The same VLANs are established in both of these configurations. In the backbone switch setup, the two switches can be on different floors. By using a backbone router in place of the backbone switch, we can form VLANs of stations in different buildings by connecting their switches to the router.

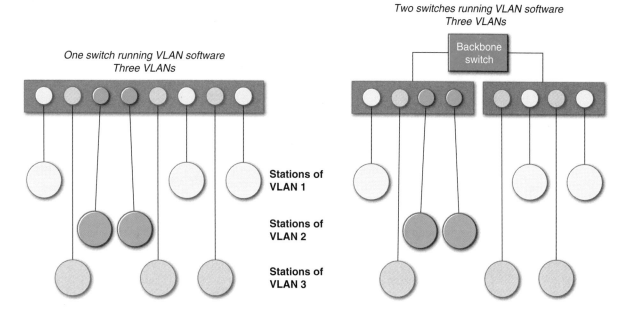

Assembling a VLAN

VLAN membership can be defined by attribute—switch port number, station MAC address, layer 3 IP address—or by frame protocols. Figure 9.14 shows two switch configuration examples. In either case, to the stations it appears as though they are on their own physical LANs.

ATTRIBUTE BASED   Switches for *attribute-based* VLANs are configured by creating *list mappings,* also called *access lists,* that comprise a table of membership attribute/VLAN associations that are stored in the switches. The switches use these to discern which ports belong to which VLANs and forward frames accordingly. There are three means for doing this:

- Mostly manual. The network administrator enters the station assignment data. This task is eased by the use of VLAN software; the administrator enters the defining characteristics—port numbers, addresses—and the software sets up the switch. Changes in membership also are manually entered.
- Partly manual. The network administrator enters the initial assignments and also defines groups into which the assignments fall. Then if a member changes groups, switch reassignments are made automatically.
- Mostly automatic. The administrator defines groups based on some characteristic. Then members are automatically added or changed based on group membership.

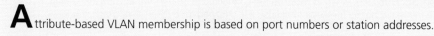

Attribute-based VLAN membership is based on port numbers or station addresses.

PROTOCOL BASED So far we have talked about attribute-based VLAN membership, determined by some station characteristic or switch port setting. Another form of VLAN that can be quite useful, though more complex in operation, is based on protocols.

Instead of funneling to a particular VLAN every frame reaching a particular port, VLAN membership can be decided on a frame-by-frame basis based on some characteristic of the frame. Thus, a station may be participating in one VLAN for some transmissions, another VLAN for other transmissions, and no VLAN for yet other transmissions. The result is called a *protocol-based* VLAN.

Protocol-based VLAN membership is defined by frame characteristics.

The most commonly used method for creating protocol-based VLANs is called *frame tagging,* for which IEEE standard *802.1q* applies. This standard modifies the Ethernet frame somewhat to include tag information, as shown in Figure 9.15. The switches use this information to transfer frames to their corresponding VLANs.

This is an easy way for one station to belong to more than one VLAN at the same time. There also is an added level of security, because each frame carries its own VLAN identification rather than simply being a function of the port used. The main drawback is that when several tagged VLANs are overlaid on the same physical internetwork, management and troubleshooting are orders of magnitude greater than for port-switched VLANs—problems may need to be traced not just down to a station but to a process that may or may not be running at the time. There also is the burden of additional processing to reconfigure the Ethernet frame.

FIGURE 9.15

Tagged Ethernet frame format

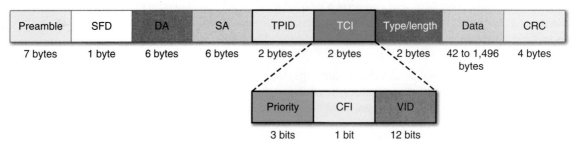

The first 20 bytes are the same as the standard Ethernet frame. Four tag bytes are inserted between the source address and the type/length field. The data field length is reduced by 4 bytes to allow space in the frame for the inserted fields. As is usual, the CRC is calculated based on all fields but the preamble and SFD.

The two added fields:

TPID: 8100H (1000 0001 0000 0000 binary) in this field identifies the frame as type 802.1q.

TCI: Carries three sub-fields:

Priority: Eight levels can be set to give precedence to frames in particular VLANs; this is useful in quality of service (QoS) situations in which minimizing delivery latency is important.

CFI (Canonical format indicator): For compatibility when switches are connected to both Ethernets and token rings — set to 0 for Ethernet. If set to 1, the frame will not be forwarded because it is destined for a token ring, which cannot accept tagged frames.

VID (VLAN ID): Identifies the VLAN to which the frame belongs — the 12 bits allow for 4,096 different VLAN designations.

One other caveat: Because a tagged frame is different from an untagged frame, the devices processing the frame must be 802.1q-compliant. If not, they will reject the frames as improper. So although tagged VLANs can be very useful, they should be used with caution and with the proper equipment.

If you would like to learn more about VLANs, visit http://www.cisco.com/en/US/docs/switches/lan/catalyst2900xl_3500xl/catalyst1900_2820/version8.00.03/scg/02vlans.html.

LAN emulation

One other pseudo-LAN type is ***LAN Emulation (LANE).*** This term is most often applied to an asynchronous transfer mode (ATM) network that, when functioning in LANE mode, can transfer traffic between Ethernet or token ring LANs. As such, the ATM network serves as a backbone. However, ATM LANEs are most commonly employed to simplify integration of Ethernet LANs with ATM networks. In either case, the process involves mapping LAN MAC addresses to ATM cells and ATM cell addresses to LAN frames. More detail is provided in Chapter 11, where ATM is discussed.

9.8 Summary

In this chapter, we looked at the many forms of LANs, from their origination to how they evolved. Along the way we saw a variety of topologies, both physical and logical. We looked at addressing considerations in general and MAC addresses in particular. Requisite hardware, including different server types, work stations, and NICs, were discussed, and we looked at the roles and functions of network operating systems. Media were described and compared.

Aside from providing a background and overview of LANs, all this served as a lead-in to Ethernet, which has become the dominant LAN technology. We described and compared in some detail the protocols and topologies under which different versions of Ethernet operate and noted how Ethernet evolved in response to business demand. This evolution embraced major improvements in media and devices, and spectacular increases in data rates from the original 10 Mbps to the latest multi-gigabit rates.

Next we explored other LAN models, beginning with token ring. Although it offered many advantages that Ethernet could not, such as predictable performance without deterioration under load, it was not successful as an Ethernet competitor. Still, token ring has an important role in LAN history and has found enough niche applications to keep it alive.

LAN performance can be improved by segmentation, a concept we examined in its various guises. We saw how different types of bridges come into play, both for segmentation and for connecting existing LANs. We also saw how backbones function to interconnect LANs, and we looked at several types.

Next we turned to FDDI, a highly robust token passing optical technology offering backbone and MAN capability. Primarily an interim system, it was instrumental in proving the viability of optical technologies for short- and moderate-span business applications.

VLANs were examined as a software solution for creating ad hoc and temporary LANs without having to physically establish those LANs. We saw various ways of setting them up and examined the implications of each method. We also discussed their versatility and importance for businesses.

Finally, we noted LANE, typically ATM based, used primarily as a method for integrating Ethernet LANs with ATM networks.

In the next chapter, we will explore circuit switching, the classic telephone company WAN technology, as it evolved over time. We also will discuss many techniques developed in that evolution, and alternative technologies as well.

END-OF-CHAPTER QUESTIONS

Short answer

1. How are LANs classified?
2. What are the layer 2 functions involved with LANs?
3. How is the uniqueness of MAC addresses assured?
4. Describe CSMA/CD.
5. How do 10BASE5 and 10BASE2 differ?
6. How does the operation of Ethernet change when a hub is replaced by a switch?
7. How does LAN segmentation improve performance?
8. Explain the operation of a learning bridge.
9. How can VLAN memberships be defined?
10. What is LANE?

Fill-in

1. In a _____ LAN, each station is an equal of any other station.
2. The OSI and TCP/IP layers of primary concern to LANs are _____.
3. Almost all LAN protocols are embedded in hardware and firmware on the _____.
4. The _____ is the physical address of the NIC.
5. The _____ mediates between the stations of the LAN and the LAN resources.
6. The simplest device for connecting two independent LANs is a _____.
7. To connect LANs with different protocols, a _____ bridge can be used.
8. _____ is a fiber-optic token passing dual ring.
9. A _____ accomplishes in software what otherwise would require physically reconfiguring LANs.
10. Four major benefits of VLANs are _____, _____, _____, and _____.

Multiple-choice

1. In a dedicated server LAN
   a. a server also can function as a station
   b. a print server is required
   c. at least one server must be a file server
   d. stations can take on server duties
   e. all of the above

2. A network interface card
   a. has ports to accommodate connectors for the medium being used
   b. plugs into the system board
   c. may take the form of a PC card
   d. must be installed in every node of a LAN
   e. all of the above

3. MAC addresses are
   a. flat
   b. hierarchical
   c. determined by the network administrator
   d. software based
   e. geographically based

4. With Microsoft Windows Server and Novell Netware
   a. small segments are installed on each station
   b. the complete NOS is installed on the file server
   c. the station segment incorporates a redirector
   d. network disk access, file storage, and server memory are managed
   e. all of the above

5. The standard Ethernet frame
   a. has a maximum of 1,500 bytes
   b. prevents collisions by using tags
   c. depends on p-persistence
   d. prevents one station from monopolizing the LAN
   e. none of the above

6. A 1-persistence strategy
   a. means that a station can transmit at any time
   b. requires a station to wait a random amount of time after sensing an idle medium
   c. requires a station to transmit immediately after sensing an idle medium
   d. is a special case of p-persistence where $1 - p = 1$
   e. none of the above

7. Switch-based Ethernets
   a. eliminate collisions
   b. can connect more than one pair of stations at a time
   c. are a simple, inexpensive upgrade from hub-based Ethernets
   d. are the configuration used by Ethernets beyond 10BASE2
   e. all of the above

8. With a token ring LAN
   a. collisions are impossible
   b. star-wiring is typical
   c. stations contend for access
   d. performance drops linearly with load
   e. both a and b

9. In a collapsed backbone
   a. the backbone is contained in a router
   b. individual LANs connect via bridges to the backbone
   c. there is a single source of failure
   d. no more than six LANs can be connected
   e. both a and c

10. A VLAN
    a. is a permanent reconfiguration of LAN membership
    b. is rarely used in business applications
    c. can cause congestion if not sized properly
    d. may be difficult to manage
    e. both c and d

True or false

1. The vast majority of business LANs are server-centric.
2. Ethernet LANs require NICs, but token ring LANs do not.
3. LAN stations are computers, but LAN servers are not.
4. A NOS is to the LAN as an OS is to the computer.
5. File servers cannot act as print servers.
6. Windows XP and Mac OS incorporate the basic functions of a NOS.
7. Star-wiring is the required configuration for switch-based Ethernets.
8. Bus-wired LANs use more cable than star-wired LANs.
9. Each LAN segment must be a complete, independent LAN.
10. Attribute-based VLAN membership is based on port numbers or station addresses.

Exploration

1. Compare the features and costs of the latest versions of Microsoft Windows Server and Novell Netware. You can start your search at http://www.microsoft.com/ and http://www.novell.com/.
2. Draw a diagram of a typical office floor and make two copies. On one, draw a cable layout for a bus LAN; on the other, draw a cable layout for a star-wired LAN. Measure the total amount of cable required for each.
3. Create a graphic representation of the evolution of Ethernet. Incorporate a timeline showing when each version came out, overlaid with a bar chart showing the speed of each. Based on the result, show what you believe will be the next two points on your representation.

THE MOSI CASE

Part 1: As the business grew, the paperwork burden became onerous and call volume increased beyond the abilities of the schedulers to provide timely responses. Part of the problem was the time spent writing down care needs and searching through various service provider lists. Also burdensome was the repetitive paper processing required of the schedulers and accountant. Further, the two social worker owners found it increasingly difficult to keep tabs on the business. To facilitate document transfer and sharing among the staff and management, and to pave the way for a database application and electronic data processing, they believe a local area network is required.

You have been asked to address this issue, recommending what type of LAN(s) to install, in what configuration, with what media, running at what speed, and at what cost. The system must be able to handle transaction volume without bogging down and be capable of easy upgrade and expansion when warranted by additional growth of the business. To accomplish this task, you intend to develop a table that shows the results of your investigation. Before you do so, what questions would you ask of the managers, employees of MOSI, or other parties? Think about what you need to know before you investigate options.

Part 2: Adding the LAN and a database application did wonders for MOSI's efficiency and capacity to handle service requests. Accordingly, the owners feel ready to expand the business to capture the demand that they were unable to handle before. They are considering hiring additional personnel, creating a marketing department and a legal department, and reconfiguring the scheduling and accounting operations as departments. Many more fee-for-service care providers will be added to the list. MOSI understands that the LAN as it exists will not be up to the task. Once again, they have asked you to investigate alternatives. Would it make more sense to expand the current LAN to cover all personnel, or to have interconnected department LANs? What is the business case for either decision? Before you reflect on these issues, what questions would you ask of the managers, other employees of MOSI, and other parties? Think about what you need to know before you investigate options.

MOSI also is considering creating an in-house staff of care providers for those outpatients who can travel to their facility—physical therapists, social workers, counselors, and transporters. This will require taking another floor in the building they are in. To investigate the feasibility of this plan, the owners have established a committee comprising an accountant, a scheduler, a lawyer, and one of the owners. One of the issues they face is how to provide this new staff, which would be on a separate floor in the building, with access to appropriate company databases. What would you suggest to aid the committee in their work? Before you answer, what questions would you ask of the managers, other employees of MOSI, or other parties? Think about what you need to know before you investigate options.

10

Circuit switching, the telcos, and alternatives

10.1 Overview

The first communications facility that could rightfully be called a wide area network (WAN) was the ubiquitous telephone system. From its early beginnings in 1877, the telephone network quickly grew to provide communications globally. To appreciate how rapidly this growth took place, consider that at the end of the Second World War in 1945 about 50 percent of U.S. households had telephone service. Just 10 years later the number was 70 percent, and by 1969 it had reached 90 percent.

Such rapid growth required significant technological innovation for efficient media utilization, increased transmission speed, and improved automation for call connection. Addressing this need was the Bell Telephone Laboratories, established in 1925 by the dominant U.S. telephone provider at the time, the American Telephone & Telegraph Company (AT&T). Bell Labs assembled the top-notch scientific talent needed to tackle these issues. The availability and reliability of the telephone system is a testament to their success.

In this chapter, we will examine the basic architecture of the telephone system, how multiplexing techniques were used to reduce the enormous amount of wire and fiber that would otherwise be required, the way the architecture has changed in response to greater traffic volume and demand for non-voice traffic, and the alternative services that arose.

10.2 The evolution of telcos in the United States

To better appreciate the structure and technologies of the telephone system and how it was instrumental in the development of telecommunications and computer networking, it is helpful to consider how it evolved from its inception. Let's take a look at the technical and commercial history of the telcos in the United States.

A summary of telco technical history

Commercial telephone service in the United States began in 1877 with the formation of the Bell Telephone Company by the telephone's inventor, Alexander Graham Bell, and his two financial supporters, Gardiner Hubbard and Thomas Sanders. A year later, the first telephone exchange opened in New Haven, Connecticut, licensed by the Bell Company.

Exchanges soon were added, providing more widespread service. By 1881, telephone exchanges operating under Bell Company licenses were in service in towns across the country, prompting Bell to change the company name to American Bell Telephone Company. Within a few years, American Bell took ownership of most of its licensees. That conglomeration came to be known as the Bell System.

To facilitate interconnection of the Bell System exchanges, American Bell formed the American Telephone & Telegraph Company (AT&T) in 1885 as a wholly owned subsidiary. It was given the job of installing and running a nationwide long-distance telephone network. At the end of that century, AT&T acquired its parent, American Bell, thus becoming the parent of the Bell System.

The first interconnection, completed in 1892, linked New York City and Chicago. Unfortunately, the line could only handle one call at a time at a very expensive rate of $9 for the first five minutes. (Based on relative consumer price indexes (CPIs), $9 in 1892 was the equivalent of over $209 in 2007.) In the same year, the first device to automate the process of making a telephone connection between two subscribers, the automatic circuit switch as developed by Almon Strowger, was installed (see Chapter 1, "Introduction").

Over the next quarter century, AT&T continued to add long-distance connections between major population centers in the United States. However, truly long-distance connections spanning the continent from the east to west coasts had to await the invention of the electronic vacuum tube by Lee De Forest in 1906. The tube was the basis for the first practical amplifiers developed to boost electrical telephone signal strength sufficiently to allow signals to travel the thousands of miles between the coasts. As a result, AT&T was able to open the first of many transcontinental lines in 1915.

HISTORICAL NOTE
Lee De Forest

Lee De Forest, born in Iowa in 1873, was an electrical engineer and prolific inventor. Considered one of the fathers of the electronic age, he died in 1961, having patented over 300 electronics-related inventions.

The first intercontinental telephone service began in 1927 between New York City and London using radio transmissions. Only one call could be placed at a time, and the cost was $75 for the first three minutes. (Again based on CPIs, the call cost of $75 in 1927 was over $885 in 2007 dollars.) Despite the high cost, businesses found the service quite valuable.

Transatlantic telephone service soon expanded, but it was not until 1934 that the first transpacific service was initiated, between the United States and Japan. This service also used radio waves and was limited to one call at a time, with a cost of $39 for the first three minutes. ($39 in 1934 was equal to about $598 in 2007.) It is interesting to note the sizable drop in cost in just seven years, even though the distance involved was considerably greater.

These first intercontinental connections were of relatively low quality, suffering from electromagnetic interference, inconsistent signal quality caused by atmospheric variations, and a lack of security (the airborne signals could easily be intercepted). Significant improvement was achieved with the laying of the first transatlantic telephone cable in 1956.

Not only did call quality improve, but the cable was able to handle 36 simultaneous calls at a significantly lower cost of only $12 for the first three minutes. ($12 in 1956 equaled a little more than $91 in 2007.) Similar improvements were achieved on transpacific calls in 1964, with the laying of an undersea cable between Japan and Hawaii that connected to an existing cable between Hawaii and the U.S. mainland.

Further improvements in signal quality and reductions in costs were made as fiber-optic cable began replacing copper cable. AT&T installed the first commercial fiber-optic cable for telephone use in 1977. By the mid-1980s, fiber-optic cable had proliferated throughout the telephone network and had become the cable of choice for trunk lines. In 1988, AT&T installed its first fiber-optic transatlantic cable, capable of carrying 40,000 calls simultaneously; today's version handles over 1,000,000 such calls. A transpacific cable followed in 1989.

In order to better take advantage of the near-universal availability of fiber-optic cable, BellCore, the research arm of the local Bell telephone companies, began work in 1985 on a new way to package and transmit information over fiber. The result was the Synchronous Optical Network (SONET) that became the standard fiber-optic transmission method. Currently, SONET can achieve transmission speeds of 40 Gbps with extremely high reliability over single-mode fiber.

A summary of telco commercial/business history

As we saw, the telephone system in the United States began with creation of the Bell Telephone Company in 1877. This led to the formation of AT&T in 1885, whose charge was the development of a nationwide long-distance network. Over the years, AT&T also began to manufacture telephone equipment and to engage in research and development of products and services, eventually becoming the single source for all telephone-related service in the United States.

From about 1907 until its break-up in 1984 by the U.S. government, AT&T and its local telephone companies operated as a government-sanctioned monopoly. For most of that time, not only were other companies not permitted to provide local or long-distance telephone service, they also were prohibited from even attaching their own telephone equipment to the AT&T telephone network.

Over those years, lawsuits challenging the monopoly arose; the most significant result was the *Carterfone decision of 1968* by the Federal Communications Commission (FCC), the federal agency responsible for regulating communications services and technologies in the United States. This decision allowed users to connect their own telephone equipment to the public telephone system for the first time.

Subsequent challenges further eroded the AT&T monopoly—for example, by allowing competition for long-distance telephone service. The final deregulation and deconstruction of AT&T, however, began as an antitrust suit filed by the U.S. Department of Justice in 1974. The suit dragged on until 1982 when AT&T agreed to a settlement, which went into effect on January 1, 1984, and is called the *consent decree of 1984.*

The decree wrought major changes in how telephone service was provided in the United States. AT&T was divested of its 23 local telephone companies, known as the *Bell operating companies (BOCs).* These were grouped into seven *regional Bell operating companies (RBOCs)*—Ameritech, Bell Atlantic, Bell South, Nynex, Pacific Telesis, Southwestern Bell, and US West. For example, Wisconsin Telephone, Michigan Bell, Illinois Bell, Indiana Bell, and Ohio Bell BOCs became the RBOC Ameritech.

The RBOCs provided only local telephone service, whereas AT&T was limited to long-distance service. Although the RBOCs continued to be monopolies whose rates were subject to approval by government regulators, long-distance service was no longer regulated;

any company wishing to provide long-distance service could be in the telephone business and set its own rates.

Over time, through mergers and acquisitions, the seven RBOCs have become three (see "Historical note: seven RBOCs become three") and provide more than local service.

HISTORICAL NOTE
Seven RBOCs become three

Since their creation in 1996, through mergers and acquisitions the original seven regional bell operating companies (also called RBOCs or baby bells)— Ameritech, Bell Atlantic, Bell South, Nynex, Pacific Telesis, Southwestern Bell, and US West—have become three. Here is what happened:

- **1996:** *Bell Atlantic* merged with *Nynex*—the combine was called *Bell Atlantic*.
- **1998:** SBC Communications (which had changed its name from *Southwestern Bell* in 1995) merged with *Pacific Telesis* (PacBell)—the combine was called SBC.
- **1999:** Qwest Communications merged with *US West*—the combine was called **Qwest.**

SBC merged with *Ameritech*—the combine was called SBC. (As part of the deal, the Ameritech wireless division first was sold to GTE.)
- **2000:** Bell Atlantic merged with GTE—the combine was called **Verizon.**
- **2006:** *Bell South*, the sole surviving original RBOC, was purchased by the new AT&T—the result was called **AT&T.** (The new AT&T was formed in 2005 when SBC acquired AT&T, but it took the name AT&T instead of keeping the name SBC.)

So, the original seven baby bells are now three: AT&T, Quest, and Verizon.

To define and delineate the difference between local and long-distance service, the geographic area covered by each RBOC was divided into regions called *local access and transport areas (LATAs).* Telephone service within a LATA (intra-LATA) was defined as local, and service between LATAs (inter-LATA) was defined as long distance. Intra-LATA service was provided by *one* telephone company, called a *local exchange carrier (LEC),* or *common carrier.* To handle long-distance calls, *interexchange carriers (IXCs)* connect the LATAs. Because of their definition, if the line between two LATAs runs down a street, a call from one side of the street to the other must go through an IXC and is not considered a local call.

LATAs do not necessarily fall along state boundaries; some LATAs cover parts of more than one state, whereas other states contain more than one LATA. There are now approximately 160 LATAs.

Intra-LATA phone service is local; inter-LATA service is long distance.

The *Telecommunications Act of 1996* aimed at increasing telephone service competition further. Congress took note of changes that had occurred in technology since 1984 and the effect they were having on the telecommunications market place. In response, they viewed both local and long-distance services as part of a larger telecommunications offering that also included newer services such as mobile telephony, database resources, and video services. As one result, the Act allowed any company to provide of any of those services, intra-LATA or inter-LATA.

For a newcomer to the business, called a *competitive local exchange carrier (CLEC),* a potentially insurmountable hurdle was infrastructure—phone lines and switching offices—that could be prohibitively expensive to construct and that could face impasses in securing rights-of-way. Cognizant of this, the Act provided that the RBOCs, now also called *incumbent local exchange carriers (ILECs)* would continue to own and operate the local infrastructure but would have to provide access to that infrastructure to the CLECs at rates below market. In that way, ILECs would still make money from access fees, but CLECs would be able to provide a variety of services and still have room in the cost structure for a profit margin.

AMPLIFICATION

Adding to acronym confusion, some publications interpret ILEC as *independent* local exchange carrier. It often is unclear from this usage whether they are referring to both *incumbent* LECs and *competitive* LECs, or to just one or the other. To avoid misunderstanding, we use ILEC to refer to incumbent and CLEC to refer to competitive.

10.3 Public switched telephone network architecture

The telephone system as we now describe it is referred to as the *public switched telephone network (PSTN). Public* connotes that it is available to anyone who pays to use it; *switched* means that by switching, end-to-end circuits are formed to connect any customer to any other customer; and *network* emphasizes that it consists of interconnected nodes. The overall network is a hierarchical structure that facilitates the interconnection of local exchange carrier networks with interexchange carrier networks. As a result of this structure, a long-distance call, for example, may require the services of three carriers: two LECs (one on either end of the connection for local access) and an IXC for the long-distance interconnection between the LECs (see Figure 10.1).

FIGURE 10.1

Connections for a long-distance call

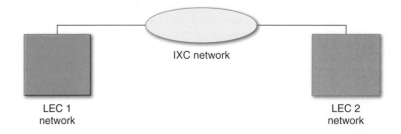

LECs

As we have seen, LECs provide local telephone service: the connection from each home or office to the telephone system. These are the familiar wires often seen on telephone poles in suburban areas that are known as *local loops* or *subscriber lines.* (See "Technical note: local loops and trunks.") They terminate in a switching facility variously called a *central office,* an *end office,* or a *local exchange.* There, local loops typically terminate at switches that interconnect subscribers according to the telephone numbers dialed. This point of entry into the telephone system, formally known as a ***Class 5 telephone office,*** forms the first part of the five-level telephone network hierarchy. Class 5 offices always are owned and operated by LECs.

E very local loop is connected to a Class 5 telephone office.

To facilitate the switching process, AT&T introduced the 3-3-4 telephone-numbering plan (actually an addressing scheme) for North America in 1947. The first three digits are the area code, the next three are the local exchange, and the last four are the line within the exchange (see Table 10.1).

TABLE 10.1   The 3-3-4 Telephone numbering plan

Segment	Meaning
3-digit area code	Designates a specific geographic region, such as a city, part of a city, or state, depending on population.
3-digit exchange (prefix)	Originally specified a particular switch in the exchange to which the local loop was connected. Now, with ***local number portability (LPN)*** that allows a phone number to be used at any switch within a LATA, it is simply a set of numbers called a prefix.
4-digit line number	Specifies the local loop on the Class 5 switch to which the subscriber is connected.

TECHNICAL NOTE
Local loops and trunks

L ocal loops consist of twisted-pair wires, each loop identified by a unique telephone number. Typical local loop telephone service, known as ***plain old telephone service (POTS),*** uses analog signals to and from the Class 5 end office. The signals represent either a voice call or data masquerading as voice coming through a modem. The bandwidth of analog signals on the local loop may vary considerably, perhaps occupying a range from 0 Hz to 50,000 Hz. At the end office, however, frequencies in the arriving signal are restricted to a range of 300 Hz to 3,400 Hz, a bandwidth of 3,100 Hz.

Because the process of restricting the frequencies is not perfect, an additional range of frequencies is assumed to exist in the restricted analog voice signal, bringing the total bandwidth allocated to the local loop to 4 kHz.

Trunks, on the other hand, have very wide bandwidths, suitable for carrying a large amount of data at high speeds. Depending on the situation, a trunk may be twisted-pair wire, coaxial cable, multimode, or single-mode fiber-optic cable. In today's telephone systems, most trunks are single-mode fiber-optic cables that offer a tremendous bandwidth.

Calls are routed at the Class 5 office according to the following scheme:

- Directly to the dialed subscriber if both are connected to the same switch
- Over an interoffice trunk to another switch if the dialed subscriber is connected to another Class 5 office in the same LATA
- Over a trunk connection to a Class 4 office if the dialed subscriber is connected to a Class 5 office in another LATA

A *Class 4 office (toll center)* is owned and operated by a LEC and is the second layer in the telephone network hierarchy. It is the switching center through which any long-distance call, as well as any call that is subject to message unit charges, is routed. The Class 4 office typically serves a large city or several small cities and generates customer billing information. From there, calls may be routed to a *Class 3 office (primary center)* that serves large metropolitan areas.

The primary center can be owned by either the LEC or an IXC; when both the LEC and the IXC place their equipment in the same primary center, it is referred to as a *tandem office.* From there, if the call requires the services of a long-distance carrier, it is connected to a *Class 2 office (sectional center)* that handles calls for a very large geographic area. At this point, the call is handed off to the IXC that has been specified by the caller—that is, the caller's long-distance company.

From the Class 2 office, the call may be routed to a *Class 1 office (regional center),* which handles calls from multiple states. The call may be switched to another regional center over interconnecting trunks; from the last regional center in the route, it is switched down through the various telephone offices until it reaches the destination Class 5 office to which the called party is connected. Note, however, that it is not always necessary for a telephone call to traverse all the levels of the hierarchy; in many cases, some of the levels can be skipped, reducing the number of telephone offices involved. (See Figure 10.2.)

FIGURE 10.2

The telephone network hierarchy

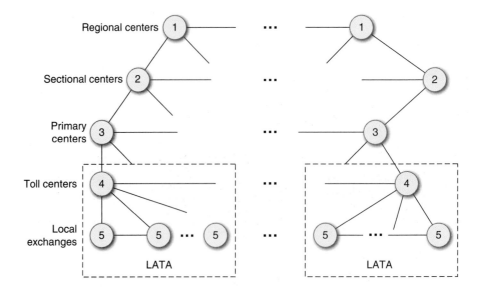

IXCs

As a result of the deregulation of the telephone system, it is now possible for a customer to select from among many long-distance carriers. Because all subscribers are connected to LECs, the various IXCs must link to each of the LECs. This means that each IXC must have a network presence—called a *point-of-presence (POP)*—in each LATA. POPs are switches that the IXC provides to connect to the LEC. These may be placed (***collocated***) in the LEC's toll center or connected by trunks, leased from the LEC, that run from the toll center to the IXC's own switching office. (Recall that when equipment is collocated, the toll center is called a tandem office.) See Figure 10.3.

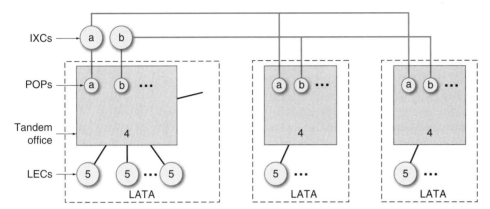

FIGURE 10.3

The IXC connection (with collocated POPs)

10.4 Efficient use of trunks via multiplexing

As we have seen, a call between parties connected to different Class 5 switches must be routed between the switches over a trunk line. At any instant in time, many such calls need to travel on the same route. If a trunk could carry just one call at a time, a tremendous number of trunks would be needed to accommodate the potentially large volume of simultaneous calls. Not only is this impractical from a physical viewpoint, but even if we did install those lines, call volume varies widely, so much of the time many would go unused—not a wise business solution. Multiplexing is therefore employed so that each trunk can carry many simultaneous calls. In this section, we will look at how the telephone companies do this. (For a more thorough discussion of multiplexing, see Chapter 6, "Communications connections.")

T-1 trunk circuits

Prior to 1960 or thereabouts, analog signals were used throughout the telephone network. At that time, frequency division multiplexing (FDM) was applied to the interoffice trunks to achieve a reasonably efficient level of usage. Subsequently, the telephone network was shifted to digital signaling in all but the local loops, where analog signals still dominate— converting local loops to digital would have required replacing millions of analog telephones with digital phones, an extremely costly course of action. At the Class 5 end office, analog signals from the local loops are converted to digital signals for transmission over the trunks, and digital signals from an end office to the local loops are converted to analog signals. (Chapter 4, "Encoding," has a more detailed discussion of analog to digital conversion and vice versa.)

Conversion from analog to digital is accomplished by pulse code modulation (PCM); each analog phone call is converted into a digital stream of 8-bit samples repeated 8,000 times per second, for an overall rate of 64,000 bits per second. For transmission, the digital streams of 24 calls are merged via ***time division multiplexing (TDM)*** onto a single pair of wires. This is called a ***T-1*** circuit. (T-1 is a full duplex circuit that uses two twisted wire pairs, one for sending and one for receiving. TDM is applied in both directions.)

Specifically, to create the T-1, one sample (8 bits) from each of 24 calls is interleaved with the others to form a *frame* to which a synchronization bit, the *framing bit,* is added, for a total of 193 bits per frame (see Figure 10.4).

FIGURE 10.4

The T-1 frame

24 8-bit slots plus a 1-bit framing slot; 193 bits total
The T-1 rate: 8,000 frames per second × 193 bits per frame = 1.544 Mbps

The consecutive samples of each call occupy the same slot position in successive frames, thus creating a channel (a logical path), for each of the 24 calls. This matches the DS-1 signal level (see "Technical note: the T-1 carrier system and the DS hierarchy"). Because of the speed of the T-1, to the callers the connection appears to be continuous.

Why 8,000 frames per second?

According to the Nyquist sampling theorem, every sample must be delivered across the trunk at the rate of 8,000 per second. Because each frame carries one sample of each call, the *frame rate must match the sample rate*—hence 8,000 frames per second, giving a cumulative T-1 rate of 1.544 Mbps: $(8 \times 24 + 1) \times 8,000$.

T-1 is a North American telephone specification. The European standard essentially follows the same scheme but multiplexes 30 channels (individual calls) instead of 24, for a cumulative data rate of 2.048 Mbps. This is called E-1.

TECHNICAL NOTE:
The T-carrier system and the DS hierarchy

In practice, the terms *DS-1* and *T-1* often are used interchangeably. However, they are not the same. DS-1 is a signal level (the DS stands for digital signal), one of a hierarchy of digital signal levels that begins with DS-0, whereas T-1 is a communications channel that can carry DS-1 signals.

To understand the difference, let's look at some of the hierarchy. DS-0 is an 8-bit signal transmitted at 8,000 bps, for a total of 64 Kbps of voice (digitized via PCM) or digital data. When we multiplex 24 DS-0s, the resultant signal is a DS-1, which has a combined rate of 1.536 Mbps. This signal can be carried over a T-1, whose 24-slot frames coincide with the 24 multiplexed DS-0s.

For framing purposes, so that the receiver can correctly demultiplex the frame, T-1 adds 1 frame synchronization bit per frame—hence 8 Kbps, resulting in a T-1 total rate of 1.544 Mbps.

T-1 is married to DS-1, but not the other way around. That is, if you contract for T-1 you get DS-1—and this is typically how DS-1 service is arranged—but DS-1 signals can be carried over any digital communications channel: T-1, PRI-ISDN, HDSL, microwave, or even a fiber-optic line.

Now what about that hierarchy? If we multiplex 96 DS-0s, we get DS-2. Multiplexing 672 DS-0s (often denoted as 28 DS-1s) gives us DS-3. 4,032 DS-0s provide DS-4. When carried by the T-system, the corresponding Ts are T-2, T-3, and T-4.

T-1 applications expand

Initially, the telephone companies used T-1 circuits only for trunk lines. However, by the early 1980s businesses were demanding faster computer connections to the telephone network than were available at the time, an opportunity the phone companies seized by supplying T-1 circuits to connect businesses directly to the telephone network, skirting the local loops. However, this was not without difficulties (see "Technical extension: installing T-1 circuits").

Despite fairly high installation cost and rather long delays before installation could take place, T-1 became quite popular because of its relatively high speed and ability to take the place of 24 of a company's separate lines. Even today, T-1 is a very common circuit, widely used by many companies to connect to an ISP for access to the Internet and as connections between the nodes of data networks—for example, frame relay. T-1 also is used in private (non-telco) networks, such as on campuses where much of the cabling is within private grounds, and even in internal corporate networks.

TECHNICAL EXTENSION
Installing T-1 circuits

Two problems made installation of T-1 circuits difficult and costly—finding the necessary wire pairs and conditioning the line. Sometimes overcoming these problems was not possible, making T-1 unavailable.

T-1 needs two twisted wire pairs. Typically, these are taken from one of the 25-pair bundles running into the business building. Installers need to find available pairs and test them to see if they will support a T-1 circuit. Although it sounds simple, it is a time-consuming process that is not always successful. Available pairs may be in poor condition, connections and splices may have deteriorated, and bridge taps (see Chapter 6) may

still be present. Any of these conditions can render pairs unusable.

After suitable pairs are found, the distance to the end office must be determined. For proper T-1 signal strength, repeaters are needed at least every 6,000 feet, and the first and last repeaters in the path must be no more than 3,000 feet from the end-connection points.

T-1 was successfully installed in a great many locations, but often considerable technician time was involved, resulting in long waiting times before customers could be accommodated. Installation cost also could be considerable, especially in difficult installations.

Configurations

The T-1 can be used in one of two configurations: *channelized* and *unchannelized.* When configured to carry phone calls as described earlier, we say that the T-1 is channelized— each call occupies one of the 24 channels. This is an effective way for companies to provide employee phone service; it obviates the need for a local loop for each phone. Further, the 24 channels can be allocated dynamically as needed, so that they usually can serve many more than 24 phones, although no more than 24 calls at one time. Typically, dynamic allocation is done by a *private branch exchange (PBX)* on the business premises. (PBX is discussed shortly.)

A T-1 circuit also can be used in an unchannelized mode that makes 1.536 Mbps of capacity (framing bits are excluded) available to an application. This is common practice when the T-1 is used to interconnect nodes of a data network, discussed in subsequent chapters.

DSU/CSU

For T-1, bits are encoded with either AMI or B8ZS (see Chapter 4), which must be specified when the T-1 is established so the circuit-terminating equipment can correctly interpret the bits. Because the equipment that the T-1 is connected to may not be using the same coding or framing structure, for compatibility a device called a ***Data Service Unit*** or ***Digital Service Unit (DSU)*** sits between the T-1 and the customer equipment. The DSU converts the T-1 digital format to the digital format used by the customer equipment. In addition, when a T-1 circuit is leased, the telco requires the user to connect to the T-1 via special ***customer premises equipment (CPE)*** called a ***Customer Service Unit (CSU)*** (see Figure 10.5). The purpose of this requirement is twofold:

- The CSU protects the telephone network against damage from faulty devices connected to it by the customer.
- The CSU allows the telephone company to test the condition of the T-1 remotely, which may save the expense of sending a technician to the customer's premises. (See "Technical note: loop-back testing").

FIGURE 10.5

DSU/CSU

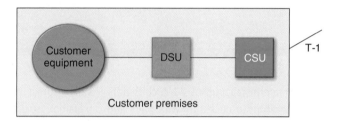

Customer premises

In-band and out-of-band signaling: implications

A curious thing about the T-1 structure is that the entire 24-slot capacity of the frame is used to carry calls; there is no provision within the frame for carrying telephone control/management information. For example, how can a customer using call waiting service be notified when there is a second caller?

The only recourse is to take time slots from customers to carry that information—this is called ***in-band signaling.*** That is, control/management information is sent in the bands used by the customers. In the call waiting example, a time slot of the first caller is taken to send a notifying beep about a second call, which momentarily interrupts the first call, not to mention the annoyance of the beep to the caller.

TECHNICAL NOTE
Loop-back testing

- A technician at the phone operations center sends a command through the T-1 to put the CSU in loop-back mode; if successful, the CSU will return all the bits sent to it (that is, it loops the bits back).
- The technician sends a test pattern to the CSU and examines the returned bits. If they match exactly what was sent or they contain fewer bit errors than the line specifications allow, the line is good and the problem must be due to non-T-1 issues.
- If the loop-back command does not go through or if the bit errors exceed the line allowance, the line is bad and the telco will have to make repairs.

On occasion, more control information must be sent than can be accommodated by a single slot. To provide a general way of sending such information along T-1 lines, the telephone network implemented an in-band scheme called *bit robbing*—taking bits from customer time slots and grouping them to form control codes that are interpreted by the telephone switches. For example, in one scheme, 1 of the 8 bits in each of the 24 time slots is stolen every sixth and twelfth frame—a pattern known as the *Extended Super Frame (ESF).*

Because the 8 bits generally represent digital voice samples, robbing a bit reduces the fidelity of the reproduced sound somewhat. However, it has been found that the ear is not overly sensitive to this degradation and there is therefore no significant impact on telephone calls that are truly voice calls.

The picture is entirely different if the call is that of a computer sending data via a modem. Here, having one bit robbed even occasionally is one robbed bit too much. To avoid this problem, modems do not normally place data in the eighth bit position. This leads to a maximum possible data rate of 56,000 bps (7 bits/slot $\times$ 8,000 slots/second). The actual achievable data rate on a telephone line is guided by the requirements of Shannon's relationship (see Chapter 4) and may result in a lower rate. Either voice-wise or data-wise, in-band signaling is not a customer-friendly technique.

Recognizing the shortcomings of in-band signaling, the telcos moved to *out-of-band signaling* in newer services. This provides management/control data with its own band (time slot) within the structure of the service and so has no impact on the user's communication. We will see examples of this when we discuss ISDN and SONET.

T-3 trunk circuits

In time, as telephone traffic increased, the telcos were forced to better utilize their interoffice trunks. This led to a line called T-3, which increased transmission density by multiplexing together 28 T-1 circuits to achieve a cumulative rate of 44.736 Mbps (often referred to by its rounded value of 45 Mbps). (The European version of the T-3 is the E-3, a multiplex of 16 E-1s for a cumulative data rate of 34.368 Mbps.)

Whereas a T-1 can carry the equivalent of 24 simultaneous calls, the T-3 can carry 672 (which is 24 $\times$ 28). However, just as T-1 frames, based on a sampling rate of 8,000 samples per second, have to be delivered at the same rate (8,000 frames per second), so too do the T-3 frames, based on the same sampling rate—they must travel at 8,000 frames per second. This means that the bit duration for T-3 is much shorter than for T-1.

For substantial distances, moving data at T-3 rates over twisted-pair or coax cable was problematic. In addition to the same pair availability and conditioning issues of T-1, there also was a problem of inadequate medium bandwidth. This made T-3 service costly and, for some routes, impossible.

Luckily, a new technology came to the rescue: optical fiber cables using light as the signal carrier. This enabled far higher speeds over much longer distances without the need for repeaters. It eventually resulted in a complete revamping of the copper-based multiplexing schemes that had led to the T-1 and T-3 and the building of a new telephone network infrastructure based on optical fiber. This architecture was called *Synchronous Optical Network (SONET).* Another consequence was that no further substantial effort was made to extend the T-3 to a T-4 and beyond. We will examine SONET later in this chapter.

PBX

A PBX (private branch exchange) is a small version of the Class 5 office, and it performs many of the same switching functions. A T-1 connection is brought from the local end office to the PBX. The PBX de-multiplexes the 24 telephone channels and switches each of the channels to the appropriate telephone handset. If the handset requires analog signals, the PBX also performs digital-to-analog conversion first. For digital handsets, the handset itself performs the digital-to-analog conversion.

A PBX can provide additional cost savings by switching intra-office calls itself without the need to resort to the telco. Thus, if two employees within the building need to converse, the PBX connects them directly. Without the PBX, the calls would have to go first to the telco network, which would simply route them back and, of course, charge a fee for the service. PBXs also can provide such features as intercom facilities and abbreviated dialing (that is, using less than the entire called telephone number). However, technically knowledgeable personnel are needed to keep the PBXs up to date (as phone assignments change) and running.

PBX alternative

For small businesses that may not be able to justify the expense of a PBX or may not want to maintain the equipment, many LECs provide similar services for a fee. An example is Centrex, short for *centr*al office *ex*change. It functions like a PBX but is owned and operated by a telco.

Switching equipment at the central office is used to provide PBX-like service for telephones at a company. No switching equipment is owned by the company or needed at the company premises. Using such a service also can make good business sense if a company is spread over a number of buildings, which otherwise would require multiple PBXs. Further, it can make the many sites appear as just one to an outside caller, who would need but one telephone number to reach any of the sites.

10.5 ISDN: an alternative digital phone system

By the late 1960s, it was apparent that data transmission had become as important as voice transmission. Yet data transmission over the telephone network, the main data communications vehicle at the time, was constrained to relatively slow rates by the analog nature of the local loop serving residential and business subscribers.

Applying Shannon's theorem to the local loop and the standard telephone connection at the central office shows that the maximum data rate is approximately 35,000 bps. (See Chapter 4 for details.) Telephone networks beyond the local loop operate digitally. There, far higher data rates (T-1 and above) are possible.

The goal of an *Integrated Services Digital Network (ISDN)* was to provide digital access directly from the customer's premises to the telephone network at high (for the time) data rates and, furthermore, to treat voice and data in the same way—as digital data. For a variety of reasons, ISDN was slow to catch on in the United States until the introduction of the Internet pressed demand for high-speed access in the mid-1990s. By then, however, a new technology called *digital subscriber line (DSL)* quickly overshadowed ISDN. Nevertheless, ISDN can still be a useful technology in some instances—for example, in providing a secondary (backup) connection between two nodes when the primary connection fails. For completeness, we provide a summary of ISDN in Appendix H.

10.6 DSL: re-using the local loop to greater advantage

The limitation in providing ever-higher data transfer rates to customers via the telephone system has been the local loop, the so-called *last mile.* In an era when the Internet is used to download multimedia-rich content such as MP3 music files, video clips, and graphics-laden Web pages, the low speeds available via the traditional telephone modem just don't suffice. As a result, many consumers have acquired broadband high-speed access via the cable TV systems that either were already installed in many locations or were easily installable.

To compete, the telcos developed a class of technologies known as ***digital subscriber line (DSL).*** DSL comes in several versions that, as a group, are referred to as ***xDSL;*** the letters replacing *x* indicate the version, most notably *A* for *asymmetric, S* for *symmetric, H* for *high bit-rate,* and *V* for *very high bit-rate.* We will explore ADSL and HDSL in detail, and we will note the pertinent characteristics of the others.

ADSL

ADSL is designed to provide high-speed Internet access to the home user. In designing this technique, a major objective was to provide service over the existing local loop, thus avoiding the expense of additional wiring while allowing voice service to continue on the same local loop at the same time as computer communication.

As we have seen, at the end office the standard telephone system limits signals on the analog local loop to a spectrum of 0 to 4,000 Hz. But in fact, the local loop can support a much wider bandwidth, with signal frequencies up to about 1.5 MHz. By using the entire bandwidth, considerably faster transmission speeds can be realized. This is accomplished by detaching the end office bandwidth limiting equipment from the local loop, which instead is connected to a ***digital subscriber line access multiplexer (DSLAM).*** At the customer's end, the local loop is terminated in a signal splitter that permits a phone and a computer to connect to the same line, a filter that blocks data bands from the phone connection and keeps data signals from interfering with phone calls, and an ADSL modem to connect to the computer for digital and analog conversion. A similar setup is used at the telco end office. (See Figure 10.6.)

FIGURE 10.6

DSL connections

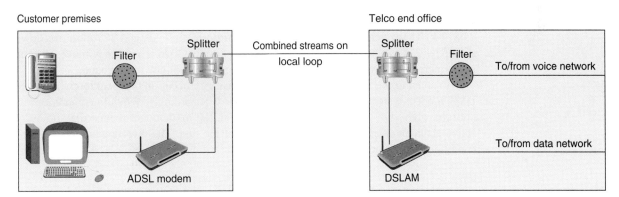

There are two standards for provision of ADSL service: ***carrierless amplitude/phase modulation (CAP)*** and ***discrete multitone (DMT).*** CAP, a proprietary standard developed by AT&T, is the earlier and relatively simpler scheme and is easier to implement than DMT. Currently, DMT is the ANSI standard and performance-wise the preferred technique. Unfortunately, the two are not compatible.

Other modulation techniques include Discrete Wavelet Multitone, Simple Line Code, and Multiple Virtual Line. DSL is defined by the ITU-T standards body. Their Web site is http://www.itu.org. Additional information can be found at the DSL Forum Web site, http://www.dslforum.org/.

CAP

Using frequency division multiplexing (FDM), CAP divides the local loop into three logical channels. The first 4 kHz are reserved for voice, as with standard phone service; the band from 25 kHz to 160 kHz is used for upstream transmission (to the end office); and the band from 240 kHz to as much as 1.5 MHz carries downstream traffic. As the actual upper limit depends greatly on a variety of factors, including line length, wire quality, and noise, it may be significantly lower than 1.5 MHz, but it cannot be higher. Frequencies between these bands are called guard bands; they serve to separate the different signal components to avoid interference. (See Figure 10.7.) CAP is less able to adjust to local loop line conditions than DMT.

FIGURE 10.7

ADSL bandwidth allocation

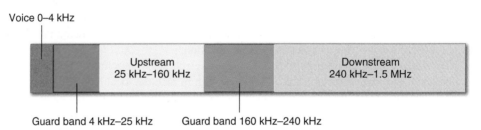

Voice 0–4 kHz

Upstream 25 kHz–160 kHz

Downstream 240 kHz–1.5 MHz

Guard band 4 kHz–25 kHz   Guard band 160 kHz–240 kHz

We see that the upstream and downstream bandwidths are not the same, hence the term "asymmetric" in ADSL. The reasoning behind this is that ADSL is intended for connecting to the Internet. In this usage, upstream communications typically are short, primarily e-mail and requests for Web pages and file downloads—these do not require much bandwidth or speed; downstream communications, the responses to the upstream requests, tend to be much larger—these do benefit from wider bandwidth and higher speed.

DMT

DMT uses FDM and quadrature amplitude modulation (QAM) in combination. First, FDM subdivides the total available local loop bandwidth into 4.312-kHz channels, a number of which are allocated for voice and data. A typical design uses the first six channels (0 Hz to 25.872 kHz) for voice, the next 25 channels for upstream data, and 225 more for downstream data. As with CAP, this is an asymmetric design. QAM is applied within each channel to increase its bandwidth; the result is a channel capacity of 15 bits/baud.

To adapt to the variety of line conditions that may occur on the local loop, the ADSL DMT modem tests the loop and adjusts the speeds accordingly. When line conditions are poor, or when they deteriorate during operation, the modem can reduce the number of active channels, thereby adapting to the state of the line. The reverse can be done when conditions are better.

HDSL

In the early 1980s, businesses began to clamor for higher speed connections to the telephone network than were available. Although the telephone companies had been using the high-speed T-1 connection internally for some time, providing it to customers was challenging because of the limited distance that a T-1 signal could travel before it needed to be repeated. Installing repeaters was not just costly—it was not always practical to place them where they were needed. ***High bit-rate DSL*** technology, originally developed by Bellcore, was introduced as a solution, providing T-1 data rates over distances up to 18,000 feet without repeaters, compared to the 3,000- and 6,000-foot limitations of T-1.

Maintaining unrepeated signal strength over that distance requires either a much larger bandwidth or a variety of signals whose bandwidth demands are lower. (The encoding schemes used for T-1, most commonly AMI and also B8Zs, operate at a relatively high baud rate and consequently require a wide bandwidth. This is what limits unrepeated T-1 distances.)

With local loop bandwidth fixed, the 2B1Q coding scheme, which operates at a significantly lower baud rate than AMI or B8ZS, was chosen for HDSL. ANSI standard HDSL uses two wire pairs for full duplex operation at a data rate of 784 Kbps on each pair, providing T-1-like speed; unlike ADSL, HDSL provides the same data rate in both directions (that is, it is a symmetric DSL).

This design is more suitable for businesses, for which upstream and downstream traffic needs are likely to be the same. At each end of the connection, the wires terminate in an HDSL modem that operates at the T-1 speed of 1.544 Mbps. Note, however, that there is no provision for analog voice, as there is with ADSL.

A more recent variation of HDSL, HDSL-2, can operate in full duplex mode over only two wires. However, it requires better phone lines and has a maximum distance of about 10,000 feet.

SDSL

Symmetric DSL is a rate-adaptive version of HDSL, also with equal upstream and downstream bandwidth. It uses the same 2BQ1 encoding and also has no provision for analog phone service. It has found a market as a WAN technology for small to medium businesses, competing well on a cost basis with leased lines and frame relay.

VDSL

Very high bit-rate DSL is an asymmetric design that achieves high data rates over local loops by considerably tightening line length limits. Actual rates are highly dependent on length, with a maximum of about 55 Mbps downstream for lines of no more than 1,000 feet, but down to 13 Mbps for lines over 4,000 feet. Like ADSL, upstream rates are much lower, ranging from about 1.5 to 2.3 Mbps. Downstream and upstream traffic travels in separate frequency bands.

Another significant difference from the symmetric DSLs is that bandwidths are reserved for standard phone service and ISDN. The data channels occupy their own separate frequency bands. This means that VDSL can be overlaid on existing phone or ISDN services.

10.7 Broadband cable and alternative telephone service

Although ADSL allowed the telephone companies to dramatically increase the access speed to the Internet over the local loop, the service has some shortcomings:

- Because of distance limitations and other telephone network issues, ADSL service is not available to all who may want it.
- Actual speed achieved varies with line conditions. Maximum downstream speed is on the order of 1 to 3 Mbps. Although this is considerably faster than dialup, it is not always sufficient for large data downloads of multimedia files (such as movies).

The business of cable TV began as a way of providing television broadcasts for people who either lived too far from the TV broadcast antennas or whose reception was compromised by obstructions (such as tall buildings or mountains). In order to overcome these problems, very tall antennas were erected that were capable of obtaining strong signals over the air from the TV broadcasters. Those signals were carried over coax to a distribution facility called the ***head end.*** From there they were distributed via coax to homes, the signals being amplified periodically along the way to overcome attenuation. These were called *community antenna TV (CATV)* systems.

With deregulation of telephone service in 1984, cable TV providers realized that by virtue of having already wired millions of customers, they could legally offer telephone services to their existing customer base. However, CATV carried transmission in only one direction: from the head end to the customer. This simplex system first had to be upgraded to the duplex operation required for phone calls. Amplifiers had to be bi-directional, and any uni-directional amplifiers had to be removed.

In the process, cable companies began replacing coax cable from the head end to the neighborhood distribution point with optical fiber, leaving coax in place from that point to customer homes. Aside from the added expense of running fiber right up to the customer premises, a decoder would have to be placed at each home rather than just one at each distribution point. This was deemed too expensive.

After a duplex cable system was in place, high-speed broadband Internet access also could be offered. Generally, all that was needed at the customer site was a cable modem.

Cable modems

Cable TV uses FDM to divide the roughly 750 MHz of coax bandwidth into channels of 6 MHz each. TV channels commonly occupy frequencies from 54 MHz to 550 MHz; this is called the *video band.* The bandwidth on both sides of the video band is used for upstream and downstream communications paths. For the same reason that ADSL allocates different bandwidth/speeds to the upstream and downstream channels, cable operators also provide more downstream bandwidth/speed than they do upstream.

Cable modems have two drawbacks:

* In the typical setup, an Ethernet interface on the cable modem is connected to the customer computer or a wireless router, either via at least Cat 5 UTP cable. The data rate on the Ethernet connection is usually a nominal 10 Mbps; however, because Ethernet is a shared LAN, actual data rates vary depending on how many others are concurrently using the shared cable (that is, how many are connected to the Internet via the same distribution point, which can cover a building or a neighborhood) and can be much lower. Even at best, data rates rarely exceed 6 to 7 Mbps; at worst they may drop below 2 Mbps.
* Any time connections are shared, security may be an issue.

In comparison, ADSL is a dedicated connection whose speed is not affected by other users in the system, and because the connection is not shared, security of transmitted data is far less of a problem. Of course, connecting either cable modems or ADSL modems wirelessly has other security implications.

On balance, with appropriate firewalls on the cable connection and with a responsive cable operator who adjusts overall system speed as new users are added to the network, cable modem transmissions are about as secure as ADSL and data rates are almost always significantly higher. On the other hand, typical monthly charges for cable are substantially greater.

Standards still an issue

Unfortunately, as of this writing there is no standard for cable modem construction and operation. If you change from one cable operator to another, you are likely to need a different modem. To remove the onus from the subscriber, cable operators usually include a modem as part of the subscription. When you terminate the service, you must return the modem or incur a charge.

To address compatibility, an industry trade group, ***CableLabs,*** has crafted a standard that it would like all cable modem manufacturers to adopt. Called ***Data Over Cable Service Interface Specification (DOCSIS),*** it is slowly finding acceptance within the industry.

Cable for telephone service

Cable TV operators now provide the full range of local and long-distance telephone services at competitive rates. In fact, by offering to bundle cable TV, high-speed Internet access, and telephone services, they are, in some cases, severely undercutting the traditional telephone companies.

Cable phone service is carried by ***Voice over Internet Protocol (VoIP)*** technology. This is discussed in Chapter 13, "TCP/IP, associated Internet protocols, and routing."

10.8 SONET: speeding up the telephone system

The growing dependence of business on its computers and the data networks that connect them drove the need for ever-faster connections. Using copper with its fairly limited bandwidth and inherent noise, the telephone companies that very often provided the WAN connections found it increasingly difficult to raise data rates; practically speaking, the fastest copper wire speed available from the telcos tops out with T-3 (about 45 Mbps).

With the advent of fiber-optic cable using light signals as carriers, the telcos began to re-engineer their networks to take advantage of this new medium. In the process, they also decided to rectify many of the shortcomings of their copper-based networks; one in particular was the lack of strong in-band or an out-of-band signaling capability. The result was the ***Synchronous Optical Network (SONET),*** proposed and drafted as a telephone network standard by Bellcore. It was accepted and approved in 1988 by the CCITT and in late 1989 by ANSI.

AMPLIFICATION

The ***Comité Consultatif International Téléphonique et Télégraphique (CCITT),*** which began in about 1960, was an international organization for communications standards functioning within the intergovernmental ***International Telecommunication Union (ITU).*** In a 1992 reorganization, the functions of CCITT were subsumed by the T division of the ITU (ITU-T), also known as the Telecommunication Standardization Sector. CCITT no longer exists as an entity.

Until SONET, not all telephone companies followed the same standard. (Despite the dominance of AT&T and the baby bells, there always were other telcos in operation.) It could happen that when two telephone companies needed to interconnect their lines, incompatibilities prevented them from doing so—the so-called ***mid-span problem.*** As an example, for two carriers to provide a continuous T-1 connection, in which each one supplies a T-1 from their end of the span, the two segments must be compatible to be connected mid-span.

"Synchronous" in SONET refers to the notion that all of the communications devices making up the SONET network, no matter where they are located, take their clocking from a single time source. One increasingly common method for doing this relies on the ***global positioning system (GPS),*** a collection of satellites that provides timing and location data globally.

Beyond helping us find our way in unfamiliar areas, the GPS also provides a highly accurate timing signal, based on an atomic clock, to anyone with an appropriate antenna. That signal is available everywhere on earth, making it possible to use the same clock for all SONET devices. Prior to SONET, communications system devices generally used separate clocks, which complicated bit recognition and TDM. SONET greatly improved the reliability of the network while vastly simplifying it.

Physical elements of a SONET system

Like the POTS network, SONET is based on time division multiplexing. Hence, it is constructed of a combination of TDM multiplexers and regenerators. Two types of multiplexers are defined: an *edge mux* and a *core mux.* The edge mux (also known as an *STS multiplexer*) interfaces to the user at the "edge" of the SONET system, whereas the core multiplexer (also known as an *add/drop multiplexer* or *ADM*) mixes and redirects traffic within the SONET system (at the core).

The physical SONET system is composed of three parts (regions)—a *section,* a *line,* and a *path.* Each of these has particular duties and responsibilities:

- A *section* consists of any two devices directly connected by an optical fiber. For example, an ADM mux directly connected to an STS (synchronous transport signal) mux by a fiber link is a section.
- A *line* consists of any two muxes that communicate directly with each other either over a fiber cable or through one or more regenerators.
- A *path* connects two STS muxes, either directly over a fiber connection or via any combination of ADM muxes and regenerators; that is, a path consists of sections and lines. It essentially constitutes an end-to-end transmission system: A user injects information into the SONET at one end of a path via an edge mux, and the information eventually exits the SONET at its destination at the other end of the path via another edge mux. (See Figure 10.8.)

FIGURE 10.8

A basic SONET

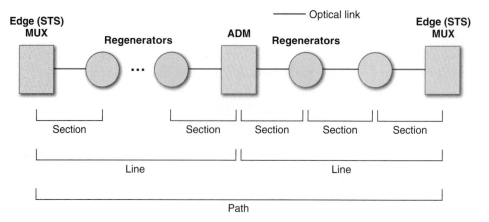

The SONET model architecture

The SONET model architecture comprises four layers, all of which are sublayers of the OSI-TCP/IP physical layer. They are: Path, Line, Section, and Photonic. Their responsibilities are as follows:

- Path. Responsible for optical signal transmission from STS mux to STS mux—that is, from edge to edge within the SONET system. Path protocols are implemented in STS muxes.

- Line. Takes care of signal transport across a physical line—that is, between multiplexers. Line protocols are implemented in STS muxes and ADMs.
- Section. Moves signals across a physical section, between each pair of devices. Section protocols are implemented in STS muxes, ADMs, and regenerators.
- Photonic. The optical parallel to the electrical physical layer. It deals with the physical details of the fiber-optic links and uses NRZ encoding (see Chapter 4) for light signaling. Photonic protocols are implemented in every SONET device.

Frames

To allow the devices that make up the regions to control and communicate with each other, the SONET frame is partitioned into three parts, each set aside for one of the regions: *section overhead, line overhead,* and *synchronous payload envelope (SPE).* The SPE is further divided into *path overhead* and *synchronous payload.* The overhead sections correspond to the SONET architecture. The synchronous payload is the actual information that the frame is to transport.

For compatibility between SONET and the existing telephone structures based on the T-carrier system, the basic SONET frame was designed to carry exactly one T-3 transmission stream. (Because the T-3 comprises 28 T-1s, this design easily accommodates T-1s as well.) The T-3 frame is embedded in the SONET frame as the synchronous payload. But to match the T-3 data rate of 44.736 Mbps with a frame that has many more overhead bits, the SONET data rate has to be higher—51.84 Mbps—which is the slowest SONET data rate.

The SONET frame is visualized as a matrix of nine rows and 90 columns, each cell containing 1 byte. The first three columns carry section and line overhead, and the fourth column is path overhead; these provide for control and management data that is not present in the T-carrier frames, a considerable enhancement in terms of service provisioning. The remaining 86 columns carry the synchronous payload, each of whose cells is a data time slot. (See Figure 10.9.)

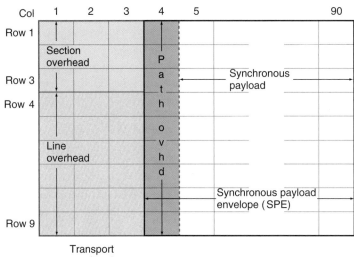

FIGURE 10.9

Representing the SONET frame

SONET frames are transmitted at the same 8,000-frames-per-second rate as are T-1 frames. Whereas each byte in the T-1 frame is one time slot (and can represent a voice sample), in the SONET frame only the synchronous payload carries user data (and potential voice samples). The cells (bytes) are transmitted one bit at a time, row by row from left to right. Frames are transmitted one after the other without a break.

SONET can operate at data rates far beyond the 51.84-Mbps base rate. Higher speeds are achieved essentially by taking two or more SONET frames that each carry a T-3, "gluing" them together, and transmitting the combined structure at the same overall rate—8,000 glued frames per second. Actually, frames are glued by interleaving columns. Thus, the first column comes from the first SONET frame, the second column from the second SONET frame, and so on for as many as are to be glued. This is done by the STS multiplexers.

To maintain the 8,000-frames-per-second rate, carrying three T-3s in one glued-together SONET frame requires tripling the data rate of the single SONET frame, resulting in a data rate of 155.520 (3 × 51.84) Mbps. The same 8,000-frames-per-second overall data rate requirement carries through to all SONET frames (all T-3 multiples). Thus, the difference between the basic SONET frame and the higher-speed SONET frames is simply the size of the frame and the bit duration. All SONET frames still are conceptualized as containing nine rows, but the number of columns increases as frames are glued together.

AMPLIFICATION

We have seen that telcos convert analog voice signals to their digital equivalents by sampling the voice signals 8,000 times a second, and that for the destination to reconstruct the conversation correctly, T-3 frames must arrive at the same rate— 8,000 frames per second. Because SONET frames carry T-3s or their equivalent, they must repeat at 8,000 frames per second, no matter how big the frames become through gluing. The data rate increases accordingly.

STS and OC

SONET was designed as a light-based single-mode optical-fiber system. However, most user information sources today exist in electrical form, so data streams entering a SONET system reach an edge (STS) mux as electrical signals. The STS mux itself processes data electrically; it is only when all processing is complete that it converts the multiplexed signals into light signals for transmission over the SONET system. The process is reversed for light signals reaching an STS mux on their way out of the SONET system.

Because both electrical and light signals are involved, two naming systems are used: a signal in electrical form is called a *synchronous transport signal (STS),* and in optical form it is called an *optical carrier (OC).* The *basic SONET signal,* carrying one T-3 or its equivalent, is designated electrically as *STS-1* and optically as *OC-1.* As it happens, a SONET frame also is referred to as an STS frame; the basic SONET frame, then, is called an STS-1 frame.

In general, designations are of the form STS-n and OC-n, where the "n" designates the number of T-3s or equivalents carried by the signal and therefore also indicates the width (capacity) of the SONET frame (in multiples of 90 columns). For example, a SONET signal carrying three T-3s is called an STS-3. The OCs, referring to the same signals but in light form, use the same n's. So, for example, the OC equivalent of STS-3 is OC-3. The STS/OC numbers represent a *hierarchy of signal levels,* which indicates various SONET capacities. Manufacturers did not find it feasible to implement every possible level. The common implementations are listed in Table 10.2.

An interesting rule of thumb: The bit rate of an STS signal can be approximated by dividing its designation by 20. As examples, for the STS-48, 48/20 is 2.4 Mbps; for STS-192, 192/20 is 9.6 Gbps.

TABLE 10.2 Common SONET implementations

SONET signal	Bit rate (Mbps)	Capacity (T-equivalents)*
STS-1/OC-1	51.840	1 DS-3 (28 DS-1s)
STS-3/OC-3	155.520	3 DS-3s (84 DS-1s)
STS-12/OC-12	622.080	12 DS-3s (336 DS-1s)
STS-48/OC-48	2,488.320	48 DS-3s (1,344 DS-1s)
STS-192/OC-192	9,953.280	192 DS-3s (5,376 DS-1s)
STS-768/OC-768	39,813.120	768 DS-3s (21,504 DS-1s)

*See "Technical note: the T-carrier system and the DS hierarchy"

Notice that the levels are even multiples of each other. For example, the STS-3 rate is three times the STS-1 rate—in other words, three STS-1 channels can be combined (multiplexed) into one STS-3, the STS-12 rate is four times the STS-3 rate (12 multiplexed STS-1s), and so on.

All multiplexing derives from STS-1 signals (and is done by STS multiplexers). For example, for four STS-3s to be multiplexed into an STS-12, they must first be demultiplexed into 12 STS-1s, which then can be multiplexed into an STS-12. (Also see "Technical note: concatenated frames.") In the future, with advances in technology, higher capacities are sure to be implemented.

TECHNICAL NOTE
Concatenated frames

SONET frames can carry signals whose data rate exceeds that of an STS-1. But the frame cannot be formed by gluing multiple STS-1s, because no single STS-1 can carry the signal. Instead, to handle a signal whose base rate is at or near an STS-n rate, the entire STS-n frame is treated as an entity.

Without concatenation, each STS-1 component would have its own section and line overhead. With concatenation, that overhead is needed only once, because it applies to the entire frame entity. The unneeded overhead space is used for additional user payload. (As a result of these modifications, the STS-n signal cannot be demultiplexed into n STS-1s, as would normally be the case.)

As an example, using this technique, a concatenated STS-3 can carry ATM cells, whose base data rate is 155.52 Mbps.

Managing SONET: out-of-band signaling

As we saw (refer to Figure 10.9), the frame reserves space (actually, time slots) for out-of-band management, making it simple for the section, line, and path network components to communicate with each other and for network devices to report their conditions. It also provides a means for operating and controlling the network remotely. These functions are specifically referred to as *operation, administration, maintenance, and provisioning (OAMP)* capabilities for network management. (See "Technical note: OAMP.")

One very important consequence of OAMP is that frame header information can be used by the ADMs to add (merge) signals from different sources into a path and remove signals from a path without having to demultiplex (separate out each data stream) and remultiplex (reconfigure) the entire signal, as would otherwise be the case. The headers enable the ADMs to identify individual data streams within the signal, so the signal can be reorganized on the fly.

Out-of-band signaling allows network operators to provide a far greater array of end user services. SONET has thus gone a long way toward rectifying the T-system's initial total lack of such facilities. The many users who still connect to the network via a true T-line will continue to lumber under its restrictions until they upgrade to SONET connections. Recall, however, that the lowest upgrade is to STS-1/OC-1, which provides T-3 speed. If this speed is not needed, remaining with T-1 could be more cost effective.

TECHNICAL NOTE
OAMP

Out-of-band overhead simplifies frame and network management. The three components—section, line, and path—each have specific functions:

Section. Contains information required for section-to-section communication, data for framing and performance monitoring, a voice channel with which maintenance personnel can communicate while working on devices on each end of the section, and a channel for transferring section-specific OAMP information.

Line. Contains information required for the ADMs to communicate with each other so that they can control the line portion of the communication transmission. This includes a channel for transferring line-specific OAMP information and line performance monitoring information, as well as another voice channel for maintenance personnel.

Path. Enables end-to-end monitoring of the payload and its performance as it travels through the network, ensures that the correct connection was made, identifies the payload type (T-3 or 28 T-1s, for example), and provides a user channel for network operator information. Unlike the section and line segments, path is carried within the payload because it is created or looked at only when the payload enters or exits the SONET network. In contrast, section and line data must be processed and re-created every time the frame travels through a regenerator or an ADM.

Configuration and reliability

SONETs can be configured as linear (point-to-point or multipoint), mesh, or ring networks. Rings, which can be unidirectional or bi-directional, are by far the most common, and of those, the unidirectional topology is most often used; that is the one we will focus on.

The unidirectional ring topology, compared to the other possibilities, requires a minimum amount of optical fiber. This is because typically, to provide full duplex operation on other topologies, a second set of fibers is required—one set for each transmission direction. A unidirectional ring obviates that need; in effect, the single fiber provides full duplex operation, with all nodes transmitting and receiving on the same fiber.

To provide greater reliability should there be a break in the path, a second fiber ring is employed (still less fiber than a second set of dual fibers). Theoretically, to minimize the effects of cable damage, it is preferable for the second fiber to be run along a different physical path. Practically speaking, however, it is much simpler and cheaper to run both in the same cable bundle. This does increase the risk that if one fiber is accidentally cut, both will be, but the risk is generally deemed acceptable given the cost savings, especially because of the self-healing capability of the ring (described shortly).

SONET rings use a variety of strategies to provide high levels of network integrity. Commonly, one of the two fibers carries all traffic between the nodes on the ring, say in a counterclockwise direction. This ring is designated the ***working ring.*** The second fiber carries an exact copy of the data sent on the working ring, but in the opposite direction: clockwise, to follow our example. It is called the ***protection ring.*** SONET devices can automatically detect ring failure, for instance as caused by a break in the working fiber. In that case, devices switch to the protection ring.

If both fibers are cut, as might happen when a cable is severely damaged, the devices at each end of the fault quickly loop the traffic from the working ring onto the protection ring, thus bypassing the fault and re-creating a continuous path connecting all nodes. Restoration within 50 ms is not unusual. This is called ***ring wrapping.*** (See Figure 10.10.) SONET rings are therefore called ***self-healing.*** When the fault is repaired, normal ring operation recommences automatically.

FIGURE 10.10

SONET ring wrapping

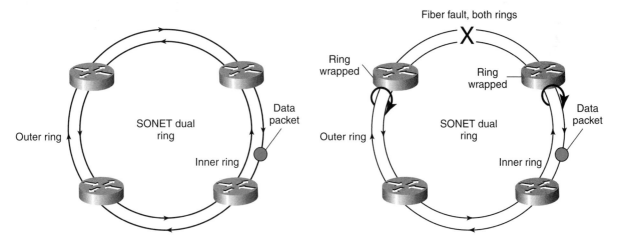

Linking SONET rings

Small SONETs can be installed locally, on site in a company building or campus. They also can have broader spans, serving as a metropolitan area network, and even broader as a network that spans a region. Any of these SONETs can be interconnected via their ADM multiplexers. By linking the rings, connectivity can be maintained over a wide area while still keeping all transmissions within a SONET structure.

10.9 Summary

We began this chapter with a brief summary of the technological and business history of the telephone systems in the United States. From this, we can understand why the telephone networks have played and continue to play a vital role in the telecommunications industry. We saw how communications capabilities grew in response to demand, by now a familiar picture. The result was a change from a purely analog system to an all-but-the-local-loop digital system, along with a shift from FDM to TDM. We saw the development of the T-carrier system and how it improved telecommunications capabilities, but we also saw how its limitations led to the much higher performing SONET system.

Along the way, the consent decree of 1984 forced AT&T to divest itself of local phone service; 12 years later, the Telecommunications Act of 1996 opened the way for competition on both the local and long-distance sides of phone communications and led to a flurry of CLECs and independently owned IXCs and to a significantly diminished role for the once-mighty AT&T. It also paved the way for competition in dialup Internet access.

We learned the basics of T-system service, its advances over POTS, and its drawbacks. We saw how PBXs owned by companies can replace the functions of a Class 5 switching office and how the phone companies offer services that create quasi-PBXs in their own switching offices.

ISDN was proffered as a better digital transmission system than the analog phone system for data transmission. Although it never became the blockbuster that the phone companies hoped it would be, it did play a role in the continuing evolution of digital communications.

DSL came to be the high-speed connection service that enabled the telcos to utilize the capacity of the local loops that pure phone service and dialup modems did not. In its variety of versions, it has been a rapidly growing means for broadband connection to the Internet and a fairly straightforward way for the telcos to use existing infrastructure to compete with the burgeoning cable modem services.

Cable modems came into the picture when the cable companies seized the opportunity to utilize their existing cable system to provide Internet access to the home, by converting their systems from simplex to duplex operation. After that was done, they were also able to take advantage of the deregulation of the telephone industry beginning in 1984 by offering phone service over the same cable system that served TV. Although slow to catch on, that service is growing rapidly.

Finally, we looked at SONET, the telcos' light signal–based system for very reliable high-speed transmission of voice and data. This was made possible by advances in optical system technology and the vast networks of fiber-optic cables that were installed in the 1990s.

In the next chapter, we will look at how packet switched WANs operate and explore a variety of their implementations.

END-OF-CHAPTER QUESTIONS

Short answer

1. What was the result of the consent decree of 1984?
2. What is a LATA?
3. How do local loops differ from trunk lines?
4. Describe the DS hierarchy and how it relates to the T-system.
5. Explain the functions of a DSU/CSU.
6. What is the impact of the provision of out-of-bound signaling in a transmission system?
7. What affects the availability and speed of ADSL? of cable broadband data service?
8. Describe the STS hierarchy and how it relates to OC designations.
9. What happens to the SONET data rate as frames are "glued" together? Why?
10. Why is SONET called self-healing? How does self-healing work?

Fill-in

1. _____ provides local phone service.
2. _____ interconnect LATAs to provide long-distance phone service.
3. Local loops terminate in _____.
4. To make the entire T-1 frame available to an application, it is run in a/an _____ configuration.
5. A _____ is a small version of a Class 5 telephone switching office that can be owned by a business.
6. Four versions of DSL are _____, _____, _____, and _____.
7. In the typical setup, a cable modem is connected to the customer computer via _____.
8. SONET user data is carried in the _____.
9. The _____ ring and the _____ ring are the two components of a unidirectional SONET ring configuration.
10. If both SONET ring fibers are cut, _____ bypasses the fault.

Multiple-choice

1. The Telecommunications Act of 1996 was aimed at
   a. increasing competition in telephone service
   b. breaking up AT&T
   c. insuring that a fiber-optic infrastructure would be created
   d. separating mobile telephony from wired telephony

2. The public switched telephone network
   a. is a hierarchical structure
   b. facilitates interconnection of LECs with IXCs
   c. carries local phone service
   d. all of the above

3. A T-1 line
   a. is designed to carry only data signals
   b. uses a 24-bit frame
   c. runs at a rate of 8,000 frames per second
   d. has an overall rate of 56 Kbps

4. ADSL
   a. takes over the entire bandwidth of the local loop for data transmission
   b. requires a filter to remove data signals from phone calls
   c. allocates approximately 750 MHz of bandwidth to both upstream and downstream traffic
   d. runs on fiber links

5. Before cable TV systems could offer broadband data access, they had to
   a. install fiber to the home
   b. convert to an all-digital system
   c. replace simplex operation with duplex operation
   d. all of the above

6. Cable modems
   a. utilize Ethernet on the customer side
   b. have widely variable data rates, from under 2 Mbps to over 6 Mbps
   c. should not be used without firewalls
   d. all of the above

7. SONET
   a. tops out at the T-3 rate of about 45 Mbps

   b. has strong out-of-band signaling capability
   c. uses a single clocking source for all communications devices
   d. both b and c

8. SONET rings
   a. can be linked to provide wide-area SONET coverage
   b. can be installed locally in a company building or campus
   c. are usually based on single-mode fiber
   d. all of the above

9. Concatenated SONET frames
   a. are simply "glued" basic SONET frames
   b. utilize unneeded overhead space for user data
   c. make use of in-band signaling
   d. all of the above

10. The SONET STS hierarchy
   a. is made up of multiples of STS-1s
   b. has a minimum data rate equal to the T-1 rate
   c. deals with optical signals
   d. applies only to ring configurations

True or false

1. After the Telecommunications Act of 1996, RBOCs became known as CLECs.
2. Local loops terminate in a central office.
3. For efficiency, trunk lines now use FDM.
4. T-1 circuits can directly connect businesses to the telephone network, bypassing the local loop.
5. Although ISDN largely has been surpassed, it is still useful in particular applications.
6. xDSL takes advantage of excess capacity on trunk lines.

7. A SONET ADM can merge or remove signals from different sources without demultiplexing the entire signal.
8. The basic SONET frame was designed to carry one T-3 transmission stream.
9. A SONET frame reserves 4/9ths of its capacity for section, line, and path overhead.
10. Over 95 percent of the SPE is for user data.

Exploration

1. Investigate the availability of ADSL at different specific addresses in your home town. Can you find areas where it is and is not available? Why might this be?
2. Compare availability, cost, and data rates for HDSL, SDSL, VDSL, T-1, and T-3 in your college's area.

3. Contact businesses in your area to find some that have installed PBXs and others that have not. Can you discover how those decisions were made?

CASE   BROADBAND FOR THE HOME

Your friend has been using dial-up service to access the Internet. For some time, her main usage was for e-mail and instant messaging, with occasional forays to Web sites, for which dial-up was fine. Lately, however, she has become interested in Web sites with much graphic, video, and music content, and she often downloads files. With her dial-up connection, this has proved to be tedious and, for some sites, even impossible. She wants to move to broadband, but not having a technical background, she has turned to you for advice. Which broadband method would you recommend? Why? Think about what you need to know before you investigate options. Write down your questions, make up reasonable answers, and then provide what you believe to be the best solution for your friend. As a means of justifying your solution, make up a table comparing alternatives.

THE MOSI CASE, CONTINUED

The company's growth plans have paid off. MOSI now has agreements with five area hospitals, resulting in a significant increase in call volume and placements. To make information transfer more efficient, management is considering connecting to these hospitals via broadband, so that placement requests can be transmitted and confirmed electronically. MOSI believes that this will make it easier for the hospitals to handle patient discharge needs, further improving their satisfaction with MOSI's services and, along with it, creating increased business volume. At the same time, the telephone burden of the schedulers and hospital personnel should be reduced.

If this move is successful, MOSI believes they will be able to attract other hospitals to collaborate with MOSI. You have been asked to investigate the possibilities. Before you do, what questions would you ask of the managers, other employees of MOSI, the hospitals, or other parties? Think about what you need to know before you investigate options. How would you take into consideration the possibility that even more hospitals may reach agreements with MOSI in the future?

11

Packet switched wide area networks

11.1 Overview

A wide area network (WAN) interconnects computers and related equipment over distances that extend beyond the corporate walls. WAN interconnections are extensive, giving WANs global coverage. In this chapter, we will focus on *packet switched WANs,* which we discussed briefly in Chapter 8, "Comprehending networks." Here we will go into more detail.

Packet switched WANs made their mark in data communications, supplanting the common carrier circuit switched networks in that market. In Chapter 8, we saw that the bursty nature of computer communications makes circuit switched networks ill-suited to most data exchange—slower, more costly, and wasteful of capacity. Further, packet switching enables common carriers to use their resources for many customers in a shared mode that, as we shall see, is more efficient than the simple time division multiplexing (TDM) used for circuit switching. As with circuit switching, customers have their own connections to the packet switched network, but within the network itself, packets from many customers share the links.

Any WAN, packet switched WANs included, has four basic components:

- Nodes. Devices that can process data. Nodes that provide access to the WAN are called *access devices* or *edge switches.* In businesses, these typically are *routers,* also called *edge routers* to clarify their position as the businesses' connections at the edges of the WANs.
- Switches. Nodes internal to the WAN that connect links to move traffic over its paths.
- Links. The media between the switches over which traffic flows. *Link* also refers to two switches and the medium between them.
- Programs. The components that run the nodes and therefore the WAN. Programs may be implemented in hardware or firmware, or they may reside in switch memory.

We also can think of a packet switched WAN as a communications network that transports data among some combination of the computers that people use and the computers that provide services such as database access. These computers are called *end systems* because they are at the ends of a communications chain.

To effect these connections, other computer-based equipment move data between the end systems and each other. These nodes are called *intermediate systems.* When the end systems are remote from each other, the intermediate systems of a packet switched WAN come into play, such as switches, routers, and even LANs.

Packet switching comes in two service flavors: ***connectionless*** and ***connection-oriented.***

- **Connectionless service**
  No formal arrangement is made with the destination node regarding the message to be sent. Packets making up the message are simply given to the network by the sending node. This is similar to the way in which the postal system handles mail: A letter is deposited in a mail box without regard to whether the recipient is willing or able to accept the message—that is, no connection is established with the addressee.

  Similarly, just as the postal service tries its best to deliver the mail but does not guarantee success, so, too, does connectionless service try its best, but it does not guarantee successful message delivery. Therefore, it is called a ***best-effort*** communications system. For example, the routing function in the Internet layer of the TCP/IP model, called ***datagram service,*** is connectionless.

- **Connection-oriented service**
  The receiving node is engaged at the outset. The receiver becomes a partner in the process, providing feedback to the sender that allows for a far greater level of error checking and reliability. For example, the routing function in an asynchronous transfer mode (ATM) network uses a connection-oriented service called ***virtual circuit service.***

For either service flavor, issues of traffic control, reliability, congestion, and error handling need to be considered. These, together with cost, provide a basis for choosing the type of service that best fits an organization's needs.

11.2 Switches, nodes, and links

Switches, nodes, and links together make up the fabric of a WAN. Links may be fiber optic, twisted pair, coax, or microwave, all of which are used.

Switches

Switches are intermediate devices that operate at the OSI-TCP/IP data link layer, network layer, or both. (See Figure 11.1 and "Technical note: Switches and routers.") As such, they do not examine the data carried by the frames; they need to look only at header information.

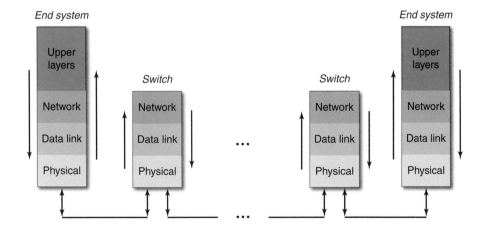

FIGURE 11.1

Switches and the data link/network layer

There are two basic switch types: ***store-and-forward*** and ***cut-through.*** Packet switched WANs can intermingle the two types.

- **Store-and-forward**

    A store-and-forward switch reads the entire incoming packet and stores it in its memory buffer, checks various fields (for example, to see whether the packet has been damaged in transit), determines the ***next hop*** (the next directly connected switch to send the packet to, called the ***forwarding link***), and finally forwards it.

    The "store" requirement means that a packet arriving at a switch whose memory is full must be discarded because it cannot be read. Because that packet will have to be retransmitted, there is a double wasting of bandwidth: once to send the original packet and again for transmitting a replacement. To minimize this problem, store-and-forward switches are configured with considerable memory. In addition, flow control measures designed to restrict switches from using congested links are implemented—it is these links where discards are most likely to happen.

AMPLIFICATION

A congested link is the result of a congested switch—that is, a switch that is either very busy or has no buffer memory left. When reference is made to a congested link, it actually refers to two switches and the line connecting them.

- **Cut-through**

    In contrast to store-and-forward, a cut-through switch begins forwarding the bits of a packet as soon as the next hop is known, without waiting for the entire packet to arrive—the bits "cut through" the switch.

    Cut-through switches move data without the delay of store-and-forward, but because they cannot see the whole packet at once, they will forward damaged frames. Because of this, using cut-through switches in a noisy network will result in a lot of wasted bandwidth—not a good idea. On the other hand, in a highly reliable WAN, cut-through switches can greatly improve overall throughput with rare penalty from forwarding faulty packets.

AMPLIFICATION

We recall from Chapter 5, "Error control," that error check calculations are based on almost the entire frame, so the whole packet has to be held in memory for the calculation to take place. Thus, error checking by cut-through switches is not feasible.

Furthermore, even if an error could be discovered without holding the packet, by then at least part of the packet would already have been forwarded anyway.

Generally, WAN switches are linked in a partial mesh (see Figure 11.2)—all switches will have direct links to many other switches, but, except for very small WANs, no switch has a direct link to every other switch. Otherwise, an enormous number of links would be needed, a prohibitively costly proposition. (Recall that a full mesh of N devices requires $(N)(N-1)/2$ links.)

TECHNICAL NOTE
Switches and routers

The distinction between a switch and a router is not always obvious. Part of the problem is that the terms sometimes are used interchangeably; another part is that the terms refer more directly to particular functionality than what to call a device.

At the LAN level, switches generally refer to hub replacement devices that can directly connect to LAN stations. As such, they operate at the data link layer (more specifically, at the MAC sublayer of the data link layer).

The devices used at the company site to connect to external networks are usually called routers. They operate at the network layer and are able to select routes over which to send packets.

The definitions are fuzzy because:

• Even at the intra-company level, there are layer 3 switches that encompass some routing functions.

• The intermediate nodes in a WAN, which also operate at the network layer, are referred to as switches in many references and as routers in others.

• Some specific routing devices have "switch" as part of their name (an example is an ATM switch).

To simplify matters, we will use the term *switch* as a generic reference in most of our WAN discussions. Functionally, these devices switch frames and packets from link to link, although they do so based on various forms of routing information. We will see examples of routing procedures. Bear in mind these two functions of WAN switches as you read through the chapter.

FIGURE 11.2

Graphical representation of a packet switch

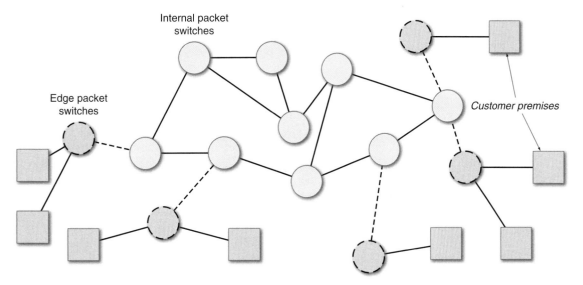

This partial mesh has several paths between any of the edge switches.

The partial mesh design means that packets must travel through a number of intermediate nodes and their associated links to reach their destinations, except for those very few where there are direct links. So the question becomes, what path should packets be sent over?

This is precisely the reason for and major function of the switching nodes: to best determine and implement the movement of information through a network when direct connection between the end nodes may not exist. If every node were connected to every other node, switching would be a simple matter of sending the data out the appropriate port. When there are many connections and paths between end nodes, determining the best path is vital to efficient functioning of the internetwork.

Best path calculation utilizes sophisticated logic embodied in *routing algorithms.* There are several such algorithms, each with characteristics that make it suitable for one network or set of transmission requirements, but perhaps not for another. It may be that the complete end-to-end path for a given message is determined in advance—each of the message's packets follow that route; this is the case in virtual circuit packet switching. It also may be that each step of the path is determined independently on the fly for each packet; this is what is done in datagram service. Let's look at these two possibilities more closely.

Datagram service

A datagram service is a connectionless network layer service that provides *best-effort* packet transmission. When best effort is sufficient, network layer services are all that is needed. Examples of applications for which best effort commonly suffices are Internet video and voice (Voice over IP) and notification messages (for example, to play a tone or tune when e-mail arrives). When the WAN is the Internet, the TCP/IP network layer protocol *IP (Internet protocol)* provides datagram service. (IP is discussed in Chapter 13, "TCP/IP, associated Internet protocols, and routing.")

If guaranteed delivery is required, the end systems must be put in play. Normally, this is done by bringing the transport layer into the picture for end-to-end error control and packet sequencing. Applications such as e-mail, Web browsing, and file transfer are likely to depend on guaranteed delivery.

On the Internet, *TCP (transmission control protocol)* is the transport layer protocol commonly used for delivery guarantee, packet sequencing, and elimination of duplicate packets. (This also is covered in Chapter 13.) As an example, file transfer typically invokes *FTP (file transfer protocol),* an applications layer protocol. FTP supplies end-to-end reliability and uses TCP services for actual packet transfers.

As we saw, in datagram service no paths are predetermined, each packet being treated independently with next hop calculated at each switch. To enable next hop determination, packet headers contain full information about the intended destination. Hop selection is based on one or more metrics, such as distance, cost, load, and link availability. All else being equal, the link that brings the packet closer to its destination is chosen. Typically considered as well are congestion or switch loading, the idea being to avoid heavily congested links. This has another implication: For a switch to know the condition of its forwarding links, it must receive status information from them.

Although it is possible, and even probable when networks are lightly loaded, that all packets from a single source follow the same route, this is a happenstance rather than a requirement. Different paths can be selected or not at any point in the network from among the many next hop choices. The great advantage of this is *robustness.* As long as any path exists between two end points, they can communicate; congested and failed links can be routed around.

Robustness comes at a cost:

• **Delay**

Next hop decisions take time. Each switch's decision-making adds to the total transit time.

• **Re-sequencing**

A packet may find itself on a route experiencing unusual delays or on a longer route attempting to avoid congestion, whereas a later packet from the same message may sail right through on some other route. Then it could arrive at the destination before the earlier packet, out of sequence.

For a message to make sense, all its packets must be put in proper sequence at the destination node. This means that they must be stored until all have arrived, which delays actual receipt of the message. The sorting process itself also takes time. Finally, if many such messages are arriving, the storage buffers can fill, congesting the node.

When best effort suffices, the flexibility of robustness is almost always worth the cost.

Virtual circuit service

A *virtual circuit (VC)* imitates a circuit switched connection in that it seems to behave as though a dedicated connection exists, although it does not. What does exist is a *dedicated route*. When a VC is set up, the sequence of next hops to create a single path from one customer to another is determined in advance of regular data transmission and is used for all packets between those customers. In this way, a dedicated route is analogous to a dedicated connection. (See "Technical note: Virtual and switched circuits compared.")

TECHNICAL NOTE
Virtual and switched circuits compared

Except in the local loop, common carriers operate a digital system based on TDM. When a circuit switched connection is set up, the customer is allocated a definite fixed time slot on every link making up the end-to-end common carrier connection, whether used or not. (See Chapters 8 and 10.)

VCs are set up on data networks, whose providers operate a digital network based on STDM. A customer's packets travel along the links of the preselected path. Every switch in the path will forward packets only when it is appropriate to do so. This depends on such factors as overall traffic on the next link, the size of a particular packet (in a variable packet system), and the priority of the packet's data. Although the entire path between end points is predefined and every packet follows the same route, each packet is switched individually and may experience significant delay at any node along the way.

A VC requires that customer data be divided into packets, whereas a circuit switch allows the data to flow as one continuous file. Hence, the factors that can delay packets in a VC are irrelevant to a switched circuit, where no significant delay is added at each node.

VCs have a number of advantages over datagrams:

- VCs are connection oriented and therefore offer more error checking and reliability.
- Because all packets of a message follow the same path, packets cannot arrive out of sequence.
- Packets travel through a VC packet switch faster than through a datagram packet switch because no packet-by-packet routing decisions have to be made.
- Each packet carries less addressing overhead than is required in a datagram packet switch (discussed later).

In a virtual circuit, the route is dedicated, not the connection.

Virtual circuit path demarcation

When a virtual circuit is established, the network assigns a separate and unique ***virtual circuit number*** to each link that makes up the path. Figure 11.3 illustrates this with three nodes connected by two links. Here, a VC number of 7 is assigned to the first link and 23 is assigned to the second. Subsequently, all packets of the VC will be identified by VC7 as they traverse the first link and VC23 as they traverse the second.

FIGURE 11.3

Virtual circuit number assignment

Each switch in the path enters into its routing table the unique VC number and next hop link (actually the outgoing port number) of the path. This associates the packets of a message and their VC number. (Figure 11.4 has more a detailed example and explanation.)

AMPLIFICATION

Links are connected to a node via ***ports.*** This is the same idea as connecting devices to a PC—a printer is connected to a parallel port or a USB port. To send a packet out on a particular link, the packet actually has to be sent to the switch port to which the link is connected. Each of the many ports associated with a node is identified by a hardware address called a ***port number.***

Just as with datagram service, when a packet arrives, the switch looks up the outgoing port number in its routing table. However, that table is considerably smaller than the corresponding routing table for datagrams, because the latter must provide rows for all the possible destination routes of a packet, whereas the former needs to hold only the much smaller number of virtual circuit identifiers. Therefore, VC next hop lookup, and therefore switching, is significantly faster than for datagram service.

FIGURE 11.4

Virtual circuit setup and circuit numbers

Connection view

Assume that Node A is connected to Router 1's Port 12 and Node B is connected to Router 2's Port 24.

Port 12 — Node A — Router 1 — Port 23 Port 15 — Router 2 — Port 24 — Node B

Packet numbering view

From Node A to Node B:
Node A(VC10) ⟶ Router 1(VC150) ⟶ Router 2(VC410) ⟶ Node B(VC410)

From Node B to Node A:
Node B(VC18) ⟶ Router 2(VC205) ⟶ Router 1(VC123) ⟶ Node A(VC123)

Virtual circuit setup

For packets from Node A to Node B:

- Node A sends a VC setup request to Router 1, specifying VC10 for packets that it sends on the circuit and VC123 for packets that it receives on that circuit.

- Path calculation by Router 1 indicates that Port 23 is the best to send out packets from VC10 and assigns VC150 to those packets. So Router 1 enters in its table for Port 12: VC10 in — Port 23 out — number VC150, meaning *switch any packet numbered VC10 coming into Port 12 to outgoing Port 23 and change its virtual circuit number to VC150.*

- Path calculation by Router 2 indicates that Port 24 is the best for outgoing packets for VC150 and assigns VC410 to those packets. So Router 2 enters in its table for Port 15: VC150 in — Port 24 out — number VC410, meaning *switch any packet numbered VC150 coming into Port 15 to outgoing Port 24 and change its number to VC410.*

- Node B accepts the circuit and notes that packets it receives have number VC410.

For packets from Node B to Node A on the same circuit:

- Node B notifies Router 2 that it will use VC18 for packets that it sends on the circuit.

- Router 2 assigns VC205 to those packets. So Router 2 enters in its table for Port 24: VC18 in — Port 15 out — number VC205.

- Router 1 uses Node A's requested number VC123 for those packets. So Router 1 enters in its table for Port 23: VC205 in — Port 12 out — number as VC123.

In addition, the VC identifiers themselves are fairly small, but destination addresses are quite large. Taken together with their fewer number of rows, we see that VC routing tables need considerably less space to accommodate their data than do datagram routing tables. Further, the VC packet header does not have to include actual destination addresses (the VC number suffices), which reduces header overhead. By comparison, we saw that datagrams must include full destination addresses because each packet requires a separate routing decision at each switch.

As always, there is a downside. The VC's switching speed advantage is offset when there is congestion on a next hop link or when a next hop link is down, because there is no way to route around the problem. This can result in the VC being unavailable for some time.

For datagram service, switches calculate next hop independently for each packet. For virtual circuit service, all next hops are determined in advance.

Switched and permanent virtual circuits

There are two types of virtual circuits—switched and permanent. The difference is that a *switched virtual circuit (SVC)* is temporary and a *permanent virtual circuit (PVC)* is not.

A PVC is a path between two predefined end points, set up by a network administrator well in advance of any data transmission. After it is set up, it is always "on" and available, but it can be used only between its two predefined end points. To communicate with another end point, a different circuit is needed. What's more, if the PVC fails, ongoing transmission will be interrupted and further transmission will not be possible until it is repaired or another circuit is established. Thus, a PVC behaves very much like its telephone analog, the dedicated (leased, private) line.

An SVC is similar to a telephone dial-up connection. The originating device sends a *call setup* packet to the originating switching node. The network attempts to set up an SVC (path) to the destination node; if successful, the customer is notified and given the originating VC number. Then transmission can begin. When the circuit is no longer needed, the originating device sends a *call termination* packet to the originating switch; the tables of the switches in the path are cleared of the VC number and next hop ports.

When there is fairly continuous or regular need for the VC, a PVC makes sense because there is just one setup. When transmissions are more sporadic, an SVC is more cost effective because switch memory is not tied up with VC numbers and next hop port numbers.

11.3 WAN technologies

Packet switched networks were developed to overcome the shortcomings faced by computer data transmission over traditional telephone networks. As we have seen, telephone networks are built around circuit switching and TDM. Although they perform well for their originally intended purpose, voice communications, they are overly restrictive and expensive for computer data communications.

In the mid-1960s, businesses increasingly turned to computers for all sorts of data processing. Concomitantly, the need for long-distance computer communications grew dramatically, bringing to the fore the limitations of telephone networks. Growing pressure from the business world was one of the primary motivations to improve the situation.

At about the same time, the U.S. Department of Defense, also increasingly dependent on computers, was looking for a more robust communications environment to provide reliable connections among its many incompatible systems and for continued operation in case of an attack on its communications facilities.

The result of all this was packet switching based on statistical time division multiplexing (STDM), which was applied to and tested in the ARPANET. It quickly became obvious that this was just the technology needed to revolutionize the way networked computers communicated. Various private companies experimented with it by building private packet switched networks. As these originally were intended only for computer communications, they were called *data communications networks.*

This was soon followed by attempts to create a public packet switched network that would be to computers what the public telephone network was to telephones. Called *public data networks (PDNs),* they were extremely popular during the 1970s and 1980s. It was not until the growth of the Internet, beginning in the early 1990s, that they were finally eclipsed.

In the following sections, we will examine three of the most important packet switched WAN technologies: X.25, frame relay, and ATM. Let's look at their evolution.

X.25

Although the 1970s saw a proliferation of packet switched networks, there were no standards for implementing the technology or for connecting to those networks. That made it difficult and unwieldy for users to take advantage of their benefits. What was needed was a common standard that would make connecting a device to a public or private packet switched network, or interconnecting packet switched networks, as simple as connecting a telephone to a telephone network.

With this in mind, the United Nations organized a study group to develop a common standard for interfacing to a packet network. The result, issued in 1976, was called *X.25*. It has been revised a number of times, the last in 1992.

For the most part, X.25 has been superseded by other network technologies and thus is correctly considered to be an obsolete technology. But it is the base from which modern networks evolved. By understanding it, we can see why later systems took the paths they did and we can gain some insight into how they work, always worthy goals. For those reasons, we spend some time discussing X.25.

HISTORICAL NOTE
CCITT/ITU

The International Telegraph Union, precursor of the **International Telecommunication Union (ITU)** that we know today, began in 1865. In 1947, the Telegraph Union became an agency of the two-year-old United Nations. Twenty-six years later, it was renamed the International Telecommunication Union, organized into three sectors—radio communication (ITU-R), telecommunication development (ITU-D), and telecommunication standardization (ITU-T).

The **Comité Consultatif International Téléphonique et Télégraphique (CCITT)** began in 1960 as an international organization for communications standards functioning within the ITU. In a 1992 reorganization, the functions of CCITT were subsumed by the ITU-T sector.

Each sector is further subdivided into study groups focused on particular communication technology issues. Every group is identified by a letter of the alphabet, which carries over to the standards that the group promulgates. Thus, the international standard recommended by the ITU-T group X for interfacing to a packet switched network was named X.25.

For more information about the ITU, visit

http://www.itu.int/home/index.html.

RELIABILITY   X.25 was designed with a very high level of reliability in mind. After all, it was felt that a network's first responsibility was to deliver transmissions accurately. The copper media in use at the time was very electrically noisy, with bit error rates ranging from 1 in 100 to 1 in 1,000 (see "Technical note: BER and BERT"). To account for this, X.25 was designed to be relentless in checking packets as they flowed through the network. Each switch performs error checking, requesting retransmission of every faulty packet. This continues until every packet passes the checks or there are so many retransmission requests that the network concludes that there is a fundamental problem requiring the attention of network management.

TECHNICAL NOTE
BER and BERT

A common measure of the quality of a medium using digital signaling is the *bit error rate (BER).* BER measures the average number of faulty bits received for a given number of bits sent. Thus, a BER of 1 in 100 indicates that for every 100 bits sent, it is likely that one bit will arrive with errors. The BER of a medium can be determined by using a *BERT (bit error rate tester).* A BERT sends streams of known bit patterns through the system and examines the received data streams to calculate the BER. The smaller the BER, the more reliable the transmission system.

DTE AND DCE   There are two X.25 devices involved in connecting a node to a packet switched network: *data terminal equipment (DTE)* and *data circuit-terminating equipment (DCE).* The DTE is an end communications device, such as a computer or a terminal. It is connected to the DCE that, in turn, is connected to the X.25 network.

The X.25 interface is based on virtual circuits. The link connecting the DTE and the DCE is one leg of a VC that extends through the X.25 network to the destination DTE. Because a physical link can carry more than one VC, each must have an identification number that uniquely identifies a particular transmission. X.25 combines a *Logical Group Number* (4 bits) together with a *Logical Channel Number* (8 bits) to create a 12-bit identifier. Theoretically, one physical link could carry up to 4,096 (2^{12}) VCs. The number a given link actually can carry depends on the characteristics of the link itself. (See Figure 11.5.)

FIGURE 11.5

X.25 interface specification

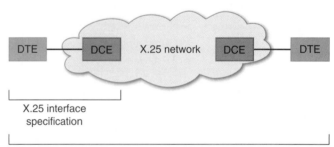

X.25 interface specification

Virtual circuit (one of up to 4,096 possible VCs)

INTERFACE SPECIFICATION   The X.25 specification requires that data exchanged between the DTE and DCE be in packet form. Messages larger than can be carried by the maximum packet size must be segmented. Segmentation is a reasonable process if the DTE is an intelligent device (computer based). However, in the 1970s many organizations connected remotely to mainframes over the telephone system using *dumb terminals.* Dumb terminals do not have processing capabilities and memory, so they could not create packets or connect to packet switched networks.

As a remedy, ISO defined specification *X.3* for a *packet assembler/disassembler (PAD)* to sit between any non-packet-capable device and the DCE and handle segmentation. Along with X.3 came *X.28,* specifying the interface between the DTE and the PAD. (See Figure 11.6.)

To require one PAD for each dumb terminal would be cost prohibitive for businesses. Hence, the PAD was designed to accommodate multiple terminals by establishing a separate

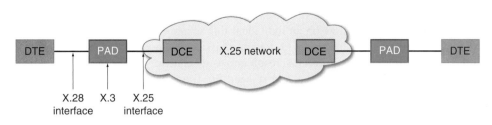

FIGURE 11.6

X.3, X.25, and X.28
interface specifications

VC for each one connected. In this way, as many as 4,096 terminals—the number of VCs
possible over one X.25 link—could be connected through one PAD. In effect, the PAD acts
like a multiplexer (see Figure 11.7).

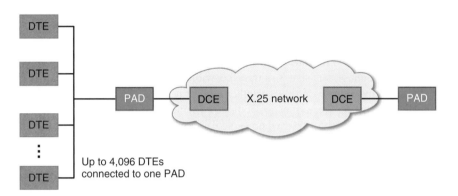

FIGURE 11.7

The PAD as a multiplexer

PROTOCOL LAYERS   X.25 defines a three-layer protocol stack. The first three layers of
the OSI architecture, which arrived about 10 years later, are similar.

- **Layer 1: physical**
  Named *X.21,* layer 1 specifies X.25's own unique electrical and mechanical interfaces. The most common physical interface specification is *EIA/RS 232-C,* the same
  as the serial port on the typical PC. (EIA/RS is the Electronics Industries Association
  of America/Radio Standard.)

- **Layer 2: data link**
  Layer 2 calls for the widely used high-level data link control (HDLC), a full-duplex
  protocol that provides a great deal of error checking and flow control in the DTE-
  DCE link. X.25's configuration is called *link access procedure—balanced (LAPB).*
  Balanced means that devices can act independently as senders and receivers at will,
  as opposed to one primary device that initiates communication (the rest being secondary), which is unbalanced.
       The data link layer encapsulates user data between a header and a trailer. The
  resulting protocol data unit (PDU) is illustrated in Figure 11.8.

Flag	Address	Control	Data	FCS	Flag
8 bits	8 bits	8/16 bits	x bits	16 bits	8 bits

FIGURE 11.8

X.25 LAPB frame
(data link PDU)

- **Layer 3: packet layer**
  The packet layer manages packet exchanges (routing) between DTEs over a VC.

THE DATA LINK LAYER   LAPB carries out error checking and flow control over an
individual link using information in the header control field. ACKs are sent for error-free

frames. If an error is detected, LAPB discards the frame and sends information that triggers a retransmission. Packet flow on an individual link is monitored. If flow is too heavy, a supervisory message tells the sender to stop transmissions temporarily, preventing overload.

Discards and retransmissions can result in out-of-sequence frames. A destroyed ACK will cause the sender to time out and re-send the frame, also producing a duplicate. Accordingly, LAPB must keep track of frames. To do so, the sending node assigns each frame a unique number, held in the control field.

THE PACKET LAYER   The packet layer is what gives X.25 its unique characteristics. Whereas the data link layer manages data flow across an individual link, the packet layer is responsible for end-to-end flow, from the originating node to the ultimate destination. To accomplish this, the packet layer adds its own header-encapsulating the data sent by the DTE to the DCE.

X.25 CONCLUSIONS   X.25 was introduced to provide a cheaper, more flexible data transmission alternative to the traditional telephone network. By virtue of using STDM, X.25 allowed computers to transmit at various data rates based on need while paying only for the actual amount of data sent. Contrast this with the telephone networks, for which cost was determined by connection time (whether used or not), the distance between the sender and the receiver, and the fixed transmission rate (whether the full rate was used or not).

Designed in the early 1970s when typical links were copper based and electrically noisy, X.25 went to great lengths to ensure reliable communications. But the error checking involved to accomplish this, done at both the data link and packet layers, created a processing bottleneck at each node. Furthermore, X.25 was designed around the relatively slow links of the day: data rates were generally limited to no more than 64 Kbps.

In its day, X.25 served the data communications community well. Over time, the demand for transmission of ever-greater amounts of data at ever-higher data rates outstripped X.25's capabilities. This impelled the development of new packet switching paradigms. In the next sections, we will see how the technology evolved to meet the needs of today.

TECHNICAL NOTE
Summarizing the pros and cons of X.25

Pros

- Provides very reliable transmission because of emphasis on error control at multiple protocol layers.
- Has relatively low cost.
- Allows two devices of differing speed capabilities to communicate because packets are temporarily stored at each transit node, allowing the network to compensate for speed differences. This offers a great deal of flexibility compared to circuit switching, wherein sender and receiver speed must be identical (there is no buffering).

Cons

- Very slow—measured by today's needs and standards. Extensive error checking and flow control at each node delay forwarding. Significant speed increase is unlikely.
- High-cost equipment—compared to other methods. High-speed CPUs and very large buffers and disks needed to accommodate required node storage and processing.

For more details about X.25, see Appendix I, "Some details of X.25 and frame relay operations."

Frame relay

The explosion of computer-based data and the growing need to transfer data between remote computers combined to put a strain on the capabilities of X.25 networks.

During the 1980s, higher-quality (less electrically noisy) links and better digital transmission equipment and techniques greatly reduced the bit errors of communications lines. This permitted network designers to streamline the operation of X.25 by vastly reducing the amount of error correction performed. The result—*frame relay.*

Frame relay networks perform neither error correction nor error recovery. End users decide whether they need error correction. If they do, they must provide it by running higher-level protocols such as TCP on top of frame relay. Further, whereas X.25 provides robust flow control via the sliding window mechanism (see Chapter 7, "Digital communication techniques"), frame relay provides none. Thus, each frame relay node is relieved of a great deal of processing, so packets breeze through the network at far higher speeds than are achievable with X.25—up to 2 Mbps, compared to X.25's 64 Kbps.

To achieve greater efficiency from network resources, frame relay also packages user data differently. With X.25, all packets within a given network must be of one size (although different networks can use different sizes). If more data than will fit in one packet has to be transmitted, it must be split up over several packets. Likewise, if the data is smaller than one packet requires, the packet is padded with bits to fill it out. This one-size-fits-all approach is not efficient: Splitting data over a number of packets increases overhead (aside from processing, each additional packet has its own overhead), and padding causes the network to carry useless bits.

Recognizing this, frame relay designers opted for variable size frames that could be aligned more closely with data needs, ranging from a minimum of 5 bytes to a maximum of 8,192 bytes, excluding the start frame and end frame flags. (The Frame Relay Forum industry standards group recommends frames of no more than 1,600 bytes.) This made sense from the perspective of reducing overhead and wasted capacity, but it was not without a cost—the additional processing needed at each node to handle the different frame sizes.

X.25 requires all packets in one network to be the same size. Frame relay allows variable size frames within the same network.

The data link layer header differs from that of X.25 in the elimination of the control field—no longer needed because error control is dropped—and the increased size of the address field—to provide the network layer functions that were combined into the data link layer. (See Figure 11.9 and compare to Figure 11.8.)

Flag	Address	Data	FCS	Flag
8 bits	16/32 bits	x bits	16 bits	8 bits

FIGURE 11.9

Frame relay hybrid data link header

HISTORICAL NOTE
Why is it called frame relay and not packet relay?

Because frame relay networks reduced the complexity of network and data link layer services, the two layers were combined into one hybrid data link layer, resulting in a two-layer architecture, data link and physical. This led to the name frame relay, as opposed to packet relay. Here's why:

• At the data link layer, protocol data units are called frames; at higher layers, they are called packets. (To add a bit more to the nomenclature confusion,

packet are called *cells* in ATM networks and *datagrams* in IP networks.)
• Switches that make next hop decisions at the network layer are called packet switches because the unit they base switching on is the packet.
• Frame relay networks make switching decisions at the (hybrid) data link layer, where the unit is the frame. So they use frame-based switches; hence the name frame relay.

HOW FRAME RELAY WORKS Frame relay, derived as it is from X.25, also is a connection-oriented network using virtual circuits. Two components of the address field, *data link connection identifier (DLCI) upper* and *DLCI lower* identify a particular circuit. Combined, their 10 bits can demarcate 1,024 virtual circuits per link. The *extended address (EA)* bits can increase this number to 4,119,304. (See Figure 11.10.)

FIGURE 11.10

Inside the frame relay address field

DLCI upper	C/R	EA	DLCI lower	FECN	BECN	DE	EA	Address extension	D/C	EA
6 bits	1 bit	1 bit	4 bits	1 bit	1 bit	1 bit	1 bit	6 bits	1 bit	1 bit

Two of these can be added, providing up to 12 more address bits

DLCI: Data link connection identifier.
C/R: Not used; originally meant for running over ISDN. Can be used as desired in a given network.
FECN: Forward explicit congestion notification.
BECN: Backward explicit congestion notification.
DE: Discard eligible.
EA: Extended address indicator.
 If EA=1, the header ends here — the address is defined by the DLCIs.
 If EA=0, the header has another 8 bits, 6 of which are appended to the DLCIs to increase the address space. One or two address extensions can be added.
D/C: Data control indicator.

The typical connection to the frame relay network is via a leased line, say T-1, from the local telephone company. The customer's computer (DTE) is connected to a *frame relay assembler/disassembler (FRAD),* which is connected to the leased line that in turn is connected to the frame relay point of presence (POP). (See Figure 11.11.) The FRAD can connect end networks of many different types to a frame relay network. Operating in full

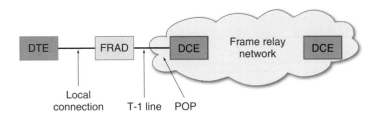

FIGURE 11.11

Connecting to the frame
relay network: an example

duplex mode, the FRAD converts data units coming from one end network into frame relay frames, and reverses the process for frame relay frames headed for that end network.

To avoid overwhelming the network in the face of heavy demand (because flow control is not part of frame relay), three mechanisms are used in conjunction with the *discard eligible (DE), forward explicit congestion notification (FECN),* and *backward explicit congestion notification (BECN)* bits. When congestion is high, frames are discarded until the situation is alleviated. The first frames discarded are those marked DE. At the same time, nodes in the network notify each other of building congestion via the FECN and BECN bits. For more detail on this process, see Appendix I.

DATA RATES AND GUARANTEES   Frame relay *service level agreements (SLAs)* are contracts that specify a guaranteed data rate, called the *committed information rate (CIR).* An SLA allows exceeding the rate for a period of time as long as the average excess rate is not greater than the *committed burst size (Bc),* which also is part of the contract. Contract cost depends on those rates. (Appendix I explains CIR and Bc in greater detail. Also, see "Business note: One CIR strategy.")

Business NOTE   One CIR strategy

Public frame relay networks provide transmission services for a fee. A major part of that fee is the CIR—the higher the CIR, the greater the cost. An interesting strategy that some customers use to reduce cost is to specify a CIR of 0 bps. This means that any data sent is eligible for discard should the network experience congestion.

At first glance, this may seem like a strange strategy for a business that relies on the network. However, frame relay networks may be designed with substantial spare capacity so that often no frames have to be discarded. If you are a risk taker, this is a strategy for you. (Not every frame relay provider allows this, but many do.)

FRAME RELAY CONCLUSIONS   Frame relay was designed to eliminate the processing burden imposed on X.25 because of the state of the communications links of the time. Significant improvement in the communication links and better transmission techniques meant it was no longer necessary to impose as severe and time-consuming error correction and flow control on the network. This in itself allowed frame relay networks to improve data throughput by an order of magnitude when compared to X.25. Additional throughput improvements were achieved by introducing variable frame sizes, extending the maximum frame size, and consolidating the network and data link layers. As a result, frame relay networks place the burden of achieving reliable communications on the user.

TECHNICAL NOTE
Summarizing the pros
and cons of frame relay

Pros

- Variable size frames—provide more efficient use of network capacity.
- Significantly higher throughput than X.25.
- Availability of SLAs with committed information rates.
- Continued use of virtual circuits.
- Low cost and high available speeds—can make its use feasible in place of leased lines.

Cons

- Unreliable "best-effort" communications.
- Variable frame size—increases complexity of processing frames and makes it not very suitable for multimedia.

Asynchronous transfer mode

As we have seen throughout the text, technology marches on, most often in response to consumer pressure. Although frame relay was a significant improvement over X.25, the growing diversity and volume of data sources drove further refinements in the design of packet switched networks and their underlying technology. Adding to the pressure for improvement was the fact that different networks were needed to handle different data types.

At the time, it was quite common for large companies to build private networks for their own use. Typically, this meant a traditional telephone network for voice and a separate network for data. It was not long before company accountants took note of the expense of this dual requirement and began pointedly to question it. After all, a network is a network! Or so it seemed.

That presumption became a reality in the late 1980s with *asynchronous transfer mode (ATM),* the network technology that converged the telephone and data networks into one to provide the best features of both. By the time the ATM designers went to work, they had the advantage of a new connection medium: optical fiber. Compared to copper media, fiber has an extremely high bandwidth and is almost noise free. This makes it marvelous for carrying data at very high rates. Even the copper networks were greatly improved, reducing their noisiness considerably. Relatively noise-free networks meant that error correction, and even some error detection, could be dispensed with. Removing these tasks reduced the ATM processing burden, and therefore processing time, even further than frame relay.

FROM A FRAME TO A CELL All network nodes are computers, highly specialized and tuned for the functions they perform. Converting the software they run into hardware results in much faster execution than running software code. Because of manufacturing issues, producing such firmware is practical only if the required processing is relatively simple.

As one means of simplifying processing so as to take advantage of firmware speed, the designers of ATM mandated that all frames be the same size regardless of which network ATM runs on. Contrast this with frame relay's variable size packets, and with X.25's allowance of different sizes in different networks, although they must be the same size within any one network.

After the decision to fix frame size was made, the next question was what that size should be. Here are the considerations:

- **Hardware Processing**
  Hardware is most efficiently built for small frame processing.

- **Traffic**
  High speed and low latency are requisite to successfully handle time-sensitive traffic. Whereas e-mail is not greatly affected by speed or delay, digitized sound—whether for voice conversations or for streaming audio—and video are very sensitive to delays. Natural-sounding conversations and audio transmissions depend on fast, low-latency delivery, as does smooth full-motion video.

  Small frames reduce the chance that time-sensitive traffic will experience delays, because a video or voice packet will not have to wait long while a non-video or non-voice packet is being transferred by the network.

- **Efficiency**
  Large frames utilize a network more efficiently; small frames increase network overhead—each frame, regardless of size, adds to overhead, so the more frames it takes to handle a transmission, the greater the overhead.

When these considerations were assessed, the first two were deemed more important. The third was less significant because ATM networks run at very high speeds, with data rates of up to 622 Mbps over fiber-optic cable and 155 Mbps over Cat 5 UTP. High speed reduces the impact of extra overhead.

The conclusion was to fix frame size at 53 bytes. To distinguish the ATM frame from those of other systems, it is called a *cell.*

ATM has fixed-size 53-byte cells and uses specialized hardware to handle cell processing, greatly speeding data flow through the network.

THE ATM CELL   The ATM cell is divided into two logical parts: a 5-byte header and a 48-byte payload. (See Figure 11.12.) As with all frames, the header is used for traffic control and the payload carries user data.

ATM networks, like X.25 and frame relay networks, are connection oriented based on virtual circuits. At any point in time, many virtual circuits are concurrently in use. Many of these share the same physical transmission path. To distinguish the virtual circuits on a transmission path, they are assigned VCIs.

For efficiency and robustness, ATM bundles several VCIs into one *virtual path,* labeled by the VPI. If a link in a physical path goes down, the entire bundle is rerouted—every circuit in the bundle follows the same new path. This is much quicker than rerouting each individual virtual circuit.

ATM OPERATION   Like frame relay, ATM assumes that the networks it runs on are extremely reliable; hence, neither control flow on virtual circuits nor error detection or correction are provided. The one exception is errors that affect the integrity of the cell header, thus ensuring that data never is delivered to an incorrect destination.

CLASS OF SERVICE AND QUALITY OF SERVICE   Speed increase alone is not sufficient for effectively transporting the variety of traffic types that ATM was intended to handle. In addition, different traffic streams must be processed differently—some delay in delivering

FIGURE 11.12

The 53 byte ATM cell

NNI cell:

VPI	VCI	PT	CLP	HEC	Payload
12 bits	16 bits	3 bits	1 bit	8 bits	384 bits

5 bytes ——————— 48 bytes

Note: In the **UNI cell**, the 12-bit VPI segment is replaced by:

GFC	VPI
4 bits	8 bits

VPI: Virtual path identifier
VCI: Virtual channel identifier
PT: Payload type
CLP: Congestion loss priority
HEC: Header error control
GFC: Generic flow control

The **NNI (*network-to-network interface*)** cell header is for traffic between two ATM switches.

The **UNI (*user-to-network interface*)** header is for traffic between a user device and an ATM switch. The UNI VPI field is reduced to 8 bits, so there are fewer virtual path numbers. This reflects the fact that the number of (virtual) connections between an end user device and an ATM switch is much smaller than the number between two ATM switches. The GFC bits were intended for end user flow control, although that never was implemented; GFC is simply padded with 0s.

AMPLIFICATION

An ATM virtual circuit is identified by the combination of VPI and VCI. Theoretically, A UNI can support 16,777,216 virtual circuits (2^{24}). An NNI can support 268,435,456 virtual circuits (2^{28}). The actual number of virtual circuits depends on the capacity of the physical transmission path, a much smaller number.

e-mail is relatively unimportant, whereas delays, especially variable delays, in voice or video delivery are critical.

ATM distinguishes traffic flow types by defining four *Classes of Service (CoS)* that broadly capture the nature of different types of traffic and the special requirements the network must provide:

- *CBR (Constant Bit Rate)*
  CBR is meant for sources that generate a steady flow of data and that require delivery with very little delay and almost no delay variability—typically uncompressed voice and video. Similar to a dedicated link, CBR guarantees that a specific bit rate will be maintained.
- *VBR (Variable Bit Rate)*
  The opposite of CBR, the bit rate can vary from moment to moment. Most often, traffic of this type is produced when data is compressed to reduce its size to decrease transmission time. VBR guarantees that a specific throughput level will be maintained. For example:
  - Voice can be compressed by removing silent moments; because silence occurs at varying times, a variable bit rate results.

- Digital movies are often compressed through the use of a *lossy* compression scheme called *MPEG.* The bit rate varies according to the images compressed, available network bandwidth, and the required quality of the compressed video stream.

AMPLIFICATION

A lossy compression scheme actually discards some of the original data in an attempt to meet a user-specified percent reduction in size. The hope is that by carefully choosing the data to discard, the resulting information may be adequate to the task after it is uncompressed.

- ***ABR (Available Bit Rate)***
  ABR provides a guaranteed minimum level of network capacity, but it allows the sender to increase the data rate if the network has additional capacity available at that moment. This is attractive for bursty interactions such as those involved in client/server applications.
- ***UBR (Unspecified Bit Rate)***
  UBR service simply uses whatever capacity the ATM network has available at the moment and makes no guarantee of any service level. It offers a best-effort attempt to transmit the user's data. Thus, it is suitable for applications that are not time sensitive, such as file transfer.

TECHNICAL NOTE
Summarizing the pros and cons of ATM

Pros

- High-speed performance from hardware-based switching.
- Fixed-size cells (frames) that simplify switch processing.
- Use of virtual circuits.
- All data types handled, including time-sensitive data.
- High-speed, robust data transport.
- QoS support.
- Scalable—from small, relatively low-speed to large, very high-speed networks.

Cons

- Small cells—greater total overhead to transmit a flow.
- Very complex, and therefore harder to administer.
- Cell loss—cells dropped when network is congested.
- More expensive than other choices.
- Evolving protocols—different ATM switches may be incompatible.
- Competition from high-speed (gigabit and 10 gigabit) Ethernet.

Within each class, ATM allows specifying the service level that the network is to provide for a particular connection—the ***Quality of Service (QoS).*** The user decides what is tolerable in terms of cell loss (from discards by the network during periods of congestion), cell delivery delay, and the degree of variation in the delay of successive cells. By carefully controlling these quantities, ATM can successfully provide transport for a large mix of data types.

ATM CONCLUSIONS ATM designers considered the drawbacks of frame relay for transporting time-sensitive data such as voice and video, and the predicament of needing different networks for different data types. They designed ATM to overcome those problems, taking advantage of significant improvements in communications hardware and transmission media. The result was the convergence of all types of data onto one high-speed network, thereby reducing overall costs and the manpower of maintaining multiple networks.

ATM uses very small fixed cells that can be processed rapidly by ATM switches, thereby avoiding delays caused by queue buildups at the switches. The connection-oriented virtual path design of ATM is conceptually the same as used by X.25 and frame relay; although significant changes improved efficiency and robustness, the heritage of those techniques continued.

11.4 Summary

In this chapter, we explored wide area networks—networks that extend beyond the corporate wall—in their packet switched forms. We saw how packet switching grew as a solution to the drawbacks of circuit switching for data transmission, and how their development followed two approaches—connection oriented and connectionless. Within the networks themselves, we looked at store-and-forward and cut-through switches, next hop determination via routing algorithms, and link/node congestion considerations.

In the model architecture layer view, we examined IP at the network layer and TCP and UDP at the transport layer. We also delved into virtual circuits in their switched and permanent modes, how they are set up, and how they operate to deliver packets.

With that background, we looked more closely at the evolution of three key packet switching technologies—X.25, frame relay, and ATM. As we have done throughout this text, we followed an evolutionary progression to see not just how each technology works, but how each approached solutions to the problems of their predecessors in dealing with the demands of the time.

In the next chapter, we will focus more closely on the Internet, which makes extensive use of these WAN technologies.

END-OF-CHAPTER QUESTIONS

Short answer

1. What is a wide area network? How do packet switched and circuit switched WANs differ?
2. Distinguish between connectionless and connection-oriented service.
3. Compare store-and-forward switches with cut-through switches. What are the advantages and disadvantages of both?
4. What is the relationship between WAN robustness and delay? Illustrate with connection types.
5. Illustrate virtual circuit setup and circuit numbers.
6. What is the role of PAD in an X.25 network?
7. What are the pros and cons of X.25?
8. What are the pros and cons of frame relay?
9. What are the pros and cons of ATM?
10. How did ATM lead to network convergence?

Fill-in

1. The computers people use are called _____ systems, whereas other computer-based equipment that move data between them are called _____ systems.
2. Connection-oriented service also is called _____.
3. Three components of the fabric of a WAN are _____, _____, and _____.
4. The first standard for implementing packet switched networks was _____.
5. Frame relay packet size is _____.
6. ATM packet size is _____.
7. Maximum data rate of X.25 is _____.
8. Maximum data rate of frame relay is _____.
9. Maximum data rate of ATM is _____.
10. ATM, X.25, and frame relay all are _____ oriented based on _____ circuits.

Multiple-choice

1. Which of the following are basic WAN components?
   a. nodes
   b. switches
   c. links
   d. programs
   e. all of the above
2. A connectionless service
   a. requires a formal arrangement between the originating and destination nodes
   b. guarantees delivery
   c. requires routing decisions at each switch
   d. is also called TCP
   e. is like a telephone call

3. Best-effort delivery
   a. is a characteristic of connection-oriented service
   b. is a characteristic of connectionless service
   c. means nodes request retransmission of faulty packets
   d. starts with a sender/receiver setup
   e. none of the above

4. Packet re-sequencing
   a. is a consequence of virtual circuits
   b. is never needed for connectionless service
   c. can result from congested links
   d. occurs when the original transmission rate is low
   e. requires matching sender and receiver data rates

5. A major design goal in X.25 was
   a. high reliability
   b. low latency
   c. fast transit
   d. backward compatibility
   e. all of the above

6. Packet size
   a. is fixed at one size in all frame relay networks
   b. is fixed at one size in all X.25 networks
   c. is fixed at one size in all ATM networks
   d. cannot vary between X.25 networks
   e. all of the above except a

7. Frame relay
   a. requires virtual circuit service
   b. has more packet overhead than ATM for large flows
   c. is better for streaming video than ATM
   d. performs significant error correction
   e. none of the above

8. ATM
   a. requires virtual circuit service
   b. has more packet overhead than frame relay for large flows
   c. is better for streaming video than X.25
   d. performs no data error correction
   e. all of the above

9. Virtual circuit identifiers are needed
   a. to route packets on a connectionless service
   b. to distinguish flows on the same physical path
   c. to keep flows synchronized
   d. for packet re-sequencing
   e. to operationalize UDP

10. The actual number of virtual circuits supported on an ATM network is
    a. 2^{28}
    b. 2^{24}
    c. dependent upon the speed of the switches
    d. dependent upon the capacity of the physical transmission path
    e. determined by the cell size

True or false

1. Packet switched WANs made their mark in voice communications.
2. Packet switched networks provide both connection-oriented and connectionless services.
3. For proper operation, a cut-through switch needs large buffer memory.
4. In a virtual circuit, the connection is dedicated, not the route.
5. To connect to an X.25 network, both a DTE and a DCE are needed.
6. The X.25 interface is based on virtual circuits.
7. X.25 copied the physical, data link, and network layers from OSI.
8. Frame relay networks focus on error correction and recovery.
9. The ATM cell is always 53 bytes, excluding a 5-byte header.
10. X.25, frame relay, and ATM all are versions of datagram service.

Exploration

1. Search the Web for X.25 service providers. How many did you find? What do they offer? Where are they located? What conclusions can you draw from your findings?
2. Search the Web for frame relay service providers. How many did you find? What do they offer? Where are they located? What conclusions can you draw from your findings?

3. Search the Web for ATM service providers. How many did you find? What do they offer? Where are they located? What conclusions can you draw from your findings?

CASE MAKING A BUSINESS CASE FOR BROADBAND

For a company seeking a high-speed broadband WAN link, the two major options are circuit switching and packet switching. How would you make a business case for moving on each option? What do you see as the critical success factors for each?

THE MOSI CASE, CONTINUED

In Chapter 10, "Circuit switching, the telcos, and alternatives," you investigated MOSI's options for circuit switched broadband connections to five area hospitals so that placement requests can be transmitted and confirmed electronically. MOSI also wants to consider connections to a packet switched network. What are their options? Would you recommend datagram or virtual circuit service? Are either frame relay or ATM viable options? Make the business case for the one you recommend.

What do you need to know about MOSI's operations before you start your investigation? In addition to their current status, how would you take into consideration the possibility that even more hospitals may reach agreements with MOSI in the future?

Internetworking and the Internet

12.1 Overview

Simply put, an ***internetwork*** is a group of connected autonomous networks. By virtue of this interconnectivity, the group can function as a single network, and the individual networks of the group can continue to operate independently as well. Connections are made by a variety of devices, such as switches, routers, and gateways.

Different kinds of networks and even individual computers can be interconnected. Internetworks range from a local group formed by a company's internal networks to a global interconnection of networks. A prime example of the former is an ***intranet*** and of the latter is the Internet, which connects thousands of commercial, academic, and government networks and millions of nodes worldwide.

Company internets (notice the lowercase *i*) and intranets typically revolve around LANs; their interconnection simplifies data and resource sharing and network management. For connections between the networks of a company that has different geographical locations, wide area networks (WANs) come into play. The same is true for different companies that need to interconnect with each other—for example, companies that form strategic partnerships, business-to-business links, and other forms of temporary and permanent alliances. When these networks use the TCP/IP protocols, they are called ***extranets.***

The high-speed local area networks (LANs) and WANs of today have made practical the expansion of internet usage from data transmission to such wide-bandwidth-demand applications as multimedia downloading, real-time audio/video streaming, and two-way video conferencing. This has caused a tremendous surge in popularity and usage, not only on the commercial side with applications such as e-commerce, but also for the great populace of individuals who make frequent use of the Internet (notice the uppercase *I*).

Although the concept of an internetwork is relatively straightforward, creating one requires paying attention to many interrelated factors—primarily cost, reliability, compatibility, management, and security:

- **Cost** involves initial setup, ongoing fees for WAN links, technical support, and maintenance of local installations.
- **Reliability** means having the service operational when needed. This may require building in redundancies so that the internetwork can keep running in the event of various failures. It also speaks to needing some amount of flexibility so that networks can be reconfigured as necessary without major disruptions.

An intranet is a particular kind of company-owned in-house network—one that uses the same TCP/IP protocols as the Internet. Even when connected to the Internet, intranets are not accessible by the general populace and are protected by firewalls to keep them secure. Intranets are designed to be reachable only by employees who have proper authorization.

An extranet is like an intranet in that it is private, designed to be accessible only by persons with proper authorization. However, it comprises connections between the owner company and networks of participating organizations, such as suppliers, outsourcers, and the like. This enables them to communicate with the company's internal resources, typically through its intranet. Extranets commonly use public carriers for connections to the participating organizations via the Internet.

- **Compatibility** deals with being able to connect networks and devices that may be running on different media, with different protocols, and at different speeds.
- The ability to **manage** the internetwork is paramount. For company-owned internetworks, management is the province of the company.
- **Securing** internetworks is a quest that is levels of magnitude greater in scope and difficulty than securing intranets, or isolated LANs or computers. After a doorway to a company's networks is created, however protected, there always is a chance that someone will find a way to open it.

In previous chapters, we dealt with several of these issues as they pertain to LANs and WANs. In this chapter, we focus on the Internet as the premier internetwork of today. Management and security are topics large enough to warrant entire books on either subject. We cover the pertinent aspects of these topics in Chapter 15, "Network security," and Chapter 16, "Network management."

12.2 History of the Internet revisited, very briefly

The beginning of the Internet is usually traced to its precursor, the ARPANET, but a case can be made that the impetus dates back to October 1957 when the USSR launched the Sputnik satellite. Sputnik was the first artificial object to orbit the earth and, to the U.S. Department of Defense, a worrisome step that led to the creation of the *Advanced Research Projects Agency (ARPA).*

From this agency grew the *ARPANET project*, whose initial concern was interconnecting independent (mostly mainframe) computers. Later, the goal became development of a robust internetwork that would keep the military's communications flowing in the face of a variety of attacks and outages and, as importantly, also could deal with a complicated communications picture in which many incompatible networks were in play. The ARPANET created what was the basis for the Internet that followed. Interesting glimpses of the key people involved and major milestones leading to the Internet are discussed in Chapter 1, "Introduction." A more comprehensive history is at www.isoc.org/internet/history/brief.shtml.

12.3 Internet topology and access

The topology of the Internet, which comprises millions of interconnected hosts, local and wide area networks, is a pseudo-hierarchical structure based on links among different levels of *service providers*—the organizations whose nodes and links supply all the interconnections. The main hierarchy has international Internet service providers (IISPs) and national service providers (NSPs) at the top (most NSPs also are IISPs), regional service providers (RSPs) next, and local Internet service providers (ISPs) at the bottom. However, many providers at the same and different levels also connect directly to each other, bypassing traditional hierarchical form. In addition, local providers have points of presence in telephone switching offices to offer dial-up access, thus bringing some portion of the phone system into the picture. Figure 12.1 has a general view of this topology.

FIGURE 12.1

The basic topology of the Internet

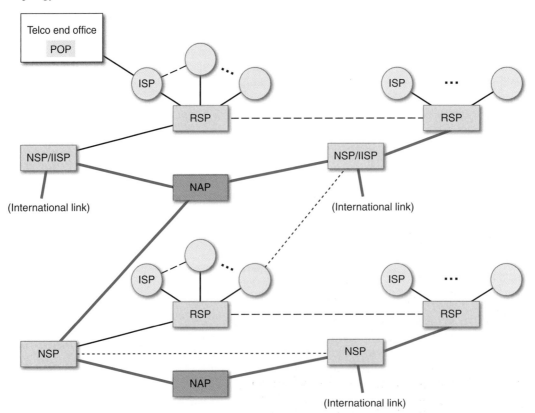

NSP: National service provider; may also provide links to other countries (IISP)
NAP: Network access point
RSP: Regional service provider
ISP: Internet service provider (local)
POP: Point of presence

We can see from the figure that the Internet has both hierarchical and non-hierarchical aspects. At the top, the NSPs form what is called the *Internet backbone,* in essence the core topology of the Internet; it extends worldwide. NSPs are private companies that own and maintain the backbone networks. The backbone shown in Figure 12.1 is, of course, greatly simplified, but it illustrates the concept—basic global interconnections are provided by the NSPs linked to each other through *network access points (NAPs)*. NAPs, also privately owned and usually by companies other than the NSPs, are switching stations, albeit quite complex ones.

As the figure shows, some NSPs also connect directly to each other, bypassing the NAPs and the hierarchy as well. To do so, the NSPs establish *peering points* in their switching offices—conceptually, these are like the POPs of the telco end offices to which interexchange carriers (IXCs) connect. NSP/IISPs also are linked to those in other countries to form a global backbone.

One step down in the hierarchy are the RSPs. They connect hierarchically to the NSPs through routers (not shown in the figure), but they also can connect through routers directly to each other. One more level down are the ISPs that hierarchically link to the RSPs and, if they are geographically close, directly to each other. Some also connect directly to NSPs, again sidestepping the hierarchy. As you might expect, the farther up in the hierarchy, the faster the links and the greater their capacity—their media are almost always fiber optic.

Individuals link to the Internet via their local ISPs. Businesses can do the same. ISPs support many connection types, including dial-up, cable modem, DSL, ATM, frame relay, and Ethernet, although not all ISPs support all types. Some large organizations can connect directly to an RSP as well.

Although this brief discussion does not fully illustrate the complexity of the backbone and its interconnections, it does contain the essence of the architecture. Suffice it to say that there are many thousands of links and interconnects in the United States alone; then multiply that manyfold to cover the rest of the world.

12.4 Internet2 and Abilene

Internet2 is a nonprofit development project of an academic, industry, and government partnership led by over 200 universities. It was formed to create advanced technologies and applications that can be adopted by the Internet, and it will eventually lead to the Internet of the future. Its formation and constituency harks back to the similar consortium that led to the development of today's Internet.

A related development is Abilene, a high-speed wide-bandwidth optical backbone network designed to support Internet2. Participating in Abilene's creation and operation are Indiana University, Juniper Networks, Nortel Networks, and Qwest Communications in partnership with Internet2.

As part of the future of network communications, both Internet2 and Abilene are discussed in Chapter 18, "The future of network communications," along with vBNS.

12.5 The World Wide Web

The *World Wide Web* (or just "the Web") is to the Internet what a database application is to a database—that is, just as the database application is one means for us to access the database, so the Web is one means for us to access the Internet—note that we're talking about an interface here, not about physical connections. (See "Historical note: How the World Wide Web evolved" for a little background.)

Web browser software has simplified the process of finding information on the Internet by providing easy-to-use interfaces to the Web. Of the variety of Web browsers on the market, the most popular are Microsoft Internet Explorer, Netscape Navigator, and Mozilla Firefox. Using a browser, we can go to millions of Web sites—collections of files (pages) organized by links among them via a structure called hypertext—comprising

HISTORICAL NOTE
How the World Wide Web evolved

The World Wide Web often is said to have its beginnings in March 1989 with a publication by Tim Berners-Lee called *Information Management: A Proposal*, in which he proposed a global system for managing and transferring information over a complex internetwork via hypertext linking. This itself was based on his earlier work with Robert Cailliau that produced Enquire, a hypertext system for sharing work among the researchers at CERN.

But it could be said that the foundation of the Web appeared 44 years earlier, when, in an article entitled "As We May Think," published that July in the *Atlantic Monthly*, Vannevar Bush described his creation, Memex (short for memory extension), a mechanical device that could make and follow links from one microfiche document to another—in effect, hyperlinking.

In any event, in 1990 Berners-Lee wrote the first World Wide Web server, named httpd, and the first client, named WorldWideWeb, a hypertext browser/editor. The program was made available on the Internet in the summer of 1991. He went on to found the World Wide Web Consortium (W3C) in 1994, whose members work to develop recommendations and standards for the Web and the Internet. Among his most valuable and providential ideas was to make his concepts freely available without royalties and to require the same of the Consortium. From there, the Web (and its underpinning, the Internet) grew by leaps and bounds to what

we know it as today; and growth has not stopped. Although many others have since played significant roles in the Web's development, it is no stretch to consider Berners-Lee the father of the World Wide Web.

End notes

Tim Berners-Lee, born in 1955, is a British computer scientist who worked at many institutions including CERN, the European Particle Physics Laboratory in Geneva, Switzerland. While there, he published his seminal work on the creation of the World Wide Web.

Robert Cailliau, born in 1947, is a Belgian computer engineer who was instrumental in many of the developments surrounding the Web and the Internet.

CERN, as quoted from the "about CERN" link on their home page, http://public.web.cern.ch/public/, ". . . is the European Organization for Nuclear Research, the world's largest particle physics centre . . . a laboratory where scientists unite to study the building blocks of matter and the forces that hold them together." It might seem odd that on its home page it also bills itself as the place "where the Web was born!" but not when you consider that Tim Berners-Lee was working there when he came up with his ideas about the Web.

Vannevar Bush, 1890–1974, was an American engineer who held a variety of positions in research institutes and governmental agencies as well as a professorship at MIT.

billions of pages. **Hyperlinks,** addresses that take us from page to page and site to site, make traversing the Web straightforward. Yet as anyone who has done so can attest, although the process is simple, finding the information you want may not be. With so many interconnections, it's easy to get lost, or at least sidetracked.

12.6 The client/server model

Client/server is a ubiquitous model in networking. The name refers to the association between entities on a network, the client requesting services and the server providing them. Although it is sometimes described as a relationship between hardware devices—as in client computer and server computer—it more accurately indicates a relationship between processes—that is, how different types of software running on network devices interact. Here are some examples:

- You request a customer record via a relational database application on your network computer. If that record is stored in a file on a network database server, your application (client) sends the request to the server's database application (server), which in turn transmits the record to your application.
- When you go to a Web site, your browser software (client) requests Web pages from the site's Web server software (server).
- You can download a file from a server on the Internet by using an FTP (file transfer protocol) client that requests the file from a server running FTP software (part of the TCP/IP protocol suite).

In any of these examples, the corresponding computers involved can be referred to as client and server machines, but the operative components are processes (software). Interestingly, an application can be both a client and a server, one time requesting services and another time providing them. This is quite common in peer-to-peer networks in which, if so set up, any device can play any role, depending on the applications involved. It happens on server-centric networks as well.

AMPLIFICATION

To reinforce the notion that client/server is a software model and not a hardware model, consider that if an application on your machine requests data that is provided by another application on your machine, the client/server model still holds. However, it is common for networked computers to be thought of as separate devices; quite typically, network servers are computers running dedicated service-providing software.

Client software requests services; server software provides services.

An important point to note is that, although client/server may seem analogous to the master/slave relationship typical of mainframe computing, there is a significant difference: Server software in the client/server model does not control the network, as is the case with master software in the master/slave model. Rather, servers and clients operate independently and are joined only in their request-response relationship.

Because these operations are software based, the client/server model provides an architecture that is highly flexible and scalable, especially compared to the older mainframe/terminal-based architectures that were the mainstay of computing before the 1980s. This is the major reason for their growth in popularity. Now, from LANs to the Internet, client/server holds sway.

There are many specific client/server architectures. Describing them is beyond the scope of this text. If you wish to pursue this topic, a good place to start is http://www.sei.cmu.edu/str/descriptions/clientserver_body.html.

12.7 The challenge of internetwork addressing

The Internet would not be the success it is without standardized protocols and procedures. Among the most important are those that resolve the location of each device. To send a message from one computer to another, the system needs to know where the recipient machine is and be able to distinguish it from among all the devices on the Internet.

As we have seen, computers on a shared medium LAN have unique physical flat addresses that make recipients easy to identify. When we move up to internetworking, flat addresses are insufficient because they do not contain any location information that tells us where a particular machine may be. Without this knowledge, the system would have to search every network that was part of the internetwork until the one containing the recipient machine was found. Given the size, activity, and growth of internetworks in general and the Internet in particular, this would take inordinate amounts of time—clearly not practical.

Internetwork addressing needs a hierarchical scheme, with at least one level identifying a particular network of the internetwork and another the physical machine address. In the Open Systems Interconnection (OSI) model architecture, the MAC sublayer of the data link layer handles physical addresses while the network layer handles logical network addresses.

The Transmission Control Protocol over Internet Protocol (TCP/IP) model architecture follows the same pattern, although the labels may be different—corresponding to the data link is the data link or link layer, and corresponding to the network layer is the network or internetwork layer. (In some references, the physical and data link layers are combined into one layer called network interface or network access.)

Hierarchical addresses

This section offers a brief review of hierarchical addresses, more thoroughly described in Chapter 6, "Communications connections."

The postal system uses hierarchical addresses, comprising ZIP codes, states, cities, streets, and names, among other identifiers. This scheme allows the post office to route mail in stages—to general areas of the country, then to more local areas, and so on to the final destination. In the same way, hierarchical network addresses comprise groupings, or segments, that allow the system to route messages to general areas, particular networks and subnetworks, and finally to the destination machine. It is the network layer of OSI, or the internetwork layer of TCP/IP, in which these addresses are constructed and with which messages are routed.

In contrast to a physical address, which refers to a particular device, a network address is logical in that it refers only to the network in which the device resides. The network address changes when the device is moved to a different network.

Here is an analogy: An automobile VIN stays with the automobile and is like a physical address. The license plate is state-specific, hence logical. If you register the vehicle in a different state, the VIN does not change but the license plate does.

12.8 Addressing in the Internet

On January 1, 1983, the ARPANET officially adopted TCP/IP as the standard communications protocol, replacing NCP (network control protocol). This was a major step toward the Internet we know today. It is why the Internet uses the TCP/IP model architecture, which groups application functions into a single applications layer and puts communications functions in the other layers. (In the OSI model architecture, the layers above transport focus on applications, whereas those below session deal with communications aspects.) See Figure 12.2.

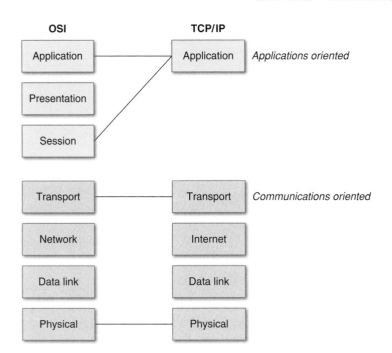

FIGURE 12.2

Model architectures

For the Internet, the ***IP (Internet protocol) address*** (which is in the internet layer), is used to identify a device. An IP address is different from a medium access control (MAC) address. The latter is a data link layer physical address of a device on a LAN. The former is *associated* with a machine, which may or may not be on a LAN, is a *logical* address at the internet layer, and may be changed without effect on the physical address.

An IP address can be *static,* assigned by a network administrator and fixed on the device until changed by the administrator, or it can be *dynamic,* assigned to a device by a protocol process when the device links (logs on) to the Interent. In the latter case, the IP address assignment is temporary and therefore likely to be different each time the device links. Dynamic IP addresses are recycled—released when a device disconnects and thus available for assignment to another connecting device.

IP addresses are used by the Internet to route packets. Even though every IP address is unique over the entire internetwork, to reach an actual device there must be a mapping of its IP address to its physical address. That is, the IP address, which after all may not remain the same, needs to be *associated* with the device's physical address. There are several protocols to do this. The most popular for the Internet are ***address resolution protocol (ARP),*** its companion, ***reverse ARP (RARP),*** and the newer ***dynamic host configuration protocol (DHCP).*** These are discussed in Chapter 13, "TCP/IP, associated Internet protocols, and routing."

AMPLIFICATION

Actually, for internal internetworks that have no connection to any external networks, IP addresses need to be unique only within their own self-contained internetwork. When they are connected to external internetworks, such as the Internet, IP addresses must be completely unique worldwide. The Internet Engineering Task Force (IETF) has set aside a number of IP addresses strictly for private internal use.

The domain name system

IP addresses used by network devices are numeric in form. As such, they have no obvious connotation to people. Alphabetic names are more meaningful and are what we usually think of when we want to visit a particular Web site, say www.icann.org, or when we send an e-mail message, perhaps to myfriend@ispconnection.com. On the Internet, the alphabetic version of an IP address is called a ***domain name.***

Every domain name and e-mail address is globally unique and has a one-to-one relationship with a unique IP address. To translate a domain name or e-mail address to an IP address, the Internet uses the ***domain name system (DNS).***

When you type a domain name in a browser's address line, the DNS translates that name into an IP address that the Internet uses to route the transmission. For example, the IP address of the ICANN Web site (www. icann. org) translated into a notation called ***dotted quad*** (dotted decimal) is 192.0.34.65. (Because computers ultimately work in bits, expressing the 32-bit dotted quad in decimal notation actually is another convenience for people.) The translation process is called *resolving the domain name.*

The same process applies to e-mail addresses. A computer program called a ***mail transfer agent*** sends e-mail from one computer or mail server to another. These agents use the DNS to find out where to deliver the e-mail.

Consider that at any given moment there are millions of Web site visits and e-mail transmissions, that domain names frequently are added, removed, and changed, and that there are billions of active IP addresses and names. Keeping track of all this, let alone translating, is a monumental endeavor. Yet when you visit a site or send an e-mail, translation happens almost instantaneously. How is this managed?

The DNS actually is an interconnected hierarchical system of high-speed servers running distributed domain name databases. When translation is needed, the system searches its databases to find the IP address associated with the name and relays it back to the device in question.

Keeping the DNS databases up to date is a huge job. To structure the process, some form of centralized organization is needed that, among other things, is responsible for distributing domain names and IP addresses and insuring their uniqueness. This requires that domain names be registered, a process that involves making an application to a ***domain name registry.*** These days, there are several registries, but in the beginning there was just one. (See "Historical note: Domain name registries.")

As you might suspect, the DNS and its operations are considerably more complex than the brief overview presented here. If you would like more information, http://www.internic.net/faqs/authoritative-dns.html provides detailed explanations without getting overly technical.

Domain names and the parts of a URL

A ***uniform resource locator (URL)*** is a symbolic means for specifying a Web resource, the Web server on which the resource resides, and the protocol that will be used to retrieve the resource. The components of a URL are separated from each other by one or more forward slashes (/), dots, and sometimes colons. To understand a URL's components, let's start with the example in Figure 12.3A. Interpreting the components is easier if we first read from right to left, then left to right.

- The rightmost segment, *.edu,* is called the ***top-level domain (TLD).*** The TLD in this example is assigned to educational institutions and is one of the original TLDs. The other five are as follows:
  - *.com* for commercial enterprises
  - *.gov* for government sites

- *.net* for organizations providing network services
- *.mil,* used by the military
- *.org* for non-profit organizations and those that do not fit the other designations

Over time, the characterizations of .com, .org, and .net blurred. Now they are referred to as **generic TLDs (gTLDs).**

The TLD concept is important for making efficient the translation of URLs into the machine-readable form used by routers and switches. Partitioning the DNS database by TLDs and distributing the partitions across different servers speeds up the process of searching the database, because each database partition is relatively small.

A. http://   www   .baruch .cuny   .edu
    protocol server name   subdomain domain top-level domain

B. http://www.baruch.cuny.edu /careers   /students   /index.htm
               directory in www   subdirectory in careers   file in students

C. http://www.uts.edu .au/
        country code for Australia

FIGURE 12.3

Domain name and URL components

- To the left of the TLD, and separated from it by a dot, is the **domain name** (also called **second-level domain**) *.cuny.* This one is assigned to the City University of New York (CUNY). The combined domain name, *.cuny.edu,* specifies a particular network, an autonomous system (AS) within the Internet. That name must be registered to ensure its uniqueness. (See "Business note: The naming quandary.") Notice that as we move to the left we go from the more general to the more specific in identifying the location of the resource.

HISTORICAL NOTE
NATO's domain name

Early on, NATO petitioned for a *.nato* TLD. For a short time, it was implemented, but it was soon replaced by *.int* for international (intergovernmental) organizations. Subsequently, NATO changed its domain name to nato.int.

- Continuing to the left, we have the **sub-domain name** *.baruch.* This narrows the location of the resource server. In this example, baruch is a subnetwork within the cuny.edu domain. (Baruch College is one of the senior colleges in CUNY.)
- To the left of the sub-domain name is *www,* the name of the server (also called a host) that holds the requested resource. Based on what we have already learned from the other parts of the URL, we can see that *www* is a server at Baruch College.

It is common practice to give the name *www* to the server that hosts Web documents, most likely because it appears to stand for the World Wide Web, but this is by no means required. Rather, it is simply a convenient symbolic name for this type of server. Here is an example of a URL without a *www* component: *http://zicklin.baruch.cuny.edu,* home page of the Zicklin Business School at Baruch College; *zicklin* is the name of a server in the *baruch* sub-domain.

The registered domain name owner is free to decide what to name servers in that domain and, in fact, what to name the subdomains. Of course, other issues apply, such as copyright infringement, trademark protection, and poaching. For example, if we register the domain name "ismine.com" and then use as a server name PepsiCola, creating *PepsiCola.ismine.com,* which is technically possible, we would undoubtedly be enjoined by PepsiCo, Inc.

Taken together, the top-level domain, the domain name, the sub-domain name, and the server name are the symbolic representation of the server's IP address. Although this completely specifies the location of the server, it does not explicitly specify the file we want that is on that server—a specific Web page. What is needed is the path on the server to the file—particular directories and the file name. This information is appended to the right of the TLD, separated from it by a slash (/). Figure 12.3B illustrates this. Here we see:

- */careers,* a directory in the *baruch* subdomain where Web files for the college's Career Development Center are stored.
- */students,* a subdirectory of *careers* where files specific to students are stored.
- */index.htm,* one of those files. The file extension .htm indicates that the file is written in hypertext markup language (HTML). You also will find the extension .html used for files of this type.

As it happens, index.htm and index.html are default file names that are automatically searched for if no file name is given. Thus, if you see a URL that ends after the TLD or after a subdirectory name, the extension /index.htm or /index.html is assumed.

Finally, the URL must inform the server of the protocol the client will use in the interaction. This is the leftmost segment of the URL. In this example, we see ***http:// (hypertext transfer protocol),*** a common Web protocol. Http defines the actions taken in response to particular requests. For example, when you enter an http URL in a browser, a command is sent to the site's Web server to download the Web page.

Http is the protocol most widely used on the Web by browsers. This protocol and others are part of the application layer of the TCP/IP suite.

In the http protocol, each command is performed independently without reference to or even awareness of preceding commands. Thus, it is a "stateless" protocol, which makes it difficult to create sites that interact with users beyond clicking on links.

To overcome this limitation, such software as Java is used to write very small text files, known as *cookies,* to the client's hard drive. The cookies contain "state" information that allows a server application to understand the sequence of http requests that make up a continuous exchange.

By itself, http does not prevent unauthorized access to the information that is exchanged during the client/server interaction. For sites such as banks that require secure transmissions, unreachable without appropriate passwords and protected from prying, an *s* is added, as in https://. This indicates that the site is secure because transmissions are encrypted. Encryption is discussed in Chapter 15, "Network security."

Another commonly employed protocol is ***ftp (file transfer protocol),*** used for uploading and downloading files to and from ftp servers. In ftp URLs, the server name typically is ftp as well, although as with www, that name is not required.

One other identifier is shown in Figure 12.3C, where we see the URL of the home page of the University of Technology Sidney. This is an example of a URL with a country identifier, here *.au* (Australia). The country designation is part of the top-level domain (.edu), though separated from it by a dot. Taken together with the TLD, here ucs.edu, this is called a ***country code top-level domain (ccTLD).*** There are over 240 ccTLDs. For a full list, visit http://www.iana.org/cctld/cctld-whois.htm.

Business NOTE | The naming quandary

As the Web has grown, so has the demand for domain names. One result is that the meanings behind the original TLDs have become somewhat diluted because they are so broadly used. To remedy this situation, seven new TLDs were proposed:

- .aero: reserved exclusively for aviation-related organizations
- .biz: for businesses worldwide
- .coop: for cooperative businesses
- .info: despite its name, an unrestricted domain under which any person, group, or organization can register a name
- .museum: for museums and related associations and professionals
- .name: personalized domain names for individuals
- .pro: for medical, legal, accounting, and engineering professionals

All are operational except .pro, which is still in registry negotiations. (For more information, visit http://www.internic.net/faqs/new-tlds.html.) It is interesting to note that the new TLDs are not restricted to the "dot and three letters" format of the original TLDs.

One quandary for new and existing companies is which TLD to use. If you already have a *.com* TLD, should you also register the same name with a .biz TLD, or if you are an airline, with a .aero TLD? Similarly, if you are a new company, which TLD makes the most business sense, or should you register with several? In either case, you may be concerned that a customer might not search on one or another and so not find you.

Another quandary is name confusion. For example, suppose your company, with the domain name xyzname.com, finds that there is another company with domain name xyzname.biz. Customers who are looking for your site may instead go to the other one. Trademarks also are at stake. Would Kleenex, which registered Kleenex.com, be happy to see another company register Kleenex.biz? To handle this and other similar issues, ICANN has established the **Uniform Domain-Name Dispute-Resolution Policy (UDRP),** which all registrars follow. (For the complete policy, visit http://www.icann.org/udrp/udrp.htm.)

Ipv4

IP addressing began with the ARPANET and went through three versions from the early 1960s until 1981, when IPv4 became the standard that is still in force. A hierarchical scheme that supported rapid growth of the Internet, it is slowly but surely reaching the end of the road.

When a two-level IP addressing hierarchy (network address/host address) was being contemplated, the question was how to split the number of bits reserved for addresses—how many for the network address and how many for the host address. This was an issue because different organizations had different addressing needs, so any one split would likely not serve most companies well. For example, a company with few hosts would not need many bits for host addresses, whereas a company with many hosts would need a lot more.

Taking this into consideration, the reasoning was that three different splits were logical:

- For the few organizations needing a great many host addresses, allocate a few bits for network addresses and many for host addresses.
- For the many more companies with many hosts, allocate more bits for network addresses but still leave many bits for host addresses.
- For the great many organizations with very few hosts, allocate more bits for network addresses and only a few for hosts.

Following this logic, three arrangements, called ***classes*** of addresses, were created.

HISTORICAL NOTE
Domain name registries

From the earliest days of the ARPANET, there was a clear need for an organized means of assigning host IP addresses to ensure their uniqueness. Initially, that task was undertaken voluntarily by Jon Postel, who gave each ARPANET host a file (host.txt) that contained the addresses of all the hosts on the ARPANET.

Soon after the system was in place, its operation was turned over to the Stanford Research Institute (SRI). Although it worked for a few years, the system did not scale well; handling growth became problematic. The solution came in 1983, when Paul Mockapetris proposed a design for the architecture of the domain name system (DNS). At that time there were about 500 hosts in the ARPANET.

The maintenance of the entire incipient Internet and the DNS stayed under contracts from the Department of Defense until 1984, when military use was split from the ARPANET and named MILNET. In that year alone, the number of hosts doubled. Within two years, the networks of the National Science Foundation (NSFNET) were made available to educational institutions; by 1990, NSFNET replaced ARPANET. A year earlier, Tim Berners-Lee had laid the foundation for the World Wide Web, and this became the spur to the rapid growth of the Internet.

Postel's task grew to be too large, so he formed the **Internet Assigned Numbers Authority (IANA),** which he headed. A division of IANA, the **Internet Registry (IR),** took over the job of name and address assignments. Tragically, Postel died prematurely in 1998.

By the fall of that year, the government concluded that a dedicated organization was needed, and so by a contract from the U.S. Department of Commerce the **Internet Corporation for Assigned Names and Numbers (ICANN)** was created to be the central registry and to deal with protocol and parameter issues for the Internet.

Over the years, in addition to its role in assigning and managing domain names and IP addresses, ICANN undertook to create new top-level domains and distribute the registration work by adding other registries. Continuing with the idea of a hierarchical organization, four **regional Internet registries (RIRs)** were created. In alphabetical order they are: *American Registry for Internet Numbers (ARIN.net)*, *Asia Pacific Network Information Centre (APNIC.net)*, *Latin American and Caribbean Internet Addresses Registry (LACNIC.net)*, *and Réseaux IP Européens (RIPE.net)*. These, in turn, have created many subregistries to handle the growing volume of work. All remain centrally coordinated to ensure domain name and address uniqueness.

End notes

Jon Postel, 1943–1998, was a computer scientist who was involved in many of the earliest and subsequent developments of the ARPANET and the Internet.

Paul Mockapetris, a computer scientist credited as the inventor of the DNS, made many contributions to the technology of the Internet. He worked on the DNS with Jon Postel.

Accordingly, the most widely used type of IPv4 is called *classful addressing.* Consisting of 32 bits arranged in the dotted quad format, it comprises three *unicast* (from one source to one destination) classes, labeled A, B, and C.

These are two-part (network/host) addresses that split the 32 bits as follows: class A 8/24; class B 16/16; class C 24/8. The splits include class identifier bits (also called prefixes) in the network address part of the split.

Two other categories were defined: D is for *multicasting* (from a source to multiple destinations), and E is reserved for experimentation. Although these sometimes are referred to as class D and class E, neither is a classful scheme.

Table 12.1 illustrates the classes and their address ranges. We see that Class A, with only 126 addresses in the network segment, was meant for the very few networks that have very large numbers of hosts. Class B has many more network addresses (16,382), each with many host addresses (65,534), and therefore was aimed at medium-size networks; Class C, with a very large number of network addresses (2,097,150) and very few host addresses for each (254), was meant for small networks. These classes account for 87.5 percent of the potentially available addresses.

TABLE 12.1   IPv4 classful addressing

IPv4 has a 32-bit address space arranged in four 8-bit sections called a dotted quad. The 32 bits are viewed as two segments, the first being a network address and the second a host address. In this table, the prefix (leftmost bits), which identifies the class and is not part of the network address, is shown in bit-notation; the other two columns show the number of addresses possible in each segment. Note that no address with all 0s or all 1s is allowed, hence the subtractions of 2. (See "Technical note: Address ranges for IPv4 networks" for more details.)

Class	Prefix	# of Networks	# of Hosts
A	0	$2^7 - 2 = 126$	$2^{24} - 2 = 16{,}777{,}214$
B	10	$2^{14} - 2 = 16{,}382$	$2^{16} - 2 = 65{,}534$
C	110	$2^{21} - 2 = 2{,}097{,}150$	$2^8 - 2 = 254$

Classes D (multicast) and E (reserved) are not segmented into networks and hosts. Class D addresses begin with 1110, and class E addresses begin with 1111; both allow for $2^{28} = 268{,}435{,}456$ addresses.

As an organizing scheme, classful addressing made sense, but it has a significant limitation—it wastes a lot of addresses. Here's an example of why: When an organization applies for an IPv4 address, it receives a network address that carries with it a block of potential host addresses whose size depends on the address class. The organization creates its own host addresses within the block.

Now suppose a company has 1,300 hosts; they would need either six class C addresses or one class B address. Six class C addresses can handle a total of 1,536 hosts (6 × 256), meaning that 236 addresses go unused. Rather than dealing with six network addresses, the company might prefer one class B address. That would make the situation much worse—because the address can handle 65,534 hosts, 64,234 addresses are unused.

All of these unused addresses are associated with the company's block(s); hence, they are unavailable to others and so are wasted. Even with the relatively few wasted class C addresses of this example, if you multiply by the millions of organizations with such addresses, the loss becomes enormous. And what about many millions of small businesses that may need only a handful of addresses?

When IPv4 was introduced, wasted addresses were not much of a concern. But the demand for IP addresses has grown by leaps and bounds along with the phenomenal growth of the Internet. This made wasted addresses problematic, hastening the day when there are no more addresses to give out. To forestall IPv4 obsolescence, ***classless addressing*** was implemented. This is discussed in a subsequent section.

TECHNICAL NOTE
Address ranges for IPv4 networks

The prefixes noted in Table 12.1 are the most significant (leftmost) bits in the 32-bit dotted quad. From these and the network/host segmentation, we can see the decimal and binary range of values in each class.

Class A uses 1 bit for the class identifier and reserves 7 bits for network addresses, leaving 24 of the 32 bits for host addresses. This would seem to give us $2^7 = 128$ network addresses, but because we do not permit an address of seven 0s or seven 1s, 126 possibilities remain. Of the $2^{24} = 16,777,216$ seeming possibilities for hosts, we again eliminate all 0s and all 1s, leaving 16,777,214. Similar calculations apply to class C.

Translating to binary, we see that the first quad begins with 00000001 (decimal 1) and ends with 01111110 (decimal 126). Because host addresses account for the rest, we can see that the entire Class A decimal range is 0.0.0.1 to 126.255.255.254. Continuing in this manner, we can construct the ranges for classes B and C.

Class	Net address range, binary	Full address range, decimal
A	**00**000001 to **01**111110	1.0.0.1 to 126.255.255.254
B	**10**000001 to **10**111110	128.1.0.1 to 191.254.255.254
C	**110**00001 to **110**11110	192.0.1.1 to 223.255.254.254
D & E addresses are not classful		
D	***1110***0001 to ***1110***1111	*225.0.0.0 to 240.255.255.255*
E	***1111***0001 to ***1111***1111	*241.0.0.0 to 255.255.255.255*

Note

Decimal	Binary	Decimal	Binary	Decimal	Binary
1	**0**0000001	192	**11**000000	241	11110001
126	**0**1111110	223	**11**011111	254	11111110
128	**1**0000000	225	**111**00001	255	**1111**1111
191	**1**0111111	240	**111**10000		

Classful addresses, networks, subnets, and masks

When a company is assigned a classful address, what it receives is a ***network ID.*** The corresponding network address is the network ID with host address all 0s. This identifies the network itself and is used by routers outside the company to direct IP packets addressed to the company. It is not assignable to any company host (recall that no host address can be all 0s).

As we've just seen, how many potential host addresses are included in a network address depends on the address class. Beyond host addresses, it often makes sense for a company to subdivide the classful network address into ***logical IP networks.*** Whereas the network address is, in essence, how the company network is known to the outside world, logical networks are how the company can organize its own hosts.

The company can create *subnets*—internal logical networks with their own subnet addresses—by assigning hosts to groups with their own subnet addresses. This adds another level to the address hierarchy—network address, subnet address, host address.

There are many ways to organize subnets: by department, by location, by building, by LAN, or some combination of these, among others. Aside from internal organization, a major advantage to subnetting is that the company can be connected to the Internet with a single IP address rather than one for each of its subnetworks. Not only is this a more efficient use of IP addresses, but it also means that an organization can have better control over how it subdivides and manages its networks.

To separate network, subnet, and host addresses, *masks* are used—bit patterns applied to entire addresses to isolate their components. Masks have the same number of bits arranged in the same dotted quad segments as the IP address, but they consist only of 1s and 0s—for example: 11111111.11111111.00000000.00000000, or in decimal notation, 255.255.0.0. Bitwise multiplication of the address by the mask (equivalent to applying the "and" operator) captures address parts where mask bits are 1 and ignores parts where mask bits are 0. Here is an example:

Address 130.57.110.9 in binary is: 10000010.00111001.01101110.00001001

Mask 255.255.0.0 in binary is: 11111111.11111111.00000000.00000000

Multiplication: 10000010.00111001.00000000.00000000

captured   *ignored*

(the network ID)   (host addresses)

Internet routers easily identify the class of an IP address by looking for the bit patterns shown in bold in "Technical note: Address ranges for IPv4 networks." When the class is identified, a *network default mask* is applied.

The three classful default masks are:

Class A: 255.0.0.0   Class B: 255.255.0.0   Class C: 255.255.255.0

In the preceding example, the two leftmost address bits are 10, a class B address. The default mask 255.255.0.0 is applied, revealing the network address (the network ID with host address all 0s):

10000010.00111001.00000000.00000000, or 130.57.0.0 in decimal notation

This network address is assigned to the edge router of the organization. When a packet reaches any router, it applies the appropriate mask. If the resulting network address is not that of the router, it passes the packet to the next hop router. (Chapter 13 explains Internet routing in more detail.)

If the network address is the router's address, a *subnet mask* is applied. This works the same as a network default mask, except that a subnet address comprises the network address with the additional bits of the subnet address appended and the remaining bits (host address) all 0s. The total number of bits in the combined network and subnet addresses is indicated by a */n* notation at the end of the address.

In the preceding example, if the */n* address were 130.57.110.9/*19*, the subnet address would be determined by the 3 bits following the 16-bit network address, in their place within their 8-bit quad. Thus, we have:

Address: 10000010.00111001.**011**01110.00001001   (130.57.110.9)

Subnet mask: 11111111.11111111.**111**00000.00000000

Multiplication: 10000010.00111001.**011**00000.00000000

(the subnet address, 130.57.96.0)

After the subnet address is defined, host addresses can be assigned. For example:

10000010.00111001.**011**00110.00001111   (130.57.102.15)

We also can see that 3 subnet bits can be used to define as many as eight (2^3) subnets within the same network address, and the 13 remaining bits in the class B address can define up to 8,190 ($2^{13} - 2$) host addresses for each subnet. If more subnets are desired, more bits can be assigned as subnet addresses. For example, with 4 subnet bits, up to 16 subnets can be defined, each with as many as 4,094 ($2^{12} - 2$) hosts. Similar calculations can be made for other numbers of subnet bits and other address classes.

AMPLIFICATION

Newer routers can handle *subnet* addresses that are all 0s or all 1s, but older routers cannot; they are restricted to $2^3 - 2$ or 6 subnet addresses in this example. Note that host and network addresses still must adhere to the "no all 0s or all 1s" rule.

Classless addresses, subnetting, and supernetting

Although subnetting makes more efficient use of IP addresses and results in fewer wasted, it would seem that the problem could be solved completely with classless addressing, because all of IPv4's address space of 32 bits would be available without restriction. That would mean that 4,294,967,296 (2^{32}) addresses could be created, or about twice as many as are available with classful addressing.

Unfortunately, it's not that simple. In order to avoid hopelessly complicating Internet routing, not to mention exceeding the capacity of the Internet routers to hold routing tables as large as would be required, some addressing hierarchy must be incorporated and restrictions must be placed on possible bit combinations. Yet there seems to be some merit to the idea, especially if there were many fewer restrictions than with classful addressing. This leads us to the scheme called *classless inter-domain routing (CIDR).*

The compromise that CIDR makes is that it allows any number of leftmost bits to be assigned as a network address. That means that this address can be allocated to organizations based on the number of hosts their networks have to support instead of being restricted to a class designation. CIDR also is not limited to network addresses (plus prefixes) of 8, 16, or 24 bits.

Currently, network addresses ranging from 13 to 27 bits are used, corresponding to addresses with as few as 30 hosts ($2^5 - 2$, because 5 bits of the 32 remain after a 27-bit network address) to those with as many as 524,286 ($2^{19} - 2$ for the 19 bits remaining after a 13-bit network address). Hence, network address assignments can be more in line with an organization's needs.

Albeit an improvement over classful addressing, CIDR is not perfect. Using our 1,300 host example, a block of 2,048 addresses is needed, which requires 11 host bits ($2^{10} = 1,024$; $2^{11} = 2,048$). The 11-bit host address space wastes 748 addresses (2,048 − 1,300) instead of 64,234, a vast improvement, though still imperfect.

SUBNETTING By employing subnetting on top of CIDR, we can improve efficiency in a way similar to what we did with classful address subnetting. To indicate the number of network address bits, CIDR appends /*n*. In the preceding example, /11 would be appended to the dotted quad. The external router mask would be adjusted accordingly.

Because network address lengths are variable, correspondingly variable subnet masks are used to separate network and host addresses. Subnetting is accommodated with CIDR in the same manner as with classful addresses. If, as in the prior example, 3 bits are needed for subnets, the /11 would be changed *internally* to /14 and the subnet mask would be adjusted accordingly.

Because of its increased flexibility, CIDR is used by the gateway routers on the Internet backbone and is expected to be used by ISP routers as well. Older routers do not support CIDR. As it stands now, the Internet is a mix of old and new. From a current business perspective, it makes sense to purchase CIDR-capable routers if replacements are needed.

SUPERNETTING   CIDR provides a hierarchical scheme that in a sense parallels subnetting but is applied to routing outside the organization and therefore is called *supernetting.* This is a method of *route aggregation,* whereby a single high-level routing table entry represents many lower-level routes. (Think of the telephone hierarchy, in which one area code represents many local prefixes, which in turn represent many individual phones.)

This means that the Internet backbone routers need many fewer entries than otherwise would be the case. Each of those entries represents blocks of addresses that can be assigned to the large ISPs that, in turn, can allocate smaller blocks to the smaller ISPs, and from there to the organizations. Supernetting eases the table size requirements of the routers at each level because they need hold many fewer entries, and it adds some degree of efficiency, as does subnetting.

Even with CIDR, supernetting, and subnetting, the Internet is running out of addresses. You may hear this predicament stated as, "the Internet is running out of domain names." That is not the case. We are sure that imagination can produce an endless supply of names. The problem is how to find numerical IP addresses to associate with those names. It is the IP addresses that are in short supply.

This foresight led to the development of IPv6, formally adopted in 2003 and expected to be fully implemented during 2008, as a replacement for IPv4. IPv6, also called IPng (Internet Protocol next generation) by some, was recommended by the IPng Area Directors of the Internet Engineering Task Force in 1994 and made a proposed standard the same year by the Internet Engineering Steering Group. Four years later, the core protocols were issued as an IETF Draft Standard.

IPv6

Several major goals were realized in the design of IPv6:

- Increasing the number of IP addresses available
- Improving routing in the Internet
- Improving authentication and privacy
- Adding quality of service capability

To increase the number of addresses, IPv6 uses a 128-bit address sequence instead of 32. Aside from adding addresses, this allows for additional levels in the addressing hierarchy that, in turn, make improved routing efficiency possible. IP header extensions are used to support several options, including address type, confidentiality, authentication, and integrity.

Quality of service (QoS) levels are achieved by labeling added to IP packets to provide for level of service requests—for example, normal handling, priority, and real-time (which labels particular packets as belonging to the same "flow" and hence to be delivered in succession in real time, as with video).

IPv6 addresses

As with IPv4, for human convenience IPv6 addresses are not referenced in bit notation, but unlike IPv4, instead of a dotted quad there is what we may awkwardly call a coloned octal (eight segments separated by colons) with each segment comprising two bytes, resulting in a 128-bit address (8×16).

Each of the segments typically is written in hexadecimal rather than decimal notation. (Hexadecimal is a base 16 number system.) Because one hexadecimal digit represents 2 bytes, an IPv6 address still has 32 characters, but they are hexadecimal characters. Further notational simplification is gained by eliminating leading 0s in a section and by using a single 0 to represent a section of all 0s. Here is an example:

A1B9:CC5F:000D:0037:FF0E:3945:0000:2A4D becomes

A1B9:CC5F:D:37:FF0E:3945:0:2A4D

If there is a single run of consecutive 0s, the 0s can be eliminated completely. For example:

BB12:0:0:0:E3CC:0:A111:7273 becomes

BB12::::E3CC:0:A111:7273

However, only one string of 0s can be eliminated in a given address.

IPv6 accommodates CIDR addressing simply by appending a /n to the address, where n is the number of bits in the CIDR prefix. To denote a 35-bit prefix in the preceding address, we would write:

BB12::::E3CC:0:A111:7273/*35*

The intricacies of IPv6 addressing are beyond the scope of this text, but let's look at the basics in comparison to IPv4.

- An IPv6 address is associated with a node's interface rather than the node itself. Each interface belongs to one node, but a node can have more than one interface, and any of the interfaces can be used as the node address. Further, an interface can be assigned more than one of any of the three IPv6 address types: *unicast, multicast,* and *anycast.*

  Unicast and multicast are the same as in IPv4. Anycast is a new type: A packet will be sent to one member of an anycast group (the closest one, where closest depends on the routing protocol being used), rather than to all members as with a multicast group.
- The 128-bit address is four times that of IPv4, but the number of possible combinations is enormously larger: 3.4×10^{38} vs. 4.3×10^{9} (2^{128} vs. 2^{32}) or almost 29 times larger. But as with IPv4, addressing is not unfettered. Rather than classes, however, IPv6 adds levels to the addressing hierarchy. This speeds routing at the cost of eliminating some address possibilities.
- The packet header is substantially simplified compared to IPv4. (See Figure 12.4.)
- QoS options have been added, with provision for 15 levels. (See Chapter 13.)
- Extension headers are defined to specify packet options, separate from and in addition to the IPv6 header. Unlike the 32-bit IPv4 options field, they do not have length limits so they can carry as few or as many options as needed. Most of these options are ignored by the Internet routers until the final destination is reached. This means that they usually do not add to the routing burden or slow down the switching process.

  The types currently provided for are: authentication for packet integrity; encapsulation for packet privacy; packet segmentation and assembly alternatives; destination options; extended routing; and hop alternatives. Each type has several possibilities.

12.9 Moving from IPv4 to IPv6

Because the differences between IPv4 and IPv6 are substantial, the Internet cannot be changed from one to the other overnight. To permit gradual cutover and to allow for variations in timing, three methods have been developed that permit functioning in mixed IPv4/IPv6 environments. These are called *dual stack, tunneling,* and *translation.*

FIGURE 12.4

IPv6 and IPv4 packet headers

Comparing the IPv6 and IPv4 packet headers, we see that the former is significantly simpler. Yet IPv6 is more flexible, has greater address space, and provides for more options via extension headers.

IPv6

IP version 4 bits	Packet priority 4 bits	Flow label 24 bits	Payload length 16 bits	Next header 8 bits	Hop limit 8 bits	Source address 28 bits	Destination address 128 bits

IP version: IPv6 is backward compatible with IPv4; this section indicates which is being used.

Packet priority: Fifteen levels; the higher the level, the higher the priority.

Flow label: Used to number, and therefore identify, packets that are part of a given "flow." These are handled specially by the routers, providing real-time delivery capability.

Payload length: The number of bytes in the packet following the header; this allows lengths of up to 65,536 bytes to be specified (2^{16}).

Next header: The type of the header in the overall packet immediately following this header — allows for extension headers. (If an extension header is used, it goes between the transport header and the IP header — by noting the next header within the packet, this field indicates whether an extension header is inserted — see below.) If there is no extension header, then is the type of the header in the transport layer: namely, TCP or UDP.

Hop limit: Each time a node forwards the packet, the hop limit is reduced by one. If the number reaches zero, the packet is discarded.

Source address: Where the packet originated.

Destination address: Where the packet is to be delivered, unless source routing is used, in which case it is the address of the next hop router.

Total IPv6 header length is fixed at 320 bits (40 bytes). However, up to six extension headers can be added.

With no extension header

Layer 2 header	IPv6 (layer 3) header	Layer 4 header

With one extension header

Layer 2 header	IPv6 header	Extension header	Layer 4 header

IPv4

IP version 4 bits	Header length 4 bits	Diff svcs 8 bits	Total length 16 bits	ID 16 bits	Flag 3 bits	Seg offset 13 bits	Time to live 8 bits	Protocol 8 bits	Header chksum 16 bits	Source addr 32 bits	Dest addr 32 bits	Options 32 bits

Header length: The number of 32-bit words in the header — allows calculation of the header end, necessary because the number of options is variable. With no options, the header is 160 bits, the minimum header length.

Differentiated services: To specify how the IP datagram is handled (class of service for QoS). This was the Type of Service field before IntServ and DiffServ QoS.

ID: To identify packets into which the original IP packet was segmented.

Flag: Indicates whether the packet was segmented.

Segment offset: Place marker for reassembling the segments.

Time to live: Counter to prevent packets from cycling around the Internet; formerly specified in seconds, now a hop count.

Protocol: The protocol used in the data field of the packet.

Header checksum: Interestingly, some header values may change at each packet switch; if so, checksum must be reset.

Options: Allow for specifying a limited number of options; seldom used.

Dual stack

The word *stack* refers to the IP protocols used by the network nodes—routers and hosts. Dual stack nodes contain the stacks for both IP versions. Before sending a packet, the sender queries the DNS system for the destination address: If an IPv4 address is returned, an IPv4 packet is sent; if an IPv6 address is returned, an IPv6 packet is sent. (See Figure 12.5A.) When the changeover to IPv6 is complete, the IPv4 stack can be deleted.

FIGURE 12.5

Transitioning from IPv4 to IPv6

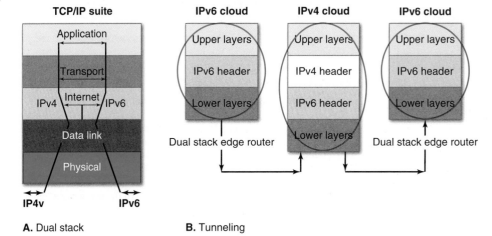

A. Dual stack B. Tunneling

One drawback of this method is that each of the dual stack nodes must have an IPv4 address, which means that the IPv4 address scarcity is not alleviated until the changeover is completed. Another is that processing through the two stacks adds to switching time.

Tunneling

A packet from an IPv6 node or region of IPv6 nodes (also called a cloud) may have to travel across an IPv4 cloud or node to reach another IPv6 node. The edge IPv6 router at the IPv6/IPv4 cloud border must give the packet an IPv4 address.

To maintain the integrity of the IPv6 packet, the router encapsulates it into an IPv4 packet; at the IPv4/IPv6 border, the IPv4 edge router decapsulates the packet. In effect, an IPv4 tunnel is created through which the IPv6 packet can travel in the IPv4 cloud. (See Figure 12.5B.) For this to work, the edge routers must be dual stack, but the others need not be.

This method avoids having to assign IPv4 addresses to IPv6-only nodes within a cloud, but it has the drawback of additional processing at the borders.

Translation

If an IPv6-only host needs to transmit to an IPv4-only host, the latter will not understand the packets. Tunneling will not help, because after the encapsulating header is removed, the IPv6 packet remains. At the least, the edge router has to convert the IPv6 header into an IPv4 header. This can get considerably more complicated if the processes running on the end node involve the IP protocols themselves.

Many countries are involved in IPv6 development and deployment. For further information, see http://www.ipv6forum.org/.

12.10 Summary

We began by defining internetworks (internets) and intranets. Company internets and intranets commonly comprise interconnected LANs. The Internet, on the other hand, the largest of the internets, goes far beyond the corporate domain, with global reach and linkages among every type of network. The growing availability of broadband connections has made multimedia, real-time audio and video streaming, and two-way video conferencing a practical reality, even for individuals in their homes.

We looked at the topology of the Internet and found a pseudo-hierarchical structure, with high-speed backbone providers (NSPs) linked to regional providers (RSPs) that in turn are linked to local providers (ISPs), but we also saw direct links between providers at each level that skirted the hierarchy. For businesses, the key factors to assess in choosing vendors and service providers to establish internetworks are cost, reliability, compatibility, management, and security.

We explored the World Wide Web (the Web), saw how it evolved, and examined its relation to the Internet. Then we looked at the client/server model, ubiquitous in networking, where we noted that it actually is an association between processes, not hardware—client software requests services, whereas server software provides services.

Next we examined the components of URLs and looked at addressing issues. We delved into IPv4 addressing, including classful and classless addresses, subnetting, and supernetting. We saw how addresses are handled by the domain name system and how the growing inadequacy of IPv4 has led to IPv6. Last, we examined the options for moving from IPv4 to IPv6.

In the next chapter, we will look more closely at a number of the protocols of the TCP/IP architecture and at the ins and outs of Internet routing.

END-OF-CHAPTER QUESTIONS

Short answer

1. Describe and contrast internets and intranets.
2. How do cost, reliability, compatibility, and security factor into creating an internetwork?
3. Illustrate and discuss the topology of the Internet.
4. What is the Web and how does it relate to the Internet?
5. Describe the client/server model.
6. How does internetwork addressing differ from LAN addressing?
7. What is an IP address? How is it used?
8. What is the function of the domain name system?
9. Describe the parts of a URL.
10. What are the advantages and drawbacks of classful addressing?

Fill-in

1. An _____ is a group of connected autonomous networks.
2. The _____ was the basis for the Internet that followed.
3. _____ are user interfaces to the Web.
4. _____ are addresses that take us from page to page and site to site.
5. _____ requests services and _____ provides services.
6. A _____ address has no location information.
7. To route packets properly, the Internet needs to deal only with _____.
8. The alphabetic version of an IP address is called a _____.
9. Translating a domain name into a dotted quad is called _____.
10. The original TLDs are _____.

Multiple-choice

1. NSPs connect directly to each other through
   a. POPs
   b. RSPs
   c. Peering points
   d. ISPs
   e. NAPs

2. Addresses that take us from page to page and site to site are called
   a. IP
   b. Hyperlinks
   c. ISPs
   d. Multilinks
   e. Domain names

3. The client/server model refers to a relationship between
   a. hardware devices
   b. software processes
   c. peers
   d. controllers
   e. domains

4. Internetwork addresses must be
   a. flat
   b. recursive
   c. hierarchical
   d. integrated
   e. bipolar

5. IP addresses are
   a. in the transport layer
   b. in the data link layer
   c. in the internet layer
   d. part of the MAC address
   e. always static

6. Every URL
   a. is globally unique
   b. has a many-to-one relationship with an IP address
   c. must be registered
   d. is independent of the domain name system
   e. all of the above

7. The 32-bit IPv4 address
   a. allows for 2^{32} unique addresses
   b. must use classful addressing
   c. always begins with a host address
   d. is more efficient than an IPv6 address
   e. has six classes

8. Class A, B, and C IPv4 addresses
   a. are based on allocations to host and network addresses
   b. exclude subnetting
   c. waste many addresses
   d. do not allow for addresses created by a company
   e. eliminate the need for masks

9. A major goal of IPv6 is
   a. avoiding the need for routing in the Internet
   b. better authentication and privacy
   c. eliminating QoS
   d. increasing the number of IP addresses available
   e. b and d only

10. The IPv6 packet header
   a. is more complex than the IPv4 header so as to accommodate added functionality
   b. is designed to handle flows
   c. eliminates hop counts
   d. reduces the IPv4 payload length limit to speed transmission rate
   e. all of the above

True or false

1. NSPs form the Internet backbone.
2. Abilene is intended to support Internet2.
3. IPv4 is running out of domain names.
4. Every domain name must begin with www.
5. Moving IPv4 to classless addressing is all we need to do to avoid running out of addresses.
6. Multicasting is provided for under both IPv4 and IPv6.
7. The more host addresses allowed for, the fewer network addresses available.
8. Masks consist only of 1s and 0s.
9. Edge routers can make use of subnet addresses.
10. CIDR allows any number of leftmost bits to be assigned as a network address.

Exploration

1. Investigate your school's IP addresses. Are they IPv4 or IPv6? If IPv4, what class? If IPv6, are extension headers used? What are your department's host addresses? Is subnetting used? What masks are in place?
2. Compare the dual stack, tunneling, and translation methods for moving from IPv4 to IPv6.

Can you think of situations in which each would be preferable?
3. Visit four company Web sites. Identify each component of their home page URL's links one and two levels down from their home page. At least one of the four should be located in a country other than your own.

CASE   IP MIGRATION

The Bigger is Better Corporation (BiBc) began operating with four LANs and 300 hosts. For Internet access, they acquired two Class C IPv4 addresses. As the company grew, it added LANs and hosts; now it has 3,100 hosts in 35 LANs. To accommodate Internet access, they released their Class C addresses, replacing them with one Class B address. Now they are contemplating two possible changes to improve flexibility: introducing subnetting and moving from IPv4 to IPv6. What factors should they consider in deciding which option to choose? For the move to IPv6, which transition method would you suggest?

One IT employee suggested that rather than taking either step now, BiBc should wait a few years until IPv6 is more widespread, and then move to it. Do you agree? Which of the three possibilities do you think is the one to choose? Would you change your mind if you also learned that BiBc is contemplating merging with the Much Bigger Corporation (MBc), an international organization with over 50,000 hosts worldwide? Why or why not?

THE MOSI CASE, CONTINUED

MOSI has been looking at various WAN strategies to interconnect their three sites, and to provide links for their feeder hospitals as well. They are considering throwing the Internet into the blend of WAN services they already contract for. However, they are unsure of how to go about evaluating their options. In particular, they do not feel ready to move to IPv6, but they do not know if an IPv4 classful address or a classless address makes more sense. Should subnetting be considered as one of the decision factors?

What questions would you ask to help you advise MOSI? Should they consider other options as well? What advice would you give them?

CHAPTER 13

TCP/IP, associated Internet protocols, and routing

13.1 Overview

The Transmission Control Protocol (TCP) and the Internet Protocol (IP) were originally developed to support the nascent ARPANET. As the ARPANET grew into the Internet, so did the number and variety of protocols that define the actions and procedures on which it runs. The resulting suite of protocols came to be called TCP/IP, which also is the name of the five-layer Internet model architecture.

We looked at the development of the Internet and TCP/IP in Chapter 12, "Internetworking and the Internet," and others, and we have compared it to the OSI model architecture. In this chapter, we will focus on particular protocols of the suite, where they come into play, and how they operate.

We consider the TCP/IP architecture to be a five-layer model, of which the top three layers (application, transport, and internet) are most common in the Internet. In practice, the bottom two layers (data link and physical) can draw from a variety of protocols, much as the often-used OSI model does (discussed in Chapter 1, "Introduction," and Chapter 9, "Local area networks"). As far as TCP/IP is concerned, it makes no difference.

Dozens of protocols are defined within the TCP/IP model; we will explore the more prominent ones found in the top three layers. These are listed in Table 13.1.

TABLE 13.1   Major TCP/IP protocols

Layer 3: Internet

IP; ARP and RARP; DHCP; ICMP; IGMP

Layer 4: Transport

TCP; UDP

Layer 5: Application

HTTP and CGI; FTP; SNMP; SMTP, POP, and IMAP; Telnet and SSH; VoIP; H.323

Visit http://www.protocols.com/pbook/tcpip1.htm for a full list of TCP/IP and OSI protocols.

TCP and IP are protocols. The term TCP/IP refers to both a suite of protocols and a model architecture.

13.2 Layer 3 (internet/network) protocols

IP

Node-to-node communication between two directly connected devices is handled by the data link layer. One step up is node-to-node communication in which the nodes are not directly connected. (See "Technical note: Clarifying some terminology.") This is the province of layer 3, the internet layer, wherein we find *Internet protocol (IP)*. One of the core protocols, IP primarily is concerned with layer 3 addressing and routing for datagram packet transmissions. (See "Technical note: Why IP addresses?")

TECHNICAL NOTE
Clarifying some terminology

The terms *node* and *host* sometimes are used confusingly when speaking of networks in general and the Internet in particular. The basic distinction is that a node is any device on the network, whereas a host is an end user device, which is one type of node. Switches and routers are other examples of node types.

We can distinguish among node types by the layers at which they operate. Hosts, as end user nodes, generally need to be able to run the entire protocol stack, hence layers 1 through 5 (in the TCP/IP model). Switches and routers, which are concerned with sending packets along particular routes, never run end user applications and therefore do not need to go above layer 3 (network).

For two directly connected nodes, layer 2 (data link) is sufficient because no routing is required. Hence, we have nodes that are layer 2 switches. When intermediate devices come between two communicating nodes, layer 3 is required, so we have layer 3 routers and the so-called layer 3 switches. When end-to-end services are needed, layer 4 (transport) comes into the picture, a particular case of host-to-host.

In some references you will find three communications categories, called node-to-node (layer 2), host-to-host (layer 3), and end-to-end (layer 4). This is somewhat misleading. More accurate, although admittedly more cumbersome, is directly connected node-to-node (layer 2), node-to-node connected through intervening nodes (layer 3), and host-to-host where the hosts are end points of the communications (layer 4).

Routing deals with switching decisions—that is, where to send the packet next on each step of its journey. The total path from source to destination is a series of *hops*—each hop is a direct connection between two switches. Because any switch is likely to have a number of next hop possibilities—one connection to each of its immediate neighbors—the question is, how are next hop decisions arrived at?

TECHNICAL NOTE
Why IP addresses?

Recall that the Internet comprises a great number of *autonomous* (independent) interconnected networks. There is no requirement for any of them to use a particular addressing scheme. Organizations tend to use the technology that best suits them. Hence, there are many different addressing structures in play in the vast Internet.

It is not reasonable for a node in one autonomous network to know and be able to handle the addressing schemes of the nodes in all the other networks it may communicate with. Even if we assume that they do know and can interpret every scheme, it would take an inordinate amount of memory and processing time to route a packet.

Clearly the Internet would not be able to operate under those conditions. Instead, what is needed is a common addressing scheme overlaid on whatever other scheme is used. As it happens, all participants in the Internet agree to use IP addressing as that overlay.

Routing decisions for IP packets typically are made on a local neighbor basis. That is, the decision is based on some neighbor-performance metric and not what happens beyond. However, for local decisions to make sense, the ultimate destination must be known. Otherwise a series of local choices could result in endless loops or branches from which the destination node cannot be reached. That means that IP packets must carry full destination addressing information.

Another view of this is that what makes a next hop choice best depends on the conditions at each of the neighboring switches. But their conditions depend on those of their neighbors, and so on down the line. So it could be argued that local next hop decisions, in effect, are global.

Whichever way the decisions are viewed, IP routing is very flexible. For any router, the next hop choice can change from moment to moment according to network conditions. For example, packets can be routed around links that are down or congested.

There are many IP routing algorithms for path determination. One way to categorize them is as belonging to one of two general classes: *link state* and *distance vector.* Link state algorithms are concerned with conditions between a router and the possible next hop routers—that is, the state of the links; distance vector algorithms look at possibilities for the total path from source to destination. Both base hop decisions on some form of distance measure, where distance can be cost, time, number of hops, and so on. Within each category there are many different specific algorithms. Four popular ones are discussed in section 13.5.

A detailed discussion of routing algorithms is beyond the scope of this text. If you wish to pursue this topic, a good source is http://www.cisco.com/univercd/cc/td/doc/cisintwk/ito_doc/routing.htm.

ARP and RARP

For IP networks in general and the Internet in particular, knowing a host's IP address, which is a logical address, does not mean that its address within the network is known; similarly, knowing an address within a network does not mean that the IP address is known. Converting or relating one to the other is called *address resolution.*

AMPLIFICATION

Quite often, the address of a machine within a company network is a physical hardware address—the MAC address on the NIC of the machine—when the network in question is a LAN, which usually is the case. However, it is possible that the machine is not a LAN device—for example, it is on an ATM network—in which case its address is logical, but still directly associated with the machine. In either situation, address resolution is required to relate an IP address to the machine address.

Address resolution protocol (ARP) converts a given IP address into a machine address; *reverse address resolution protocol (RARP)* converts a machine address into its associated IP address. Actually, ARP and RARP can resolve any of the internet layer addresses, not just IP addresses. So ARP can be looked at as translating layer 3 addresses into layer 2 (usually MAC sublayer) addresses, whereas RARP translates layer 2 addresses into layer 3 addresses. Because of the fantastic volume of traffic on the Internet, their most common use involves IP addresses. ARP and RARP packets use the same header, shown in Figure 13.1.

Bits:

ht 16	pt 16	hal 8	pal 8	oc 16	sha 32	spa 32	dha 32	dpa 32

FIGURE 13.1

The ARP header

ht: Hardware type—the hardware interface (Examples: Ethernet, ATM, frame relay, fibre channel)
pt: Layer 3 protocol type (Example: IP)
hal: Hardware address length—number of bytes
pal: Protocol address length—number of bytes
oc: Operation code—the packet's purpose (Examples: ARP request, ARP response, RARP request)
sha: Layer 2 source hardware address (Example: Ethernet MAC address)
spa: Layer 3 source protocol address (Example: an IPv4 address)
dha: Layer 2 destination hardware address
dpa: Layer 3 destination protocol address

ARP converts IP addresses to their associated machine addresses; RARP converts machine addresses to their associated IP addresses.

ARP and RARP come into play to dynamically discover the requisite addresses. When a host or Internet router needs to find a machine address, it sends an ARP broadcast request packet that contains its own machine and IP addresses and the IP address of the destination. Because IP addresses are unique, only the destination device will see its own address and will send an ARP response packet with its machine address back to the source. Hosts and routers build their IP/machine address tables in this manner, so the next time the host can simply look up the address.

DHCP

To carry out the process of assigning host IP addresses and other transmission parameters to the devices in an autonomous network, *dynamic host configuration protocol (DHCP)* is employed. Dedicated DHCP servers run the protocol software. Although "dynamic" is part of its name, there actually are three address allocation schemes: manual, automatic, and dynamic.

- **Manual address allocation.** IP-machine address associations are manually entered into the DHCP server table by a network or server administrator. A host whose machine address is in the table is given its tabled IP address when logging on to the network. Only those hosts with table entries will get IP addresses and be fable to log on successfully.
- **Automatic address allocation.** Instead of entering specific IP addresses, the administrator enters an address range. The first time a host logs on, the DHCP server permanently assigns to it an address within the range. Because only the range is entered, the administrator's job is easier.
- **Dynamic address allocation.** This scheme is similar to automatic except that, instead of a permanent address assignment, an IP address is assigned every time a host logs on, so it is likely to be different each time; in some setups the IP address is changed at various time intervals during a logon session. Dynamic assignment considerably eases administrator work where there are frequent host changes, which is typical of large business networks. Dynamic allocation also is commonly used by ISPs for dialup connections, because permanent address assignment does not make sense—such assigned addresses would be unavailable to anyone else, even when those hosts were not logged on.

In addition to host IP addresses, DHCP servers also send what are called *TCP/IP stack configuration parameters* to the hosts. Examples of these are subnet masks, IP addresses for various servers, printers and other network devices, and default routers.

ICMP

For hosts to be informed of problems with their transmissions, messages must be transmitted to them by the parties discovering the problems. There also must be a means of transmitting actions to be taken in response. The following are examples:

- A router informs a host that the destination of a packet is unreachable.
- A host is told by a router to slow down its rate of packet transmissions (called *source quench message*).
- When a router decrements a packet's hop count to zero, a "time to live exceeded" message goes to the original sender.

The mechanism for doing these and similar functions is the *Internet control message protocol (ICMP).*

ICMP messages are embedded in IP packets. The two major parts of a message are a *type number* that indicates the kind of message and a *code number* that indicates the specific message within the type. For example, the "destination unreachable" message is type 3; code possibilities include 0 (network unreachable), 1 (host unreachable), and 2 (protocol not supported). Some types are just single messages: Source quench is type 4 and code is 0. Perhaps somewhat ironically, because these are layer 3 datagram messages, their delivery is not guaranteed. ICMP versions match IP versions. Thus, for IPv4 there is ICMPv4; for IPv6 there is ICMPv6.

IGMP

Although the abbreviation is similar to ICMP, the *Internet group message protocol (IGMP)* is quite different. IGMP is the mechanism that supports IP multicasting, providing temporary "host group" addresses, adding and deleting members from a group.

To form a multicast host group, each member is given the same IP address—an IP datagram with that address goes to all members of the group. The group may be temporary or permanent. Members of a temporary group receive a temporary multicast address. Members of a permanent group receive a permanent multicast address. *Note that these are in addition to the normal unique IP host addresses.* A host can belong to more than one group. Hosts do not need to belong to a group to send it a multicast message, but they do need to belong to a group to receive one.

13.3 Layer 4 (transport) protocols

TCP

Transmission control protocol (TCP) is one of the main protocols of the Internet and, as noted previously, was first developed along with IP to support packet transmissions over the ARPANET.

TCP is connection oriented, guarantees end-to-end packet delivery, guarantees correct ordering of segmented (fractionalized) packets, and can provide reliable delivery for datagrams, thus overcoming the limits of "best effort delivery" provided by layer 3.

On transmission, TCP divides messages that are too large for IP to handle into segments and numbers them so that correct ordering can be achieved at the recipient. Transmission requirements may dictate that a long message be divided into separate segments. Because of variable delays over a wide area multi-path network such as the Internet, or because some segments may be damaged and require retransmission, the segments comprising a message might not arrive at the receiver in the same order as they originally were transmitted. For the receiver to reconstruct the message properly, the original sequence of segments must be reconstructed.

For reliability, TCP end receivers send acknowledgments back to the sender. If an acknowledgment is not received within a given amount of time, the packet is presumed not delivered and is re-sent. Packets with checksum failures are not acknowledged and eventually are retransmitted. TCP also has a number of mechanisms for flow control, chief among which is sliding window (discussed in Chapter 7, "Digital communication techniques").

TCP works quite well for reliable data transmission. However, for applications that depend on speedy packet delivery in steady streams, TCP can be problematic. One problem is slow-down due to router processing requirements. Another is that if a packet from a segmented group is lost or proves defective, subsequent packets are withheld from the application until a replacement is received—a necessity for guaranteed proper packet order. All this means that for real-time, streaming audio or video, or voice transmission, TCP does not do. For those applications, dropped packets are less of a problem than halts waiting for retransmission. This brings us to UDP.

AMPLIFICATION

*S*treaming means transferring data in such a way that it can be processed as a steady, uninterrupted flow. If data are received at a faster rate than necessary for processing, they can be buffered at the receiver and processed as needed. But if the delivery is too slow or not steady, the flow will be interrupted and the result will not be smooth.

UDP

UDP (user datagram protocol) is the second of two protocols available at the TCP/IP transport layer. Whereas TCP is a reliable protocol, UDP is not; TCP is connection oriented, and UDP is *connectionless.* Although TCP may be the more familiar protocol, UDP is no less important or useful.

UDP handles the *segments* of a transmission at the transport layer in a way that mirrors how IP handles *datagrams* at the IP layer; that is, it treats each segment as independent of any other segment and provides no flow or error condition processing. Just as we saw that datagrams are packets at the IP layer that are sent without prior connection setup, unlike TCP, UDP also does not set up a connection between the end parties prior to transmission. Thus, UDP is a *best effort* delivery service: Neither delivery nor packet ordering are guaranteed.

Eliminating those mechanisms makes UDP significantly faster than TCP. Therefore, it usually is more appropriate where timeliness is more important then error processing or where lost datagrams are not an issue. For example, in SNMP, a lost datagram is simply replaced later by more up-to-date data. In addition to streaming applications, UDP is used for name/address retrieval in the DNS, for carrying Voice over IP (VoIP) packets, and for many online games. (UDP and TCP are discussed further in Section 13.6.)

A consequence of UDP being connectionless is that an application cannot hand UDP a large file and expect UDP to divide it into appropriate sized segments, each with a sequence number for reassembling the file. Therefore, only applications that generate small messages or files that match the size of one user datagram should use UDP as the transport protocol. This does not preclude the use of UDP for sending large quantities of data. It simply means that UDP is appropriate for use with applications that inherently generate data as individual small units. For example, even though we may think of streaming video as a very large file, it is actually composed of individual *video frames* that can fit into single datagrams.

What, then, does UDP actually do? The answer is, very little. Its one main function is to add a transport header to the data segment that contains the destination and source port addresses. Together with the destination and source IP addresses added by IP, they form the destination and source sockets, respectively, that serve to uniquely identify the processes that are engaged in a communication session.

13.4 Layer 5 (application) protocols

HTTP and CGI

We are most familiar with *hypertext transfer protocol (HTTP)* as the leftmost part of a URL (http://) that indicates the protocols (service) being used on the Web page. It is most commonly used to view Web sites and to retrieve a variety of data types from a Web server. Http only describes how the browser and Web server interact with one another and the format of the messages they exchange. Http uses the services of TCP and IP to actually move data between the browser and the server. Specifically, http at the Web server operates over the well-known TCP port 80.

Although http contains the word *hypertext* in its name, it is quite capable of dealing with a wide variety of data types that have nothing to do with hypertext, including video and mp3 files. Http was, however, tailored to the needs of hypermedia, in which frequent interactions with the server are needed as the user clicks from link to link. By specifying the data type in the http message header, http can transport any data type. As long as the client has the appropriate software, say to view an image or run a video, the data can be acted on. Software for a particular data type may be part of a standard browser or integrated into a browser via a plug-in. It also may be installed separately and associated with the data type, invoked automatically when that type is downloaded.

Http is *stateless,* meaning that each request is treated without any reference to previous requests. It also is *connectionless,* in that no connection is maintained between client and server after the request is carried out. Interactions between client and server are by request/response messages: The client issues a request to the server, and the server responds with the appropriate data.

The client does not know how the server obtained the requested information, nor does it care. This allows for some flexibility in how the server responds to client/browser requests. For example, a common browser request is to see a particular Web page. Web pages are generally constructed using HTML and are *static* in nature. That is, the content does not change in response to any external conditions such as the time of day or the identity of the user.

Yet it often is convenient or necessary to construct a Web page on the fly—for example, when a user request requires access to a database or when the response depends on the results of a calculation. These are *dynamic* Web pages. Accessing a database or producing dynamic Web pages requires running a server-side program. This is where the ***common gateway interface (CGI)*** comes into play.

CGI defines how a Web server can supply input information to a program it is running, how the program must return its results to the server, and how a dynamic document is to be constructed as a result. CGI is independent of any programming language. It simply defines an open standard that allows Web servers and server-side programs to interact. The programs themselves can be written in any programming language that supports the CGI standard. Thus, CGI comes into play whenever there is a dynamic interchange between a user and the Web server. Examples include database access requests, forms processing, online games, and user-specific Web page delivery.

FTP

File transfer protocol (FTP) establishes rules for transferring data between an ftp server and a client. You can *download* a file from an ftp server, and you can *upload* a file to an ftp server. In this respect it is similar to http, but there is a major difference: With http, you can interact with the data, but ftp is strictly for data transfer. Ftp is used to download large data sets where the receiver is interested in the data but not concerned with presentation.

In many instances, you need a password to log on to an ftp server before you can move data in either direction. However, many ftp servers have public directories that anyone can access by "anonymous" logon. In either case, transfers can be initiated by line commands, but most often small graphical user interface programs are used, because they are much simpler, more convenient, and do not require any knowledge of ftp commands.

SNMP

Simple network management protocol (SNMP) is designed to assist in managing networks remotely by enabling monitoring and controlling of network nodes, collecting performance data, and administering cost, configuration, and security measures. SNMP is implemented on a network device by a software module. Remote management, especially in large networks, is accomplished via a *network management system (NMS)* that utilizes SNMP's protocols and features. An NMS is a hardware/software combination that aids in network management using data provided through SNMP. Network management is discussed in Chapter 16.

SMTP, POP, and IMAP

Simple mail transfer protocol (SMTP), post office protocol (POP), and ***Internet message access protocol (IMAP)*** all deal with e-mail. E-mail clients, software for sending, receiving, and organizing e-mail, utilize SMTP, POP, and IMAP. There are many such clients. Some, such as Eudora, are standalone programs; others are integrated into software suites, as exemplified by IBM's Lotus Notes; still others are part of an operating system, as is Microsoft's Outlook Express.

SMTP handles *sending* e-mail. When you connect to the Internet to send e-mail messages, your client software uses your connection provider's SMTP server to send your messages. (See "Business note: An e-mail complication.")

POP and IMAP handle *receiving* e-mail. POP is a very simple protocol that downloads e-mail to the inbox of your computer's e-mail client. You can set it up to leave e-mail on the server even after it is downloaded, or not. Other manipulations depend upon your e-mail client. POP comes in several versions, the latest of which is POP3.

IMAP, a much more comprehensive alternative to POP, also is considerably more complex; version 4 is the latest. Here are some of the capabilities of IMAP that POP does not have:

- Multiple clients can connect simultaneously to the same mailbox.
- Clients can utilize and manipulate multiple mailboxes and folders on the same server, including renaming, transferring e-mail among the mailboxes, and access to public (shared) mailboxes.
- Clients can initiate searches of e-mail on the server in addition to local (inbox) searches.
- Clients can operate in a "connected" mode, whereby the connection to the server is maintained. POP, by contrast, typically disconnects as soon as e-mail is downloaded and reconnects for the next download request. IMAP response, therefore, is more rapid.

POP is the most common protocol for receiving e-mail and is almost always what is used in homes, small businesses, and for remote connections to company e-mail. IMAP is most often found in large networks where employees need ready access to company e-mail systems. For a given client, you use either POP or IMAP, not both. Which one to use depends on the e-mail servers you are working with.

Business NOTE   An e-mail complication

If you have a business e-mail address that you also use off-site, it is common practice that you must use your own ISP's SMTP server, rather than that of the business, to send e-mail. In principle, this has to do with offloading externally created e-mail transmission from the business server. Some ISPs will not allow you to send e-mail if you use a "from" e-mail address different from what you get from the ISP, even though you can receive e-mail to that different address. This can complicate the business on-site/off-site e-mail scenario.

Telnet and SSH

Telnet originally was designed to emulate a computer or terminal connected to a mainframe via a phone line (the name is an abbreviation of *telephone network*) so as to make it appear as though a direct connection was in place. Another of the client/server software protocols, it was widely used for command-line login between Internet hosts and for execution of various line-by-line commands. But because telnet sessions are not encrypted, they are vulnerable to hacking. As a result, telnet is being replaced by *secure shell (SSH),* which provides encrypted communications between two hosts over unsecure networks, such as the Internet.

VoIP

Voice over Internet protocol (VoIP) is designed to carry voice over packet switched IP networks. We usually think of it as telephone calls over the Internet, but the methods apply to any IP network, including those internal to a company. The precursor of today's VoIP dates back to 1973, when *network voice protocol (NVP)* was used experimentally to carry voice over the ARPANET. VoIP is discussed further in Section 13.8.

H.323

H.323 is part of a group of standards (H.32x) that cover multimedia communications over a variety of network types. Originally designed to handle multimedia communications over LANs, which have no inherent quality of service (QoS) capability, it has been put forth by the ITU-T as an expanded *Recommendation* to include such communications over any IP network, the Internet included. Because vendors whose products comply with H.323 can be assured of interoperability, it has grown considerably in popularity.

AMPLIFICATION

The International Telecommunication Union is an organ of the United Nations. ITU-T is the telecommunications standardization sector of the ITU. Standards published by the ITU-T are called Recommendations (the R is always capitalized).

13.5 Internet routing

Packets on the Internet must find their way from source to destination; most often this involves traversing many switches, routers, and even whole networks. Various schemes are employed to determine which path (route) from among the many possibilities a packet should take. As discussed earlier, procedurally this is called *routing,* and each step along the way is called a *hop.*

Implicit in this definition is that there is some choice involved in moving a packet through an internetwork—that there are alternate routes between source and destination. We saw that such choice requires layer 3 addresses. Protocols that support such addresses are called *routing protocols.* Some, typically those that broadcast messages, are not choice dependent—because the packets must go to all in the broadcast list, there is no routing choice.

There are many routing protocols and techniques and many ways to categorize them. Whichever ones are used, routers routinely use *lookup tables* that indicate where to send each packet next. These tables cannot be global, because to contain all the possible routes through the Internet they would have to be gigantic, and even if they could be accommodated, they would have to be continuously updated across the entire Internet, which would generate enormous traffic loads. Therefore, methods have been developed that require much less information for any given table.

Within these techniques, tables can be *static* or *dynamic.* Static tables are created and maintained manually by administrators and are sensible only for small networks where changes are rare. In dynamic routing, tables are created and maintained by the routers themselves, using information carried by special routing packets and periodically sending out control packets providing or requesting addressing information updates. This is typical of the Internet, where routing also depends on whether the IP addressing scheme is classful or classless. (See Chapter 12.)

Here are some categorizations:

- Routing may be ***predetermined*** or determined ***on the fly.*** Predetermined routes are selected in advance for a particular group; each packet of the group follows the same path through the Internet—a connection-oriented virtual circuit approach. This contrasts with on the fly, in which each packet's next hop is determined individually at each router—a connectionless approach.
- A commonly used routing tactic in the Internet is called ***next hop routing.*** A table needs to contain only those entries that tell a router where to send a packet next; it neither needs nor has information as to ultimate destination, complete paths, or even the hop beyond the next one. Yet each next hop moves the packet on its way to its final destination. This approach considerably reduces routing table size because, in the scheme of things, there are far fewer next hops from any given router than if other addressing information had to be included.
- The router table for ***network-specific routing*** has a list of layer 3 addresses from which to choose in making a routing decision. A similar technique is ***host-specific routing,*** in which host addresses are tabled. However, this is used only in very restricted routing scenarios and not for general Internet routing because, as noted, it is not feasible to maintain tables with all Internet host addresses.
- We saw that routing techniques can be classified as ***link state*** or ***distance vector:*** the former apply to next hop routing and the latter to full path routing. Link state protocols make use of various link metrics (see the next section) in making a next hop decision; distance vectors rely on total trip hop counts. An exception is the ***interior gateway routing protocol (IGRP),*** a Cisco protocol that uses a combined metric of link delay (latency) and bandwidth.
- One of the most useful ways to categorize the algorithms that carry out routing protocols is as ***interior*** or ***exterior,*** which raises the question: What defines interior and exterior?

  In this context, it is instructive to consider the Internet as comprising many independent networks and independent self-contained groups of networks—for example, the private networks of an organization. These are called ***autonomous***—they operate and are managed *independently* and are in the *interior* of (internal to) the organizations. (In fact, different autonomous networks within an organization need not be running the same protocols.)

  Routing protocols used within autonomous networks, also called autonomous systems, are known as ***interior routing protocols,*** also called ***interior gateway protocols (IGP).*** The mechanisms that implement them are interior routing algorithms. Connections between two autonomous networks are made by routers at the network edges, called border or edge routers. Because they go outside each individual network, they are external to them. Hence they use ***exterior routing protocols,*** also called ***exterior gateway protocols (EGP),*** implemented by exterior routing algorithms. This extends to connections among many autonomous systems.

  Now let's look at the most popular protocols for each.

Interior routing

OSPF   The most popular of the interior routing protocols, especially for large networks, is *open shortest path first (OSPF).* This is a link state next hop technique that typically uses Dijkstra's algorithm to determine the next hop. (For an algorithm definition and links, see http://www.nist.gov/dads/HTML/dijkstraalgo.html. You can find Java applet demos of the algorithm at http://www-b2.is.tokushima-u.ac.jp/~ikeda/suuri/dijkstra/Dijkstra.shtml.)

The basic idea is that the next hop whose "distance" is shortest is the one to choose. What makes this algorithm so flexible is that distance can be defined in many ways. For example, for each next hop choice: If link cost is used, then shortest path becomes least cost path; if the inverse of link speed is used, then shortest path becomes quickest path.

Other metrics include the inverses of link load, link delay, bandwidth, and reliability. Of course, this amounts to local optimization and so does not guarantee that the total trip will be "shortest," but the algorithm is simple to implement and next hop choice can be made very quickly. It also enables routers to route around problem links. OSPF2 is the latest version for IPv4; for IPv6 there is OSPF3.

RIP   Not as popular as it once was, *routing information protocol (RIP)* is a dynamic distance vector method based on hop counts. It still is quite common for the smaller of the autonomous systems noted earlier. The Bellman-Ford routing algorithm used in the early ARPANET is still used for RIP. (For details on Bellman-Ford, see http://www.laynetworks.com/Bellman%20Ford%20Algorithm.htm.)

In some implementations, Dijkstra's algorithm is used instead. In essence, each router creates a table that lists every network within the system that it can reach and how many hops it takes to do so—these are the distance vectors. Routing decisions are based on minimizing hop counts.

Although RIP works well in small autonomous systems, it does not scale well because the routing tables grow rapidly and because the vectors must be refreshed frequently to keep pace with changes; the larger the table, the greater the refresh traffic and update work.

Another problem for large networks is a drawback of all distance vector techniques: Hop counts are not always the desired way to route packets. For example, the smallest hop count path may include links with large latency, low reliability, high cost, and so on. This usually is not a major concern within small autonomous systems, but it is quite important for the Internet. The latest version for IPv4 is RIP2, and for IP6 it is RIPng.

Exterior routing

BGP   *Border gateway protocol (BGP)* is the major exterior routing protocol of the Internet—the one most likely to be used in border routers to interconnect autonomous systems, including ISPs and NSPs, to route packets among them. BGP is the only current exterior protocol that can effectively handle internetworks the size of the Internet. It also supports CIDR (classless inter-domain routing—see Chapter 12).

BGP also can be used as an interior protocol, as is done in some very large corporate networks. To distinguish uses, BGP used within an autonomous system is called IBGP (interior BGP), and EBGP (exterior BGP) when used between systems. In common usage, BGP by itself means EBGP.

When two autonomous systems are running different protocols, their border routers provide the translation services necessary to make the connection work. Typically, for example, an organization will have a gateway connecting it to the Internet—that gateway is likely to be a border router running BGP. The latest BGP is v4, which supports both classful and classless addressing.

BGP tables are based on *path vectors,* which are similar to distance vectors but with a major difference: Distance vectors are hop count based; path vectors are *policy based.* This means that factors other than or in addition to hop counts can be incorporated by the network administrator, who can require that particular metrics be used in path determination.

Usually these metrics are based on particular business policies, hence the name *policy based.* For example, path selection can be based on the protocol used in the packet's data field, or certain paths can be specified to be used or avoided depending on the relative locations of the source and destination. This requires that in addition to the next hop, router tables also contain the paths to the destination router—the path vector.

13.6 UDP and TCP revisited

We have seen that the internet layer deals with packet delivery between nodes that are not directly connected, whereas the data link layer handles directly connected nodes. Not accounted for by these two layers is *process-to-process* communication—that is, between two applications running on different hosts that are end points in a communications chain (end-to-end). This is the responsibility of the transport layer in general and TCP in particular.

Two main delivery protocols come into play:

- TCP, complicated but reliable
- UDP, simple but unreliable

To know which to use, we need to know what *reliable* and *unreliable* mean. The straightforward answer is that a reliable service guarantees delivery and an unreliable service does not. Generally speaking, the Internet is unreliable at the internet layer because IP is an unreliable service. So:

- When reliability is not needed, IP and UDP are used.
- When reliability is needed, IP and TCP are used.

A major consideration in the design of any internetwork is how to handle flow, congestion, and error control—at each hop (point-to-point) and/or at the end points (end-to-end). Flow control prevents a sender from overwhelming a receiver by sending data too fast for it to process. Congestion control deals with "traffic jams" that can occur at any node in an internet, such as when a router fed by many links experiences heavy transmissions from those links. Error control is concerned with discovering and correcting faulty packets.

As the ARPANET was evolving into the Internet, these design issues were at the forefront. The conclusion favored minimal control at the hops, where routing takes place and where no addressing information above layer 3 is needed, and overall control at the end points, where layer 4 addressing is required to identify the end hosts. That is why at the internet layer we have IP as the protocol for packet forwarding and at the transport layer we have TCP, which was given the responsibility for end-to-end delivery.

Finding the delivery target—ports and sockets

Host-to-host delivery needs just one identifier (that of the host), but because any host is likely to be running several processes at the same time, process-to-process delivery needs two identifiers—one for the host the process is running in and one for the process itself. The host identifier is its IP address, and the process identifier is a *port number;* taken together, they form a *socket address* or, simply, a *socket.* (We say that the IP address and a port number are *bound* together to form a socket.)

TECHNICAL NOTE
Ports and sockets

Every host has two kinds of ports: physical (hardware) ports, to which devices are attached, and virtual ports, which are numbers that keep track of processes. For an Internet connection, the socket is a virtual identifier, the virtual connection to a process running in a host. It is a combination of the (virtual) port number and the IP address (also virtual). A hardware port is simply where a cable or wireless transceiver is plugged in to the host, and it is not related to addressing.

Ports are given two-byte numbers and therefore have possible values of 0 to 65,535. These are divided into three ranges defined by IANA. Port numbers from 0 to 1,023 are assigned to specific processes; these are the so-called *well-known ports.* Here are some examples:

For UDP:	69 TFTP (trivial file transfer protocol)
	161 SNMP
For TCP:	20 FTP
	23 Telnet
	25 SMTP
	35 DNS
	80 HTTP

Port numbers from 1,024 to 49,151 are not assigned, but their use must be *registered* to avoid duplication. Ports 49,152 to 65,535 are neither assigned nor registered; as the so-called *dynamic range,* these can be used by any process.

SOCKETS IN ACTION   Sockets are created by the processes that need them. In doing so, a process specifies the address domain (which for us is the Internet) and socket type (datagram, stream, or raw). Datagram sockets read an entire message transmission as it is received—they use UDP; stream sockets view transmissions as character (byte) streams and use TCP; raw sockets are used by applications such as ICMP that communicate with IP directly without the TCP or UDP—raw sockets are not supported by every service provider.

To communicate with each other, processes must have the same type and domain so that their sockets are compatible.

To make a request, the client (source) must know the address of the server it needs, but before the server receives a request, it does not know or need to know that the client even exists. Therefore, for the server to address a reply appropriately, the request packet must carry a source port number, which becomes the destination port of the reply. TCP makes use of port numbers to create a connection. Now let's see how this works.

In the discussion that follows, keep in mind that uniqueness is maintained by sockets—the binding of port numbers to IP addresses. Although we speak of ports, it is the sockets that ultimately come into play. The TCP connection is between the sockets defined at each end of the transmission (the client and the server, or the local host and the foreign host).

To communicate, a host application opens (defines) a port and then uses it to send data from it and look for data delivered to it. Because at any moment there can be thousands of processes running on various client hosts sending packets to a server, each client is free to select port numbers at random from the *dynamic range* to identify each of its processes. However, in most instances server port numbers cannot be random—that is, if the port numbers that a server associates with a process also are random, clients would not know what number to use.

Within an autonomous network, there is no restriction on port numbers—any numbers can be used as long as they remain local to that network. Under other circumstances, such as for experimentation or to restrict access to selected users, the well-known port numbers are not used. However, applications that are to be available to anyone and that use popular protocols such as http and ftp must use their well-known port numbers.

Server ports, then, generally are from the well-known predefined range. For example, a client can be running multiple browser copies and will associate a different random port number with each, but the server always will be using port 80 for http requests.

With this background, let's investigate UDP and TCP further.

TECHNICAL NOTE
Is it multiplexing or is it not?

Ports allow many client processes to run over a single end-to-end connection, the packets of each process being properly identified by their sockets. Some references call this **transport layer multiplexing,** in which they say several client process packets are multiplexed by their port numbers. The packets also carry server port numbers, which is said are used to demultiplex by sending each process's packets to the appropriate server port.

A more straightforward definition of multiplexing is combining several low-speed transmissions into a high-speed stream, or splitting a high-bandwidth channel into several lower-bandwidth subchannels. The common element here is simultaneous transmission, actual (as with FDM and WDM) or virtual (as with TDM and STDM).

UDP

As we saw, UDP is an unreliable connectionless transport service. Packets are not numbered and may be delivered out of sequence, late, or even not at all. Further, there is no provision for acknowledgments. All this makes UDP sound rather useless, but the upside is that it is very simple, fast, and has little overhead (see Figure 13.2).

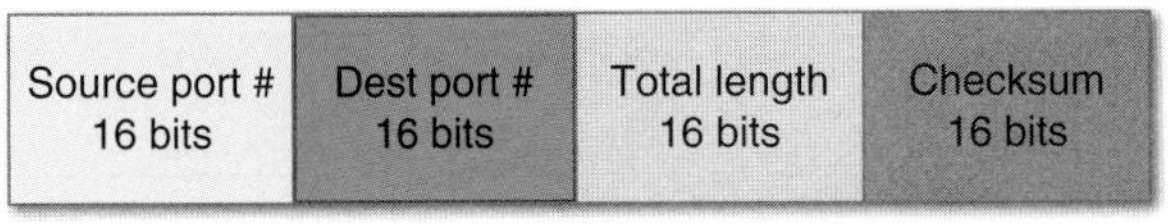

FIGURE 13.2

The UDP header

Source port # 16 bits	Dest port # 16 bits	Total length 16 bits	Checksum 16 bits

Port numbers: 16 bits can hold values from 0 to 65,535, which is why IANA port number designations have that range.

Total length: The number of bytes of the total datagram, hence 0 to 65,535.

Checksum: An optional field; if used, the server can determine whether a packet is erroneous. This does not mean that a message is sent back to the source.

Applications that do not need reliability can use UDP, as can applications that themselves provide flow and error control, because they don't need the transport (TCP) services to duplicate their efforts.

TCP

As a reliable, connection-oriented transport service, TCP is the opposite of UDP. A connection is established in a three-step process called a three-way handshake:

1. Host 1 (say, the client) sends a connection request packet to host 2 (say, the server). Included is a random sequence number used to rule out duplicate packets and to learn whether a packet is lost.
2. The server sends a confirmation packet to the client that carries another random sequence number for the same reason and often information about the connection as well. (Sometimes a separate packet is sent for the latter purpose.)
3. The client confirms receipt and the connection is considered established.

Connection termination happens separately in each direction. For example, the client sends a termination packet to the server, which is acknowledged. This ends the connection from client to server but not from server to client, which the server can keep open to send packets to the client. (Note how this differs from a physical connection, in which, when either party breaks the connection, it is terminated for both.)

On the sender side, TCP is handed data by the applications layer, divides it into appropriately sized segments, adds its header, and sends to the internet layer where it is encapsulated in an IP datagram. At the receiving end, sequencing, acknowledgments, and error control are exercised by that host's TCP, which eventually sends error-free properly sequenced packets up to its application layer.

Sequence numbers and acknowledgments also are used for sliding window flow control. Figure 13.3 shows the TCP header. Compare this with the UDP header in Figure 13.2.

Error control

Error control is explored in Chapter 5, "Error control," and Chapter 11, "Packet switched wide area networks." To reprise briefly here, we note that TCP error control relies on checksums, acknowledgments, and timeouts. Acknowledgments are sent by the receiving end for successfully received error-free packets or groups of packets, but no notice is sent for missing or erroneous packets. Instead, the sender sets a timer for each packet transmitted. If an acknowledgment is not received before it times out, the sender assumes retransmission is required, and so sends the packet(s) again.

Congestion control

Congestion is a function of queuing at the Internet routers. A packet arriving at a router is queued in an input buffer where it waits for one-at-a-time processing. After processing, it is queued in an output buffer where it waits for transmission to its next hop. The entire process, from input arrival to output to next hop, is called *forwarding.*

FIGURE 13.3

The TCP header

Source port 16 bits	Dest port 16 bits	Seq # 32 bits	Ack # 32 bits	Hdr len 4 bits	Rsvd 3 bits	ECN 3 bits	Ctrl 6 bits	Window size 16 bits	Chksum 16 bits	Urgent pointer 16 bits	Options 0 to 352 bits

Port numbers: Values from 0 to 65,535, as in the UDP header.

Sequence number: For ordering packets.

Acknowledgment number: For the return message.

Header length: The number of 32-bit (4-byte) words in the header (TCP headers always are multiples of 32 bits); serves as a data offset that indicates where the data that follows the header begins.

Reserved: Set to 0.

Explicit congestion notification (ECN): An optional field; set to 0 if not used. ECN attempts to avoid congestion before it gets out of hand. Details are beyond the scope of this text.

Control: Each of the 6 bits signals a different control condition.

Window size: For sliding window flow control.

Checksum: For error detection.

Urgent pointer: If set, points to the sequence number in the last byte in a segmented group of urgent data.

Options: Each option must begin at the start of a byte; padding (0s) must be added to insure that the TCP header is a whole multiple of 32 bits.

It is the nature of queuing systems that when the arrival rate (into a queue) is low compared to the service rate (processing and transmission), the queue remains small. But as the arrival rate approaches the service rate, the queue builds up rapidly; when the arrival rate equals or exceeds the service rate, the queue becomes infinite in very short order. Picture traveling on a highway with heavy but moving traffic. Then there is an accident that closes one lane. Very quickly, traffic backs up for miles.

When packets arrive at a router at a rate close to its processing speed, the incoming buffer will quickly fill up. Subsequent packets will be discarded—the incoming link is congested. A similar situation can occur in the output buffer. There, delay in transmission is due to congestion on one or more of the next hop links. As congestion increases, throughput decreases.

AMPLIFICATION

Throughput is the amount of data received in a given amount of time, often expressed in bits per second or, for particular networks, packets per second. Because packet sizes are not constant from system to system, or even within many systems, bits per second is a better measure for comparison purposes.

Router congestion results when the packet arrival rate approaches or exceeds the router's forwarding capability—hence, the links connected to the router are congested. By extension, network congestion results when the network load (number of packets in process) approaches or exceeds the network's processing capability.

There are several methods for dealing with congestion. They can be classified by when they are applied: before buildup causes congestion (preventive control, or avoidance), and after congestion occurs (remediative control, or recovery).

To a large degree, controlling congestion means controlling flow. (We saw node-to-node flow control in action in Chapter 7.) The principle is that by controlling flow, you control congestion. Before the fact, flow control attempts to prevent buffer overflow by anticipating a problem; after the fact, it attempts to reduce input so the router can catch up with the demand.

Flow control alone is not always sufficient. For example, if a router drops a packet, the sender will retransmit it; if there is delay in the network and an acknowledgment is late (past the time out), the sender will retransmit it. Both these scenarios mean added traffic on the network—more load that can lead to more congestion, which means more retransmissions, and so on.

TCP deals with congestion by extending the sliding window concept. Instead of the window size being set solely by the receiver, congestion is accounted for by the sender. The result is two possible window sizes: the receiver window and the congestion window. The sender uses the smaller of the two. A commonly used method allows the sender window size to build up rapidly to a point, then grow slowly until a timeout occurs, after which the window is quickly reduced. Subsequent timeouts cause further reductions.

Here is an example. When a TCP connection is first established, the sender window is set to the maximum packet *segment* size—the size of the TCP packet, header plus data, that is sent to the internet layer for IP encapsulation. As part of connection establishment, the sender and receiver agree on a segment size.

The window size is doubled when the packet is acknowledged, doubled again for the next acknowledgment, and so on for each successive acknowledgment—an exponential rate of growth by which window size increases rapidly. Oddly, this process is called *slow start.*

When the *threshold* window size—the maximum window size allowed, also agreed on at connection establishment—is reached, the window is increased by just one segment for each acknowledgment. This is so regardless of how many packets the acknowledgment is for. If there is no acknowledgment before a timeout, the threshold is reduced to half the last window size, the window is reset to the beginning (the maximum segment size), and the process starts again.

13.7 Quality of service on the Internet

The innate meaning of *quality of service (QoS)* for any communications system is that it provides an acceptable level of network performance relative to application need. QoS also refers to a formal contract between a business and a communications provider detailing the levels of service that will be provided, under what conditions, and at what cost. This is called a *service level agreement (SLA).* In this chapter, we will focus on QoS in the Internet. QoS for other communications systems, such as frame relay and ATM, have some similar considerations and some that are different.

For the Internet, QoS has to do with servicing packet *flows*—the packets created by segmenting a given stream of bytes from an application or process. Packets with the same source and destination sockets belong to a flow.

QoS has several components, primarily bandwidth, latency (delay), jitter, and packet loss. Related measures are reliability, sequencing, error rate, data rate, and throughput. How critical these components are to QoS depends not only on their own contribution to performance, but on what is important for the process in question.

- Bandwidth is a measure of the capacity of the system. For QoS, the issue is the bandwidth needed by an application relative to what is available in the network.

- Latency is caused by congestion, directly or indirectly. A congested router will hold packets longer; packets may take alternate longer routes to avoid congestion. When delays in a flow are variable, the packets do not arrive at the destination with the same timing they had when they were first transmitted. This is called *packet jitter* and is different from signal-level jitter, which is the result of instantaneous phase shifts.
- Packet loss occurs when packets are discarded or corrupted in their journey through the Internet.
- Reliability involves ensuring that all packets are delivered intact to their appropriate destinations. This means that corrupted or discarded packets must be retransmitted, which as we have seen can lead to extended delays in completing delivery of a flow.
- Dropped or rerouted packets from a flow are not likely to arrive in their original order. Waiting for out-of-sequence packets and processing to sequence them adds to the time until the complete flow can be delivered to the host. Even if a flow is delivered in stages, packets in the sequence that follow a missing or late packet cannot be delivered until that packet arrives.
- Erroneous packets are those that become corrupted during transmission. Reliability requires detection and correction.
- Data rate refers to the speed with which bits traverse a link or channel. A related performance measure is throughput.

Let's look at some common applications and see how these components relate to QoS:

- E-mail and file transfers should be reliable, complete (lossless), and error free, but bandwidth, latency, and jitter are relatively unimportant.
- When a browser fills a screen with a Web page, blank or incomplete areas are not well tolerated, but although they can be annoying, slow screen fills are less important. Screens usually are filled in sections rather than a full page at a time, which is not a problem. Greater bandwidth minimizes these issues.
- If you are streaming audio to your computer, latency and jitter can result in very distorted sound, but a few skips (lost packets) here and there may not be too bad. Here too, greater bandwidth yields better results. On the other hand, if you are downloading a data file, a few skips render the result useless. Although it can be frustrating to wait for slow downloads caused by limited bandwidth, it is not disabling.
- Streaming video is very sensitive to jitter and delays, which can cause artifacts, freezes, and image breakups. It requires fast throughput and significant bandwidth, especially when color is involved, so that motion appears continuous. A few dropped packets here and there may be tolerable.
- Video conferencing demands high bandwidth so that audio and video are delivered smoothly. However, it may be acceptable to have less than full-motion video as long as audio quality is high, thereby reducing bandwidth needs.
- One could say that Internet telephony (VoIP) can tolerate some small delays and a few voice disruptions because the listener can wait a bit for a reply or ask the caller to repeat the message. On the other hand, that would not be considered very good QoS, especially because VoIP service often is compared to PSTN (public switched telephone network). More problematic is jitter, which can render calls unintelligible.

Achieving QoS

There are all sorts of traffic flows on the Internet. Increasing QoS for one flow generally means reducing it for another. We know that some processes need higher QoS than others, but sometimes we must limit the tradeoff so as not to deteriorate service too greatly for the latter. Improvements in QoS can be gained by controlling its components according to what is important for the flow in question. Generally this means managing router queues, setting priorities, and controlling throughput on a policy or class basis.

PRIORITIES AND QUEUE MANAGEMENT   We saw that when a router's incoming buffer is full, subsequent packets are rejected. Because the packets arriving at the end (tail) of the queue are discarded, this is called *tail drop.* In this mode of operation, no consideration is given to the QoS needs of the packets involved; in fact, even if the whole queue contains low-service-need packets, new arrivals, high need or not, still will be dropped.

We could ease the tail drop QoS problem by establishing separate router queues, assigning packets to them by service need. But that requires more buffer space and more processing; even so, the high-need queue could fill up. A more effective method is to anticipate congestion by discarding packets from the buffer before it fills—congestion avoidance.

That is the idea behind *random early detection (RED),* which randomly deletes packets from the buffer before it fills when arrival rates are picking up. TCP's congestion window will shrink when packets are dropped, which will lower the transmission rate, reducing congestion likelihood.

RED does not address QoS directly because random discard could drop packets with any QoS need and because high-need packets still can be queued behind those with low need. To deal with that problem, *weighted RED (WRED)* is used. This selects packets to delete based on *IP precedence* (priority, service class), thus making room for arrivals with higher need while not discarding similar packets already in the queue.

The IPv4 header has a differentiated services field that carries service class parameters, and the IPv6 header has a priority field. The edge routers assign IP precedences to packets and move them into the Internet. Core routers running WRED use those precedences to manage traffic.

WRED deals with how packets get into a router queue, but not with how they get selected for service. Although deletion based on weighting increases the likelihood of higher-priority packets being in the queue, standard *first come first served (FCFS)* processing does not follow through. Instead, higher *priority first* service is needed.

Priority first can be achieved in two ways:

- By ordering the queue so that the highest priority packets are in the front and then using FCFS, or, equivalently, establishing multiple priority-based queues and taking packets from the queues in priority order
- By removing packets out of the queue in priority order regardless of where in the queue they are

In regard to processing, ordering the queue—which can be done by simple insertion techniques for each arrival—is easier and more efficient than priority removal, which involves searching the entire contents of the queue each time.

POLICY AND CLASS METHODS   As often is the case, QoS methods began as proprietary schemes; these were implemented on manufacturer's routers as added features. When QoS grew in importance as a business issue, standards were pursued. In 1997, the Internet Engineering Task Force (IETF) published the flow-based QoS scheme *integrated services (IntServ),* followed two years later by the class-based *differentiated services (DiffServ).* We summarize them next.

IntServ   A key concept in IntServ is capacity (bandwidth) reservation. Using the *resource reservation protocol (RSVP),* capacity for a given flow is requested for an entire end-to-end route before the flow begins transmitting. There are three possible classes of responses to the request, two if that capacity is available and one if not:

- **Guaranteed.** No packet loss, specified maximum delay and jitter, guaranteed bandwidth. This class requires that the capacity is available over each hop of a predetermined route.
- **Controlled.** Uses statistical time division multiplexing (STDM) to attempt to provide the same service on a heavily loaded route that would be expected on a lightly loaded route. There is no guarantee, but this class typically provides a constant level of service for a given flow. There may be some hops where bandwidth is (temporarily) less than originally requested.
- **Best effort.** Operation without reservation, as though IntServ was not in effect. No bandwidth is reserved.

Each requesting flow is assigned to a response class. Each router in the path must implement IntServ and use three output queues, one for each class. Substantial router processing is required because IntServ does not aggregate flows by response class, operating instead on individual flows.

Furthermore, routers in an RSVP route have to coordinate with each other to set up the reserved bandwidth path and must remember information about flows on that path. Hence, as the load (number of flows) increases, processing burden grows considerably—therefore, IntServ does not scale well. On the other hand, it can offer QoS guarantees to flows for which capacity is able to be reserved.

DiffServ   The primary impetus behind DiffServ was to alleviate the processing burden of IntServ. Consequently, DiffServ aggregates flows at the edge routers by type of service and marks the ***differentiated services (DS)*** IPv4 header field accordingly—the marks are called ***differentiated services code points (DSCPs).***

AMPLIFICATION

DS is an 8-bit field, 6 bits of which are used for DSCPs. The first DSCP bit is the In/Out Profile (based on data rate; packets below a predefined rate are marked In, otherwise Out—should drops be necessary, Out packets are discarded before In packets; also see RED and WRED). The next 5 bits specify service type (enough for 32 types).

The core routers need only act on a next hop basis according to the code points. They do not have to analyze flow requirements individually or keep track of flow states along a path as IntServ does. (We might say, then, that DiffServ is a stateless policy and IntServ is stateful.) With DiffServ, the majority of the processing load is at the edges rather than on all the routers in the path, which makes it readily scalable.

Based on the code points, ***forwarding behavior*** (router actions) on the aggregated flows are defined by what are called ***per hop behaviors (PHBs),*** which are loaded into the routers. This is both an advantage and a drawback of DiffServ. PHBs are described according to one or more flow requirements for bandwidth, delay, jitter, packet loss, and so on. Yet because DiffServ is per hop and stateless, it cannot guarantee a particular end-to-end QoS level as IntServ can. Despite code points, a packet still can be forwarded to a congested router and be rejected or experience excess delay. Still, the simplicity of DiffServ is appealing and has led to widespread use. Some go so far as to say that it will overtake and replace IntServ, which they say is on its last legs. That remains to be seen.

Whatever the case, the fact remains that both methods have advantages and significant drawbacks. Perhaps the future belongs to a technique that combines their best features, providing guarantees where warranted without necessitating a large processing burden. One possibility for this is a scheme called ***multiprotocol label switching (MPLS)***, originally designed as a routing protocol but increasingly being applied to QoS.

MPLS for the Internet   MPLS originally was designed to relieve the switching burden in the Internet by creating what amounts to virtual circuits. Along the way it was realized that MPLS also could be used for improving QoS. Of the main QoS parameters (bandwidth, latency, jitter, packet loss, and so on), MPLS can deal with two: latency and jitter. If appropriate bandwidth is available, latency and jitter are the most important parameters for streaming applications and fast Web response. MPLS improves the performance of these parameters by combining packet labeling with layer 2 switching and layer 3 routing. This speeds up switching across the Internet.

All the routers involved must be MPLS enabled. Those at the edge are called ***label edge routers (LERs);*** those in the Internet core are called ***label switched routers (LSRs).*** Packets reaching non-MPLS routers will be rejected as nonconforming.

TECHNICAL NOTE
When is it switching, and when is it routing?

Switching and routing are among the more confusingly applied terms in computer communications. In layer 2 and layer 3 router processing, routing is the method of determining the next hop router; switching directs the packet to the appropriate router output port—the one linked to that next hop router. (To hold the packet until it can be transmitted, there may be a single output buffer or multiple port-based buffers.) Both routing and switching are functions performed by routers.

Bits in a 32-bit MPLS header are marked (labeled) by an LER according to policies for specific applications. Then, based on the labels, the LSRs create ***forwarding equivalency classes (FECs),*** which they use to direct packets through the Internet over explicit paths called ***label switched paths (LSPs).*** Because traffic in an FEC follows a particular path, MPLS makes a good combination with DiffServ, which itself is not path oriented; MPLS adds path capability to the DiffServ QoS.

IP packet header analysis is done just once, at the LER. This too complements DiffServ, whose flow aggregation also takes place at the edge routers. The LER encapsulates the IP packet with the MPLS header, which is positioned as a prefix to the IP header. Hence, it appears to be inserted between the normal layer 3 IP header and layer 2 data link header (see Figure 13.4). Because of this, MPLS sometimes is called a layer 2.5 scheme. Once encapsulated, the packet enters the ***MPLS domain*** (the collection of LSRs in the Internet).

FIGURE 13.4

The MPLS header

Label 20 bits	CoS 3 bits	Stack 1 bit	ttl 8 bits

A. The MPLS header

Label: The MPLS label.

CoS (class of service): Carries packet priorities. Originally, it was designated as an experimental field. With 3 bits, 8 classes can be specified.

Stack: Indicates which packet is at the top of the labeled stack and which is at the bottom.

ttl (time to live): Copied from the IP ttl field.

| Layer 2 hdr | MPLS hdr (top of stack) | ... | MPLS hdr (bottom of stack) | Layer 3 IP hdr |

B. Positioning of the MPLS header

MPLS also can use RSVP to query MPLS routers to determine whether there is sufficient bandwidth on a path to support a particular flow; if the response is positive, the class of service (CoS) and labels can be assigned so the flow uses that path. This adds to the QoS capabilities of MPLS combined with DiffServ.

As you can imagine, QoS is a complex topic. If you would like to delve further, visit http://www.cisco.com/univercd/cc/td/doc/cisintwk/ito_doc/qos.htm.

13.8 VoIP

Voice over IP, also called IP telephony, is a method for transmitting voice over any IP network, of which the Internet is the most commonly used. To make VoIP practical, several issues need to be addressed:

- Customers expect VoIP to behave like a telephone call over the PSTN, which is a circuit switched service, but IP is a packet switched service, which potentially is more problematic for QoS.
- If severe enough, latency and jitter will render IP telephony unusable.
- Sequencing the packets in a flow would appear to be paramount—out-of-order packets would render the conversations unintelligible. Yet there can be no waiting for replacement packets or out-of-order packets to arrive before forwarding a completely sequenced message, because that would stop the flow. Hence, we must live with dropped packets, ignore complete sequencing, and use UDP to maintain flow.
- As with telephone calls, connect, use, and disconnect are required.

In the end, the main problem for VoIP is congestion, a traffic volume vs. bandwidth issue. If there is no congestion, VoIP calls can proceed smoothly. When congestion enters the picture, the other problems come to the fore. To handle these issues, a combination of hardware and software supported by several protocols is employed:

- Voice is digitized by an ***analog to digital converter (ADC);*** the process is reversed by a ***digital to analog converter (DAC).*** These are required at each end of the conversation.

They may be standalone devices (in one box) that a standard phone is plugged into, put on a card in a computer, or built into a digital telephone. Together the ADC/DAC is called a *codec (coder/decoder).*

- Compression techniques can be used to reduce bandwidth requirements of a flow.
- Connection-oriented communications make use of *signaling* to exchange information for connection establishment (call setup), maintenance, and termination and to provide the familiar dialing capability, ring tones, and busy signals. VoIP makes use of several signaling-related protocols to do this:
  - *H.323.* Part of an ITU-T applications layer suite of protocols (H.32x) originally designed for multimedia communications.
  - *Session initiation protocol (SIP).* Comes from the IETF and was specifically designed for VoIP. Despite its name, it handles call maintenance, termination, and the other signaling features, along with initiation. It also is used for interactive multimedia sessions.
  - *Media gateway control protocol (MGCP)* and *megaco.* The older MGCP functions within an autonomous system to make it appear as a single VoIP gateway. Physically, a *call agent* (also called a *media gateway controller*) sets up and terminates calls via a *media gateway* that converts voice to packets and back and operates during the call. MGCP provides the supporting protocols.

    Megaco is similar to MGCP. Both are gateway protocols that allow interconnection of IP and non-IP networks, such as the PSTN. Megaco has more features and can operate as a general-purpose gateway protocol.

    MGCP is detailed by the IETF in RFC 3435; megaco, a joint development by the IETF and the ITU-T, is defined by the former in RFC 3525 and by the latter in H.248.

QoS issues fall under the heading of *call transport.* As you would expect, protocols in this category are in the transport layer and deal with latency, jitter, packet loss, and sequencing. Taken as a group, they are *real-time transport protocol (RTP), real-time transport control protocol (RTCP),* and *secure RTCP (SRTCP).* RTP numbers and time stamps each voice packet so that the end host can assemble the voice packets in sequence and know if packets are lost. This is the answer to an apparent contradiction—VoIP cannot wait for packet sequencing, so assembly comprises forwarding packets as they are received, but ignoring (dropping) out-of-sequence packets. The time stamps enable sequence recognition so that only those out of sequence will be dropped.

Together with H.323 or SIP, RTP is used for "push to talk" cell phone systems as well as for VoIP. RTP utilizes UDP at the transport layer and also runs in conjunction with RTCP. The latter is a mechanism for out-of-band control data for the RTP flows, including information on the QoS parameters. SRTCP adds encryption and authentication to RTCP, useful for some multimedia applications but not generally used for VoIP.

No end-to-end transport protocol can guarantee real-time delivery, RTP included. However, RTP's timestamps, which can be used to synchronize streams, take a step in that direction and therefore have found use for real-time flow transport—for example, for VoIP. Nevertheless, it remains unreliable in the sense that it must ignore out-of-sequence packets to maintain flow and thus cannot guarantee total QoS.

Why VoIP makes business (and even personal) sense

VoIP has many compelling attributes that are contributing to a rise in popularity:

- Calls using VoIP are not tariffed (as PSTN calls are), are not subject to the government-mandated surcharges, and make no distinction between local and long distance, even worldwide. That makes them considerably cheaper than other calling services.

- VoIP requires a broadband connection, nearly ubiquitous in the corporate world and increasingly common in private residences. If the connection already is installed, VoIP can be added for very little expense.
- Incoming phone calls can be automatically routed to your VoIP device wherever you are, as long as you have broadband Internet access. This is a boon for employees who travel between corporate locations or make business trips. (Broadband access is increasingly common in hotels, often at no charge.)
- Most VoIP providers include integrated voice mail and e-mail services. Some also are capable of data transfer and video transmission during a phone call.

    Several companies are in the VoIP business. Some, such as Skype and Vonage, are free for calls between computers of their own customers. This requires only a sound card (universal in PCs of the last few years) and an inexpensive microphone, plus the provider's software, also free. They charge a relatively small monthly fee for VoIP calls from standard or digital telephones (a codec is built in to the latter and must be added to the former) to any other phone of either type or to a computer-based phone.

- Telephone companies offer VoIP, usually over their DSL links. Packages include various land line and VoIP combinations.
- Cable companies provide VoIP through their cable networks, but cable broadband is more likely to be found in homes than in the corporate world. Packages cover television service and VoIP.

Why VoIP may not make sense

With all of its many attractive features, VoIP is not yet a perfect communications system:

- Despite the various QoS techniques that are employed, VoIP still cannot guarantee QoS. When Internet loads are heavy, latency, jitter, and dropped packets can become problematic. This is especially so when satellite links are involved.
- VoIP calls will be stopped at the corporate firewall unless *session border controllers* are installed. This not only is an added expense, but it also may leave an opening that can compromise internal network security.
- There may be connection or continuity problems when a call is routed from one VoIP provider to another, because there are many proprietary systems at play.
- Conventional phone lines are powered by the phone companies, which have backup systems at their central offices. That is why phones usually continue to operate even when there is a general power outage. VoIP phones run over networks powered by the electrical companies. In a power failure, they do not work. Of course, business computers and PBXs also run on electrical company power. Backup power systems keep them running in a power failure, but these systems primarily are for orderly shutdown and, in any case, do not extend beyond the company wall.
- Emergency calls (911, called e911 on mobile phones or VoIP) can be a problem. With a land line, the 911 system automatically locates the calling address. This is not so simple on an IP network. Most VoIP providers cannot provide geographical location information, although they are working on a solution. This is less of a corporate issue than a personal one, though.

    In the end, as with all networking and telecommunications issues, whether VoIP makes sense depends on how the pros and cons trade-off in a given situation.

13.9 Summary

Two protocols, TCP and IP, were originally developed to support the ARPANET, but as it grew into the Internet, the two protocols grew into a suite of protocols called TCP/IP, which also is the name of the five-layer Internet model architecture. They have become de facto standards in the Internet. In this chapter, we explored the major protocols of the suite in relation to the architecture layers in which they reside. The layer 3 protocols are concerned with Internet addressing and address resolution, the layer 4 protocols deal with packet transport, and the layer 5 protocols handle applications support.

We saw why IP addresses, or at least an addressing system that pays attention to the challenge of internetwork addressing, as IP does, are needed. By looking at particular protocols, including ARP, RARP, and DHCP, we saw how this works. We also explored the differences between connection-oriented TCP and connectionless UDP at the transport layer, and how they relate to IP.

We discussed the ins and outs of Internet routing, including various routing protocols, looked in depth at the workings of TCP and UDP, and delved into quality of service on the Internet. This included discussions of both policy and class methods—IntServ, DiffServ, and MPLS.

Finally, we looked at VoIP, saw how it works, and discussed when it might or might not make sense to deploy.

In the next chapter, we will explore three basic categories of wireless networks—local area, personal area, and wide area—and their links to the wired realm. We also look at two wireless networks of a different sort—cellular telephony and satellite systems.

END-OF-CHAPTER QUESTIONS

Short answer

1. What is the difference between a connection-oriented protocol and a connectionless protocol? Which transport layer protocol is connection oriented and which is connectionless?
2. Http is referred to as the basis for exchanging information over the Web. Why?
3. What is a hop?
4. Why are local next hop decisions, in effect, global?
5. Contrast link state and distance vector algorithms.
6. How does dynamic address allocation of DHCP work?
7. Compare TCP and UDP.
8. How do router tables work?
9. How do interior routing protocols and exterior routing protocols differ?
10. Explain ports and sockets.

Fill-in

1. The _____ layer handles communications between two directly connected nodes.
2. _____ is concerned with layer 3 addressing and routing for datagram packets.
3. The three allocation schemes of DHCP are _____, _____, and _____.
4. Three layer 5 protocols that deal with e-mail are _____, _____, and _____.
5. Procedurally, _____ is concerned with finding paths to traverse the Internet.

6. OSPF is a _____ distance routing technique.
7. _____ is the major exterior routing protocol of the Internet.
8. Port numbers from 0 to 1,023 are called _____.
9. Congestion is a function of _____.
10. The main components of QoS are _____, _____, _____, and _____.

Multiple-choice

1. The top three layers of the TCP/IP model architecture are
   a. transport, data link, application
   b. internet, network, transport
   c. application, presentation, session
   d. transport, application, internet
   e. physical, data link, network

2. A host is
   a. a router
   b. any device on a network
   c. an end user device
   d. a switch
   e. all of the above

3. FTP
   a. is one protocol that establishes rules for transferring data between a server and a client
   b. is commonly used to download large data sets
   c. can only be accessed with a password
   d. can be used in place of http for Web page access
   e. a and b only

4. SMTP handles
   a. sending e-mail
   b. receiving e-mail
   c. sending and receiving e-mail
   d. sending instant messages
   e. sending and receiving instant messages

5. POP and IMAP handle
   a. sending e-mail
   b. receiving e-mail

   c. sending and receiving e-mail
   d. sending instant messages
   e. sending and receiving instant messages

6. SSH
   a. provides for communications over a secure network
   b. encrypts communications to send over an unsecure network
   c. sends unsecure transmissions over secure networks
   d. cannot be used on the Internet
   e. has been replace by Telnet

7. Predetermined routing
   a. means routes are determined on the fly
   b. is a connection-oriented virtual circuit approach
   c. can route around congested links
   d. is required for every packet
   e. cannot be used with packet flows

8. Autonomous networks
   a. cannot be made up of groups of networks
   b. require exterior routing protocols
   c. comprise independent networks and independent self-contained networks
   d. within an organization must use the same protocols
   e. management depends on the exterior networks they are attached to

9. Link congestion
   a. is a function of queuing at the Internet routers

b. worsens as packet arrival rate approaches router switching rate
c. can result in discarded packets
d. is handled under TCP with a sliding window
e. all of the above

10. VoIP
a. is affected by latency and jitter
b. resequences out-of-sequence packets
c. relies on TCP to control packet flow
d. is a connection-oriented service
e. is independent of bandwidth

True or false

1. TCP and IP are protocols; TCP/IP is a protocol suite and a model architecture.
2. Switches and routers need at least four of the five model layers.
3. Next hop decisions always are based on transit time.
4. ARP converts physical addresses to IP addresses.
5. With automatic address allocation, the administrator only needs to enter an address range in the DHCP server.

6. ICMP is a mechanism for hosts to be informed of problems with their transmission.
7. IGMP supports IP multicasting by providing temporary host group addresses.
8. CGI provides the rules set under which http operates.
9. Http is stateless and connectionless.
10. MPLS can deal with latency and jitter, but not packet loss and bandwidth.

Exploration

1. We state, "it could be argued that local next hop decisions, in effect, are global." Make that argument and illustrate it with examples.
2. Find three router manufacturers that are rated highly by Fortune and Forbes. Compare their offerings by type, variety, capability, protocols, and cost. Which one would you choose to provide edge routers for your company? Why?

3. How many providers of VoIP can you find? Compare services and costs for several major and minor providers. Search for reliability ratings and customer satisfaction for each one.

14

Wireless networks

14.1 Overview

Wireless communication has a long history, with its beginnings in radio transmission first demonstrated in 1895 by Marconi. In recent years, wireless computer-based networks have seen a rapid increase in growth and interest. As often happens in such a situation, there currently is a sometimes confusing mix of methods, protocols, standards, and proprietary schemes that changes daily. In this chapter, we will explore three basic categories of wireless networks—local area, personal area, and wide area—and their links to the wired realm. We also will look at two wireless networks of a different sort—cellular telephony and satellite systems.

Wireless networks employ electromagnetic waves, primarily radio waves and microwaves, to carry transmissions over the air or through the vacuum of space using antennas to transmit and receive signals. For transmission, the electromagnetic carrier is modulated to represent the data signal. On receipt, it is demodulated to extract the data. By appropriately using carrier frequencies and multiplexing, many transmissions can take place at the same time without interfering with each other.

In regard to size and span, wireless networks run the gamut from very small, short-range personal area networks to medium-range local area networks to satellite-based networks that can span the globe and reach into space. They have certain commonalities but also several differences, as do wired networks.

14.2 Wireless local area networks

A *wireless local area network (WLAN)* uses radio wave carriers to transmit signals among its nodes. Most WLANs operate in 2.4 GHz and 5 GHz bands. These, together with the 900 MHz band, are the three *industrial, scientific, medical (ISM)* bands that are unlicensed in the United States and most other countries. They are defined within the *national information infrastructure (NII)*—a collection of network types that includes radio and television networks, the public switched telecommunications network, and private communications networks. The ISM bands are referred to collectively as *U-NII,* the *U* denoting "unlicensed." (See "Technical note: The radio spectrum.") WLANs typically share the networking burden with their wired counterparts, enhancing them by providing flexibility and mobility for connecting users to wired networks, especially in the world of business.

In addition, WLANs offer:

- Easy creation; no cables need to be pulled, and WLANs can be connected wirelessly to wired LANs
- Access to corporate networks in places where wiring is not feasible or is overly costly
- Simple connection, usually automatic, for spontaneous participation
- Within range, mobility and unconstrained physical configuration

Of course, there are drawbacks as well. Among them are:

- Possible interference from electromagnetic radiation in the relevant ISM bands
- Potential for eavesdropping and security breaches
- Limited data rates compared to wired networks
- Incompatibilities due to the number of proprietary schemes in the market

AMPLIFICATION

As stated on their Web site (http://www.fcc.gov/aboutus.html), "The Federal Communications Commission (FCC) is an independent United States government agency, directly responsible to Congress. The FCC was established by the Communications Act of 1934 and is charged with regulating interstate and international communications by radio, television, wire, satellite and cable. The FCC's jurisdiction covers the 50 states, the District of Columbia, and U.S. possessions."

The FCC issues and can revoke licenses for use of particular ranges of the communications spectrum. Since 1994, it has generally held auctions whereby organizations bid for licenses. In some recent instances, notably giving digital channels to analog TV stations, the bidding process has not been used.

If you would like to learn more about the FCC, visit http://www.fcc.gov.

WLAN topology

The fundamental structure of a WLAN is called a *basic service set (BSS)*. The minimum BSS has two stations. Computers in a WLAN, which can be any combination of mobile or fixed units, are called *stations.* Some make a fine distinction between a mobile station and a portable station: The latter can be moved from place to place within range of the WLAN but is stationary when operating; the former can operate while moving. A fixed station does not move at all.

A BSS can be an independent standalone LAN, as can any LAN, in which case its stations can communicate only with each other—this is called an *independent basic service set (IBSS,* or an *ad hoc network).* Figure 14.1 illustrates an IBSS that also includes a server. An IBSS does not need a dedicated server, although it can have one or more. Without a server, it operates as a peer-to-peer LAN. This is analogous to LANs in the wired world.

FIGURE 14.1

A WLAN IBSS

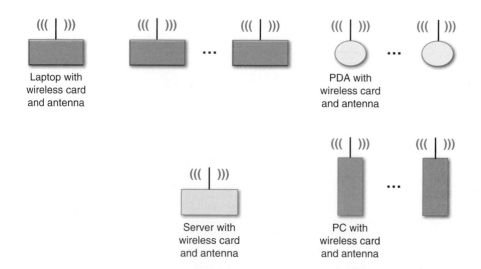

A BSS can include an *access point (AP)*—a node connected wirelessly to the BSS stations and by wire to the organization's wired networks through a LAN or backbone. Without an AP, the BSS is isolated (its stations cannot communicate with any outside the BSS), which may or may not be desirable.

When a group of people who can come to a common meeting place need to share information with each other on a temporary basis, an IBSS makes sense, especially if they all do not have access to each other's machines through the company's networks. Still, a more common practice in business is to set up a BSS to include at least one AP. This enables mobile users to connect to corporate networks while operating wirelessly in the BSS; at the same time, it does not impinge upon the freedom of BSS participants to come and go at will (see Figure 14.2).

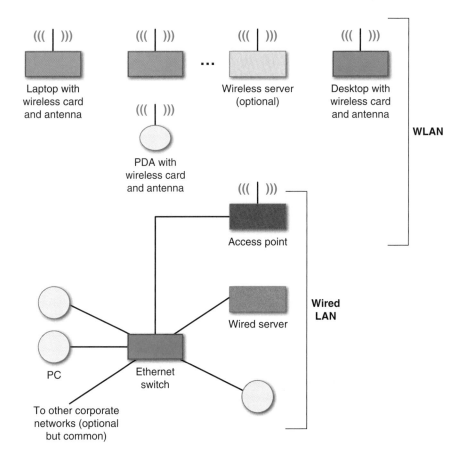

FIGURE 14.2

A WLAN BSS with an access point

An AP makes the BSS part of the organization's infrastructure; hence, such a BSS is called an ***infrastructure BSS.*** (Usually, when the term BSS is used, it refers to an infrastructure BSS. We have already used IBSS to mean an independent BSS.) An AP also can connect to another local AP, to broadband via DSL or cable modems, or to corporate WAN links via routers, thus extending the reach of the BSS.

Neither BSSs nor IBSSs need servers. If they do have them, they usually are stationary units, but they do not need to be. Although not common, a server in a BSS can function as an access point, in which case it is both wireless and connected by wire to the corporate networks, and therefore stationary.

BSSs are the basic building blocks of extended WLANs. When two or more BSSs are connected to the same wired LAN (the typical case) or backbone via their APs, they can be connected to each other. The wired portion is called a ***distribution system (DS),*** because it distributes communications between the BSSs. The combination of the DS and the BSSs is called an ***extended service set (ESS).*** Figure 14.3 illustrates this setup.

FIGURE 14.3

A WLAN BSS and ESS

For simplicity, laptops in this diagram represent the variety of wireless devices that can comprise a BSS.

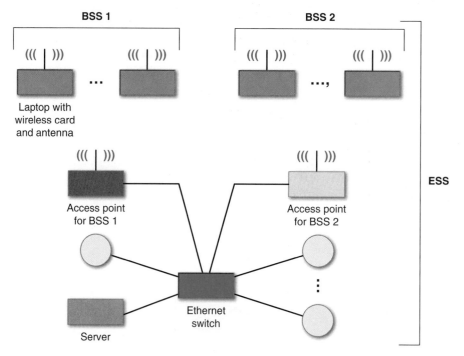

The DS provides the following services that allow stations to participate in and move about an ESS:

- **Association.** Before a station can participate, it must associate itself with the BSS access point. A station can associate with only one AP at a time, so the AP knows where the station is. This is a dynamic affiliation because stations can enter and leave a BSS, physically or by booting up or shutting down.

  A station moving only within one BSS is said to have ***no-transition mobility.***

- **Disassociation.** When a station leaves a BSS or shuts down, its affiliation with the AP is dropped. The AP also can disassociate a station. After it is disassociated, the station cannot participate in the WLAN.

- **Re-association.** A station can move between BSSs of a single ESS. To accommodate this, the DS switches the station's association from the AP of the BSS it is leaving to the AP of the BSS it is entering.

  A station moving between BSSs of a single ESS is said to have ***BSS transition mobility.***

- **Distribution.** When a station in a BSS needs to communicate with one in another BSS of the same ESS, the DS distributes the transmission from the AP of the former to the AP of the latter, which sends it to the destination station.

- **Integration.** The DS integrates communications between the stations of the ESS and the wired LANs or other wired connections of the corporate networks.

- **Inter-ESS movement.** A station can move from one ESS to another. Called ***ESS transition mobility,*** it is not supported directly. The station will be disassociated from an AP in the ESS it leaves and has to re-establish a connection via the association process in an AP of the ESS it moves to.

The DS also provides services specific to stations:

- **Authentication.** Before a station can associate with a BSS, it must identify itself. This is authentication. One version, called ***open system authentication,*** is simply a means of station identification and is never denied. The other, called ***shared key***

authentication, is meant to control access and requires the station to possess a secret key in order to be authenticated. The key is distributed via the Wired Equivalent Privacy (WEP) algorithm, discussed in Chapter 15, "Network security."
- **De-authentication.** When a station leaves a BSS or is disassociated by the AP, its authentication is terminated.

Protocols

The *de jure* standards for WLANs are contained in the IEEE 802.11 specifications, which define two protocol sets:

- **Client/server.** The typical LAN paradigm, also is followed for WLANs, which therefore employ many of the other 802.x LAN protocols as well.
- **Ad hoc.** Designed for small coverage areas with nodes operating without a server or an AP. This IBSS setup also is the Bluetooth paradigm, a wireless personal area network model.

IEEE 802.11 was ratified in 1997. Information about the IEEE 802.11 working group is at http://grouper.ieee.org/groups/802/11/.

WLAN protocols and mechanisms are in the lowest two layers of the model architectures: physical and data link. As you would expect, the physical layer defines electrical and spectrum specifications and bit transmission/receipt; data link is responsible for frame assembly, node-to-node error control, physical addressing, inter-node synchronization, and medium (channel) access.

The physical layer actually is divided into an upper sublayer (physical layer convergence procedure—PLCP) and a lower sublayer (physical media dependent—PMD). Let's look at physical layer transmission methods first.

PHYSICAL LAYER The physical layer of 802.11 defines four transmission methods: one infrared and three radio frequency—frequency hopping spread spectrum (FHSS), direct sequence spread spectrum (DSSS), which includes high rate DSSS (HR/DSSS), and orthogonal frequency division multiplexing (OFDM). For nodes to communicate, each must use the same transmission method.

Infrared As its name implies, signals are carried by infrared light, which has a very short useful range—no more than about 5 or 6 meters (roughly 15 to 20 feet). Most commonly found in devices such as TV remote controls, wireless connections between keyboards and computers, and the like, its major advantages are:

- It works in electrically noisy environments without interference.
- Signals can reflect off walls, floors, ceilings, and fixtures to reach their target.
- It is very inexpensive.

However, its disadvantages include the following:

- Very limited span
- Line-of-sight requirement
- Inability to penetrate solid (opaque) objects

These disadvantages make its use for WLANs rare, except for some instances of Bluetooth.

(From another perspective, however, inability to penetrate opaque objects is an advantage—infrared signals cannot be intercepted (eavesdropped) beyond the walls as radio frequency signals can.)

The relevant group for infrared devices is the ***infrared data association (irDA),*** which has defined three physical layer protocols:

- IrDA-SIR (serial infrared, also called slow infrared) which supports data rates up to 115 Kbps

- IrDA-MIR (medium infrared), with data rates to 1.15 Mbps
- IrDA-FIR (fast infrared), supporting data rates to 4 Mbps

We have included infrared in this chapter for completeness, but because it is not in widespread use in the corporate network world, we do not develop the topic in detail. For more information, visit www.irda.org.

FHSS *Frequency hopping spread spectrum (FHSS)* gets its name from the way it works. An FHSS data signal has a narrow bandwidth, only a small portion of the 2.4 GHz WLAN spectrum. The entire spectrum is utilized by constantly shifting the signal from *frequency* sub-band to frequency sub-band—that is, *hopping*—to *spread* the signal across the *spectrum*. This minimizes interference and eavesdropping, because the signal stays in a sub-band only for a very short time.

The hopping sequence, timing, dwell time (length of time the signal stays in one sub-band), and station synchronization are established and maintained by one station that acts as a master. Every participating station follows the same hop sequence, so transmissions appear to take place over a single virtual communications channel. As a further measure against interference, an adaptive version of FHSS enables the master to sense sub-band activity and skip those sub-bands where activity is detected.

FHSS is not common in business WLANs, but it is in Bluetooth and HomeRF networks, which are best for personal application. These (especially Bluetooth) are becoming more popular, with many players entering the field. For that reason, we discuss FHSS and Bluetooth further in section 14.3.

DSSS *Direct sequence spread spectrum (DSSS)* spreads the signal over the entire 2.4 GHz spectrum by substituting a redundant sequence of bits called a ***chipping code*** for each bit of the signal to be transmitted. Because the data rate of the chipping code is sufficiently higher than the original signal bit rate, there is no delay in signal transmission: For a chipping code with k bits, the DSSS data rate is k times the original signal data rate. If the code rate were not fast enough, at the least the original signal would have to be buffered to slow transmission speed to the DSSS rate. A detailed discussion of chipping codes is beyond the scope of this text.

The redundancy in the chipping sequence makes the signal less vulnerable to interference, because the receiver can use the redundant bits to correct bits damaged in transmission. (Review the discussion of forward error correction in Chapter 5, "Error control.") However, because each signal bit covers the entire 2.4 GHz spectrum, a within-range FHSS system can corrupt the DSSS transmission as the FHSS hops around the same frequencies. On the other hand, if adaptive FHSS is within range, it will not transmit at all because it will sense activity on every sub-band. This is another reason why FHSS is rarely found in the business environment.

DSSS is most often used in 802.11b WiFi at an 11-Mbps data rate and in 802.11g WiFi at data rates below 20 Mbps. These are discussed shortly.

AMPLIFICATION

WiFi (wireless fidelity) is a name for 802.11b and g products trademarked by the Wireless Ethernet Compatibility Alliance (WECA), a non-profit organization founded in 1999. WECA seeks to certify product compliance and interoperability. Those that pass WECA's tests can display the WiFi logo.

OFDM *Orthogonal frequency division multiplexing (OFDM)* is similar to FDM, except in the latter, signals from multiple sources are transmitted at the same time, with each assigned a separate frequency sub-band; in the former, all of the sub-bands are used by a single source for a given amount of time, somewhat analogous to TDM's time slots.

The signal is modulated onto the sub-band carriers, which are spaced orthogonally. A simplified description of this is that the carrier frequencies are produced in such a way that the peak amplitude of each frequency coincides with the minimum amplitude of the adjacent frequency. Each demodulator is aligned to see only the frequencies in a particular carrier sub-band.

The complexities of OFDM also are beyond the scope of this text. If you wish to pursue the topic, a good place to start is http://www.palowireless.com/ofdm/tutorials.asp.

802.11: a, b, g, AND n The original IEEE *802.11* standard (1997) ran at up to 2 Mbps over either infrared (although you would be hard-pressed to find one) or the 2.4 GHz ISM band. The *802.11b* modification (1999), the original WiFi standard, represented a major jump in speed, running at 11 Mbps on the 2.4 GHz band. Using DSSS modulation, it has a span of about 300 feet. The speed jump and its relatively low cost made it very popular in the marketplace.

802.11a (2001) delivered even greater speed, 54 Mbps, but on the 5 GHz band instead of the 2.4 GHz band and using OFDM instead of DSSS. Although the higher speed was attractive, the higher frequency meant much shorter span, down to about 60 feet. It also meant that line of sight was generally required and that its signals were more easily absorbed by walls, furniture, and the like.

802.11a requires several more access points to cover the same area as 802.11b. On the other hand, the 5 GHz band is much less crowded than the 2.4 GHz band, which is used by everything from portable phones to microwave ovens; so interference with the "a" modification is less likely than with "b."

Because the "a" and "b" versions use different bands and run at different speeds, they are not compatible. Although there are wireless cards that can convert from one to the other, the release of *802.11g* (2003)—which also runs at 54 Mbps using OFDM, but in the same 2.4 GHz band as "b" and is backward compatible with "b"—took much of the play out of the "a" market.

The latest development, *802.11n* (2006), operates in the same 5 GHz band as "a" but uses a spatial multiplexing technique called *multiple input/multiple output (MIMO),* with which many data streams can travel over the same frequencies while carrying different information using multiple transmitter and receiver antennas and special encoding techniques called space-time block codes. This allows data rates of at least 100 Mbps and possibly as much as 600 Mbps.

For additional information, see http://www.enhancedwirelessconsortium.org/. According to this Web site, "The Enhanced Wireless Consortium (EWC) was formed to help accelerate the IEEE 802.11n development process and promote a technology specification for interoperability of next-generation wireless local area networking (WLAN) products."

DATA LINK LAYER The data link layer, as with all 802 LANs, is subdivided into logical link control (LLC) and media access control (MAC). When an ESS is created, its component BSSs appear to the LLC layer to be a single IBSS. This means that any station in the ESS can communicate with any other of those stations and even can move between BSSs, transparently to LLC.

A station's physical address is the 48-bit MAC addresses of the (wireless) NIC. In common with all 802 MAC addresses, it goes in the packet header as the source address

TECHNICAL NOTE
802.11 working groups and protocol release dates

(Those without dates are in progress.)
- a: 5 GHz, 54 Mbps, OFDM (2001)
- b: 2.4 GHz, 11 Mbps, DSSS (1999)
- c: Wireless bridges (2001)
- d: International compatibility for 802.11b (2001)
- e: Quality of service (2005)
- f: Interoperability of APs (2003)
- g: 2.4 GHz, 54 Mbps, OFDM (2003)
- h: International compatibility for 802.11a (2003)
- i: Encryption methods for WLAN security (2004)
- j: Incorporation of Japanese extensions of 802.11a (2004)
- k: Radio resource management (2005)
- l: Reserved designation
- m: Standards maintenance
- n: 5 GHz, to 600 Mbps, MIMO (2006)
- o: Reserved designation
- p: WAVE—wireless access for vehicular environment
- q: Designation reserved
- r: Fast roaming VoIP
- s: ESS mesh networks
- t: WPP—wireless performance prediction
- u: Internetworking between 802.11 networks and any attached networks
- v: Management for 802.11 wireless networks
- w: Protected management frames for data integrity, authenticity, and confidentiality
- x: Reserved designation
- y: Opening the 3.65–3.7 GHz spectrum to 802.11 networks
- z: None yet

along with the destination MAC address—that of the recipient node. A frame check sequence is attached as a trailer. Medium access itself, however, is different from that of legacy Ethernet CSMA/CD. Instead, CSMA/CA is used.

Avoiding collisions: CSMA/CA Because signals travel over a common shared medium (the air), collisions are possible. Carrier sense is required as part of collision avoidance, but the nature of wireless transmission and range considerations means that carrier presence can be hidden.

Collision detection is problematic as well. To sense a collision, a station must "hear" it. But in radio frequency systems, the noise of a collision can be masked by the transmission or hidden by distance, so collision detection is not reliable. This renders CSMA/CD infeasible. Instead, a collision *avoidance* scheme called ***carrier sense multiple access with collision avoidance (CSMA/CA)*** is used in somewhat modified form from that used in wired LANs. Focusing on coordinating transmissions, it is referred to as ***distributed coordination function (DCF),*** although it is not unusual to find it called CSMA/CA anyway. With DCF, collisions still are possible, but less likely. (See "Technical Note: CSMA/CA and DCF.")

Time-sensitive transmission: PCF Voice and video do not tolerate latency well, especially when it is variable. Hence, DCF, which by design introduces delays by distributing access control to the stations, is not a suitable mechanism. Instead, ***point coordination function (PCF)*** is used. PCF utilizes the BSS access point as a single point of control for medium access. The access point polls the stations in a fixed order, giving each one a chance to transmit. This means that maximum latency is both predictable and guaranteed, and variability is minimal. Of course, as the number of stations grows, that maximum increases, so it may become too long to be useful for voice and video transmissions.

When PCF is employed, it almost always is an added option rather than a replacement of DCF. Only one of these modes operates at a time, with DCF typically the default and PCF being invoked as needed.

TECHNICAL NOTE
CSMA/CA and DCF

With CSMA/CA, before a node can transmit it must sense the medium (air) for activity; if none is heard, it waits an additional random amount of time and, if the medium still is inactive, transmits. One modification is that when a packet is received error-free, the receiving node sends back an ACK (also following the CSMA/CA sensing scheme before transmitting the ACK).

If the ACK frame is not received within a timeout period, a collision is assumed and the packet retransmitted, following CSMA/CA. Of course, it may be that the ACK was involved in a collision, rather than the original packet. It also may be that there was no collision but that the medium became busy so the ACK could not be sent before the timeout.

Despite CSMA/CA, collisions can occur because of the *hidden node* problem. Two nodes that are within range of the access point may be out of range of each other, and therefore unknown to (hidden from) each other. When sensing for activity, the one cannot hear the other and may believe there is no activity, yet if both transmit they will collide at the access point.

To handle this, *request to send (RTS)* and *clear to send (CTS)* are incorporated into the protocol. After finding no activity and before transmitting, the node sends an RTS frame to the destination, which, if available, responds with a CTS frame. Any other nodes hearing an RTS or a CTS will not attempt to transmit for an amount of time that is specified in the RTS and CTS frames, even if the medium is inactive. This gives nodes a chance to communicate without running afoul of hidden nodes and gives hidden nodes a chance to communicate without colliding with others.

The CA process, combined with explicit ACKs and the RTS/CTS procedure, provides a reasonable mechanism for medium sharing and collision avoidance. On the other hand, it adds overhead to the process. This means that 802.11 will always be somewhat slower than the equivalent 802.3 wired LAN.

14.3 Wireless personal area networks

To accommodate data sharing and connectivity needs of small, often impromptu groups of people and for what we might call personal connectivity, the *wireless personal area network (WPAN)* comes into play. The "personal" in WPAN refers to its very limited span, so the devices are "close to a person."

The predominant WPAN technology today is *Bluetooth,* which connects laptops to printers and other peripherals, devices such as hands-free phone headsets, PDAs, mp3 players, cameras, and so on, in an ad hoc network. As such, it has limited use in the corporate world and, as its generic name implies, is much more likely to be used by individuals.

Nevertheless, as a rapidly growing technology it is a ripe field for OEMs (original equipment manufacturers) and applications and peripherals.

Bluetooth

Bluetooth is a relatively new technology, not even a decade old. (A brief history: Early 1998, SIG formed; 1999, version 1.0 released; 2000, first consumer products marketed; 2004, version 2.0 released.) First created by Ericsson Mobile Communications, it was named for Harald Bluetooth, a Viking chieftain whose real name was Harald Gormsson and who, history tells us, had nary a blue tooth.

In Chapter 8, "Comprehending networks," we saw that Bluetooth uses radio waves for transmission over a very short range, on the order of 30 to 40 feet. Recent developments have extended the range to nearly half a mile under the right atmospheric conditions by increasing transmission power and using special antennas. This is far beyond the range originally intended in Bluetooth's design.

The original impetus for its design was to replace the clutter of desktop cables by enabling wireless connection between keyboards and computers, computers and printers, headphones and sound cards, and the like. Before long, that concept expanded to the creation of a *personal area network (PAN),* a mini-network among devices in close proximity.

The basic Bluetooth PAN is called a *piconet,* which needs at least two active members and can have up to eight. (Three bits are reserved in the Bluetooth packet for a member dynamic layer 2 address—simply a number from 0 to 7.) There can be additional devices on standby. Piconets are established automatically on the fly—as a device enters a piconet with fewer than eight active members, it is given an address—and members can come and go at will; in a full piconet, a standby can become active when an active member leaves.

When a piconet is formed, the first member assumes the role of master; the others act as slaves. All communications travel through the master regardless of whom they are sent by or sent to. A piconet member can be mobile or stationary. Mobile members can move within a piconet as long as they do not go out of range.

Piconets can be linked through their masters to form internetworks called *scatternets.* This enables the individual piconets to communicate with each other while still operating as independent networks. When the masters are appropriately placed, a scatternet can cover a much larger span than a piconet. For convenience, we repeat the illustration shown in Chapter 8, here as Figure 14.4. In 14.4C, we see that a slave can be a member of more than one piconet at a time.

Let's see what is behind the workings of Bluetooth.

PROTOCOLS   Bluetooth is based on the IEEE 802.11 standard, as WLANs are, and operates in the same ISM 2.4 GHz band as 802.11b and g. However, Bluetooth does not use the 802.x LAN protocols because it is not designed for LAN communications or for large-scale data transmissions.

Because the ISM band is unlicensed, many devices use it, including portable telephones, remote baby monitors, and microwave ovens, to name a few. This creates a so-called noisy environment that potentially could cause considerable interference. To avoid this and to render eavesdropping ineffective, Bluetooth does not operate on a single carrier frequency. Instead, the 2.4 GHz band is divided into 79 sub-bands (channels) of 1 MHz each, beginning at 2.402 GHz and ending at 2.480 GHz. Then, at the physical layer (in Bluetooth parlance called the *baseband* layer), Bluetooth uses FHSS, choosing from 32 hopping sequences to jump rapidly from channel to channel. The master determines the hopping sequence. (In some countries, numbers other than 32 are used, but 32 is the most common.)

Radio wave communication

Master: ● Slave: ○

FIGURE 14.4

Piconets and scatternets

A. The smallest piconet—one master, one slave

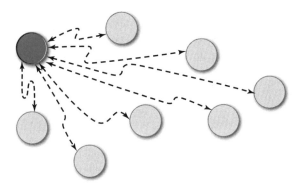

B. The largest piconet—one master, seven slaves (in addition, there may be standby nodes, not shown)

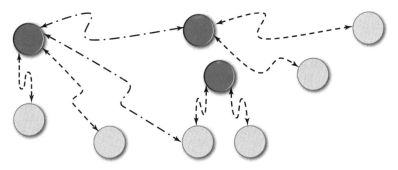

C. Linking three piconets to form a scatternet

AMPLIFICATION

In somewhat of a departure from model architectures, Bluetooth's *radio layer* lies below the baseband (physical) layer, although some references make it part of the physical layer. Also, taken together, the radio through data link layers are called the Bluetooth *transport layers.*

The following are two major advantages of FHSS:

• Interference with and from other spread spectrum networks within range is reduced—the narrow band signals will interfere only if they are on the same sub-band at the same time.

- Eavesdropping prevention is enhanced, because an intercepted signal will be only a very small portion of the transmission—whatever is on the particular hop.

The more FHSS systems that are within range of each other, the more likely is some interference from hop overlap. Interference also can come from full-band systems.

To enhance interference avoidance and anti-eavesdropping effectiveness, packet size is very small and hopping frequency is very fast, so the chance of any one packet being damaged, being overheard, or containing information useful to an eavesdropper is quite small. 802.11 specifies at least 2.5 hops per second—the Bluetooth hop rate is 1,600 per second. Forward error correction also is employed, which usually is able to correct those packets that are damaged.

A newer development is *adaptive frequency hopping (AFH),* which further reduces interference among other devices using the 2.4 GHz band. AFH detects the frequencies being used by other devices and skips them in the hopping sequence. If any of those devices is using the full band, AFH will not transmit at all.

In addition to controlling the hopping sequence, the master maintains clock synchronization for all piconet members. Even when there is no activity on the piconet, the master continuously sends out timing signals to keep members synchronized. Standby members too are synchronized but do not have Bluetooth addresses. When an active member leaves, its address is transferred to the next standby member, which thereby becomes active. An active member that leaves can become a standby or can depart the piconet completely.

For transmission and receipt, multiplexing is used. Time slots are set up and filled by the master, usually on a one-packet one-timeslot basis, although as many an five slots can be taken by a single packet. *Asynchronous connectionless (ACL)* protocol is used for single-channel data transmission; *synchronous connection-oriented (SCO)* protocol is used for up to three simultaneous synchronous audio channels (voice) or one channel that supports simultaneous synchronous audio and asynchronous data.

Versions 1.1 and 1.2 have nominal data rates of 7,231 Kbps, although in use, speeds are usually around 500 Kbps. Version 2.0, which incorporates *enhanced data rate (EDR),* is rated at 2.1 Mbps, although operation on the order of 1.5 Mbps is more likely. A penalty for the added speed of version 2.0 is higher power consumption, important for portable devices. However, the claim is that because the data rate is about three times that of the earlier versions, the shorter transmission time more than offsets the increased power draw. (For additional information, see "Technical note: The Bluetooth protocol stack.")

PROFILES Currently, there are 13 profiles defined for Bluetooth, and many more are in the development stage. These profiles delineate the way Bluetooth members communicate with each other. Examples are the *generic access profile (GAP)* and the *service discovery profile (SDP),* which works together with the *service discovery application profile (SDAP).*

GAP is a foundation profile, the basis for all the others because it delineates how to set up a link between devices. No matter what else a Bluetooth device may implement, GAP is required to ensure compatibility so that piconet members can communicate with each other even if they are using other profiles as well, some or all of which could even be generic. SDP procedures allow devices to query each other to see what services are offered, whereas SDAP indicates how SDP is to be used.

For a complete list of profiles, see http://www.palowireless.com/infotooth/tutorial/profiles.asp.

TECHNICAL NOTE
The Bluetooth protocol stack

The Bluetooth core specification describes the protocol stack of the radio layer, the baseband layer, and the data link layer, in which resides the *logical link control and adaptation layer protocol (L2CAP).* Above the core are the profiles that define protocols for particular Bluetooth services and features. The baseband layer supports *synchronous connection-oriented (SCO)* channels for real-time voice traffic by reserving bandwidth, and *asynchronous connectionless (ACL)* channels for best-effort data traffic. L2CAP handles data packets of up to 64 kilobytes.

802.15.1 In 2002, the IEEE released the 802.15.1 standard for a WPAN that is fully compatible with Bluetooth. The IEEE and the Bluetooth Special Interest Group (SIG) collaborated in the development process, which included the IEEE licensing portions of the technology from the SIG.

Also operating in the 2.4 GHz band, 802.15.1 "defines specifications for small-form-factor, low-cost wireless radio communications among notebook computers, personal digital assistants, cellular phones and other portable, handheld devices, and connectivity to the Internet." (See http://standards.ieee.org/announcements/802151app.html.) This provides an additional resource for Bluetooth developers and legitimizes Bluetooth technology as a *de jure* standard.

For more information about the IEEE WPAN working group, visit http://ieee802.org/15/index.html. For more information about Bluetooth, visit http://www.bluetooth.com/bluetooth/, the official Bluetooth Web site, and https://www.bluetooth.org/, the official Bluetooth membership site. To learn more about the Bluetooth SIG, visit http://www.bluetooth.com/Bluetooth/SIG/.

14.4 Wireless metropolitan area networks

The IEEE 802.16 standards delineate the *wireless metropolitan area network (WMAN),* also called *WiMAX,* as a high-data-rate broadband system that can operate over substantial distances—as fast as 70 Mbps and ranging more than 30 miles. Because WiMAX uses the same logical link control as the other 802 networks, including WiFi (802.11), they all can be linked via routers or bridges. In particular, WiMAX and WiFi networks can interconnect.

AMPLIFICATION

The name *WiMAX* derives from Worldwide Interoperability for Microwave Access and is a certification given to products that pass tests for conformity with 802.16.

The original 802.16 standard specified line of sight on the 10–60 GHz band. The "a" version lowered the band to 2–11 GHz, which is mostly unlicensed worldwide. The lower frequencies also enabled relaxing the line-of-sight requirement.

WiMAX

WiMAX is considered to be particularly applicable to providing wireless access in metropolitan areas by providing four functionalities:

- **High-speed connectivity** for businesses in a metropolitan region as an alternative to contracting for wired services.
- **Last-mile broadband** connection to data networks and the Internet without the need for telco last-mile local loops.
- **Hot spot (hot zone)** coverage for mobile applications to connect mobile devices to the APs of service providers. This standard, introduced by the 802.16e working group in 2005, is called the *Air Interface for Fixed Broadband Wireless Access Systems.*
- **Backhaul alternative** for transmitting from a local or remote network to a main site and as a linking service to extend the reach of and connectivity to cellular networks. For example, wired backhaul connects the APs of wireless networks to the company core networks and from APs to service provider networks.

    Backhaul also is used to describe the roundabout route that may be taken by a phone call because the more direct route is unavailable—a call that goes from the calling party to one or more non-direct switching offices, then back to a more direct office, and finally on to the called party. Wireless backhaul has the potential to be much more cost effective and easier to install.

WiMAX also is applicable to providing coverage in remote or rural areas where cabling is limited or non-existent, and where it is too expensive or physically problematic to install cable for the relatively few potential users. In cabled areas, it could compete with DSL and cable modems.

The proponents of WiFi (802.11) claim it to be a feasible alternative for many of these functions. Using high-gain antennas to extend span, WiFi can manage last-mile connectivity. Deployed in a mesh network design, WiFi can extend its reach to provide hot zone coverage for metropolitan area mobile users. (WiMAX can be deployed in a mesh design, too.) In these applications, the "g" version of 802.11 is most appropriate because its data rate is much higher than the "b" version, its market penetration is far greater than the "a" version, and OFDM can cope better with potential interference than the "b" version's DSSS.

WiMAX standards in other countries

The ETSI (European Telecommunications Standard Institute, http://www.etsi.org/) released *HiperPAN (high performance radio PAN), HiperLAN (high performance radio LAN),* and *HiperMAN (high performance radio MAN).* These are compatible with IEEE's 802.15 PAN, 802.11 WiFi (WLAN), and 802.16 WiMAX (WMAN), respectively.

KTTA, the (South) Korean Telecommunications Technology Association (http://www.tta.or.kr/English/new/main/index.htm) developed *WiBro (wireless broadband),* compatible with both WiMAX and HiperMAN.

Two good sources for additional information about WiMAX are:

- The WiMAX Forum (http://www.wimaxforum.org/home/), "an industry-led, non-profit corporation formed to promote and certify compatibility and interoperability of broadband wireless products."
- The IEEE working group on WMAN standards (http://www.ieee802.org/16/).

14.5 Cellular telephony

Although various types of mobile communications have been with us for many generations, including the walkie-talkies of the 1940s and mobile radio phones of the 1950s, it
was not until 1983 that what we call cellular telephony became available commercially.
The first cell phone was demonstrated in 1973 by Motorola (it weighed almost 2 pounds),
but it took 10 years for the technology to become commercially available. The Motorola
DynaTAC, marketed in 1983, weighed one pound and cost about $4,000, which is about
$8,100 in 2006 dollars based on the Consumer Price Index.

In the years since, cellular phones (or, more commonly, "cell phones") have grown
from an expensive, small-market, limited-use device to an inexpensive worldwide phenomenon. In fact, there are more cell phones than land line phones in many countries, and
it is no longer uncommon for cell phones to be the only phones that people have.

A cell phone is a low-power transmitter/receiver (transceiver) for voice and data, communicating wirelessly through a collection of stationary ground-based sites called *base
stations,* each of which is linked to its nearest neighbor stations. The term *cellular* refers to
the base station coverage areas, called cells.

Cells are a construct to enable efficient use of the available wireless frequencies. For
all earthbound wireless transmission, the common medium is air. To circumvent much of
the interference that could result from simultaneous transmissions over the air, govern-
ments everywhere regulate how the wireless frequency spectrum is used. In the United
States, that is the responsibility of the FCC.

The FCC has partitioned the available wireless frequency spectrum into a number of
subgroups called *frequency bands.* The more bands available for a particular wireless
service, the greater the number of users who can use the service simultaneously.

Frequency bands are allocated based upon their particular characteristics and the
needs of various services that use them. Overall, there is more demand for dedicated frequency bands than there are appropriate bands available. This is particularly true for the
rapidly expanding mobile telephony services.

The FCC allocates bands vary sparingly, which leaves cell phone providers to resolve
for themselves how to use their bands most effectively. That is precisely the essential problem faced by cellular telephony: how to provide mobile telephone service to the greatest
number of users with the limited frequency allocations given them by the FCC. (In other
countries, the problem is the same; only the governing agencies differ.)

Here is an example of the problem: Suppose a mobile wireless telephony provider
were allocated eight frequency bands. The simplest use of these bands would limit the
number of simultaneous calls to eight. This is obviously not a feasible business proposition. Instead, if the provider could divide its coverage area into independent geographical
areas and reuse the eight frequencies within different areas, the picture would improve
considerably. How to reuse bands among the areas revolves around avoiding interference
among the signals.

We call the independent geographical areas cells. In essence, a cell is simply a logical
way of thinking about covering a region. As it happens, a hexagon is the ideal cell shape
for covering a region without gaps or overlaps. It is important to note that signal transmission patterns do not conform to hexagons. Nevertheless, hexagons are a convenient, commonly used conceptualization.

The trick is to assign individual frequency bands to each cell in such a way that, at the
very least, no two adjacent cells use the same frequency—otherwise, their signals could
interfere with each other. This is not a trivial task. The solution depends on the propagation
characteristics of the frequencies, as well as the terrain and other obstructions. Keys to the
solution are: signal power, placement of a cell's base station, and antennas and cell size.

Base station power is low, typically on the order of a few watts (see "Technical note: Base station power levels"), to keep neighboring cells from interfering with each other. This means that cells, especially non-adjacent cells, can use the same frequencies as each other (called frequency re-use), which allows many more simultaneous phone calls than would otherwise be possible.

The base stations are connected to and controlled by stationary *mobile switching centers (MSCs)*, also called *mobile telephone switching offices (MTSOs)*, which establish call connections, coordinate all base stations, provide links to the wired telephone network and the Internet, and keep calling and billing records. When a call is initiated, a connection is established between the caller's phone and the base station of the cell that the caller is in.

As the caller begins to move out of range of that cell, the base station senses the drop in signal power and relays that information to the MSC. The MSC automatically "hands off" the call to the base station of the cell that the caller is moving into. In a newer procedure, *mobile assisted handoff (MAHO)*, the MSC has the cell phone (or other mobile unit) report signal strength on a set of frequencies in the new cell. Handoff is then to the strongest frequency.

The call may be to another cell phone (which may or may not be moving from cell to cell as well) or to a land line. In any event, the MSC plays a key roll and is both a wired and wireless component of a cellular system.

TECHNICAL NOTE
Base station power levels

Base station power is measured in two confusingly named ways: *effective radiated power (ERP)*, which measures the directional characteristics of transmitting antennas, and *actual radiated power (ARP)*, which is the power of the transmitted signals. Although the FCC allows ERPs up to 500 watts per channel (as a function of tower height), most non-rural ERPs are no more than 100 watts per channel.

ARP is much lower than ERP; typically, ARP is on the order of 5 to 10 percent of ERP (a function of antenna type). For example, an ERP of 100 watts produces an ARP of about 5 to 10 watts. When cells are subdivided to expand system capacity, as is common in densely populated urban areas, even lower ERPs are used—10 watts per channel is not atypical—producing an ARP of 0.5 to 1 watt. Power levels even lower than these are not unusual.

Some references say that base stations are located at cell (hexagon) centers; others say that they are at the cell vertices. Actually, these amount to the same thing—it is a question of viewpoint. From a geographic viewpoint, base stations are located at cell vertexes; from a coverage viewpoint, base stations are centered in the cells.

Figure 14.5A shows this arrangement. The black outlined hexagons A, B, C, and D are the geographic areas. Base station 1 is located at the common vertex of A, B, and C; base station 2 is at the common vertex of B, C, and D. The blue dashed outlined hexagon is the coverage area of base station 1 and the black dashed outlined of base station 2. Figures 14.5B and 14.5C illustrate base station locations from the coverage (B) and geographical (C) viewpoints. Conclusion: Where the base stations are located with respect to hexagonal cells is actually a viewpoint question.

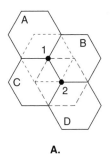
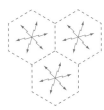

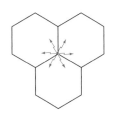

A.   **B.** Coverage viewpoint   **C.** Geographical viewpoint

FIGURE 14.5

Geographical and
coverage hexagons

Coverage (availability of service) is a constant issue for cell phone users. Most coverage problems have more to do with antenna/base station locations relative to conditions and surroundings than with cell phone technology itself. Cell size, and therefore the number and proximity of base stations, varies depending on several factors related to coverage. Some common factors include:

- **Terrain.** Signals travel farther over level terrain—larger and fewer cells are needed.
- **Density of buildings and other structures.** Many structures can block signals—smaller and more cells are needed.
- **User population density.** More users require more stations to prevent overload and the inability to get a connection—smaller, more numerous cells are needed.
- **Allowable antenna placement.** Municipalities generally restrict sites where antennas and antenna towers can be located; this is critical for providing coverage—without a tower, there is no coverage.

Basic operation

Making a call from a cell phone begins with a connection setup procedure:

- When the cell phone is turned on, it *searches for service;* in other words, it looks for a *broadcast signal* from the base station of the phone's service provider that is within range—in the same cell and not blocked by structures or signal interference.
- The broadcast signal contains message protocol information that is used by the phone to send a *registration message* to the base station, which relays it to the MSC.
- The MSC *authenticates* the phone and tells the base station to send the phone a *service signal.* (See "Technical note: Cell phone identification and authentication.")
- If the cell phone does not receive a service signal, this means that there is no base station in range, all channels are busy, or the phone did not authenticate. In any of these cases, no link is established.
- Otherwise, the phone is on standby, ready to receive a call or make a call by transmitting a number to the base station.
- When making a call, the base station relays that number to the MSC, which locates the called party.
- If the call is to another cell phone, the MSC pages the cells to find the called phone; if the call is to a land line, the MSC connects to a telco switching office, which processes the call.
- For any call, the MSC assigns a pair of frequency channels to the cell phone—one for send and the other for receive. At that point, the call is set up. If the called phone is available, a ring tone is heard. Otherwise, a busy signal is heard.
- After they are connected, the phones remain connected until transmission is terminated or the call is dropped (interrupted by moving into a non-covered area within a cell or region, or by interference). When the call ends, the connection is released.

Competing service providers agree to handle each other's calls, thereby enabling connections to be made between phones of different providers.

TECHNICAL NOTE
Cell phone identification and authentication

Three identifying numbers are associated with a cell phone, the first two of which are used in rendering service to the phone:

- **Cell phone telephone number (CTN),** the 10-digit number used to call the phone
- **Mobile identification number (MIN),** a 10-digit number derived from the telephone number, coded into the phone when the service is activated
- **Electronic serial number (ESN),** a 32-bit number coded into the phone by its manufacturer
- In addition, each cell phone **service provider** (carrier) has a **system identification code (SID),** a five-digit number assigned to it by the FCC.

When a cell phone *searches for service*, it is looking for the SID of the carrier contracted to provide service to that phone—SIDs are continuously transmitted by the base stations. If the SID cannot be found, a *no service* message will appear on the phone's screen. If it is found, the phone transmits a registration request to the base station, which forwards it to the MSC. The MSC *authenticates* the phone by comparing the phone's MIN with the carrier's database of authorized phones. If found, the MSC tells the base station which pair of frequencies to use for sending and receiving messages for the phone and to send a *service signal* to the phone. The MSC also uses the MIN to determine which cell the phone is in and to follow the phone from cell to cell as the call is handed off.

Generations and systems

FIRST GENERATION   The first-generation cell phones (1G—early 1980s), were analog systems of voice channels multiplexed by a *frequency division multiple access (FDMA)* technique called *advanced mobile phone system (AMPS).* (See "Historical note: Cells and AMPS.") Problems were typical of analog-based communications: noise and poor voice quality. In addition, coverage was limited, cells had relatively little capacity, and it was easy to tap into the airborne signals to discover a phone's code number and use it for making calls—fraud was rampant.

SECOND GENERATION   To overcome those problems, second-generation cell phones (2G—late 1980s to 1990s) introduced digital service. Three different schemes are considered to be 2G: *digital AMPS (D-AMPS), personal communications system (PCS),* and *global system for mobile communications (GSM).*

D-AMPS is a digital version of AMPS, based on *time division multiple access (TDMA),* that uses the same 850 MHz cellular band as AMPS. TDMA is a digital TDM system that divides the cellular band into multiple time slots that then can be allocated to individual calls. The first TDMA system in the United States was called North American Digital Cellular (NADC). That name has been dropped.

HISTORICAL NOTE
Cells and AMPS

In the 1960s, Bell Labs proved the concept of using hexagonal cells for mobile communications. Each cell would have a radio transmitter to communicate with moving vehicles. As a vehicle moved out of a cell, communication would be transferred to the next transmitter. This system evolved into AMPS, which began operating in 1983.

To ensure competition, every market area was federally mandated to have two licensees, each with their own network, using the same 416 channels in the 850 MHz band. To avoid interference, each base station had to use a subset of the channels different from those used by the nearest stations. Because not all channels could be used at any one site, the number of channels available for calls in any cell was significantly reduced.

The 850 MHz band, also known as the **cellular band** and the **AMPS band,** oddly is sometimes referred to as the 800 MHz band. It has an overall spectrum of 824 to 894 MHz, of which 824 to 849 MHz is assigned for mobile unit to base station transmissions and 869 to 894 MHz for base station to mobile unit transmissions. The 806 to 890 MHz frequency band, originally assigned to UHF TV channels 70 to 83, could no longer be used for over-the-air TV signals.

AMPLIFICATION

The terms *FDM* and *FDMA* can be confusing, because both refer to frequency division as a technique for simultaneous sharing of bandwidth by multiple devices. With FDM, the bandwidth is divided into frequency sub-bands, which are used to multiplex analog transmissions. FDM operates at the physical layer. FDMA, popular for some cell phone carriers that used the AMPS and D-AMPS systems and now used together with CDMA for GSM, is a data link protocol that uses FDM to achieve its multiplexing goal. When a cell phone call is set up, two sub-bands are reserved—one for sending and one for receiving. After the sub-bands are assigned, they are not available to any other cell phone until the call ends or is dropped.

Confusion regarding TDM and TDMA is resolved in the same way. TDM multiplexes transmissions by slicing the entire bandwidth into time slots, which are assigned to particular devices. Each device uses the entire bandwidth of its slot. As is the case with FDM, TDM is a physical layer protocol. TDMA is a data link protocol that uses TDM for multiplexing. TDMA also is popular with some cell phone carriers using D-AMPS and GSM and some using CDMA. When a cell phone call is set up, two time slots are assigned—one for sending and one for receiving. The slots are not available to any other cell phone until the call ends or is dropped.

A *voice coder (vocoder)* built into the cell phone transforms spoken voice (analog) into digital data. Vocoders are like the codecs used for analog to digital conversion in wired networks. AT&T and Cingular used TDMA at one time.

When AMPS was first designed, it was intended to be installed in automobiles—not a bad idea because early units were quite heavy and cumbersome, much better suited to be mounted in an automobile than to be carried around. The design of PCS, on the other hand, was meant from the start to be a personal system for any sort of mobile use. Hence, beyond mobile calling capabilities it also includes features such as caller ID, e-mail, and paging, with self-contained phone books, call logs, calendars, and games.

PCS uses a different multiplexing scheme than TDMA: *code division multiple access (CDMA).* CDMA is a digital system that combines DSSS (to create multiple channels) with chipping codes that allow multiple conversations to be carried across the same channels.

PCS occupies the 1,900 MHz band, which is divided into 1,850 to 1,910 MHz for mobile unit to base station transmissions and 1,930 to 1,990 MHz for base station to mobile transmissions. Sprint and Verizon use CDMA.

GSM was developed in Europe and has since spread to many parts of the world. (See "Historical note: The development of GSM.") GSM runs in four different bands—two in Europe and some Asian countries, and two primarily in the United States and Canada. GSM uses a combination of FDMA to divide each band into channels and TDMA to create time slots within each channel. It is incompatible with D-AMPS TDMA.

GSM operates in the 900 MHz and 1,800 MHz bands in Europe and Asia and in the 850 MHz and 1,900 MHz band in the United States, where it is used for digital cellular and PCS. The four GSM bands are divided into the following mobile unit to base station and base station to mobile unit sub-bands:

Europe and Asia:
- 900 MHz: 890–915 MHz mobile to base; 935–960 MHz base to mobile
- 1,800 MHz: 1,710–1,785 MHz mobile to base; 1,805–1,880 MHz base to mobile

United States:
- 850 MHz: 824–849 MHz mobile to base; 869–894 MHz base to mobile
- 1,900 MHz: 1,850–1,910 MHz mobile to base; 1,930–1,990 MHz base to mobile

The European and U.S. GSMs are not compatible. AT&T, Cingular (now the new AT&T), Nextel (now merged with Sprint), and T-Mobile use GSM.

HISTORICAL NOTE
The development of GSM

For some time in Europe, 1G analog systems were operating in many countries, and most of those systems were incompatible with each other. Realizing that this was an intolerable situation, the 1982 **Conference of European Posts and Telegraphs (CEPT)** set up the **Groupe Spécial Mobile (GSM)** to create a uniform system for all of Europe. Incorporating the TDMA digital concept, they handed their findings to the ETSI, which released GSM.

At that point, though the letters remained the same, the meaning of GSM was changed to **Global System for Mobile communications.** It is mandated as the only system in Europe and has become the preferred system in many other countries as well, including Australia, Russia, and several countries in Africa and the Middle East. This uniformity has made advances in overall coverage and service much simpler than in the United States and other countries where there are competing standards. GSM has a presence even in those countries where it is not dominant, including the United States.

The 2G systems generally work well, but their data throughput is not particularly fast, running at no more than 20 Kbps. This is suitable for short text messages and push-to-talk walkie-talkie service, but streaming video and audio are problematic.

Some modifications boosted data rates of the different 2G systems variously to 30–90 Kbps (sometimes labeled *generation 2.5* or *2.5G*), but although this allowed slow Web browsing and downloading of short video clips, voice clips, and ring tones, it was only a small step. On the other hand, all 2G systems employ powerful authentication schemes based on the ***cellular authentication and vector encryption (CAVE)*** algorithm that are far superior to those used in wireless networks. As a result, most of the fraud prevalent in the 1G systems disappeared.

If you would like to learn more about the CAVE algorithm, visit http://www.geocities. com/rahulscdmapage/Documents/Authentication.pdf.

THIRD GENERATION Third-generation (3G) technologies addressed the speed shortcoming, providing data rates of 144 Kbps to over 2 Mbps. As a result, a panoply of service possibilities became practical, such as Web browsing and Web-based applications, multimedia (including audio and video streaming), and e-mail with or without attachments. The phones that take advantage of this technology are called ***smart phones.*** These either are cell phones with PDA features or PDAs with cell phone features.

Of course, speed is one thing, but memory and online costs are others. At this point in cell phone and PDA development, memory limitations and cost make cell phone performance less satisfactory than the always-on Internet, full Web browsing, and downloading that we experience with computers with broadband connections. On the other hand, 3G speeds make it possible for laptops to get broadband connections via cell phone PC cards instead of depending on WiFi or WiMAX hot spots. Connection cost, charged at cell phone rates, still is a limiting factor, however.

The evolution of 3G and beyond Three technologies currently provide 3G service: UMTS, derived from GSM, a wide-band code division technique more accurately called WCDMA; CDMA2000, an improvement of 2G code division multiple access; and TD-SCDMA, which combines time division and synchronous code division.

By dint of already having a mandated uniform system (GSM), Europe was in a position to lead the way in uniform 3G service for Europe and potentially the rest of the world. Their scheme, ***universal mobile telephone service (UMTS),*** was designed to run over existing GSM networks. It is likely that UMTS will replace GSM as it matures. The CDMA camp responded with CDMA2000, which has two rather awkwardly named versions: ***1xEV-DO (evolution-data only)*** and ***1x-EV-DV (evolution-data and voice).***

Modifications to the 3G systems have boosted data rates as high as 14 Mbps (sometimes called *generation 3.5* or *3.5G*). It is not likely to be long before fourth-generation (4G) technology becomes practical. Early forays point to data rates of between 100 Mbps and 1 Gbps. At those speeds, full-motion video conferencing, video on demand, and even VoIP become feasible.

Radio frequency radiation and cell phone safety

From time to time, articles appear that discuss the potential hazards to human health of radio frequency (RF) radiation from cell phones and base station transmissions. Whether RF from any source constitutes a hazard depends on the power of the radiation. Apart from anecdotal evidence, several studies have shown that the power levels used in cellular systems are below the levels that can cause harm to humans. At this juncture, the evidence points to the safety of cellular devices. However, long-term-exposure studies still are ongoing. Further, none of the studies has been claimed to be definitive as yet.

The following is quoted from "Radio Frequency Safety," by the Office of Engineering and Technology of the FCC (http://www.fcc.gov/oet/rfsafety/cellpcs.html).

A question that often arises is whether there may be potential health risks due to the RF emissions from hand-held cellular telephones and PCS devices. The FCC's exposure guidelines, and the ANSI/IEEE and NCRP guidelines upon which they are based, specify limits for human exposure to RF emissions from hand-held RF devices in terms of specific absorption rate (SAR). For exposure of the general public, e.g., exposure of the user of a cellular or PCS phone, the SAR limit is an absorption threshold of 1.6 watts/kg (W/kg), as measured over any one gram of tissue.

Measurements and computational analysis of SAR in models of the human head and other studies of SAR distribution using hand-held cellular and PCS phones have shown that, in general, the 1.6 W/kg limit is unlikely to be exceeded under normal conditions of use. Before FCC approval can be granted for marketing of a cellular or PCS phone, compliance with the 1.6 W/kg limit must be demonstrated. Also, testing of hand-held phones is normally done under conditions of maximum power usage. In reality, normal power usage is less and is dependent on distance of the user from the base station transmitter.

14.6 Satellites

Before satellites and cable TV, radio and television signals were broadcast over the air, to be picked up by antennas. Unimpeded signals of these types tend to travel in straight lines. Because of the earth's curvature, this means that eventually they head off into space.

Signals sent by broadcast radio, which operates at lower frequencies than TV, reflect off the ionosphere and can be picked up in places on earth well beyond ground-based line of sight (although this does not mean that radio signals could circle the globe). Actual distance depends, among other things, on signal power, interference from other signals, and atmospheric conditions.

TV signal frequencies, on the other hand, are too high to reflect off the ionosphere—they require earth-bound line of sight. This meant that wireless TV broadcasting had strict distance limits; transatlantic or transpacific broadcasting, for example, was not possible, nor were long-range wireless transmissions in any of the higher spectra.

AMPLIFICATION

The ionosphere is a region of ionized particles in concentric bands above the earth. Fluctuating in height and degree of ionization with the time of day and season of the year, it can be as low as about 30 miles and as high as about 400. The lower regions are strong reflectors of radio frequencies of 1 to 3 MHz.

It was not a stretch to imagine that if a way could be found to reflect or retransmit higher-frequency signals heading off into space, the ground-based line-of-sight dilemma could be overcome. The idea of using satellites as communications relay stations to do this is quite simple: Signals from one location on the earth are sent to an orbiting satellite (*uplink*) that is in line of sight with the sending station. The satellite retransmits the signals back to another earthbound station (*downlink*) in a different location that also is in line of sight with the satellite. Of course, there is a lot more to it, but this is the essence of the process.

By the late 1950s, the possibility of artificial earth-orbiting communications satellites was drawing interest. But first, the practicality of putting an artificial satellite into orbit had to be resolved. The Russian Sputnik 1, launched on October 1, 1958, and several others that followed demonstrated that it was feasible to launch satellites into orbit and that radio frequency transmissions from satellites to earth worked. Although they were not communications satellites in the sense of relaying signals from one earthbound location to another, they were the starting point.

In 1960, an experimental satellite called Echo 1 was put into a low earth orbit by the United States. Although it was only a metallicized balloon that reflected radio frequency signals, it was the first satellite that tested the possibility of relaying communications from one ground-based location to another. It led the way for Telstar 1 and Relay 1 in 1962, which went beyond simple reflection by incorporating receivers, repeaters, and transmitters. Today, hundreds of communications satellites are in orbit, used for purposes as varied as TV broadcasts, Internet transmissions, global positioning systems (GPS), and satellite radio (XM and Sirius).

For an interesting and more detailed history of communications satellites, see the NASA document "Communications Satellites: Making the Global Village Possible," by David J. Whalen, http://www.hq.nasa.gov/office/pao/History/satcomhistory.html.

Lines of sight and orbits

Although the limits are being extended, line of sight still is required from the earth transmitter to the satellite, from the satellite to the earth receiver, and indeed from one satellite to another. If the earth stations cannot "see" the satellite, or if satellites cannot see each other, there cannot be successful transmission between them.

From the earth, a primary factor is the satellite's orbit. Echo 1, for example, circled the earth about once every 90 minutes in its orbit 1,600 kilometers (about 994 miles) above the earth; from its altitude, it could see about one-ninth of its earth latitude track at once. That meant that it could be seen from one spot on earth for only about 10 minutes per orbit ($90 \times 1/9$).

Satellites in *geosynchronous earth orbits (GEOs)* match the rotation of the earth, so to an observer on the ground, they appear to be stationary—they always are in line of sight. At 35,786 kilometers (about 22,240 miles) above the earth, the GEO orbit is far higher than those of almost all other communications satellites.

The orbit is centered over the equator and covers a surface from about 75 degrees north latitude to 75 degrees south latitude (called an *equatorial orbit*). Because of the extreme altitude, there is considerable delay in round-trip signal time—almost 1/8-second uplink and the same downlink, plus processing time to regenerate the signal and change its frequency band. Total round-trip time is about 1/4 second.

No single GEO satellite (nor any satellite, for that matter) can see around the globe at once. A GEO satellite can see about 35 to 40 percent of the earth within its latitude bands, so it takes at least three GEOs for global coverage (see Chapter 8). To achieve sufficient capacity, many more than three GEOs currently are in orbit, but there is a limit to how many can be in that orbit before they start interfering with each other; GEOs are not the entire solution.

Satellites in several lower orbits (*medium earth orbits (MEOs)* range from about 5,000 to 15,000 kilometers, or roughly 3,100 to 9,300 miles, above the earth, and *low earth orbits (LEOs)* range from altitudes of 100 to 2,000 kilometers, or almost 100 miles to a bit over 1,240 miles) provide additional coverage.

None of these are synchronous orbits, so the satellites do not appear stationary. Parades of satellites (called *constellations*) must be used. With the minimum number of satellites needed for a continuous connection, as one satellite begins to move out of sight, the next one is just appearing. Transmissions from the departing satellite are handed off to the incoming one. Constellations at various altitudes circle the globe.

All these orbits are nearly circular and in line with various latitude bands that, for reasons of the physics involved, cannot cover high-latitude (polar) regions. A different type, the *highly elliptical orbit (HEO),* ranges in altitude from only 500 kilometers to as far as 50,000 kilometers (under 311 miles to over 31,000 miles), providing coverage for the other areas. One version of a HEO is called a *Molniya orbit,* after the Russian military Molniya communications satellite launched in 1962 that followed a highly elliptical orbit to provide polar and high-latitude coverage.

Many companies have tried to get into the communications satellite business; most have failed. Some very small companies are in operation, with just one or a handful of satellites. Here is an overview of the more important attempts, successful and not.

Little LEOs and big LEOs

The earliest LEOs, Telstar and Relay, actually had somewhat elliptical orbits that went into and out of the Van Allen radiation belts. Later LEOs were in circular orbits, some not exceeding 500 miles are below the belts, and others are in and above the belts.

Little LEOs are satellite constellations that use the VHF band (30–300 MHz) for data-only transmissions. Big LEOs provide both voice and data services in frequencies above 1 GHz.

In the United States, the FCC licensed five organizations to operate little LEOs:

- **ORBCOMM (http://www.orbcomm.com/).** Orbcom received a 48-satellite LEO data-only license in 1994 and has since launched 35 satellites, of which 30 are operational.
- **E-SAT (http://www.dbsindustries.com/index.html).** Originally licensed in 1998 by EchoStar, the company is now a joint venture between EchoStar and DBSI. It has permission to launch six LEO satellites for data-only transmissions.
- **Final Analysis (http://www.finalanalysis.com/).** Formed in 1993, Final Analysis acquired a LEO license in 1998. They claim to be developing FAISAT, a 32-satellite data-only LEO system, but it is not operational.
- **Leo One.** This company received a license for a 48-satellite LEO in 1998, but the company appears to be defunct.
- **Volunteers in Technical Assistance.** Also licensed in 1998, this company is defunct.

The state of these licensees illustrates the technical and financial difficulties of forming a LEO constellation. Not only is the launch process very expensive, so is ground support for satellite control and for transmitting/receiving bases, maintenance, replacement, and operation. This is even more the case with big LEOs, whose constellations and ground support are extensive. Their saving feature to date has been voice-based services.

Two big LEOs are operating:

- **Iridium (http://www.iridium.com/).** Conceived by Motorola, Iridium had a promising but shaky start, filed for Chapter 11 bankruptcy in 1999, and ceased operating in 2000 after having launched a complete constellation of 66 satellites supported by a network of ground stations and inter-satellite links for bona fide global voice and data service worldwide. (*Complete constellation* means there are enough satellites in the constellation for global coverage.)

  While in bankruptcy, they were deciding how to de-orbit the satellites, which they could no longer afford to maintain; the Department of Defense came to their rescue. Then a group of investors bought their assets and kept the name. (The name comes from the element iridium, which has atomic number 77. Iridium's original license and plan called for a 77-satellite constellation.)

  Iridium is now an ongoing commercial venture.

- **Globalstar (http://www.globalstar.com).** This LEO also had a rocky beginning, having lost 12 satellites in one launch attempt in 1998. They now have a 48-satellite constellation and hundreds of ground stations for voice and data coverage over a large portion of the globe. Although not as extensive as Iridium, Globalstar is their only real competitor so far.

MEOs

More difficult to realize than LEOs because of their higher altitudes, there is only one MEO that claims to be poised for operation, but as yet it is still in the planning stage. Called New ICO, it is a London-based company formed from ICO Global Communications that declared bankruptcy in 1999, only two weeks after Iridium. They intend to use Boeing Satellite Systems, Inc. (http://www.boeing.com/defense-space/space/ bss/factsheets/601/ ico/ico.html) to launch their satellites.

GEOs

Intelsat (http://www.intelsat.com/index_flash.aspx) is a prime and founding player in GEO communications satellites. In 1962, President John F. Kennedy signed the Communications Satellite Act, whose goal was the establishment of a satellite system in cooperation with other nations. Accordingly, Congress created the Communications Satellite Corporation (Comsat), which in 1964 was joined by agencies from 17 other countries (later growing to 143) to form the International Telecommunications Satellite Consortium (Intelsat). Less than a year later, Intelsat 1 (Early Bird) was launched into a GEO, the world's first communications satellite. On July 20, 1969, Intelsat transmitted live TV images of the first moon landing and Neil Armstrong's walk on the moon. Intelsat went private in 2001, becoming Intelsat Ltd.

Another successful GEO satellite company is the London-headquartered Inmarsat (http://www.inmarsat.com/), whose GEO constellation provides mobile phone, fax, and data services globally except for the polar regions. The satellites can be reached directly from mobile equipment and indirectly through the Internet.

Inmarsat began in 1979 as an international government organization (IGO) called the International Maritime Satellite Organization. (The United States' Comsat was a member.) Its mission was to provide the maritime industry with satellite communications for managing ships at sea, including handling safety and distress situations. From there it expanded into land-based and air communications, launching a growing number of satellites. In 1999 it went private. Inmarsat now offers BGAN (broadband global area network), which provides simultaneous voice and data, including text and streaming IP, anywhere in the world.

Both Intelsat and Inmarsat also have LEO satellites in operation.

Frequency bands

Communications satellites use microwave signals in a range from 1.5 GHz to 30 GHz. There are five frequency bands, each with two frequencies—one for uplink and one for downlink. See Table 14.1.

TABLE 14.1 Uplink and downlink satellite frequencies

Band	Uplink (GHz)	Downlink (GHz)
L	1.6	1.5
S	2.2	1.9
C	6	4
Ku	14	11
Ka	30	20

If you would like to learn more about communications satellites, visit http://sulu.lerc. nasa.gov/rleonard/index.html#section1.

14.7 Security

In today's networked world, security is a primary consideration. Whether transmissions are confined to wired systems or make use of wireless air and space, we want delivery to the intended recipient without interception or compromised privacy. Wired and wireless security have many aspects in common. Wireless security bears the additional burden of its transmissions being more easily captured, which forces added emphasis on ways to make transmissions unreadable to the interceptor.

Security has assumed such import that we devote a separate chapter to the subject.

14.8 Summary

Wireless transmission is not a new phenomenon, having begun with radio as early as 1895. Wireless computer communication, on the other hand, is relatively new. The aim is to provide mobility with the same speed and security as wired networks. In this chapter, we looked at various wireless communications methods, saw how they work, and examined how close they come to that aim.

All wireless networks employ electromagnetic waves, primarily radio and microwaves, and use antennas to transmit and receive signals. Wireless LANs employ two different unlicensed bands, namely 2.4 GHz and 5 GHz. They can be set up as independent LANs, called basic service sets, or via access points to corporate wired networks. The latter also can be connected to each other, using the wired portion as a distribution system.

We looked at the client/server and ad hoc LAN protocol sets, delving into their capabilities and drawbacks. This included examination of FHSS, DSSS, and OFDM. We explored the IEEE 802.11 WLAN versions a, b, g, and n and looked at the collision/avoidance issues.

Next we discussed wireless personal area networks, typified by Bluetooth. We saw how Bluetooth works, and we discussed its configurations, protocols, advantages, and limitations. By way of comparison, we investigated the IEEE 802.15.1 WPAN standard, which is fully compatible with Bluetooth.

We looked into wireless metropolitan networks, typified by IEEE 802.16 and the WiMAX certification. This included a brief foray into WiMAX standards in other countries.

Cellular telephony in all its aspects and configurations was explored in some depth, including its generational development and safety issues. This was followed by satellite communications, the different orbits, and their characteristics. We also saw the limited progress that has been made so far in achieving actual working systems of the different types.

In the next chapter, we will look at network security, challenges to which can come from internal and external sources. We will survey security issues and provide details in those areas most relevant to businesses today: attacks on corporate networks and protecting corporate transmissions from meaningful interception.

END-OF-CHAPTER QUESTIONS

Short answer

1. What are the ISM bands? How and by whom are they defined?
2. What are the advantages and disadvantages of WLANs?
3. What is a distribution system? An ESS? How are they set up? Illustrate.
4. Contrast FHSS and DSSS.
5. Why is CSMA/CD infeasible for WLANs? What is used instead?
6. Describe the topology of cellular phones and include illustrations.
7. What are the steps of the cell phone connection setup?
8. Compare the four satellite orbits.
9. What line-of-sight requirements apply to communications satellites?
10. List the five frequency bands used for communications satellites.

Fill-in

1. A wireless local area network (WLAN) uses _____ to transmit signals among its nodes.
2. The _____ is the fundamental structure of a WLAN.
3. An _____ makes a BSS part of the organization's infrastructure.
4. _____ and _____ WLANs both run at 54 Mbps, whereas _____ runs at 11 Mbps.
5. Interference in the 5 GHz band is _____ likely than in the 2.4 GHz band.
6. The Bluetooth hop rate is _____.
7. The _____ IEEE standard for WPANs is fully compatible with Bluetooth.
8. _____ are areas where mobile applications can connect mobile devices to the APs of service providers.
9. _____ establish cell phone call connections, coordinate all base stations, provide links to the wired telephone network and the Internet, and keep calling and billing records.
10. The orbital speed of a satellite in a LEO orbit is _____ than one in a MEO orbit.

Multiple-choice

1. The minimum BSS
   a. has at least three stations
   b. must include an access point
   c. can operate as a peer-to-peer LAN
   d. can communicate with the organization's wired LANs
   e. all of the above

2. The *de jure* standards for WLANs
   a. are not part of any 802 specifications
   b. define both client/server and ad hoc protocol sets
   c. involve the first three layers of the model architecture
   d. do not allow for an infrared carrier
   e. have no provision for error control

3. The 802.11g specification
   a. runs in the same 5 GHz band as 802.11a
   b. has the same data rate as 802.11a
   c. suffers less from interference than 802.11b
   d. is compatible with the 2.4 GHz 802.11b
   e. all of the above

4. WLANs
   a. cannot use CSMA/CA because of the hidden node problem
   b. use DCF to remove the possibility of collisions
   c. can add PCF for time-sensitive transmissions
   d. dispense with ACKs
   e. dispense with time outs

5. Bluetooth
   a. is a WPAN
   b. has at least one piconet
   c. runs in a master/slave mode
   d. can form scatternets
   e. all of the above

6. WiMAX
   a. is a high-data-rate baseband system
   b. cannot be linked to WLANs or WiFi
   c. can have a range of over 30 miles
   d. requires line of sight for all versions
   e. has nominal speeds of up to 2.1 Gbps

7. Base stations
   a. are switching centers that coordinate cell phone calls
   b. provide links to land lines for cell phone callers
   c. are arranged in hexagonal coverage zones
   d. use high-signal power to extend reach
   e. all use the same signal frequencies

8. 3G cell phone service
   a. is based on a global uniform standard
   b. is fast enough for full-motion video conferencing and video on demand
   c. achieves increased speed at the expense of dropping authentication
   d. has data rates of 144 Kbps to over 2 Mbps
   e. currently is offered only in Europe

9. Using satellites as communications relay stations
   a. requires geosynchronous orbits
   b. eliminates signal noise
   c. boosts data rates to wired equivalents
   d. does not work for TV or radio signals
   e. can overcome ground-based line-of-sight requirements

10. To provide continuous communications with satellites in non-GEO orbits
    a. a constellation of satellites is required
    b. handoffs from one satellite to the next are unnecessary
    c. as few as three satellites suffice
    d. altitudes must vary
    e. the sky must be cloudless

True or false

1. Wireless networks employ electromagnetic waves, primarily radio and microwaves, to carry transmissions over the air or through the vacuum of space.
2. An independent basic service set (IBSS) is an ad hoc network.
3. A station moving only within one BSS is said to have transition mobility.
4. FHSS is commonly found in the business environment.
5. WiFi is a WLAN standard.
6. Bluetooth is based on the same 802.11 standard as WLANs.
7. Cell phone radiation has been found to be harmless over the long term.
8. Radio signals reflect off the ionosphere, thereby overcoming ground-based line-of-sight limitations.
9. The lowest satellite orbits provide the simplest communications schemes.
10. Three GEO satellites can cover the entire earth.

Exploration

1. Find statistics on trends in the installation of WLANs over the last several years. How many manufacturers (not distributors or retailers) are in the WLAN business?
2. GPS popularity is growing rapidly. Find as many applications of GPS as you can. For three manufacturers of GPS devices, compare their offerings with regard to capability, portability, applications and features, and costs.
3. Search the Web to find companies that provide satellite communications services. For each, list their service types, coverage, costs, orbits, number of satellites, and availability.

THE MOSI CASE, CONTINUED

As MOSI has grown, it has needed to create a series of ad hoc committees to work on various short-term projects to deal with expansion and reorganization planning. The project teams typically involve personnel from various departments. To facilitate the work of these groups, MOSI has been setting up VLANs, but as the number of projects has increased, doing so has become rather burdensome to the IT group. To alleviate that issue, IT has suggested incorporating WLANs into the corporate network infrastructure. MOSI has formed another committee to investigate that option, and you are leading that committee.

Which MOSI employees would you like to be on this new committee with you? What questions should be answered to enable your committee to assess the situation properly? Would you support the move to WLANs? Do you believe that WLANs could reduce IT's burden? Do you think WLANs should supplant all VLANs?

In a related development, MOSI is considering providing its field workers with wireless access to appropriate corporate databases. Before creating a project to do so, MOSI has asked you to consider the feasibility of such a plan. Do you believe it is worth pursuing? How would you expect it to affect the daily operations of MOSI?

CHAPTER

15

Network security

15.1 Overview

Network security covers a wide range of concerns, including physical intrusion and disruption, software-based mischief and assaults, unauthorized transmission capture, and even terrorist attacks. Thwarting such challenges, which can come from internal and external sources, is the goal of network security.

This subject is too broad in scope for reasonable coverage in a single, or even several, chapters. Many books deal with the full range of network security issues, and several focus on security with regard to particular arenas, such as the Internet, wireless, or wired networks. Two excellent full-coverage books that focus on network security are noted at the end of the chapter.

In this chapter, we will survey security issues and provide details in those areas most relevant to businesses today: attacks on corporate networks and protecting corporate transmissions from meaningful interception. Both fall under the broad heading of *intrusion,* which we define to mean any unauthorized activity on corporate or wide area networks with the intent to disrupt operations or to alter stored data or transmissions in any way.

Consider that security is not an all-or-nothing proposition. Dealing with it adequately is an ongoing task that is bound to be substantial in terms of time and cost. From the corporate perspective, before security measures are modified, enacted, or even contemplated, it is wise to undertake a *risk assessment* (also called *risk analysis*). This will identify the types of threats faced, their likelihood of occurrence, and the probable cost to the company of various security breaches should they be successfully carried out.

The analysis can be used to determine the personnel needed to monitor the networks and contain threats, the methods, hardware, and software best suited for the tasks, and an appropriate budget. The implication is that security is policy based, hence company specific. (See "Business note: What is a corporate security policy?") There is no "one-size-fits-all" solution. Further, risk assessments and policies must be revisited regularly to keep them up to date, and the security methods employed must be relevant and effective.

In small companies, network security is likely to be part of the network management job. In large companies, network security usually is a separate undertaking. Whatever the case, there are many clear areas of distinction between network management tasks and network security functions; there also are many areas of overlap. Hence, even when separated departmentally, close coordination and cooperation is paramount. (See "Business note: Network security and the smaller firm.")

Intrusion is any unauthorized network activity.

Security should be policy based and company specific.

 **Business NOTE** | **What is a corporate security policy?**

A corporate security policy lays out the rules and regulations for access to, protection of, and use of company assets and resources, including information and information systems. It focuses on security from two viewpoints: keeping intruders out of internal systems and external transmissions, and preventing employees from compromising the corporation, either internally or externally. Collaterally, it includes rules for the safekeeping and privacy of customer data.

Network security is an important dimension of a security policy.

To develop an appropriate policy, a risk assessment must be undertaken first. This will provide the corporate-specific information on which the policy will be based. Neither carrying out an assessment nor creating a policy is easy; both take significant time and resources, yet both are critical to the life of the company and should not be treated lightly. Furthermore, both must be revisited regularly to keep them up to date and relevant.

15.2 Security perspectives

Not every network disruption is a security breach. Power outages due to acts of nature, damage from accidents, and equipment failures can interrupt or shut down a network. Such eventualities should be considered as part of a risk assessment, and action plans should be developed to cope with them, but they are not security issues per se. To clarify thinking, it is useful to consider security issues from several perspectives: by source, by type of threat, by intent, by method, and by target:

- **Source.** Internal (by company employees) or external attacks; by an individual or a group.
- **Type.** Physical or electronic theft (illegal or unauthorized downloads or uploads).
- **Intent.** Mischievous (pranks) or malevolent (disruption of service, physical damage, file corruption, records theft); random or focused.
- **Method.** Breaking and entering, hacking, spoofing, denial of service.
- **Target.** Corporate networks, wireless networks, the Internet.

Business NOTE | Network security and the smaller firm

One might think that the network security needs of a smaller firm are less stringent than those of a complex, large-scale corporation. This is not necessarily so. To a great degree, it depends on the firm's customers.

The smaller firm that has or is seeking large businesses as customers must meet the security mandates of those businesses. A collaborative business relationship that necessitates data sharing could call for more thorough measures than otherwise would be contemplated. If the small firm cannot demonstrate the rigor required to secure corporate data and systems, including those that are used to transmit data from one to the other, the likelihood of successful collaboration is small.

From another perspective, smaller companies must protect their assets and resources from misuse and intrusion, whether participating in a smaller-smaller combine or operating as network/data standalones. Although smaller and less varied systems may present a less complex picture, their security goals are the same.

Prevention in brief

Network attacks from internal sources are addressed by monitoring and limiting access:

- **Monitoring.** It is increasingly common for employee activity to be monitored. This includes requiring access codes to enter certain areas, with comings and goings recorded, reading e-mail or scanning it for particular words or phrases, and mounting video cameras in sensitive locations. The latter two and similar measures carry with them privacy considerations, which must be addressed in any security policy. As part of the monitoring process, *activity logs* are kept. These enable trace-back to the sources of internal attacks or other breaches.
- **Limiting access.** Physical access is restricted by requiring codes, tags, or biologics (such as thumb prints and retina scans) to enter locked areas, using *thin clients* in place of full-blown desktop computers, and bolting down equipment. Electronic access is controlled by passwords or biological signatures for permission to use equipment and files, limiting rights to particular networks, database resources, and other company assets. In this light, we see that *authorization* for specific users to access specific resources is an important part of policy development.

Network attacks from external sources are addressed by devices and software:

- **Devices.** The principal corporate blockade is the firewall, a device set up to refuse entry to internal networks based on particular criteria. Other common devices are proxy servers, which sit between user requests and the actual internal servers. Devices are effective to the degree that the software they are running is effective.
- **Software.** Programs implementing various protocols are used to secure transmissions on their journey through external networks from authorized sender to designated receiver. They include encryption techniques and tunneling and encapsulation methods. Virus detection and removal software, anti-spam, anti-spyware, and virus blockers also fall into this category.

In general, we can say that security measures take two basic routes:

- **Proactive.** Cordoning off corporate networks to prevent attacks before they take hold; for example, running firewalls. This is of paramount importance, given that the Internet itself has no such access restrictions or content filtering.
- **Reactive.** Invoking procedures to remove threats after they appear; for example, using virus removal software.

Intrusion detection

The primary *intrusion detection systems (IDSs)* in use today focus either on network data flows or host activity. The aim of both is to detect security threats, whether arising internally or externally.

Depending on the protocol layer at which they are operating, network based IDSs monitor packets by inspecting layer headers or applications data. They usually signal the network administrator (send alarms) when breaches are attempted; they also can isolate or quarantine the attempts.

A host-based IDS monitors activity on the host machine (for example, download attempts), watching for valid security certificates, signatures of known threats, and access to suspicious sites. When a threat is identified, notification usually appears to the machine's user; some more sophisticated systems notify the network administrator as well, but such action is more likely to be the province of a complete network management system that includes intrusion detection software.

Actions include isolation and quarantine of suspected files, prevention of access to particular sites, and refusal to download or install certain files. When acting in this mode, an IDS also is an *intrusion prevention system (IPS).*

In the remainder of this chapter, we will explore firewalls, Internet security, encryption, virtual private networks, authentication, wireless security, and some laws and regulations. We leave discussions of physical intrusion and its prevention to other sources.

15.3 External attacks and firewalls

Conceptually, a firewall screens traffic coming into one network from another. Typically, the former is the corporate network and the latter is the Internet, although any WAN applies. The firewall, which comprises hardware and software, sits between them. Its purpose is to prevent intranet access by unauthorized parties and to stop transmissions that could harm or compromise corporate data, confidentiality, or resource functioning—intrusion prevention. Firewalls themselves do not address viruses, spyware, spam, and the like, although it is possible to include such software in a firewall package.

Corporate firewall devices are dedicated computers, typically without keyboards or monitors, although firewall software can run in a standard PC or router. Whatever the case, they are not usually used for anything but firewall functions. Although home PCs with Internet connections may run firewall software in the PCs themselves or in broadband routers or modems, this is not sufficient for the corporate scene.

Properly installed firewalls are connected to but not part of any internal networks. This prevents transmissions from bypassing them to get to those networks directly. Accordingly, there should not be any "back doors" to the internal networks, because these can be used to evade the firewalls.

AMPLIFICATION

A *backdoor* is a purposely created route to one or more corporate networks that bypasses IDSs. It allows company IT personnel to work with the networks, a good thing. On the other hand, if a backdoor is discovered, it gives hackers the same direct access. Hence, backdoors should be kept to a strict minimum, used discreetly, and closed when no longer needed.

Firewalls operate by examining packets, taking action based on what they find. They can be classified by how deep into the packet they look:

- *Packet-filtering firewalls* run on corporate border routers, the primary entry points to company networks. Layer 3 (network) headers of all packets coming from external networks are checked. Because these firewalls are network layer devices, unchecked packets can reach no higher than the data link layer before being stopped. Traffic from the Internet is routed by IP (network layer) addresses. That is why network layer packet filtering routers are the principal corporate firewalls.
- *Circuit-level firewalls* delve into the transport headers, monitoring connection-oriented session (circuit) establishment attempts by TCP (which is in the transport layer).
- *Application firewalls* look all the way into application-layer packet data for program-specific software.

Because each of these firewall types functions by filtering based on packet characteristics, the general label of *packet-filtering firewall* often is applied to any of them. There also are firewalls that incorporate the operations of all three types in one device. These are called *multilayer firewalls.*

Filtering modes

Admit/deny decisions are determined by a variety of criteria called *rules,* loaded into the firewall router by the network administrator. Rules can be based on one or more combinations of:

- IP addresses or domain names
- Port numbers
- Protocols
- Circuits or sessions
- Applications
- Other packet attributes, such as specific data patterns, words, or phrases

Firewalls operate in one of two filtering modes, with action rules established accordingly:

- **Deny all but explicit.** Transmit only those packets that meet specific rules for acceptance.
- **Pass all but explicit.** Transmit any packets that do not match specific rules for denial.

The security needs (policy) of the company in question determine which mode to use. The more secure is "deny all but explicit," because there will be no unexpected through-traffic. This policy focuses on what is allowable and does not need to consider what is not. A potential drawback is that a packet that would be acceptable but is not covered by the rules list will be denied.

With a "pass all but explicit" policy, the emphasis is on which traffic should be denied, everything else being passed. This is more risky, because new threat traffic not in the denial list will be passed until explicitly excluded; that cannot happen with the "deny all but explicit" policy. In either case, rules must be kept up to date for the filters to be effective.

Which packet characteristics can be applied in defining particular rules depends on the layer at which the firewall is operating. Whatever the case, bear in mind that, in order to be useful, a firewall has to block packets before they reach the network operating system, which is an entry point into the internal corporate networks. This means they must operate at least as low as at the network layer. Such a firewall has its own network-layer software so that the NOS never sees the rejected packets. If circuit-level and applications firewalls are used without network-layer packet filters, they leave open a doorway into the corporate networks.

Regardless of firewall activity, IP addresses can be spoofed—changed to that of a trusted host—to hide the host they actually are coming from. This can trick the firewall into passing harmful packets.

Stateful and stateless operation

Circuit-level firewalls that incorporate stateful operation are more efficient than those that do not. The state of the connection—relevant aspects of each approved connection-oriented session—is stored in a router table. Although the initial setup for validating a connection is processing-intensive, after the profile of an allowed session is established, subsequent packets are quickly processed. A table lookup is all that is needed to see whether a packet belongs to one of the pre-validated sessions, a process called *stateful inspection.* This is much simpler and faster than comparing every packet to the entire rules set.

If the stateful table is full, new requests cannot be processed. To alleviate this possibility, stateful routers are configured with a lot of memory, and table entries are erased when a session ends or when some pre-set period of time passes with no activity on a session. There are no guarantees, however. If session demands are heavy, the table may fill up anyway.

Stateful operation can be incorporated in network-layer packet filters. A state table holds the attributes of approved network-layer parameters, to which packets are compared. As you might imagine, stateless firewalls do not maintain state tables and so must treat each packet independently, without regard to prior experience.

15.4 Security attacks via the Internet

The Internet is wide open in the sense that it is up to the users to address security issues, and not the Internet itself. Particular ISPs may provide some value-added services aimed at securing transmissions or examining traffic for specific threats or junk e-mail, but in the end the user is responsible for dealing with the variety of threats posed.

Malware

Software aimed at network or computer-related disruption of one sort or another is called *malware.* Examples include viruses, denial-of-service attacks, and Web site substitution or alteration. These and others generally are laid to the door of hackers who, with mischievous or malicious intentions, perpetrate malware attacks. Let's look at the more prevalent varieties of malware.

VIRUSES   There are many hundreds of viruses in circulation throughout the Internet, and new ones are created every day. Like a biological virus, a computer virus spreads by infection. To do this, it places executable program code into a file on a computer, thus infecting the file. When the file is executed, the code reproduces itself and infects other files on the computer.

Damage is done by the actions the viruses take. Virus programs corrupt computers in ways ranging from simply displaying messages or pictures to modifying or erasing files, some even going so far as wiping out all files, reformatting drives, and crashing the machine. Viruses can be carried to other machines via infected files that are transmitted from one computer to another, thereby extending their range.

WORMS   Like viruses, *worms* are self-replicating, but unlike viruses, they can propagate on their own (viruses need to attach themselves to other programs to reproduce and do their dirty work). Worms usually are designed specifically to travel along with transmissions, thus spreading rapidly. Each machine they move to sends out worm transmissions, so the overall effect on the Internet is a rapid and significant increase in traffic and bandwidth usurpation. Hence, worms tend to aim more at network disruption than damage on an individual computer.

E-mail is a common transit medium for worms. A common worm trick is to send e-mail messages to everyone in your address book and then, of course, to everyone in the address books of all the computers it reaches. Those e-mail messages may contain the virus as well, or they may just be annoying e-mail that wastes your time and fills up your mailbox.

TROJAN HORSES   Like the Trojan horse of mythology, the gift to Troy that Greek soldiers hid in to secretly enter Troy and subsequently defeat the Trojans, *Trojan horse malware (trojan)* hides within or disguises itself as legitimate software. Trojans cannot run on their own; they must be specifically executed. This happens when the user unsuspectingly activates a program believed to be something else. For example, an e-mail message may say to click on an attachment to see a picture, take advantage of a special offer, get a message from an old acquaintance, validate your bank account, download a screensaver, or the like. Some trojans will pop up a message saying your computer has been infected and to click on the link to remove the infection. Responding to any of these activates the trojan.

Trojans differ from viruses and worms in that they do not reproduce themselves. Formerly, their principal means of spreading was e-mail. More recently, viruses, and especially worms, have been designed to carry trojans, thereby providing easy rapid transit from machine to machine. Even so, trojans must be specifically activated.

SPYWARE   As its name implies, *spyware,* also referred to as tracking software, watches your activity on the computer without your knowledge or consent. Spyware captures what it sees, and the record of your activity, even down to keystrokes, can be transmitted over the Internet to other parties.

Some spyware is relatively harmless, such as spyware that sends Web site visit information that is used to improve advertising campaigns or site design. Other more annoying spyware will pop up ads, presumably focused to your interests. Privacy and confidentiality may be compromised, though, even when the spyware creators claim that no personal information is involved. More malicious hacker spyware seeks to steal credit card information, bank account numbers, passwords, and the like. Spyware usually does not replicate itself. Rather, it is carried along on particular files. Web pages are common carriers of spyware.

ADWARE   Adware is similar to spyware in that it tracks your usage, particularly of the Web, and presents advertisements based on that usage. Some consider adware to be another form of spyware, not to be tolerated. Others view it as more benign, not even belonging to the malware category, because its intent is not malicious and typically depends on user consent. For example, many programs are offered in a "paid mode" or a free "sponsored mode." The latter will come with adware that presents advertisements as you use the program, to which you have consented in return for getting the program for free. On the other hand, consent may be embedded in the "terms of use" that you must agree to in order to use the software, free or paid.

DEALING WITH MALWARE   Firewalls can stop many malware attacks. Properly configured e-mail servers are good at catching spyware and adware and can incorporate scanning software to trap viruses and worms that come in as attachments. It's also a good idea to have anti-malware software installed on end user machines.

Some ISPs' e-mail systems scan attachments in your outgoing mail before it is sent, to prevent malware you may have from spreading, and scan incoming attachments to save your machine from infection. Operating systems can be set to block pop-ups, thereby subverting some adware, but unless exceptions are specifically listed or you take specific steps, all pop-ups will be blocked, including those you might want to see.

Typical spyware and adware programs operate after the fact, on your initiation or at preset times. Discoveries can be deleted or quarantined. Most anti-virus software checks incoming traffic on the fly and can be run on command as well.

Whether firewall-, server-, or computer-based, anti-malware software must be kept up to date to stay on top of the daily barrage of new and modified malware. Updating includes both the file of known malware and the detection engine embodied in the software.

Denial-of-service attacks

Hackers use ***denial-of-service (DoS) attacks*** to shut down particular resources by overloading them, thereby denying their services to legitimate users. The typical DoS attack is against a company's Web servers, especially those used to fulfill online requests for goods or services. Although not designed to destroy files or steal data, they can result in great cost to the companies attacked, for lost business and for the time and resources needed to restore operations.

There are several forms of DoS attacks, the most common being:

- **TCP-based SYN flood.** This attack takes advantage of TCP's handshaking procedure for setting up a session. Normally, a session request consisting of a SYN packet segment is sent to the server, which assigns a sequence number to the packet, reserves space (queues the request) in a session table, sets a timer, and sends a SYN/ACK back to the requester. The requester returns an ACK and the session is established.

  For a DoS attack, the requester sends a great many session requests, each with a different bogus IP address. When the SYN/ACKs go out, they cannot be delivered and will not generate a response. The result is a great number of half-open connections—open from the server side but not from the sender side. Even though eventually these requests would time out, if the flood is sufficient the session table will fill, stopping the server. Depending on its buffer management, the server even may crash.

- **UDP-based flood.** Counterfeit UDP packets requesting delivery to an application are sent to randomly chosen ports on the server. UDP looks for the application the packets are trying to reach, but because the packets are phony, it will not be found. A "destination unreachable" ICMP message will be sent out. If enough UDP packets are sent, the host will be tied up attempting to process the requests. In addition, the volume of incoming packets and outgoing messages uses up significant link bandwidth.
- **Broadcast attack (Smurf attack).** This method engages many hosts to unknowingly bombard one other host. The attacker sends a broadcast ICMP echo request that goes to many hosts, using as the source IP address that of the host to be attacked. Every host that responds to a broadcast request will therefore reply to the one host, which is quickly overloaded. In addition, the traffic usurps the bandwidth available to the single host.

A number of older attacks no longer affect newer systems, devices, and operating systems, but still can be troublesome for older ones. These do not depend on floods as much as they attempt to exploit weaknesses in protocol implementations.

One type uses invalid packets to stymie the IP packet reassembly procedure. Reassembly depends on knowing where in the packet the data begin (offset value). By setting the offset values so that packet assembly is impossible, the host crashes in the attempt. The *teardrop attack* sends packets whose offset values overlap. The *bonk attack* uses offset values that are too large and therefore do not point to legitimate packet sections. Newer systems ignore such invalid packets.

A similar idea is the *ping of death* attack, which sends an ICMP echo request with an IP packet larger than 65,535 bytes maximum size. When that packet becomes part of reassembly, the buffer overflows, crashing the computer. Newer systems discard oversized packets.

Another type of invalid packet is one whose source and destination IP addresses are the same, confusing the host. For example, if the packet is a SYN request, the machine tries to set up a connection with itself. This is called a *land attack.* Newer devices will ignore packets like these.

DISTRIBUTED DENIAL-OF-SERVICE ATTACKS With a distributed denial-of-service (DDoS) attack, the actual attack is one of the DoS attacks, but many hosts are unknowingly enlisted in the process. Thus the attack is distributed, coming from numerous sources. A common method for carrying out a DDoS attack involves sending trojans to a great number of computers. When activated, the trojan installs code that lets the computer be controlled by a remote host—that of the attacker—who sends the code that carries out the attack. The target is rapidly flooded by attacks from the unsuspecting hosts which, because they are unaware of what they are doing, are called *zombies.*

DEALING WITH DoS AND DDoS ATTACKS Denial of service is difficult to deal with. Often the attack is recognized only after it does its damage and the attacked services are shut down. Then the only recourse is to restore the system. If the attack is recognized while it is ongoing, it may be possible to block it before shutdown. If shutdown occurs, a means to block the flood still must be found. Otherwise, shutdowns will be repeated.

Some specific measures can be taken beforehand:

- SYN floods can be handled if border routers and other nodes are configured to limit the number of half-open sessions and to keep time-outs short. Still, repeated attacks can slow down responses substantially, even if shutdown is prevented.
- UDP floods can be reduced by closing unused UDP ports at the firewall. Similarly, requests for unused UDP services can be blocked at the hosts.

- Broadcast attacks can be eliminated by configuring devices to not respond to broadcast requests, but this also prevents responses to legitimate requests.
- Teardrop, bonk, ping of death, and land attacks, as well as their variants, are best dealt with by updating systems and software, as they have been designed to deal with such vulnerabilities.

Social engineering

Much security breach activity focuses on obtaining confidential, personal, private, or other sensitive information. Tricking people or systems into providing such information is called *social engineering.* For example, a person claiming to be a representative of a bank, police department, social agency, or the like phones you and in the course of conversation gets you to reveal your social security number, a bank account number, or even passwords—this is called *pretexting.*

Pretexting has nothing to do with texting—the sending of text messages on a cell phone. Rather, the word comes from "pretext"—a deception, a claim to be someone you are not or to represent something or someone you do not.

Similarly, a system may be fooled into admitting traffic that seems to come from a trusted source, although it does not. Quite commonly, attempts at social engineering that are carried out via the Internet use a number of schemes that fall under the headings of spam, spoofing, and phishing.

SPAM   *Spam* is bulk e-mail—that is, e-mail sent to a very large number of addresses. Spam may be solicited. For example, you sign up for a free e-magazine, and in the registration process you are asked if you want to receive e-mail from sponsors, related publications, interested parties, and so on. In some cases you choose the ones you want (opt in); in other cases you deselect the ones you do not want (opt out). Then you become part of the mass e-mailings along with others who have made the same choices. This soon can result in much more e-mail than you were expecting, but as long as no private information is being sought to use for nefarious purposes, such spam is not social engineering. Unsolicited spam is another story.

SPOOFING   Unsolicited spam not only is annoying, it often is dangerous. *Spoofing* refers to falsifying source addresses to lure you into revealing information that you shouldn't. The following are examples of spoofing as methods of social engineering:

- An e-mail message with a return address that was spoofed to a known address (changed to that of a person you know) may trick you into opening a malware attachment labeled as a picture of a friend.
- An e-mail message that seems to come from a bank where you have an account (even including the bank's logos and formats or a link to a legitimate-looking home page) warns you that your account may have been compromised and asks you to send your account numbers and passwords for verification purposes.
- An e-mail message appears to come from your credit card company, asking for passwords and account numbers for confirmation.

PHISHING   Trolling for personal or private information by randomly sending out spoofed spam is called *phishing.* Clues to its bogus nature are that often such e-mail appears to come from banks or credit cards that you have no connection with, appears to come from someone who is in your address book but is not a person you normally correspond with, uses an unusual usage or spelling of your name, or includes a subject with odd spellings or symbols.

Other phished social engineering lures are e-mail messages that offer steeply discounted drugs (frequently with no prescription required) or other amazing bargains, solicitations seeming to come from well-known charities or from someone offering an incredible monetary return from a small investment, and notifications that you have won some lottery or prize. All you need to do, they say, is reply with some confidential information or transfer some small amount of good faith money from your bank account. At the least, you will lose that money. At worst, you will become a victim of identity theft.

Business NOTE | Spoofing caller ID

A prankster makes random phone calls to many parties, spoofing the caller ID to be your phone number. If any of the called parties returns the call, they go to you.

Annoying? Yes. But now suppose you get a phone call that your caller ID says comes from your bank. The caller says that a computer malfunction has damaged your records, asks you for your account number, social security number, and password to verify your account. Because the call appears to come from your bank, you supply the information—but the ID was spoofed, you become the victim of identity theft, and your bank account is emptied. Even worse, credit cards are opened in your name and maxed out, bank loans are obtained, and your credit rating crashes.

Suppose you are the bank. Do you bear any liability? Are there measures you should have or could have taken to prevent your customer from account loss? What verification do you require before you let a major transaction take place? How might this inconvenience your legitimate customers? What are the legal ramifications you may have to deal with? What impact might news of this have on your bank's reputation? On customer loyalty?

DEALING WITH SOCIAL ENGINEERING The best way to avoid being duped is to be on guard. Never open an e-mail message whose source or subject looks suspicious in any way, or at least don't open any attachments they contain. Such messages may have subjects with misspellings or interspersed symbols designed to fool spam filters. If you get unexpected messages that seem to be from someone you know, send an e-mail message to that person asking for verification that they did indeed send it before opening any attachments. Be wary of messages with no subject. Keep your scanning software up to date.

Even if it seems that there could be a legitimate reason for you to be contacted by a business, bank, or other financial institution, never supply any information unless you initiate the responding message and send it to the address you know to be legitimate, rather than simply replying. Do the same for replies by phone.

Packet sniffers

A packet sniffer is a device for eavesdropping on network traffic. It also includes software to discover the protocols being used and thereby interpret the overheard bit stream. In the hands of network administrators, packet sniffers are useful tools to help them discover and locate the causes and sources of potential problems and current faults in their networks. In the hands of hackers, they are tools to help them break into the networks and their attached systems. After they are in, they can steal sensitive data and disrupt system functioning.

DEALING WITH HACKER PACKET SNIFFING   For intranets, securing wire closets and unused network connections will reduce physical tie-ins. But many sniffers can detect the electromagnetic radiation (EMR) produced by electrical and wireless transmissions and thus capture the bit streams. Currently, optical systems, which do not produce EMR, are too costly as replacements for all electrical systems. On the Internet, what amounts to wire tapping is pretty much a free-for-all. Hence, the best prevention is encryption to render intercepted data meaningless.

15.5 Proxies

A *proxy* is a stand-in or intermediary for something else. For example, if you own stock in a company and do not attend the annual meeting, you will be asked to give your proxy to someone who will vote your shares for you.

There are many types of proxies in networking. The most common is the *proxy server.* As its name implies, it is a stand-in for another server. Following the client/server model, a client requesting a file that resides on a particular server actually gets connected to the proxy server, which requests the file from the other server and supplies it to the original client. Thus, the proxy server acts as an intermediary, sitting between the client and the requested server. The original client is never connected directly to the target server, thus providing a measure of security. Although proxy servers can represent any server type, typically they act for Web servers.

A full discussion of the variety of network proxies is beyond the scope of this text. For additional information, a good place to start is http://compnetworking.about.com/cs/ proxyservers/a/proxyservers.htm. Another good source is http://en.wikipedia.org/wiki/ Proxies. For an interesting site, go to http://webproxies.net/.

Why proxy servers?

Proxy servers perform many useful functions in their roles as guardians of corporate networks and as a means of enhancing network performance:

- **Security.** When a client request is connected directly to a server, a doorway to the corporate networks is open. The disconnect created by the proxy keeps that doorway closed. Proxy servers work with firewalls and can even be installed in the same box. In addition, they can incorporate anti-malware software, thus enhancing the security provided by firewalls and PC software.
- **Performance.** Proxy servers can be equipped with a sizable cache (memory). As files are requested, copies are kept in the cache for some time. If the files are requested again, they can be supplied directly from the cache instead of the proxy having to go to the server to retrieve those files. This improves performance, especially when the requested file is a commonly sought Web page that would take significant additional time to retrieve from the target server each time. To keep the cache from overflowing, files are deleted based on last access time, request frequency, and file size, giving recent and routinely requested files preference for continuance in the cache.
- **Filtering.** Proxy servers can filter content—especially common for Web pages—to remove sensitive or offensive material before providing the pages or blocking the pages altogether. Although in some cases this has led to anti-censorship arguments and complaints about infringement on freedom of speech, it is one means of ensuring privacy.
- **Formatting.** Web proxies can reformat pages to fit particular devices, such as the small screens of PDAs or cell phones.

Bypassing the proxy server

Proxy servers take time to do their jobs. In some cases, such as when trusted clients need access to particular servers, performance is improved if the proxy can be bypassed. The *common gateway interface (CGI)* provides a mechanism for direct transactions between clients and servers. For example, a CGI running on a company gateway allows requests to connect directly to a Web server. This can provide access for particular users to a site that is otherwise blocked. Care must be taken to keep the bypass concealed to prevent hacking into the site.

15.6 Encryption

The idea behind encryption is a simple one—obfuscate the data so that it will not be intelligible to anyone but the intended recipient, who has the means to decrypt it. The original unencrypted document is called *plaintext;* the encrypted document is called *ciphertext.* The word "cipher" derives from various languages, all of which give it the meaning of zero, empty, or nothing.

This is an idea that existed long before computers entered the picture. But now, with the Internet and so many other interconnected networks, the ease with which data can be sent around the world—subject to being intercepted in the journey—makes encryption ever more important.

Encryption is done by algorithms—manipulations based on rules to disguise the plaintext. For example, we could replace each letter of the alphabet by the one that follows it, except for "z," which we would replace with "a." This is called a *substitution code,* one symbol being substituted for by another.

Of course, this example is much too simple to be useful. The algorithms actually used are very complex and are based on long bit strings called *keys.* Applying a key to plaintext converts it to ciphertext. Depending on the encryption method, the same or a different key translates the ciphertext back into plaintext.

Key systems

Most relevant to computer communications are *key ciphers,* in which mathematical algorithms use keys to encrypt plaintext and decrypt ciphertext, thus ensuring *privacy.* Two versions of key ciphers are asymmetric and symmetric.

ASYMMETRIC KEYS *Asymmetric* denotes that there are two different keys in play, one that is *public* and one that is *private.* The way asymmetric key systems work, both must be used to complete the transmission. Here's how:

Suppose A wants to send ciphertext to B. B publishes a public key, which A uses to encrypt the plaintext. After it is encrypted, it can be decrypted only with B's private key, which only B has. Thus, even if A's transmission is intercepted, it cannot be understood.

A similar process can be used to send a *digital signature,* which provides *authentication* (assurance that a message actually is from the party it appears to be, not spoofed) and *non-repudiation* (prevents the sender from claiming it did not send the message). For A to send a digital signature to B, A publishes a public key and uses A's own private key to encrypt a message. B uses A's public key to decrypt. Because only A could have encrypted the message with A's private key, B is assured that it did indeed come from A. Of course, anyone who picked up the public key could decrypt the signature, but because its only purpose is to validate the sender, no harm is done.

For secure encryption and authentication, both methods are used together. First, A encrypts messages using A's private key, and then A encrypts it again using B's public key.

When the ciphertext reaches B, B's private key is applied to decrypt, and then A's public key decrypts again, thus re-creating the original plaintext and verifying the sender.

The tradeoff for the improved security of asymmetric key systems is the added computation involved. For networks where security is of high importance, the tradeoff is a good one. Otherwise, symmetric keys can be used.

SYMMETRIC KEYS *Symmetric* means that the sender and receiver use the same key, the sender to encrypt and the receiver to decrypt. Because there is only one key, it must be kept private from everyone but the authorized sender and receiver.

A major weakness of symmetric keys comes from the problem of getting a key to the receiver. If the receiver is nearby, the sender can carry a disk with the key to the receiver. But if the receiver is at some distance, the disk must be physically shipped or the key electronically transmitted. Either way, there is some risk of interception. Symmetric keys work best for internal use within company networks, or via a third-party key manager.

KEY MANAGEMENT VIA THIRD PARTIES Key-based systems, whether asymmetric or symmetric, face the problem of reliable key exchange. Unless each party to a transmission has the appropriate keys and no one else has them, the systems will fail. Even in asymmetric key systems, which rely on public as well as private keys, keeping a public key from being truly public is a good idea. Currently, the most reliable method for online key exchange is based on *digital certificates.*

DIGITAL CERTIFICATES A digital certificate is a copy of a key that is digitally signed by a trusted third party, called a *certificate authority (CA)*. The certificate verifies that the key it contains is genuine and comes from the named source, thus assuring the party that receives the key that it is authentic.

In practice, a number of steps are involved:

1. A sender applies to a CA for a certificate.
2. The CA transmits its public key to the applicant.
3. The sender uses the CA's public key to encrypt its own key and sends it to the CA.
4. The CA issues a certificate, which contains a serial number, the name and key of its owner (sender), the certificate's valid dates (from/to, after which it expires), the name and digital signature of the CA, and the algorithm used to create the CA's signature.
5. The sender transmits the encrypted message, with the certificate attached, to the recipient.
6. The recipient uses the CA's public key to decrypt the certificate, uncovering the sender's key and using it to decrypt the message. The recipient can use that same key or its own certificate to send a reply.

The most widely used standard for digital certificates is ITU-T X.509; version 3 is the latest release. (See http://www.itu.int/rec/T-REC-X.509/en.) Properly employed, a digital certificate prevents the use of bogus keys to impersonate a source. However, in many instances senders do not keep their certificates up to date, and recipients use the keys they contain even though they see a warning message that the certificate has expired. This is not unusual when the message comes from a trusted source—but is it really from that source? That's a risk you take when you accept an expired certificate.

Currently there are six international CAs: VeriSign, Thawte Consulting, Società per I Servizi Bancari (SSB) S.p.A., Internet Publishing Services, Certisign Certification Digital Ltda, and BelSign. In fact, anyone can set up a CA. Although this does not make much business sense on a national or international level, it can be a good idea for a corporation to set up its own CA for internal use.

BREAKING THE KEYS Keys can be broken by using mathematics or by brute force. In the former, various mathematical techniques use partial knowledge of the ciphers and look for weaknesses that help uncover the keys. Three such schemes are called *linear cryptanalysis, differential cryptanalysis,* and the *Davies attack.*

Brute force relies on computer power to run through every possible bit combination in the key to discover the one that is used. As computers gain power, keys must be lengthened to be effective; that is, they must be made sufficiently long so that even the fastest computers cannot, on average, discover the key in a usefully short time. (We say "average" here because it is always possible that a key can be stumbled upon relatively quickly.)

SOME KEY CIPHER SYSTEMS There are a large number of encryption systems—algorithms for using keys to encrypt plaintext and decrypt ciphertext. This section includes the most common.

DES, Triple DES, and AES *Data encryption standard (DES)* was published by IBM in 1975 and became a U.S. Federal Information Processing Standard (FIPS) in 1976. It uses a 56-bit key cipher and the *data encryption algorithm (DEA).* Although it sufficed for a short while, as computer power grew its key was able to be broken without much difficulty by brute force attacks.

To solve this problem, *triple DES (TDES)* was published by IBM in 1978, in conjunction with *triple DEA.* TDES is a block cipher that applies three 56-bit blocks consecutively to create a 168-bit key. Parity bits added to each block increases their size to 64 bits, so the total key is 192 bits. A later version, called *3TDES,* follows the same consecutive process but is even more secure because it uses a different key at each step instead of just one for all steps.

The DES improvements come with a cost—relatively long computation time to encrypt and decrypt. To alleviate that dilemma, *advanced encryption standard (AES)* was created. AES is a consecutively applied square block cipher with fixed-block size of 128 bits and possible key sizes of 128, 192, and 256 bits. The design of its computational complexity is such that it is much faster than any of the DESs, but at the same time it is more secure, especially when the longer keys are used.

HISTORICAL NOTE
Rijndael

Two Belgians, Vincent Rijmen and Joan Daemen, created an encryption method they called Rijndael and published it in 1998. They also submitted it as a proposed standard to the U.S. National Institute of Standards and Technology (NIST), one of many examined in the search for an AES. It was adopted as FIPS 140-2 by NIST in 2001.

PGP and S/MIME   E-mail is at once a great convenience and an easily sniffed medium. Encryption helps ensure that e-mail is not readable by someone other than the intended recipient. Two commonly employed encryption schemes are *pretty good privacy (PGP)* and *secure multipurpose Internet mail extensions (S/MIME).*

PGP, which provides both encryption and authentication, is an implementation of several other encryption algorithms. It is designed to facilitate key exchange and digital signature verification. Although it can be used for encryption in general, its most common use is for e-mail.

PGP originally was designed by Phil Zimmerman and released in 1991. It has since been worked on by others as well, with an eye toward maintaining interoperability with older versions, and has become an Internet standard called OpenPGP. For more information, see http://www.pgp.com/ and http://www.philzimmermann.com/EN/background/index .html.

MIME is a nearly universally used Internet Engineering Task Force (IETF) standard for formatting e-mail sent over the Internet, almost always in conjunction with simple mail transfer protocol (SMTP). The extensions that MIME provides enable e-mailing data that is not part of the ASCII code set. In addition to e-mail, MIME is used by Web browsers for pages that are not created using HTML. IANA now controls MIME functioning. You can register a media type for inclusion in MIME by applying to IANA at http://www.iana.org/ assignments/media-types/.

MIME does not incorporate encryption. For that purpose, there is S/MIME, which also provides digital signatures and has become a standard. S/MIME uses a public key encryption scheme originally created by RSA Data Security. It also is possible to use PGP instead of S/MIME to encrypt MIME.

RSA's Web site is http://www.rsasecurity.com/. For further information about MIME and S/MIME, see the Internet Mail Consortium's site at http://www.imc.org/.

SSL, TLS, HTTPS, and HTTP-S   Netscape (http://www.netscape.com/) developed *secure sockets layer (SSL),* a connection-oriented protocol to provide encryption and authentication, primarily to protect communications between Web clients and servers. When an SSL-secured Web page is accessed, the protocol notification portion of the URL is *https.* All current Web browsers and servers incorporate SSL; 3.0 (1996) is the latest version.

Transport layer security (TLS), developed by an IETF workgroup that was established in 1996, was intended to be the successor to SSL. (See http://www.ietf.org/html .charters/tls-charter.html.) Although it is based on SSL 3.0, the two are not compatible. Newer browser versions support TLS in addition to SSL.

Secure Web browsing can also be ensured via *secure http* (s-http, http-s, or shttp). This provides the same type of security as https, but it is an independent connectionless protocol that does not run on SSL or TLS.

15.7 Virtual private networks

A *virtual private network (VPN)* is a way to transmit secure data over a network that may not be secure. This can be an internal company network; more commonly it is a public network, most often the Internet. As its name implies, a VPN acts as though it was a dedicated private network, but it is not. Instead, the sender's VPN software encrypts the packet's data and source address. The receiver decrypts the packet and runs a checksum. Because the source address is included in the encryption and checksum calculation, a spoofed IP address will cause the checksum to fail. If the checksum fails, the packet is discarded.

VPNs are created by *tunneling,* a technique to send one network's packets through another network using secure protocols, without those packets having to conform to the other network's protocols. To do so, one network's packets are encapsulated within the protocols of the other network. Encapsulating protocols are removed on exit.

The most frequently used protocol set is *IPsec.* Less frequently used protocols are:

- *Point-to-point tunneling protocol (PPTP).* Developed by the PPTP Forum, PPTP is used with the *generic routing encapsulation protocol (GRE)* to create a secure version of the point-to-point protocol (PPP). For details, see http://support.3com.com/infodeli/tools/remote/general/pptp/pptp.htm.
- *Layer 2 tunneling protocol (L2TP).* To carry PPP sessions, L2TP is used to construct a VPN by creating a tunnel. Combining the features of PPTP and L2F (Cisco's layer 2 forwarding), it is being worked on by the IETF. Because L2TP lacks provision for confidentiality, it is joined with IPsec to fill the gap. For details, see http://www.cisco.com/univercd/cc/td/doc/product/software/ios120/120newft/120t/120t1/l2tpt.htm#wp5939.
- *Multiprotocol label switching (MPLS).* MPLS is designed to emulate a circuit switched network in a packet switched network. MPLS is discussed in Chapter 13, "TCP/IP, associated protocols, and routing." Additional information can be found at IETF's MPLS working group, http://www.ietf.org/html.charters/mpls-charter.html.

IPsec

As we have seen, IP is not a secure protocol. But IP is commonly used for packet exchange over the Internet. When those packets must be secured, *IPsec,* a protocol set operating at the network layer, can be employed. Developed by the IETF, IPsec is a group of open standards commonly used to create VPNs. For additional information, see http://www.cisco.com/en/US/products/sw/iosswrel/ps1835/products_configuration_guide_chapter09186a00800ca7b0.html.

There are two IPsec modes:

- **Transport.** The layer 3 payload (the transport header and everything it encapsulates) is encrypted, but the IP header is not. This mode normally is used for protected end-to-end communication between two hosts.
- **Tunnel.** Both the layer 3 payload and the IP header are encrypted. This mode normally is used for protected transmission between two nodes, one of which is not a host—that is, between two routers, a host and a router, or two firewalls.

In either version, the IPsec *authentication header (AH)* creates a *hash value* from the packet's bits. The receiver uses that value to authenticate the packet. Any modification of the original packet will result in a different hash value and the packet will be discarded. Therefore, the AH also provides *integrity assurance*—assurance that the packet, including its original headers, was not modified.

AMPLIFICATION

Created by a *hash function* operating on a string of bits, a *hash value* is a unique result that can be used to identify the string—if any bits in the original string are changed, the function will produce a different value.

The AH does not provide confidentiality, however. That is the job of the second part of IPsec, the *encapsulating security payload (ESP)*, which encrypts the packet to provide privacy. Newer ESP functionality adds authentication and integrity.

IPsec requires that the sender and receiver use the same public key. Therefore, without proper key management and security, IPsec is useless. For key management, the *Internet Security Association and Key Management Protocol (ISAKMP)* is used. Although ISAKMP manages key exchange for a communications session, it does not establish the keys themselves. Other protocols are used for that purpose—most frequently paired with ISAKMP is *Oakley.*

For details on Internet key exchange protocols (IKE) in general and ISAKMP and Oakley in particular, visit http://www.cisco.com/univercd/cc/td/doc/product/software/ios113ed/113t/113t_3/isakmp.htm.

A weak spot in end-to-end VPNs

Whatever the protocols used, traffic traveling in a VPN tunnel carries packets with confidentiality assured by encryption, content integrity verified by hash keys, and end-point authentication from digital signatures. A potential weak spot is at the end points. If one is hacked into, traffic can be read before the VPN process takes place or after the packet emerges from the tunnel.

15.8 NAT

Network address translation (NAT) originally was designed as a short-term solution for the dwindling availability of IPv4 addresses. (The long-term solution is IPv6.) To do this, NAT maps a single public IP address to many internal (private) IP addresses. Because these internal host addresses are strictly local and host packets must go through NAT for translation of their private addresses to the public IP address, they do not have to be globally unique. Furthermore, with a NAT-enabled border router, there is no direct route between an external source and an internal host.

With proper protocols installed in the NAT router, internal hosts gain a measure of security from malicious external sources. In addition, unless specific TCP and UDP protocol support is included, the NAT router will obstruct TCP connection attempts and UDP traffic initiated from outside the organization.

Because NAT mapping changes IP addresses, it can interfere with IPsec—the hash values will indicate that the packet has been altered. There are two solutions to this dilemma:

- Run NAT before hashing by IPsec.
- Use products from companies that are designed to handle both NAT and IPsec without conflict.

15.9 Wireless security

Attacks on wireless networks have the same goals as attacks on wired networks: disruption of service, interception or corruption of private or sensitive data, and mischief. Aside from being targets themselves, wireless networks attached to distribution systems are tempting targets as possible backdoors into the wired networks.

Security measures for wireless networks must address the same issues as wired networks: confidentiality, integrity, and authentication. What complicates matters is the fact that wireless transmissions are receivable by anyone within range.

WEP and WEP2

When the IEEE 802.11b WLAN standard was published in 1999, it included *Wired Equivalent Privacy (WEP).* The implication of its name is that it provides the same security protection that is available for wired LANs, but it falls short. As a MAC sublayer protocol, WEP encryption applies only between stations, or between a station and an access point. End-to-end protection is not part of the standard. WEP encryption will prevent loss of confidentiality from what we may call casual eavesdropping. However, all members of a WLAN share the same static 40-bit key, which is concatenated with a 24-bit *initialization vector (IV)* to produce a 64-bit encryption key. At only 64 bits, this key is fairly easy to crack. Hence, a dedicated eavesdropper can compromise confidentiality without much effort.

Even more to the point, although the IV is randomly generated and can be different for each frame, it is put into the frame as plaintext so that the receiver can perform the same concatenation with the shared key and thereby decrypt the frame. Thus, the IV can be intercepted and read directly.

A later version, called *WEP2,* increased the shared key size to 104 bits, producing an encryption key of 128 bits when concatenated with the 24-bit IV. With the desktop computing power available today, cracking a 128-bit key is not much of a challenge, either.

WPA, WPA2, and 802.11i

To overcome the deficiencies of WEP, the IEEE 802.11i subgroup began working on a better scheme. Rather than wait for its completion, the Wi-Fi Alliance (http://www.wi-fi.org/) released *Wi-Fi protected access (WPA)* in 2002. This version implemented many of the features that were to be included in the full 802.11i protocol set. Because WEP was WiFi certified by the Alliance, they incorporated WEP compatibility into WPA while adding significant enhancements:

- Key size was increased to 128 bits and IV size to 48 bits, for a total of 172 bits.
- Data encryption was improved by using the *temporal key integrity protocol (TKIP),* which changes the key dynamically before encryption. Thus, every data packet is encrypted with its own unique key.
- Provision for user authentication was made via an IEEE 802.1X authentication server, which distributes different keys to each user and controls access to LAN ports. Port-based network access is controlled by authenticating attached LAN nodes. Authentication failure will close the port to the node in question.

When *802.11i* was released in 2004, it was certified by the Wi-Fi Alliance as *WPA2* and became the official 802 replacement for WEP. In addition to the features of WPA, 802.11i replaced WEP's (and WPA's) RC4 stream cipher with the *advanced encryption standard (AES)* block cipher discussed earlier, bringing it up to the federal standards specified in FIPS 140-2. (See http://www.rsasecurity.com/rsalabs/node .asp? id=2250.)

A more secure means for key exchange also was incorporated. (See http://www .embedded.com/showArticle.jhtml?articleID=34400002.)

WPA is a good choice for home and home office networks, much preferred over WEP; WPA2 is the choice for corporate environments.

15.10 Compliance and certification standards for computer security

Security standards exist in many realms. As with all standards, compliance and conformance is not legally mandated or guaranteed. However, it is becoming more common for businesses to demand compliance and conformance in the products and systems they use. Given the current climate, this trend surely is sensible. We will cover some of the more prevalent security compliance standards in this section.

Common criteria

Currently the most comprehensive international standard for computer security is the **Common Criteria (CC),** officially named ISO/IEC 15408. The CC grew out of three similar but separate standards:

- **Trusted Computer System Evaluation Criteria (TCSEC),** the U.S. standard, also called the Orange Book, issued in 1985 by the U.S. National Computer Security Center.
- **Canadian Trusted Computer Product Evaluation Criteria (CTCPEC),** the Canadian standard, published in 1989 by the Canadian government.
- **Information Technology Security Evaluation Criteria (ITSEC),** the European standard, created by a consortium of France, Germany, Great Britain, and the Netherlands, released in 1990.

The CC, released in 2004, was an international effort that combined the pre-existing standards into a unified document that enabled interested parties to evaluate products by just one standards set. Rather than providing the security standards themselves, the CC comprises guidelines for creating two basic documents that can be used to establish security specifications and to evaluate and compare product claims:

- **Protection profile (PP)** for specifying security requirements and identifying devices that meet those requirements. The PP focuses on users or customers of security products.
- **Security target (ST)** for specifying security requirements and functions for a product or system, called the **target of evaluation (TOE).** The ST is a guide for evaluators determining compliance of hardware and software to ISO/IEC 15408 and can be used by developers during creation and design to ensure compliance of the finished products.

The CC also provides items to support the writing of PPs and STs:

- **Security functional requirements (SFRs)** are derived from a list of security functions from which the document creators can choose. The choices go into the PPs and STs.
- **Security assurance requirements (SARs)** is another list that describes the steps to take in developing hardware or software to make sure compliance will be met by the final product. Choices depend on what is being developed. These choices go into the STs.
- **Evaluation assurance levels (EALs)** are indicators of the assurance testing that has been performed. Levels range from 1 to 7, representing increasing scrutiny for validation of TOE security claims. (The CC notes that assurance is relative to TOE claims and does not guarantee performance against all possible threats.)

AMPLIFICATION

Issued jointly by ISO and the International Electrotechnical Commission (IEC), the latest version of ISO/IEC 15408 was published in 2005, in three parts. For complete information visit the ISO or the IEC Web sites: http://www.iso.org/iso/en/Catalogue DetailPage.CatalogueDetail?CSNUMBER=40612&ICS1=35&ICS2=40&ICS3 or http://www.iec.ch/cgi-bin/procgi.pl/www/iecwww.p?wwwlang=e&wwwprog=seabox1.p&progdb=db1&seabox1=15408.

Latest activities and news, as well as other references, can be found at "the official Web site of the Common Criteria Project": http://www.commoncriteriaportal.org/.

FIPS

FIPS-1, officially named *Security Requirements for Cryptographic Modules* when published by the U.S. National Institute of Standards and Technology (NIST) in 2001, is a standard used to certify cryptographic modules. The latest version, FIPS-2, was a joint effort of NIST and the Canadian Communications Security Establishment (CSE).

FIPS is intended to assess product ability to protect government IT systems using four increasingly stringent levels of encryption and security. More and more, it is being adopted by corporations that must safeguard sensitive data, including compliance with Sarbanes-Oxley (http://www.sarbanes-oxley-forum.com/) and HIPAA (http://www.hhs.gov/ocr/hipaa/).

Products that pass FIPS testing are given *validation certificates* for the level certified. Certificates are published on the NIST Web site along with the version certified, instructions for enabling FIPS mode, product-specific details about roles and authentication, approved and unapproved cryptographic functions, critical security parameters, and other related information. Because NIST is an independent agency, its test results are an excellent guide to security products and its Web site a reliable source for locating products of interest.

For a list of FIPS 140-1 and FIPS 140-2 validated vendors' modules, see http://csrc.nist.gov/cryptval/140-1/140val-all.htm.

15.11 Cyberlaw

Succinctly defined, *cyberlaw* refers to legislation and regulation as applied to computer-assisted communications. As is often the case with technological developments, the technology changes faster than do the laws and regulations. Consequently, legislation designed to deal with older means of communication, primarily print and telephone, does not apply well to high-speed networks, associated databases, and the Internet.

Much of what has made its way into regulations of one sort or another has to do with how networks, particularly the Internet, are used—that is, for what purpose—rather than the networks themselves, but even then, clarity and direct relevance have yet to appear to any great measure. One good source to begin an exploration is http://bubl.ac.uk/LINK/i/internetregulation-law.htm, which has links to a variety of sources of more or less applicable regulatory information.

One issue that currently is being debated rather hotly is *net neutrality*. As it is defined at http://www.google.com/help/netneutrality.html, "Net neutrality is the principle that Internet users should be in control of what content they view and what applications they use on the Internet." The debate centers around whether net neutrality should be preserved or replaced with a tiered structure of fees and access that depend on factors such as bandwidth and availability. As this is critical to what the Internet of the future will look like, we discuss net neutrality in Chapter 18, "The future of network communications."

15.12 Summary

Network security concerns cover such wide-ranging issues as physical intrusion and disruption, software-based mischief and assaults, unauthorized transmission capture, and terrorist attacks. Thwarting such attacks, which can come from internal and external sources, is the goal of network security. In this chapter, we explored the issues most relevant to business today, namely attacks on corporate networks and protecting corporate transmissions from meaningful interception—in other words, intrusion detection and prevention.

We saw that, although there are principles that are generally applicable, to be most effective security should be policy based and company specific. We also saw that in developing a policy, it is useful to look at security issues from several perspectives—by source, by type of attack, by intent, by method, and by target.

We explored different types of firewalls, how they function, their effectiveness in preventing external attacks, and their impact on processing time. We also looked at the Internet as a source of a variety of attacks, including malware, viruses, worms, Trojan horses, and spyware. Then we outlined what can be done about them, both pre- and post-infection.

Denial-of-service attacks are another class of security problems. We saw how a number of them operate, what they do, and how to deal with them. Next we looked at the techniques of social engineering—pretexting and, especially via the Internet, spam, spoofing, and phishing. We also looked at packet sniffers and discussed what they can do and how they can be foiled.

We explored proxy servers as an effective security measure, acting as intermediaries between the client and the target server. In addition to security, they can improve network performance and response time, and they can filter content as well.

We went into some detail to explain the options and functioning of encryption systems. Then we described virtual private networks and network address translation. We examined the added complications of security for wireless networks and where we stand so far in achieving the same level of protection as we do for wired networks.

Finally, we looked at computer security compliance and certification standards, followed by a brief foray into cyberlaw.

For further reference, the following are two excellent, full-coverage books on network security:

- Bragg, Roberta, Mark Rhodes-Ousley, and Keith Strassberg. *Network Security: The Complete Reference.* McGraw-Hill, 2003.
- Kizza, Joseph Migga. *Computer Network Security.* Springer, 2005.

In the next chapter, we will discuss network management—in particular, the management of corporate networks and their connections to public data networks. Also discussed are the management of LANs and VLANs that are isolated from other networks for reasons of security or because they are used for purposes that do not require interconnecting them.

END-OF-CHAPTER QUESTIONS

Short answer

1. What is a risk assessment? What is a corporate security policy?
2. What is a firewall? What can it do? What can't it do?
3. What are "deny all but explicit" filtering and "pass all but explicit" filtering? Which is more risky? Why?
4. Describe the actions of Trojan horses. How do they differ from viruses and worms?
5. What is a denial-of-service attack? What are their most common forms?
6. Contrast spam, spoofing, and phishing.
7. How do proxy servers enhance security?
8. How do virtual private networks provide for secure data transmission?
9. NAT, originally designed as a short-term solution for the growing shortage of IPv4 address, can be used to improve internal host security. At the same time, NAT can conflict with IPsec. How can this be dealt with?
10. Compare WEP, WPA, and 802.11i.

Fill-in

1. Five perspectives on security issues are _____, _____, _____, _____, and _____.
2. Network attacks from internal sources are addressed by _____ and _____, whereas those from external sources are addressed by _____ and _____.
3. Three firewalls that examine packets are _____, _____, and _____.
4. _____ are malware that can replicate on their own.
5. Another name for tracking software is _____.
6. _____ are devices for eavesdropping on network traffic.
7. A _____ can transmit secure data over an unsecure network.
8. A potential weak spot in end-to-end VPNs is _____.
9. _____ is a federal standard used to certify cryptographic modules.
10. Legislation and regulation applied to computer-assisted communications is called _____.

Multiple-choice

1. Network-based intrusion detection systems
   a. monitor download attempts
   b. check for valid security certificates
   c. inspect layer headers
   d. send alarms to notify the network administrator
   e. both c and d

2. Host-based intrusion detection systems
   a. monitor download attempts
   b. check for valid security certificates
   c. inspect layer headers
   d. send alarms to notify the network administrator
   e. both a and d

3. Viruses
   a. are one form of malware
   b. use executable program code
   c. spread by reproduction
   d. can erase files and crash computers
   e. all of the above

4. Flood denial-of-service attacks
   a. can take advantage of the TCP handshake session setup procedure
   b. use the well-known ports for counterfeit UDP packets
   c. are foiled by increasing available bandwidth
   d. are stopped by pinging
   e. all of the above

5. Encrypted data
   a. can be read by anyone with a substitution code
   b. requires two keys to interpret
   c. can provide digital signatures
   d. eliminates the need for secure Web sites
   e. is another name for ciphertext

6. Asymmetric keys
   a. are more difficult to get to the receiver than symmetric keys
   b. use different public and private keys
   c. require digital certificates
   d. cannot be combined with digital signatures
   e. are less effective for authentication than symmetric keys

7. Virtual private networks
   a. must be created with point-to-point tunneling protocol
   b. frequently make use of IPsec
   c. discard packets with checksum failures
   d. all of the above
   e. b and c only

8. WEP2
   a. provides the same wireless security as is available for wired LANs
   b. is less effective than WiFi protected access
   c. uses 128 bits for encryption
   d. uses 172 bits for encryption
   e. is no longer used

9. The Common Criteria for computer security
   a. is a required standard
   b. specifies the security protocols to be used
   c. provides guidelines for establishing security specifications
   d. does not allow for product comparisons
   e. applies only in the United States

10. Legislation and regulation
    a. for computer-assisted communications lags technological change
    b. designed for print and telephone applies to high-speed networks as well
    c. is perfectly suited for the Internet
    d. dealing with satellite transmissions conflicts with that dealing with cell phones
    e. all of the above

True or false

1. Intrusion is any unauthorized network activity.
2. A generic security policy will suffice for almost all companies.
3. Firewall devices are dedicated computers.
4. Properly configured e-mail servers are good at catching spyware and adware, and they can incorporate scanning software to trap viruses and worms that come in as attachments.
5. The most important factor in dealing with malware is keeping the software up to date.
6. Currently, the most reliable method for online key exchange is based on digital certificates.

7. PGP and S/MIME are commonly used for encrypting e-mail.
8. Because WEP was certified by the Wi-Fi Alliance, they incorporated WEP compatibility into WPA.
9. Temporal key integrity protocol is an advanced feature of WEP.
10. FIPS-2 is being adopted by corporations that must comply with Sarbanes-Oxley and HIPAA.

Exploration

1. Look for anti-spyware programs on the Web sites of the companies that produce them. Create a table showing the company, product, actions, and cost. Which would you choose? Search the Web for reviews of these programs. Does what you find change your choice?

2. Investigate third-party key management companies. What services do they provide? At what costs?
3. Go to the Wi-Fi and WiMAX Web sites. What do those organizations do? How do they differ?

CASE   **SECURING WIRELESS NETWORKS**

Data-R-Us, Inc. (DRU) provides data warehousing, backup, and recovery services for a wide range of businesses. Along with its internal wired infrastructure, DRU employs wireless networking extensively, internally for its in-house employees and externally for its large cadre of traveling sales agents, troubleshooters, and support technicians. WLANs, Bluetooth, WiFi, and WiMAX all are part of DRU's operation. With so much information being sent over the air, security is a particular concern.

What do you think of the variety of wireless technologies DRU uses? Would security issues be easier to handle if the variety was reduced? Would doing so affect DRU's business model?

You have been hired to assess the situation. What questions would you ask to get the information you need? Who would you like to interview? What do you see as reasonable options?

THE MOSI CASE, CONTINUED

MOSI patient records include a considerable amount of confidential information. Because MOSI's networks are connected to the outside world, external intrusion always is a concern. Internal intrusion cannot be overlooked, either. Aside from the patient records that MOSI keeps, confidential patient data is transmitted between MOSI and its feeder hospitals, between MOSI and various insurance companies, and between MOSI and government oversight agencies. Field agents remotely transmit and receive considerable amounts of data to and from the corporate databases.

Outline the specific patient security issues MOSI faces. Describe the security policy you would recommend that MOSI employ. Is HIPAA a factor? How do the types of networks involved influence the policy? What triggers should invoke a policy review? How can MOSI determine whether the policy is being properly carried out?

CHAPTER

16

Network management

16.1 Overview

It is easy to say that *network management* deals with managing networks, and of course, it does. But the term is not as monolithic as its name implies. For a small business with simple networks, it may mean an occasional visit by a trained technician to handle a particular problem, make sure the networks are running properly, or install some upgrades.

At the other end of the spectrum are complex networks in large-scale firms that are attended to by an entire department. Specialists coordinate closely with network security personnel and use sophisticated hardware and software management systems for real-time performance, traffic monitoring, and troubleshooting. They have a cadre of technicians to carry out proactive measures, perform routine maintenance, resolve problems, and install upgrades.

From a business perspective, whether we are dealing with simple or complex networks, their management should be a centralized operation. The networks we are concerned with managing are corporate networks and their connections to public data networks (PDNs). Also included are LANs and VLANs that are isolated from the others for reasons of security or because of uses that do not require interconnection.

PDNs are privately owned and operated WANs that provide public access and charge fees for connection services. They are commonly used by corporations to extend the reach of their own networks. Often, corporations do not own their own WANs; they are managed by the WAN owners, who are responsible for link maintenance, upgrades, and problem fixes. Problems within the corporate network are the province of corporate network management.

It is possible, however, for a corporation to own and manage its own WAN. For example, it may have networks in different locations that it connects via microwave, or via leased lines or its own cables run over leased rights-of-way such as along railroad lines or highways. Managing such a WAN follows the principles that this chapter covers, but on a larger and more complex scale that is beyond the scope of this text.

An organization's own internal networks routinely comprise multiple LANs interconnected by internal routers. The routers see these networks simply as connections and move transmissions among them via network layer protocols, typically those of the TCP/IP suite. When TCP/IP is used, this collective internal network is called an *intranet.*

Intranets that have external connections reside behind the corporate firewalls and are accessible only to authorized employees. A company also may have one or more *extranets.* These provide limited access to specific parts of an intranet to people outside the corporation. Here are two examples: A company may set up an extranet between itself and key suppliers to automate order/re-order inventory processing. Or a company may provide access to those parts of its network that provide particular information services to specified customers.

As long as there have been networks, there has been network management. Initially, the greatest task faced by network managers was getting a variety of often incompatible networks and legacy systems to talk to each other. This was made more difficult by the fact that different expertise often was needed for the different systems, and it was not likely that the same technician could work with all of them. Later, as outdated systems were replaced, compatibility was kept in mind, so the task load shifted to keeping complex interrelated systems running smoothly.

For some time in the 1990s, the makers of expensive management consoles—automated *network management systems (NMSs)* claimed to be capable of monitoring and managing entire corporate networks—pushed companies to purchase those systems, ostensibly to simplify network management. Companies that installed them soon learned that simplification often was a myth. The NMSs were not necessarily compatible with all the corporate equipment and the (proprietary) monitoring devices they contained, and they were complicated to master.

Disillusionment put a damper on that business until late in the decade when manufacturers made their consoles more versatile and compatible. The more complex the networks, the more a company will benefit from NMSs whose size, reach, and capabilities are tailored to the organization's needs.

16.2 People and systems

Networks are managed by people using various hardware and software tools and management systems. Even though comprehensive NMSs routinize and automate many management activities, the ultimate responsibility for managing networks rests with people. In a small company with few networks, the management job may be given to one or two network administrators. In a large company with complex networks, administrators usually are accounts managers (who handle passwords and access rights), technicians (who resolve faults and perform upgrades), and upper-level managers (who oversee operations on a department level). (See "Business note: Who are these people?")

At either extreme and in between as well, technology is employed to help with the job of management. So we use databases to track access rights, usage, and passwords, sniffers to monitor traffic; hardware and software modules installed in network devices to provide activity data and respond to commands; and NMS consoles to integrate and coordinate the lot.

No matter how automated a company's network management system is, the ultimate responsibility for network management rests with people.

Business NOTE

Who are these people?

The titles of people engaged in network management often are used in confusing ways. The fact is that there are no universally agreed upon definitions, so you will find titles and job descriptions varying from company to company. In broad terms:

Network administrator: someone who manages a network. This follows from the definition of an administrator as a manager. Accordingly, we also have systems administrators and database administrators. Interestingly, some references use the term *network manager* to denote a network administrator, whereas others reserve that term for the NMS and associated software.

So what does a network administrator do? In a nutshell, a network administrator is responsible for all aspects of the operation of corporate networks, although others may carry out the actual tasks. More specifically, responsibilities include:

- Network installation, management, and control (access)
- Network setup, maintenance, and security (In large corporations, security often is a separate, though coordinated, operation.)
- Software licensing and acquisition, application installation, distribution, and upgrading (This may be the responsibility of an applications administrator.)
- Performance and activity monitoring and performance tuning
- Network design and reconfiguration, VLANs, LAN segmentation, extranets, intranets, and WAN interfaces

- Storage management, backup, and restore (For network attached storage and storage area networks—database administrators may be involved.)

Even this is not an exhaustive list. Obviously it takes more than one person, so the network administrator functions primarily as a director and overseer of the management activity, except in small companies where the administrator, perhaps with a couple of staff members, does the job. Personnel will include engineers, technicians, and other technically trained people.

Systems administrator: someone who is hands-on in the running of the networks, often with an engineering background, and often supervising technicians.

And what does a systems administrator do? In general:

- Firewall configuration, password assignment, and management of user accounts
- Acquisition, installation, and maintenance of network hardware, software, and operating systems
- Backup and recovery operations
- E-mail address assignment

You can see that there is overlap in these lists. In fact, actual responsibilities and titles are very organization-dependent. Regardless of title and purview, network personnel need to work hard at keeping up to date with rapidly changing technology so as to remain an effective and efficient arm of the business.

Planning and process issues

SCOPE   Perhaps the biggest issue in planning for network management is deciding what network devices to manage, how closely they should be managed, and by corollary, what not to manage. It may seem appropriate to say that every device should be managed, but there is a cost associated with the decision—the more that are managed, the more it costs in every dimension: time, equipment, people, money.

In general terms, first priority goes to critical systems, those that are most important to the functioning of the business—for example, a bank's transaction processing systems are managed very closely. The next priority goes to those whose malfunctioning is disruptive but not disabling to the business—a company's online ordering system would be managed closely. Last are those where faults cause little to no disruption to the business—for example, an employee's login from a desktop machine is managed lightly, most likely on an after-failure basis via a Help desk.

Deciding which network devices to manage and how closely to manage them is more directly a business decision than a technology decision.

HETEROGENEITY Network hardware and software are most likely heterogeneous—the products of different manufacturers even for the same type of device, possibly based on different standards, different versions of the same standards, or even proprietary standards. There also may be software or hardware installed by employees apart from what is "authorized." In some companies, this is the responsibility of an applications management group; in others, it falls under the network management umbrella.

Part of network management is a design role—presenting the case for reducing variety to an acceptable minimum as systems are replaced and upgraded. Another part is seeing what needs to be done in the face of heterogeneity to manage the existing systems according to what needs managing and how closely. And still another is a discovery and enforcement function to remove unauthorized products and prevent their installation.

SIZE AND COMPLEXITY The larger and more interconnected the networks, the more difficult they are to manage. Network management needs to keep networks trim and fit, avoiding unneeded interconnections, blocking unused ports to reduce intrusion risk, considering segmenting LANs as traffic patterns emerge, and balancing connectivity needs with options for providing for those needs—for example, running new cabling or adding wireless facilities. The problem of managing heterogeneity is compounded as network size and complexity grows.

INTERMITTENT FAILURES One of the more frustrating and time-consuming situations, both for the network managers and the affected parties, is discovering the sources and causes of intermittent failures—seemingly random packet loss, odd instances of dropped connections, arbitrary login rejections, and the like. By logging alarms and notifications, NMSs may help to isolate these problems, but because systems appear to be operating normally when the faults are not occurring, these failures are orders of magnitude more difficult to deal with than what might be considered to be "catastrophic failures"—crashed routers or cable breaks, for example, which are down for the count.

16.3 Structuring network management

There are two major incompatible protocol sets for structuring and managing networks: *simple network management protocol (SNMP)* and the *common management information protocol (CMIP).* The former is a TCP/IP layer 5 protocol, the product of the Internet Engineering Task Force (IETF); as its name implies, it is simpler than the latter, which is an OSI layer 7 protocol. Thus far, SNMP is much more popular and the one to which the following discussion applies.

SNMPv3 is the latest version, first published as a request for comment (RFC) in 1998 and released as a full version in 2002. (For additional information, see http://www .cisco.com/univercd/cc/td/doc/cisintwk/ito_doc/snmp.htm#xtocid8 and http://www .snmplink.org/.)

The degree to which a network or intranet can be managed depends upon which of its components are *managed devices*—the computers, hubs, switches, routers, and the like that have *network management modules (NMMs)* installed in them. These modules provide software *agents* that monitor their devices, collecting information about their device states and the packets they process.

SNMP provides a structure for information exchange between the managed devices and the manager. There are two types of information: generic data commonly defined for any device following the TCP/IP protocol suite (for example, a device's IP address) and device-specific data particular to the device itself (for example, a configuration parameter).

Individual types of information are called *objects;* for example, an object may be the counter of a particular packet type. The collection of objects is called a *management information base (MIB).* MIB2, the latest version, was published in 1991 as RFC 1213. Objects, also called MIB objects and managed objects, are defined in the *structure of management information (SMI)* standard, version 2 of which was released by the IETF in 1996 as RFC 1902. (For additional information, see http://www.ietf.org/rfc/rfc1213.txt? number=1213 and http://www.ietf.org/rfc/rfc1902.txt.)

The objects, generic and device-specific, are contained in *MIB modules.* Device manufacturers provide MIB modules for their devices. The modules incorporated in a managed device determine what it can report and how it can be controlled. By combining particular generic and specific modules in various devices to be managed, the network management system can be tailored to the company's needs.

It is important to note that SNMP specifies the functionality of MIBs but not the actual objects—these are defined by the manufacturers in accordance with the needs and capabilities of their devices. This is a much more flexible arrangement, and it is one of the reasons the protocol is called simple. (In earlier versions, there were no local MIBs. The local agents transmitted all data to a single "central" MIB every couple of minutes.)

In operation, an agent sends data to SNMP manager software when polled, at predetermined intervals, or when a problem arises or is impending. Based on agent reports, the manager software can send control messages to the devices. An NMS can perform most routine operations automatically.

Manager-initiated communications follow a "fetch/store" (also called "get/set") object-oriented model comprising two basic types of commands: *fetch* (read data from the device) and *store* (write data to the device). The former retrieves data collected by the device agents concerning its condition and information about the packets it sees; the latter acts to control the device by resetting counters or re-initializing the device. Using these simple command types combined with the objects in the MIBs circumvents the need for a large collection of specific commands and replies. This is another reason the protocol is "simple."

Each MIB object has a unique name that the manager uses when sending a fetch or store command. Here is an example: A device may have a MIB status object that counts the number of frames reaching the device that fail their frame check—let's call it "failchk." To read the count, the manager sends a *fetch failchk* command, to which the device responds by sending the counter value. Then the manager resets the counter by sending a *store failchk* command with value 0.

Aside from responding to manager-initiated communication, devices also may send data periodically at preset intervals, and when some fault (failure) occurs or is about to occur. Fault alert messages are called *alarms.* Alarm types also are pre-defined in the MIB.

In a basic setup, the manager can request agent information only from managed devices that are on the same network as the manager. For devices on other attached networks, ***remote monitoring (RMON)*** is required. This can be accomplished with a module running RMON protocol software. The RMON protocol, which is an extension of SNMP, defines statistics that can be passed between managers and remote devices, and functions that can be activated for control purposes. The latest version, RMON2, was released in 1997 by the IETF as RFC 2021.

Quite often, RMONs are installed in routers, particularly backbone and border routers. In this way, a single RMON can report activity on all the managed devices in the networks directly attached to the router. The collection and analysis of RMON data is accomplished by what are called ***probes.*** In addition to traffic monitoring, probes can send alarms about impending or actual faults. See Figure 16.1 for a general overview of a managed network structure.

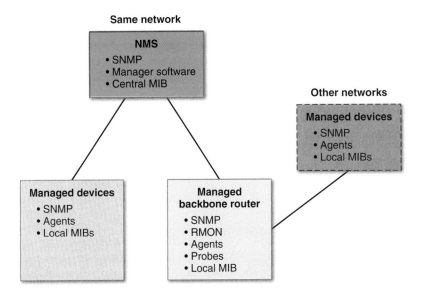

FIGURE 16.1

Managed network structure

16.4 Concerns of network management

What usually comes to mind as the principal network management job is discovering, locating, and resolving faults. Besides actual failures, faults can be symptoms of unusual activity caused by a variety of problems that eventually can become failures or can cause failures in other parts of an intranet. If a problem spot can be identified before that state is reached, correction usually is simpler.

This points to the importance of *monitoring* network performance. As examples, monitoring might indicate:

* The need for *load balancing* to reduce traffic on overutilized segments by increasing it on underutilized segments
* *Unusual activity* at a node, which could be caused by chatter (spurious transmissions) from a failing, though not yet failed, connection
* Opportunities for *segmentation* to better contain traffic and improve link utilization
* The necessity for *bandwidth management* to prevent congestion from shutting down a link

As with most network-related areas, monitoring is not an all-or-nothing proposition. Monitoring can range from continuous to occasional, depending on the nature and importance of the systems and devices in question. Continuous monitoring is not, and in fact cannot be, done exclusively by people; that is where an NMS comes in.

On the other hand, no matter how automated a system is, people are indispensable. They can react to alarms and take action for those that cannot be handled automatically, they can review NMS tracking statistics to spot potential problem areas and then take proactive steps to ward off impending failures, and they will be constantly engaged for limited periods of time when serious problems are occurring.

16.5 FCAPS

A commonly used model for network management is ISO's *FCAPS,* an acronym that comes from the five management areas on which it focuses: *fault, configuration, accounting, performance,* and *security.* These employ:

- **Managed objects (MO).** As noted previously, these are the information types that managed devices collect and respond to. The collection of MOs for a device forms a MIB, so a managed device in a network is defined by its MIB as a set of managed objects.
- **Network elements (NE).** This is another name for managed device–addressable and manageable network equipment running management modules utilizing MIBs.
- **Element management system (EMS).** An EMS manages one or more types of NEs.
- **Network management system (NMS).** This is the hardware/software platform (console) that integrates information from the EMSs, issues commands to NEs, and performs diagnostics. It incorporates a user interface that presents information in a form meaningful to people and provides for command issuance, typically via a graphical user interface (GUI).

Let's look at the five FCAPS management areas more closely.

Fault management

Fault management aims at discovering, locating, correcting, and logging failures and conditions that are likely to lead to failures. When the problem is in a managed device, discovery usually comes from an alarm sent by the device indicating failure or abnormal activity, but it also can result from predictions made by analyzing data coming from the devices to detect trends that have led to failure in the past.

Taking proactive measures then can prevent failure or at least keep the network running at a reduced capacity until further steps are taken. Fault notification also comes from a call to the Help desk, especially when the fault is not in a managed device or when an NMS is not used. (IETF RFC 3887 defines the Alarm MIB, a component that describes management objects for modeling and storing alarms.)

Locating a fault is another matter. It is not necessarily the case that the device experiencing a problem is where the fault lies. For example, a failed switch port may first be reported as a "failure-to-connect" notice from a LAN station. An NMS has the capability of querying devices in an orderly fashion, beginning with the reporting device and tracing back to where the fault lies.

Correcting the fault may require nothing more than the NMS sending a command, which may even happen automatically, or as much as dispatching technicians to trace and resolve the problem in coordination with personnel at the console.

Logs are an important part of fault management. Whatever resolution process is followed, a log entry is made. As the logs build, they create a highly valuable source of company-specific information—a database that tracks faults, corrective steps, and results. The database is used:

- As a *lookup reference* to see how to resolve faults that recur.
- To *discern patterns* that show areas that need attention—for reconfiguration or upgrading.

- To *predict* when the next failure might occur so that proactive steps can be taken.
- For a *history* of faults and the steps taken to correct them.

Calculations carried out on the data compiled from log entries can indicate the service levels of the managed devices and of the intranet as an entity. This information also can be used in decisions about when to replace and when to upgrade devices and software.

Configuration management

The configuration of a device refers to its hardware components and its software; the configuration of a network indicates its physical and logical topologies and protocols. Keeping configuration documentation current is vital to the network management operation.

NMSs routinely store configuration information for all the managed devices. As configurations are changed, information is added via queries to or messages from the device agents—typically an automated process. Manually recorded data may be necessary as well. The information allows tracking of configuration histories and also provides the up-to-date data necessary when fault resolution is required and when upgrades are being considered. Imagine trying to isolate a problem when the information you are using shows connections that no longer exist or does not show all connections that are in place.

Aside from logging, configuration management pertains to:

- *Upgrading or updating* software in attached devices. This may be done remotely from a server. If not, support personnel must visit each machine.
- *Overseeing* hardware modification, replacement, addition, relocation, and removal.
- *Reconfiguring* networks.

Accounting management

The fundamental goal of accounting management is the *efficient allocation of resources*. One activity is adding and deleting individual user accounts and creating and revising group memberships. Groups, which comprise individual users, are established based on some commonality—the department they work in, the functions they perform, the responsibilities they have, and so on.

Each group has resource access rights assigned to it, such as the ability to attach to specific databases and operations allowed on those databases. For example, a group of online order-takers may have rights to read from and write to customer accounts and inventory databases, but not rights to add to stock counts, reorder items, or remove customers.

A group's members automatically acquire its rights. In addition, particular members may be given other rights or may have certain rights restricted. In the order-taker example, perhaps a new employee will not be able to update a customer file without receiving a clearance code from a supervisor. Rights such as these are established by accounting management but are operationalized by the software in question—for example, a database application will monitor user rights.

Accounting management also handles password and login name assignment, distribution, and removal. Passwords and login names can be required to start a workstation, to connect to particular networks, to use external links, to run specific software, and so on.

Other forms of resource control include:

- *Chargebacks* to user accounts—a fee for using specific resources, which may be assessed against an individual's account or a group's account.

- *Quotas* on device loading—access limits based on the combined usage of a resource at any particular time.
- *Bandwidth restrictions* at particular times of the day or for particular kinds of traffic.

AMPLIFICATION

Fees charged against a budget may be actual dollars or "funny money," which is a non-cash charge. In either case, the real or funny money budget has a limit that, when reached, prevents further use of that resource unless funds are added. Overruns may occur when unusual events, such as catastrophic failure, lead to unexpected expenditures, or simply because of improper budget allocations to begin with or poor use of funds. Regardless of the cause, a request for additional funds usually requires a review that itself may lead to discovery of areas whose management could be improved.

An NMS-based accounting management system can collect statistics on the usage of managed resources. These can be used to modify allocations, increasing or reducing allowances to better manage those resources, correct imbalances, or evaluate usage patterns to look for potential misuse. They also can be used for cost analysis and containment and to determine the most appropriate budget for networking and how those dollars should be distributed most effectively.

One useful measure is **total cost of ownership (TCO),** which indicates the annual cost for keeping a network component (and by extension, a network segment, a network, and an entire intranet) operational. This includes the direct costs of repair or replacement, upgrades, and support personnel, and the indirect costs of time or production lost because of failure.

Performance management

Performance management seeks to keep the networks running as efficiently as possible. Performance is measured by such variables as throughput, resource utilization, transmission error rates, network latency, mean time before failure, and mean time to repair (see "Technical note: Performance measures").

Data on these variables can be collected by the management system. When particular measures fall below par or fail to meet established values or standards, corrective action is indicated. This means working in conjunction with fault and configuration management to uncover the causes of the decline and determine whether they are temporary, and then deciding how best to improve them.

In a manner similar to trend analysis for fault prediction, analysis of performance data can show trends that reveal when steps need to be taken to keep the networks running smoothly. For example, device capacity or bandwidth may need to be increased because throughput is dropping, error rates are increasing, response time is slowing, or resource utilization is at its limits.

A more inclusive performance measure is called **service level,** which refers to a package of functionalities called **quality of service (QoS).** This comes into play most often when a company contracts for services, such as frame relay, leased line, Internet access, or Web hosting. It takes the form of a **service level agreement (SLA),** a contract between the customer and the service provider by which the latter commits to guaranteeing particular levels of service for a stipulated price.

Throughput is the number of bits per second received at the destination node. Throughput cannot exceed channel capacity, but it may be less, sometimes much less. That is, because throughput measures the actual number of bits received per time, throughput falls if a channel is congested, even though its native data rate is unchanged. For example, throughput of a traditional 10-Mbps Ethernet never reaches 10 Mbps—and because of collisions, the more heavily loaded it is, the lower the throughput.

Generally speaking, when throughput drops below a pre-established critical value, action is required to restore network performance.

Resource utilization is the percentage of a resource's capacity used by the packets it is processing. Although we want high utilization to get the most out of a resource, we also want some reserve capacity to handle unusual temporary loads. A device continuously operating at or near capacity could be an indication of traffic problems or the need to upgrade. A resource whose utilization jumps significantly for an extended period is another indication of potential problems.

Error rate is the number of erroneous bits received as a proportion of the total number of bits sent, also called the **bit error rate.** Wired networks operate at much lower bit error rates than wireless networks. That is why self-correcting codes are preferred for wireless networks and repeat requests are used for wired networks. (See Chapter 5, "Error control.")

Latency is the time between packet transmission and receipt; it is a measure of the responsiveness of a network, or concomitantly, a measure of delay. Because data cannot move from point to point instantaneously, every network has some measure of latency. This is called **propagation delay**—the time it takes for a bit to travel from sender to receiver.

From a performance perspective, we need to consider two questions:

- Is the measured latency acceptable?
- Is the latency variable?

In packet switched networks, variable latency is caused by delay differences among each of the packets of a flow. Some may take different routes and some may encounter congestion. This can cause latency to vary from packet to packet. The quality of streaming digital video and audio rapidly deteriorates in the face of variable latency. The result is skipped sounds, unintelligible speech, jerky video, frozen frames, and artifacts (pixelation). For any type of transmission, a trend of increasing latency is an indication of a problem.

Mean time before failure (MTBF) is the average length of time before a network component fails. Eventually, any device will fail. If accurate statistics are kept, critical devices usually can be replaced or serviced before they fail.

Mean time to repair MTTR is, according to one definition, the length of time between when notification of a failure is received and when the device is back in service; in another definition, the time starts when the failure occurs. The latter includes the time it takes to realize that there is a failure, called **response time.**

For critical components, such as backbone routers, minimizing response time is vital. To keep MTTR low for such devices, it makes sense to have backup units that can be put into service quickly, reducing the pressure to repair the failed device and the time that the network, as opposed to the device itself, is not working. For example, a router failure can bring down a collapsed backbone—the backbone is the network component while the router is the device.

Also included is the possibility (not guaranteed) of exceeding those levels for short periods under certain conditions. For example, for a frame relay line, the guaranteed service level is called the committed information rate (CIR)—a specific bandwidth or data rate—and the higher service level is called the burst information rate (BIR).

The same idea can be carried into the organization by treating internal network operation as though it were a contracted SLA. In effect, that pseudo-SLA sets the performance levels considered to be appropriate, thereby providing benchmarks against which actual performance can be measured. As noted, when measures trend toward failing to meet benchmarks, corrective action can be initiated. This should prompt a review to make sure that the SLA is properly set. Still, a continuing downward trend in service, as opposed to a temporary slowdown, is indicative of performance problems, regardless of what the SLA calls for.

Security management

From the network management perspective, security management means controlling access to network resources, including the networks themselves and the data they contain. Originally, SNMP did not provide much in the way of network security. Version 3 addressed many security issues by incorporating authentication of data source, checks for data integrity, and encryption. Security methodologies relevant to network management and SNMP are discussed in Chapter 15, "Network security."

16.6 Business considerations

Business decisions regarding internal resources and systems usually are made on a cost/benefit basis. Network management is an expensive proposition. Aside from the requisite hardware and software, a significant number of support personnel is needed, many of whom are highly salaried engineers. The expense side also includes the costs of various kinds of downtime weighted by their likelihood of occurrence. Generally speaking, these calculations are fairly straightforward.

For the benefit side of the ratio, valuing network management is another matter. Even though it is apparent that the business cannot run without its networks (especially complex intranets) running smoothly, this does not mean that the value of network management is the value of the entire business. Complicating the calculation is the relationship between network management effectiveness and downtime costs—more effective management will reduce both the frequency of downtime and the time to restore operations when there is a problem.

Faced with this difficult issue, experience tells us that businesses tend to go in one of two directions:

- View network management as a cost center. The result is budgeting as little as possible to get by. This can lead to large, unexpected expenses when major problems arise that more expedient management could have prevented.
- View network management as the most important information system component, especially when combined with security management. The result is overinvestment in complex NMSs, large inventories of spare equipment that becomes obsolete without ever being deployed, and very large staffs.

We do not pretend to resolve this issue here, but the key is to match network management to the business's workflow and network complexity. This means that each contemplated network management function should be incorporated only if it directly addresses a business problem. In other words, whether a function is selected for inclusion should be driven by its business case.

Business NOTE — Open network management

The trend toward open software and open platforms has been growing. These terms derive from the notion of *open source*, which means a computer program whose actual programming (source code) is freely available for viewing and modification by others. Thus, the code develops as an effort of a community of interested persons rather than as proprietary corporate software.

In effect, open source is not owned by anyone but instead is in the public domain. (This is different from freeware, which also is available without charge or with non-mandatory requests for donations, but is owned and distributed by its creator and not subject to modification by anyone else.)

In line with the open source trend, an open network management system has been created, called OpenNMS. To quote from their Web site:

OpenNMS is the world's first enterprise grade network management platform developed under the open source model. It consists of a community supported open-source project as well as a commercial services, training and support organization.

For details on the platform, how open sourcing works for its development, how to obtain the system, and how to participate in its development, visit their Web site: http://www.opennms.org/index.php/ Main_Page.

16.7 Summary

Network management covers a broad range of activity, from managing very simple networks in small firms to very complex interconnected networks in large-scale firms. Accordingly, personnel vary from one or two technicians, in-house or contracted for from an outside firm on an as-needed basis, to a full-blown department whose personnel have a wide variety of specialized skills. In this setting, we looked at the issues involved with managing corporate networks and their connections to public data networks.

We distinguished between the people (network administrators, systems administrators, and other support personnel) and the network management systems (hardware and software to support the management activity).

We saw that the biggest issue in planning for network management is deciding what network devices to manage, how closely to manage them, and what not to manage. That decision should be guided by how crucial particular systems and devices are to the functioning of the business, and the dimensions of time, equipment, people, and money.

We saw how to structure network management, especially with regard to the commonly used SNMP. This included looking into hardware devices and software. Aside from fault detection and resolution, we noted the importance of monitoring network performance as a preventive measure to provide alerts predictive of actual failures. In addition, monitoring provides information as to when load balancing, segmentation, and bandwidth management are called for.

We looked at ISO's popular FCAPS network management model in some detail. Finally, we delved into the business considerations in developing a network management plan.

In the next chapter we look at the issues involved with the planning and design of modern networks. Resolving these issues requires a careful, systematic approach, as does any systems development project. We explore the steps involved, along with the systems development life cycle, its analog, the network project development life cycle, and project management.

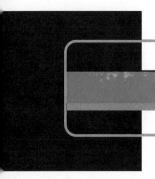

END-OF-CHAPTER QUESTIONS

Short answer

1. Discuss the range of network management functions and personnel.
2. What are the responsibilities of network administrators? Of systems administrators?
3. "Deciding which network devices to manage and how closely to manage them is more directly a business decision than a technology decision." Explain.
4. What makes intermittent failures so difficult to deal with? How can the causes of such problems be isolated?
5. Describe how SNMP provides for structuring and managing networks.
6. Where do MIB objects come from? How do they work?
7. Why would network administrators be concerned with load balancing, segmentation, and bandwidth management?
8. What is FCAPS?
9. What are the concerns of configuration management?
10. Discuss the cost/benefit issues of network management.

Fill-in

1. A _____ is a hardware/software device that automates network management.
2. Planning for network management must include consideration of _____, _____, _____, and _____ issues.
3. Two major protocol sets for structuring and managing networks are _____ and _____.
4. Computers, hubs, switches, routers, and the like that have network management modules installed in them are called _____.
5. The _____ command reads data from a device, whereas the _____ command writes data to a device.
6. An _____ module is used for a manager to request agent information from a device on an attached network.
7. The ISO model for network management is _____.
8. The collection of managed objects forms a _____.
9. FCAPS deals with _____, _____, _____, _____, and _____.
10. _____ is the annual cost for keeping a network component, or an entire network, operational.

Multiple-choice

1. Network management systems
   a. easily integrate all management functions
   b. are not customizable to specific corporate needs
   c. are automated systems for monitoring and managing corporate networks
   d. function without action by management personnel
   e. are an inexpensive means of network management

2. Networks are managed by
   a. remote
   b. NMSs
   c. hardware and software
   d. people using various technology tools
   e. OEMs

3. Heterogeneous hardware and software
   a. should be replaced by homogeneous hardware and software
   b. exclude unauthorized devices
   c. present a design issue for network managers
   d. cannot be managed
   e. are rarely found in today's network environments

4. SNMP
   a. is an OSI standard protocol
   b. is more complex than CMIP
   c. is the most popular protocol set for managing networks
   d. is required by every NMS
   e. is a TCP/IP layer 3 protocol

5. An agent sends data to SNMP management software
   a. when polled
   b. at predetermined intervals
   c. when a problem is impending
   d. when a problem arises
   e. all of the above

6. Monitoring network performance can indicate
   a. the need for bandwidth management
   b. opportunities for segmentation
   c. unusual node activity
   d. the need for load balancing
   e. all of the above

7. As part of fault management, logs serve
   a. as a lookup reference
   b. to discern patterns indicative of reconfiguration needs
   c. for failure prediction
   d. all of the above
   e. none of the above

8. Service level
   a. is an inclusive measure of total cost of ownership
   b. is concerned with QoS
   c. is involved with SLAs
   d. all of the above
   e. b and c only

9. Open network management
   a. is an old idea that has not found traction in network management
   b. is not related to open source
   c. is an idea that as yet has no available product
   d. is the same as freeware
   e. none of the above

10. Security management
    a. is the concern of the security department and not network administrators
    b. is not addressed by SNMP
    c. means controlling access to network resources
    d. means controlling access to network-accessible data
    e. both c and d

True or false

1. Network management should be a centralized operation.
2. A corporation owns its LANs but cannot own and manage its own WAN.
3. The biggest issue in network management is deciding which NMS to purchase.
4. Planning for network management only requires determining which devices should be managed.
5. Network management modules provide software agents that monitor devices.
6. SNMP supplies a structure for information exchange between managed devices.
7. SNMP defines and supplies the MIB objects.
8. Accounting management is concerned with the efficient allocation of resources.
9. To include downtime cost in a cost analysis, the likelihood of occurrence must be taken into account.
10. Businesses tend to view network management as a cost center.

Exploration

1. Compare the products of the major companies providing NMSs.
2. Find the salaries of network administrators in at least three of the Fortune 500 companies. How do they compare with the salaries of CIOs, CFOs, and COOs?
3. Look into open network management systems. Describe their development over the last few years. What do you predict for their future?

THE MOSI CASE, CONTINUED

Currently, MOSI has a network management group and a network security group. They cooperate with each other but operate more or less independently. MOSI is thinking about combining them into one group but is not sure if that is a good idea—and if it is, MOSI is not sure which group should take precedence. That is, should the network group subsume the security team, or vice versa?

As the CIO of MOSI, you are asked for a report that would clarify the situation. What questions would you ask to provide the information you need for the report? Whom would you like to question? Are the two choices MOSI presented the only ones that should be considered? Your report must end with conclusions and recommendations. Write that section.

CHAPTER 17

Planning, designing, and implementing a network

17.1 Overview

In the preceding chapters, we looked at communications from an historical and developmental perspective—how technologies developed in response to market-driven performance demands and attempts to overcome technological limitations; how shortcomings of particular methodologies moved developments in response to competitive pressures; that most often, advances in data networks and computer communications are the result of business decisions. This led to an investigation and understanding of today's prevalent technologies.

In that journey, we discovered that there are many network types, media types, and protocols available to us. Now we are faced with the question of choice: Whether we need to upgrade or expand existing networks, or build or contract for one from scratch, how do we decide what is most appropriate? We must embark on a network design and implementation project.

The planning and design of modern networks is a very challenging and complicated undertaking that demands the application of a careful, systematic approach. In essence, this is no different from any systems development project, and so it involves the same steps: planning, analysis, design, development, testing, implementation, and maintenance. This is the *systems development life cycle (SDLC).* By analogy, we have the *network DLC.*

One other important consideration—*should the project be done in-house, or should it be outsourced?* The answer depends on two main factors:

- Are the in-house personnel up to the task? That is, do they have the requisite skills and experience?
- Are the appropriate in-house personnel available? Assuming the staff is capable, do they have the time needed to devote to the project?

Answering no to either of these questions means that outsourcing is the better choice. However, the initial query does not have to mean an all-or-nothing proposition. For example, we could design the project in-house, purchase the equipment and software, and outsource the installation. We might do everything but cabling. We may just write a *request for proposal (RFP)*—a detailed description of the project requirements that serves as a solicitation to vendors to bid on the project—and outsource the entire job.

The in-house/outsource question is an important one. Delving into it in great detail is outside the scope of this text, but for the essential points, see "Business note: In-house or outsource your network project?"

Regardless of how the project is undertaken, we must be sure that it is properly managed so that it yields the best possible outcome. One of the greatest causes of project failure is insufficient attention paid to its management.

It is the goal of this chapter to provide general guidelines to follow to achieve the establishment of successfully operating networks.

Business NOTE

In-house or outsource your network project?

Whether outsourcing is an all-or-nothing choice for a company or one in which some part of the project will be handled in-house and the rest outsourced, the considerations that go into making the decision are the same:

- **Skills and experience.** Do your employees have the abilities needed for the project or the portion you want to do in-house? This is the first question to ask, because if the answer is no and you do not wish to or are not in the position to hire a complete staff, outsourcing is the only alternative.
- **Availability.** Assuming you do have the requisite staff, are they available for the time required to see the project through?
- **Hires.** After the network is completed, will you need to supplement the in-house staff with new hires for operation and maintenance? If the new or expanded network will require additional support staff, consider hiring them before the project begins and then making them part of the project team. Even if implementation is outsourced, they can help with the network plan, design, and RFP.
- **Control and predictability.** You have greater control over the project when it is done in-house. This includes quality, timeliness, and cost. Outsourcers are beholden to you according to the terms of your contract, but they also are beholden to other customers. When problems arise, delays in other projects are incurred, or costs escalate, outsourcers are less likely to be as responsive to you as your in-house staff, especially

if your project is relatively less important to them than others they are working on. Changing outsourcers mid-project may not be feasible, and even if it is, the disruption will likely cause delays and entail additional expense.

- **Dependency.** Will you be dependent on the outsourcer for maintenance, upgrades, troubleshooting, and the like? This can be an issue if you do not have the personnel to oversee the network and will not be hiring the staff to do so. If you choose a contractor that uses industry-standard hardware and software (highly recommended), you do not need to be too concerned about this, assuming your chosen contractor is reliable and likely to remain in business.
- **Contract.** If any part of the project is outsourced, read the contract completely and carefully. Make sure you understand the contractor's and your responsibilities for network completion and for some period of time after it is up and running. If cable installation is outsourced, the contractor should have to test the installation to demonstrate that it performs as specified. All cables must be properly labeled so that they are easily identified as to type and run. When completed, the entire network should be tested and certified before acceptance.

In the end, the choice may come down to management philosophy, especially when all other factors are more or less equal. Nevertheless, those factors should be considered first so that philosophy does not overrule common sense.

17.2 Planning

First things first

Unless we are talking about a trivial network, a network project is not a solo operation. Before we even think about planning, we must assemble the project team. That team should comprise people with a variety of skills, talents, and positions in the organization. Typical would be network engineers, technical support people, a strong project manager, and, vitally important, representative end users.

Furthermore, we presume that the project's existence owes to a management directive. Therefore it also must have a sponsor—someone who is a liaison between the project manager and upper management and who will support the project and its goals. Finally, there must be a secured budget that covers all phases of the project through implementation, a time frame for project completion, and an understood budget for operating the network (cost of ownership/cost of operation). It is crucial that this last point is carefully determined and made clear at the outset, for over time the cost of ownership/operation will far exceed the cost of design and implementation.

Determining ownership/operating cost is not a subject for this text. Suffice it to say that a good design will keep that cost as low as possible.

A network design and implementation project begins with assembling an appropriate project team.

On to the plan

In the planning stage, we first must determine the scope of the project—what it will include and, importantly, what it will not. Scope must take into account not only the capabilities of the network, but the budget and the time frame we have to meet. The plan will be based on that scope.

It may be tempting to begin by looking at the array of available technologies, but that is not a good place to start. Every project has what are called ***critical success factors.*** For a network project, they begin with what the business needs the network to do—after all, the *raison d'être* for the network is to support the goals and policies of the business. So, we start with a question: *What purpose is the network to serve?* Looked at more directly from the business perspective, the question becomes: *What are the business functions that the network needs to support?*

Unless we clearly understand the role the network is to play in the organization, the project is likely to fail, or at the least produce a result that does not meet the expectations of the stakeholders. More specifically, here is what we need to find out:

- What communications and data services are to be provided?
- Who are the users and where are they located?
- What applications are to be accommodated?
- What do users expect regarding application availability and response times?
- What is the nature and quantity of data to be handled?
- What level of reliability is needed?
- How is a major network disaster to be handled?
- What provisions need to be made for future expandability?
- How will the network and its components be managed?
- What will be the costs for acquisition, installation, and operations?

The answers to these questions and their relative importance to the organization form the business and technological requirements of the network—the basis upon which any successful network plan is built. We also must be aware that as the plan is developed, there is likely to be some give and take—tradeoffs to be considered among project scope, budget, personnel, and time frame. This is one area where the project sponsor plays a key role.

Project scope rests on the base of the purpose the network is to serve.

Let's expand a bit on what some of these queries mean.

Assess user needs

Traditionally, systems design projects have a high rate of failure: not finished on time; over budget; not as functional as planned; or even cancelled outright. Network projects are no different. Too often networks are designed by engineers who focus on building a sophisticated technological creation without much regard for how and by whom the network will be used. The result is a network that does not meet the needs of the organization.

To avoid this outcome, it is imperative to engage the end users at the earliest possible point in the planning cycle. They best know how they will use the network, what applications they will be running, and how they would like those applications to perform over the network. Their input should drive the choice of network type (for example, LAN vs. WAN), wired or wireless, network technology (for example, ATM or IP), network topology (ring vs. mesh), and security level required.

Although end users can and do provide valuable input for the technical team members, they may put forth requirements that are unrealistic from a technical or economic point of view. However, by involving them early, end users' expectations can be realistically incorporated, and their buy-in to the project for any compromises that have to be made can be obtained. The latter is another crucial piece—without end user buy-in, the project ultimately will not fare well.

It is vital to understand end user requests and requirements, but they must be assessed in terms of feasibility and business-critical functionality—a key part of determining project scope.

APPLICATIONS SURVEY   Having established user needs, the network designers should have a complete list of applications to be run on the network. It is up to the network design team to assess the characteristics of each application and their impacts on the network design.

- An e-mail application requires much less of network devices (for example, routers and switches) than does a streaming video application.
- Some applications can tolerate short interruptions in service and others cannot.
- Some applications may require an entirely different type of network than is being built (for example, one that is circuit switched rather than packet switched), which means that they cannot be accommodated in the plan, that other applications must take their place, or that the plan must be revised to provide for them.

- Applications often use particular protocols and require specific network interfaces. For example, one may interface to the network via a 10BASE-T Ethernet connection using a PLC (programmable logic controller) application protocol, whereas another may require an EIA-232 interface and a telnet application protocol.
- Some required applications that were developed in the past may use protocols and programming structures that are not supported by current systems (so-called *legacy* systems). Should they be dropped, replaced, or supported in other ways?

The point is that on investigation, business and technological requirements may significantly alter the direction of the proposed network design. It is far easier to change a design while it is still in the planning stage than after it is built. In general, the farther along in the project you go, the more difficult and more costly it is to make modifications.

 Network design depends heavily on the applications to be run on it.

USER LOCATIONS/TIME ZONE SURVEY A network that provides connectivity for users who all reside in one building and will not need to access outside facilities is very different from one that must provide connectivity to users who are all over the globe. Such differences determine which network technologies are suitable, the types of communications links that are available, the capacity of network switches/routers and the associated links between them, the nature of disaster recovery capabilities, and the development and operating costs involved.

If the entire user community is located in one building or on a campus whose premises are privately owned, and all their networking is strictly in-house, one or more local area networks might do the job. If some external interaction is required, the addition of a link to the Internet might suffice. If the corporate user community is widely distributed geographically, a metropolitan or wide area network will be necessary.

We can appreciate the impact that the geographic location of the user community has on network design by comparing the two following e-mail scenarios:

1. **Problem:** A company has 500 employees in three locations on the east coast of the United States: 200 in New York City, 100 in Boston, and 200 in Washington, D.C. The company wants to network the three locations to allow its employees to exchange highly sensitive e-mail over its own private network. The greatest traffic load on the proposed network is anticipated to occur between 9 A.M. and 10 A.M. Monday through Friday when all the employees access the network to retrieve the bulk of their e-mail.

   Plan considerations: Because the users are spread over a relatively large geographic area, a wide area network (WAN) is appropriate. Because all the users are within the same time zone, they will be accessing the network at the same time. To provide quick response times, the network will have to be sized to accommodate this peak flow of e-mail messages. After the peak hour, traffic on the network will be substantially lower, leaving it underutilized and thus wasting valuable resources.

   Possible alternate solution: Have the employees retrieve their e-mail on a staggered time schedule, thus eliminating the major surge in usage. This solution requires a change in work habits and eases the network design problem. Whether that is an acceptable change depends on the company and its employees.

2. **Problem:** Another company faces the same problem as the first one, except that its 500 employees are located in three more dispersed sites: 200 in New York City (eastern time zone), 100 in Chicago (central time zone), and 200 in Seattle (Pacific time zone).

   Plan considerations: Because the users are spread over a relatively large geographic area, a wide area network is once again appropriate. In this scenario, however, the users are not within the same time zone, so their e-mail retrieval will be staggered across a three-hour time span. The network does not need as great a capacity for the e-mail surge as in the first example, so less is unused and component costs are lower. In effect, the time zones create the staggered schedule suggested as a possible alternate solution to the first problem.

Of course, there are more network factors involved than e-mail access, but these scenarios illustrate the point by showing how different conditions yield different requirements that lead to different solutions.

Beyond capacity and speed, the user community members' locations also dictate the types of communications links available. For example, if the members are spread over different continents, both undersea cables and satellite links become alternatives.

Also bear in mind that regardless of what may seem to be the best solution technically, every type of communications media and service will not be available in all geographic regions. So the best may have to be abandoned in favor of the best that's available.

User locations and dispersion may obviate or favor particular solutions.

Traffic analysis

The next step is a detailed traffic pattern analysis. This will further crystallize the network architectures, technologies, and types of communications links that are appropriate to consider.

The analysis should identify all significant traffic sources. Because traffic is generated by applications, this is tantamount to analyzing the data transmission characteristics of those applications and their users. Be sure to include sources outside the network whose traffic is simply passed through the proposed network on its way to other destinations.

To proceed:

- Estimate the network capacity required by each source, in terms of expected data rates and variations. For sources whose data rates are sporadic, ascertain peak and average rates. Consider them together with data rates from sources whose transmissions are relatively continuous, to size network nodes and connections correctly.
- Include scalability. The demands made on a network are not static. Incorporate future plans that could affect data rate requirements. For example, the traffic produced by an e-mail application will vary with the number of employees. If significant growth in number of employees is likely, capacity to support the increased load should be part of the design.

  Aside from planned changes, organizations often tend to grow in unexpected ways. Network designers should anticipate this by creating a scalable structure—one that can be expanded readily by adding resources (such as nodes and links). This avoids having to replace the whole network prematurely, a very costly undertaking.

- Assess application traffic patterns. These are as important as the quantity of data generated.

    - **Local or distributed.** Local traffic is confined to a specific (geographic) part of the network; distributed traffic travels throughout the network.

        For example, a company's engineers use the network to exchange CAD (computer aided design) drawings only within their own department, hence affecting just their local portion of the network and its capacity needs. The company's auditors and accountants are in many sites. They exchange large financial reports daily, which travel throughout the network. Their traffic has quite a different impact than that of the engineers.

    - **Client/server, terminal/host, server/server.** Application structure greatly influences traffic patterns. Client/server architecture typically generates relatively little traffic from the client side, but very substantial traffic from the server side. The same is true of terminal/host applications. In addition, rapid response time often is critical for them; this has its own impact on network design. Server/server applications usually produce a large amount of traffic in both directions.

        Any applications that have other unique interaction mechanisms should also be taken into account.

    - **Quality of Service (QoS).** Application assessment must include the delivery demands made of the network. Is packet loss acceptable? Must data units (packets, cells, frames, datagrams) arrive within some specified time of each other?

To ensure that the network designed will function as intended, traffic patterns, largely determined by requisite applications and their usage, must be fully understood and accounted for.

Reliability assessment

Computer communication has become central to the operation of most businesses, whether on automated teller machines (ATMs) networks operated by banks, corporate networks that support the flow of business-critical information, wireless networks that enable mobile connectivity, or the Internet that makes e-commerce possible.

HOW CRITICAL   For many business processes, networks are not involved in mission-critical operations; loss of communications for a little while may be annoying, but not very burdensome or damaging to the bottom line. For many other business processes, however, the networks involved must be up and running continuously, every moment of every day. Failure, even for short periods, can lead to serious business disruptions and the potential loss of considerable sums of money. We can imagine the catastrophes that could ensue if critical networks like those used by air traffic controllers were to break down. Ensuring that networks are always available demands highly complex designs that will cost considerably more to produce and operate.

MAINTENANCE IMPLICATIONS   Whether continuous operation is required or not, various portions of the network will have to be taken offline at times for routine maintenance and servicing. Network designs must provide a means for doing this without incapacitating the entire network or negatively affecting important user traffic. This may be as simple as making particular routes or services unavailable for a short time, typically late at night or very early in the morning when they are not likely to be needed, or as complex as incorporating fully redundant systems and routes that can be engaged to keep all communications and services running continuously.

Up-time and down-time considerations   No matter what the system or its uses, it is not realistic to expect that it will perform flawlessly all the time. Therefore, as part of the planning phase an assessment must made as to how much of an interruption is tolerable. This typically is specified as the yearly percentage of up-time that is expected of the network. For example, a reliability of 99.99 percent (called four 9s) means a network is operational and continuously available for all but a total of 53 minutes per year at most.

This may not seem like a long time, especially when spread out over a year, but for some critical applications it may be too much. Achieving four 9s reliability is extremely difficult and costly. Imagine what must be involved for business processes that require a five 9s (99.999 percent); this translates to a downtime of no more than 5.3 minutes per year! In fact, whether such reliability can actually be achieved is subject to some debate in the industry.

Even for four 9s, network planners and designers must fully understand and carefully weigh the consequences of network failure against the cost of providing a particular level of reliability. It is pointless to aim for a reliability level whose costs significantly exceed its benefits. Also bear in mind the possibility that, whatever the cost, the reliability level demanded may not be achievable at all. These issues must be evaluated and decided on in the planning stage of the project.

Reliability options   Generally speaking, a reliable network design will not allow any one device or link failure to crash the network—no ***single point of failure (SPOF).*** To achieve this, redundant devices, alternative communications paths, or a combination of both must be included in the plan.

Network recovery procedures also must be part of the initial plan. In the most catastrophic instance, in which an entire network or a significant part of it fails, a ***disaster recovery plan*** must be in place so that restoration can begin without undue delay. At the extreme, this may entail having in place a geographically and/or operationally isolated duplicate network running in parallel to the primary network. In a catastrophic failure of the primary, operations can be switched to the duplicate.

A less costly alternative is to back up business-critical data and software on a regular basis (daily, weekly, or as the business operations demand) and store the backups in a highly secure and physically robust location. There are commercial providers that have such facilities and handle the process for a fee. This is different from and in addition to the routine backup/restore facilities that every network should have. Coupled with this, arrangements can be made to temporarily use the network facilities of vendors specializing in providing such services.

Arrangements need to be made in advance of need and should be part of the plan. Then, if a catastrophe occurs, backed up data and applications can be retrieved and installed on the temporary network, thus enabling the business to continue operating, though perhaps with only the most necessary and critical services.

As always, the extent of the measures to be taken depends on business requirements and a cost/value tradeoff calculation.

The degree of reliability sought and the extent of the measures taken to achieve it depend on careful assessment of business requirements and cost/value tradeoff calculations.

Standards

When you are considering network technologies, their status should be taken into account. Is the technology proprietary, or does it follow industry standards?

Proprietary technology is owned by a specific vendor who controls how it operates and interacts with other devices. If there are special functions or features that are absolutely needed, proprietary may be the only way to go. In general, though, a proprietary solution can be problematic, because:

- It limits the company's ability to easily replace a device or system with one from a different vendor.
- It means reliance on the sole vendor for updates and upgrades.
- It may limit interconnectivity between the proposed network and existing ones.
- The sole vendor might go out of business, leaving you with a network that is difficult to manage and maintain.

Unless there is some specific business requirement that can be met only by the proprietary technology, the wisest course is to avoid it. Even where a business need seems to require proprietary technology, serious consideration should be given to long-term consequences. It may prove to be far better to modify or relax the seemingly requisite business aspect driving the perceived need than to rely on proprietary technology. The decision should be based on careful consideration of the alternatives.

Of course, business need must be the driver for determining technological requirements, and not the other way around. But it is not unusual for the technology choice to be based on an incomplete understanding of the relationship between that need and the available technology. That is one reason why the project team must include many stakeholders—management, technologists, and end users.

The alternative to proprietary technology is technology that follows industry standards. Throughout this text, we have seen many examples of *de jure* standards published by organizations such as the IEEE, ISO, and the ATM Forum, and *de facto* standards exemplified by the TCP/IP protocols. Conformant hardware and software from different manufacturers will be much more likely to interoperate, offer reasonable assurance that similar technology and upgrades will continue to be produced for some time (postponing obsolescence), and comprise a competitive market that will keep costs down.

Network performance, maintenance, and long-term cost issues almost always point to the use of industry-standard products as the wisest choice.

The plan

The end result of the planning process is a detailed description of the functions and characteristics of the proposed network—the ***network technical architecture.*** Although much of this derives from the business requirements that impelled the plan, information from industry—hardware and software suppliers, systems engineers, and network installers—is essential in its formulation. After all, they are in the best position to know whether the business requirements are consistent with available technologies. This provides not only a reality check, but also data to derive an initial cost estimate.

17.3 Designing

With the plan in hand, the design process may begin. This means translating the plan into actual capabilities built from real devices and particular network architectures. The planning stage examined *potential* technologies and approaches; the design stage is where we drill down through the generalities, develop the specific network structure and its protocols, and choose actual technologies.

Investigate available technologies

The capabilities and suitability of the choices that can fulfill the plan requirements must be investigated in detail. For example, if a WAN is called for, traditional technologies such as ATM or frame relay can do the job. However, high-speed switched Ethernet recently has been viewed as a reasonable, low-cost WAN alternative. Before that decision can be made, there are various aspects of Ethernet as a WAN technology that must be clearly understood.

Continuing with this example, we see that Ethernet has not yet developed a good way to handle QoS, or comprehensive methods to shift from one communications link to another if the first link is broken. Whether Ethernet's shortcomings are important in a particular instance depends on how the various technologies match up with needs defined in the plan's functional requirements. Rarely will there be an ideal match, but by diligent investigation, a reasonable choice can be made.

The more cutting edge the technology is, the higher the risk to use it, but if it works as expected, the longer it is likely to be serviceable.

Work with vendors to determine equipment capabilities

Even if we limit our technology to industry standards, it does not follow that every manufacturer's products implement them the same way. Several standards incorporate options; which ones are followed is up to the vendor. Some specifications are open to a degree of interpretation. So, after we have chosen the network design, we still must investigate how each of the considered vendors have implemented the products that we need to fulfill the design.

AMPLIFICATION

We use the term *vendor* as a general reference to denote an OEM (original equipment manufacturer), a distributor, a contractor, an installer—that is, any external business entity with expertise in network component creation, supply, installation, or maintenance.

Implementation variations can lead to operational problems when equipment from different manufacturers is interconnected. The full range of capabilities expected of our network may not be completely realized due to these variations.

Maintenance and support may be more difficult as well. For example, even though industry standards include specifications for remote device management, not all equipment contains that feature. In that case, control requires a trip to the device itself. In large networks comprising many devices spread over a large geographic area, this issue is particularly important.

Only by studying the detailed specifications of a manufacturer's equipment can we determine whether it meets the requirements of the proposed network.

Select a vendor

The result of our vendor investigations is a short list from which we will select one or more. That selection should consider the following:

- **Vendor reputation.** A vendor whose products have had wide distribution and who has been in business for many years will have developed a reputation within the industry. Ask for a list of customers, and contact them to see how satisfied they are with the vendor, the products, the service, and the support. Because networks are designed to operate for many years, it is important to know how long the vendor will support those products and troubleshoot problems even as new versions are produced and older ones are discontinued. And what about upgrade and replacement policies?
- **Vendor stability.** How sound is the vendor's business? No matter how good the reputation, if the business is at risk, it may not survive long enough to provide support when it is needed. The network technology business is particularly volatile. Manufacturers come and go, merge, or are acquired by other companies. This lends even more credence to the importance of focusing on industry-standard technologies—if our vendor does go out of business, we have a much better chance of being able to substitute another vendor's products without much difficulty.

Assessing vendors with respect to these two criteria may result in a pared-down short list. From those remaining, we can set up a grid to compare their offerings, pricing, and contracts. For fairly simple networks, this is a straightforward matter. For more complex networks, selection usually is better handled by an RFP providing potential vendors with specific requirements and inviting them to bid on the project.

No matter how thoroughly vendors are investigated, choice is never risk-free. However, due diligence can reduce the risk considerably.

17.4 Other important design considerations

In addition to network technology and device selection, other considerations must be part of a successful design. The major ones are outlined in this section.

Security

As we know, networks can be vulnerable to unauthorized access and activity from outside and inside the organization. Even those who have access rights can engage in harmful pursuits, accidentally or maliciously. When access is gained by whatever means, it is possible to disrupt network functioning, do all sorts of damage to files and applications, and read, retrieve, alter, use, or distribute private data.

In Chapter 15, "Network security," we saw examples of some of these nefarious deeds: denial-of-service attacks, adulteration of transmitted data, alteration of databases, Web site defacement or replacement, eavesdropping, and stealing sensitive data. To circumvent these activities, data and resources must be secured and, to the extent feasible, unauthorized access prevented. Measures such as activity monitoring should be considered as well.

Securing a network is a multifaceted undertaking that has significant impact on its design. The usual measures involve incorporating firewalls, proxy servers, and access controls. Devices to handle these functions are placed at many points within the network and operate together with specialized software that functions throughout the network. This adds substantial complexity and cost.

To establish appropriate levels of security, all potential threats and ways to infiltrate the network must be examined, culminating in a risk analysis that assesses threat probabilities, severity of likely damage, and cost to prevent each one. The analysis is a basis for determining which threats warrant mitigation and to what degree—ultimately a business decision.

As an illustration of network implications of a security decision, consider using encryption to prevent data adulteration and unauthorized viewing. This common and sensible process can profoundly influence network design—strong encryption results in larger files that use more of the network's resources and affects protocol choice. The particular impact depends on what and how much data needs to be encrypted and where in the network it will be done. Then, too, encryption/decryption schemes require considerable processing, which can slow the flow of data through the network.

Ultimately, which security threats to mitigate and to what degree is a business decision.

Addressing

Every device in a network must have a unique address so it can be referenced by other devices. If networks are to be interconnected, more than a single address is needed—for example, an Ethernet MAC address (physical) and an IP address (logical). Obtaining and assigning logical addresses is crucial to the smooth operation and maintenance of the network. If IP address assignment is automatic via a dynamic host configuration protocol (DHCP) server, placement and location of the server is an important consideration for network traffic flows and routing.

In addition to basic IP addressing consideration, decisions must be made about subnetting and IP version. The addressing scheme selected will affect the ease and efficiency of routing and switching. As with most network issues, it is best to decide on addressing at the outset of the design process.

Addressing schemes affect traffic flow, an important design factor.

Cabling plan for the wired world

Cable layouts and runs require careful consideration during the planning and design stage. For example, if a building is to be provisioned with Ethernet local area networks (LANs), how the cabling is arranged throughout the building will determine the number and locations of hubs and switches. A good plan will ensure that the cabling scheme will accommodate rearranging user equipment and make the system readily maintainable. Typical in-building cabling designs use structured vertical and horizontal cabling schemes.

For management efficiency and flexibility, structured cable plans are the norm.

Wireless to wired in-house connections

Wireless LANs are becoming a natural part of the corporate network scene. Whether set up as an ad hoc wireless LAN (WLAN) for the duration of a project, a means of providing access where there are no cables and no plans to add them, or a convenience for employees who move about the building regularly, WLANs assume greater importance when they are connected to the corporate wired networks. Part of planning an in-house wired network involves providing that connectivity.

We saw in Chapter 14, "Wireless networks," that the key to providing access to the corporate wired networks is the number and locations of access points, those devices that live simultaneously in the wireless and wired worlds. Generally, it is preferable to handle management, provisioning, and configuration centrally. On the other hand, authentication and intraWLAN and interWLAN traffic control normally are localized functions. Although providing for in-house wireless is not in itself a complex undertaking, it always is better to think about what might be needed beforehand, during the network planning stage.

Accommodating WLANs is part of the wired network design process.

An iterative process

A key point of the network planning and design process is that it is iterative. We begin with user-provided initial needs, incorporate security and other considerations, and generate a requirements document. This is refined by working groups that look at the consequences of the initial requirements and modify them accordingly. Feedback at every stage is vital. This means that any of the individual processes may be repeated several times until a consensus is reached and a final design document is generated.

TECHNICAL NOTE
A wireless design project

The lack of cables in the wireless network itself may seem to imply that the design for such a network is much simpler than for a wired one. Actually, except for not having to develop a cabling plan, there is no procedural difference. Thus, design team composition, end user needs, business goals, traffic analysis, reliability, addressing options, security, standards, vendor due diligence and selection, and testing are the same as for wired network projects. Of course, product types, network locations and restrictions, and usage are specific to wireless and so will differ in the details of wireless vs. wired specifications. Nevertheless, the planning and design processes are equivalent.

17.5 Design testing and finalization

Building any sizable network is an expensive, time-consuming proposition. Therefore, it is prudent and necessary to test the proposed design prior to actual implementation. Any flaws that are detected are more readily corrected at this point than after the network is installed.

Testing

An excellent way to test the design is by using network simulation software. This allows you to set up the planned network virtually and put the design through its paces on a computer. The software produces statistics that indicate overall network performance as well as what is happening at each of the various network nodes.

It takes relatively little time to run many usage, loading, and failure scenarios, thus giving designers a very good idea of how the network will behave under various operating conditions—including the very ones that formed the basis for the design in the first place. If design modifications are indicated, they can be made using the software tools that are part of the simulation packages and tested again.

Network simulation software enables thorough testing of a great many network usage scenarios in a short time.

Finalizing

After thorough testing and modification as appropriate, it is time to finalize the design. The result is the final ***technical architecture.*** This is the blueprint from which the actual network is built and the documents to purchase and install the network—***contract specification documents***—are created. There are two versions of the latter: ***information for bidders (IFB)*** and ***request for proposal (RFP).***

Information for bidders

When an organization's own experts or the consultants it hires for assistance can completely design every facet of the network, down to the specific selection of every piece of equipment and the placement of every wire, a completely specified design document for potential bidders—the IFB—can be issued. The IFB provides prospective vendors the entirety of information regarding what they are expected to provide.

The advantage of this approach is that the organization knows in advance precisely what it will be getting, assuming the vendor lives up to the contract. The disadvantage is that, should anything in the design turn out to be incorrect or overlooked, the organization must bear the responsibility and cost for corrections.

Generally speaking, large and technologically complex networks do not lend themselves to this approach, because usually only the vendors know enough about their equipment capabilities and quirks to reasonably put a working design together. Furthermore, the rapid pace of technological change can mean that by the time vendors are asked to bid on the project, the organization's design may have become obsolete, or at least less capable than what was thought possible. This type of approach therefore works best for relatively simple networks and those that will use very stable and well-understood technologies.

Request for proposal

An RFP is an offering to vendors to present a solution to a set of requirements. Unlike an IFB, an RFP does not have complete and detailed information about the network to be furnished. Rather, it contains as much, or as little, information as the organization deems suitable.

If the organization wants a network built around the newest and most promising technology, for which there is yet not a great body of detailed information or designers with such experience, it will specify a general set of *functional requirements*—what the network will run and how it will be expected to perform; the overall design is left to the vendors. If the organization has decided what technology and/or type of network architecture it wants, it will provide more detailed requirements, which constrains the designs that vendors will offer.

By using an RFP, the organization looks to the vendors to propose their own solutions, for a price, and bid on the job. For fairly complex jobs, the organization will hold a bidders' conference, at which prospective bidders can raise question about details and clarify points that may be ambiguous or subject to interpretation. After all the bids are in, the "best" vendor can be chosen. Because the design will be crafted by the successful vendor as detailed in his proposal, if problems occur in executing the design, the onus for making corrections falls on the vendor. For this reason, the RFP is preferred for complex undertakings. Because these are the most common network systems in question, the RFP is the more common technique.

The RFP is preferable for complex projects; the IFB is better suited to simple, stable networks.

17.6 Implementation

Creating and installing the actual network, particularly for large and technologically complex designs, is a major challenge for even the most seasoned network specialist. It is not unusual for the most professional, well-conceived design to produce surprises and unintended consequences during implementation. For example, the design may have called for ATM switches from two manufacturers, both of whom follow the ATM standards. Yet the vendors' implementations may prevent the switches from working together, something that usually cannot be completely determined until they are actually installed.

To mitigate the challenges and problems that might arise, it is wise to consider and deal with the following items early on in the project:

- **Vendor and contract details.** Large network projects usually require the services of many vendors—cabling, equipment, software, facilities, and room tempering providers, among others. To avoid a management nightmare, an organization can hire one *general contractor (GC)* to provide all the required services and assume responsibility for the entire project. Among other things, the GC has to hire and coordinate *subcontractors*—various vendors the GC engages to supply services to satisfy the requirements of the contract.

  When the project is finished, the organization is left with myriad products, hardware and software, that it has to live with for many years. Therefore it is crucial that the contract itself be very precise with respect to:

  - Criteria for appropriate installation—for example, equipment on concrete pads, or wiring on cable ladders.
  - Temperature control where needed to ensure that equipment does not exceed rated operating temperature.
  - Complete documentation as to everything that was installed, including wiring diagrams.
  - Fully labeled cables, outlets, and wire closet patch panels.
  - Warranty durations and start dates (immediately upon purchase under the contract or when the project is completed).
  - Hardware and software maintenance provision responsibilities and costs.
  - Software ownership.
  - Personnel training in the use, maintenance, and modification of software and hardware.

- **Pilot installation.** Especially for large or complex projects, it is good practice to install a small representative portion of the network to allow the implementers to proof their design, develop smooth implementation procedures, and deal with bugs and unexpected results that may crop up. It is far easier to fix problems at this stage than it is when the entire network has been constructed. It is not a stretch to make a pilot installation mandatory for all but the simplest network project.

- **Testing, testing, and testing.** To ensure that the network will perform as intended, it is absolutely necessary to perform testing at each step of the way:

  - **First article testing**, a comprehensive test that is particularly valuable if a piece of equipment or software has been produced specifically for the project. It ensures that required functions are met and that equipment is constructed from suitable materials and is appropriate for the environment in which it is to be placed.
  - **Factory acceptance testing** for each item as it leaves the factory, to ensure that it meets its stated specifications.
  - **System acceptance testing**, which comprehensively checks the entire system in its final configuration by putting the network through its paces to demonstrate that all components, software, and cabling work together and that the network performs as expected under a variety of arbitrary traffic loads.

- **User expectations.** Employees must be trained in the use of the network. At the same time, they must be made aware of the capabilities of the system. It is common that no matter what the network can do, user expectations seem to out-pace its capabilities. Educating the user community is the best way to manage their expectations and ensure that they will be satisfied with the new facility.

- **Network deployment.** The final stage of the project is to put the network into production and, if it is a replacement, to cut over from the current system. Care must be taken to deal with unexpected problems. Unfortunately, in spite of extensive testing, it is never possible to fully anticipate what will happen when any large, complex network is put into operation. This indicates that appropriate support personnel must be available to deal with problems as they arise and that, in case of major difficulties, a fallback plan is in place for a rapid return to the old system.

Implementation is fraught with details and snags. Careful oversight is indispensable.

17.7 Operational verification

Successful deployment does not end the network design effort. Networks are always in transition as new applications are added and user patterns change. Therefore, it is important to monitor the network on an ongoing basis to determine whether changes are indicated. This is part of standard network management in general, but here we talk about the implications for network design in particular.

Periodically, a formal evaluation of the network should be undertaken to ascertain the following:

- Network performance compared to expectations
- Reliability and whether up-time objectives are being met
- User satisfaction with network response times and application handling
- Changes in average and peak traffic loads, higher or lower
- Suitability of points-of-presence locations
- Handling of wireless interconnects if part of the design, or changes if they need to become part of the design

Monitoring the network also points to impending problem areas and helps gather information on specific problem incidents. The monitoring system should allow the generation of *trouble tickets,* succinct descriptions of network problems and error conditions that will be forwarded to technicians for resolution. A database should be maintained of all trouble tickets generated and their resolution for an overall analysis of the network.

Networks always are in transition as applications and traffic patterns change. Monitoring is essential to signal where and when upgrades or modifications are needed.

17.8 Upgrading the network

As networks are dynamic entities, they require continuous care. Although monitoring gives us a picture of network behavior over time that we use to determine when we must install faster switches, links, and more nodes, some modifications are more subtle. For example, the need to upgrade switch or router software is not likely to be indicated by monitoring. Equipment vendors periodically change device software and may drop support for older versions.

Replacing or upgrading network software can be a particularly difficult and treacherous undertaking for an organization. How can the new software be installed without interrupting service? What happens if an unexpected problem arises that causes parts of the network or the whole network to crash? If the network was initially designed to consider such situations, the impact of these problems may be greatly or entirely reduced. In any case, before attempting to upgrade software, a thoroughly thought-out fallback plan must be in place.

Upgrades must be carefully planned and executed so as not to disrupt the network unnecessarily. Include a fallback plan.

17.9 Summary

In this chapter, we examined the steps to be taken when building a communications network. Just as preparing to build an edifice requires a carefully crafted plan, so too does building a network. Initially, requirements for the network must be derived from the user community: The various applications they will use and how each will impact the network must be studied and understood. Network and application experts must assess the users' expectations of the network capabilities and performance in light of available technology and cost and manage their expectations accordingly.

After the functional requirements are finalized, specifications are prepared, as either an IFB—a complete design that vendors can bid on to implement—or an RFP—functional requirements for which vendors submit proposals for design and implementation. In either case, sufficient consideration must be given to the implementation, testing, and continuing evolution of the network after it is built. Formal monitoring helps deal with problems that may arise and recognize changing traffic and usage patterns that will guide designers in how to best upgrade the network.

In the next chapter we explore some of the relevant emerging networking and computer communications technologies. We look at several prominent issues in the field and discuss the work that is being done to resolve these issues. This provides insight into the why and wherefore of the directions the development of future methodologies is taking.

End note

Although this chapter focuses on network projects, many of the considerations are similar to those of general technology project management. If you would like to delve into that topic further, three excellent books are:

Schwalbe, Kathy. *Information Technology Project Management*, 4th edition. Course Technology, 2005.

Marchewka, Jack. *Information Technology Project Management: Providing Measurable Organizational Value*, 2nd edition. John Wiley & Sons, 2006.

Gray, Clifford F. and Erik W. Larson. *Project Management: The Managerial Process,* 3rd edition. McGraw-Hill, 2006.

END-OF-CHAPTER QUESTIONS

Short answer

1. What factors should be considered in the in-house/outsource network design project decision?
2. What are the principal critical success factors for a network project?
3. What does a disaster recovery plan entail?
4. Why should industry-standard hardware and software be specified? When should it not?
5. What is the difference between the network plan and the network design?
6. What is an RFP and when should it be used?
7. What is an IFB and when should it be used?
8. What are the functions of a general contractor? Why would we want one?
9. Describe three types of implementation testing.
10. What is the purpose of operational verification?

Fill-in

1. A network design and implementation project begins with _____.
2. Project scope indicates _____.
3. The result of an applications survey is _____.
4. A _____ is when malfunction of one device or link can crash the network.
5. _____ are in the best position to know whether the business requirements are consistent with available technologies.
6. Securing a network usually involves incorporating _____, _____, and _____.
7. The blueprint from which the actual network is built and the contract specification documents are created is the _____.
8. The _____ provides all the required services and assumes responsibility for the entire network implementation.
9. A _____ plan provides for alternate means of handling traffic should the network be disrupted during upgrading.
10. A _____ plan provides for continued operation of critical business functions should there be major network outages.

Multiple-choice

1. Most network projects
   a. are solo operations
   b. require a team of engineers
   c. do not need a project manager
   d. should be done by a multi-skilled and talented team
   e. do not need to bring in end users until after installation

2. Business and technical requirements
   a. are the basis from which the network plan is built
   b. may need modification as the plan is developed
   c. take scope, budget, personnel, and time into consideration
   d. must serve user needs to be successful
   e. all of the above

3. Network design depends heavily on
   a. the applications to be run on it
   b. the locations of the users
   c. traffic analysis
   d. reliability assessment
   e. all of the above

4. The network technical architecture
   a. is a drawing of the cabling plan
   b. must be based on the OSI model
   c. is a detailed description of the functions and characteristics of the proposed network
   d. should always be provided by the vendors
   e. cannot be changed after it is approved

5. When multiple vendors are employed
   a. there may be compatibility problems in their equipment
   b. specific expertise from specialists can be incorporated
   c. maintenance and support is easier
   d. a single contractor should oversee their work
   e. all of the above

6. Establishing appropriate security levels
   a. requires eliminating all potential threats
   b. means that low-risk threats should be ignored
   c. is ultimately a business decision
   d. is solely the domain of the network security division
   e. all of the above

7. Addressing schemes
   a. are not relevant to traffic flow considerations
   b. do not need to be considered until implementation
   c. require only physical address designs
   d. can be changed at will
   e. none of the above

8. Testing
   a. is required only after the network is set up to make sure it functions properly
   b. is carried out throughout the design process
   c. is not reliable when carried out via simulation software
   d. can point out failures but cannot signal the need for design changes
   e. none of the above

9. Large network projects
   a. usually require the services of many vendors
   b. leave the organization with myriad products, hardware, and software
   c. can benefit greatly from a pilot installation
   d. need thorough testing
   e. all of the above

10. Network upgrading or modification
    a. should not be necessary for many years with a properly designed network
    b. can be a particularly difficult undertaking
    c. should be done only if there is a parallel network that can carry the load during the process
    d. should be considered on a daily basis
    e. is indicated only by the results of network monitoring

True or false

1. A network design project needs a team manager but not a project sponsor.
2. Traditionally, systems design projects have a high rate of failure: not finished on time, over budget, not functional as planned, or even cancelled outright.
3. End users should be engaged at the earliest possible point in the planning cycle.
4. The network must be able to handle every end user request.
5. The later in the project a change is made, the easier it is to do.
6. With due diligence, vendor choice can be made risk-free.
7. Only horizontal and vertical structured cable plans should be considered.
8. Accommodating WLANs is part of the wired network design process.
9. Trouble tickets are generated by network monitoring systems.
10. The best network designs usually contain compromises between what is desired and what is feasible.

Exploration

1. Investigate the offerings of several vendors of network equipment and solutions services. What information can you get from their Web sites? Rank the sites by how informative they are. Which vendors would you select for a small network project? A medium project? A large project? Why?
2. Consider network simulation software. Describe the capabilities of the various packages available. What are their costs? Which would you choose? Look for reviews that comment on their effectiveness, capabilities, and flexibility.
3. Failure rates for systems projects in general and network projects in particular are rather high, despite the fact that such projects have been carried out for many years. Why do you suppose that is? Find examples of network projects that succeeded and projects that failed. What factors do you suppose led to each outcome? Are there commonalities among these factors that you think could be predictive of success or failure?

MOSI has gone through a long period of growth. The company now has substantial operations in all boroughs of New York City. They use a variety of networks extensively, internally in each location and for connections among the locations. They also link to major feeder hospitals. But despite MOSI's dependence on networks, monitoring has been sporadic.

The CEO believes it is time to review MOSI's network implementations and strategies, especially because a small but growing number of complaints is being registered about the capabilities and response times of some of these networks. In addition, the CEO is becoming concerned about security breaches. Because MOSI's databases contain a great deal of confidential information, any significant incursions would seriously undermine MOSI's credibility.

How would you suggest that MOSI proceed? Write an annotated outline of the steps you think MOSI should take and explain the significance of each step. Include a ranking of which tasks should be tackled first, which next, and so on. Explain your rankings.

18 The future of network communications

18.1 Overview

In the realm of computer-based technology in general, it is safe to say that the future is faster, smaller, cheaper. We expect the networks and computer communications sectors of that realm to follow those trends and some others as well.

In this chapter, we will discuss some of the newer relevant emerging technologies. Rather than trying to prognosticate beyond the "safe" comment we began with, we will look at several issues and the developments in various networks and communications techniques that are attempting to resolve them. The following are among the most prevalent:

- Increasing network speed and capacity
- Distributing and broadening access
- Improving communications reach
- Continuing convergence of methodologies

Let's look at some specific technologies and see how they address these quests. This will give us an idea of where we might be headed.

18.2 Fiber to every home and office

We have seen the advantages of data transmission over fiber-optic media compared to copper media—very high bandwidth, immunity to electromagnetic interference, and minimal signal attenuation. We have also noted its expense and the specialized expertise it takes to install the media and maintain the systems, and the electrical-light-electrical conversions that must take place at all the switching and end points of the transmission paths.

In the United States, there is a significant amount of long-distance fiber-optic cabling, much of it installed during the dot-com boom, a period of incredible investment in technology from about 1996 to 2001. It was followed by the dot-com bust, during which many overhyped, overfinanced, underperforming firms failed.

As a consequence, much of the fiber was dark (unused) until the past few years. Now, more and more has been lit and even added to, replacing and supplementing wire media for long-haul and medium-haul transmission. This trend is global, but converting the last mile has lagged. This gap is beginning to be addressed in the ***fiber to the home (FTTH)*** evolution, perhaps more properly termed *fiber to every home and office,* which many call "true broadband."

The last mile, also called the local loop, refers to the link between customer premises and the closest telephone switching office. The term is a metaphor, not an actual physical distance. Activity is growing in alternatives to the local loop for last mile connectivity.

Why fiber?

The demand for rapid data transmission continues to grow, especially in many business applications. Filling that demand calls for high-speed, symmetric, wide-bandwidth systems. On the home consumer side, cable TV companies are beginning to face competition from telephone companies that are laying fiber-optic cable to carry voice and television signals. Home and business demand also is growing for video and audio streaming and fast image transfer.

The existing global wire media infrastructure, much of which is quite old, is becoming increasingly taxed—in some areas overtaxed. Significant improvement requires major additions and overhaul. As one salient argument goes, if you have to add infrastructure, it might as well be fiber.

The business case for converting to fiber can be made if the cost and demand picture is right—increasingly it is. Bundled services for voice, Internet access, music, and video are growing in popularity. When that video is HDTV and real-time full-motion conferencing, bandwidth is even more critical. These kinds of services are not handled well by legacy copper networks designed as single-service systems.

Perspective

Properly designed fiber-optic systems can handle the full variety of current services and more. Single-mode fiber is not only the medium of choice for long haul, but it must be considered for the last mile as well, especially when that last mile is the link of a high-demand business. Less expensive solutions for less demanding needs combine single-mode fiber to a distribution point, from where it is split off to several multimode fibers or copper to the end users.

The light-electricity conversion issue is another question. It increases complexity and cost, and decreases overall speed. It will be resolved completely when light-based computers are produced. That is a longer-term proposition. In the meantime, optical switch development, key to creating optical networks, is progressing and fiber-optic build-out is taking place. More on this in the next section.

For a more detailed discussion of FTTH, see the tutorial on the International Engineering Consortium Web site at http://www.iec.org/online/tutorials/fiber_home/topic01.html.

For an overview of current FTTH activity, see the Fiber to the Home Council Web site at http://www.ftthcouncil.org/.

18.3 Optical networks

We have seen that much of the long-haul networks already are light based, running over fiber-optic cables, making use of dense wavelength division multiplexing (DWDM) to maximize efficiency. The goal is to move forward to *all optical networks (AON).*

We know that networks depend on switches, so it follows that optical networks depend on optical switches. Two types currently available are *optical-electrical-optical (O-E-O)* and *optical-optical-optical (O-O-O)*—the middle letter refers to the switch itself, the outer letters to the input and output. There is more than one technology being worked on for both of these categories. (See "Technical note: Optical switches.")

TECHNICAL NOTE
Optical switches

Late in 2005, a group of electrical engineers at Stanford University announced that they had developed a means of switching a laser beam on and off at speeds as fast as 100 billion times a second. This compares with current market devices that switch at rates of no more than 10 billion per second. Importantly, the chip to do this was made with standard chip-making processes, implying that the cost of producing such chips will quickly become competitive after routine volume manufacturing processes are adapted.

The chips achieve those speeds by transmitting or blocking a continuous laser-generated light beam, thus providing "on/off" states that can be interpreted as bit values. At such rapid switching speeds, the possibility of extremely high data rates between interconnected devices, including those inside computers themselves, becomes feasible, provided that light-detector capabilities are developed to work at those switching speeds. This would lead the way to creating very-high-speed routers, which in turn would boost network speeds and be the next step in developing an all-optical network.

Owing to their speed and avoidance of electrical conversion, it may seem at first glance that O-O-O switches are the better choice. That is not necessarily the case. O-E-O switches are intelligent—capable of multiplexing and demultiplexing. Because there are as yet no optical computers, current O-O-O switches are not intelligent.

This is a definite downside for carriers providing high bandwidth to businesses, because they depend on multiplexing to maximize the efficiency of their links. For them, O-E-O switches make the most sense, particularly at the network edges. On the other hand, core carriers that transport already-multiplexed signals intact are better off with O-O-O switches. So mixed buildouts are desirable for the time being.

O-E-O switches have downsides too. The electrical part of the switch is significantly slower than the optical part, and processing to convert incoming light signals to electrical signals and back to light for transmission takes time. Neither of these is part of O-O-O switch operation. When muxing/demuxing is added to the mix, we can understand the relative slowness of O-E-O switches.

Perspective

As development proceeds, electronic components will be replaced with optical components. When intelligent O-O-O switches and optical computing become practical, the network picture will change. Natural evolution will move networks from semi-optical to all optical. At that point, transport, switching, and bandwidth management will be completely optical—the AON. These networks will be much faster by dint of eliminating the need for electrical/optical conversions.

For additional information, see the All-Optical Networking Consortium Web site at http://www.ll.mit.edu/aon/.

18.4 Power line networks

For electrical power delivery, power lines already form a vast network grid, both externally (owned by electric utilities) and internally within corporations and homes. The idea behind power line networks is to utilize appropriate segments of the electrical grids to deliver data, thus obviating the need for adding data cabling where it does not exist or where what does exist is insufficient. At this juncture, transmission speeds are relatively low, however.

The process of delivering data over power lines is called ***power line communications (PLC).*** Narrowband systems are meant for internal business and home networks; broadband systems are designed for electric utility distribution systems, including long-haul power lines. Both carry data as digitally encoded analog signals.

In either system, when data are carried from or through power distribution centers, an addressing mechanism must be provided to prevent the data from being delivered to anyone on the grid but the intended recipient. This is not different in concept from the need for addressing in any multi-path network, but the addresses and addressing systems themselves are not yet standardized. So far, most installations have been used by utilities for monitoring electricity usage and power systems conditions. However, there is growth potential for all the typical Internet applications.

Standards

The standards picture is incomplete, with several organizations working on various PLC aspects. As is often the case with emerging technology, currently there is no single standard that guarantees compatibility among different providers and across platforms. Here are three of the most relevant:

- ***IEEE P1901,*** whose work is saddled with the long but descriptive name *Draft Standard for Broadband over Power Line Networks: Medium Access Control and Physical Layer Specifications*, deals with broadband systems. P1901 is a working group for developing a standard. (http://grouper.ieee.org/groups/1901/)
- The ***European Telecommunications Standards Institute (ETSI)*** is promoting standards for interoperability between in-house and external power line networks, although there is no agreed-on standard for either type of network as yet. (http://www.etsi.org/)
- The ***Universal Powerline Association (UPA)*** is, in their words, "the first truly global and universal PLC association to cover all markets and all PLC applications . . . to promote among government and industry leaders the tremendous potential of PLC technologies to build a global communication society." The UPA develops specifications to submit as proposals to standards bodies, for interoperability (compatibility among connected equipment) and coexistence (non-interference between different applications and technologies on the same system). (http://www.upaplc.org/page_viewer.asp?category=Home&sid=2)

A DOWNSIDE   One concern voiced about PLC is the potential for interference with radio frequency broadcasting. We know that varying electrical current produces electromagnetic radiation. Power lines, strung in long straight lines, are great radiators. When that radiation is in the same frequencies as radio broadcasts, interference can result. This is a potential issue for all-wireless communications.

A major organization focused on the issue is the ***International Special Committee on Radio Interference (CISPR)*** (http://www.iec.ch/zone/emc/emc_cis.htm), a member committee of the ***International Electrotechnical Commission (IEC)*** (http://www.iec.ch/). The ***American National Standards Institute (ANSI)*** (http://www.ansi.org/) contributes standards to CISPR.

Perspective

It is likely that if PLC over external power grids does grow for data communications, it will be in areas where there is a dearth of communications cabling but a reasonably extensive and reliable power grid. In those areas, it could compete with wireless, because it does not require location and construction of wireless base stations, antennas, and distribution points. Perhaps the greater penetration will be for internal applications, where connecting to the company networks would mean simply plugging a device adapter into an electrical wall outlet.

18.5 Power over Ethernet

Instead of sending data over power lines, *power over Ethernet (POE)* does the reverse. It is meant to provide up to 48 volts of electrical power over standard unshielded twisted pair (UTP) LAN cables to network-attached devices such as laptop computers, VoIP-ready digital telephones, wireless access points for connecting wireless LANs (WLANs) to the company-wired infrastructure, and even IP video cameras for remote security coverage. This eliminates the need for locating devices near electrical outlets or installing additional outlets to provide power for them.

The current IEEE POE standard is *802.3af*. It details limitations on how and over what the power can be delivered. For safety and to comply with regulations, either two or four wire pairs are used to carry the current. The amount of power available to any one device depends on how many devices on the same network are drawing power, but it is currently limited to about 15 watts at no more than 350 milliamps. The powered devices must be compliant to the standard—a sensing component in the power source will not deliver power to noncompliant devices.

Enhancements to the standard will increase the power available and the number of devices that can be attached, although there are limits on the amount of power the cabling itself can handle before failing.

There are two power source types: mid-span and end-span. Mid-span devices are meant for adding POE to legacy LANs; they are connected between the LAN switches and the devices to be powered. End-span devices are used in new installations and are integral to the switches.

Perspective

The 802.3af standard was published in 2003, but so far there has not been an installation boom. It seems likely, though, that with the increasing penetration of IP devices into the corporate infrastructure and the fact that the majority of network devices need both network connectivity and power, POE is a natural complement. With enhancements to the standards and improvements in the equipment, significant growth is likely. (For additional information about the standard, see http://www.ieee802.org/3/af/.)

18.6 100 gigabit Ethernet

The latest commercially available Ethernet is rated at 10 Gbps. Several standards have been released by the IEEE. They differ in media (mostly various versions of fiber-optic cable, but there also are two potential standards for copper cable) and span. The IEEE created the *Higher Speed Study Group (HSSG),* which originally was to consider 40 gigabit Ethernet, but has decided to focus on 100 gigabit instead. They expect to be able to create a standard that will operate at distances greater than 9.6 kilometers (about 6 miles) on single-mode fiber. Optimistically, the standard may be ready by 2009. Commercial products, mainly 100 gigabit Ethernet switches and routers, would follow some time after that.

Perspective

At 100-Gbps speeds and spans of more than 9.6 km, Ethernet becomes a viable option for metropolitan area network (MAN) links and one that is likely to be a cost-effective choice as volume adoption and production kicks in. Once again, what began as one of the oldest LAN technologies forges ahead, continuing Ethernet on its seemingly never-ending growth path.

18.7 vBNS, Internet2, Abilene, and NGI

In the early 1990s, the National Science Foundation was becoming concerned about the impending inadequacy of NSFNet, the high-speed interconnections among various U.S. research institutions, especially those housing NSF-supported supercomputing facilities. To improve the situation, in 1995 they commissioned MCI WorldCom to build a much more capable network. It was named the *very high-performance Backbone Network Service (vBNS)*. Initially it was built on ATM, but over the years vBNS has grown into two networks running in parallel. One of them is based on OC-12 and OC-48 SONET with IPv4 as an overlay network. The other remains ATM based at 622 Mbps but with IPv6.

A completely separate entity, *Internet2* is an alliance of over 200 U.S. universities that are involved with learning and research projects requiring wide bandwidth links. Many high-tech companies have signed on as sponsors. Hence, Internet2 focuses on providing appropriate infrastructure to support the work. Among these projects are investigations into ways to use the Internet and Internet2 infrastructures for education. Unlike vBNS, Internet2 sees its developments as leading to an eventual Internet replacement.

In their words:

> . . . working with industry and government, Internet2 develops and deploys advanced network applications and technologies for research and higher education, accelerating the creation of tomorrow's Internet. . . . [Internet2 is] a cost-effective hybrid optical and packet network . . . designed to provide next-generation production services as well as a platform for the development of new networking ideas and protocols. With community control of the fundamental networking infrastructure, the new Internet2 Network will enable a wide variety of bandwidth-intensive applications under development at campuses and research labs today. (http://www.internet2.edu/)

In a time frame similar to vBNS, members of the Internet2 group were working on a different high-performance backbone. Called *Abilene,* it was first implemented in 1999. Their intention was to provide a test bed for Internet2 researchers that was more like the Internet than was vBNS. Hence, it was not intended to be a vBNS competitor or replacement.

Abilene began with an OC-48 SONET backbone and IPv4 as an overlay network, similar to one of the vBNS networks. However, Abilene is a much more distributed network, covering over 13,000 miles. Now the backbone capacity has been increased to OC-192, creating a 10-Gbps network. It is accessible by Internet2 institutions.

In their words:

> Abilene is a proving ground for high-bandwidth technologies. The cross-country backbone is 10 gigabits per second, with the goal of offering 100 megabits per second of connectivity between every Abilene connected desktop. (http://abilene.internet2.edu/)

Another development project was the *next generation Internet (NGI)* initiative. It began with a 1996 announcement by President Clinton that was based on statements from a number of government and congressional advisory groups, academia, and other interested parties. NGI was officially launched in 1997 with the publication of an implementation plan. The plan's goals were similar to Internet2, in that NGI aimed at developing a replacement for the current Internet. NGI was designed as a five year project to supplement the other projects taking place—vBNS, Internet2, and abilene. (For more information, see http://www.nitrd.gov/ngi/pubs/concept-Jul97/pdf/ngi-cp.pdf and http://ecommerce.hostip .info/pages/794/Nest-Generation-Internet-Initiative-NGI.html.)

Perspective

These four initiatives, vBNS, Internet2, Abilene, and NGI, have the same goal: improving the speed of and access to interconnected computer communications. NGI ended in 2002; currently the first three are available only to the researchers and institutions involved in the work. Eventually their findings will lead to faster service, wider bandwidths, and better quality of service (QoS) for all of us.

18.8 Net neutrality

One of the hot-button topics being debated globally and likely to be pushed in one direction or the other for some time is *net neutrality.* The term refers to the idea that usage of the Internet's "pipes" should be the same regardless of destination and application, and not partitioned based on cost/price models for link speed and bandwidth. In other words, network access providers should not be able to discriminate against users on the basis of applications or the bandwidth they need. On one side of the debate are several of the companies that own the networks over which data flow; on the other are a mélange of ISPs, companies that make heavy use of the Internet in their business models, particularly content providers, and public interest groups. The issue and its many sub-issues are argued fervently, often couched in terms as dramatic as being a debate over the future of the Internet.

Opposing net neutrality

Highlighting and supporting the anti-neutrality arguments is the Net Competition organization (http://www.netcompetition.org/). Their fundamental argument is that competitive choice is better than government regulation. The latter refers to efforts in the U.S. Congress and governmental bodies of other nations to pass legislation mandating net neutrality.

You can get a sense of their position from a sampling of their slogans:

Free market Internet vs. socialized Internet
Net design flexibility vs. net design rigidity
Freedom to choose vs. non-discrimination mandate

These come from their claim that those who argue for net neutrality are falsely describing the current Internet as neutral when it is not. Examples to prove this contention are described in a page on their site called Debunking Net Neutrality Myths: http://www. netcompetition.org/docs/pronetcomp/debunking-myths.shtml. They bolster their general proposition that the Internet is not now neutral and it should not be forced to become so.

Here are the members who "support the mission and efforts of the NETCompetition. org e-forum":

American Cable Association

Cellular Telecommunications Association

National Cable and Telecommunications Association

US Telecom Association

AT&T

BellSouth

Cingular

Comcast

Qwest

Sprint

Time Warner Cable

Verizon

Verizon Wireless

WCA International

Favoring net neutrality

No less passionate than NETCompetition.org is an opposing organization whose Web site is http://www.savetheinternet.com. They claim to be doing nothing less than fighting for Internet freedom, as exemplified by stating that net neutrality "prevents companies like AT&T, Verizon and Comcast from deciding which Web sites work best for you—based on what site pays them the most."

To reinforce their claim, they have a list of what they see as the consequences of abandoning net neutrality, called "How does this threat to Internet freedom affect you?" (http://www.savetheinternet.com/=threat), which includes a list of "past abuses."

Their coalition has a membership of several hundred, arranged in several categories:

Not-for-profit organizations

Small businesses

Individuals and educators

Church affiliates

Internet service providers

Video gamers

Blogs and web sites

Perspective

It is difficult to claim that the Internet, in its current form, is fully neutral. However, when talking about neutrality, the question to ask is, to which part of the Internet do you refer? On one hand, we know that there are different price structures for different access speeds—dial up, slower and faster broadband. On the other hand, anyone (individual, group, company) that puts up a Web site now is assured that the site can be accessed by any of these means regardless of site ownership or content. But if access providers could charge more for high-speed access to a particular site, or differential fees to various sites, that is a different story.

There now are some situations in which differential pricing and access hold sway. Although statements to that effect made by the NETCompetition forum are eminently rational and reasonable sounding, it is clear that dropping any guise of neutrality will drastically alter the Internet as we now know it, and most likely not for the better.

That fact notwithstanding, there is no reason to believe that net neutrality must be an all-or-nothing proposition. The solution we are headed for likely will present infrastructure providers with equitable means of recouping their investments without unfairly burdening or discriminating against particular classes of users. This will be increasingly important as Web trends demand more and more bandwidth and Internet usage continues on its global growth path. The journey to that point is probably going to be on a rocky road, though, especially as it will involve coordination and cooperation among many countries.

18.9 The Web 1, 2, 3

In a word, the Web we are most familiar with is *pages*—on a vast array of independent sites with all sorts of content. Retrospectively, we can call it *Web 1.0*. More recently there has been a groundswell of material describing *Web 2.0*. The difference between the two is mostly one of application—affiliations that bring otherwise independent sites or content together, sometimes called mashups. For example, real estate sites will automatically add a Google map of the area to their information on a house you are interested in, zoomable right down to the block it's on and perhaps even with a satellite image of it as well. Some pundits label the proliferation of podcasts and blogs as Web 2.0. Others include within the Web 2.0 universe sites that aggregate in one place content from disparate sites.

Web 3.0 is an incipient movement in another direction—the so-called *semantic Web.* The idea is to provide mechanisms for the Web to derive meaning by interpreting the nature of your requests and responding accordingly. In other words, instead of supplying data passively as is now the case, Web 3.0 will process it actively. This may mean combining data from various sources and presenting it in a format suited to the user, or taking action based on gathered information. Some examples:

- Advances over traditional searching would produce better results in less overall time. Now searches list sites whose content contains particular phrases or keywords, the results of which you have to wade through to perhaps find what you're looking for and perhaps not. Instead, semantic processing would be able to answer questions directly:
  - I'm looking for a house for sale by owner in a town in the Northeast with a population of no more than 100,000, top-rated school systems, and an asking price of no more than $400,000.
  - Who are the people who contributed the most to the development of the Internet and what did they do?
  - What's the best way to cook a turkey in a gas oven for someone who's never cooked before?
  - What are the most popular freeware packages for Web page development and how do they compare with open source and commercial packages?
- Network-attached surveillance systems would interpret what they "see" to determine whether there is a threat and, if there is, what kind of threat. Then they would automatically take appropriate action and notify the authorities as well.
- Automated Web searching could be invoked to gather specific detailed data for research projects, simply by describing the project and the data needed.

Perspective

Thinking about these possibilities and others, we can see that they all revolve around adding intelligence to Web applications, which will bring along much richer content. As such enhanced applications grow in number and capability, so will the demand on the support infrastructure—primarily the Internet. Thus, the success of Web 3.0 will depend on the sort of backbone growth presaged by vBNS, Intenet2, and Abilene, along with similar improvement in the links connecting the backbone to regional and local service providers, including the beginnings of all-optical networks. Importantly, last-mile limitations must be conquered as well.

18.10 Local loop bypass technologies

The classic local loop is the wire link between customer premises and the nearest telephone switching office. Because of its origin in voice phone calls, the local loop has a relatively limited bandwidth and, DSL notwithstanding, presents a bottleneck in the quest for high-speed network connectivity. In addition, it can be an expensive link and, in many developing countries, one that is unreliable and with limited availability.

These factors point to pressure to replace, or at least provide solid alternatives to, the local loop. Four technologies have the potential to do so: power line communications, cable TV systems, FTTH, and wireless technologies including cellular networks, WiFi, WiMAX, and satellites. For now, cable TV has a bandwidth advantage, especially with much of their copper infrastructure being replaced by fiber.

Perspective

For any of these technologies to be feasible for bypassing the local loop, they have to become faster and more robust. Cellular also must get a lot cheaper. We know that faster and cheaper are hallmarks of technological progress, so that can be expected. Of course, which technology will win out, at least for the time being, is an open question.

Power line communication seems to have tremendous growth potential in developed countries where the power grids are extensive. But those are the same countries where other communications technologies, in particular, optical systems, also are widespread. Furthermore, the latter technology does not suffer from the problem of creating electromagnetic radiation interference.

For Internet access, wireless local loop bypass already has made inroads for data communications. Except for cellular, bypass relies on VoIP for voice and WiFi/WiMAX for data; Internet QoS is improving, although it still is not as good as it is on wired networks.

The greatest potential for wireless local loop is in developing countries where the wired infrastructure is poor. Building a wireless infrastructure has considerable cost advantages over building a wired one, especially for ground-based (rather than satellite) systems. Although they have great potential for coverage, satellite systems are expensive to create and maintain. Their upside is better for developed countries than for developing ones.

18.11 Computer-telephone integration

Cell phones run on cellular networks, which interconnect with landline phone systems. WiFi allows computers wireless access to the Internet and corporate infrastructure networks. Now you can reach the Internet without a direct connection, via WiFi or WiMAX and over the cellular network with a cellular card plugged in to a laptop. Conversely, with WiFi you can make VoIP phone calls from your laptop and even your WiFi-enabled cell phone without recourse to the wired phone or cellular networks; with appropriate routers, wired phones also can be reached.

New cell phones are being developed that will connect via WiFi to enable you to make VoIP calls from the phone, bypassing the cellular networks altogether. This doesn't make the cellular service providers happy, but some of them feel that anything that increases use of cell phones is good for all concerned parties.

For both the cell carriers and traditional phone companies, WiFi and WiMAX hotspots are a threat to their profitability and recovery of the billions they have invested in the infrastructure that WiFi and WiMAX bypass. As yet, the coverage areas of both the latter are more limited and spotty than cellular coverage, but installations are growing. Overall, land lines are on the losing side of this competition.

Currently in the United States, cell phone growth has reached a point at which there are more cell phones in use than wired phones. Partly responsible are the increasing functionality and improving reliability of cell phones and cellular networks, which have led to another growing trend: for many people, cell phones are their only phones. These phenomena are true in many other countries as well, especially those where the wired phone systems are not particularly dependable or robust.

Perspective

Whether a "phone" or a "computer," devices are getting smaller and more integrated. One of the limits on computer shrinkage is the minimum size needed to accommodate fingers to work the keyboard. As voice recognition and interpretation technology improves, this restriction will be eliminated.

There is no reason to assume that computers the size of today's cell phones with the capacity of today's laptops will not be produced in the relatively near future. We are heading toward a time when a single pocket-sized device will serve for voice and data communications, and computation. And as hotspot coverage improves, much of that communication will take place over the Internet.

One wrinkle is that WiFi uses unlicensed spectrum, which means that the potential for interference is high. Cellular systems use licensed spectrum to avoid that problem, but that is one of the factors that raises their costs. WiMAX is based on both licensed and unlicensed spectrum, but the infrastructure to support it is cheaper than what is needed for cell phones. WiMAX also has much greater span than WiFi. That makes WiMAX a possible competitor to WiFi, especially in areas where spectrum use is high.

18.12 The mainframe redux

Mainframe computers, all but written off a few years ago, are making a solid comeback in certain business-related arenas. Examples are the increasingly popular large data centers, especially those that run data warehouses from which data marts are created frequently, and data call centers that are the underlying support for banking and credentialing operations. In those usages, mainframes provide rapid communication and data transfer across many attached networks—distributed infrastructure supplemented by distributed data.

Mainframes are readily scalable, increasingly fast, and highly reliable. The mainframe network model has moved from a primarily IBM-centric one based on systems network architecture (SNA) to an Internetwork model based on IP or the TCP/IP protocol stack. This presages a move toward Web services for handling online business transaction processing and online analytic processing. To implement these usages, mainframes need to interface with LAN technologies, especially 10-Gbps and faster Ethernet, and handle virtual LAN (VLAN) pipes with requisite encryption services.

Perspective

This is yet another trend that will demand ever greater performance from networks within the corporate walls and throughout the WANs of the world—faster data transmission, better QoS, increased reliability, and higher levels of security. As has typically been the case, demand for increased services and improved performance is pushing developments in network infrastructure and support technology.

18.13 Summary

In this chapter, we have taken a brief look at some of the trends in computing as they relate to networks and computer communications. What it all boils down to is the continuing quest for faster, more reliable systems that operate with fewer and fewer transmission errors and provide greater access globally while reducing costs. That might seem like a tall order, but in the context of technology it is a reasonable expectation, continuing a long-standing trend.

Which technologies will dominate remains to be seen. Because of the increasing demand for mobility—on-the-go computing—it is rather evident that wireless products and applications will assume a greater role and share of the communications realm than they now do. Nevertheless, wired systems will not go away and will continue to predominate for fixed-platform networks because of their greater speed, security, and reliability.

END-OF-CHAPTER INVESTIGATIONS

Instead of the usual mix, this chapter ends with questions that require investigation, analysis, and some amount of pondering to reach conclusions. First review the chapter material on the subjects posed. Then look for sources that provide you with additional information and opinions and form a judgment as to the reliability of those sources. Finally, form your own conclusions and respond to the questions concisely, supporting your opinions with the information you have found.

1. What does CISPR have to say about interference from electromagnetic radiation emanating from power line communications (PLC)? What methods can you find to counter their concerns? Which organizations or companies favor PLC? Which oppose it? Based on your findings, do you favor expanded use of the technology or not?

2. Imagine that fiber to every home and office is a reality. What kinds of applications do you foresee becoming popular that now are either very limited in scope or not possible? Which providers do you think will be the most active in this movement?

3. Many companies have installed fiber-optic cable within their buildings for particular high-demand applications. Where is fiber most likely to be used? Do you foresee fiber replacing copper for more applications? Will faster Ethernet versions affect the choice? What about new installations?

4. What do you think is the future of power over Ethernet? Will it become a popular technique, a niche technology, or a passing fad? Do you envision it as a more relevant option for home or for business?

5. Evaluate the pro and con sides of the net neutrality controversy. Which do you think is more credible? If you were the arbiter who had to decide how it would be handled, what would you recommend? How would the global Internet picture look if some countries mandated neutrality and others did not?

6. Network data security depends on encryption and encapsulation procedures. Encryption strength depends on algorithm quality and key size. These are under continual development. The most common security encapsulation procedure now is VPN based on IPsec. VPN/SSL is another option. Which of these is growing rapidly and which is not? Why do you suppose that is? Compare new installations of frame relay, ATM, and VPN for intersite communications. What trends do you find?

7. How do you see the Web evolving? Which capabilities do you expect to become dominant? What infrastructure improvements will be required to support them?

8. Would corporations be interested in the local loop bypass technologies mentioned in this chapter when they already have direct links via T-line (T/DS), SONET (OC/STS), frame relay, and ATM methodologies? Whether or not they will be, do you believe there is a significant market for them elsewhere? What would that market be?

9. Where is the growth in mainframe demand and usage coming from? Who are the mainframe manufacturers competing in those markets? What alternatives are offered? What mix do you expect will emerge?

Appendix A

Sine waves: basic properties and signal shifting

Basic properties

The properties of the sine wave stem from a study of trigonometry undertaken by the Greeks a few thousand years ago. Working with parcels of land, the Greeks needed to accurately define their dimensions; they defined many geometric shapes, one of which was the right triangle, in which two sides are perpendicular to each other and the third side connects the two, as shown in Figure A.1. Sides P and B meet in a right angle (90 degrees); side A is called the hypotenuse, and the angle it forms with side B is labeled θ, as shown in the figure.

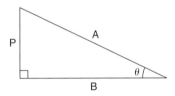

In mathematics, it is more usual to label a right triangle as ABC, but for reasons that will become clear as we proceed, we will use the above labeling, which is more pertinent to communications.

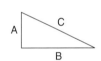

The Greeks defined quantities that relate the angles of the right triangle to ratios of the sides. One such quantity is the **sine,** which relates the angle θ to the ratio of the opposite side and the hypotenuse. Referring to Figure A.1, we have:

$$\sin\theta = P/A \qquad (1)$$

The value of angle θ can be measured in units of *degrees* or, more typically for communications, in units of *radians*. The two units are directly related. A full circle has 360 degrees, or 2π radians; a half circle has 180 degrees, or π radians; a quarter circle has 90 degrees, or $\pi/2$ radians; one degree equals $\pi/180$ radians; and so on.

Another way to see the relationship between angles, sines, and triangle sides is to embed the right triangle in a circle whose radius is A, the hypotenuse of the right triangle, as shown in Figure A.2.

Suppose we increase the angle θ so that the point (vertex) at the intersection of sides P and A moves around the perimeter of the circle in a clockwise direction until it reaches the $\pi/2$ radians (90-degree) point. *(Note that, for clarity, we have marked the angle measurements on the circumference of the circle, but each such mark refers to the angle θ as formed by A and B.)* As we do so, side P gets longer until it is the same length as the hypotenuse A, the radius of the circle. At that point, because $P = A$, we have:

$$\sin\theta = P/A = 1 \quad \text{so} \quad \sin(\pi/2 \text{ radians}) \quad [\text{or } \sin(90°)] = 1$$

FIGURE A.2

Right triangle in a circle

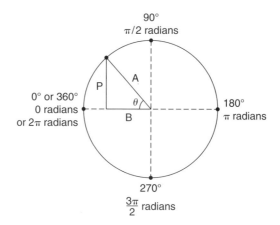

We also can see that as we increase θ further, P decreases until we reach $\theta = \pi$ *radians*, at which point P's length is zero. So now we have:

$$\sin\theta = P/A = 0 \quad \text{because} \quad P = 0 \quad \text{so} \quad \sin(\pi \text{ radians}) \quad [\text{or} \sin(180°)] = 0$$

As we continue to increase θ, we see P again lengthening until we reach $3\pi/2$ *radians*, and then P shortening once more as we reach 2π *radians*:

$$\text{so} \quad \sin(3\pi/2) = 1 \quad \text{and} \quad \sin(2\pi) = 0$$

To understand how the circle relates to the familiar sine wave pattern, imagine a blue ink pen at the end of triangle side A; then let's see how the circle develops as we increase θ and so move around the circle. In Figure A.3, the top row shows the circle's development in quarters, and the bottom row shows the picture that emerges if, when we reach π *radians*, we flip the perimeter and begin drawing it in the opposite direction. A picture of a sine wave emerges (see Figure A.3). Note that by using various ovals instead of circles, we can trace sine waves with a variety of shapes. All follow the same basic repetitive cyclical pattern.

FIGURE A.3

Moving around a circle to create a sine wave

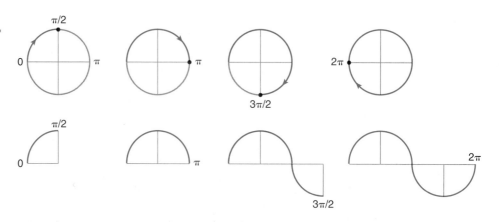

We can add a time element to this picture. Instead of simply saying, let's increase θ, we can explicitly factor time into the sine relationship by saying that θ moves at a rate of ω *radians per second*. Thus, at any time t we have $\theta = \omega t$ *radians*, and we can rewrite the sine equation (1) as:

$$\sin(\omega t) = P/A \tag{2}$$

More commonly, this equation is expressed in terms of P. Solving (2) for P gives us:

$$P = A \sin \omega t \tag{3}$$

Now if we think about a sine wave representing an electrical signal, *the length of line* P *corresponds to the amplitude (or strength) of the signal at time* t, and *the length of line* A *is the maximum amplitude (or strength) of the signal.*

Replacing P in (3) by $S(t)$, which more directly refers to the strength of a signal S at time t, we finally arrive at what we will call *the equation that describes the sine wave:*

$$S(t) = A \sin \omega t \tag{4}$$

To gain a more intuitive understanding of the sine wave, we need to consider how its shape changes as we vary the parameters that dictate its shape—***amplitude, frequency,*** and ***phase.***

Amplitude is the height of the sine wave (hence the strength of the signal) at any moment in time. Amplitude A in (4) is the *maximum* value that the sine wave $S(t)$ attains, which we can see happens when $\omega t = \pi/2$ and $3\pi/2$. ω is the rate at which angle θ ($= \omega t$) changes. In other words, the *angular rotational speed* ωt of sine wave $S(t)$ indicates how quickly θ is changing. When θ rotates through 2π radians, the process begins anew and the pattern repeats.

The *length of time* it takes θ to rotate through 2π radians is called the *period* of the sine wave, typically measured in units of seconds. The number of times the angle θ rotates a full 2π radians in one second is called the *frequency* of the sine wave, and each complete rotation is called a *cycle*. Frequency is then a measure of the number of cycles completed in a second. One cycle per second also is called one Hertz (Hz) in honor of the eminent physicist Heinrich Hertz. For example, if θ rotates through 100 complete revolutions of 2π radians in one second, the sine wave's frequency is 100 Hz.

We can relate frequency f, the period T, and the angular rotational speed ω of θ. First, because T is the time it takes the sine wave to complete one cycle, the angle θ at that point in time is equal to 2π *radians*. Thus:

$$2\pi(= \theta) = \omega T \tag{5}$$

Solving (5) for ω:

$$\omega = 2\pi/T \tag{6}$$

Next, how many cycles does a sine wave complete in one second? The answer is, however many periods fit into one second. If there are T seconds in one cycle, there are $1/T$ cycles in one second—and as we have seen, the number of cycles per second is the frequency of the sine wave. Hence:

$$f = 1/T \tag{7}$$

Combining (6) and (7):

$$\omega = 2\pi/T = 2\pi f \tag{8}$$

By including time t explicitly as before, (8) becomes:

$$\omega t = 2\pi f t \tag{9}$$

Finally, we can use (9) to replace ωt in equation (4), the sine wave as a function of time, giving us:

$$S(t) = A \sin 2\pi f t \tag{10}$$

This is the equation typically used in communications to represent a sine wave with maximum amplitude A and frequency f.

Figure A.4 depicts how the sine wave varies with time for two values of frequency, $f = 1\,\text{Hz}$ and $f = 5\,\text{Hz}$.

FIGURE A.4

Comparing frequencies

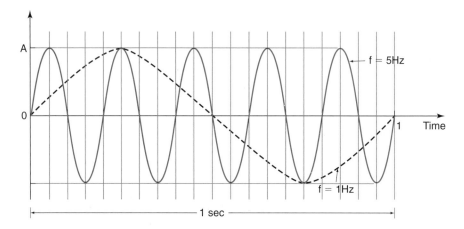

The remaining characteristic of sine waves is the *phase*.

In equation (10), there is the presumption that we start looking at the sine wave at time $t = 0$, which we call the time origin. We might ask, however, whose time origin are we referring to? Is there one time origin from which all of us calculate time in equation (10)? We also could ask: If, in fact, sine waves represent signals that we wish to view, how do we know *where* to locate the time origin?

The answer to all these questions is that *there is no single universal time origin*, that each of us considers $t = 0$ to be the instant that *we* begin our observations. This means that an ongoing sine wave may appear somewhat different to each of us, that difference being the point along the curve that the wave has reached when we start our observation. So in actuality, $t = 0$ is a convenience that we adopt.

Figure A.5 shows how the same sine wave may appear to two different people who start viewing the sine wave at different points in time. Each person considers the time origin to be that instant at which observation began.

Now if we look at equation (10), we see that when we substitute $t = 0$ the result is $S(t) = 0$. How, then, can we account for the different appearance of the sine wave at those various arbitrary time origins? We introduce *an angle offset*, φ, called the *phase (angle)* of the sine wave. Thus, a more complete equation of a sine wave that accounts for all three characteristics—amplitude, frequency, and phase—is:

$$S(t) = A\sin(2\pi ft + \varphi) \tag{11}$$

After we establish a time origin, we can look at the wave at different time points. If we want to compare two sine waves, we can establish one as the reference, with origin $t = 0$, and see what phase the second has reached at various time points compared to the first wave.

To simplify this comparison, suppose the two sine waves have equal peak amplitudes and frequencies. Figure A.6 shows us that if the second wave's origin is later than the reference wave's origin, the second is lagging in phase. By the same token, if the second wave's origin is earlier, it is leading in phase. Note that lagging and leading are determined solely in relation to what the time origin is considered to be—theoretically, sine waves go on forever, so where we choose to start looking is the key.

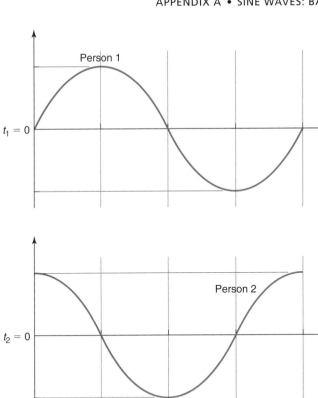

FIGURE A.5

Comparing phases

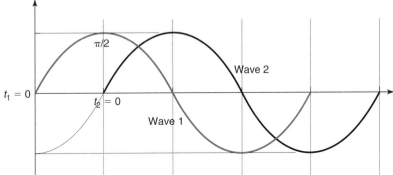

FIGURE A.6

Phase lag/lead

Also useful is the comparison of phase positions of each sine wave at given points in time. Figure A.6 also shows that the two sine waves are $\pi/2$ radians (90 degrees) out of phase—wave 1 is at its $\theta = \pi/2$ point when wave 2 is at its $\theta = 0$ point. The difference can be accounted for in equation (11) by assignment of the appropriate value to the phase angle, φ. In this example:

$$S_2(t) = A\sin(2\pi f t_1 + \pi/2)$$

Finally, we come to the cosine. Trigonometrically, the cosine of an angle is the ratio of the adjacent side to the hypotenuse; using Figure A.1:

$$\cos\theta = B/A \tag{12}$$

If we look again at Figure A.2, we see that if we reduce θ, the vertex moves counterclockwise around the perimeter, and B increases until when $\theta = 0$ side B equals side A, the radius of the circle. In equation (12), we have:

$$\cos 0 = 1$$

If we increase θ, the vertex moves clockwise and B decreases, reaching 0 when $\theta = \pi/2$. Again using equation (12), we have:

$$\cos \pi/2 = 0$$

At these same two points, the sine values are:

$$\sin 0 = 0; \quad \sin \pi/2 = 1$$

So we see that the cosine lags the sine by an offset of $\pi/2$ radians. We could, therefore, express the cosine as:

$$\cos\theta = \sin(\theta + \pi/2)$$

Shifting the spectrum of a signal

It often is the case that a signal's spectrum is not in the same frequency range as that of the transmission system we wish to use. For example, with frequency division multiplexing (FDM), we divide the system's bandwidth into sub-bands whose spectra will usually not match those of the signals we wish to multiplex.

In general, if signal and system bandwidths are compatible and we can shift the signal frequencies so that signal and system *spectra* also are compatible, we can send our signals over the transmission system. This is accomplished by applying some basic trigonometry. (For a refresher on basic trigonometry, visit http://www.sosmath.com/trig/trig.html.) First we will look at what the trigonometry reveals; then we will see how to apply the result.

We use the trigonometric identity:

$$\sin U \cos V = \tfrac{1}{2}[\sin(U + V) + \sin(U - V)] \tag{13}$$

Here, U and V are two arbitrary trigonometric angles. Note that $\cos V$ and $\sin V$ are actually the same signal observed at different time origins—that is, at different phases. Specifically, $\cos V$ lags $\sin V$ by $\pi/2$ radians (90 degrees):

$$\cos V = \sin(V + \pi/2)$$

As we see from (13), multiplying $\sin U$ by $\cos V$ gives us two new sinusoids, $\sin(U + V)$ and $\sin(U - V)$, whose angles are the sum and difference of the original angles U and V.

Now suppose that U is an angle whose frequency component is in the spectrum of a signal. By choosing an appropriate V, we can change (shift) the frequency component of angle U to whatever value we desire; in particular, we can choose a V that will shift the frequency component of U into one that lies within the spectrum of the system.

To see how this works, let's first replace the angles U and V with their time-dependent forms that reveal the frequency components, as is commonly done in dealing with communications systems. We have:

$$U = 2\pi f_U t \quad \text{and} \quad V = 2\pi f_V t$$

where f_U and f_V are the frequency components associated with U and V. Substituting these forms for U and V into the identity equation (13) gives us:

$$\sin(2\pi f_U t)\cos(2\pi f_V t) = \tfrac{1}{2}\left[\sin(2\pi f_U t + 2\pi f_V t) + \sin(2\pi f_U t - 2\pi f_V t)\right]$$

We can simplify the right side of this equation a bit by factoring out the $2\pi t$ terms, giving us:

$$\sin(2\pi f_U t)\cos(2\pi f_V t) = \tfrac{1}{2}\left[\sin 2\pi t(f_U + f_V) + \sin 2\pi t(f_U - f_V)\right] \qquad (14)$$

Now let's use an example to see how this manipulation helps us shift a signal's spectrum. Suppose the lowest frequency of that spectrum is 1,000 Hz and we call that frequency f_U (that is, $f_U = 1,000\,\text{Hz}$), and the system's frequency spectrum starts at 5,000 Hz. Equation (14) tells us that by choosing $f_V = 4,000\,\text{Hz}$ (1,000 + 4,000 = 5,000), we can shift f_U to the system's starting frequency of 5,000 Hz, as follows:

$$\sin(2\pi 1{,}000t)\cos(2\pi 4{,}000t) = \tfrac{1}{2}\left[\sin 2\pi t(1{,}000 + 4{,}000) + \sin 2\pi t(1{,}000 - 4{,}000)\right]$$
$$= \tfrac{1}{2}\left[\sin(2\pi t 5{,}000) + \sin(-2\pi t 3{,}000)\right]$$
$$= \tfrac{1}{2}\sin(2\pi 5{,}000t) + \tfrac{1}{2}\sin(-2\pi 3{,}000t) \qquad (15)$$

Now compare the signal we started with, $\sin(2\pi 1{,}000t)$, with the first term of equation (15), $\tfrac{1}{2}\sin(2\pi 5{,}000t)$. We see that the frequency component, $f_U = 1{,}000$, is replaced by a frequency component of 5,000. This is the result we are after—shifting the original frequency component from 1,000 Hz to 5,000 Hz!

But what about the second term of equation (15)? It is superfluous because the original signal component is represented adequately by the left term alone; we can get rid of it.

To apply this trigonometric result, we use an electronic device that multiplies our sinusoid waveforms, resulting in the composite sinusoid represented by equation (15). Then we eliminate the second term sinusoid by using an electronic filter to screen it out, leaving us with the shifted frequency sine wave that we need. Thus, we have shifted the original sine wave signal to lie within the system's spectrum.

Note that in our example we chose a multiplier frequency that caused the signal's shifted frequency component to coincide with the lowest frequency of the system's bandwidth. We could, however, shift the signal into any part of that bandwidth simply by choosing the appropriate multiplier.

Two points remain. First, in the shifting process, the amplitude of the shifted signal is reduced by half. If we need to restore it to the strength of the original unshifted signal, we can send it through an amplifier.

Second, in the example, we shifted the frequency of just one signal component. In practice, we need to shift all the frequencies in the signal's spectrum. To do so, we expand the process accordingly. Making use of the fact that any signal is a sum of sinusoids, we can express a general signal $m(t)$ as:

$$m(t) = A\sin 2\pi f_A t + B\sin 2\pi f_B t + C\sin 2\pi f_C t + \cdots + Z\sin 2\pi f_Z t + \cdots$$

Here $A, B, C, \ldots, Z \ldots$ are the maximum amplitudes of the component sine waves (in our first example, the maximum amplitude of U implicitly is 1, but it could have been any other value), and $f_A, f_B, f_C, \ldots, f_Z \ldots$ are their corresponding frequency components.

We can shift the entire spectrum of $m(t)$ by multiplying it by the cosine of a suitable angle V, just as before:

$$m(t)\cos(2\pi f_V t) = \frac{1}{2}[A\sin 2\pi f_A t + B\sin 2\pi f_B t + C\sin 2\pi f_C t + \cdots + Z\sin 2\pi f_Z t$$
$$+ \cdots][\cos(2\pi f_V t)] + \cdots$$
$$= [A\sin 2\pi f_A t][\cos(2\pi f_V t)] + [B\sin 2\pi f_B t][\cos(2\pi f_V t)]$$
$$+ [C\sin 2\pi f_C t][\cos(2\pi f_V t)] + \cdots$$
$$+ [Z\sin 2\pi f_Z t][\cos(2\pi f_V t)] + \cdots \qquad (16)$$

We see that each of the terms in (16) is of the form $\sin U\cos V$ and therefore can be manipulated as before by using the trigonometric identity of equation (13). This results in a pair of terms for each component similar to those of equation (15). Hence, as before, by using our electronic multiplier device and filtering out the second term of each resulting component pair as we did above, we are left with:

$$\frac{1}{2}A\sin 2\pi t(f_A + f_V) + \frac{1}{2}B\sin 2\pi t(f_B + f_V) + \frac{1}{2}C\sin 2\pi t(f_C + f_V)$$
$$+ \cdots + \frac{1}{2}Z\sin 2\pi t(f_Z + f_V) + \cdots \qquad (17)$$

in which each frequency component has been shifted by the appropriate amount, f_V, and the second terms (of form $f_X - f_Y$) filtered out. As before, if need be we can send the shifted composite signal through an amplifier to restore the original strength.

We shifted our signal's spectrum to fit it into the system's spectrum for transmission. When it arrives at its destination, we must shift it back to restore it to its original spectrum. Amazingly, this is done by multiplying the shifted signal by $\cos 2\pi f_V t$, exactly as we did to shift it in the first place!

Let's see how this works. If we multiply any component of the shifted signal in (17), say the B component $\frac{1}{2}B\sin 2\pi t(f_B + f_V)$, by $\cos 2\pi f_V t$, here's what happens (again using the identity in (13)):

$$\left[\frac{1}{2}B\sin 2\pi t(f_B + f_V)\right][\cos 2\pi f_V t]$$
$$= \frac{1}{2}B\left[\frac{1}{2}\sin 2\pi t(f_B + f_V + f_V) + \frac{1}{2}\sin 2\pi t(f_B + f_V - f_V)\right]$$
$$= \frac{1}{4}B[\sin 2\pi t(f_B + 2f_V) + \sin(2\pi t f_B)] \text{ (the } +f_V \text{ and } -f_V \text{ in the second term cancel)}$$
$$= \frac{1}{4}B\sin 2\pi(f_B + 2f_V)t + \frac{1}{4}B\sin 2\pi f_B t \qquad (18)$$

We see that the second term of equation (18) is the sine wave B component shifted back to its original frequency f_B. As before, we use a filter, this time to remove the first term component, and, if need be, we amplify the signal to restore it to its original strength.

In addition to its use in FDM, as mentioned, frequency shifting also is used for amplitude modulation (AM), frequency modulation (FM), and phase modulation (PM) and is crucial for successful operation of all these techniques.

Appendix B

Electricity

What is electricity?

Matter, the material of the observable universe, is composed of atoms that in turn are composed of smaller particles including protons, neutrons, and electrons. We picture atoms as having protons and neutrons at the center (nucleus), with electrons circling around them, similar to the way the planets orbit the sun.

Electrical forces are associated with electrons and protons. Like magnets, these act in opposite directions: An electron and a proton will attract each other, and two electrons or two protons will repel each other. We call proton forces positive ("+") and electron forces negative ("−").

In most atoms, there are equal numbers of protons and electrons, so the forces are in balance and the atom is stable. Hydrogen, the simplest atom, has just one proton and one electron (and therefore an atomic number of 1). All other atoms are more complicated, with many protons, neutrons, and electrons. Carbon, for example, has six protons and six electrons (atomic number 6); copper has 29 protons and 29 electrons (atomic number 29). Most matter is made up of combinations of atoms called molecules.

Suppose we apply a negative electrical force to some material, say a length of copper wire. The force would repel the (negative) electrons of the atoms of the wire. If the force is strong enough, it can actually push some electrons of the wire's atoms out of their orbits and cause them to flow away from the force. This leaves those atoms with more protons than electrons, so they are positively charged.

The opposite happens if we apply a positive electrical force. Because a positive force would attract the (negative) electrons, the electrons would flow toward the force instead of away from it. A natural question that arises is, doesn't a flow of (positive) protons also result when negative or positive electrical forces are applied? The answer is, it could, but for the strength of the forces used in computer communications, the protons hardly budge. That is because protons are very much heavier than electrons and also are much more strongly bound within the atom. Therefore, considerably greater electrical forces than we use in computer communications are needed to nudge them loose.

The free electrons, without protons to balance them, are negatively charged and are attracted by the positively charged atoms, so they flow toward them. We call this flow of electrons *electricity* and the process of electron flow *conduction*. As long as the electrical force is maintained, the flow of electrons continues and we have an *electric current*.

How strong the current is depends in part on the strength of the force we apply. It also depends on how tightly or loosely the electrons are bound to their orbits. Material whose electrons are loosely bound flow rather easily in the face of a force; they are called **conductors**. The looser a conductor's electrons, the better an electrical conductor it is. Most good electrical conductors are made of metal such as copper and aluminum.

Material whose electrons are tightly bound are called ***insulators***—the more tightly bound an insulator's electrons, the better it resists conducting electricity. Rubber, plastic, and air are examples of insulators.

Another sort of material falls in between. Although they usually act as insulators, we can make them act as conductors. Called ***semiconductors,*** they are the basis of the chips used in computers and other advanced electronics.

We think of electricity as moving between two points instantaneously. When we flip on a light switch, for example, the light comes on without apparent delay. In fact, although electricity flows very quickly, approaching the speed of light, it does not appear instantly at all points along a conductor when we turn on the current.

If we could slow down the flow and watch it develop, this is what we would see: First, the external electrical force that starts electrons moving is applied. The electrons closest to the force, say on one end of a wire, are the ones that move first. As they move, they bump into the atoms of the wire. That bumping, together with the force of repulsion between electrons, pushes electrons off their orbits in their atoms. This continues down the length of the wire, thus creating the flow.

Even though this happens at the nearly the speed of light, until the bumping and repelling action reaches a particular section of the wire, there is no flow in that section. This is a simple but extremely important concept that comes into play in dealing with signal flow and other aspects of computer communication.

Resistance and energy loss

Resistance is the opposition to electrical flow. Because of resistance, electrical energy is lost to the production of heat. Here's a quick explanation: As electrons flow along a wire, they bump into the atoms of the molecules that make up that wire. This bumping transfers some of the electrons' energy to the atoms, similar to the way a bowling ball transfers some of its energy to the pins it knocks down.

The atoms' motion, in turn, transfers energy to the molecules of the conductor, which vibrate in response. We perceive that molecular motion as heat.

An object's heat is defined as the total kinetic energy (that is, energy of motion) of its molecules. An object's temperature is defined as the average kinetic energy of its molecules. Anything that makes an object's molecules move faster raises its heat (and therefore its temperature). So, for example, chemical reactions, nuclear reactions, sunlight, and electrical energy all can cause an object to heat up.

The more bumping, the more electron energy is transferred, so the greater the electrical energy lost to heat production.

For a given current, the better the conductor, the less bumping, so the less energy lost to heat production. *For a given material,* the stronger the current, the greater the energy loss to heat production.

An electric toaster works on this principle. We force current through a fairly poor conductor, resulting in much electron "bumping," thereby producing the heat that toasts our bread. For electricity used in computer communications, we want to have wires that are very good conductors, so that we do not lose much energy to heat.

We also can infer that the longer a wire, the more bumping will take place, so the greater the energy loss.

Remembering that energy loss is called attenuation, we see that signals attenuate less in better conductors and more in longer conductors. To a degree, we can extend the length of our wire before attenuation becomes too severe by increasing the power of the signal carrying current, but if we force too much electricity through our wire, it may burn up.

We can calculate the resistance R of a piece of wire with this formula:

$$R = \rho l / a$$

In this formula:

- ρ is a constant related to the wire's material (such as copper or aluminum)—the more resistant to electrical flow the material is, the higher the value of ρ.
- l is the length of wire in meters.
- a is the cross-sectional area of the wire (a measure of thickness) in square meters.
- R is measured in ohms.

Area a is calculated as: $a = \pi d^2/4$, where d is the cross-sectional diameter of the wire (another measure of thickness—see Figure B.1). So by substituting for a, we also could express the resistance formula as $R = \rho l / \pi d^2$.

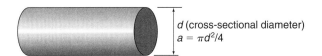

d (cross-sectional diameter)
$a = \pi d^2/4$

FIGURE B.1

Diameter and area

It is useful to understand the relationships illustrated by the formula, because that will help us understand how different wire types and wiring schemes affect our communications abilities. Looking at the formula, we can see that for a given thickness of wire, the longer it is the greater its resistance. On the other hand, for a given length of wire, the thicker it is the lower its resistance. So we can look at this formula as telling us how thick a wire we need to span a given length without its resistance exceeding some desired value.

Wire manufacturers label wires by thickness (called *gauge*). The ***American Wire Gauge (AWG)*** system is a commonly used standard for categorizing wire. Tables show the AWG numbers associated with resistance per unit length of wire (often per meter or per kilometer) based on wire diameter (often in millimeters) or cross-sectional area. In this system, the lower the number the thicker the wire, hence the lower the resistance. For example, an AWG 12 wire (diameter 2.05 mm) is thicker than an AWG 16 wire (diameter 1.29 mm). So too, then, an AWG 12 wire will be less resistant to current flow (.005 ohms per meter) than an AWG 14 wire (.012 ohms per meter) of the same length.

Electricity, magnetism, and radiation

If we send a steady (DC) current through a wire, it produces a magnetic force that encircles the wire and an electrical force that is perpendicular to the wire. These forces radiate out from the wire to the surrounding area. The space they cover is called a field; hence we have magnetic force fields and electrical force fields. These fields are perpendicular to each other and to the direction of the electrical flow. (See Figure B.2.)

Now suppose we send a current through another wire, which we lay parallel to the first. The magnetic fields created in the two wires will repel each other if the current is flowing in the same direction in both wires and attract each other if the current is flowing in opposite directions. So what we can see is that these magnetic forces interact *without any direct connection between the wires.*

Instead of DC, suppose we send AC through one wire and nothing through the other wire. The changing current in the first wire produces a changing magnetic field that produces a changing electrical field that in turn produces a changing magnetic field and so on, spreading out as they go, perpendicular to each other and to the original current. These

FIGURE B.2

Electric and magnetic
fields

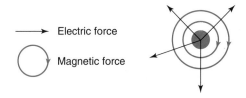

End view of wire: electrical flow into page

Electric force

Magnetic force

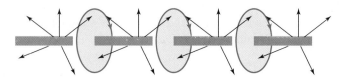

Side view of wire: electrical flow left to right

spreading fields are coupled, resulting in electromagnetic waves. When these waves intersect the second wire, they induce a current in that wire. If our changing current is carrying
signals, the current induced in the second wire will mimic the signal patterns in our wire,
again without any direct connection between the two.

This is the principle on which antennas are based, and it explains how signals in one
wire can interfere with signals in another wire. So, to send signals over the air or through
space, we want to maximize the electromagnetic radiation (EMR) radiated by our wire. On
the other hand, for wired transmission systems we want to minimize, if not eliminate altogether, radiation from our wires or radiation impinging on our wires.

Remember that radiation-induced patterns are possible only if the electricity in one
wire is continuously *changing* in magnitude or direction or both, but because such changes
are a requirement for using electricity to create signals, radiation is a phenomenon that we
have to deal with one way or another. And like the speed of electricity, the speed of radiation cannot be faster than the speed of light.

Thermal noise

Thermal noise is caused by the random motion of electrons in the conducting material.

Thermal noise can be expressed by this equation:

$$N = kTB$$

where N is noise power in watts per Hz of bandwidth, k is Boltzman's constant
(13.8×10^{-24} joules per degree Kelvin), T is temperature in degrees Kelvin, and B is
bandwidth in Hz.

Noise power also can be expressed in voltage—specifically root mean square voltage,
by this formula:

$$V = (kTBR)^{1/2}$$

where R is resistance in ohms.

Appendix C

Light

Explaining what light is has been a quest for centuries. Even today, there is no universal definition. Instead, there are three: light as rays (descriptive optics), light as waves (wave optics), and light as particles (quantum optics). Each definition can explain different light phenomena, but none alone can explain all. All three play a role in communication by light.

Light as rays: reflection and refraction

Light rays are subject to phenomena called **reflection** and **refraction.** If we ignore the forces of gravity and magnetism, which also can affect the way light travels, then when moving through a consistent medium light travels in a straight line. However, when a ray of light strikes the surface of another medium, it may *refract* (bend) at the interface, continuing its journey on a somewhat different line, or it may *reflect* off the surface.

Reflection

Think of the surface of a mirror as a flat plane, and imagine a line perpendicular to that plane. The angle from the perpendicular at which a ray of light strikes the mirror is called the **angle of incidence,** and the angle at which it is reflected, also relative to that perpendicular, is called the **angle of reflection.** If the angle of incidence is zero degrees (that is, if the incident light ray is perpendicular to the mirror's surface), the light ray is reflected directly back on the path it came from, so the angle of reflection also is zero. At angles not perpendicular to the surface, the angle of reflection will equal the angle of incidence, but the reflected ray will travel in the opposite direction. (See Figure C.1.)

FIGURE C.1

Reflection

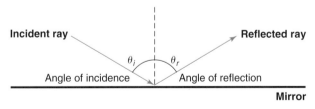

When reflecting off a plane surface, the angle of reflection equals
the angle of incidence: $\theta_r = \theta_i$

The surface does not need to be a mirror or even a flat plane for reflection to occur. Whether a ray of light reflects off a surface depends on the angle of incidence and the composition of the medium.

Refraction

We usually think of light as traveling at a constant speed—the speed of light!—or about 186,000 miles per second (almost 300,000 kilometers per second). But as it happens, that speed is a maximum, occurring when light travels through a vacuum. Light actually travels at slower (and different) velocities in different media. The more *optically dense* a medium is, the slower light travels through it.

When a ray of light passes from one medium to another at an oblique angle, where these media have different optical densities, the change in speed of the light ray as it crosses the boundary causes it to **refract** (bend) at the boundary. For example, a ray of light passing from the air into a lake at an angle not perpendicular to the surface of the lake will bend at the lake's surface. (That is why when you look at a fish swimming in a lake, it appears to be in a somewhat different place than it actually is.) Furthermore, the ray will bend toward the perpendicular if the second medium is optically more dense and away from the perpendicular if it is less dense. Because air is less optically dense than water, the light ray in this example will bend toward the perpendicular. (See Figure C.2.)

FIGURE C.2

Refraction

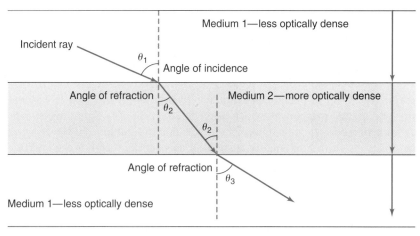

Notes:
- Because medium 1 (top and bottom) is less optically dense than medium 2, an incident ray traveling from 1 to 2 will refract toward the perpendicular ($\theta_2 < \theta_1$); when traveling from 2 to 1, it will refract away from the perpendicular ($\theta_3 > \theta_2$).
- Angle of refraction θ_2 becomes the angle of incidence for angle of refraction θ_3.

The angle of the ray in the first medium is the **angle of incidence,** and the angle in the second medium is the **angle of refraction.** When the angle of incidence is zero degrees, so is the angle of refraction—there is no bending. Otherwise, the greater the difference in densities, the greater the amount of refraction.

INDEX OF REFRACTION   For investigating the behavior of light in various media, it is useful to have a measure of how much a medium will refract a light beam. That measure is called the **index of refraction,** calculated as the ratio of the velocity of light in a vacuum to the velocity of light in the medium. This relationship is:

$$n = v_v/v_m$$

Here v_v is the velocity of light in a vacuum and v_m is the velocity of light in medium m.

It has become traditional to label the velocity of light in a vacuum with the symbol c rather than v_v. So, our equation becomes:

$$n = c/v_m$$

From this we can see that the index of refraction of a vacuum is 1 ($n = c/c$), whereas the index of refraction of any medium is always greater than 1 because v_m is always less than c.

For example, light traveling through a typical fiber-optic cable (described in the following sections) may slow down to about 200,000 kilometers per second. The index of refraction of that fiber, then, is:

$$n_{\text{fiber}} = 300,000/200,000 = 1.5$$

For comparison, air has an index of refraction of about 1.0003 and water about 1.33.

The relationship between angles of incidence and refraction was formalized by Willebrord Snell (1580–1626), a Dutch mathematician, in a formula now called Snell's law, which states:

$$n_1 \sin \theta_1 = n_2 \sin \theta_2$$

Here n_1 and n_2 are the indices of refraction of media 1 and 2, θ_1 is the angle of incidence, and θ_2 is the angle of refraction. By transposition, this formula becomes:

$$n_1/ n_2 = \sin\theta_2 /\sin\theta_1$$

From this we can see that there is an inverse relationship between refraction indices and angles of refraction. For example, if $n_1 < n_2$ (n_1 is less optically dense than n_2), then $\sin\theta_2 < \sin\theta_1$ (light from 1 to 2 will refract toward the perpendicular).

TOTAL INTERNAL REFLECTION   An interesting phenomenon important in communication over optical fiber is ***total internal reflection.*** Suppose we have rays of light traveling in a more optically dense medium hitting the boundary of a less optically dense medium. As we increase the angle of incidence, the angle of refraction also will increase, approaching 90 degrees. When the angle of incidence reaches a point at which the angle of refraction equals or exceeds 90 degrees, total reflection results (see Figure C.3). That angle of incidence is called the ***critical angle***—it depends on the relative densities of the two media.

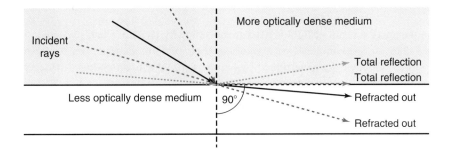

FIGURE C.3

Total internal reflection

Conclusion: if we want to keep a beam of light completely contained within an optical fiber, its angle of refraction must be such that we have total internal reflection.

Snell's law (expressed as $n_1/n_2 = \sin \theta_2/\sin \theta_1$) gives us another insight into total internal reflection. As we saw earlier, the critical angle for the *refracted* ray is 90 degrees. The angle of incidence needed to achieve at least 90-degree refraction depends on the relative indices of the core and cladding. So the most we can say as a general statement is that *the angle of incidence must be such that the angle of refraction is at least 90 degrees.*

Suppose n_1 and n_2 are the indices of refraction of the core and cladding, respectively; θ_1 and θ_2 the angles of incidence and refraction. If we substitute 90° for θ_2 in the equation, the relationship becomes:

$$n_1/n_2 = \sin 90°/\sin\theta_1 = 1/\sin\theta_1$$

Because $\sin \theta_1 < 1$, we must have $n_1 > n_2$. That is, the core must be more optically dense than the cladding. We do not want to make the core too dense, however, because that will slow down the light ray speed too much; typical values are $n_1 = 1.48$, $n_2 = 1.46$.

Light as waves: wavelength and color

Wavelength plays a significant role in determining the characteristics of electromagnetic radiation; for example, wavelength determines the color of the light we see. (See Figure C.4.) Because of this, we often refer to light by its wavelength rather than its frequency.

FIGURE C.4

Wavelength and color

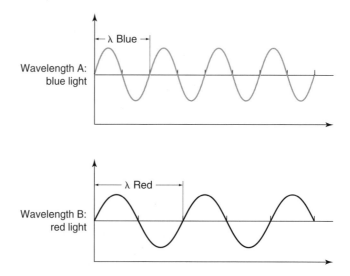

Color, frequency, and wavelength

The frequency of a beam of light is determined solely by its *source* and *remains constant*. When the beam is generated, we could say that its color depends on its frequency. However, color actually is determined by *wavelength*, which *can change*—it depends on the medium the light is traveling in.

We can see this in the wavelength equation:

$$\lambda = v_m/f$$

where λ is wavelength, v_m is the speed of light in medium m, and f is its frequency as generated.

The more optically dense a medium is, the slower the velocity of light. In a vacuum, all electromagnetic radiation travels at "the speed of light," nearly 300,000 meters per second. This is a maximum speed; in other media, electromagnetic radiation, including light, travels at different, somewhat slower, speeds.

Because frequency does not change, the equation tells us that wavelength λ must decrease proportionally. (The reverse applies when traveling in a less dense medium.) This means that when a beam of light passes from one medium into another of different density, its color changes!

The longest wavelength of visible light is about 760 billionths (760×10^{-9}) of a meter (red light); the shortest is about 400 billionths (400×10^{-9}) of a meter (violet light). To more easily refer to such small numbers, we often measure wavelength in nanometers, where 1 nanometer (1 nm) equals one billionth of a meter (10^{-9} meters). Thus we would say that *visible* light has a wavelength range of about 760 nm to 400 nm.

Infrared light, which we cannot see, has longer wavelengths than visible light, ranging from about 780 nm to 1 mm. By its name, it seems that infrared light is one "color," implying one wavelength. Namewise it is one color, but bear in mind that the color "infrared" comprises a range of wavelengths. *This is important, because infrared light is what is used in optical communication systems, and in those systems we can use different wavelengths in the infrared range to carry signals simultaneously.*

Other phenomena of the wave theory of light

The existence and properties of light waves were first proposed in 1865 by British mathematician and physicist James Clerk Maxwell, although it took 20 more years before his proposition was verified by another physicist, Heinrich Hertz.

Maxwell not only demonstrated that light is waves of radiated energy, he also made the startling discovery that light is a form of electromagnetic energy, just like the radiated electricity described in the discussion of the properties of electricity in Appendix B. Furthermore, he determined that light waves, like all electromagnetic waves, can be described by sinusoids. According to this theory, what distinguishes what we call light from other electromagnetic radiation is simply the frequencies of the sinusoidal waves!

With wave theory we can explain *constructive and destructive interference*. As two beams of light (two sinusoidal waves) cross each other, where the sinusoid peaks meet, their power adds and a bright spot occurs (constructive interference); where the peak of one meets the trough of the other, powers subtract and a dark spot results (destructive interference).

We also can explain ***diffraction*** of light in the same way. As a beam of light passes the edge of a suitably small surface, the various sinusoids that make up the wave reflect off the edge at different angles. These reflections of the same beam interfere with each other, producing a series of light and dark portions that appear to have bent around the edge.

One more property of light waves is ***coherence.*** A beam of light from ordinary sources such as light bulbs or the sun consists of waves that have no fixed relationship to each other; they do not have any internal order and their sinusoid waves are not aligned or in phase with one another. This kind of light is called ***incoherent.*** *Coherent* light has waves that are parallel and in phase with one another. Coherent light is much more useful for communications than incoherent light.

Light as particles: photons and color

Quantum theory tells us that light consists of particles called ***photons,*** which have characteristic energy content. Quantum optics tells us that the color of light produced by a photon, say from a laser, is related to its energy. In previous sections, we saw that the color of a light wave is related to its wavelength. How are photon and wave phenomena interrelated?

The energy of a photon depends on its frequency, as shown by the formula:

$$E = hf \qquad (1)$$

where E is the energy (measured in *joules*) of a photon in a light beam of frequency f (in Hz) and h is Planck's constant (6.63×10^{-34} joule-seconds).

Making use of the wavelength formula:

$$\lambda = v_m/f \qquad (2)$$

Along with formula (1), we can relate the wavelength and particle theories of light, as follows. Solve the photon energy formula (1) for f (resulting in $f = E/h$) and substitute that result for f in the wavelength equation (2). The result is:

$$\lambda = hv_m/E \qquad (3)$$

relating the wavelength of a beam of light to the energy of the beam's photons. In (3) we see that wavelength is inversely related to photon energy. That is, the greater the energy, the shorter the wavelength, and vice versa.

By solving (3) for E, we can see this relationship from the energy view:

$$E = hv_m/\lambda \qquad\qquad (4)$$

Because wavelength also determines color, we see in (4) how photon energy is related to color.

Quantum theory also tells us that if the right beam of light hits the right kind of metal, electricity can be produced. The photons of the light beam knock electrons off the atoms of the material, which propagate along as a flow of electricity.

The number of electrons knocked off their atoms is proportional to the amount of light, and the energy of the electrons depends on the frequency of the light for a given material. Below a threshold frequency, no electrons are freed no matter how bright the light is; above that threshold, electrons always are freed, no matter how dim the light.

The amount of light energy transferred to an electron is the energy of the photon. Called the **photoelectric effect,** this was first explained by Albert Einstein. Interestingly, Einstein won a Nobel Prize (in 1921) for his work on the photoelectric effect and not for his famous theory of relativity!

How lasers work

Quantum mechanics tells us that the electrons in an atom can be in different energy states. At their lowest (normal) energy states, called the **ground atomic state,** the atom is stable. At higher energy states, called **excited atomic states,** the electrons are unstable and want to release their extra energy so they can return to the ground state, or at least to a lower excited state. The energy released in this process is electromagnetic, in the form of photons of light.

The emitted light from a collection of photons can be *incoherent* or *coherent.* Coherent photons, having the same frequency and phase and moving in the same direction, reinforce each other to create a very powerful beam of light. (Incoherent photons, not being in step, do not reinforce each other.)

Light emitting diodes (LEDs) produce incoherent light; lasers produce coherent light. In LEDs, excited electrons drop to the ground state randomly; hence, photons are emitted at random times and in random directions, producing incoherent light. This process is called **spontaneous radiation.** Lasers are designed to produce coherent light of specific wavelengths, by a process called **stimulated radiation.**

For communications, incoherent light serves well only for short distances and relatively low speeds. Coherent light is needed for long-distance, high-speed optical communications systems, the very application in which lasers are coming into force.

One photon is a very small, weak amount of light. To be useful for communications, we need our lasers to produce a huge quantity of specific wavelength photons at the same instant. How do we make this happen?

We start with a **lasing material,** called an **active medium.** Lasers have been constructed from many different active materials, including carbon dioxide (the gas that makes soda fizz), helium-neon gas (helium floats balloons and neon lights store signs), artificial rubies (not the type you would want to wear as jewelry), and, most useful and common for communications, **semiconductors** (what you find in computers and other electronic devices).

The first step is to boost most of the electrons in the lasing material into an excited state by adding electrical or photon energy; that is, we use an **energy pump** to create a **population inversion**—a condition in which there are more atoms in an excited state than in the ground state. When we have an inversion, at least one electron will drop to the ground state, releasing its excess energy as a photon, and this photon can stimulate other electrons to do the same. But we must control the process if we want our photons to be released en masse and to produce coherent light.

When an emitted photon stimulates an excited electron to release a photon, the first photon is not destroyed. Instead, we have two photons in play, and they will have the same frequency and phase. This is because the frequency of the emitted photons is a function of the difference in energy levels of the excited and ground states: $f = (E_e - E_g)/h$, where E_e is the excited state energy, E_g is the ground state energy, and h is Plank's constant. Hence, boosting the electrons to the same excited energy level causes the photons they emit to all have the same frequency.

These electrons, in turn, can stimulate other electrons, producing the same double-photon releases in a chain effect, all with the same frequency and phase, though not moving in the same direction. To sustain the process, we need to keep the photons in play. We also need to focus them so they move in the same direction. Both of these are accomplished by placing mirrors at either end of the lasing material, to trap and focus the photons.

The distance between the mirrors depends on the photon wavelength that we want to create. We saw that the relationship between a photon's energy and its wavelength is $\lambda = h v_m/E$ and that the energy of a photon is the difference between its excited and ground state energies ($E_p = E_e - E_g$). So the wavelength of the photons we are creating is $\lambda = h v m/E_p$.

As they reflect back and forth off the mirrors, the photons are directed and also stimulate other electrons in the lasing material, resulting in a cascade of a huge number of coherent photons. For the laser light to escape the trap and send forth its rays, one of the mirrors is only partially reflective, so that light of the proper wavelength will refract through it. Only those waves with the appropriate angle of incidence will refract out, thus creating the coherent focused laser light beam. See Figure C.5.

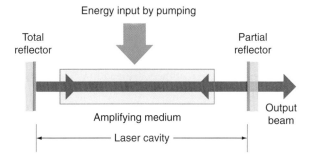

FIGURE C.5

Producing a laser beam

Separating the wavelengths of light

Light is the name we give to a range of wavelengths in the electromagnetic spectrum. Sunlight, for example, covers the visible light portion of the spectrum, representing the colors from red to violet. If we put a prism in the sunlight, the various wavelengths in the light are separated and we see all of its component colors.

This happens because at the boundary between two media, the shorter the wavelength, the greater the refraction. Hence, violet refracts more than blue, which refracts more than green, and so on to red which refracts the least. So, the prism provides *angular separation* of the components of light—the separation angle measures how much a component bends compared to a line perpendicular to the medium boundary.

When it comes to the longer wavelength portion of the electromagnetic spectrum that is used for telecommunication—the infrared range from about 800 nm to 1,600 nm—

prisms are not precise enough, nor is reliance on refraction. Instead, *diffraction* is used to create the angular separation (also called *dispersion*) of light components. For wavelength division multiplexing, the greater the dispersion, the easier it is to separate individual channels.

Diffraction is a property described by the wave explanation of light. When light strikes an edge or passes through an aperture whose size is near the wavelengths of the light, it bends (diffracts); rather than the result of crossing the boundary between two media, diffraction is a phenomenon caused by the interaction of the light beam with a physical object. Just as with refraction, the amount of diffraction depends on wavelength. Also, depending on the physical dimensions of the edge or aperture, constructive and destructive interference effects will produce bright and dark spots, lines, rings, or spheres.

To utilize this phenomenon, **diffraction gratings** are employed. Diffraction gratings used in telecommunications come in several designs, but all are some configuration of closely spaced parallel ridges or slits. We can see the effects of a diffraction grating in visible light by moving the shiny side of a recorded-on CD in a beam of light; the colors we see are the result of the light diffracting off the tracks burned into the CD (typically spaced at about 625 tracks per millimeter).

Perhaps the most common diffraction grating used in telecommunications is based on Bragg's law, expressed by the equation $n\lambda = 2d \sin \theta$, where λ is wavelength, d is the distance between surfaces, θ is the angle of incidence, and n is an integer; the physical dimensions of the surfaces must be close to the wavelengths of light. (English physicists Sir W.H. Bragg and his son Sir W.L. Bragg developed the law in 1913 to explain why the surfaces of crystals reflect x-ray beams only at certain angles of incidence. It has since been applied to dispersion effects in gratings. See the next section, "Deriving Bragg's law.")

Gratings using this principle are called *Bragg diffraction gratings*, which can be visualized as a series of semi-circular bumps.

DERIVING BRAGG'S LAW   Using a Bragg diffraction grating element as an example, we can see how Bragg's law is derived. In Figure C.6, which depicts one of the semi-circular bumps, we see two parallel, incident, in-phase rays striking the Bragg grating element (represented by the curved line). Ray 1 must travel farther than ray 2 before striking the element, as shown by the dashed line AC. If ray 1 is to remain in phase with ray 2, the extra distance must be an integer multiple n of the wavelength λ. This tells us that

$$n\lambda = AC \tag{5}$$

FIGURE C.6

Deriving Bragg's law

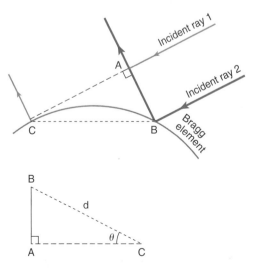

By drawing a line from point B, where ray 2 strikes the element, to point C, where ray 1 strikes the element, we see that we have formed a right triangle, ABC, redrawn below with the angle AC-BC labeled θ. The hypotenuse BC, labeled d, is the distance between the struck surfaces. The curvature of the Bragg element is such that for the rays to remain parallel,

$$AC = 2AB \qquad (6)$$

Substituting (6) in (5) gives us

$$n\lambda = 2AB \qquad (7)$$

Now in the triangle we can see that $\sin \theta = AB/d$. Solving for AB gives us

$$AB = d \sin \theta \qquad (8)$$

Finally, substituting (8) in (7) gives us $n\lambda = 2\,d \sin \theta$, which is Bragg's law.

Appendix D

Optical fiber: testing and optical link loss budgets

Testing

Fiber-optic links typically extend many kilometers in today's complex networks. The fibers, usually placed in conduits or ducts to protect them from the environment, often are not easily accessible. How, in such circumstances, do we go about determining the cause and location of a fiber link problem? The answer is a very versatile instrument, the ***Optical Time Domain Reflectometer (OTDR).*** It is so versatile that it is often the only instrument a professional will require. With access to only one end of what may even be a very long fiber link, the OTDR can determine all of the following:

- The attenuation of the fiber and/or the various sections of the link
- The light loss due to splicing
- The light loss due to connectors
- The length of the link and the distance from the end of the fiber to various parts of the link, such as splices

The OTDR usually provides a graphic depiction of these characteristics that can be saved for future reference.

Good network management practice requires the OTDR to be used on a fiber link that is initially installed, not only to insure that it is operating properly but also to establish a record of the link's characteristics. Subsequently, if a problem arises on the link, a new OTDR test can be performed and the result compared to the original reading. By noting any changes in the two readings, it often is possible to diagnose and locate the problem, enabling a technician to resolve it quickly.

The OTDR works on the principle of reflection and refraction of light through the fiber. For example, to determine the length of the cable, the OTDR directs a short burst of light into the fiber and measures how much time elapses until it detects the reflection of some of the light from the far end. The total length of the fiber is calculated from the elapsed time based on the speed of light in the fiber, which is derived from the index of refraction of the fiber core, available from the fiber manufacturer. The simple relationship of distance (d), speed of travel (v), and trip time (t) is:

$$d = vt$$

Given the index of refraction (n) of the fiber core, we have:

$$n = c/v_m$$

where c = speed of light in a vacuum and v_m is the speed of light in the core.

Putting the two relationships together yields:

$$d = ct/2n$$

Based on the same reflection/refraction principle, the OTDR can determine where a fiber is cut, where a splice exists, how much light loss it produces, and the location and light loss due to any other interruption in the fiber.

Optical link loss budget

Optical fiber cables attenuate light rays, splices and connectors cause light losses, light sources produce light of a certain power, and optical detectors need a certain amount of light power to function properly and recognize signal elements. How do we go about choosing, contracting for, or designing a fiber-optic system that will perform successfully in view of these various factors? The answer is by constructing an *optical link loss budget.* Here is a summary of the steps involved, followed by an example:

1. Start with the length of fiber-optic cable required to span the distance between the light source and the optical detector.
2. Based on this distance, determine whether multimode or single-mode fiber is required.
3. For the selected optical fiber type, obtain the light loss per kilometer from the manufacturer of the fiber.
4. Determine the number and type of splices that will be required to achieve that length of fiber run, and tabulate the loss per splice.
5. Ascertain the number of connectors the fiber link will require, and tabulate the loss per connector.
6. Sum up all the light losses incurred by the fiber-optic link.
7. Choose a light source of sufficient power to allow the light signal that arrives at the optical detector to have at least 10 dB more power than the minimum required by the optical detector you will need to choose. *Do not,* however, over-specify the power of the light source, as light detectors are very sensitive and can be blinded or damaged by light beams that are too strong.

Example

A fiber link is to be designed having the following requirements:

* The link length is 70 km.
* The link requires a single-mode fiber of 0.20 dB/km attenuation.
* The link includes three fusion splices with light loss of 0.1 dB per splice.
* The link includes two mechanical splices with light loss of 0.2 dB per splice.
* There is a connector with a light loss of 1 dB at each end of the link.
* The receiver sensitivity is −36 dBm at 1,550 nm.

To determine the required laser light output power in dBm, we construct the following optical link loss budget table.

Link element	Loss per element instance	Loss calculation	Total loss per element	Cumulative loss
Transmitter connector loss	−1 dB	$(1)(-1)$ dB	−1 dB	−1 dB
Fiber-optic attenuation	−0.20 dB/km	$(2)(-.20\text{ dB/km}) \times (70\text{ km})$	−28 dB	−29 dB
Fusion splices	−0.1 dB	$(3)(-0.10)$ dB	−0.30 dB	−29.30 dB
Mechanical splices	−0.2 dB	$(2)(-0.20)$ dB	−0.40 dB	−29.70 dB
Receiver connector loss	−1 dB	$(1)(-1)$ dB	−1 dB	−30.70 dB
10 dB additional loss for good design (safety margin)	−10 dB	−10 dB	−10 dB	−40.70 dB
Total cumulative losses (l_c)	—	—	—	−40.70 dB
Receiver sensitivity (R_s), dBm	−36 dBm	N/A	N/A	−36 dBm
Transmitter laser output power (P_o), dBm	Calculated value: 4.7 dBm (=3 mW)	$R_s = P_o + L_c$ or $P_o = R_s - L_c$: $P_o = -36\text{ dBm} - (40.70\text{ dB})$ $= 4.7\text{ dBm}$	—	—

Appendix E

Error detection and correction techniques

Computing parity

To count the number of 1-bits, computers use the *exclusive or (XOR)* operator for even parity and the *negative exclusive or (NXOR)* operator for odd parity. The following rules apply:

$$0 \text{ XOR } 0 = 0; \quad 0 \text{ XOR } 1 = 1 \quad 1 \text{ XOR } 0 = 1; \quad 1 \text{ XOR } 1 = 0$$
$$0 \text{ NXOR } 0 = 1; \quad 0 \text{ NXOR } 1 = 0; \quad 1 \text{ NXOR } 0 = 0; \quad 1 \text{ NXOR } 1 = 1$$

The operators are applied to the bits two at a time; the value resulting from the first two bits is XOR'd with the next bit; that resulting value is XOR'd with the next bit, and so on. With even parity and no errors, the final result of the XORs will be 0; for odd parity, the final result of the NXORs will be 1. Here is a stepwise example with even parity:

$$\text{Bit string } \mathbf{1\,0\,1\,0}\text{: } \mathbf{1} \text{ XOR } \mathbf{0} = 1; 1 \text{ XOR } \mathbf{1} = 0; 0 \text{ XOR } \mathbf{0} = 0$$

The string is considered to be error-free.

$$\text{Bit string } \mathbf{1\,0\,1\,1}\text{: } \mathbf{1} \text{ XOR } \mathbf{0} = 1; 1 \text{ XOR } \mathbf{1} = 0; 0 \text{ XOR } \mathbf{1} = 1$$

The string is considered to be erroneous.

Checksum

To calculate a checksum, the sender separates the bits of a frame into equal segments; these are added, the sum is complemented, and the result is the checksum value, which is placed in the frame's frame check sequence (FCS) field.

To implement checksum, we need to consider the size of the FCS field, which in turn dictates the number of bits in the checksum. If the size of the FCS field is fixed at k, the number of bits in the checksum is k. Typically, checksums are 16 bits long, although an 8-bit size is used as well.

Each segment is required to have the same number of bits as the checksum, but when the segments are added, because of possible carries the result can have more than k bits. To handle this, the segment sum, called a *partial sum,* is limited to k bits; any extra bits from the carries are added to the first (rightmost) bit of the partial sum to produce the *final sum,* which then is complemented. That result is the checksum, placed in the FCS field.

Here is a short example to see how the checksum procedure works. Suppose we have an 8-bit FCS field and a 32-bit frame that we group into four 8-bit segments.

	1 1 1 1 1 1 1 1 *carries*
segments	1 0 1 0 0 1 0 0
	0 0 1 0 1 0 0 1
	0 1 0 1 0 1 0 1
	1 1 0 0 0 0 1 0
the *partial* sum is:	**1 1 1 0 0 1 0 0**

Because the sum must have the same number of bits as the segments (here 8), the last carry, *1*, is not brought down to the left as with standard addition. Instead, it is added it to the rightmost digit of the sum. We find the new sum and take the complement of it to produce the checksum:

$$
\begin{array}{ll}
1\,1\,1\,0\,0\,1\,0\,0 & \textit{partial sum} \\
1 & \textit{last carry} \\
\hline
1\,1\,1\,0\,0\,1\,0\,1 & \textit{new sum} \\
\end{array}
$$

checksum: **0 0 0 1 1 0 1 0**   *complement of new sum*

Cyclical Redundancy Check

The basic steps of the cyclical redundancy check (CRC) technique, illustrated graphically after this description, are:

1. The sender constructs a frame of n bits, of which m bits are for the message—everything sent (including headers and data) except for the CRC—and $n - m$ bits are reserved for the CRC FCS. The CRC is set to zero.
2. The m-bit string is divided by a divisor one bit longer ($n - m + 1$) than the CRC. This produces a remainder of $n - m$ bits, which is the CRC; that value replaces the zero bits in the CRC FCS field. (It is possible that after the calculation, the CRC is still zero; that is, the result of the division has no remainder. This does not affect the operation of the technique.)
3. The receiver uses the same divisor and repeats the division, but on the *entire n-bit* frame, including the CRC.
4. If the remainder of this division is zero, the frame is considered to be error-free; otherwise it is deemed erroneous.

A key determinant of the effectiveness of CRC is the divisor. A properly chosen divisor will produce very accurate error detection. Divisor size is a significant component of the choice: For a CRC of k bits, an appropriate $k + 1$-bit divisor will miss only one error in 2^k. The most commonly used CRC sizes are 12, 16, and 32 bits: Ethernet and token ring LANs use 32-bit CRCs. With appropriate divisors, these will miss one error in 4,096, one in 65,536, and one in 4,294,967,296, respectively. Again we face a tradeoff—accuracy versus number of overhead bits added and computational effort.

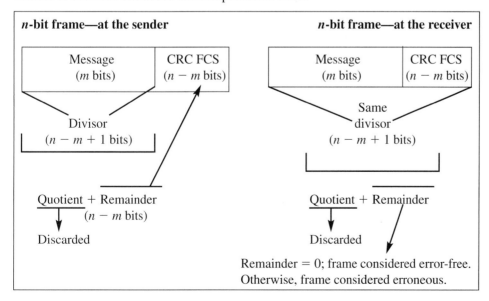

CRC—sender and receiver

Computing CRCs

CRC computations can be viewed in terms of binary arithmetic with no carries (equivalent to modulo 2), or in terms of polynomials. These are illustrated in the following sections.

CRCS VIA MODULO 2 DIVISION At the sender, we first enlarge the frame to create space for the $n - m$ FCS bits by shifting the original frame $n - m$ bits to the left. In binary form, this is accomplished by multiplying the original frame by 2^{n-m}. For example, suppose we have a 6-bit original frame $F_o = 101011$ and a 2-bit FCS; the total frame size, then, is 8 bits. We multiply F_o by 2^{8-6}, that is, by $2^2 = 4$ (which is 1 0 0 in binary):

$$
\begin{array}{r}
1\,0\,1\,0\,1\,1 \quad (\boldsymbol{F_o}) \\
\times\ 1\,0\,0 \quad (\boldsymbol{2^2}) \\
\hline
0\,0\,0\,0\,0\,0 \\
0\,0\,0\,0\,0\,0 \\
1\,0\,1\,0\,1\,1 \\
\hline
1\,0\,1\,0\,1\,1\,\underline{\mathbf{0\,0}} \quad \textit{(original frame shifted two to the left; two 0s in the FCS)}
\end{array}
$$

Next, we divide the enlarged frame by our $n - m + 1$ bit divisor D producing quotient Q and remainder R. These two steps can be expressed as:

$$F_s = 2^{n-m}F_o/D = Q + R$$

Last, we add the remainder to the shifted frame, producing the transmitted frame F_t:

$$F_t = F_s + R$$

At the receiver, the received frame F_r, which hopefully is the same as the transmitted frame, is subjected to the same divisor. That is:

$$F_r/D = Q + R$$

If the remainder R is zero, the frame is considered to be error-free.
Example:

$$\boldsymbol{F_o}\text{: } 101011;\ \boldsymbol{D}\text{: } 101$$

Shift F_o two to the left as in the above example, resulting in 10101100.
  Then by modulo 2 division (binary arithmetic with no carries):

$$
\begin{array}{r}
1\,0\,0\,0\,1\,1 \quad \textbf{\textit{Quotient Q}} \\
1\,0\,1\,\overline{)\,1\,0\,1\,0\,1\,1\,0\,0} \\
\underline{1\,0\,1} \\
0\,0\,1\,1\,0 \\
\underline{1\,0\,1} \\
0\,1\,1\,0 \\
\underline{1\,0\,1} \\
1\,1 \quad \textbf{\textit{remainder R (the CRC)}}
\end{array}
$$

Add R to the shifted F_o:

$$
\begin{array}{r}
1\,0\,1\,0\,1\,1\,0\,0 \\
1\,1 \\
\hline
1\,0\,1\,0\,1\,1\,1\,1 \quad \textit{the transmitted frame } F_t
\end{array}
$$

At the receiver, the received frame F_r undergoes the same division. If there are no transmission errors, F_r will be equal to F_t.

Assuming that to be the case, the division is:

```
                  1 0 0 0 1 1    Quotient Q
          1 0 1) 1 0 1 0 1 1 1 1
                 1 0 1
                 0 0 1 1 1
                     1 0 1
                     0 1 0 1
                       1 0 1
                           0    remainder R is zero
```

It is left as an exercise for the reader to try an example where the received frame contains an error.

CRCS VIA POLYNOMIALS The polynomial method of the CRC technique is simply another view of the same process; hence, it follows the same steps. The difference is that instead of working with bit values directly, their place values are converted to polynomial exponents of a dummy variable, as follows.

At the sender, the original frame (excluding the CRC bits) is examined to construct a polynomial whose exponents are the powers of 2 represented by the positions of the 1-bits in the frame.

For example, if the original frame F_o is 101011, then using x as a dummy variable, the polynomial $P(x)$ is:

$$x^5 + x^3 + x^1 + 1 \quad \text{(Note: } x^0 = 1\text{)}$$

The divisor polynomial $D(x)$ is created from the binary divisor in the same way in which $P(x)$ is created.

To shift $P(x)$ to make room for the FCS, we multiply $P(x)$ by x^{n-m}. To compute the CRC, we divide the shifted polynomial by our divisor, $D(x)$, producing a quotient $Q(x)$ plus a remainder $R(x)$. As before, the remainder is the CRC and it is added to $P(x)$; the result is returned to binary form to create the full n-bit frame to be transmitted (F_t). So we have:

$$x^{n-m}P(x)/D(x) = Q(x) + R(x) \quad \text{and}$$

$$F_t = P(x)x^{n-m} + R(x) \quad \text{converted to binary form}$$

At the receiver, the received frame F_r is transformed into a polynomial in the same way as at the sender, and that polynomial is divided by the same divisor $D(x)$. If the remainder of this operation is zero, the received frame F_t is considered to be error-free. Here is the modulo 2 example carried out with polynomials:

Shifted frame: 1 0 1 0 1 1 0 0

$$P(x) = x^7 + x^5 + x^3 + x^2$$
$$D(x) = x^2 + 1 \text{ (converted from 101)}$$

```
              x^5 + x + 1                   quotient Q(x)
  x^2 + 1) x^7 + x^5 + x^3 + x^2
           x^7 + x^5
                     x^3 + x
                     x^2 + x
                     x^2 + 1
                           x + 1   remainder R(x)
```

Converting the quotient and remainder to binomial form results in 100011 and 11, respectively, which we can see are the same results that we obtained in the modulo 2 view. The remaining steps of the CRC procedure follow in the same way. We leave these calculations to the reader for an exercise.

Relating modulo 2, binary arithmetic without carries, and XOR

Binary arithmetic without carries is equivalent to modulo 2 division. We recall that modulo division (mod) produces the remainder of a division as a whole number; if there is no remainder, the modulo result is zero. For example, $9 \bmod 5 = 4$; $9 \bmod 9 = 0$. The only results producible by modulo 2 division are 1 and 0. Thus, $1 \bmod 2 = 1$; $2 \bmod 2 = 0$; $3 \bmod 2 = 1$; $4 \bmod 2 = 0$; and so on.

Binary arithmetic *without carries* also produces either 1 or 0 as a result. For example, in addition without carries, operations are strictly bitwise:

$$
\begin{array}{llll}
\text{A:} & \begin{array}{r} 1\,0\,1 \\ +\,0\,1\,1 \\ \hline 1\,1\,0 \end{array} & \text{B:} & \begin{array}{r} 1\,1\,0 \\ +\,1\,1\,1 \\ \hline 0\,0\,1 \end{array}
\end{array}
$$

In the same way, subtraction without carries is strictly bitwise, with no signs:

$$
\begin{array}{ll}
\begin{array}{r} 1\,0\,1 \\ -\,0\,1\,1 \\ \hline 1\,1\,0 \end{array} & \begin{array}{r} 1\,1\,0 \\ -\,1\,1\,1 \\ \hline 0\,0\,1 \end{array}
\end{array}
$$

The equivalent bitwise modulo operations (from right to left) are:

A: $1 \bmod 1 = 0$; $0 \bmod 1 = 1$; $1 \bmod 0$ defined as $0 \bmod 1 = 1$

B: $0 \bmod 1 = 1$; $1 \bmod 1 = 0$; $1 \bmod 1 = 0$

These apply to subtraction as well.

We obtain the same results from using the exclusive or (XOR). Thus (again bitwise from right to left):

A: $1 \text{ XOR } 1 = 0$; $0 \text{ XOR } 1 = 1$; $1 \text{ XOR } 0 = 1$

B: $0 \text{ XOR } 1 = 1$; $1 \text{ XOR } 1 = 0$; $1 \text{ XOR } 1 = 0$

So we see that binomial arithmetic without carries, modulo 2 division, and XOR are equivalent operations on binary data.

As an interesting extension, we can see that these techniques give us an easy way to compare two bit strings of the same length. In particular, wherever the bit values are the same, the modulo result will be zero; where they differ, the mod result will be one. For example:

$$
\begin{array}{r}
1\,0\,1\,0\,1\,0\,1\,0 \\
1\,0\,0\,1\,0\,0\,1\,0 \\
\hline
0\,0\,1\,1\,1\,0\,0\,0
\end{array}
$$

We see that the 1s in the result indicate which bits have different values in the two strings. It would seem that this would give us an easy error-detection method and an error-correction method; if we knew which bits were 0s instead of 1s and vice versa, we simply could change their values. We send the frame twice and have the receiver do the bitwise comparison, thus revealing whether there was a transmission error and which bits were erroneous.

Alas, this is not a practical procedure. First, error detection requires sending twice the volume of data, an enormous load on the transmission system. Second, although we would be able to see that the strings differed, we would not be able to tell whether the errors were in the first string, the second string, or both. Still, such comparisons are useful in constructing *Hamming codes,* explored next.

Hamming codes

One possibility for using Hamming codes relies on the concept of *Hamming distance.* If we compare two bit strings of equal length, the Hamming distance is defined to be the number of bits in which they differ, which we can calculate with XOR.

As an example:

$$
\begin{array}{r}
1\,0\,1\,1\,0\,1\,0\,1 \\
\text{XOR} \quad \underline{1\,0\,0\,1\,1\,1\,1\,0} \\
0\,0\,1\,0\,1\,0\,1\,1
\end{array}
$$

There are four **1**s *in the result, so the Hamming distance is* **4.**

To see how we might put this measure to use, let's start with a 3-bit message block and assume that the only legitimate messages we can send are 000 and 111. Now suppose the receiver gets the string 010, a faulty message. The Hamming distance between 000 and 010 is 1, whereas the distance between 010 and 111 is 2. Hence, the receiver would change the code to 000, the one with the minimum Hamming distance.

Let's extend this example to use all eight possibilities for a 3-bit message block. This adds a level of complication: We must add redundant bits, because if we don't, any 3-bit message is "legitimate," even if the received bits are different from what was sent. In Chapter 5, "Error control," we saw that we need to add enough redundant bits to satisfy $2^r \geq m + r + 1$, where m is the original number of bits and r is the number of redundant bits, thus creating a codeword. For our 3-bit message example, we need a 6-bit codeword ($2^3 \geq 3 + 3 + 1$). Here is one possible codeword table for the eight 3-bit message combinations:

Message block	legitimate codeword	
0 0 0	0 0 0 0 0 0	In this example, the message blocks are embedded after the first 0 of the codeword.
0 0 1	0 0 0 1 0 0	
0 1 0	0 0 1 0 0 0	
0 1 1	0 0 1 1 0 0	
1 0 0	0 1 0 0 0 0	
1 0 1	0 1 0 1 0 0	
1 1 0	0 1 1 0 0 0	
1 1 1	0 1 1 1 0 0	

Now suppose the receiver gets the bit string 0 1 0 1 1 0; this is not one of the legitimate codewords, so it must be in error. We can calculate the Hamming distance between that string and each of the legitimate codewords. Then we can choose the codeword whose Hamming distance is least, and correct the received string accordingly.

The following table shows the Hamming distance between each legitimate codeword and the received string 010110:

block	codeword	H-distance	
0 0 0	0 **0 0 0** 0 0	3	
0 0 1	0 **0 0 1** 0 0	2	
0 1 0	0 **0 1 0** 0 0	4	
0 1 1	0 **0 1 1** 0 0	3	
1 0 0	0 **1 0 0** 0 0	2	
1 0 1	0 **1 0 1** 0 0	1	*This is the minimum Hamming distance, so*
1 1 0	0 **1 1 0** 0 0	3	*we change the received string to 0 1 0 1 0 0.*
1 1 1	0 **1 1 1** 0 0	2	

We can see that this method is not foolproof. With a 6-bit codeword, we can account for $2^6 = 64$ states, although we need just eight for our 2^3 possible messages. If we get any of the 48 codewords not in the list, we call the transmission faulty, but we do not know whether that error is due to just one faulty bit or several. That is, the "minimum distance codeword approach" assumes that the fewest bit errors occurred, which is not necessarily the case. With this simple approach, there is no way to know. Furthermore, we may receive a codeword that is faulty because one or more of its bits flipped to the pattern of another legitimate codeword, but not the one we originally sent. This error will go undetected. We need to make our error correction more general.

Also in Chapter 5, we saw:

- If two legitimate codewords are Hamming distance H apart, it takes H single bit flips to convert one to the other.
- The error detection and correction abilities of a codeword set depend on the set's Hamming distance H_d, defined as the minimum H over all possible 2-codeword combinations in the set.
- To *detect* e errors, we need a codeword set whose H_d is $e + 1$, because in such a set e bit errors cannot change one valid codeword into another—at least $e + 1$ flips would be needed to do so.
- To *correct* errors, we need a codeword set whose H_d is $2e + 1$, because with such a set, even if there are e bit errors, the received erroneous codeword is still closer to the originally transmitted codeword than any other codeword in the set. If we want to be able to correct all possible bit errors in a frame of size d, then e in the above must equal d.

Here are some examples:

Given the codewords: 000000 101010 010101 111111

We have $H_d = 3$. Therefore, this code can correct 1-bit errors ($H_d = 2e + 1$: $3 = 2 \times 1 + 1$).

Given the codewords: 0000000000 1010101010 0101010101 1111111111

We have $H_d = 5$. Therefore, this code can correct 2-bit errors ($5 = 2 \times 2 + 1$).

Single-bit error correction: a robust technique using Hamming codes

With the simple "minimum distance" codeword criterion, we achieve a modest level of error correction accuracy. To make full use of the redundant bits, we need to consider where they should be placed—proper placement enables accurate detection and correction of faulty single bits.

Suppose we have an m-bit message to which we add r redundant bits, creating a codeword of $n = m + r$ bits. For single-bit errors there are n possibilities—one in each of the n bit positions—any of the m message bits and any of the r redundant bits. We want the redundant bits to point to where the bit error is, so they must be capable of pointing to n bit-places. In addition, if there are no errors, we want all the r bits to be 0. Therefore, the redundant bits must be able to express at least $n + 1$ values—one for each of the n bit positions plus all 0s when there is no error.

As we have seen, these requirements tell us how many redundant bits are needed: Because r bits can express 2^r values, r must satisfy $2^r \geq n + 1$, or, equivalently, $2^r \geq m + r + 1$.

To see how the redundant bits can convey error location information within a codeword, let's use an example. Suppose we have an 11-bit message. Our inequality tells us that we need 4 redundant bits: ($2^4 \geq 11 + 4 + 1$). In a 15-bit codeword (11 message bits and 4 redundant bits), then, we need to place the 4 redundant bits in such a way that the *location* of a single bit error, if any, is revealed by the value of those 4 redundant bits. We place the redundant bits in positions that are powers of 2; for the 15-bit codeword, that means positions 1, 2, 4, and 8. The message bits occupy the remaining positions (see the following illustration).

position:	15	14	13	12	11	10	9	**8**	7	6	5	**4**	3	**2**	**1**
bits:	m11	m10	m9	m8	m7	m6	m5	**r4**	m4	m3	m2	**r3**	m1	**r2**	**r1**

In binary, we see that the r-bits are in positions represented by a single 1-bit:

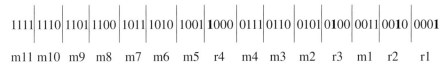

1111 | 1110 | 1101 | 1100 | 1011 | 1010 | 1001 | **1000** | 0111 | 0110 | 0101 | **0100** | 0011 | **0010** | **0001**

m11 m10 m9   m8   m7   m6   m5   r4   m4   m3   m2   r3   m1   r2   r1

The reason this works lies in how we use the redundant bits. Each of these bits takes on the value of either 1 or 0, as do all bits. Together we want the 4 redundant bits to take on the value of the errant bit's position (as a binary number). For example, if message bit m10 in position 14 (binary 1110) is faulty, we want the redundant bits r4 r3 r2 r1 to take on the value 1110. For this to happen, we need redundant bit r1 to always be a 1 whenever the faulty bit in the codeword is such that its binary position has a 1 in its least significant bit position, that is, r4 r3 r2 *1*. Similarly, we want r2 to be a 1 if the errant bit's binary position value has a 1 in its next-to-least significant digit, that is, r4 r3 *1* r1. Likewise, we want r3 to be a 1 if the errant bit's binary position has a 1 in its third bit, that is, r4 *1* r2 r1, and r4 to be a 1 if the errant bit's binary position has a 1 in its fourth bit, that is, *1* r3 r2 r1. Thus, the redundant bits "monitor" those positions where their 1-bit values appear.

In the example, r3 monitors m2, m3, m4, m8, m9, m10, m11—those message bits that have a 1 in the third bit of their binary position. Likewise, r2 will monitor m1, m3, m4, m6, m7, m10, m11, and so on. (Notice that r's may share responsibility for monitoring message bits.) When it comes to monitoring the status of the redundant bits, however, we have a dilemma: A redundant bit would need to monitor itself, clearly nonsense. This problem also is resolved by the same positioning of the redundant bits—here, at positions 1000, 0100, 0010, 0001. When the receiver repeats the calculations, if the error is in a redundant bit, that bit will always calculate to a 1 and all other redundant bits will always calculate to a 0. To illustrate, we show an example of the sender setup and calculations followed by the receiver calculations, repeating some items shown previously for ease of reference:

position:	15	14	13	12	11	10	9	8	7	6	5	4	3	2	1
bits:	m11	m10	m9	m8	m7	m6	m5	r4	m4	m3	m2	r3	m1	r2	r1

1111	1110	1101	1100	1011	1010	1001	**1000**	0111	0110	0101	**0100**	0011	**0010**	0001
m11	m10	m9	m8	m7	m6	m5	r4	m4	m3	m2	r3	m1	r2	r1

Monitor assignments:

r1: m1(3), m2(5), m4(7), m5(9), m7(11), m9(13), m11(15)
r2: m1(3), m3(6), m4(7), m6(10), m7(11), m10(14), m11(15)
r3: m2(5), m3(6), m4(7), m8(12), m9(13), m10(14), m11(15)
r4: m5(9), m6(10), m7(11), m8(12), m9(13), m10(14), m11(15)

Now that we have set up the codeword process, we determine what values to give to the redundant bits by parity. Using even parity and the 11-bit message 1 0 1 0 1 0 0 0 1 0 1, we show the r's in the bit positions they monitor, with asterisks to indicate those r's where the message bit in that position is 1. Parity values for the r's are in their bit positions, italic and bold.

message:	1	0	1	0	1	0	0		0	1	0		1		
bit position:	15	14	13	12	11	10	9	**8**	7	6	5	**4**	3	**2**	**1**
parity for r1:	r1*		r1*		r1*		r1		r1		r1		r1*		*0*
parity for r2:	r2*	r2			r2*	r2			r2	r2*			r2*	*0*	
parity for r3:	r3*	r3	r3*	r3						r3	r3*	r3	*1*		
parity for r4:	r4*	r4	r4*	r4	r4*	r4	r4	*1*							

Putting the r-bits into the message gives us our codeword (r's emphasized):

1 0 1 0 1 0 0 **0** 1 0 1 **0** 1 **1 0 0**

To see how this works, suppose in transit the bit in position 5 flips from 0 to 1. The received codeword would be 1 0 1 0 1 0 0 1 0 1 1 1 1 0 0. The receiver repeats the parity calculations for this entire codeword:

codeword:	1	0	1	0	1	0	0	1	0	1	1	1	1	0	0	**new**
bit position:	15	14	13	12	11	10	9	8	7	6	5	4	3	2	1	**parity**
parity for r1:	r1*		r1*		r1*		r1		r1		r1*		r1*		r1	**1**
parity for r2:	r2*	r2			r2*	r2			r2	r2*			r2*	r2		**0**
parity for r3:	r3*	r3	r3*	r3						r3	r3*	r3*	r3*			**1**
parity for r4:	r4*	r4	r4*	r4	r4*	r4	r4	r4*								**0**

The redundant bit set is 0101, which translates to decimal 5—bit position 5. To correct the codeword, we simply flip bit 5.

Suppose the received codeword was correct. Examining the preceding table shows that with the 5th bit equal to 0, the new parity would be 0000—no error.

The actual calculations use the XOR operator to combine redundant and message bits:

r1: r1 XOR m1 XOR m2 XOR m4 XOR m5 XOR m7 XOR m9 XOR m11

r2: r2 XOR m1 XOR m3 XOR m4 XOR m6 XOR m7 XOR m10 XOR m11

r3: r3 XOR m2 XOR m3 XOR m4 XOR m8 XOR m9 XOR m10 XOR m11

r4: r4 XOR m5 XOR m6 XOR m7 XOR m8 XOR m9 XOR m10 XOR m11

A comparison with the prior illustration shows that this produces the same result.

Appendix F

Echoplex and beyond

An interesting example illustrating how need drives technology and technological limitations drive development came about historically at the intersection of asynchronous and synchronous communication technologies.

To deal with bit errors that arise during transmission, asynchronous communication typically adds a parity bit to each character that is sent. As we explained in Chapter 5, parity, although better than nothing, is not a very effective means of detecting such errors. One computer vendor devised a clever yet simple scheme that greatly improved error detection by enlisting the human being at the terminal.

As each character is typed at a terminal, it is sent to its display so the user can see what was typed, and it is simultaneously sent to the remote computer. But if there is a transmission error, what the user sees is not what the remote computer receives. If the error was not detected by the parity check, the user would not know there was a problem, because the correct character is displayed at the terminal. To reduce the possibility of such errors, the former Digital Equipment Corporation (DEC), a maker of a very successful line of minicomputers, introduced a technique called *echoplex.*

Here's how it works: When a keystroke is typed on the terminal, it is sent to the remote computer but not displayed simultaneously on the terminal. Instead, the terminal waits for the remote computer to regenerate the character and send it back (echo it) to the terminal for display. The user can see if the correct character is displayed and if not, knows there was a transmission error. For this to work well, the round trip time has to be very small; if the delay is significant, many additional characters may have been typed before any are displayed, possibly resulting in a confused and disoriented user.

When DEC initially introduced echoplex, the terminal and remoter computer were typically connected together through the telephone system. In this mode, the connection is, practically speaking, equivalent to a direct wire that can transmit the typed character immediately without significant delay. Although this meant that the process was technically sound, connection costs proved to be extremely high. Occurring before deregulation of the telephone industry, the cost of either long-distance dial-up connections or dedicated lines was very dear.

High cost was one of the major drivers for developing alternate means to the telephone system for computer communication. The result, in the late 1970s, was data communications networks, also called packet networks because of the way they handled data. These networks used synchronous framing, with typical frames consisting of 128 bytes (1,024 bits). They cost far less to use because they were attuned to how computers talk to each other (discussed in Chapter 6, "Communications connections"). Generally, unlike the telephone system, the cost of using a data network was not dependent on the distance between the sender and receiver nor on the amount of time the two were connected. Instead, charges were based on the amount of data sent.

In order to use data networks, the sender and receiver had to be capable of utilizing synchronous frames. This precluded using asynchronous terminals to realize the cost savings provided by the data networks. However, the demand from the asynchronous terminal community, who represented what was then a prevalent means of communications, grew so strong that a work-around was developed. A device, called a PAD (Packet Assembler/Disassembler), was placed between the asynchronous terminal and the data network.

The terminal would continue to send a character at a time, but the characters were intercepted by the PAD where they were buffered until enough characters arrived to fill the required packet (for example, 128 bytes) or a special character such as "enter" was received or a "timeout" occurred. Only then were the characters sent on to the destination. In a similar fashion, when a packet arrived for the terminal, the PAD would disassemble the packet into individual characters and forward them to the terminal. Thus, the terminal was actually unaware that it was not connected to the destination directly.

This solution was workable as long as the destination did not actually need to see each character immediately as the sender typed it. The additional few seconds of time delay was then insignificant. However, when a terminal operating in echoplex mode was connected to the data network, things did not work smoothly. If the PAD held on to each character until a whole frame's worth was collected, sent, and echoed back, nothing was displayed on the terminal for a long period of time. If, on the other hand, the delay was short-circuited by arbitrarily filling the PAD with extraneous characters (say, blanks) except for the one character typed, most of the cost advantage and efficiency of the data network would be lost because of the extremely high overhead. The upshot was that DEC terminals in echoplex mode could not generally connect via data networks.

Appendix G

Communicating with light: some early efforts

Claude Chappe (1763–1805)

Chappe, a French inventor, worked with his four brothers on visual "telegraphs." Their synchronized pendulum system (1791) comprised two structures about 10 miles apart, each with a pendulum clock divided into 10 numbered parts. After synchronizing the clocks, the sender blasted a sound when his clock pointed to the number to be sent; on hearing the sound at the other structure, the operator read his clock, presumably pointing to the same number. Keeping the clocks synchronized was extremely difficult, and even so, the time it took for a sound signal to travel 10 miles could mean the wrong number was read.

Almost a year later, Chappe used a tall structure with five panels that could be opened or closed, providing 32 combinations that allowed for a simple binary code. Faced with an impending revolutionary war, the French government demanded more. Under pressure, Chappe responded with a tower using a long four-position cross-arm with a smaller seven-position indicator arm at each end, providing 196 combinations. In 1792, a chain of telescope-equipped towers (reports vary from 15 to 22 towers) were built from Paris to Lille (about 120 miles). In ideal conditions, messages could be relayed in only eight minutes (versus 30 hours by horseback). Their first use was in 1794, informing Parisians about the recapture of Condé-sur-l'Escaut from the Austrians less than an hour after it occurred.

For more details about Chappe's work, along with illustrations of some of his creations, go to http://people.deas.harvard.edu/~jones/cscie129/images/history/chappe.html.

John Tyndall (1820–1893)

Tyndall, an Irish scientist and inventor, observed that a visible light beam did not scatter when passing through highly filtered air or extremely pure water, even seeming to disappear when viewed from the side. This led to his discovery that light is visible in all directions only when it bounces off particles in the air or water—the so-called Tyndall effect—and that the light is scattered differently by particles of different sizes. By noting that light at the blue/violet end of the spectrum is scattered by much tinier particles than light at the red end, he explained why the sky appears blue. (Some of those blazing red sunsets we see are the result of pollution particles in the air scattering light at the red end of the spectrum.)

Most significantly for developments in optical communication, Tyndall made use of the lack of scatter in an appropriate medium and the concept of total internal reflection to create a "light pipe," demonstrated with a torch for the light source and a stream of water (the light pipe) along which the torchlight flowed. Even now this technique is used to illuminate water fountain streams. Tyndall's work was a very early precursor to today's light-based transmission systems, which use the same principles to create optical fiber light pipes.

Alexander Graham Bell (1847–1922)

Bell, the Scottish inventor famous for his role in the invention of the telephone with his assistant Charles Sumner Tainter, also invented the *photophone* for transmitting sound on a beam of light! Speaking into a megaphone aimed at a selenium crystal mirror caused it to vibrate in tune with the voice sounds. Sunlight shining on the mirror captured the vibrations because they affected the amount of light reflecting from it. This modified sunlight flashed to the same type of mirror at the receiver's photophone. Because the electrical resistance of crystalline selenium varies with the amount of light striking it, variations in the received sunlight caused current in the crystal to vary the same way. Changing the current back into sound reproduced the speaker's voice, thus transmitting voice through the air via light beams. In 1881, they sent a message between buildings more than 600 feet apart.

Although this extremely creative system suffered from its dependence on strong sunlight and its limited range, it was a clear precursor to today's optical communications systems, which are based on variations in light beams. Ironically, although Bell is remembered for the telephone, he considered the photophone to be his greatest invention.

Appendix H

ISDN

ISDN comes in two flavors: *Basic Rate Interface (BRI)* and *Primary Rate Interface (PRI).* BRI is intended for residential use, PRI for business use.

BRI

BRI ISDN uses digital signals between the customer's premises and the central office and requires the use of two local loops: one for sending data to the central office, the other for receiving data from the central office. Both of the local loops are divided into three logical channels: two *bearer (B) channels* that operate at a data rate of 64 Kbps, and one *delta (D) channel* that operates at a data rate of 16 Kbps. The B channels carry user data, and the D channel is used mostly for the control and signaling of the two B channels—*out-of-band* signaling.

Note that the speed of an ISDN B channel (64 Kbps) corresponds exactly to the data rate of a digitized voice channel (a DS-0). This is no coincidence; it is a result of the need to carry either voice or data in the same fashion (that is, an *Integrated Services Digital Network*).

B channels

The B channels are *dial-up* connections and can be used to connect to any other party on the telephone network in exactly the same way as a regular telephone connection. In fact, ISDN BRI service provides the customer with two independent telephone numbers: one for each B channel. However, the ISDN B channels differ from a regular telephone connection in the following ways:

- The B channels use digital signals; a standard telephone uses analog signals and cannot be directly connected to a B channel. Either an ISDN telephone is needed, or a device called a *Terminal Adapter (TA)* must be used between the ISDN line and the standard telephone handset. The TA also can be used to connect any other standard non-ISDN telephone device (such as an answering machine) to the ISDN line.
- The power to operate a regular telephone handset is provided by the telephone system; the power to operate an ISDN telephone must be supplied at the customer's premises. The major significance of this is that during an electrical power outage at the customer's premises, a standard telephone typically will continue to operate, whereas the ISDN telephone will not. This suggests that it may not be a good idea to rely solely on an ISDN telephone, as it may not be usable during emergencies.
- As was mentioned, an ISDN connection is created by dialing the remote party's telephone number in exactly the same manner as is done with a regular telephone

connection. However, to effect a dial-up connection via a standard telephone line can take up to 30 seconds; to effect an ISDN dial-up connection usually takes less than one second. The significantly faster ISDN connection time makes it possible for ISDN to be used for backing up a primary dedicated connection.

To achieve faster operation than is afforded by a single B channel, the two B channels can be *bonded* together to provide a composite data rate of 128 Kbps. In fact, the two B channels can be bonded and un-bonded on demand because of the out-of-band signaling available on the D control channel.

Here is an example of how this feature can be used: Suppose you have BRI service at home, and you decide to connect your PC to the Internet at the highest possible data rate of 128 Kbps using the two bonded B channels. If these were two standard telephone circuits, normally you would not be able to receive an incoming call because both telephone circuits would be busy.

Even if you had call waiting service, you could not switch one of the lines temporarily from the Internet connection to the incoming call because the call waiting signal in the standard telephone connection is an in-band signal that would interrupt the Internet connection, dropping it entirely. Because of this, modems attached to standard phone lines generally are configured to disable call waiting before they attempt to make the dial-up connection. However, with ISDN, notification of an incoming call is sent on the D channel without interfering with the ongoing transmissions on the two B channels.

You can decide whether to accept the incoming call over one of the two B channels. If you do, the two B channels will be un-bonded, reducing your Internet connection to just one B channel at a data rate of 64 Kbps, while the other B channel would be used for the incoming call. When you finish your conversation, you can choose to re-bond the two B channels.

D channel

The D channel, operating at 16 Kbps, is intended for out-of-band control and signaling of the two B channels. After a connection on one of the B channels is in place, there is often very little further activity on this channel. To allow the most efficient utilization of the connection, it is possible to use the idle capacity of the D channel for *data-only* applications. The data is sent as packets with the understanding that if there is a need for signaling or control information to be sent, the packet transmission will be interrupted temporarily until the D channel once more becomes idle.

BRI interface at the customer's premises

At the customer's premises, the two local loops terminate in a device called a ***Network Termination 1 (NT1)***. The NT1 assures that the 2B+D channels share the line without interfering with one another and also provides power to the line. When the TA and NT1 are packaged together, the device is referred to as an ***ISDN modem.***

PRI

For business applications, there is primary rate interface ISDN service. PRI consists of 23 B channels and one D channel. The D channel runs at 64 Kbps (compared to 16 Kbps for the BRI D channel). The higher speed is needed to control the larger number of B channels in PRI. Otherwise, all of the B and D channel characteristics described for BRI apply to PRI service.

PRI interface at the customer's premises

The total of 24 64-Kbps channels is strikingly similar to the structure of the T-1. This not by coincidence. PRI ISDN service is often delivered to the business premises as a T-1 circuit.

ISDN equipment

Telephone equipment that can be directly connected to the ISDN line, such as a digital telephone, is designated as *TE1 (Terminal Equipment 1),* whereas standard (analog) telephone equipment is designated as *TE2 (Terminal Equipment 2).* TE2 equipment must be connected to the ISDN line through a TA.

Appendix I

Some details of X.25 and frame relay operations

X.25

X.25 is based on a 3-layer architectural model that preceded the OSI model. The three protocol layers are: physical, data link, and network (also called packet). The physical layer is similar to those of the OSI and TCP/IP model architectures. The data link and network layers, however, have unique features designed to deal with the noisy and poor quality of the copper media of the 1970s.

In that regard, both the data link and network layers incorporated extensive error checking. When errors did occur, correction was by retransmission. In fact, both the data link and network layers use the same error detection/correction methods. The difference is that the data link focuses on individual links while the network layer focuses on end-to-end problems. In essence, the network layer incorporated what we think of today as functions of the OSI and TCP/IP transport layer.

Layer 2, data link

The data link layer of X.25 uses a version of HDLC (High-level Data Link Control) known as LAPB (Link Access Protocol Balanced). There are three types of control fields: information, supervisory, and unnumbered. Figure I.1 depicts the *information* control field, indicated by a 0 in the first bit position. It is used to send user-originated data. The 3-bit N(S) and N(R) fields store the unique frame sequence numbers: N(S) is the number of the frame being sent; N(R) is the number of the next frame expected by the receiver.

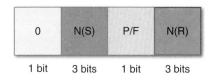

FIGURE I.1

X.25 LAPB information
control field

A special feature of LAPB, and of HDLC in general, allows the receiver to "piggyback" an acknowledgment (ACK) on a message to the sender. This is far more efficient than separate ACK messages. LAPB also uses timers for every sent frame. If the timer expires before the sender receives an ACK, the sender assumes the packet was lost and re-sends the frame in question. In fact, the timer process does question why there was no ACK (destroyed packet, destroyed ACK, processing problem), so once the time expires, the packet will be re-sent even if it was received in good shape.

THE SUPERVISORY FRAME The *supervisory* frame can carry one of four messages, indicated by the value of the 2-bit S field (see Figure I.2):

- S = 00: Receiver Ready (RR)—indicates receiver status when there is no user data to send back. The N(R) field plays the same role described in the previous section.

FIGURE I.2

FIGURE I.2

X.25 LAPB supervisory
control field

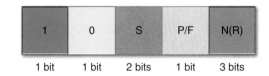

1	0	S	P/F	N(R)
1 bit	1 bit	2 bits	1 bit	3 bits

- S = 01: Reject (REJ)—a negative acknowledgment (NAK). The N(R) field specifies the rejected frame(s).
- S = 11: Selective Reject (SREJ)—a NAK used when the communication arrangement in the network is as follows: Discard only the errant frame, but not any subsequent frames that are intact. Here, N(R) specifies the specific frame that was damaged and that should be re-sent. (This contrasts with the go-back-n procedure, wherein all frames following a faulty one are discarded.)
- S = 10: Receiver Not Ready (RNR)—sent when the receiver has no user data to send back but needs to tell the sender to stop transmitting. When conditions permit accepting frames again, it sends an RR frame.

TECHNICAL NOTE
The size of N(S) and N(R)

The number of bits allocated for N(S) and N(R) determines how many frames can be sent prior to receiving an ACK. For example, if 3 bits are allocated, up to seven frames ($2^3 - 1$) can be sent without acknowledgement, after which the link sits idle. This undesirable situation usually is caused by a very busy receiver. It should not happen frequently for properly sized network nodes, but when it does, a backup of frames waiting to be sent results, wasting valuable link resources.

We could ease the burden on the receiver by allocating more bits to N(S) and N(R), but this increases the size of the control field and with it the frame overhead. In practice, 3 bits generally works fine.

There is a situation for which 3 bits is always inadequate: geosynchronous satellite links, which have a round-trip transmission time of about .25 seconds plus processing time at the satellite. For a typical link speed of only 56 Kbps and frame size of 1,024 bits, the transmitting earth station will have sent the maximum number of outstanding packets allowed (seven) in just 0.128 seconds ([1,024/56,000]*7), well before it will have received an ACK from the satellite, preventing further transmission for the time being. At higher bit rates, the problem is even greater.

To remedy the situation, the number of bits allocated for N(S) and N(R) is increased to 7, allowing 127 frames ($2^7 - 1$) to be sent before requiring an ACK. Within the greater amount of time it will take to send all 127 frames, the satellite will have sufficient time to send an ACK, thus enabling the earth station to continuously send frames.

THE UNNUMBERED FRAME The role of the unnumbered frame is to control and manage the operation of the link connecting two nodes. The meaning of the frame depends on the value of the M bits. As is shown in Figure I.3, the M bits are not contiguous, but they are interpreted as one 5-bit field. Hence, there are 32 possible control messages.

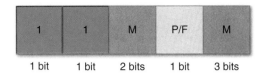

FIGURE I.3

X.25 LAPB unnumbered control field

Here are a few examples:

- M = 11 001: Reset (RSET)—for the sender to reset the value of N(R) in the receiving station.
- M = 10 001: Frame Reject (FRMR)—for the receiver to report that it has received a frame with a serious error that will not be correctable by simple retransmission of the frame.
- M = 11 101: Exchange ID (XID)—for a node to identify itself and its characteristics to its neighbor node.

Layer 3, packet/network

The packet layer gives X.25 its unique characteristics. Whereas the data link layer manages data flow across an individual link, the packet layer manages data flow from the originating node to the final destination node—end-to-end. To do this, it adds its own header—see Figure I.4.

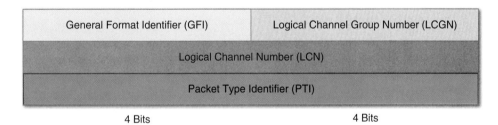

FIGURE I.4

X.25 Packet header

The packet layer is a connection-oriented network interface that performs the functions typical of the OSI network layer:

- Managing permanent virtual circuits.
- Setting up and terminating switched virtual circuits.
- Routing packets and managing routing tables.
- Controlling the flow of packets through the network.
- Multiplexing packet streams from different users over a shared physical connection via logical channels.
- Ensuring end-to-end integrity of individual packet streams. (An individual packet stream consists of the packets that make up a message or file that one user is sending across a shared physical connection. The packet stream flows via an assigned virtual circuit over the shared connection.) Note the similarity of these functions with functions that are typically thought of as the domain of the OSI Transport layer.

We can see how the packet layer performs several of its functions by looking at some of the fields in its header:

- General Format Identifier (GFI)—a 4-bit field used to indicate whether a packet contains user or network control information and the configuration of the control information packet.

- Logical Channel Group Number (4 bits) and Logical Channel Number (8 bits)—two fields used together to form the *Logical Channel Identifier (LCI),* which identifies one of a possible 4,095 virtual channels assigned to a user on the shared physical connection between the DTE and the DCE. (Channel 0 is reserved for network use.)
- Packet Type Identifier (PTI)—an 8-bit field identifying the packet's function. For example, if the least significant bit is 0, the packet is carrying user data; the meaning of the other bits is shown in Figure I.5. Notice the similarity of this field to the LAPB information control field (Figure I.1). In fact, the two have similar functions: The latter protects packets traveling across a single link between DTE and DCE; the former, in this example, protects the packets of a single originating user transmitting over an assigned virtual circuit.
- P(S)—at the packet layer, a field that is associated with a particular user's data stream and is different for each virtual circuit. Thus, the packet layer can track a given user's packets end to end. Whereas the value of P(S) stays the same end to end, N(S) changes every time the packet travels over a new link. The same is true for N(R) and P(R). Note the similarity to the mechanism used at the data link layer.

FIGURE I.5

PTI field when least significant bit = 0

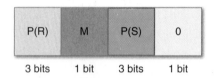

P(R)	M	P(S)	0
3 bits	1 bit	3 bits	1 bit

There are some 20 packet types in all that are used to either send user data or control the end-to-end connection.

Frame relay

Just as the telephone networks serve phone users according to various fee structures, frame relay networks serve data terminals according to various fee structures.

Congestion control: discarding excess frames

The frame relay network decides which frames to delete to clear congestion by checking the discard eligible (DE) bit in each frame: If set to 1, that frame is eligible to be discarded first; if set to 0, it will be discarded only if the congestion has not been cleared by discarding the discard-eligible frames.

The DE bit is set to 1 in two ways:

- A user may elect to do so.
- According to the **Service Level Agreement (SLA).** For a fee, a user is guaranteed a particular throughput level, with compensation given if it fails to do so. The DE bit is set to 1 for frames whose data rate exceeds the guarantee.

The SLA throughput guarantee is called the **Committed Information Rate (CIR).** The network will discard other users' DE frames to ensure that the CIR is achieved. It also will accept higher throughput rates if it has the capacity to handle the extra data. Two other throughput levels are part of the SLA:

- Committed Burst Size (Bc)—the CIR rate can be exceeded for some period of time such that the average excess rate does not exceed the Bc rate.
- Excess Burst Size (Be)—the user can exceed the Bc up to a point called Excess Burst Size, but any Be bits are discard eligible.

COMMITTED INFORMATION RATE STRATEGY   Frame relay networks are services offered by network providers to the public, and they are therefore available to any organization for a fee that depends on the data rates contracted for.

In view of the fact that the higher the CIR contracted for, the greater the cost (a strategy some customers take), with providers that agree, is to choose a CIR of 0 bps. This means that any data sent is immediately discard eligible. Although this may seem strange for a business that relies on the network, the fact is that the networks are designed with a great deal of spare capacity. So, most of the time no frames will be discarded. In practice, the strategy works well much of the time. If you are a risk taker, this is for you.

Congestion control: notifying users

Another way that frame relay networks deal with congestion is user notification via the *forward explicit congestion notification (FECN)* and *backward explicit congestion notification (BECN)* bits. If a frame making its way through the network encounters congestion, the node the frame is headed for (the forward direction) is notified by the network setting the FECN bit to 1. On the other hand, if the congestion is in the opposite direction to the frame's travel (the backward direction), the network sets the BECN bit to 1. The nodes may use this information to throttle the amount of traffic they inject into the network; however, this is voluntary and may be ignored.

Discarding frames: beyond congestion control

Although frame relay networks do not correct errors or ask the sender to retransmit faulty frames, they nevertheless do not want to pass along corrupted information. Hence, frames are discarded if an error is detected via the *frame check sequence (FCS)* field. If error correction is required, the user has to implement it by providing appropriate higher-layer functions. Importantly, *the network does not provide any notification when it deletes a frame.*

Because of these procedures, frame relays are known as **unreliable networks,** also called **best-effort networks.** This is not to imply that they are risky; quite the contrary: A well designed frame relay network works very well most of the time.

Glossary

1000BASE-CX: A standard for gigabit Ethernet connections with copper twinax or quad cabling, with a maximum span of about 25 meters.

1000BASE-LX: A fiber-optic gigabit Ethernet standard using 1,300-nm signals, with a maximum span of 300 to 550 meters with multimode fiber and over 3 kilometers with single-mode fiber.

1000BASE-SX: A fiber-optic gigabit Ethernet standard using 850-nm signals, with the same span limits as LX.

1000BASE-T: A standard for gigabit Ethernet over copper wiring. It requires unshielded twisted pair (UTP) category 5, 4B/5B encoding, and has a maximum span of 100 meters.

1000BASE-X: A gigabit Ethernet standard over fiber with 8B/10B encoding, with three options: 1000BASE-CX, 1000BASE-LX, and 1000BASE-SX.

100BASE-FX: The multimode fiber-optic version of 100BASE-TX standard.

100BASE-T4: A fast Ethernet specification designed to run on unshielded twisted pair (UTP) Category 3.

100BASE-TX: Refers to official designation of fast Ethernet and runs over two pairs of category 5 or above cable.

10BASE2: A variant of Ethernet that uses thin coaxial cable terminated with bayonet Neill-Concelman (BNC) connectors.

10BASE5: An original "full spec" variant of Ethernet cable, using special cable similar to RG-8/U coaxial cable, with transmission speed of 10-Mbps data rate, baseband signaling, and a 500-meter maximum segment span.

10BASE-FL: Most commonly used 10BASE-F specification of Ethernet over optical fiber, with 10 megabits per second baseband.

10GBASE-X: 10 gigabit Ethernet.

1-persistence: A protocol used to determine when an Ethernet node can transmit on a shared medium: if the medium is busy, wait until the medium is idle; if the medium is idle, transmit.

1xEV-DO (evolution-data optimized): A 3G CDMA standard.

1x-EV-DV (evolution-data and voice): A 3G standard that addresses both data and voice.

3TDES: Follows the same consecutive process as TDES but is even more secure because it uses a different key at each step instead of just one for all steps.

802.1d: It is the IEEE MAC Bridges standard that includes Bridging, Spanning Tree, interworking for 802.11 and others. It is standardized by the IEEE 802.1 working group.

802.1q: An IEEE standard for frame tagging.

802.3a: A thin coax version of Ethernet released in 1985 by IEEE.

802.3ab: Defines gigabit Ethernet transmission over unshielded twisted pair (UTP) category 5, 5e, or 6 cabling. It is also known as 1000BASE-T.

802.3ac: The IEEE standard, with max frame size extended to 1,522 bytes (to allow "Q-tag"). The Q-tag includes 802.1Q virtual LAN (VLAN) information and 802.1p priority information.

802.3ae: An IEEE standard for 10 gigabit Ethernet. It operates in full-duplex mode at 10 Gbps up to 40 kilometers using single-mode fiber and up to 300 meters using multimode.

802.3af: The IEEE Power Over Ethernet (POE) standard.

802.3u: An IEEE standard for Ethernet with transmission speed of 100 Mbps. It is also known as Fast Ethernet.

802.3x: A collection of IEEE standards defining the physical layer and the media access control (MAC) sublayer of the data link layer of wired Ethernet.

802.3z: An IEEE standard for gigabit Ethernet over optical fiber and shielded twisted pair (STP). It provides for full-duplex transmission from switch to end station or to another switch and half-duplex over a shared channel using the CSMA/CD access method.

802.5: An IEEE standard for a token ring local area network access method, which is widely implemented in token ring.

802.11: A family of IEEE standards for wireless LANs that were designed to extend 802.3 (wired Ethernet) into the wireless domain. The 802.11 standard is more widely known as "Wi-Fi" because the Wi-Fi Alliance, an organization independent of IEEE, provides certification for products that conform to 802.11.

802.11a: A WLAN standard, which offers a maximum data rate of 54 Mbps, but suffers from lack of backward compatibility with the 802.11b standard.

802.11b: A standard for WLAN, which operated at a maximum data rate of 11 Mbps in the 2.4 GHz band. It's an extension to 802.11.

802.11g: A WLAN standard that works in the 2.4 GHz band but operates at a maximum raw data rate of 54 Mbit/s or about 19 Mbit/s net throughput.

802.11i: An IEEE standard security protocol for 802.11 wireless networks that was developed to replace the original WEP protocol. It was certified by the Wi-Fi Alliance as WPA2.

802.11n: An enhancement to the IEEE 802.11 wireless network standard that increases transmission speeds to 108 Mbps and beyond. It operates in the 5-GHz band, but uses a spatial multiplexing technique called multiple-input and multiple-output.

Abilene: High-performance backbone network created by the Internet2 community.

ABR (Available Bit Rate): A service used in ATM networks when source and destination don't need to be synchronized. ABR does not guarantee against delay or data loss.

Absorption: The process whereby the incident particles or photons of radiation are reduced in number or energy as they pass through matter, i.e., the energy of the radiation beam is attenuated.

Access device: Node that provides access to the WAN.

Access list: A table of membership attribute/VLAN associations that are stored in the switches.

Access point (AP): A node connected wirelessly to BSS stations and by wire to the organization's wired networks through a LAN or backbone.

ACK: See **Acknowledgement.**

Acknowledgement (ACK): A packet or signal used to indicate that the frame was received correctly.

Activity logs: Enable trace-back to the sources of internal attacks or other breaches.

Ad hoc network: A wireless network connection that is established for the duration of one session and requires no base station.

Adaptive frequency hopping (AFH): Improves resistance to radio frequency interference by avoiding crowded frequencies in the hopping sequence.

Add/drop multiplexer (ADM): A multiplexer that mixes and redirects traffic within a SONET system.

Address resolution protocol (ARP): A standard method for finding a host's hardware address when only its network layer address is known, i.e., converts a given IP address into its associated machine address.

Address Resolution: Finding a host's hardware address when only its network layer address is known, or viceversa (as in RARP).

ADSL (Asymmetric Digital Subscriber Line): A form of DSL, a data communications technology that enables faster data transmission over copper telephone lines than a conventional voiceband modem can provide. It is usually used as a service to provide high-speed Internet access to the home user.

Advanced encryption standard (AES): An encryption algorithm for securing sensitive but unclassified material by U.S. government agencies and, as a likely consequence, may eventually become the de facto encryption standard for commercial transactions in the private sector.

Advanced mobile phone system (AMPS): An analog cellular mobile phone system in North and South America and more than 35 other countries. It uses FDMA transmission in the 800-Mhz band.

Advanced Research Projects Agency (ARPA): An agency of the United States Department of Defense, ARPA underwrote development for the precursor of the Internet, known as ARPANET.

Agents: Network management software modules having local knowledge of management information that translate that information into a form compatible with SNMP.

Alarms: Fault alert messages.

All optical network (AON): A communications network working completely in the optical domain that uses optical switches connected by optical fibers.

Alternate mark inversion (AMI): An encoding method in T1 and E1 transmission in which consecutive 1s have opposite voltage polarity in order to maintain 1s density for synchronization purposes. All 0s, on the other hand, are always sent as 0 volts.

Alternating current (AC): An electric current that reverses its direction at regular intervals.

American National Standards Institute (ANSI): Oversees the development of voluntary consensus standards for products, services, processes, systems, and personnel in the United States.

American Standard Code for Information Interchange (ASCII): Uses 7 bits to represent all uppercase and lowercase characters, numbers, punctuation marks, and other characters. *Extended* ASCII uses 8 bits.

Ampere (A): A unit of electric current (electron flow) or pressure.

Amplifiers: A device that takes in a given electric signal and sends out a stronger one. Amplifiers are used to boost electrical signals in many electronic devices, including radios, televisions, and telephones.

Amplitude modulation (AM): The transferring of information onto a carrier wave by varying the amplitude (intensity) of the carrier signal.

AMPS band: The 800-MHz band used by advanced mobile phone service (AMPS).

Analog information: Information that is continuous; that is, any piece of information that can take on any of an infinite set of values is said to be analog.

Analog signaling: A signal which changes continuously and can take on many different values. The analog signal, in effect, is an analog to the real physical quantity (e.g., music) it is representing.

Analog signal: Any time continuous signal where some time varying feature of the signal is a representation of some other time varying quantity.

Analog to digital converter (ADC): An electronic integrated circuit that converts continuous signals to discrete digital numbers.

Anycast: Communication between a single sender and the nearest of several receivers in a group.

Application firewall: Limits the access that software applications have to operating system services, and consequently to the internal hardware resources found in a computer.

ARPANET project: See **ARPANET**.

ARPANET: A computer network developed by the Advanced Research Projects Agency of the U.S. Department of Defense. ARPANET was the predecessor of the Internet. Its objectives were to allow continuous communications among dissimilar networks and, in the event that portions of the networks were disabled (possibly due to military or nuclear weapon attack), to enable communications to continue.

ASCII character: See **American Standard Code for Information Interchange.**

Asynchronous communication: Refers to digital communication (such as between computers) in which there is no timing coordination between the sending and receiving devices as to when the next character will be sent. The start and end of each character are signaled by the transmitting device— character at a time transmission.

Asynchronous TDM: See **Statistical TDM.**

Asynchronous transfer mode (ATM): A cell relay, packet switching network, and data link layer protocol that encodes data traffic in small (53 byte) fixed-sized cells.

Attenuation: A form of distortion in which signal energy is lost as it travels, due to the resistance of the medium to electrical flow. Attenuation is measured in decibels per kilometer (dB/km) at a specific frequency.

Authentication header (AH): Creates a hash value from the packet's bits.

Authentication: Assurance that a message actually is from the party it appears to be, not spoofed.

Authorization: Permission to use equipment and files, limiting rights to particular networks, database resources, and other company assets.

Automatic repeat request: See **Repeat request.**

Autonegotiation: An Ethernet procedure whereby connected devices agree to the transmission parameters to be used for communications.

Autonomous (independent) interconnected network: A network that operates independently according to its own set of policies.

Backbone: A high-speed communications link that is used in interconnecting LANs in many businesses, especially those that occupy several floors in a building. A backbone is also used to interconnect WANs, as is done, for example, in the Internet.

Backoff: For Ethernet networks, a random time waited by each station before beginning the carrier sense process again.

Backward error correction (BEC): Techniques in which the receiver requests retransmission when it detects erroneous data. When error rates are low or zero, BEC can be very efficient. However, if the same error occurs repeatedly, BEC techniques can never transmit the data properly. They are mostly useful for guided transmission systems.

Backward explicit congestion notification (BECN): A one-bit field in the frame relay header that signals to any node receiving the frame that congestion is occurring in the opposite direction from which the frame arrived.

Band: A contiguous group of electromagnetic frequencies or wavelengths.

Bandwidth: The data transmission capacity of a channel; the difference between the highest and lowest significant frequencies in a signal's spectrum; the difference between the highest and lowest frequencies that a communications system can handle.

Base station: A wireless communications station installed at a fixed location.

Baseband signal: A signal that includes frequencies equal to or very near zero, by comparison with its highest frequency. For example, a sound waveform can be considered as a baseband signal, but a radio signal cannot. Baseband is also used to refer to signals that have not been multiplexed.

Basic service set (BSS): In WLAN, each access point and its wireless devices.

Basic SONET signal: Carries one T-3 or its equivalent. It is called an STS-1 signal in its electrical form, and an OC-1 in its optical form.

Baud rate: A measure of the number of data elements that can be transmitted per second—the rate of change of signal elements. This is not always the same as the bit rate (bits per second), because a given symbol, or baud, may represent more than one bit.

Beam's spectrum: The array of colors that make up a beam of light. The beam can be separated to its component colors. Note that "color" is a relative term, meaning the wavelengths composing the beam. Visible light comprises the rainbow of colors. Infrared light is not a single "color" but rather has many wavelengths in its spectrum.

Bell operating company (BOC): AT&T's 23 local telephone companies in the United States.

BERT (Bit Error Rate Tester): An instrument for analyzing network transmission efficiency that computes the percentage of bits received in error from the total number sent.

Best effort delivery: Describes a network service in which the network does not guarantee that data is delivered or that a user will have a particular quality of service level or priority.

Best-effort communications system: A system that does not provide any guarantees that data is delivered.

Binary signal: A digital signal composed of combinations of two possible values, 0 and 1.

Bipolar 8-zeros substitution (B8ZS): A method of line coding used in the T-carrier system that improves sender/receiver clock synchronization by substituting for strings of eight zeros. It improved on an earlier line coding scheme known as AMI (Alternate Mark Inversion).

Bit duration: The time allowed for representing each bit by **its associated code value.** It is the inverse of bit rate.

Bit error rate (BER): The percentage of bits that have errors relative to the total number of bits received in a transmission, usually expressed as ten to a negative power.

Bit rate: The number of bits sent each second.

Bit robbing: A T-carrier system signaling technique in which the system borrows (robs) bits in the T-carrier frame that are normally used by the sender. The robbed bits allow the operator of the system to transmit management data on the T-carrier. This is a form of *in-band* signaling. The system did not initially account sending management/control data on the same connection used to send user data.

Bit stuffing: The insertion of redundant bits into data to assure the *transparency* of the communication system. It is used by bit-oriented communications protocol and is also called zero-bit insertion/deletion.

Bit synchronization: Synchronizing the sender and receiver clocks to the bit times.

Bit-oriented communications protocol: A communications protocol that considers the transmitted data as an opaque stream of bits with no semantics, or meaning.

Block code scheme: An approach to providing clocking information without incurring as big a bandwidth penalty as the Manchesters or RZ codes.

Block codes: A code with a fixed number of bytes.

Block parity check: Detects almost all single-bit and multiple-bit errors, but at the cost of added transmission overhead. Block parity check method detects erroneous frames for single-bit and multiple-bit errors, whether an even or odd number of bits have been inverted. The only exception is when precisely 2 bits in one frame and 2 bits in another frame in the same column positions are inverted, an extremely rare occurrence.

Blocking ports: The ports on a bridge that are barred from sending received data. This prevents flooding an Ethernet LAN with frames that will circulate forever due to loops created by the bridges. By contrast, the one port on the bridge that does forward frames is called the designated port. Also see **Spanning tree.**

Bluetooth: A WPAN technology that provides a way to connect and exchange information between devices such as mobile phones, laptops, PCs, printers, and digital cameras that are in very close proximity to one another.

Border gateway protocol (BGP): A routing protocol used in border routers to interconnect autonomous systems to route packets among them.

Bounded media: See **Guided media.**

Bridge protocol data unit (BPDU): A special frame sent by a bridge out of all of its ports.

Bridge tap: Connection to the local loops that was used to create a party line.

BSS transition mobility: A WLAN mobility type in which a terminal moves from a first access point (AP) to a second access point within the same extended service set (ESS).

Bus structure: A topology consisting of a single shared medium, typically coaxial cable, to which multiple devices are connected. These devices monitor signals on the medium and selectively copy the data addressed to them. Non-switching Ethernet hubs implement a logical bus topology in a star-wired network structure.

Byte stuffing: A special byte inserted before each bit sequence in the data that is the same as the flag sequence but is not a flag. The stuffed byte signals this fact to the receiver, thus maintaining framing scheme transparency. It is used in byte-oriented communications control. Also called character stuffing.

CableLabs: Cable Television Laboratories, a non-profit research and development consortium whose members are exclusively cable television system operators, also known as multi-system operators (MSOs).

Call setup: A logical connection established between the sender and receiver before any packets are sent.

Call transport: Protocols in the transport layer that deal with latency, jitter, packet loss, and sequencing.

Carrier sense multiple access with collision avoidance (CSMA/ CA): A network contention protocol that involves extended listening to a network in order to avoid collisions. It is a medium access method that is performed by each individual device and does not require a central controlling entity.

Carrier sense multiple access with collision detection (CSMA/CD): A network contention protocol that listens to a network in order to avoid and detect collisions. It is a medium access method that is performed by each individual device and does not require a central controlling entity.

Carrier: A sine wave that can be modulated in amplitude, frequency, or phase for the purpose of carrying information.

Carrierless amplitude/phase modulation (CAP): A proprietary standard implemented for provision of ADSL service.

Carterfone decision of 1968: The Federal Communications Commission decision that allowed users to connect their own telephone equipment to the public telephone system for the first time.

CBR (Constant Bit Rate): A uniform transmission rate used for connections that depend on precise clocking to ensure undistorted delivery.

CDDI: A copper wire standard of FDDI, published by ANSI and ISO, designed for either cat 5 UTP or type 1 STP.

Cell: Fixed size packet. See also **Frames.**

Cell relay: A method of statistically multiplexing fixed-length packets to transport data between computers or kinds of network equipment.

Cell switching: Using cell switches to forward fixed-length packets in a network.

Cellular authentication and vector encryption (CAVE) algorithm: A powerful authentication scheme employed by all 2G cellular systems.

Cellular band: The 850-MHz band.

Central office (CO): A facility of a telecommunications common carrier where calls are switched. In local area exchanges, central offices switch calls within and between the 10,000-line exchange groups that can be addressed uniquely by the area code and the first three digits of a phone number.

Centralized management: Control of access of all devices to a shared link by a single (central) device.

Certificate authority (CA): An organization that issues digital certificates (digital IDs) and makes its public key widely available to its intended audience.

Channelized: An architecture that transmits data in channels.

Channel: A particular path in a medium through which information is transmitted from a sender to a receiver.

Character stuffing: See **Byte stuffing.**

Character-oriented communications protocol: Views transmitted data as a stream of bytes.

Cheapernets: A nickname for 10BASE-2 Ethernets. The wiring in this type of Ethernet is 50 ohm, baseband coaxial cable, also known as thinnet.

Checksum method: An error detection method in which the sender calculates a value based on sums of the bit values of the data. The receiver makes the same calculation, and checks the calculated sum with the transmitted checksum. If they don't match, the receiver assumes the data was corrupted in transit.

Chipping code: A scheme used in Direct Sequence Spread Spectrum to spread a signal across a large range of frequencies for purposes of transmitting it securely and making it highly resistant to interference. The chipping code is a bit pattern that operates on the original data to achieve these ends.

Ciphertext: Encrypted text.

Circuit switch network: Switches create a circuit from the calling party to the called party by connecting a series of links leading from one to the other.

Circuit switching: A type of communications in which a dedicated channel is established for the duration of a transmission.

Circuit-level firewall: Delves into the transport headers, monitoring connection-oriented session (circuit) establishment attempts by TCP.

Cladding: The material that surrounds the core of an optical fiber. It is designed to redirect (reflects or refracts) light rays so that as many as possible travel through the core. Rays that do escape the core are absorbed by the cladding.

Class 1 office (regional center): Handles calls from multiple states.

Class 2 office (sectional center): Handles calls for a very large geographic area.

Class 3 office (primary center): Handles calls made beyond the limits of a small geographical area in which circuits are connected directly between class 4 toll offices, and use high usage trunks to complete connection between toll centers.

Class 4 office (toll center): The switching center through which any long-distance call, as well as any call that is subject to message unit charges, is routed. It serves a large city or several small cities and generates customer-billing information.

Class 5 telephone office: A telephone switch or exchange located at the local telephone company's central office, directly serving subscribers.

Class of Service (CoS): Captures the nature of different types of traffic and the special requirements the network must provide.

Classful addressing: Divides the entire IP address space into ranges of contiguous IP addresses called classes.

Classless addressing: Treats an IP address as a 32-bit stream of ones and zeros, where the boundary between network and host portions can fall anywhere between bit 0 and bit 31.

Classless inter-domain routing (CIDR): A relatively new addressing scheme for the Internet that allows more efficient allocation of IP addresses than classful addressing.

Clear to send (CTS): A signaling message transmitted by an IEEE 802.11 station in response to an RTS message.

Client/server: The association between software running in nodes on a network—the client software requests services and the server software provides them.

Cloud: A graphical metaphor representing a communications system (network) that sits between the end points of a transmission and through which the transmission travels.

Coax: A coaxial cable; a multi-conductor cable comprising a central wire conductor surrounded by a hollow cylindrical insulating space solid insulation, or mostly air with spaced insulating disks, surrounded by a hollow cylindrical outer conductor and finally a protective covering. Coax offers high capacity for carrying signals and is relatively immune to external sources of interference.

Code division multiple access (CDMA): A digital system that, by combining DSSS with chipping codes, allows multiple simultaneous transmissions to be carried across the same channel.

Code rate: The ratio of message bits to total bits.

Code redundancy: The ratio of redundant bits to total bits.

Codec (coder/decoder): A device that converts analog video and audio signals into a digital format for transmission. Also converts received digital signals back into analog format.

Codeword: A contiguous set of bits that together form a piece of information.

Collapsed backbone: A configuration in which LAN switches are connected to a router that has tables of LAN addresses. The router sends frames from one LAN to another according to frame destination addresses.

Collision: The result of two devices attempting to transmit data over a shared medium at exactly the same time. All shared media computer networks require some sort of mechanism to either prevent collisions altogether or recover from collisions when they do occur.

Collision window: The maximum length of time it takes to detect a collision and is essentially the twice the time it takes a for a frame to travel from one end of a shared medium LAN to the other.

Comité Consultatif International Téléphonique et Télégraphique (CCITT): An international organization established in about 1960 for communications standards functioning within the intergovernmental International Telecommunication Union (ITU).

Committed burst size (Bc): The number of bits that a router can transmit over a specified time interval when congestion is occurring.

Committed information rate (CIR): The rate at which the network supports data transfer under normal operations.

Common carrier: A government-regulated organization that provides telecommunications services for public use, such as AT&T, the telephone companies, MCI, and Western Union.

Common Criteria (CC): An internationally approved set of security standards that provides a clear and reliable evaluation of the security capabilities of information technology products.

Common gateway interface (CGI): A standard protocol for interfacing external application software with an information server. It allows the server to pass requests from a client web browser to the external application.

Common management information protocol (CMIP): A network management protocol built on the Open

Systems Interconnection (OSI) communication model.

Communications link: A line, channel, or circuit over which data are transmitted.

Community antenna TV (CATV): In broadband communications technology, multiple television channels may be transmitted either one-way or bi-directionally through an often hybrid distribution system to a single or to multiple specific locations.

Competitive local exchange carrier (CLEC): A telecommunications provider company in the United States that competes with the ILECs.

Computer operating system (OS): Software that manages the resources of a computer.

Conduction: The process of electron flow.

Conductors: Materials that readily allow electrical flow, such as copper and aluminum.

Conference of European Posts and Telegraphs (CEPT): A European organization that develops standards and defines interfaces for telecommunications systems.

Connection oriented: A communications connection that requires the establishment and termination of the connection. It is a feature of circuit switched connections and packet switched virtual circuits.

Connectionless: Describes communication between two network end points in which a message can be sent from one end point to another without prior arrangement.

Connectionless service: A communications connection that does not require the establishment and termination of the connection. It is a feature of datagram packet switched connections.

Connection-oriented service: A communication service in which a connection is set up and maintained for the duration of the communication.

Consent decree of 1984: Wrought major changes in how telephone service was provided in the United States.

Constellation: A group of satellites.

Contend (contention): A condition that arises when two or more data stations attempt to transmit at the same time over a shared channel, or when two data stations attempt to transmit at the same time in two-way alternate communication.

Contention protocol: Refers to the contention for access to a shared medium by each station. CSMA/CD falls under this protocol.

Contract specification document: Documents used in creating a contract for a project; includes an information for bidders (IFB) document and a request for proposal (RFP) document.

Control frame: Helps in the delivery of data frames and contains characters to establish and terminate a connection, control data flow, and correct errors.

Core: The central, infrared light carrying component of an optical fiber.

Core mux: A multiplexer that mixes and redirects traffic within the SONET system.

Counter-rotating: FDDI uses dual-ring architecture with traffic on each ring flowing in opposite directions.

Country code top-level domain (ccTLD): An Internet top-level domain generally used or reserved for a country or a dependent territory.

Coupling: Splicing (joining) cables and attaching cables to connectors.

Critical success factor: An aspect of a network project that must be achieved for the project to successfully meet its objectives.

Crossbar switch: Connects any two devices that are attached to it up to its maximum number of ports. The paths set up between devices can be fixed for some duration or changed when desired. Each device-to-device path through the switch is usually fixed for some period.

Crosstalk: Interference caused by electric power being coupled from one circuit into adjacent circuits within a cable. It can cause signal loss at high frequencies, measured in decibels (dB).

Current: The rate of electrical or electron flow through a conductor between objects of opposite charge, measured in amperes.

Customer premises equipment (CPE): Any terminal and associated equipment and inside wiring located at a subscriber's premises and connected to a carrier's telecommunication channel at the demarcation point.

Customer Service Unit (CSU): Protects the telephone network against damage from faulty devices connected to it by the customer, and allows the telephone company to test the condition of a T-1 remotely.

Cut-through: A packet switch wherein the switch starts forwarding a packet before the whole frame has been received, normally as soon as the destination address is processed.

Cycle: One complete series of changes of value of a persistently repeating pattern, e.g., a sine wave that starts at zero, progresses through positive and negative values, and back to zero again.

Cyclical redundancy check (CRC): A method for detecting data transmission errors. The sender uses polynomial division to produce a coefficient (discarded) and a remainder (16 or 32 bits long)—the CRC. The receiver makes the same calculation on the entire frame. If the remainder is zero the frame is considered to be error-free.

Data circuit-terminating equipment (DCE): The equipment that performs functions, such as signal conversion and coding, at the network end of the line between the DTE and the line.

Data communication: The transmission and reception of binary data and other discrete level signals represented by a carrier signal.

Data communications networks: A configuration of telecommunication facilities for the purpose of transmitting data, as opposed to transmitting voice.

Data encryption algorithm (DEA): A block cipher designed to be used by the data encryption standard.

Data encryption standard (DES): Uses a 56-bit key cipher and the data encryption algorithm (DEA). It was selected as an official Federal Information Processing Standard (FIPS) for the United States in 1976.

Data frame: A data packet of fixed or variable length, which has been encoded by a data link layer communications protocol for digital transmission over a node-to-node link.

Data link connection identifier: An address that identifies a particular permanent virtual circuit.

Data link escape (DLE) character: A transmission control character that changes the meaning of a limited number of contiguously following characters or coded representations.

Data link flow control: Flow control between any two directly connected nodes.

Data network: An informal name for a digital network used to send data. Data networks can interconnect with other networks and can contain subnetworks.

Data Over Cable Service Interface Specification (DOCSIS): A standard crafted by CableLabs for cable modem manufacturers.

Data Service Unit (DSU): A device used for interfacing data terminal equipment (DTE) to the public switched telephone network.

Data terminal equipment (DTE): An end communications device that converts user information into signals for transmission or reconverts the received signals into user information.

Datagram: A packet switching technique that, in making switching decisions, treats packets as independent units without regard to whether they are part of the same or different messages.

De facto standard: A standard that holds sway simply by force of common usage. The name derives from the Latin expression that means "in fact" or "in practice."

De jure standard: A standard produced by a recognized standards organization. The name derives from the Latin expression that means "based on law" or by right.

Decentralized management: Protocols for link sharing that the individual devices follow to manage themselves when seeking access to the link.

Dedicated route: A circuit switched connection.

Dedicated-server: A LAN classification in which the servers function only as servers, cannot operate as user stations. At least one must operate as a file server. These LANs are often called client-server LANs.

Delay distortion: Distortion resulting from non-uniform propagation speed of transmission of the various frequency components of a signal.

Delta modulation: A form of digital modulation where voltage values of an analog signal are changed into a fixed difference of value (or delta), and a plus or minus sign.

Demultiplexing: A process of separating out the data streams or individual channels of data from a single multi-channel stream.

Denial-of-service (DoS) attacks: Used by hackers to shut down particular resources by overloading them, thereby denying their services to legitimate users.

Dense wavelength division multiplexing (DWDM): A version of fiber optic communication that combines many optical channels on a single fiber, typically used to increase the data transmission capacity of previously installed fiber. Dense wave division multiplexing provides a significant increase in capacity compared to WDM.

Designated port: The port on each bridge over which frames may flow.

Destination address: The address of the intended recipient of a frame.

Differential Manchester encoding: A method of encoding data in which data and clock signals are combined to form a single self-synchronizing data stream. Mid-bit transitions provide a clocking signal and the presence or absence of start-of-bit transitions indicate bit value.

Differentiated services (DiffServ): An architecture that specifies a simple, scalable and coarse-grained mechanism for classifying, managing network traffic and providing QoS guarantees on modern IP networks.

Differentiated services code point (DSCP): A field in an IP packet that enables different levels of service to be assigned to network traffic.

Digital AMPS (D-AMPS): A digital version of AMPS, the original analog standard for cellular telephone phone service in the United States.

Digital certificates: A copy of a key that is digitally signed by a trusted third party, called a certificate authority (CA).

Digital communication: A communications format used with both electronic and light-based space systems that transmit audio, video, and data as bits of information.

Digital information: Information represented by a restricted finite set of values, often represented only in binary form.

Digital Service Unit (DSU): See **Data Service Unit.**

Digital signaling: Carrying information using a limited number of different (two or more) discrete states. The most fundamental and widely used form of the digital signal is binary, in which each of two possible states represents a binary value.

Digital signals: Digital representations of discrete-time signals.

Digital signature: Verification that a transmission comes from the apparent sender.

Digital subscriber line (DSL): Provides for digital data transmission over the wires of a local loop.

Digital to analog converter (DAC): A device for converting a digital code to an analog signal.

Digital transmission: Voice, image, data, or text transformed and transmitted as bits. Digital transmission is less susceptible to noise interference than analog transmission.

Direct current (DC): An electrical current that flows only in one direction in a circuit. Batteries and fuel cells produce direct current.

Direct sequence spread spectrum (DSSS): A modulation scheme that replaces each bit to be transmitted with a sequence of bits drawn from a chipping code.

Disaster recovery plan: The document that defines the resources, actions, tasks, and data required to manage the recovery process in the face of a major event that causes network failure.

Discard eligible (DE): A bit in the frame relay header that indicates if that frame may be discarded when the frame relay network experiences congestion.

Discrete multitone (DMT): The ANSI standard and preferred technique for ADSL service.

Distance vector routing: A routing protocol that selects the best path to a destination based on the shortest distance.

Distortion: The undesirable changes in signal shapes due to interactions between the signals, the medium, and noise.

Distributed access: The capability of communications devices to independently coordinate orderly access to the shared network.

Distributed coordination function (DCF): The basis of standard CSMA/CA access within an 802.11 WLAN.

Distribution system (DS): Enables the interconnection of access points wirelessly.

Domain name registry: An organization that manages the registration of domain names within the top-level domains for which it is responsible, controls the policies of domain name allocation, and technically operates its top-level domain.

Domain name system (DNS): The way that Internet domain names are located and translated into Internet Protocol addresses.

Domain name: The symbolic name given to an Internet site.

Dotted quad: The notation that expresses the four-byte IP address as a sequence of four decimal numbers separated by dots.

Downlink: The link from a satellite to a ground station.

Download: The transmission of a file from one computer system or web page to another.

Dual stack: Provides two discrete network layers, and can therefore communicate using either IPv4 or IPv6.

Dumb terminal: A computer display terminal that serves as a slave to a host computer. A dumb terminal has a keyboard for data entry and a video display, but no computing power of its own.

Dynamic host configuration protocol (DHCP): A set of rules used by communications devices such as a computer, router, or network adapter to allow the device to request and obtain an IP address from a server.

Dynamic range: Port numbers 9,152 to 65,535 are neither assigned nor registered. They are called dynamic range as any process can use them.

Edge mux: A multiplexer that interfaces with the user at the edge of the SONET system.

Edge routers: A device that routes data packets between one or more local area networks and an ATM backbone network.

Edge switches: See **Access devices.**

Effective radiated power (ERP): Measures the directional characteristics of transmitting antennas.

EIA/RS 232-C: The most common physical interface specification.

Electromagnetic interference (EMI): Unwanted energy induced in transmission line by radiation from external sources of electromagnetic energy.

Electromagnetic wave: A propagating wave in unguided media with electric and magnetic components, e.g., light waves, radio waves, microwaves.

Elementary signal: Basic sine wave.

Encapsulating security payload (ESP): Encrypts the packet to provide privacy. Newer ESP functionality adds authentication and integrity.

Encapsulation: The technique used by layered protocols in which a layer adds header information to the protocol data unit (PDU) from the layer above.

Encoding: The process of representing information, in a form suitable for either storage, manipulation, display, or transmission by a computer or over a computer network.

End of text (ETX): A character to represent end of text in a data frame.

End office: A central office at which user lines and trunks are interconnected.

End systems: Computers that are connected to the Internet.

Enhanced data rate (EDR): A Bluetooth specification for data transmission speed.

Equatorial orbit: An orbit in the same plane as earth's equator, or the equator of some other celestial object.

Error control: Any technique that ensures information received across a transmission link is correct.

Error correction: Techniques for correcting erroneously transmitted data.

Error detection: Techniques for detect errors in received data.

Error rate: The number of erroneous bits received as a proportion of the total number of bits sent.

ESS transition mobility: Provides for movement of a wireless station from one ESS to another.

Ethernet: The most widely installed local area network technology, originally created by Xerox and then developed further by Xerox, DEC, and Intel.

European Telecommunications Standards Institute (ETSI): Promotes standards for interoperability between in-house and external power line networks.

Extended address (EA): Refers to a frame relay address field that increases the addressing structure from a default of 2 bytes to 3 or 4 bytes.

Extended Binary Coded Decimal Interchange Code (EBCDIC): An 8-bit character encoding used on IBM mainframe operating systems. It does not allow for parity error detection.

Extended service set (ESS): Comprised of a number of IEEE 802.11 BSSs and enables limited mobility within the WLAN.

Extended Super Frame (ESF): A T1 framing standard.

Exterior gateway protocols (EGP): A protocol for exchanging routing information between two Autonomous Systems via the gateway routers of each the networks.

Extranets: A private network that uses Internet protocols, network connectivity, and possibly the public telecommunication system to securely share part of an organization's information or operations with suppliers, vendors, partners, customers or other businesses.

Fast Ethernet: A collective term for a number of Ethernet standards that carry traffic at the nominal rate of 100 Mbit/s.

Fault: An abnormal condition in a network.

FCAPS: The ISO Telecommunications Management Network model and framework for network management: Fault, Configuration, Accounting, Performance, Security.

Fiber Distributed Data Interface (FDDI): A standard for data transmission over optical fiber in a network that can extend in range up to 200 kilometers.

Fiber to the home (FTTH): The installation of optical fiber from a WAN switch directly into the subscriber's home.

File sharing: Access under specific rules to the same file by multiple users. File sharing users may have the same or different levels of access privileges.

Filter: A device that selectively sorts signals and passes through a desired range of signals while suppressing the others.

Flag: A control string, independent of character codes, used to identify both the start and end of a frame.

Flat address: With reference to a network device, a flat address does not have any information as to where the device is. A MAC address is one example.

Flooding: A simple routing algorithm in which every incoming packet is sent through every outgoing link.

Flow: The packets created by segmenting a given stream of bytes from an application or process.

Flow control: It is the process of managing the rate of data transmission between two nodes.

Forward error correction (FEC): A technique for improving the accuracy of data transmission. Extra bits are included in the outgoing data stream so that error correction algorithms can be applied by the receiver.

Forward explicit congestion notification (FECN): A bit set by a frame relay network to inform a DTE receiving the frame that congestion was experienced in the path from source to destination.

Forwarding: The relaying of packets from one network node to another node in a computer network.

Forwarding equivalency class (FEC): A term used in MPLS to describe a set of packets with similar or identical characteristics that may be forwarded the same way, i.e., they may be bound to the same MPLS label.

Frame check sequence (FCS): A calculated code used to determine (check) if the bits within a frame have been received correctly during transmission.

Frame relay: A network technology that transmits data packets at high speeds across a digital network encapsulated in a transmission unit called a frame.

Frame relay assembler/disassembler (FRAD): A communications device that converts a data stream into the format required for transmission over a frame relay network, and performs the reverse function when the data exits the frame relay network.

Frame synchronization: The process by which a receiving device can determine the beginning and end of a frame. This is typically accomplished by preceding and concluding the frame with a distinctive bit sequence that can be distinguished from the data bits within the frame. This permits the data bits within the frame to be extracted Correctly.

Frame tagging: A method used for creating protocol-based VLANs.

Frame: A data packet of fixed or variable length, which has been encoded by a data link layer communications protocol, for digital transmission over a node-to-node link. At the Data Link layer, the data packet is usually referred to as a frame.

Framing bit: A bit used for frame synchronization

Frequency bands: A group of adjacent frequencies.

Frequency division multiple access (FDMA): A method of allowing multiple users to share the radio frequency spectrum by assigning each active user an individual frequency channel.

Frequency division multiplexing (FDM): An analog multiplexing scheme in which the available transmission frequency range is divided into narrower bands. Each of these bands is used to carry a separate channel.

Frequency hopping spread spectrum (FHSS): A method of transmitting radio signals by rapidly switching a carrier among many frequency channels.

Frequency modulation: A type of modulation in which the frequency of a continuous radio carrier wave is varied in accordance with the properties of a second (modulating) wave.

Frequency: Defined for a periodic signal as the number of times the repeating pattern in the signal recurs within one second. It is denoted in cycles per second, or more formally in communications work as Hertz (Hz).

FTP (file transfer protocol): A protocol to transfer data from one computer to another over the Internet, or through a network.

Full duplex mode: A data flow mode in which information can flow in both directions at the same time.

Full mesh: Every node has a link directly connecting it to every other node in a network. Full mesh is very expensive to implement but yields the greatest amount of redundancy, so in the event that one of those nodes fails, network traffic can be directed to any of the other nodes.

Functional requirements: An initial definition of a proposed system, which documents the goals, objectives, user or programmatic requirements, management requirements, the operating environment, and the proposed design methodology, e.g., centralized or distributed.

General contractor (GC): Contractor who assumes responsibility for completing a network project, under contract to the owner, and hires, supervises, and pays all subcontractors.

Generic access profile (GAP): Ensures compatibility so that piconet members can communicate with each other even if they are using other profiles as well.

Generic routing encapsulation protocol (GRE): A tunneling protocol designed to encapsulate a wide variety of network layer packets inside IP tunneling packets.

Generic TLD (gTLD): A top-level domain used by a particular class of organization.

Geometric optics: The science that treats the propagation of light as rays.

Geostationary orbit: A geosynchronous orbit.

Geosynchronous Earth Orbit (GEO): An orbit directly above the earth's equator that matches the rotation of the earth. To an observer on the ground, a satellite in a GEO appears to be at a stationary point in the sky.

Gigabit Ethernet: Ethernet with a nominal data rate of 1,000 Mbps.

Global positioning system: A collection of satellites that provides timing and location data globally.

Global system for mobile communications (GSM): A globally accepted standard for digital cellular communication.

Graded index: An optical fiber wherein the index of refraction gradually decreases from the axis of the core to the edges of its diameterr.

Guard band: Frequency that is left vacant between two channels to account for overlap.

Guided media: A cabling system that guides the data signals along a specific path; also known as bounded media. Guided media are typically wire and optical fiber.

H.323: An ITU standard for real-time voice and video-conferencing over packet networks, including LANs, WANs, and the Internet.

Half duplex mode: A data flow mode in which information flows in both directions between the parties, but in only one direction at a time. It is useful where two-way communication is necessary but bandwidth is limited.

Half power point: The point on a frequency spectrum at which the power of a signal is equal to one half of its maximum power. Half power point is often called the $-3dB$ point because the signal is approximately 3dB less than maximum.

Hamming distance: A measure of the difference between two binary sequences of equal length; in particular, it is the number of bits which differ between the sequences.

Harmonics: In acoustics and telecommunication, the harmonics of a signal are all but the lowest component frequencies in the signal's spectrum. The lowest component frequency is known as the fundamental frequency and each of the harmonics is an integer multiple of the fundamental frequency.

Hash function: A transformation that takes a variable-size input and returns a fixed-size string, which is called the hash value. The hash value is attached to the data that are to be transmitted and is used by the receiver to determine if an error occurred during transmission.

Head end: The originating point in a communications system.

Header: Control information appended at the beginning (head) of a segment of user data, used to control, synchronize, route, and sequence a transmitted data packet or frame.

Hidden node problem: A node in a wireless network that is visible from a wireless hub but not from other nodes.

Hierarchical address: A scheme in which the address is divided into two or more parts. One part usually designates the network in which a device is located and the other part uniquely identifies that device from among the others in the network. The telephone company (using area codes), the postal service (using Zip codes), and the Internet (using IP address) use hierarchical schemes to help manage the large numbers of addresses they have to deal with.

Hierarchies: See **Tree network.**

Hierarchy of signal levels: Indicates various T-carrier or SONET capacities.

High bit-rate DSL (HDSL): A technology introduced as a solution providing T-1 data rates over distances up to 18,000 feet without repeaters, compared to the 3,000- and 6,000-foot limitations of T-1.

Higher Speed Study Group (HSSG): Created by the IEEE to evaluate the requirements for the next generation of Ethernet technology.

Highly Elliptical Orbit (HEO): An orbit characterized by a relatively low-altitude perigee and an extremely high-altitude apogee.

HiperLAN (high performance radio LAN): Radio based local area networking solutions, intended for connectivity between PCs, laptops, workstations, servers, printers, and other networking equipment.

Hop: Each intermediate node in a network that is traversed by a data packet as it makes its way to the destination node is called a hop.

Host-specific routing: The inverse of network-specific routing. The host address is entered in the routing table.

Http:// (hypertext transfer protocol): The communications protocol used by clients to connect to servers on the Web. Its primary function is to establish a connection with a Web server and transmit HTML pages to the client browser or any other files required by an HTTP application.

HTTPS (HyperText Transport Protocol Secure): The protocol for accessing a secure Web server. Using HTTPS in the URL instead of HTTP directs the message to a secure port number rather than the default Web port number of 80 and causes the data that is being transferred to be encrypted before it starts its journey.

Hub: A communication device that distributes communication to several devices in a network through the re-broadcasting of data that it has received from one (or more) of the devices connected to it.

Hybrid network: A local communication network that consists of different physical topologies or network architectures.

Hyperlink: An address that takes us from one page to another and makes traversing the Web straightforward.

Idle state signal: Sent across a communications link while the link is otherwise inactive. It is used to maintain clock synchronization and let the sending and receiving devices know that the link is still operational.

IEEE P1901: An IEEE draft standard for broadband over power line networks defining medium access control and physical layer specifications.

Impulse noise: A short burst of noise having random amplitude and bandwidth. Impulse noises are usually caused by external electrical sources, such as lighting.

In-band signaling: Transmission of control information in the same band and the same channel as is used to send user data.

Incumbent local exchange carrier (ILEC): A local telephone company in the United States that was in existence at the time of the break up of AT&T into the Regional Bell Operating Companies.

Independent basic service set (IBSS): The simplest of all IEEE 802.11 networks in which no network infrastructure is required.

Index of refraction: A physical characteristic of a material that light can pass through, defined by the ratio of the speed of light in a vacuum to the speed of light in the material. Optical fiber is usually designed to have high index material in its core and low index in its cladding.

Induced current: Electric current that originates in a conductor by a fluctuating magnetic field around the conductor. It is always weaker than the field that induced it. For example, crosstalk is the result of the magnetic field caused by one wire carrying a signal inducing the same signal in an adjacent wire.

Industrial, scientific, medical (ISM) band: A specific band of the electromagnetic frequency spectrum designated for communications. This band is open to public use and does not require an FCC license.

Information for bidders (IFB): A document that provides prospective vendors the entirety of information regarding what they are expected to provide.

Information: Any communication or representation of knowledge such as facts, data, or opinions in any medium or form, including textual, numerical, graphic, cartographic, narrative, or audiovisual forms.

Infrared data association (irDA): Defines physical specifications communications protocol standards for the short-range exchange of data over infrared light.

Infrastructure BSS: An 802.11 network comprising an access point and wireless stations.

Initialization vector (IV): A continuously changing number used in combination with a secret key to encrypt data.

Insulator: Material that resists electron flow.

Integrated services (IntServ): An architecture that specifies the elements to guarantee quality of service (QoS) on networks.

Integrated Services Digital Network (ISDN): Provides digital access directly from the customer's premises to the telephone network at high data rates, and treats voice and data as digital data.

Integrity assurance: Methods for guaranteeing that the packet, including its original headers, was not modified.

Intelligent terminal: A terminal that can perform limited processing tasks when not communicating directly with the central computer.

Interexchange carrier (IXC): Provide interstate (long distance) communications services within the U.S., which includes AT&T, MCI, Sprint, and more than 700 others. It handles calls between LATAs (local access and transport area).

Interframe gap (IFG): A very small amount of time that must pass between successive frames transmitted from a workstation.

Interior gateway protocols (IGP): See **Interior routing protocols.**

Interior gateway routing protocol (IGRP): A distance-vector routing protocol developed by Cisco Systems that works within autonomous systems.

Interior routing protocols: The routing protocols used to facilitate the exchange of routing information between routers within an autonomous system.

Intermodulation distortion: The result of mixing two input signals in a nonlinear system. The output contains new frequencies that represent the sum and difference of the frequencies in the input signals. It is also called intermodulation noise.

International Electrotechnical Commission (IEC): Prepares and publishes international standards for all electrical, electronic, and related technologies.

International Telecommunication Union (ITU): An international organization established to standardize and regulate international radio and telecommunications. It is operated under the auspices of the United Nations.

Internet Assigned Numbers Authority (IANA): The entity that oversees global IP address allocation, DNS root zone management, and other Internet protocol assignments. These operations have been assumed by a private non-profit corporation known as ICANN (Internet Corporation for Assigned Names and Numbers).

Internet backbone: The very high-speed connections through which the autonomous networks of the Internet communicate with each other.

Internet control message protocol (ICMP): A message control and error-reporting protocol between a host server and a gateway to the Internet.

Internet Corporation for Assigned Names and Numbers (ICANN): A non-profit corporation that was set up to deal with protocol and parameter issues for the Internet. It oversees global IP address allocation, DNS root zone management, and other Internet protocol assignments, having taken over the responsibilities of IANA.

Internet group message protocol (IGMP): A mechanism that supports IP multicasting, providing temporary host group addresses, adding and deleting members from a group.

Internet message access protocol (IMAP): An application layer Internet protocol operating on port 143 that allows a local client to access e-mail on a remote server.

Internet protocol (IP): The set of technology standards and technical specifications that enable information to be routed from one network to another over the Internet.

Internet service provider (ISP): A business that provides access to the Internet and may provide other services such as Web hosting.

Internet2: An alliance of over 200 U.S. universities that are involved with learning and research projects requiring wide bandwidth links.

Internetwork: An interconnected system of computer networks.

Intranet: A private computer network that runs TCP/IP protocols. It is used to share part of an organization's information or operations with its employees.

Intrusion detection system (IDS): Software that focuses either on network data flows or host activity to detect security threats, whether arising internally or externally.

Intrusion prevention system (IPS): Software that attempts to isolate and quarantine suspicious files, prevent access to particular sites, and also refuses to download or install certain files.

Intrusion: Any unauthorized activity on corporate or wide area network with intent to disrupt operations or to alter stored data or transmissions in any way.

Inverse multiplexer (Inverse mux): A device in which a high data stream is broken into multiple lower data rate flows to allow the use of lower speed communications links. The aggregate speed of the lower speed links has to be at least equal to the data rate of the original signal.

IP (Internet protocol): An Internet protocol that handles the routing of packets across packet-switched internetworks.

IP (Internet protocol) address: The logical address of a device attached to an IP network.

IP precedence: In QoS, a three-bit field in the ToS (type of service) byte of the IP header. Using IP precedence, a network administrator can assign values from 0 (the default) to 7 to classify and prioritize types of traffic.

IPsec: A security Internet protocol that provides authentication and encryption over the Internet. IPv6 supports IPsec.

Jamming signal: A high-voltage signal that is generated on an Ethernet network when a collision has been detected. It is used to notify and insure other devices on the Ethernet that a collision has occurred and that they should either cease or not attempt transmission at this time.

Key cipher: A key is a number that is used by a mathematical algorithm, the cipher, to encrypt plaintext and decrypt ciphertext.

Key: See **Key cipher.**

Label edge routers (LERs): A router that operates at the edge of an MPLS network.

Label switched routers (LSRs): A type of a router located in the middle of a MPLS network.

LAN Emulation (LANE): A standard defined by the ATM Forum that allows devices that are normally connected to a LAN to connect to an ATM network instead, without any change to either hardware or software. The ATM connected devices appear to each other as if they were still connected directly through a LAN.

Laser: A powerful, coherent beam of light from a lasing medium. An acronym for Light Amplification by Stimulated Emission of Radiation. Lasers are widely used as the light source for light transmission over optical fiber.

Last mile: The connection from a network POP (Point-of-Presence) to the end-user's location.

Latency: The time between packet transmission and receipt; a measure of the responsiveness of a network, or concomitantly, a measure of delay.

Layer 2 tunneling protocol (L2TP): A tunneling protocol used to support virtual private networks (VPNs).

Learning bridge: An Ethernet device that joins two Ethernet networks to create a much larger network. A learning bridge automatically learns the location and MAC address associated with each Ethernet device.

Leased lines: A permanent connection between two specified locations that is provided by a carrier such as a telephone company. Also called dedicated lines or private lines. Leased lines with various capabilities can be obtained and can be conditioned to enhance their transmission characteristics.

LED: Light-emitting diode (LED), an electronic device that lights up when electricity is passed through it. LEDs are used as light sources for light transmission over short span optical fiber.

Light detector: A device that is sensitive to light and will produce an electric current in its presence.

Line: In SONET, the portion of the network between any two multiplexers is referred to as a line. The line may also contain one or more regenerators.

Line of sight: Certain carriers such as microwave radiation and light travel in a straight line. In order to use these carriers for communications, the sending and receiving devices must be able to see each other, i.e., they have to be in each other's line of sight. Any obstructions that can prevent them seeing each other will therefore halt communications.

Line overhead: A group of 18 bytes in the SONET header that manages and controls the line portion of the network.

Link access procedure—balanced (LAPB): A data link layer protocol derived from HDLC that is used to manage communication and packet framing between the DTE and the DCE devices in the X.25 protocol stack.

Link state: A routing protocol performed by every switching node in the network, and concerned with conditions between a router and the possible next hop routers.

Loading coil: A metallic, doughnut-shaped, voice-amplifying device used on local loops to reduce the attenuation effects of the wire, thereby enabling a signal to travel much farther before becoming too weak.

Local access and transport area (LATA): The geographic regions covered by each RBOC.

Local area network (LAN): A computer network limited to a relatively small area, usually the same building or floor of a building. LANs are capable of transmitting data at very fast rates, and because they are usually completely on private property, they do not require connections from carriers.

Local exchange carrier (LEC): An organization that provides local telephone service within the U.S., which includes the RBOCs, large companies, and more than a thousand smaller and rural telephone companies (approximately 1,300 in total).

Local exchange: A regulatory term in telecommunications for a local telephone company.

Local loop: The physical link or circuit, that connects the demarcation point of the customer premises to the edge of the carrier, or telecommunications service provider, network.

Local number portability (LPN): Allows a phone number to be used at any switch within a LATA.

Logical bus: A topology in which devices are physically wired in star topology but their communications behaves as if they were wired as physical bus.

Logical Channel Number: A 12-bit field in an X.25 packet layer header that identifies an X.25 virtual circuit, and allows DCE to determine how to route a packet through the X.25 network.

Logical link control and adaptation layer protocol (L2CAP): A Bluetooth protocol in the core protocol stack providing data services to higher layer Bluetooth protocols.

Logical topology: Describes how flows between the devices in a network effectively behave. This may be different from how the physical wiring between the devices is laid out. See **Logical bus** for an example.

Lossy: A characteristic of a network that is prone to lose packets when it becomes highly loaded.

Low Earth Orbit (LEO): Range from altitudes of 100 to 2,000 kilometers.

Mail transfer agent: A computer program or software agent that transfers electronic mail messages from one computer to another.

Malware: Software aimed at network or computer-related disruption of one sort or another.

Managed devices: Devices such as computers, hubs, switches, and routers capable of collecting, storing, and transmitting management information that is used to remotely control and monitor them.

Management frames: Frames that carry information used in network management.

Management information base (MIB): A database of management information of objects where each object represents some resource to be managed. It is used and maintained by a network management protocol. The values of the MIB object can be changed or retrieved using protocol specific commands.

Manchester encoding: A self-clocking encoding technique used by the physical layer to encode a bit stream. Every bit includes a mid-bit voltage transition to provide clocking information to a receiving device. The direction of the transition indicates the bit value.

Mask: A group of bits used to select certain bits from another group of bits of the same size. For example, a mask is used to extract the network address from an IP address.

Mean time before failure (MTBF): The average length of time before a network component fails.

Mean time to repair MTTR: The length of time between when notification of a failure is received and when the device is back in service.

Media: Any material substance, air, or vacuum used for the propagation of signals in the form of electromagnetic, or acoustic waves.

Medium access control (MAC) address: A unique physical address for each NIC, hard-coded by the manufacturer, and read into RAM on initialization.

Medium attachment unit: A device connecting the cable to the station.

Medium Earth Orbit (MEO): Ranges in altitudes between LEO and GEO orbits.

Message switching: A method of handling message traffic through a switching center, either from local users or from other switching centers, whereby the message traffic is stored and forwarded through the system.

Metropolitan area network (MAN): A network whose reach is limited to a neighborhood or city (a metropolis). MANs are larger than LANs, but smaller than WANs.

Mid-span problem: Incompatibilities that prevents two telephone companies from interconnecting their lines.

Mobile switching center (MSC): A telephone exchange that provides circuit-switched calling, mobility management, and GSM services to mobile phones moving within the area that it serves.

Mobile telephone switching offices (MTSOs): An operations center that connects the landline public switched telephone network (PSTN) system to the mobile phone system. It is also responsible for compiling call information for billing and handing off calls from one cell to another.

Modem: A device that transforms digital signals generated by data terminal equipment (DTE) to analog signal forms and transforms a received analog signal back into digital signal for presentation to the DTE.

Modulation: The process by which some characteristic of a higher frequency wave is varied in accordance with the characteristics of a lower frequency wave.

MPEG: An ISO/ITU standard for compressing digital video. It is an abbreviation of Motion Picture Experts Group.

MPLS domain: A portion of a network that contains devices that understand MPLS.

Multicast: Communication between a single sender and multiple receivers on a network.

Multidrop network: See **Multipoint network.**

Multilayer firewall: Incorporates the operations of packet-filtering firewalls, circuit-level firewalls and application firewalls in one device.

Multimode fiber: Optical fiber designed to carry multiple light rays or modes concurrently, each at a slightly different reflection angle within the optical fiber core. Multimode fiber transmission is used for relatively short distances because the modes tend to disperse over longer lengths.

Multiplexer: A device that combines two or more sender signals for transmission on a single link.

Multiplexing: An electronic or optical process that combines a large number of lower-speed transmission lines into one high-speed line by splitting the total available bandwidth of the high-speed line into narrower bands (frequency division) or splitting the large bandwidth of an optical fiber into various colors of light (wave division), or by allotting a common channel to several different transmitting devices, one at a time in sequence (time division).

Multipoint connection: Communication configuration in which several terminals or stations share the same connection and access to the shared connection. Usually controlled by a device called the primary, the others being called secondary.

Multipoint network: A network characterized by shared communication links in which every node is attached to a common link that all must use.

Multipoint topology: Links three or more devices together through a single communication medium.

Multiprotocol label switching (MPLS): A standard technology for speeding up network traffic flow and making it easier to manage, by attaching labels to packets.

Multistation access unit (MAU): A hub or concentrator that connects a group of computers to a token ring local area network.

NAK (Negative acknowledgment): A message transmitted to the sender indicating that a packet contained errors or was corrupted during transmission.

National information infrastructure (NII): A collection of network types that includes radio and television networks, the public switched telecommunications network, and private communications networks.

Net neutrality: The principle that Internet providers should not base charges for connection capabilities on users or content.

Network: A system of interconnected, comprehending, communicating hardware and software, designed to facilitate information transfer via accepted protocols.

Network access point (NAP): A communications facility used by network service providers (NSPs) to exchange traffic.

Network address translation (NAT): Maps a single public IP address to many internal (private) IP addresses. With a NAT-enabled border router, there is no direct route between an external source and an internal host.

Network default mask: A default bit pattern applied by an Internet router that easily allows the router to identify the class of an IP address. There is one default mask associated with each of the classes of IP address (e.g., the class B default mask is 255.255.0.0).

Network ID: That part of an IP address that identifies a single network (an autonomous system) within a larger TCP/IP internetwork (Internet or intranet).

Network interface card (NIC): Computer hardware that connects to network media, wired or wireslly. It contains a unique flat address assigned by the NIC manufacturer.

Network management system (NMS): A collection of software and hardware that allows network technicians to monitor and manage entire corporate networks, usually from a remote network control facility. Often, the NMS will utilize SNMP protocols and features.

Network operating system (NOS): Software that manages communication between devices within a network. The NOS oversees resource sharing and often provides security and administrative tools.

Network technical architecture: The detailed description of the functions and characteristics of a proposed network.

Network-specific routing: A technique that treats all hosts connected to the same network as a single entity, and eliminates the need to maintain per-host routing information.

Next generation Internet (NGI): A United States government project intended to increase the speed of the Internet.

Next hop: The next router to which a packet is sent as it traverses a network on its journey to its final destination.

Noise: Electrical activity that can interfere with and distort communications signals.

Non-persistence: In CSMA/CD a station wanting access to the shared medium and having been unsuccessful in its attempt will wait a random amount of time and then sense the line again, and if it is idle, the station will send the frame.

Non-repudiation: Prevents the sender from claiming he/she did not send the message.

Non-return-to-zero (NRZ) code: A binary code in which "1s" are represented by one significant condition and

"0s" are represented by the other significant condition, with no other neutral or rest condition.

No-transition mobility: A station moving only within one BSS.

NRZ-I code (Non-Return-to-Zero Inverted): A method in which the polarity is reversed to represent successive 1 bits but no polarity is changed for 0 bits.

Nyquist's sampling theorem: Sampling at a fixed rate that is at least twice the highest signal frequency in the analog source's spectrum will result in the samples containing all the information of the original signal.

OC-1: An optical SONET line with a transmission speed of 51.84 Mbit/s. OC-1 is the lowest SONET speed and its frame was structured to carry exactly one T-3 frame or its equivalent, 28 T-1 frames.

Omnidirectional EMR: Electromagnetic radiation propagating in all directions at once.

Open shortest path first (OSPF): A hierarchical interior gateway protocol (IGP) for routing in Internet protocol, using a link-state in the individual areas that make up the hierarchy.

Open Systems Interconnection (OSI) model: A network communications model developed by ISO architecture consisting of seven layers that describe protocols for computer communications.

Operation, administration, maintenance, and provisioning (OAMP): Functions that must be performed to manage and operate a network.

Optical carrier: Light used to carry information on an optical fiber link.

Optical fiber: A thin strand of glass that can carry voice, data, or video signals in the form of light with very little loss. Optical fiber has a much larger practical capacity than wire.

Organizationally unique identifier (OUI): A 24-bit number assigned by IEEE to a company or organization for use in various computer hardware products, including Ethernet network interface cards and fibre channel host bus adapters. The OUI is combined with an internally assigned 24-bit number to form a unique MAC address.

Orthogonal frequency division multiplexing (OFDM): A method of digital modulation in which a signal is split into several narrowband channels at different frequencies.

Out-of-band signaling: The exchange of control information in a band separate from the data or voice channel, or on an entirely separate, dedicated channel.

Overhead bit: Any non-user generated bit added to frames to perform functions such as error detection and to identify particular types of frames.

Packet: A sequence of bits containing user data or network control information, surrounded by bits added by the network to maintain packet integrity and identity during transmission through a network.

Packet assembler/disassembler (PAD): A communications device that sits between a non-packet capable device (DTE) and an X.25 network node (DCE). The PAD performs the function of dividing information to be sent across an X.25 network into packets, and reassembles the received packets into the original information format.

Packet jitter: Measures the variation in arrival rates between individual packets.

Packet switched network: A digital data transmission network that transmits data in discrete units over shared links. Packet switches can operate in either a connectionless or connection oriented mode. In the first, every packet of a particular transmission may take different paths through the network to arrive at the destination; in the second, all packets of a particular transmission must take the same path through the network to arrive at the destination.

Packet-filtering firewalls: Software that is run on corporate border routers, the primary entry points to company networks, that monitors and grants or denies packet access based on company policies.

Page: A file on a Web server that can be accessed through a web browser.

PAM (Pulse Amplitude Modulation) sampling rate: The number of signal samples per second that are taken.

Parity check bit: A bit added to user generated data that allows the receiving device to check whether data has been transmitted accurately.

Partial mesh design: Some nodes may be organized in a full mesh scheme, but at least some others are not connected to every other node.

Patch cord: A length of cable with connectors on one or both ends used to join telecommunications circuits at patch panels or other interconnection points.

Path overhead: In a SONET frame, the overhead bits contained in the payload that allow the network to manage the path.

Path vector: A routing protocol used to span different autonomous systems.

Path: In SONET network, the sections and lines that connects two STS multiplexers.

Payload: The part of a SONET frame that contains user information and user overhead information.

PDN (Public Data Network): A privately owned and operated WAN that offers public access connection services for a fee. PDNs are commonly used by corporations to extend the reach of their own networks or in lieu of their own network.

Peer-to-Peer: A type of network in which each workstation potentially has equivalent capabilities and responsibilities.

Period: See **Cycle.**

Periodic waves: Waves that have a time-based repeating pattern, e.g., sine waves.

Permanent virtual circuit (PVC): In a packet switched network, a continuously dedicated virtual circuit set up by a network administrator.

Personal area network (PAN): A computer network used for communication among computer devices very close to a person.

Personal communications system (PCS): The term given to cellular phone technologies within the United States.

Phase modulation (PM): The phase of a signal is shifted from its reference value according ro a modulating function.

Phishing: Trolling for personal or private information by randomly sending out spoofed spam.

Physical star: A cabling topology in which every device is connected to a central device.

Physical topology: Describes the layout of the cables and the devices in a network.

Piconet: An ad-hoc computer network of devices using Bluetooth technology protocols to allow one master device to interconnect with up to eight active devices.

Plain old telephone service (POTS): The voice-grade telephone service that remains the basic form of residential and small business service connection to the telephone network in most parts of the world.

Plaintext: Original unencrypted document.

Point-of-presence (POP): The point at which a line from a long distance (interexchange) carrier connects to the line of the local telephone company or to the user if the local company is not involved. More generally, a point-of-presence is the location of any network node(s) with which users may connect to the network.

Point-to-point connection: A direct connection between two devices that does not include any intermediate devices.

Point-to-point tunneling protocol (PPTP): Method for implementing virtual private networks. Used with the generic routing encapsulation protocol (GRE) to create a secure version of the point-to-point protocol (PPP).

Policy based path vectors: See **Path vectors.**

Polling: The process of sending a request message to collect events or information from a network device. It is also used to control device access on a multi-point (multi-drop) link.

Port number: Identifies a particular application program running on a computer. It allows different applications on the same computer to utilize network resources without interfering with each other.

Port: A hardware port is a location on a device that allows attachment to other devices, e.g., a mouse port. A software port is a number assigned to a computer program (see port number) that allows a communication session between programs on two data communication devices.

Post office protocol (POP): An application-layer Internet standard protocol, to retrieve e-mail from a remote server over a TCP/IP connection.

Power line communications (PLC): The process of delivering data over electrical power lines.

Power over Ethernet (POE): A system to transmit electrical power, along with data, to remote devices over standard twisted-pair cable in an Ethernet network.

P-persistence: In the Ethernet CSMA/CD protocol, a strategy the attempts to reduce the occurrence of collisions: A station transmits with probability p after finding the medium idle.

Pretty good privacy (PGP): A method of encryption and authentication.

Primary colors: Colors that cannot be produced by mixing any other colors. For visible light, they are: red, green, and blue (RGB). For pigments, they are red, yellow, and blue.

Primary station: In polling, a primary station controls access by having all data transfers go through that station. It is also called master station.

Private branch exchange (PBX): Allocates phone calls on the business premises.

Propagation delay: The time it takes for a signal to travel from the source to the destination.

Propagation speed: The rate at which signals propagate in a medium.

Propagation: The movement of an electromagnetic signal from one point to another.

Proprietary: A design or specification owned by the developer, who holds the rights to its use and distribution.

Protection ring: In a dual ring system, carries an exact copy of the data sent on the working ring, but in the opposite direction.

Protocol conversion: Translates the way one protocol performs a particular function into the way a different protocol handles the function, so that devices with different protocols can understand each other.

Protocol-based VLAN: A virtual LAN configured by protocols.

Protocol: A rule or rule set. Many protocols for data communication are defined in model architectures.

Proxy server: A device that logically stands between a client and a server on the Internet. It filters all request coming from clients and responses coming from servers. The proxy evaluates each and based on a set of rules will allow or disallow the interaction. If allowed, the proxy server will talk to the client and server on behalf of the other: no direct communications takes place between the client and server.

Proxy: See **Proxy server.**

Public access carrier: A company providing WAN and MAN links for a fee.

Public data network (PDN): A packet data network operated by a telecommunications administration, or private agency, that provides data transmission services to the public.

Public switched telephone network (PSTN): A voice-oriented public telephone network. Also refers to the interconnected system of all such networks.

Pulse amplitude modulation (PAM): The amplitude of the pulse carrier is altered in accordance with some characteristic of the modulating signal.

Pulse code modulation (PCM): A digital representation of an analog signal where the magnitude of the signal is sampled regularly at uniform intervals then quantized to a series of symbols in a digital (usually binary) code.

Quality of service (QoS): Offers guarantees on the ability of a network to deliver predictable results. Refers to the ability of a network to provide higher priority services to selected network traffic over various WAN, LAN, and MAN technologies.

Quantization: The process of converting the sampled voltage values of an analog waveform into digital data.

Quantizing (or quantization) error: The difference between the actual value of a sampled analog signal and the resulting quantized value.

Quantizing noise: Errors that result from conversion of an analog signal into a finite number of digital values.

Queuing: Holding messages in some ordered sequence.

Radiation: The emission and propagation of electromagnetic energy in the form of electromagnetic waves through some medium.

Real-time transport control protocol (RTCP): Control for an RTP session by devices exchanging information about the quality of a session.

Real-time transport protocol (RTP): Defines a standardized packet format for delivering audio and video over the Internet.

Redirector: An operating system driver that sends data to and receives data from a remote device.

Regeneration: As used in communications, the process of recreating an attenuated and/or distorted digital signal. If successful, the recreated signal is identical to the original signal.

Regional Bell operating company (RBOC): The Bell telephone companies that were spun off of AT&T by court order in 1984 (the Divestiture). Also known as the "Baby Bells," the initial seven RBOCs were Nynex, Bell Atlantic, BellSouth, Southwestern Bell, US West, Pacific Telesis, and Ameritech.

Regional Internet registry (RIR): An organization that allocates and registers Internet addresses within a particular region of the world.

Remote monitor (RMON): A device for monitoring network traffic, usually from a command center.

Repeat request: Error control method for data transmission that remediates detected errors by requiring the data to be re-sent. Acknowledgments and timeouts are used to achieve reliable data transmission. Also known as automatic repeat request (ARQ).

Request for proposal (RFP): A detailed description of project requirements that serves as a solicitation to vendors to bid on the project.

Request to send (RTS): A signaling message transmitted by an IEEE 802.11 station indicating that it has data to transmit.

Resistance: The opposition of a material to the flow of electric current, measured in ohms.

Resource reservation protocol (RSVP): A set of communication rules that allows channels or paths on the Internet to be reserved for the multicast transmission of high-bandwidth messages.

Response time: The length of the time between sending a request and the display of the first character of the response at a user terminal.

Return-to-zero (RZ) code: A communications line code in which signal voltage returns to zero between each pulse.

Reverse address resolution protocol (RARP): Obtains the IP address that corresponds to a particular hardware address.

RGB: See **Primary colors.**

Ring: A topology in which each node connects only to two adjacent nodes, forming a loop. Ring networks are unidirectional—transmissions travel around the ring in one direction.

Ring wrapping: A dual ring procedure that redirects traffic from a failed portion on the primary link to the protection ring, thus keeping the ring operating.

Risk analysis (Risk assessment): Identifies the types of threats faced, their likelihood of occurrence, and the probable cost to the company of various security breaches should they be successfully carried out.

Root bridge: Continuously transmits network topology information to other bridges, using the spanning tree protocol, in order to notify all other bridges on the network when topology changes are required.

Root ports: The ports connecting the shortest paths from each bridge back to itself, calculated by the root bridge.

Route aggregation: A technique for organizing network layer IP addresses in a hierarchy.

Router: A path determination device for packets traveling between different networks that also forwards the packets to the next device along the path.

Routing: A process of selecting paths in a network along which to send data.

Routing algorithm: Calculates the output link over which to transmit an incoming packet.

Routing information protocol (RIP): Manages router information within a self-contained network, such as a corporate LAN or an interconnected group of such LANs.

Routing protocol: Used by routers to determine the appropriate data forwarding path.

Sampling: Converting analog information into a digital representation by measuring the voltage of analog signals at regular intervals.

Sampling resolution: The number of bits used in the binary representation of the actual sample values.

Satellite network: A network using radio frequencies relayed by satellite.

Scanning sequencer: The device that transfers TDM data to their corresponding time slots.

Scattering: A change in the light wave passing through an optical fiber caused by an impurity or change of density in the fiber, producing signal power loss. Scattered light can be reflected back to the source or refracted into the cladding.

Scatternet: A set of piconets connected through sharing devices.

Secondary station: Devices for data transfer that take place after getting polled by primary station.

Section: Any two devices directly connected by an optical fiber.

Section overhead: In a SONET frame, the 9 bytes of the transport overhead that supports performance monitoring and administration of a section of the SONET network.

Secure http: Provides the same type of security as https, but it is an independent connectionless protocol that does not run on SSL or TLS.

Secure multipurpose Internet mail extensions (S/MIME): A standard for public key encryption and signing of e-mail encapsulated in MIME.

Secure RTCP (SRTCP): Provides encryption, message authentication and integrity, and replay protection to the RTP data in both unicast and multicast applications.

Secure shell (SSH): Provides encrypted communications between two hosts over insecure networks.

Secure sockets layer (SSL): A connection-oriented protocol to provide encryption and authentication, primarily to protect communications between Web clients and servers.

Self-clocking codes: Codes that represent the binary bits in way that indicates bit values and provides clocking information for the receiver.

Self-healing: A SONET architecture that uses two or more transmission paths between nodes; in the event one path fails, traffic can be rerouted to the other path.

Semiconductor: Material whose resistivity, its behavior towards electron flow, can be changed by the application of light, an electric field, or a magnetic field.

Server-centric: A LAN classification in which the servers function only as servers. They are often called client-server LANs.

Service access points (SAPs): An identifying label for network endpoints used in OSI model. The SAP is a conceptual location at which one OSI layer can request the services of another OSI layer.

Service level agreement (SLA): A contract between the customer and the service provider by which the latter commits to guaranteeing particular levels of service for a stipulated price. It defines the terms of types of services, quality of services, and the customer payment.

Service level: A package of functionalities offered by a network provider.

Service provider: Vendor that supplies network, software, management, or other functions to the owners of computer and communication systems.

Session initiation protocol (SIP): An application-layer control protocol for creating, modifying, and terminating sessions with one or more participants.

Shared key authentication: A security protocol that controls access to network resources and requires each station to possess a private key in order to be authenticated.

Shielded twisted pairs (STP): Twisted pairs that are surrounded by a shield that prevents electromagnetic interference.

Signal constellation: A graphical method used to visualize the signal combinations in QAM and the bits they represent.

Signal to noise ratio (SNR): The ratio of the power (strength) of signal to the power of the surrounding noise. The larger this ratio, the more easily and accurately the signal can be distinguished from the noise. It is usually expressed in decibels.

Signals: A varying quantity in electricity, light, and electromagnetic waves in general, that can carry information.

Signal's spectrum: When a signal (analog or digital) is separated into its elementary signals, the resulting collection of sine waves is called the signal's spectrum.

Simple mail transfer protocol (SMTP): Standard for e-mail transmissions across the Internet.

Simple network management protocol (SNMP): An application layer protocol facilitating the exchange of management information between network devices. It is designed to assist in managing networks remotely by enabling monitoring and controlling of network nodes, collecting performance data, and administering cost, configuration, and security measures.

Simple parity check: A method of error detection that checks whether the sum of bits in each character received conforms to a given protocol. Simple parity check will detect any odd number of bit inversions, but it will miss any even number of bit inversions. Thus on average, it will successfully detect bit errors only about 50 percent of the time.

Simplex mode: A system in which data flows in one direction only.

Single bit error: An error in which just one bit in a transmitted frame is inverted (changed from a 1 to a 0 or from a 0 to a 1).

Single mode fiber: An optical fiber designed for the transmission of a single mode of light as a carrier and is used for long-distance signal transmission.

Single point of failure (SPOF): Using one device or communications line to perform a function. In order to ensure continuous operation, two or more devices or lines are used. Any computer or communications system that contains only one component to do a job creates a single point of failure.

Sliding window flow control: A technique to provide flow and/or error control whereby the sender is allowed to transmit only that information within a specified window of frames or bytes. The window is shifted upon receipt of proper data acknowledgements from the receiver.

Slot time: The length of time it takes a frame to travel from one end of as LAN to the other.

Smart phone: A full-featured mobile phone with personal computer-like functionality.

Smart terminal: An interface device that has both independent computing capability and the ability to communicate with other devices or systems. It is also known as an intelligent.

Social engineering: Tricking people or systems into providing confidential, personal, private, or other sensitive information.

Socket: One end-point of a two-way communication link between two programs running on a network, formed by combining an IP address and a TCP/UDP port number.

Socket address: See **Socket.**

Source address: The address of the network device that is sending data.

Spam: E-mail sent to a very large number of addresses, usually unsolicited.

Spanning tree: A method for Ethernet LANs that sets up the bridge ports so that there is only one route from each LAN to every other LAN. Redundant routes are held back until needed because of route failure.

Spoofing: Falsifying source addresses.

Spyware: Captures and records activities on an end user device, even down to keystrokes, and transmits it over the Internet to other parties.

Start of text (STX): A character to represent start of text in a data frame in some protocols.

Start/stop communication: See **Asynchronous communication.**

Stateful inspection: A process to see whether a packet belongs to a pre-validated session.

Station: Computer/host in a network.

Statistical time division multiplexing (STDM): A technique for transmitting several types of data concurrently across a single transmission cable or line.

Step index: An optical fiber in which the core refractive index is uniform throughout so that a sharp step in refractive index occurs at the core to cladding interface. It usually refers to a multimode fiber type.

Stop-and-wait ARQ. See **Stop-and-wait protocol.**

Stop-and-wait protocol: The receiver tells the sender when to transmit a single frame of data. It is also called stop-and-wait ARQ.

Store-and-forward switch: Reads the entire incoming packet and stores it in its memory buffer, checks various fields, determines next hop, and finally forwards it.

STS multiplexer: Interfaces to the user at the edge of the SONET system.

STS-1: The basic logical building block signal of synchronous optical networks.

Sub-domain name: The name associated with a network that is part of a larger network (domain).

Subnet: A self-contained network that is a part of an organization's larger network. It is distinguished by a range of logical addresses within the address space that is assigned to the organization.

Subnet mask: A mask used to determine the subnet to which an IP address belongs.

Subscriber: An individual or company that is uniquely identified within the system as a user of services.

Subscriber line: The local telephone loop.

Substitution code: One symbol being substituted for by another.

Supernetting: A way to aggregate multiple Internet address ranges of the same class.

Supervisory frames: See **Control frames.**

Switch: A device that direct messages along a particular path.

Switchboard: A switching system that connects telephones with one another. Switchboards can be either manual, mechanical, electrico-mechanical, or electrical.

Switched (SVC): In packet switching, a kind of virtual circuit that is created on demand and terminated when transmission is finished. Usually used where data transmission is sporadic.

Symmetric DSL: A rate-adaptive version of HDSL with equal upstream and downstream bandwidth.

Synchronous idle (SYN): A transmission control character used in some synchronous transmission systems.

Synchronous Optical Network (SONET): A standard for optical transport that defines optical carrier levels and their electrically equivalent synchronous transport signals, and allows for a multivendor environment.

Synchronous payload envelope (SPE): In a SONET frame, the structure that carries the payload (user data).

Synchronous payload: The actual user data that the frame is to transport.

Synchronous time division multiplexing: See **Time division multiplexing.**

Synchronous transport signal (STS): A standard for data transmissions over SONET.

System identification code (SID): A five-digit number assigned to a service provider by the FCC.

Systems development life cycle (SDLC): A written plan or strategy for developing information systems through investigation, analysis, design, implementation, and maintenance.

T-1: A full duplex circuit that uses two-twisted wire pairs, one for sending and one for receiving.

Tandem office: A central office unit used primarily as an intermediate switching point for traffic between local central offices within the tandem area.

Tariffs: Charges for the services offered by PSTNs or POTS.

TCP (transmission control protocol): One of the core protocols of the Internet protocol suite, which guarantees reliable and in-order delivery of data from sender to receiver.

Telecommunications Act of 1996: Provided major changes in laws affecting cable TV, telecommunications, and the Internet that was enacted to stimulate competition in telecommunication services in the U.S.

Terminal: An electronic device such as a computer or a workstation that communicates with a host computer or system. The terminal can send or receive data as well as display output either on screen or in a print format.

Termination: The point where a line, channel, or circuit ends.

Thermal noise: Caused by random movements of electrons in transmission media. Also called background noise, white noise, Gaussian noise, and hiss.

Thicknet: The original IEEE 10 Mbps Ethernet standard that used a bus topology comprising a thick coaxial cable. Network nodes attached via an AUI to transceivers that tapped into the bus. Also called 10Base5, thick Ethernet, and ThickWire.

Thin client: A computer that does not contain hard drives. Thin clients access programs and data from a server instead of storing them locally.

Thinnet A 10 Mbps Ethernet standard that followed the earlier Thicknet standard, it specifies the use of a thin coaxial cable. Thinnet simplified installation and reduced costs. Also called thin Ethernet, ThinWire, and 10Base2.

Time division multiple access (TDMA): A technology used in digital cellular telephone communication that divides each cellular channel into three time slots in order to increase the amount of data that can be carried.

Time division multiplexing (TDM): Combines multiple data streams by assigning each stream a different time in which to transmit data on a shared connection. TDM repeatedly transmits a fixed sequence of time slots over a single transmission channel. Also known as Synchronous TDM.

Token passing: A means of controlling network access through the use of a small packet, the token, which is circulated through the network from node to node. A node can transmit only when it holds the token. This prevents collisions.

Top-level domain name (TLD): The part of a domain name that, along with the second level name, has to be registered. Examples of TLDs are .com and .edu.

Total cost of ownership (TCO): The annual cost for keeping a network component operational.

Total internal reflection: An medium optical phenomenon in fiber optic cable that occurs when light is refracted at the core/cladding interface in such a way that it remains in the core.

Trailer: Data placed at the end of a block of data being transmitted, usually containing error detection information placed by the data link layer.

Translating bridge: Connects LANs operating under different 802.x protocols.

Transmission control protocol (TCP): Enables two hosts to establish a connection and exchange streams of data.

Transmission Control Protocol over Internet Protocol (TCP/IP): A set of protocols that defines how messages are transferred reliably through a data network, typically, but not only, the Internet.

Transparency: A concept used in layered model architectures in which each network layer operates without knowing about processes in any other layer; adjacent layers need to pass data between them according to the model interfaces. Also refers to a communication system whose operation is not affected by user data.

Transparent bridge: A computer network device that is used to interconnect several computers in a network, enabling the exchange of data among them.

Transparent system: A communication system whose operation is not affected by user data.

Transport flow control: End-to-end flow control between the initial sender and final receiver.

Transport layer multiplexing: Multiplexing of several client process packets by their port numbers.

Transport layer security (TLS): A cryptographic protocol that provides secure communications on the Internet for such things as web browsing, e-mail, Internet faxing, instant messaging, and other data transfers.

Tree network: Multiple nodes are connected in a branching manner. Also called hierarchical network.

Triple DES (TDES): A block cipher that applies three 56-bit blocks consecutively to create a 168-bit key.

Trojan horse malware (trojan): A virus that hides within or disguises itself as legitimate software and must be specifically executed to take effect.

Trouble ticket: A system for reporting or describing network problems and error conditions that are forwarded to technicians for resolution.

Tunneling: A technique used to send one network's packets through another network, often using secure protocols, without those packets having to conform to the other network's protocols.

Twist rate: The number of twists per inch in twisted pair.

Twisted pair: Wire pairs are insulated and twisted around each other in a spiral fashion.

UBR (Unspecified Bit Rate): An asynchronous transfer mode (ATM) level of service that does not guarantee available bandwidth. It is very efficient, but not used for critical data.

UDP (user datagram protocol): A communications protocol that offers a limited amount of service when messages are exchanged between computers in a network that uses the Internet protocol.

Unbounded media: See **Unguided media.**

Unchannelized: For T-1, the use of the entire frame's capacity, excluding the framing bit, without dividing the frame into time slots (i.e., channels).

Unguided media: Media, such as air, through which data signals travel with nothing to guide them along a specific path. Also called unbounded media.

Unicast: Communication between a single sender and a single receiver over a network.

Unicode Transformation Format (UTF): See **Unicode.**

Unicode: A 16-bit scheme that can represent 65,536 symbols, a number sufficient to handle the characters used by all known existing languages, with spare capacity left over for newly developed character sets.

Uniform resource locator (URL): A unique address for a file that is accessible on the Internet.

Universal mobile telephone service (UMTS): A third-generation cell phone technology.

Unnumbered frames: See **Management frames.**

Unshielded twisted pair (UTP): Pairs of copper wires twisted around each other and covered by plastic insulation but not by an outer metallic shield (as in STP). The twisting of the copper wire pair reduces the effects of interference as each wire receives approximately the same level of interference (balanced), thereby effectively canceling the interference. It is used for used for local access lines and computer LANs.

Uplink: Transmission of a signal from a ground station on earth to a satellite.

Upload: Sending data to a remote system, FTP server, or website.

Value-added service (VAS): Provides benefits to a customer that are not part of standard basie telecommunications services. An examples is voice mail.

VBR (Variable Bit Rate): In ATM networks, used for connections in which there is a fixed timing relationship between samples of a multimedia transmission.

Very high bit-rate DSL: An asymmetric design that achieves high data rates over local loops by considerably tightening line length limits.

Very high-performance Backbone Network Service (vBNS): Came on line in 1995 as part of a National Science Foundation–sponsored project to provide high-speed interconnection between NSF-sponsored supercomputing centers and select access points.

Video band: Frequencies from 54 MHz to 550 MHz.

Virtual circuit (VC): Connections between two hosts in a packet switched network. Created as a logical path between network nodes, where each packet of a transmission follows the same route.

Virtual circuit number: A 12-bit field in an X.25 PLP header that identifies an X.25 virtual circuit, and allows DCE to determine how to route a packet through the X.25 network.

Virtual LAN (VLAN): A method of creating independent logical networks within a physical network.

Virtual path (VP): In an ATM network, it provides a connection or a set of connections between two ATM switches. A VP contains a number of virtual circuits.

Virtual private network (VPN): A method for transmitting secure data over a network that may not be secure.

Visible spectrum: The region in the electromagnetic spectrum with wavelengths between 380 and 720 nanometers, comprising the rainbow of colors from violet to red.

Voice band: The frequency spectrum from approximately 300 Hz to 3400 Hz that is considered adequate for speech transmission.

Voice coder (vocoder): A device that transforms spoken voice into digital data.

Voice over Internet protocol (VoIP): Transmission of digitized and packetized voice conversations over the Internet or through any other IP-based network.

Volt: Basic unit of electrical potential.

WAN Interface Sublayer (WIS): Added to 10GBASE-X to provide compatibility between Ethernet and SONET STS-192c, which has a payload capacity of 9.58464 Gbps.

Wavelength division multiplexing (WDM): A process of creating several distinct communication channels through a single optical fiber via the use of a different infrared wavelength for each channel. In addition to increased capacity, it is possible to transmit data bidirectionally over a single fiber strand.

Wavelength: The distance a wave travels in one cycle.

Web 1.0: A general reference to the World Wide Web.

Web 2.0: A second generation of the World Wide Web that is focused on the ability for people to collaborate and share information online.

Web 3.0: The evolution of Web usage to include semantic capabilities.

Well-known ports: Port numbers from 0 to 1,023 that are pre-assigned by ICANN for use by privileged applications (applications that are to be used by a large population of the Internet) such as HTTP.

WEP (Wired Equivalent Privacy): A network security standard for wireless LANs as defined in the IEEE 802.11b specifications.

Wide area network (WAN): A communications network that spans a relatively large geographical area. A WAN can be established by linking together two or more metropolitan area networks, which enables data terminals in one city to access data resources in another city or country.

Wi-Fi protected access (WPA): A Wi-Fi standard that was designed to improve upon the security features of WEP. This version implemented many of the features that were to be included in the full 802.11i protocol set.

WiMAX: A telecommunications technology based on the IEEE 802.16 standard provides wireless data over long distances in a variety of ways.

Wireless LANs (WLANs): See **Wireless local area network (WLAN).**

Wireless local area network (WLAN): A type of local-area network that uses high-frequency radio waves rather than wires to communicate between nodes.

Wireless metropolitan area network (WMAN): A high-data-rate broadband system that can operate over substantial distances.

Wireless personal area network (WPAN): A small, short-range network using wireless connections.

Working ring: In some architectures that use dual rings, one ring is designated as the working ring and the other as the protection ring; traffic on the two rings moves in opposite directions. The working ring handles all data traffic in a counterclockwise direction and is the preferred path when both rings are operational.

Worm: Self-replicating malware that, unlike viruses, can propagate on their own. They are usually designed specifically to travel along with transmissions, thus spreading rapidly.

WPA2: A wireless security protocol that provides network administrators with a high level of assurance that only authorized users can access the network.

X.21: The interface used in the X.25 packet-switching protocol, and in some types of circuit-switched data transmissions.

X.25: The first international standard packet switching network published in 1976 by the CCITT.

X.28: Defines the DTE-DTC interface to a PAD, including the commands for making and clearing down connections, and manipulating the X.3 parameters.

X.3: Specifies the parameters for terminal-handling functions such as line speed, flow control, character echo, et al. for a connection to an X.25 host.

xDSL: Refers collectively to all types of digital subscriber lines.

Zombies: Unsuspecting hosts taken over by malware, that then are unaware of what they are being used for or that they are being used.

Index